Handbook of Analytical Studies in Islamic Finance and Economics

De Gruyter Studies in Islamic Economics, Finance and Business

Edited by
Abbas Mirakhor and Idris Samawi Hamid

Volume 4

Handbook of Analytical Studies in Islamic Finance and Economics

Edited by
Nabil Maghrebi, Tarık Akın, Abbas Mirakhor, Zamir Iqbal

DE GRUYTER

ISBN 978-3-11-058508-7
e-ISBN (PDF) 978-3-11-058792-0
e-ISBN (EPUB) 978-3-11-058517-9
ISSN 2567-2533

Library of Congress Control Number: 2019956076

Bibliographic information published by the Deutsche Nationalbibliothek
The Deutsche Nationalbibliothek lists this publication in the Deutsche Nationalbibliografie; detailed bibliographic data are available on the Internet at http://dnb.dnb.de.

Cover image: nnnnae/iStock/Getty Images Plus
Tyypesetting: Integra Software Services Pvt. Ltd.
Printing and Bindung: CPI books GmbH, Leck

www.degruyter.com

Preface

Twelve years after the last devastating crisis, there is a palpable sense of anxiety and pessimism among academics, policy makers, international organizations and general population regarding the economic and financial future. There is a sense that vital signs have deteriorated globally to the point that conditions are emerging for formation of a perfect storm. Diagnostics of the causes of the last crisis pointed to the failure of the dominant economic model, moral/ethical failure, governance failure, policy failure, regulation failure and the failure of global supervision of international finance and trade. These conditions allowed also for greed, an elemental ingredient in the application of the underlying theory of dominant economic system. Not only these failures have not been corrected in the post-crisis period, in some cases, they have been exacerbated.

With few exceptions, economies across the world are stagnating; unemployment (with few exceptions) is widespread; private investment is sluggish; productivity is declining; commodity prices are low and increasingly volatile; global debt (government and private) is growing to levels higher than that in the period of run-up to the crisis; governments have resorted to financial repression; there is large and growing corporate liquidity with (apparently) no place to go; financialization is proceeding unabated; global trade is shrinking; emerging markets, which provided a cushion to the world economy during and immediately after the crisis, are themselves facing considerable instability; inequality of income and wealth distribution is worsening across the world; poverty is spreading globally; macroeconomic policies in many countries have been unable to reverse or slow down adverse economic and financial trends; international financial institutions appear to have failed in their mandate to stabilize the global financial system or seriously challenge "beggar-thy-neighbor" policies and reignite global growth; the depth and spread of domestic and international political conflicts have intensified uncertainty across the globe; finally, adverse environmental and ecological trends, against which the humanity has been warned since the 1970s, are threatening life on the planet.[1]

Against this background, a wealth of information and research has sought to explain why the world is facing these formidable challenges and offer solutions from both inside and outside of the discipline of economics. Most of these efforts focus on reforms of the present dominant system and its underlying theory; some reforms propose deep structural changes; some reforms lie just at the margin. There is, however, one view that does not directly question either the working of the global system or the model driving it. This view transcends usual criticisms of assumptions and axioms of economics and focuses on historical, long-term trends in

1 For detail discussion see various reports of the international agencies (UN, IMF, WB, UNCTAD, ILO, OXFAM, EU and others as well as related academic books and articles published since the crisis).

https://doi.org/10.1515/9783110587920-202

the world economy. It claims that the world economy is in the negative phase of a Kondratiev cycle[2] that is predicted to peak in the 2020s.

Alternative views tend to focus on the need for rethinking the way societies have arranged economic activities and on the necessity of a new economics which change or at least modify the epistemological foundation of the discipline. These views are expressed from the inside or outside the discipline. The former includes economists who suggest deep changes such as renegotiation of social contracts to those who question the fundamental axioms of economics that have bearing on important social questions regarding morality, trust, cooperation, sharing, environmental protection, inequality, poverty, social cohesion and solidarity. Ultimately, these views focus on the conventional economics' fundamental assumptions of scarcity, rationality and self-interest.

There are of course insiders who defend, hard and fast, the dominant theory and the system that has resulted from its application. Arguing that many of these issues relate to morality, they hold that economics is not meant to address morality "economics is not a morality play. It is not a happy story in which virtue is rewarded and vice is punished. The market economy is a system for organizing economic activity – a pretty good system most of the time, though not always – with no special moral significance. The rich don't necessarily deserve their wealth, and the poor certainly don't deserve their poverty; nonetheless, we accept a system with considerable inequality because the system without any inequality don't work."[3]

---

2 Named after the Russian economist Nikolai Kondratiev (also Kondratieff) who identified cyclical patterns in the 1930s. The current phase of the 40–60 year-cycle is associated with pessimism, stagnation, unemployment, low investment, worsening inequality, polarization of the society, political conflicts and violence. See, G. Modelski and W. R. Thompson, 1996. Leading Sectors and World Politics: The Co-evolution of Global politics and Economics. Columbia, South Carolina: University of South Carolina Press; W. R. Thompson, 2009. "The Kondratieff Wave as Global Social Process. In World System History, Edited by George Modelski and Robert A. Denemark. Oxford: Eolss Publisher, pp. 174–195; and L. Grinin, A. Korotayev, and A. Tausch, 2016. Economic Cycles, Crises, and the Global Priphery. New York: Springer.

3 Paul Krugman "Economics is not a Morality Play." New York Times. September 28, 2010. There are many who disagree with this assertion arguing that, first, no argument, theoretical or otherwise, about the economy can be amoral. For example, Daniel K. Finn (The Moral Ecology of Markets, 2006, Cambridge University Press) argues that assertion about and defense of self-interest assumption and that of the market involve moral arguments. Second, it is argued that the dominant paradigm is not merely a benign exercise in abstract tool of understanding economic phenomena when its assumptions, conclusions and implications are internalized by economic agents. It can and does enormous harm (see for example, Shoshona Zuboff, 2009. "Wall Street crimes Against Humanity. Business week, March 20; see also Abbas Mirakhor, 2014 "The Starry Heavens Above and the Moral Law Within: On the Flatness of Economics'" Economic Journal Watch, vol. 11, No. 2, pp. 186–193). Even successful businessmen/capitalists who believe capitalism "is the greatest problem-solving social technology ever invented" assert that the basic economic model that has led to the present configuration of capitalism is flawed and morally bankrupt. It is argued that such a model "has profound non-academic consequences […] it gives both permission and encouragement to some of the worse

Other insiders' defence of the status quo is based on underlying thoughts traced to the neoliberal philosophy (Hayek-Rand-Freidman) and argue that economic agents have no moral obligation to do more than adhere to the rules and laws of the market society derived from the underlying social contract enshrined in societies' constitutions.[4] Other insiders to the discipline, however, argue that that the standard dominant economic theory's claim that material incentives are sufficient to elicit appropriate behavior from economic agents, and that moral rules are not necessary, is not supported by empirical evidence, and the foundation theory that advocates this notion is quite implausible.[5] The theory has no inherent set of rules that would have any inducements for individuals in a society of self-interested economic agents to have any "other-regarding" or prosocial proclivities, such as cooperation or collaboration. Indeed, the logic of the competitive model of this theory implies that it is not unusual for agents in this theory to gain by violating the laws and rules if "no one is looking" thus creating thereby pressure for others to do the same. On the other hand, they argue, the evolutionary success of human species owes much to human cooperation and collaboration in the economy as well as in the rest of the social sphere.[6]

Even in a society in which the economy is based on the dominant theory, empirical investigations have shown that many people do not cheat even if there is no

excesses of modern capitalism, and of contemporary moral and social life [...] if we internalize that most people are mostly selfish – and then we look around the world at all the unambiguous prosperity and goodness in it, then it follows logically, it must be true, by definition, that a billion individual acts of selfishness magically transubstantiated into prosperity and the common good. If it is true that humans really are just selfish maximizers, then selfishness must be the cause of prosperity. And it must true that the more selfish we are, the more prosperous we all become. Under this logical construct, the only good decision is a business decision – "Greed is good" – and the only purpose of the corporation must be to maximize shareholder value, humanity be damned. Welcome to our neoliberal world. But if instead we accept a prosocial behavioral model that correctly describes human beings as uniquely cooperative and intuitively moral creatures, then logically, the golden rule of economics must be the Golden Rule: Do business with others as you would have them do business with you. This is a story about ourselves that grants us permission and encouragement to be our best selves. It is a virtuous story that also has the virtue of being true (Nick Hanauer, 2018, "How to Destroy Neoliberalism: Kill 'Homo Economicus': Debunking the failed paradigm of traditional economics," Evonomics, October 13, 2018. Of course there are those who argue that it is a fallacy to equate self-interest with selfishness (see for example the arguments in this context the collection of papers by Paul Heyn in Are Economists Basically Immoral? Edited by Geoffrey Brennan and A. M. C. Waterman, 2008. Indianapolis, Indiana: Liberty Fund.

4 For a history of emergence of neoliberal thought in economics see, Philip Miroski and Dieter Plehwe (editors), 2015. The Road from Mont Pelerin: The Making of the Neoliberal Thought Collective. Cambridge: Harvard University Press.

5 See, for example, Samuel Bowles, 2016. The Moral Economy: Why Good Incentives Are No substitute for Good Citizens. New Haven: Yale University Press.

6 For detail see, for example, Peter Turchin, 2016. Ultra Society: How 10,000 Years of War Made Humans the Greatest Cooperators on Earth. Chaplin, Connecticut: Baresta Books.

monitoring and there are no gains (including reputational) for not cheating. There are highly successful firms in such societies that offer their employees the opportunity and the comfort of knowing that they are doing jobs that are useful to the society.[7] Similarly, empirical studies have shown that there are inventors, innovators and entrepreneurs (for example in the Silicon Valley) whose motivations transcend narrow self-interests and self-regard, and who do not behave as rational actors of the dominant economics. Their extrarational motivations include, inter alia, self-sacrifice, cooperation, collaboration, human altruism, seeking meaning in one's life, creativity and concern for future generations.[8]

These insiders firmly believe that there is no better or more viable alternative system to capitalism but insist that it is the underlying theory that has led to adverse and dire consequences facing humanity.[9] These people mount strong assault on the foundation axioms and assumptions of the theory (especially narrow rationality and pure self-interest) and offer ways to reform the theory. The foundation of their approach is the need they see in a reformed theory that has strong moral/ethical foundation in the spirit of Adam Smith.[10] They insist that not only the narrow self-interest assumption of the dominant economic theory lacks empirical plausibility, its role in capitalism must be reformed to have a moral and prosocial orientation if the collapse of the system is to be avoided. Others suggest that the laws and rules of a self-regarding capitalism, driven by the generally selfish orientation posited by the underlying theory, lead to such unequal levels of income and wealth distribution that provide the rich with political power to capture legislative power of rule-making in their favor. Then, compliance with the resulting rules gives the rich and the powerful additional and entrenched advantages to exploit. Hence, the

---

7 See, for example, Herbert Gintis, 2009. The Bounds of Reason. Princeton: Princeton University Press. See also Samuel Bowles and Herbert Gintis, 2011, A cooperative species. Princeton: Princeton University Press; Herbert Gintis, 2017. Individuality and entanglement. Princeton: Princeton University Press; and Robert Frank, 2004. What Price the Moral High Ground. Princeton: Princeton University Press, in which the author argues that morality has a productive role even in capitalism.

8 See, for example, Victor W. Hwang and Greg Horowitt, 2012. The Rainforest: The Secret to Building the Next Silicone Valley. Los Altos Hills, California: Regenwold. The authors present their study of successful Silicone valley projects and the motivations of their drivers that included venture capitalists, innovators and inventors who shared the risks of new project to create new and successful enterprises. They define "extrarational" motivations as those that transcend the distinction in the classical notion of "rational and "irrational" and which conventional does not consider as critical drivers of economic-value creation.

9 See, for example, Joseph E. Stiglitz, 2019. People, Power, and Profits: Progressive Capitalism for an Age of Discontent. New York: W. W. Norton.

10 See, for example, Paul Collier, 2018. The Future of Capitalism: Facing the New Anxieties. New York: Harper, in which the author argues that capitalism is "morally bankrupt" and can only be redeemed by reorganizing itself on an ethical/moral foundation (of The Theory of Moral Sentiments variety); but also see Branko Milanovic, 2019. Capitalism, Alone: The Future of the System that Rules the world. Cambridge: Belknap Press.

rationality of free-market individualism leads to economic, social and political disparities that leave a vast majority of the population unserved. In the absence of a third-party arbiter interested in preserving the societies' institutions that would avoid exploitation by the rich, it is free-riding, impoverishment of the major segments of the population and eventual collapse of the system that will become inevitable.[11]

It is worth noting that the dominant model's main objective is to solve the economic problem stated as "limited resources and unlimited wants" that in turn leads to the allocation problem whose solution becomes "economizing." Even within the system itself, there are increasingly vociferous debates regarding both elements of the phrase "limited resources and unlimited wants." Some argue that humanity is in a phase of post-scarcity shifting to a phase of abundance and therefore there is a need for a change in the mindset from "scarcity" to "abundance."

The scarcity model, it is argued, is "hardwired" in humans based on their millennia of past experience of not having enough (in terms of food, clothing and shelter) which, it is claimed, marked much of human history and created a base fear of scarcity, poverty and starvation that became part of the human value system. Facts have changed, however, now there is superabundance but the element of value system that persists regarding scarcity continues to create greed (in form of maximizing behavior and accumulation, without asking "why am I doing this way?" in an automatic response to the hardwired fear of scarcity that says "you better get it while you can") and wasteful consumption.[12] For example, it is argued that about 90 percent of people lived in dire poverty and at the verge of starvation in 1820. Now, however, the picture has reversed where only 10 percent of world population lives in dire poverty, not because resources are scarce but because of poor governance and the resulting civil strife. Importantly, it is noted that during this period, and all the time before it, the resources available on earth have remained constant and sufficient as they have always been. Humans have been responsible both for efficient and beneficial as well as for harmful uses of these resources. According to this view, poverty in human societies is not due to scarcity of resources but due to greed and antisocial radical individualism of some humans.

The notion that the fear of scarcity has been hardwired into the human psyche on the basis that the history of civilization is one of starvation, is itself challenged

---

11 See, for example, Daron Acemoglu, 2003. "Why not a Political Coase Theorem? Social conflict, commitment and politics". Journal of Comparative Economics, vol. 31, pp. 620–652, in which the author asserts that societies have inefficient institutions (rules and norms) and politics because these serve the interests of politically powerful segment of the society and because the society lacks an "outside agency" with the power to enforce better and more efficient institutions.

12 Much has been written in the context of discussions about the culture of excess and wasteful consumption; see, for example, Benjamin R. Barber, 2007. Consumed: How Markets Corrupt Children, Infantize Adults, and Swallow Citizens Whole. New York: W. W. Norton; and Andrew Abbot, 2014. "The problem of excess", Sociological Theory, vol. 32, no. 1, pp.1–26.

by anthropologists. John Gowdy (1998) argues that "hunter-gatherers, people who lived with almost no material possessions for hundreds of thousand years, enjoyed lives in many ways richer and more rewarding than ours. A far cry from their portrayal as primitive savages struggling to survive during every waking moment, these people had structured their lives so that they needed little, wanted little, and, for the most part, had all the means of fulfilling their needs at their immediate disposal ... The view of human nature embedded in Western economic theory is an anomaly in human history. In fact, the basic organizing principle of our market economy – that humans are driven by greed and that more is always better than less – is a microscopically small minority view among the tens of thousands of cultures that have existed since Homo sapiens emerged some 200,000 years ago ... the most important message for me from these descriptions of hunter-gatherers are that (1) the economic notion of scarcity is largely a social construct, not an inherent property of human existence; (2) the separation of work from social life is not a necessary characteristic of common production; (3) the linking of individual well-being to individual production is not a necessary characteristic of economic organization; (4) selfishness and acquisitiveness are not natural traits of our species; and (5) inequality based on class and gender is not a necessary characteristic of human society."[13]

Economists have known that the economic model supporting the present predatory economic system was morally deficient. It is argued however that "[m]orality had to be put in cold storage till abundance was achieved, for abundance would make possible a good life for all," so says Robert Skidelsky, an icon of Keynesian economics, who quotes Keynes argument that "[f]or at least another hundred years we must pretend to ourselves and to everyone that fair is foul and foul is fair; for foul is useful and fair is not. Avarice and usury and precaution must be our gods for a little longer still. For only they can lead us out of the tunnel of economic necessity into daylight." And Skidelski continues the argument that "Keynes understood that capitalist civilization had, at some level of consciousness, undertaken to license motives previously condemned as "foul" for the sake of future reward. It had struck a bargain with the forces of darkness, in return for which it would secure what the earlier ages could only dream of – a world beyond the toil and trouble, violence and injustice of life as it actually is."[14] It is not therefore that economics is just amoral, as Krugman would have it, it is

---

13 See, John Gowdy, 1998. "Back to the Future and Forward to the Past" in Limited Wants, Unlimited Means. Edited by John Gowdy, Washington, D. C.: Island Press, pp. xv–xxix.

14 See, Robert Skidelski and Edward Skidelski, 2012. How Much Is Enough? Money and the good life. New York: Other Press, p. 43. Their book, Skidelskis note, "is an argument against insatiability, against that psychological disposition that prevents us, as individuals and as societies, from Saying "enough is enough." It is directed at economic insatiability, the desire for more and more money [...] in rich and poor societies alike, insatiability can be seen whenever the opulence of the very rich runs wildly ahead of the means of existence of the many." The objective of the book is the reform of capitalism through policy changes as they argue: "Capitalism is a two-edged sword. On the one hand, it has made possible vast improvements in material conditions. On the other, it has exalted some of the most

that economics became immoral by design through a Faustian bargain that "paved the way to hell" as the famous saying has it. The book penned by Robert Skidelsky and his son Edward is a frontal assault on the second part of economics' conception of "limited resources and unlimited wants," and its slogan that wants are given, arguing that "[e]conomics – we generalize, but not grossly – conscientiously abstains from passing judgements on wants." And it is argued that the first element of clarity of thought to be sacrificed "is the distinction between needs and wants. Needs, on the classical conception, are objective; they refer to requirements of life or the good life. Wants, by contrast, are a psychological phenomenon; they are "in the mind" of the wanter. Needs and wants are independent of one another. The child needs, but does not want, his medicine; the bibliophile wants, but does not need, a first edition of Blake. A need establishes a moral claim to x, whereas merely wanting x does not. Beggars talk about their needs, never about their wants."

On Skidelskis' account, the distinction between needs and wants was not the only pre-modern concept that was discarded by economics. They add three other concepts that were discarded as well: distinction between necessities and luxuries; the concept of "enoughness"; and distinction between use-value and exchange-value. The first distinguishes between what is necessary for human life, which establishes a claim, and what are wanted but not needed (they "are an optional and possibly corrupting extra"). As to the second, "enough" for modern economists means "enough to satisfy wants." This implies that "there can be no such a thing as wanting more than enough. Avarice as a vice disappears from view." The third refers to the disappearance of "the central concept of use-value." In pre-modern thought use-value (based on Aristotle) meant the "particular contribution" of an object to life. Modern economics considers transformation of use value (defined as utility in consumption) into exchange value (defined as utility in exchange) "as only a technical problem of determining at what point consumption goods will be exchanged rather than used." Since the two are considered as two sides of the same coin, utility, gone is the metaphysical problem (which began with Aristotle) of the relation between the two and how two commodities that contribute to human life in different ways could be reduced to a common denominator: money. Skidelskis argue that "[u]nderstood in its original sense, a real usefulness rather than mere utility in consumption, use-value can no more be transformed into exchange value than color into length."[15]

To a large extent, Skidelskis views converge to the argument by other economists committed to capitalism, who advocate the need to reverse the course of "de-moralization" of economics. They suggest ways and means of policy reforms – including sharing, basic income, reducing the force of consumerism and insatiability, reducing the

---

reviled human characteristics, such as greed, envy and avarice. Our call is to chain up the monster again by recalling what the greatest thinkers of all times and all civilizations have meant by the "good life" and suggesting changes in current policy to help us achieve it." (page 3).

15 Ibid, pp. 88–91.

power of advertising, rethinking international relations within the context of reforms – that would make possible attainment of the "good life" for many rather than for the few. These views, as well as those suggested by others discussed earlier, modify rather than replace the current dominant paradigm of economics by "re-moralizing" it. There are other systems of thought where morality is not something that has to be introduced into the working of economic paradigm. Assuming economics as a discipline that deals with resource allocation, production, exchange, distribution and redistribution, there are systems of thoughts (including those based on religion) that have radically different perspectives on how societies could organize an economy in which morality is embedded, inherently integrated and organically placed at the core of its dynamic structure. Among these systems of thought is the Islamic vision where "moral universe shares a great deal with other great spiritual traditions of mankind". It has a clear vision of an economy and "has something distinctive to offer to the resolution of the myriad problems that face humanity, both in the rich and in the developing world: from poverty eradication, income inequalities, good governance in the poor countries to the problems that affect the rich world of overconsumption, alienation, and social fragmentation."[16]

The Islamic vision offers a perspective that "affirms the primacy of the moral vision that must form the basis of humankind's economic relations and transactions." It is based on a "model of human being whose economic actions are guided by both inspiration and the pursuit of virtues, and not only self-interest. And these actions take place in a framework where both the Divine and the normative human archetype are ever present." Its main source of guidance, the Qur'an, confirms the spiritually empowered human ability of attaining the "good life", a life in a "felicitous state of inner and outer plenitude if people cultivate an ethic of faith-in-action and the commitment that would imply in terms of pursuit of the virtues, not least the ideal of a Just Society."[17]

While the organizing principles of an economy and the rules governing the behavior of participants are provided in the Qur'an, emergence of a discipline whose epistemological mission would be to study, understand, explain and formalize the vision in a blueprint for communication to the wider Muslim world and others has been painfully slow. Allawi (2017) suggests two reasons: "The first is that its original exponents were untutored in the ways of the modern world and approached the problem mainly through a jurisprudential construct, with little regard for the changed circumstances of the world. The second is that they began to address these issues well after the supremacy of the Western economic model became established."[18]

16 See, Ali Allawi, 2010. "Foreword" in Abbas Mirakhor and Hossein Askari, Islam and The Path to Human and Economic Development. New York: Palgrave Macmillan, pp. ix–xii.

17 Ibid, p. xi.

18 See, Ali Allawi, 2017. "Foreword" in Abbas Mirakhor and Hossein Askari, Ideal Islamic Economy: An Introduction. New York: Palgrave Macmillan, P. ix.

The absence of an alternative blueprint of how to organize the economy according to the teachings of the belief system – whose rituals were practiced daily but not the rules that tells them how to behave in contemporary economy – created a vacuum providing fertile ground for the entry, growth and entrenchment of the powerful ruling ideology of liberal capitalism. The vehicle of globalization driven by economists and policy makers trained in economics and social sciences as taught in western universities had significant impact in Muslim societies. Importantly, autocratic and centralized systems in these countries began to dismantle as a result of which, "[h]uge fortunes were made either from abuse of licensing power or by the knocked-down purchases of state assets and land by well-connected individuals. Privatization, deregulation, and the licensing of monopolies, all played their part in the shift of economic power from a poorly managed and frequently corrupt state sector to a better managed but predatory form of liberal capitalism. The whole process was applauded by the "international community" as signalling the entry of the Islamic world into the new era of globalization and free markets. Of course, this process further distanced the Muslim world from the possibility of regenerating the bases of an Islamic economic order."[19]

Allawi, who served as the Minister of Defense and the Minister of Finance in post-war Iraq, argues that "the ethos of globalization, as it is formulated in the language of individual economic rights and freedom, is antithetical to the fundamental features of an Islamic economic and social order . . . the ideas of duty, charity, solidarity, and self-sufficiency do not sit well with the premise that it is only through cultivating and channelling selfishness and greed that economic activity can be optimized or maximized. The assumption is made that man by nature is acquisitive and predatory, and that the functions of a well-ordered economy are to direct these energies and drive into a socially productive direction. This of course does not square well with the idea that humans can perfect – or at least aspire to perfect – their qualities and that a moral imperative should underlie human action. Islam does not deny the follies and greed of human beings, but these must always be tempered by a constant questioning of the purposes of human action. Wealth-creation is a by-product of moral action and not the purpose of work."[20] However, an Islamic socio-economic "order can only be reborn if certain fundamental reforms – in fact, fundamental paradigm shifts-are undertaken" asserts Allawi, and he is not optimistic on that score because "the axes of the modern economy are so distant from the moral economy of Islam[21] that nothing

19 Ali Allawi, 2017, Ibid, p. x. See also his book: Ali Allawi, 2010. The Crisis of the Islamic Civilization. New Haven: Yale University Press.

20 Ibid, p. ix–x.

21 It is worth noting that in the context of this volume, and perhaps from the point of view of Allawi as well, the concept of "moral economy" in "the moral economy of Islam" is far more comprehensive, deeper and broader (see A. Mirakhor and H. Askari, 2017. Ideal Islamic Economy. New York: Palgrave MacMillan) than its use in western scholarship, first popularized by anthropologists, see, for example,

short of a spectacular break would suffice to bring the pendulum back into some form of equilibrium."[22]

Allawi argues that the "main features of an Islamic economy have been eroding for several centuries so that most are merely religious vestiges of a long-forgotten past [...] By the time of the 1970s, the elements of an Islamic economy were simply theoretical constructs that may have featured in the education of seminarians – but had no place in the modern economy."[23] Moreover, Allawi notes that the "weakening in the average Muslim's commitment to the idea of the moral imperative as the main driver of economic dealings is mirrored by the loss of charitable giving that lies at the heart of Islamic redistributive justice. It has become almost common place to bemoan the unwillingness of the wealthy in Muslim lands to share their wealth through charitable acts and endowment of foundations. The pages of the world's weeklies, glossies and websites are crammed with the faces of the new plutocracy of the Muslim world, most connected in one way or another to the explosion in oil wealth and the massive transfer of the world's savings to the oil producing countries [...] a great deal of it has cascaded down to various princes and potentates and the cronies and fixers who feed on the public trough. These are the new Muslim super wealthy class [...] notorious for their private indulgences and excesses, and their lack of any public spiritedness. There are no major research foundations, universities, hospitals or educational trusts that are funded by large charitable donations ... service-based charitable work is an essential element of Islamic economy, weaving, as it were, religious obligations with a strong sense of social justice and moral responsibility."[24]

Allawi suggests that bringing the Pendulum back requires "a process that could, over the period of time, engender the necessary change in perspectives and values that ultimately could shift the consciousness of Muslims towards finding a new identity in the authentic roots of their civilization. This requires two fundamental shifts in their cognition. The first is part of the worldwide phenomenon of questioning and challenging the conventional verities that have underpinned the legitimation of late capitalism. This will bracket Muslims with the growing global band of dissenters who call out the monstrous side effects of the dominant economic culture, even as it seems to be an unstoppable machine that produces a never-ending cornucopia

E. P. Thompson, 1971, "The Moral Economy of the English Crowd in the 18th Century." Past & Present, Vol. 50, pp. 76–136; James C, Scott, 1976. The Moral Economy of the Peasant. Princeton: Princeton University Press; see also, Norbert Gotz, 2015. "Moral economy: Its conceptual history and analytic prospects." Journal of Global Ethics, Vol 11, pp. 147–162.

22 See Allawi, 2017, p. x.

23 Note, in this context, the popularity of the content of the concept of Maqasid al-Shari'ah, relic of intellectual efforts of religious intellectuals of nearly a millennium ago without deep or strong root in the Qur'an, indicating the poverty of the present intellectual efforts at making the Qur'an's vision of economy accessible to humanity.

24 See Allawi, 2017, pp.xi–xii.

of goods and services."[25] The second shift proposed by Allawi is a "decisive leap in the cognitive framework of contemporary Muslims that leads them to redefine the meaning and purpose of economic transactions." This shift, Allawi argues, must begin "with the Qur'an, the bedrock of a Muslim's engagement with life and the hereafter." The Qur'an is the supreme moral arbiter for the economic conduct of Muslims" and which defines an order "that in effect replaces 'economics' with *muamalat* – or legitimate transactions and engagements between individuals, groups, institutions and states that are morally charged and bounded by rules that are transcendental in their origin and yet uniquely pertinent to the human condition."

Allawi, however, does not underestimate the challenge and recognizes it as "a long, Herculean process whereby Muslims take stock of their condition and begin to rebuild the scaffolding of a new world view from the wreckage of the past centuries; and fashion a way of escaping from the clutches of an amoral, hegemonic, economic engine. If Muslims prevail in this process, they can then rightly act as a guide and beacon to the rest of humanity. Not only would they have propounded a different way of organizing the world's economy, they actually would have made it work and succeed. But for that to happen they would need to shed centuries of accretions to their understanding of the world. They would have to re-interpret terms such as markets, exchanges, risk, money, accumulation, distribution, consumption, institutions and a myriad of others that define modern homo-economicus."[26]

The present volume is a unique collection of analytical studies that attempt to examine some of the difficult challenges to conventional wisdom described above, and offer new perspectives from Islamic finance and economics. The overall conviction is that the Qur'an contains a vision of an economy and prescribes rules (institutions) that govern allocation, production, exchange, distribution and redistribution in such an economy. The mission of the discipline of Islamic economics is, in the first instance, to extract, describe, interpret (that is an economic hermeneutic) and present this vision in a form understandable in communication of the "economic universe of discourse." This constitutes the first function of Islamic economics. Once this is achieved, Islamic economics has to engage in the presentation of an analytic framework for policy – based on the Qur'an's vision of the ideal economy – which, once implemented, allows the economy of Muslim countries to converge, asymptotically, to the ideal vision contained in the Qur'an and operationalized, to a significant extent, by the Messenger (sawa) in Medinah.[27]

---

25 This would require Muslim economists engaging with what Idris and Mirakhor call the "economic universe of discourse" (see the introductory chapter in this handbook) rather than attempting and advocating exclusivity and isolation as some advocate.

26 Allawi, 2017, pp. xiii–xv.

27 For a preliminary presentation of the vision of the Qur'an for economy, see Mirakhor and Askari, 2017. Ideal Islamic Economy. New York: Palgrave Macmillan.

The handbook sheds light on various issues in Islamic economics and finance from an analytical perspective that can serve better the evidence-based policy-making process, as well as the regulatory, investment and risk-management purposes. These studies are based on the same logical, statistical and econometric methods that many readers in conventional finance and economic analysis may also be familiar with. Arguably, the analytical framework can be invariably used in conventional as well as Islamic economics and finance as the logical foundations of these disciplines are equally amenable to analytical methods and scientific inquiry. The Handbook offers a blend of analytical evidence and insights on the internal mechanisms and modus operandi of an Islamic financial and economic system from econophysics to game theory, from Markov-regime switching models to the generalized method of moments, from event studies to dynamic panel analysis, and from data envelopment analysis to agent-based modelling, *inter alia*.

The structure of the handbook is reflective of the strong potential of Islamic finance and economics to redefine and reshape different aspects of economic life and financial decisions. The introductory part discusses the nature and methodological aspects of Islamic economics, including its logical character, coherence, and consilience, as well as a game-theoretic approach to the analysis of economic behavior. Part II examines the impact of economic uncertainty, and the role of interest rates, as well as the formulation of macroeconomic policies. Part III considers the statistical microeconomic models of asset prices from the perspectives of Islamic finance, and provides some empirical evidence on the risk and return relationship for equity portfolios. Part IV presents some analytical evidence on the role of risk-sharing finance as opposed to conventional finance based on risk-transfer mechanism, and the significance of financial consumer protection. Part V examines the properties of Islamic financial institutions and the stability of the Islamic financial system. Part VI discusses income inequality and the role of risk-shairing finance and asset-based redistribution. Finally, Part VII provides evidence on the relation between Islamic finance economic growth and human development.

In Part I, Hamid and Mirakhor discuss, in the opening chapter, the logical character and coherence of Islamic economics, and examine Islam's vision of the economy and economics, as well as the logical incoherence in mentality that retards intellectual discourse and saps the energies needed for the advancement of Islamic economics. The authors argue that Islamic economics is a concrete, systematic framework and methodology, based on certain philosophical considerations, for organizing and developing economics institutions. The framework is distinctive and unique vis-à-vis secular European ideologies, communicable to mainstream economists, and yields empirically testable propositions.

The principal objective is to extend the current consensus on Islamic economics by placing it in the context of a more general system of science, which is consistent with the Islamic and Prophetic sources. The authors argue that it would be difficult to avoid the ultimately non-Islamic dualism of fideism and scientism in the absence of an integrated approach to Islamic economics. The unique system of Islamic economics integrates the *economic* with the *intrinsic* values in a unified science of development and self-transcendence. In this regard, Hamid and Mirakhor attempt to answer some profound questions such as how and to what degree, if at all, a general question of contemporary Western economic theory can be transformed into one of Islamic Economics. Also, the question arises as to how and to what degree, if at all, a general question of Islamic Economics can be transformed into one of contemporary Western economic theory. The authors ask, for example, whether Islamic Economics can address non-trivial and important questions, ignored by the dominant paradigm of economics, including the purpose of wealth, and whether analytically and axiomatically neutral methods of standard economics can assist Islamic economics to arrive at its own systematic and coherent paradigm for analysis and policy making, and to achieve the life of security, peace and economic sufficiency that Islam promises humanity. The main thesis of this opening chapter is that the importance and relevance of Islamic Economics lies, in large measure, in the struggle to determine and articulate a type of scientific system that integrates the categories of human, economic, as well as moral, self-transcending experience into an (objective-logical) intricate and coherent whole.

In Chapter 2, Choudhury and Taifur explain that the current socio-scientific though and applications of the so-called modernity in intellectualism are erroneous in an Islamic epistemological sense. The authors present an analytical alternative in the light of consilience, meaning unity of knowledge from the monotheistic (*tawhid*) methodological worldview. It is also argued that the modern socio-scientific order rests on the forced displacement of religion from the domain of meta-science as a rationalistic choice. Yet it is not the way to understand the true reality for the future of the meta-scientific world-system, and its particularities arising from the general theory of unity in diversity of the good things of life. According to Choudhury and Taifur, the meaning of true reality is that of the primal ontological nature of reasoning in the framework of a unified worldview that explains the nature of 'everything'. Such a religio-scientific approach to meta-science comprises the methodological worldview of *tawhid* in the generality and particularities of world-systems. It is as a particular case of the world-system that economics assumes a heterodox academic perspective in the methodological study of Islamic economics.

The authors argue that the uniqueness and universality of the *tawhidi* methodological worldview in meta-science, characterized by the specificity of Islamic economics, economics, can be formalized by consilience, which reflects the organic unity of knowledge in the monotheistic sense. The unity of knowledge at work in a theory of meta-science of inter-causality between multivariates to establish a wellbeing criterion, paves the way for the coterminous theory of *tawhidi* worldview in everything. A theological and metaphysical approach to the study of Tawhid is supplanted by the phenomenological methodology derived from the Qur'anic foundation of the monotheistic worldview of the organic unity of knowledge as a symbiotic pairing in everything. No theocratic inhibition thereby exists in the derivation, formalism, and application of consilience as unity of knowledge derived from the *tawhidi* primal ontological origin of the Qur'an. The order of consilience is mapped onto the mind and matter unison of the world-system of unity of knowledge by *Sunnah*. The chapter concludes with a generalized model of the emerging meta-science on consilience for religion and science and beyond in regards to the episteme of unity of knowledge. This generalized model encompasses the abstraction and the applied domains in their continuity by recursion across the knowledge, space, and time dimensions. Hence, the end of the pursuit of generalized system is based on the mathematical continuity, by meta-scientific discursive recursion, of the multi-dimensional evolutionary learning processes of ontology, epistemology, and phenomenology.

In Chapter 3, Al-Suwailem provides some reflections on the principal properties of economics, as a branch of knowledge, that serves a better future, and argues that a coherent framework to reform the mainstream economics is yet to emerge, despite the ongoing debates on the evident failures and shortcomings of mainstream economics. Al-Suwailem also outlines a framework for a new paradigm in economics, and explains how it aligns with universal moral principles. It is argued first that the internal inconsistency of economic theory, together with its failures to predict and explain major economic events, cast serious doubts over its status as a science. Given the basic criteria for science, it is concluded that economics lacks the most fundamental criteria of science, namely the conservation principles that govern all natural phenomena. Al-Suwailem indicates that the variables in economics, which are thought to be conserved, are model-dependent and lack the power of empirical evidence. It is argued that concrete examples from economics, such as Pareto optimality, the law of markets, money, bubbles and Ponzi games, show that economic conservation laws are not applied in economics.

The chapter concludes that there is a pressing need to formulate core principles of economics within a scientific framework in order for economics to serve a better future. This framework has proved to be exceptionally valuable in the progress of science over the last four centuries. Economics can also adopt the same principles of science including the core moral values that guide economic behavior. Since these core moral values, like the Golden Rule, prudence, and modesty are shared across most faiths and cultures, they are universal in nature.

In Chapter 4, Mohamed, Mirakhor, and Erbaş analyze the comparative behaviors of Muslims and non-Muslims by employing selected behavioral and experimental games to examine the level of adherence to the rules of behavior in the society. There is an increasing interest in behavioral economics and behavioral finance, which hold the potential of providing plausible explanations to the question of how emotions affect markets but also how to enhance constructive behavioral norms. The focus in behavioral finance is made on the impact of emotions, framing bias, heuristics and market forces on investment decisions, firm behavior, market regulation, and education policy. The experimental games are based one the premise that Islamic economy is a rules-based system and the compliance to such rules of behavior does not only improve economic performance and social welfare but helps also individuals in achieving higher potentials. Indeed, the adherence to a rules-based system has the potential of reducing cognitive and psychological biases. The selected set of seven rules (Capstone Rule, Cooperation, Contract, Property Rights, Reciprocity, Golden Rule and Trust) can also be used to examine market failures such as those related to negative externalities from narrow decision-making, and can be useful also in the design of viable solutions based on ethical, social and legal considerations

The game-theoretic experiments are carried out on test subjects from diverse backgrounds, depending on age, ducation, profession and income levels in Malaysia and Singapore. The experimental results suggest that religious identity is associated with Muslims outperforming or underperforming non-Muslims in some, but not all, of the seven rules-based experiments. The priming on Muslims is conducive to increased adherence to the Rule of Contract and Golden Rule against unprimed Muslim counterparts, who tend to perform better in tests on Property Rights and Trust. However, given the similar performance of primed and unprimed Muslim segments, there is no evidence that Islamic identity affects the adherence to Capstone Rule, Cooperation and Reciprocity.

In Part II, the focus is placed on particular aspects of the Islamic economic system that reflect the impact of economic uncertainty, the implications of interest rates, and the objectives of macroeconomic policies. In Chapter 5, Maghrebi examines the relation between interest rates, unconventional monetary policies and volatility expectations in financial markets. Given the near-zero interest rates and abstinence from communication around policy meetings under the self-imposed purdah rules, it is expected that forward guidance may reduce market expectations of excessive volatility stemming from policy uncertainty. Based on the event-study methodology, the empirical evidence from unconventional monetary policies by the Bank of Japan, including zero-interest policies and quantitative easing programs, indicates that forward guidance has, indeed, some moderating effects on volatility expectations. It is state-contingent rather than open-ended forward guidance that can be more effective in reinforcing the expectations channels of monetary policy transmission and feedback from financial markets. In the absence of forward guidance, markets tend to be associated with higher levels of expected volatility and significant forecast errors around policy meetings.

During periods of financial instability, market participants are more likely to seek guidance, not so much from past information, as from forward-looking monetary policy and forward-looking volatility indices. Part of the problem associated with the limited room for maneuver in monetary policy to address the post-crisis econmic recessions stems from policy uncertainty and the anchoring of the entire financial system on interest rates. These interest rates are pre-determined rates of return that are independent of the states of nature of the real economy. Thus, in the absence of risk sharing and equity financing, the financial system is inherently biased toward the accumulation of debt, and the formation of asset bubbles leads inevitably to the perpetuation of financial crises. From the perspective of Islamic finance and economics, monetary policies based on interest rates are not permissible, regardless of the sign and magnitude of interest rates. The analytical evidence that policy uncertainty affects the formation of volatility expectations has an important bearing on our understanding of the essence of interest rates and monetary policies. Perhaps, no amount of forward guidance can eliminate the excessive amount of policy uncertainty stemming from the settting and resetting of interest rates, which can be conducive to unwarranted price fluctuations in financial assets, and shifting risk premia in the real economy.

In Chapter 6, Mahmud, Yamaguchi, and Yülek examine how macroeconomics works given given the complexities of the financial system. The analysis is based on the stock-flow consistent modelling based on Accounting System Dynamics (ASD), which can capture some of the complex dynamics of money creation in the financial system. In the Fractional Reserve Banking and Intermediation of Loanable Funds theories, the causality runs from fiat money to bank-induced money creation. In the endogenous view of money represented by the Financing-through-Money Creation, causality is reversed. The ASD approach can incorporate the complexities of money creation into macroeconomic modeling and assess the outcomes of different models of monetary creation and financial intermediation. The chapter reviews the shortcomings of Standard Macroeconomic Model (SMM) and propose ASD as an alternative approach to macroeconomic modelling. The notion of 'declining velocity of money' had severe implications for the stability of money-price linkage, which is central to the SMM approach. Other difficulties and anomalies include the protracted economic recession following the financial crisis, the inefficacy of traditional monetary responses and the failure of DSGE models in foreseeing the crisis.

It is argued that the stock-flow consistent ASD model can capture and better explain the inner workings of the real economy. The ASD allows for the simulation and assessment of the outcomes of money creation by banks. The findings suggest that fractional reserve banking can inherently cause monetary instability even when the base money, or monetary policy, is stable. Indeed, under the fractional reserve banking system, central banks simply cannot entirely control money stock. This can partially explain why (i) the quantitative easing policies recently introduced in Japan, U.S.A. and E.U. countries have all failed; and (ii) why debt is continuously mounting in these countries. The main conclusion is that these repeated failures are policy-proof, and are due to the design of the debt money system itself, which suggests that they can only be remedied by a re-design of the macroeconomic and financial system. It is argued that the public money system has the potential to provide a promising solution to the problems caused by the debt-based financial system. The main tenets of Islamic finance, including the notion of risk-sharing and prohibition of interest, are fully consistent with the principles of banking and financial practices under the public money system.

In Chapter 7, Othman argues that growth-enhancing policies pursued with the objective of achieving sustainable economic development have to focus more on the real sector of the economy rather than the financial sector. The recurrence of debt crises continues to generate serious arguments about the fundamentally instability of conventional financial systems and the effectiveness of macroeconomic policies. The study focuses on the inherent constraints and limits of standard macroeconomic policies, and the potential merits of alternative fiscal and monetary policies based on risk-sharing finance.

The chapter introduces some proposals for fiscal reform including Equity Participation Shares (EPS), which represent a risk-sharing structure capable of replacing government debt in the financing of fiscal deficit and development expenditures. The EPS instruments are asset-backed by government development projects, with a rate of return that is function of the rate of return in the real sector. The EPS issuance allows for a broader public participation in economic activities, and sharing of returns in the real economy. The simulation results based on the Malaysian economy indicate that EPS can indeed constitute a good substitute for interest-bearing government bonds, thereby gradually reducing the debt service. The interest payments, and hence government spending, can be reduced to the extent of the diminishing amounts of borrowing. Since the return on EPS-investment vehicles depends on the return on government portfolio of development projects, no costs accrue to the government out of EPS issuances. The analytical evidence suggests that EPS schemes can, indeed, promote financial inclusion as more equitable opportunities to access the wealth of the nation are provided to all segments of the society regardless of wealth and income levels. The positive distribution of income to participating stakeholders would, in turn reduce, the oligopolistic nature of rent seekers and riskless financial intermediation.

Part III presents some analytical studies in the emerging area of statistical microeconomics of asset prices and equity investment portfolios. In Chapter 8, Baaquie and Maghrebi provide a synthesis of theoretical models of the behavior of asset prices based on the formalism of statistical physics. The statistical theory of commodity prices developed in previous studies is formulated based on the microeconomic action functional. The empirical evidence from single and multiple spot prices lends strong support to the principal assumptions of the statistical formulation. Futures prices are also modelled in the context of a two-dimensional statistical field and a non-linear Lagrangian is postulated. The chapter argues that the demand and supply functions should not be defined by market forces driven by consumer sovereignty, short sales, margin trading, and scarcity of resources, but by genuine factors related to resource abundance, rational constraints on consumer behavior and asset-redistribution based on risk-sharing.

Some perspectives from Islamic finance and economics are also considered in the discussion of the statistical microeconomic modelling of asset prices. In particular, the focus is made on the role of risk-sharing in shaping the microeconomic action functional. Risk-sharing is regarded as the defining principle of Islamic finance, and future research may shed some light on its role within the unifying system and mechanisms underlying the demand and supply of securities, asset pricing, and exchange relations in the economy. Further analytical research may shed light on an integrated framework for asset pricing that unifies production, exchange and consumption, and supersedes the separate and independent modelling of supply and demand. Statistical microeconomics may provide a better understanding of the dynamics of asset prices and market forces based on an unconventional set of economic principles reflecting resources abundance, rational constraints on consumer behavior, and asset redistribution based on risk-sharing.

In Chapter 9, Sadr and Gholami argue that monitoring strategy may be part of the reasons for the insignificant share of participation from Shariah-compliant products in the balance-sheet of many Islamic banks. The empirical literature suggests that effective monitory by banks can mitigate the risks associated with profit-loss sharing arrangements and raise the bank risk-adjusted returns. Under the assumptions of efficient markets and complete information, equilibrium returns are commensurate to systematic risk. The violation of these assumptions may lead to arbitrage opportunities where assets are priced independent of the degree of risk undertaken. The benefits of risk diversification can be inhibited by the absence of timely and accurate information. Therefore, information gathering plays an essential role in investment decisions, portfolio rebalancing and proper functioning of markets in exchange economies.

The regression analysis based on pooled data on risk-sharing arrangements undertaken by the Agricultural Bank of Iran allows for tests of the hypothesis that the monitoring effects on the efficient portfolio allocation of portfolio assets are significant. The evidence indicates that the benefits that can potentially accrue from the implemention of monitoring policy are likely to exceed the incurred costs. Thus, there are strong incentives for Islamic banks to adopt monitoring policies, as information is crucial for investment analysis, portfolio rebalancing, and a better understanding of the return-generating process.

In Chapter 10, Raza, L'Huillier and Ashraf examine the empirical issue of whether the choice of weighting strategy affects the performance of Shariah-compliant equity portfolios under different market conditions. It is argued that Shariah-compliant investment guidelines, albeit explicit on the selection screens of stocks, are rather silent on the weighting methods used in the construction of Shariah-compliant equity portfolios. The market capitalization-weighted strategy and smart-beta strategies, which represent fundamental value-weighted, equal-weighted, and low-risk weighted strategies, exhibit different risk and return characteristics that cannot be ignored. Markov-regime switching models are used to capture nonlinearities in the behaviour of returns on a sample of active constituent firms from S&P 500 index, with shifts between two market regimes –high regimes for bullish markets and low regimes for bearish markets.

The empirical evidence suggests that shifts between market regimes have significant implications for Shariah-compliant equity portfolios, with asymmetric effects on the performance of market-capitalization and smart-beta portfolios. Whereas market-capitalization and fundamental value-weighted strategies perform better under bullish and less volatile markets, low-risk strategies can be useful for risk-hedging purposes with respect to bearish and more volatile periods. Thus, the existence of different regimes governing the behavior of economic and financial variables in the realm of Islamic finance is not negligible. The large family of regime-switching models can be useful in gaining a better understanding the dynamics of Islamic capital markets, and their dependence on latent states of the real economy. The econometric modelling of equity returns allows for rational rebalancing of Shariah-compliant portfolios depending on prevailing market regimes, and for rational regulation based on on a proper understanding of the complex market dynamics, and risk-hedging strategies.

In Chapter 11, Hamzah reviews the development of various structures of *sukuk* or so-called Islamic bonds, and discusses the implications of *sukuk* allocation for portfolio risks. While *sukuk* are usually regarded as Shariah-compliant alternatives to debt instruments, these particular modes of financing have nonetheless been the subject of serious criticism and suspicion about their reliance over the risk-transfer mechanism and resemblance to conventional bonds. The modelling of optimal *sukuk* portfolio is based on the mean-variance analysis, which is useful in understanding the trade-off between risk and return. The Chebyshev theorem is applied to determine the probability of default for the efficient sukuk portfolios. The notion of default is based on the premise that *sukuk* constitute a variant of fixed-income securities. The analytical evidence suggests that the probability of default increases monotonically as the proportion of debt-like *sukuk* increases and that of equity-based *sukuk* decreases.

It is noted that in Islamic finance, pre-determined rates of return are substituted by *ex-post* and observed rates of return on investment. Thus, the notion of risk-free asset with pre-determined payoffs is not permissible. But given the increasing probability of default for portfolios with higher proportions of debt-like *sukuk*, even the recourse to *sukuk* investment in pursuit of risk-free rates of return is shown to be not without risk. These analytical findings reinforce the notion that Islamic finance should be driven by instruments based on the principle of risk-sharing rather than the widespread practice of merely mimicking conventional bonds. The future development of *sukuk*, and indeed of the entire financial system, rests on a clear distinction between risk-transfer and risk-sharing, which is essential to ensure financial stability.

In Chapter 12, Sadr demonstrates that the set of *Shariah*-compliant instruments used to finance private and social enterprises are complementary and serve both the interests of investors and the welfare of unprivileged groups. It is shown that the implementation of *Shariah* rules would lead to the restructuring of the economic system in ways that integrate the financial and real sectors, and flows of income generated in the former are intrinsically linked to real assets in the latter. Thus, speculative activities are reduced, with both sectors growing in tandem ensuring thereby a stable flow of national income.

The analytical tests are based on a system of simultaneous equations, reflecting investment, capital accumulation and production functions. The simulation results, which are based on financial and economic time-series obtained from the Central Bank of Iran, the Statistical Center of Iran, and the Management and Planning Organization, suggest that the elimination of interest from the financial system is conducive to a significant value-added for the agricultural sector. Thus, a consistent and articulated transition from a *ribawi* to interest-free financial system can contribute significantly to sustainable growth in various sectors of the real economy.

Part IV considers various aspects of risk-sharing finance including asset-renting and crowdfunding, as well as financial consumer production. In Chapter 13, Beck, Iqbal, and Mutlu examine the profit-loss sharing, or risk-sharing, aspect of Islamic banking, and address the question of whether a more prominent role for Islamic banks is associated with higher intertemporal risk-sharing and consumption smoothing. The study relates the importance of Islamic banks to the degree of consumption smoothing in an economy by regressing changes in consumption on changes in income, and uses the consumption-smoothing parameter as a proxy for risk-sharing in a country. An attempt is made to test the proposition that Islamic banks operating on profit-and-loss sharing financial agreements rather than debt contracts can facilitate better intertemporal risk-sharing. Based on Penn World Tables, and the Bankscope and IBIS databases, as well as different balance-sheet measures of bank valuation, there is no clear evidence of significant relationship between intertemporal risk-sharing and the market share of Islamic banks. However, a closer examination of the composition of financing contracts by Islamic banks reveals that *mudarabah* investment accounts on the liabilities side of balance sheets have a stronger relationship with intertemporal risk-sharing.

It may not be surprising, indeed, that the contribution of Islamic banks to risk-sharing remains statistically, if not economically, insignificant. Under the current state of affairs, it is rather difficult for Islamic banks to contribute toward risk-sharing in a more meaningful manner, given the tendency to replicate conventional fixed-income financial products, and to engage in risk-transfer activities. The prevailing legal and regulatory environment is not supportive of risk-sharing finance either. Consumption smoothing is oftern understood in terms of moderating fluctuations in income with interest-bearing debt. It should be rather regarded as the natural result of differentiated governance structures that allow for broader and participatory asset holding and prosperity sharing. The governance structures can promote x-efficiency, system stability, employment and income, and can tangentially smooths consumption as well. Thus, the emphasis should be placed on the development of financing modes and promotion of regulatory measures that are more consistent with the principles of risk-sharing.

In Chapter 14, Akın and Iqbal examine the questions of whether and how different modes of financing have asymmetric effects on SMEs access to finance, and to what extent the access can affect firms in terms of performance and growth. Debt financing, or money renting, requires collateral and shifts financial risks to borrowers, creating serious constraints for SMEs. In contrast, asset renting, or leasing leading to ownership, is associated with lower collateral requirements, and it is also founded upon the concept of risk sharing. The empirical tests are based on a group of SMEs in member countries of the Organisation of Islamic Cooperation (OIC), with sample observations obtained from the World Bank Enterprise Survey database.

It appears that access to finance is more acute problem for SMEs in OIC member countries compared to their peers in the rest of the world. As financial services in these countries are dominated by the banking sector, the collateral and conditions attached to loan contracts constitute the main impediments to finance. The natural result is that many SMEs in the region remain credit-constrained, with growth potential diminished in line with limited access to finance, lower production and constrained growth strategies. Also, the availability of collateral is found to have a positive impact on SMEs' performance, which implies that leasing, as well as, *ijarah* can constitute viable alternatives to bank lending. Thus, the empirical results suggest that the renting of assets is associated with stronger benefits over money renting. Indeed, bank lending is function not only of firm characteristics, but macroeconomic conditions, institutional quality, country risk, and information asymmetries as well. Given the fact that many OIC countries have low scores in this respect, bank lending tends to depend solely on the existence of collateral and credit history, or lack thereof. In effect, bank lending may not necessarily increase even if the conditions attached with collateral are relaxed. In light of these conditions and empirical evidence, it is important to switch toward leasing-based options, which can facilitate and increase the access by SMEs to finance in the OIC member states.

In Chapter 15, Torabi and Mirakhor explore the issue of how credibility and reputation can be used to address asymmetric information problems related to crowdfunding in web-based social networks. The analysis is based on the premise that faithful agents (characterized by *iman* and *'amal salih*) and perceived to be compliant with the rules of behavior prescribed by the *Qur'an* ad *Sunnah* (operationally defined as *taqwa*), can develop also a reputation for faithfulness toward contractual obligations, trustworthiness and credibility. A game-theoretic model of equity crowdfunding is designed to examine the effectiveness of rule-compliant behavior. The likelihood of success is a function of the credibility of game participants and their faithfulness to the terms and conditions of contracts, which can reduce the degree of moral hazard (*gharar*).

The objective is to demonstrate how equity-crowdfunding contracts can be designed to eliminate moral hazard and control the adverse effects of asymmetric information. It can be shown that the aggregate net surplus, or *barakah*, from games including participants characterized by faithfulness is higher than that from games with participants deprived of such fame and reputation. Thus, it is important to define a reputation index, or benchmark for fame, for users of social networks and crowdfunding platforms, in order to assess the impact of individual levels of reputation on the crowdfunding community of financiers and entrepreneurs. It is expected that participants are sensitive to individual actions and changes in reputation. Thus, good reputation does not only reduce information asymmetry, it can also be conducive to higher aggregate net surplus in equity-crowdfunding projects. Trust is, indeed, built on good fame and reputation, which facilitates risk-sharing attitudes in society, and permits the sharing of prosperity as well.

In Chapter 16, Alaabed, Masih, and Mirakhor examine financial consumer protection through supervision and market discipline channels in dual banking systems. The analysis is based on the estimation of two-step dynamic GMM models for an unbalanced panel of conventional banks and Islamic banks in OIC member states. The main assumption is that the principles and *modus operandi* of Islamic banking have implications for the distribution of risk in the society and the nature of relations between consumers and financial institutions. It can be argued that Islamic banking is axiomatically aligned with greater financial consumer protection given the *Shariah* requirement for financial transactions to be anchored in the real economy, and its restrictions on the sale of debt and short selling, which reduce the degree of leverage and systemic risk.

The authors contend that the present configuration of Islamic banking falls short of its axiomatic potential and fails to restrain excessive risk-taking, to the detriment of financial consumers. These findings shed light on the crucial importance of Islamic banking reforms and the general framework of regulation and supervision required to strengthen financial consumer protection. There are serious shortcomings in the fulfillment of requiremens for transparency and accountability. Not only do Islamic banks fall short of their axiomatic disciplinary obligations. It is also clear that external discipline, more broadly, fails to restrain excessive risk-taking. Worse still, banks continue to amass liabilities, increasing thereby financial leverage and systemic risk. There is an urgent need for reforms to correct distortions in the present regulatory and supervisory framework, which contribute to excessive risk-taking and risk-shifting. Policies ought to be reshaped to ensure that losses are borne by those, who stand also to benefit from risk enterprises and economic activities, rather than by depositors and taxpayers. There should be a shift in focus by policy-makers toward measures that alter attitudes toward risk in the banking industry and increase disciplinary incentives for depositors.

Part V examines some operational aspects of financial institutions and the stability of the Islamic financial system. In Chapter 17, Dolgun examines the important issue of liquidity risk management and assesses the challenges faced by Islamic banks in light of Basel III regulations. It is well recognized that an efficient management of liquidity risk is central to the sustainability of bank financing activities and protection against systemic risk. The empirical analysis focuses on the relation between liquid assets and financing assets of participation banks in Turkey. The results suggest that the introduction of new liquidity regulations may have a negative and significant effects of bank financing in the real sector. This can be explained, in part, by the requirement to retain higher cash-holding rations, and to invest in high-quality liquid assets, increasing thereby the marginal costs of funds and diminishing the capacity of bank financing.

The chapter concludes that the problems of liquidity management by Islamic banks should be addressed differently from their conventional counterparts. Indeed, the evidence from stress tests indicates that Islamic banks are associated with a shortage of liquidity and unstable funding. The Basel III liquidity coverage ratio (LCR) requirements may lead to serious implementation challenges for Islamic banks. If the LCR requirements are enforced upon Islamic banks, a disproportionately larger share of bank resources would be constrained to increased cash holding due to the chronic shortage and inadequate availability of high-quality liquid assets such as *Sukuk*. These regulatory requirements are condutive to difficulties in calibrating the balance-sheet structure to suit the practices of Islamic banks. Thus, the introduction of appropriate regulatory measures based on the principle of risk sharing, can improve the ability of Islamic banks to mitigate liquidity risk and channel more financing to the real sector. Beyond the reduction of costs associated with financial regulation and bank supervision, the potential benefits of risk-sharing finance extend also to greater stability of the entire financial system.

In Chapter 18, Rafi provides an antifragility framework for risk-sharing finance. The quantitative analysis of antifragility is based on non-Gaussian probability distributions and heuristics tests. This study provides an original framework for the quantitative evaluation of risk-sharing finance by extending and mapping antifragility onto Islamic finance. Mapping a deterministic model to antifragility remains an unexplored area, not only in the domain of risk-sharing finance, but in the general domain of antifragility as well. It is possible to expand the quantitative methods for interest-free models into antifragility under the modeling restrictions defined by Taleb (2012), which are significantly more restrictive than those imposed in other deterministic models.

This study demonstrates the antifragility of an Islamic financial system. This property is important in light of mounting evidence about the fragility of debt-based conventional financial systems, which can be, as shown by Taleb (2012), mathematically quantified following the seminal work of Mandelbrot (2004). The evidence about the antifragility of risk-sharing finance is also consistent with earlier studies by Mirakhor (1993) and Mirakhor and Askari (2014) about the stability of interest-free economic systems. The inherent ability of the system to swiftly revert back to the equilibrium state follliwng exogenous or endogenous shocks implies that recourse to unconventional monetary measures may be possible. Thus, interest-free financial systems are inherently more stable than conventional systems, which are characterized by perpetual boom-bust cycles and require external stabilization measures.

In Chapter 19, Iqbal assesses branch n-etwork efficiency using the Data Envelopment Analysis (DEA) methodology. The issue is important because of the need for Islamic banks to ensure that individual branches are adequately resourced, and that the aggregate resources, available at the level of branch network, are used efficiently. The DEA approach has the merit of overcoming some of the shorcomings of efficiency ratios, parametric and non-parametric methods, and balance scoreboards. It has the potential of identifying different levels of inefficiency, thereby enabling managers to focus on the significant factors that determine efficiency and profitability.

Based on a branch network of an Islamic bank in Malaysia, the empirical evidence suggests that it is optimal to improve scale efficiency rather than managerial efficiency. However, managers need to ensure that additional resources are not associated with decreasing managerial efficiency. Due to the indivisibility of some resources, the ultimate objective is not to eliminate inefficiency, but to ensure that branches operate within a predetermined and acceptable threshold of efficiency. It can be argued that as the Islamic banking sector continues to develop as an integral part of the financial system, efficiency and profitability can provide reliable measures of development and maturity. A reliable assessment of bank efficiency depends, however, on a better understanding of the role of risk sharing in Islamic banking, and the intrinsic differences in inputs and outputs between conventional and Islamic banks. Thus, risk sharing has an important bearing on the *modus operandi,* efficiency and profitability of Islamic banks.

In Chapter 20, Ali assesses the impact of non-intermediation activities on the levels of risk and profitability in Islamic and conventional banking. The increasingly intense competition among banks has naturally reduced the ability of some banks to raise funds, and lowered their market valuation. There are stronger incentives for banks to compensate for the reduction in profits with income derived from non-intermediation activities. Islamic banks are no exception to this global phenomenon. Although the core business of banks still lies in lending activities, an increasing number of banks in South Asia have shifted to investment banking and other related activities. It is this structural shift towards non-intermediation activities that warrants further analysis of the potential implications on bank performance. The Generalized Method of Moments is used to test for the significance of interest-free and fee-based income, and to assess the impact of non-traditional activities on the relative performance of Islamic banks *vis-à-vis* conventional banks.

The empirical evidence indicates that, on average, banks remain profitable over the sample period, but the degree of variability of profits remains high. There are also positive and significant effects of non-intermediation income on bank profitability. These empirical findings suggest that income from non-interest financing has the potential of improving the profitability of banks without affecting their risk levels. An increase in total assets or capitalization is conducive to lower bank risk. However, a greater exposure to credit-driven activities increases default risk. Thus, it is important for Islamic banking to focus on risk-sharing activities, which offer viable alternatives to interest-based financing. A banking sector driven by financing strategies and *modus operandi* based on risk sharing has also the potential of contributing toward a stable financial system and sustainable economic growth.

Part VI includes some analtytical studies of the relation between income inequality, risk-sharing and asset-based redistribution. In Chapter 21, Akın, Bacha, Mirakhor, and Iqbal address the important issue of asset-based redistribution, and contend that asset-based redistribution driven by risk-sharing finance can address some of the shortcomings of income-based redistribution. The chapter examines also recent findings in wealth inequality related to interest-based debt contracts and increasing inequalities, which constitute an inherent feature of modern market economies. Wealth inequality is at alarming levels in many developing and developed countries, as well as OIC member states, where budget deficits and infrastructure projects are typically financed with further debt obligations. The issue arises as to whether risk-sharing instruments can be useful for asset-based redistribution in addressing the chronic problems of income inequality.

A stock-flow consistent macroeconomic model is developed to gauge the significance of GDP-linked *sukuk* as an effective redistributive policy tool. The simulation results indicate that redistributional benefits accrue to the lower segments of the population without deteriorating key public accounts, including budget deficit and public debt. Thus, the analytical evidence lends support to the argument that, as risk-sharing instruments, GDP-linked *sukuk* can be implemented as an effective redistributive policy instrument. However, the model outputs also highlight the importance of using the GDP-linked sukuk as a redistribution mechanism, which should be supported and complemented by other policy tools, such as the effective use of *zakah* and secondary markets for *sukuk* trading.

In Chapter 22, Aaminou and Akın explore the nexus between debt and wealth inequality by employing an agent-based macroeconomic model. The objective of the theoretical modelling of this relationship is to understand the implications of high inequality on several macroeconomic variables, and in particular financial fragility. The literature about the potential effects of interest-based debt contracts on the formation of high income and wealth is, however, still scant. Previous studies suggest that interest-bearing debt governs the formation of rents, and that rents and capital gains are mainly responsible for worsening wealth inequality. This study presents, perhaps, the first agent-based model in related literature to examine the issue of whether the interest-rate mechanism constitutes a long-term driver of inequality.

The simulation results indicate that inequality increases as the financial economy dissociates itself from the real activity over time due to the prevalence of *ex ante* interest rates in the financing of economic activities. The analysis is extended with the substitution of interest rates with *ex post* rates of return to the real economy. The theoretical evidence suggests that rate substitution can have a significant impact on the level of inequality and real GDP growth. As the economic output is partly produced through interest-based financing of economic activities, it is natural that, in the absence of redistribution policies, an interest-based economy is conducive to higher inequality, and that redistribution policies become therefore a necessity. The simulation results suggest, however, that a remodelling of economic activities governed by risk-sharing finance has the potential of reducing wealth inequality without even resorting to redistribution policies. These long-term effects can be significant, indeed, as economic growth under risk-sharing finance is inherently balanced and, thus, sustainable.

In Chapter 23, Mokhtar explores two main empirical issues related to the nature of the relationship between GDP growth and wellbeing and the main determinants of the latter. The analytical approach is based on *Ibn Khaldun*'s model of development, which focuses on the circular relation between justice, rules of behavior, political authority, wealth and the social welfare. The estimation of pooled ordinary least-squares regression models a sample of developing economies including some Muslim countries suggests, indeed, that the wellbeing depends more significantly on the stability of growth rates than their significance. Wellbeing is strongly related to growth persistence and external demand, and it is function of inclusive economic growth and quality of life. An increase in foreign direct investments, government expenditure and savings is likely to improve wellbeing. Thus, the results lend support to the argument that the Human Development Index can capture variations in living standard that measure of wellbeing using GDP per capita and purchasing power parity.

The empirical evidence reflects also the crucial role of efficient government, rule of law, government spending, transparency and accountability, as well as fiscal and trade freedom. Thus, the focus should be made on the government's ability to formulate and implement sound social and economic policies, and on the efficient allocation of public expenditure to promote the private sector. It is important for Muslim countries to promote wellbeing by addressing the chronic issues related to accountability, governance, and efficiency. Economic policies that focus solely on the immediate short-term effects on economic growth may bring little remedy to the long-term social effects of income inequality. It is only a coherent approach to development integrating the economic, social and human dimensions that has the potential to improve welfare and wellbeing.

Finally, Part VII considers the nexus between Islamic finance, economic growth and human development. In Chapter 24, Imam and Kpodar investigate the relationship between the development of Islamic banking and economic growth for a sample of low and middle-income countries. An attempt is made to answer the question of whether the development of Islamic banking is good for growth. The issue is important because Islamic banking has unique characteristics that differ from conventional banking, and appear to be better adapted to less developed economies in the Middle-East, sub-Saharan Africa and Asia.

The empirical analysis is based on System GMM estimation, which can be useful in controlling for endogeneity bias in testing the effects of Islamic banking on growth for a panel of developing economies, including OIC member states. The results show that, despite its relatively smaller size compared to the entire economy and the financial system, Islamic banking is positively associated with economic growth even after controlling for various determinants, including the level of financial depth. The results are robust across different model specifications, sample compositions, and time periods. The empirical results indicate that many Muslim countries that currently suffering from low growth may consider the design and implementation of policies that reinforce the role of risk-sharing in further developing this important part of the financial system.

In Chapter 25, Dieye provides an empirical analysis of economic stability and growth for developing countries in the Muslim world. Economic policies are traditionally based on monetary and fiscal solutions that, while providing short-term remedies to financial crises and economic recessions, tend to perpetuate the cycle of credit expansion, debt defaults, and economic austerity. The different paradigm of Islamic economics may offer, however, more viable alternative economic solutions. The new proposal for policy framework replaces traditional variables of macroeconomic adjustment with counterparts from Islamic economics, such as the rate of return to the real economy instead of interest rates.

The simulation exercise is based on the economic conditions of Senegal, the African and predominantly Muslim country, which offers an interesting example of a developing country with rich resources that can be optimally leveraged to address economic and social challenges. The evidence suggests that macroeconomic models based on the principles of Islamic economics can present a viable alternative to conventional models. The simulation results present, indeed, new perspectives on the need to reduce the propensities to consume and to import, which is in line with the Islamic rules of moderation in consumption. It sheds light also on the need for agricultural output adjustments to achieve domestic self-sufficiency, and for fiscal adjustments based on expenditures rather than taxation to attain higher levels of real GDP, total investment, and exports. Thus, the Islamic economic model allows for the formalization and quantification of the institutional and individual rules of conduct, and the assessment of the relation between behavioral rules and economic performance. The analytical framework can be also extended to examine the impact of risk-sharing finance, and the importance of the rate of return on the real sector for monetary, and fiscal policies. Islamic economics offers, indeed, new perspectives on institutional rules and behavior, which can contribute to the development of new institutional economics.

In Chapter 26, Akther-Uddin, Saiti, and Masih examine the relationship between human development, financial development, and economic growth using the dynamic Two-Step System Generalized Method of Moments for a large sample of developed and developing countries. The objective is to understand the significance of this nexus for OIC member states relative to other developing countries. It is noted that per capita real GDP growth rates in OIC-Asian countries have been rising significantly since the start of the twenty-first century, but still at slower rates than other developing countries. The estimation results suggest a positive relation between economic growth and human development indicators, such as the average years of schooling and the ratio of healthcare spending to GDP. In contrast, economic growth seems to be negatively correlated with financial development measured in terms of domestic credit to private sector and bank deposits, among others.

There are several policy implications, including the need to increase healthcare spending, and focus on investment in human capital accumulation. To avoid brain drain, it is also important to develop production and services industries to create job opportunities for graduates from institutions of higher learning and vocational schools. The focus should be made also on institutional development, macroeconomic stability, capital formation, and industrialization, which are crucial fo sustainable growth in Muslim countries. Since sustainable economic development depends on financial system stability, it is crucial for OIC countries to develop a robust Islamic finance industry based on the principle of risk-sharing, which strengthens the relation between the financial sector and the real economy.

Finally, in Chapter 27, Mydin and Mirakhor examine the issue of whether natural resources impede rather than contribute to economic growth in Muslim countries. The resource curse is descriptive of economic conditions where natural resources are negatively linked with economic development and growth. The issue is important in light of the relatively poor economic performance of oil-producing OIC member states. The literature suggests that this economic puzzle can be partly explained by institutional failure, which induces counter-productive behaviors such as rent-seeking, patronage and corruption.

The empirical evidence using the Pooled Mean Group (PMG) method for dynamic heterogeneous panels is, indeed, indicative of resource curse effects on the OIC economies. There are apparent weaknesses in the quality of institutions, which constitute the premise for resource curse. Poor institutional scaffolding naturally results in repeated policy failures and economic imbalances that tend to affect the poorest and weakest segments of society, particularly during financial crises and economic downturns. There is a pressing need to improve the quality of institutions by adopting an Islamic institutional framework that offers economic and social justice in countries that profess Islam and seek prosperity for all. In the divine teachings of Qur'an and Prophetic tradition, or *Sunnah*, lies a wealth of remedies to the resource curse and plight of oil-rich countries. The evidence of resource curse reflects fundamental problems related to the implications of faith and positive attitudes. It is natural that the concentration of power, poor governance, and lack of accountability result in increasing wealth disparities. Asset-based redistribution can provide some remedies to the resource curse. But no amount of rules and regulations can be effective without significant changes in attitudes toward wealth accumulation and income redistribution.

In light of the brief introduction of this unique collection of analytical studies, it is clear that risk-sharing constitutes a common thread that connects important issues that are germane to the ongoing debates about economic uncertainty and financial instability, about interest rates and policy uncertainty, about debt and financial crises, about financial institutions and financial consumer protection, about inequality and income redistribution, and about the relation between finance and development, *inter alia*. As risk permates many aspects of human life and economic actitivies, risk sharing can certainly play a central role in the distribution of risk in the society, and the setting of effective institutional and individual rules of behaviour that govern production, exchange, allocation, and distribution, as well as (re)distributive justice.

Thus, the principal conclusions that can be drawn from these analytical studies are broadly consistent and robust, despite differences in theoretical modelling, empirical testing, and logical analysis. The overriding objective of this *Handbook of Analytical Studies in Islamic Finance and Economics* is to rethink the role of economics from an Islamic perspective, and to demonstrate the relevance of Islamic economics as a useful field of knowledge that is amenable to the same analytical methods used to test standard economic propositions. Given the fundamentally distinct paradigms, it is natural that different logical arguments may be articulated, different solutions to the same problems of human development may be advocated, and different remedies to the same challenges of economic growth may be prescribed. As the axes of modern economy and Islamic economy remain distant, convergence necessitates a redefinition of modern homo-economicus and a profound consciousness about the moral imperative that drives human action. It is incumbent upon Islamic economics, as a discipline, to present an analytical framework of the Qur'anic vision of ideal economy that serves the purposes of an intelligible *economic universe of discourse*.

Contents

Part VII: Islamic Finance, Economic Growth and Human Development

Part I: **Logical Coherence and Consilience in Islamic Economics**

Idris Samawi Hamid, Abbas Mirakhor

Chapter 1: On the Logical Character and Coherence of Islamic Economics

1 Introduction

Even a cursory review of published research in Islamic Economics over the last decade reveals a picture of "glass half full." On the one hand, there has been an intensifying rise of consciousness regarding Islam's vision of the economy and economics and, on the other hand, there is also the emergence of a wilderness of logical incoherence with a rapidly developing "echo-chamber" mentality that impedes intellectual discourse and saps the energies needed for advancement of this nascent discipline. In this process, the guidance of the first generation of Muslim specialists in economists – e.g., Siddiqi, who suggested a research program that set a direction for future research – does not seem to have had much traction in the debate still raging among some well-known scholars about What is Islamic Economics?. Each side is pushing its own idea centered on how its view is right and everyone else's is wrong, but without the substantiation required of an intellectually honest critique. Regrettably and too often, the language used in these attacks lacks the *adab* (etiquette of discourse) urged by the *Qur'an.*[28] Each side takes positions, using *alqāb* (pejorative labels)[29] to discredit others' ideas. Hence, inter-communication among Muslim economists has become strained, impeding the search for a common language, epistemics, and logic of the ideal system of Islamic economy as envisioned in the *Qur'an* and operationalized by the Sunnah.

The vision of someone like Siddiqi who, in addressing a session of Muslim economists debating the question of definition of Islamic Economics, urged the participants to consider that "Islam is primarily about a spiritual view of life and a moral approach to life's problems, including the economic problem. The contentment Islam promised man is rooted in this spiritual framework." (Siddiqi, 2004, p. 12) In effect, Siddiqi seemed to be saying that, instead of focusing on vacuous debates about what is or what is not Islamic Economics, the focus of research should be on finding solutions to problems such as the ones he posed, e.g., "how to realize economic values and achieve Islamic ends in economic life of our times." (Siddiqi, 2004, p. 7) His vision transcended a narrow, localized and parochial position to suggest, "It is time to demonstrate how modern man can live a peaceful, satisfying life by shifting to an Islamic paradigm that values human relations above material possession." (Siddiqi, 2004, p. 13)

Siddiqi went further to suggest a methodology of proceeding with such a research program: The primary source of its logic and epistemics had to be the Qur'an. Then

28 See, e.g., Qur'an 2:83, 7:85, 16:125, and 39:18.
29 See Qur'an 49:11.

https://doi.org/10.1515/9783110587920-001

comes the Sunnah which, he emphasized, is "best understood as conduct and policy directed at realization of the objective [sic] and values in the Qur'an." After these, he suggested, "*fiqh* can become helpful." Siddiqi lamented that this order seems to have been reversed: "For many, if not most scholars, *fiqh* comes first." These sage advices were not heeded: Much of "Islamic Economics" research is anchored about what some *faqīh* (jurisprudent) has considered as the "*maqāṣid al-shariah,*" which, for most writers, is some *fiqh*-based conception of *shariah.* In turn, an equivalence is established between *fiqh* and *shariah.* This involves an apparent absence of awareness that 'shariah' is a term used by the Qur'an to establish a matter of infallibility, whereas fiqh is a product of the human mind and is fallible; for this reason, Islamic Economics must be grounded in the Qur'an and Sunnah, and then fiqh (in that order). (Note that, even here, Siddiqi's suggestion seems to entail the view that fiqh plays a necessary role in the understanding of how to structure the logic, design and implementation of policies derived from the first two sources.[30] Such a view may require some modification.)

A work that followed the order of priority suggested by Siddiqi in grounding the vision of the economy perceived from the vantage point of the Qur'an was the *Iqtiṣādunā* of the Shahīd ʿAllāmah M.B. Ṣadr (rḍw). Deeply seeped in the sciences of the Qur'an and Sunnah (as well as Islamaic/Aristotelian philosophy), Ṣadr developed i) a logic of istiqrāʾ/epagōgē (commonly translated "induction") – *al-Usus al-Manṭiqiyyah lil-Istiqrāʾ* (Logical Foundations of Induction); ii) a philosophy of Islam – Falsafatunā (Our Philosophy); followed by iii) his pioneering and highly fertile book on the ideal Islamic economy – *Iqtiṣādunā* (Our Economics).

Based on his work in logic, he understood that the axiomatic structure of the "science" of the contemporary, dominant paradigm of economics is in direct contradiction with the logic of an Islamic Economics based first and foremost on the Qur'an. One of these axioms involves the concept of "scarcity," which is considered to be so ubiquitous and central to standard economics that the latter is often called "the science of scarcity." That this axiom is in conflict with the the Qur'an was pointed out by the Shahīd. Rather, as the Qur'an repeatedly emphasizes, Allah (swt) has always and continues to create resources for the sustenance of humans with an "exact measure". The concept of scarcity within the dominant economic paradigm is thus juxtaposed with that of sufficiency of resources within the Qur'an.[31]

To be sure, the Qur'an does not reject the idea that, at the micro-level, humans do face so-called "scarcity." However, that is not due to any paucity of the resources created by Allah (swt), but rather to deliberately designed policies and instruments (e.g., legislative, political, social and administrative) governing distribution that favor one or more particular classes that continues to accumulate wealth in the face of the growing poverty of others. Some two decades after *Iqtiṣādunā* first appeared,

30 See Siddiqi (2004).

31 See, e.g., Qur'an 13:8, 15:21, 17:30, 28:82, 29:62, 30:37, 34:36, 34:39, 42:12 & 27, 54:49, and 89:16.

Hasanuzzaman (1984), referring to 41:10, suggested that Allah (swt) "has created sufficient resources for His creatures. Therefore, scarcity may be either due to lack of proper utilization of natural endowments or an imbalanced distribution". Indeed, there is much evidence from the Qur'an and Sunnah that it is not the paucity of resources but the system of distribution of resources that underlies the emergence of poverty and deprivation in societies.[32]

Contemporary scholars who have focused on the concept of scarcity suggest that there is a distinction between actual, material scarcity and the "feeling of scarcity."[33] The latter is conditioned by the mindset that tells a person how much is enough and how much is too little. Such a mindset is, in turn, conditioned by social, cultural, psychological, ideological, religious, and other elements.[34] In its primordial character, however, human nature knows when enough is enough.[35]

The concept of scarcity by itself, once internalized by a critical mass of members of a given society, has deleterious effects on efforts to deal with distributional problems: Incidence of poverty and deprivation can always be explained away by scarcity. On the other hand, the axiom of sufficiency, once accepted by a critical mass of members of a given society, would require a search for redistributive means of alleviating poverty in that society. The scarcity axiom, while damaging to social solidarity in and of itself, becomes even more onerous and strongly in conflict with the logic of Islamic Economics when combined with unlimited wants – the latter leads to insatiability, a "psychological disposition that prevents us, as individuals and as societies, from saying that 'enough is enough"), narrow self-interest, and presuppositions of restricted rationality. The result is a discipline with moral defects, such as the "coexistence of great wealth and great poverty" and "palpable economic defects," such as an "inherently unstable financial system".[36]

Sometime ago, Karl Polanyi argued that economics can be understood as having two distinct senses: formal and substantive. In its formal sense, economics derives from the logical character of the means-ends relationship. In its substantive sense,

> economics derives from man's dependence upon nature and his fellow. It refers to the interchange with his natural and social environment [...] the two root meanings of economics, the substantive and formal, have nothing in common. The formal meaning implies a set of rules referring to choice between the alternative uses of insufficient means. The substantive meaning implies neither a choice nor insufficiency of means; man's livelihood may or may not

32 See, e.g., Mirakhor and Askari (2017).

33 See, e.g., Mullainathan and Eldar (2013), p. 4. The authors define scarcity as "having less than you feel you need."

34 See for example, Barber (2007).

35 See, e.g., Gowdy (1998). The book is a collection of excellent anthropological studies on hunter-gatherer cultures in which members knew when they had enough for a comfortable life and managed their societies through sharing surpluses.

36 See, e.g., Skidelsky and Skidelsky (2012).

> involve the necessity of choice and if choice there be, it need not be induced by the limiting effect of a "scarcity" of the means.[37]

Economic thought that shares what Siddiqi suggests to be a "spiritual view of life and a moral approach to life's problems, including the economic problem," would lie within the universe of discourse of what Polanyi called the substantive sense of economics, sharing little or no common ground with the formal sense invoked by the currently dominant paradigm of economics. The argumentation advanced by some to conclude that Islamic Economics, if it is going to be effective and meaningful, has to abandon everything that "conventional," "standard," economics has to say is fallacious. Meanwhile, the voices in wilderness, such as those of Ṣadr and Siddiqi, that call for Islamic Economics to develop a language and logic of its own based on the Qur'an and Sunnah adequate to addressing the problems faced by humanity at large, go largely unheeded. To heed them, Islamic Economics needs to develop a common language[38] and logic based on the Qur'an. The present study is a modest attempt to address the logical foundations of Islamic Economics, in a manner that would perhaps lead to meaningful discourse both within and outside of the Islamic economic community aimed at addressing the issues suggested by Siddiqi.[39]

2 Universes of Discourse and Categorical Coherence

"The Islamic [sic] ummah is facing crises of types never before seen in Islamic history. The issue of how Islamic Economics should be defined ... remains unresolved."[40] A necessary, if not sufficient condition, for defining the concept "Islamic Economics" involves a determination of the logical, philosophical, and/or scientific parameters that govern i) the movement of consciousness and action within the particular sphere associated with the extension of that concept, as well as ii) the interrelation of that sphere with other general, relevant domains of human experience (e.g., realms of economic consciousness and action). This necessary condition involves, in part, determining whether the concept "Islamic Economics" is even coherent. Does the range of applicability of "Islamic" intersect with that of "economics" (in the contemporary sense of

37 See Dalton (1971) pp. 139–174. Quotations in the above paragraph are taken from p. 140).

38 On the necessity of a common language for Islamic Economics, see, e.g., Khan (2000).

39 For greater detail and technical development of this theme, see the authors' forthcoming book *The Logical Foundations of Islamic Economics: Objective Logic and Phenomenology of Consciousness and Action*. Much of this note condenses results discovered in the course of preparing that work.

40 Zaman (2017, p. 205). In the spirit of Sayyid Maududi and other contemporary, progressive thinkers, the authors would prefer to speak of, not the *Islamic*, but, rather, the *Muslim ummah* and *Muslim* history.

'economics')?[41] If not, then the concept "Islamic Economics" has no material[42] extension and remains in the realm of shadows. Determining some exact sense in which "Islamic Economics" is coherent depends, in large part, on fulfilling the necessary condition sketched above.

The distinction between Muslim and Islamic is one of the most important guiding principles of our discussion. Given a guideline, human activity, or phenomenon, it is *Islamic* only to the degree that it precisely flows from and is consistent with the framework of consciousness and praxis established by the Qur'an and the Messenger of Islam. A person, society, social or other institution, guideline, activity, or any other phenomenon is *Muslim* to the degree that it is reasonably associated with some class of self-identifying Muslims. In practice, it is possible and quite common that, in some domain of human experience, a Muslim does not behave in an Islamic manner. Similarly, it is possible that, with respect to some domain of human experience, a non-Muslim behaves in an Islamic manner and a Muslim does not.[43]

With respect to the "shadowy" nature of concepts and conceptual entities: A careful study of the proper sources for the articulation of any genuinely Islamic framework of knowing will show that, within such a framework, all thought is *concrete* (in some important sense of 'concrete' – to be discussed). That is, given an activity of conscious (e.g., rational) thinking, it has a real object; no single thought is truly *abstract* (in some important sense of 'abstract' – to be discussed) or merely subjective. However, if that conscious thinking (or pseudo-thinking) does not *shadow* (or reflect) reality in some primary, material sense, then its object remains *shadowy*. Related positions were held by Hegel (d. 1831ce) and Alexius Meinong (d. 1920ce). In traditional Islamaic philosophy,[44] such a position was systematically worked out, apparently for the first time, by Shaykh Aḥmad al-Aḥsā'ī (d. 1826ce). On the other hand, Kant's

41 In conformance with the standard convention for the use-mention distinction, we use in this study a single quote name to *mention* an expression, sentence, or other string of characters per se; we use a double-quote name to mention a concept, proposition, or other object of thought per se. We also use double quotes for the usual purpose of quoting the speech or comments of others. The context should make it clear which sense of double-quotes is intended.

42 *Material*: The word 'material' is being used in a general sense and without prejudice; i.e., it is not synonymous with 'physical' and its denotation includes what is normally called spiritual.

43 For example, there has been an effort to develop an "Economic Islamicity Index" that aims to objectively rank the nations of the world in terms of their compliance to a select set of Islamic economic principles. In a 2010 version of this project (Rehman & Askari 2010), the winner was Ireland; the first Muslim country to appear on the list was no. 33: Malaysia. Given the interwoven nature of the Islamic framework *in concreto* some of the methodology of the authors may be questioned. Still, their work illustrates an application of the critical distinction between Muslim and Islamic.

44 We use 'Islamaic philosophy' in place of the usual 'Islamic philosophy', 'Muslim philosophy', and so forth. The distinction between Islamic and Islamaic is analogous to the distinction between Hellenic and Hellenistic. Examples: ʿAlī ibn Abī Ṭālib (ʿa) articulated an Islamic, but not an Islamaic, philosophy. Moses Maimonides was an Islamaic, but not an Islamic, philosopher. Islamaic philosophy appropriates and develops a non-Islamic (Aristotelian, Neoplatonic, etc.) heritage.

(d. 1804ce) earlier, critical rejection of some variant of this position has dominated later European philosophical, logical, and scientific thinking.[45]

Let us rephrase the challenge set forth at the outset: The task at hand involves articulating the *universe of discourse* proper to Islamic Economics, in comparison and contrast with that proper to contemporary, mainstream economic theory and practice. Such an articulation is needed to provide a proper basis for answering questions such as, How, and to what degree, can the problems of contemporary economies be addressed by Islamic Economics? How, and to what degree, can analytic methods developed in conventional economics, which are ideologically conditioned by, and/or deduced from axioms specific to, the universe of discourse of the latter, be employed in Islamic Economics?

Our sights can be aimed deeper: Granting the coherence of "Islamic Economics", and given the roots of the range of applicability of "Islamic" in the Prophetic era and its sources (viz., the Qur'an and the authentic *Hadith*, i.e., those traditions which do not contradict the Qur'an): How and to what degree, if at all, can a general question of contemporary Western economic theory be transformed into one of Islamic Economics? The reverse is also important: How and to what degree, if at all, can a general question of Islamic Economics be transformed into one of contemporary Western economic theory? For example, can Islamic Economics address non-trivial and important questions, ignored by the dominant paradigm of economics, such as the following: What is the purpose of wealth? How much wealth is sufficient for a secure and comfortable life? Can Islamic Economics suggest ways and means of correcting the moral and economic defects of the forms of capitalism that dominate economies across the world, including those of Muslim nations? Can analytically and axiomatically neutral methods of standard economics assist Islamic Economics to arrive at its own systematic and coherent paradigm for analysis and policies addressed to achieving the life of security, peace and economic sufficiency which Islam promises humans?

A universe of discourse is basically a *closed* collection of objects of thought under discussion by members of an intellectual community; the objects of thought and concepts of that collection are generally understood by those participating in the discussion. For example, in the universe of discourse of natural numbers (0, 1, 2, 3, and so forth), we may say, e.g., "Every number is either even or odd." There is no need to mention the property 'natural' before mentioning the object 'number'; since the universe of discourse is closed it is understood by the participants as given that all numbers in that universe are natural. Another aspect of a universe of discourse is that it determines the *range* of concepts of objects over which concepts of properties can be *coherently* predicated. For example, given the properties even and odd (as denoted in number theory), the object of thought "This tree is even" is neither true nor false, but *incoherent*. That is, the concept "tree" (botany) and the concepts "odd" and

45 This topic is an important one for future study and exposition.

"even" (number theory) do not belong to the same universe of discourse. Hence it is incoherent to predicate evenness of a tree; to do so is to commit what is called a *category mistake*. A declarative sentence may express either a coherent or an incoherent object of thought; if coherent, that object of thought can be either true or false. Thus, within the universe of natural numbers: The object of thought "Some number is even" is coherent and true; "Every number is even" is false but still coherent. "Some tree is even" is neither true nor false but incoherent; to call a tree even is to commit a category mistake. A coherent object of thought is usually called a *proposition* in the strict sense of 'proposition'. But even incoherent objects of thought can be called propositional in form if not in content. Thus, the object of thought "Some tree is even" is propositional in form but is not, strictly speaking, a proposition *per se*.

3 Science, Intrinsic Value, and Self-transcendence

A universe of discourse is supposed to serve as an element within an overall framework of knowledge and practice, of *science*. Yet there appear to be certain limits, obstacles blocking our path forward before the task can even begin. For example: On the one hand, contemporary science in the narrow, quantitative sense has no place for *value* in any *intrinsic, self-transcending* (as opposed to *mercantile* or *quantitative*) sense. That is, values, allegedly, are not subject to scientific knowledge. Given some school of contemporary economics which, by and large, takes science in some such narrow sense as its ideal paradigm of knowing, intrinsic value would appear to lie outside of its scope, and thus, strictly speaking, outside of the range of applicability of the concept "economics". On the other hand, although any authentic school of Muslim thought does and must place significant emphasis on intrinsic values at its core, these are, in the contemporary *zeitgeist*, allegedly to be taken purely on faith and not in any manner that is scientific or which involves knowledge (as opposed to mere faith).[46] This would appear to implicate, i.e., point in the direction of the conclusion, that the ranges of applicability of "Islamic" and "economics" respectively are mutually exclusive, for i) economics aims to be scientific, but there is (allegedly) no science of value; and ii) the core characteristic of Islam and Islamicity is intrinsic value, but, again, there is (allegedly) no science of value.

Whether, and the degree to which, the contemporary discipline of economics can or should take science in some narrow, quantitative sense, as its ideal is a matter of

---

46 Yes, earlier, classical Muslim theology did develop a rationalist, scholastic framework of value based on presuppositions about, e.g., beauty and ugliness. But, as useful as they were in their own time, the degree to which the *Aristotelian cognitivism* (upon which systems deriving from that framework were based) produces genuine knowledge of the objects in its universe of discourse is doubtful; in major part for reasons that will be discussed further on.

debate. With respect to Islam, however, there can be little doubt that value[47] lies at the core of its system, its framework and methodology, of thought and action. According to one of the most famous *aḥādīth,* one oft-repeated by Muslims of every school of thought, the Messenger (ṣ) said, "Surely I was solely sent to perfect the nobilities of intrinsic moral value."

The use of 'intrinsic' in the translation above may raise concerns of anachronism. However, *akhlaq* (plural of '*khulq*' or '*khuluq*') literally and lexicographically signifies a disposition that characterizes its host in an innate, intrinsic manner. This is consistent with the standard Islamic principle that everyone and everything in existence was created with a fundamentally *good*, beautiful (*ḥasan*), *primordial nature* (*fiṭrah*).[48]

The aforementioned Hadith implicates that any and every object or mapping in the Islamic universe of discourse ultimately pertains to intrinsic moral value. However, it emphatically does not implicate, let alone logically imply, that Islam denies that there can be a science of intrinsic value, in some appropriate sense of 'science'. To assume that, because Islam's fundamental interest is intrinsic value, therefore there is no such thing as an Islamic science of value, let alone economics, is to commit a crude non sequitur. As we shall explore, a number of contemporary Muslim, as well as anti-Islamic, scholars have been misled by one or both of the following: i) the *scientism* of the currently dominant European culture that derives from the Cartesian analysis of the world, Newtonian mechanism, and Kant's rejection of the concrete nature of thought;[49] and ii) the concomitant fideism of the same culture, in conjunction with the traditional *fideism* promulgated and ossified by traditional Muslim figures such as Ghazzālī.

Ultimately, however, value and its praxis constitute a unity that is inseparable from genuine knowledge of (as opposed to mere faith in) the truth and reality that they are about. This is an important teaching of the Qur'an and the Messenger (ṣ), one that has been often obfuscated, when not altogether denied, by the Muslim and Islamaic traditions of scholastic theology and even philosophy. In the Qur'an one reads (29:43):

> And those are the symbols we propound to the people, yet no one can prehend them except the *knowers*.

The number of āyāt (*signs*, also known as *verses*) of the Qur'an, as well as *aḥādīth,* which bear upon this matter can hardly be counted.[50]

---

47 Unless otherwise specified, explicitly or by context, in the sequel we will use 'value' to mention intrinsic, self-transcending value.

48 This is related to the well-known fact that, in contrast to Christianity, there is no concept or reality of *original sin* in Islam.

49 In can hardly be emphasized enough that neither Descartes, nor Newton, nor Kant espoused scientism.

50 For an introduction to this matter, see Hamid (2011a, Ch. 2).

In the *āyah* quoted above, knowing is connected with *ʿaql* (*prehending, nexal consciousness*). And in other places throughout the Qur'an and Hadith, as will be discussed in some detail, such prehending is intimately bound with intrinsic value and its practice in a movement that is both developmental and self-transcending. It is in this context that Islam provides the foundations for a complete *system* of value. Such a system involves, not a mere articulation of some organized list of normative rules of action, but a comprehensive *phenomenology* of consciousness and praxis. Critically, the phenomenology of consciousness and praxis latent within Islam also entails a concrete framework and cogent method of knowing. Thus, an Islamic phenomenology is *scientific* in a broad sense of 'science'. It turns out that the framework and method of knowing espoused by Islam is neither Aristotelian (as adopted by traditional Islamaic civilization) nor empiricist (as espoused by mainstream contemporary European culture); rather, it is irreducibly *dialectical* in a sense that involves movement, development, and self-transcendence. The fact that it does not fit into an Aristotelian or empiricist paradigm explains, in part, why the Islamic framework of knowledge has, with some exception, been obfuscated, neglected, or denied throughout Muslim history, both traditional and contemporary.

An important entailment of the dialectical nature of the Islamic framework and methodology of consciousness and praxis is that *economic action constitutes a necessary* – although not sufficient – *condition for the cultivation and development of moral action*. Put another way, economic development, using 'economic' in some contemporary sense, cannot be decoupled from the cultivation, development, and perfection of intrinsic value that constitute the core of Islamicity. There can be no question of a bifurcation of the economic from the moral in the Islamic framework, methodology, and movement. And that dialectical movement is, again, scientific in a broad sense.

Let us return to the question of intrinsic value vis-à-vis contemporary economics. If Islam offers a perspective from above to below (moral to economic), might there be some perspective, also scientific in spirit (in the broad sense of 'science' to be discussed), commensurate with contemporary economic science, one from below to above (economic to moral)? It turns out that such perspectives do exist. An important case is the dialectic of the economic and the moral in the thought of the Italian philosopher Benedetto Croce (d. 1952ce). A related thinker, one influenced by Croce and especially Hegel, is G.R.G. Mure (d. 1979ce). It turns out that the contours of *Croce's dialectic of opposites and distincts* constitute something close to a special case of a corresponding and broader Islamic phenomenology and dialectics of consciousness and praxis. Furthermore, Mure's penetrating analysis of the nature of economic action, and its relation to moral action and intrinsic value, comes strikingly close to the Islamic position on the matter.[51] From one direction, the dialectics of Croce and Mure

51 See especially the second chapter of Mure (1958).

appears rich enough to allow for a fruitful mutual exploration without falling into the ditch of either syncretism or anachronism. From another, the dialectic of the economic and the moral, developed from a joint Islamic and appropriately chosen contemporary logical, philosophical, and scientific vantage point, can provide the context and meta-language in which the parameters of the coherence of Islamic Economics can be adequately determined and articulated.

4 Objective Logic and Phenomenology of Consciousness and Action

4.1 Objective Logic and Subjective Logic

As mentioned at the outset, our task involves the determination of the logical and scientific parameters governing the sphere (=category) particular to Islamic Economics, as well as the interrelations of that sphere with the relevant domains of human experience, particularly those of interest to contemporary economic science. Pursuit of that task involves a logical, philosophical, and scientific methodology that is sometimes called *objective logic*. Contemporary economics, as a discipline, involves a universe of discourse associated with some paradigm of logic and/or science internal to that universe. Islamic Economics, as a discipline, also involves a universe of discourse associated with some paradigm of logic and/or science internal to itself. A paradigm of logic and/or science *internal* to some universe is sometimes called its *subjective logic*.

This point can hardly be overemphasized. As William Lawvere, one of the founders of the formal objective logic known as mathematical category and topos theory, puts it (Lawvere & Rosebrugh 2003, pp. 239–240):

> The long chains of correct reasonings and calculations of which subjective logic is justly proud are only possible within a precisely defined universe of discourse, as has long been recognized. Since there are many such universes of discourse, thinking necessarily involves many transformations between universes of discourse as well as transformations of one universe of discourse into another.

Given a set of scientific axioms or presuppositions, they are specific to some specific universe of discourse (= category). The conclusions deduced from those axioms also belong to the same universe of discourse. As Aristotle discovered, deduction from first principles (= axioms, presuppositions) is always bound to and never escapes the relevant universe of discourse. It is in this respect that deductive logic is subjective. But this leaves a serious problem, one not solved by traditional Aristotelian logic. For Aristotelian logic has no solution, no precise formalism for representing or articulating objective-logical reasoning.

When an observer looks at two universes of discourse from the perspective of the subjective logic particular to one of them, particularly from that of the narrower of the two, it is easy to fall into some bifurcationist fallacy. This is, in part, because it is easy to forget that the cogency of reasoning of some subjective logic is not independent of the associated universe of discourse in which it is being employed. Even from the perspective of the broader of the two, if the factor of dialectical development and self-transcendence is left out, then, once again, it is easy to fall into a bifurcationist fallacy.

In contrast to the situation with subjective logic, an objective logic is a logic and science of bridging distinct (even apparently irreconcilable) universes of discourse and exhibiting them as a coherent, inter-related whole, and to make precise and explicit the logical rules of transformation between one and the other. This may involve development (or self-transcendence) from one universe to the higher; it may also involve decay (or self-corruption) from one universe to the lower. An example from mathematics will illustrate: A set may be said to *develop*, objective-logically, into a topological space; a topological space may be said to *decay*, objective-logically, into a set. Correlative to a set, a topological space constitutes a *broader* universe of discourse (= category); correlative to a topological space, a set constitutes a *narrower* universe (= category).

The Islamic category has its own subjective logic, as does contemporary economics. If "Islamic Economics" is coherent, then it must constitute an objective-logical system, one appropriate to i) some category of intrinsic value, as well as to ii) another category specific to economic action. The questions asked earlier may now be expressed in more general terms: Given two categories within an objective-logical system, what are the cogency conditions of the subjective logic appropriate to each category? What are the rules for transposing a problem expressed within the narrower category, and investigated via its associated subjective logic, into the corresponding problem in the broader category, and investigated via the subjective logic associated with the latter?

4.2 Two Dialectical Lynchpins

The current research of the authors into the logical foundations of Islamic Economics, based upon study of the Qur'an and Sunnah, reveals a number of dialectical lynchpins that subserve the Islamic phenomenology of consciousness and action. Together, they appear to constitute necessary and sufficient building blocks for the construction of a very concrete objective-logical system. For purposes of this note we restrict ourselves to discussion of only two of them.

One lynchpin of Islamic phenomenology is its *dialectic* of knowing and doing; more generally, of the theoretical and the practical. This is in sharp contrast to the

Western paradigm, dominant from its initial articulation by Aristotle up to the present day (in both Western and Islamaic traditions), which recognizes and builds upon a bifurcation of theory and practice. Variants of such a bifurcation set in early in Muslim history,[52] leading the gamut of its theological and intellectual thought off track ever since, vis a vis the primordial Islamic spirit. Over the course of this research, we have worked out the parameters of an Islamic phenomenological system based in large part upon certain critical, general objective-logical guidelines – each is explicitly stated in general form in the course of a crucial narration or āyah, and supported by numerous other evidences from the Qur'an and Hadith. One such guideline is the following: Through *nexal-consciousness/prehending* (*ʿaql*) the depths of *praxial-wisdom/wise practicing* (*ḥikmah*) are fathomed; through praxial-wisdom the depths of nexal consciousness are fathomed.

The importance of this particular guiding, dialectical principle for the development of any authentic, Islamic framework and methodology of knowing and practice can hardly be overestimated. Among other things, it entails a rejection of *Aristotelian cognitivism*,[53] as well as empiricism, in favor of another, dialectical approach to science.

The second lynchpin involves the dialectic of *nexal-consciousness* (*ʿaql*) and *ignorance* (*jahl*) (= *ego* (*nafs*)). The Islamic sources provide a guide in the form of one of the most important traditions for our phenomenology: The Hadith of the Troops of Nexal Consciousness and Anti-Consciousness (i.e., Nexal-Grasping and Ignoring, or Nexus and Ignorance). At first glance, the setting is a cosmological account of creation, but the phenomenological subtext is explicit: First and foremost, this Hadith provides an account of the innermost drama of the human spirit. Following is an excerpt. As reported by the great-grandson of the Messenger (ṣ), the Imām Jaʿfar al-Ṣādiq (ʿa):

> Surely God created Nexal-Consciousness – and it is the first of all spiritual things[54] – from the light of the right of the ʿArsh (Empyrean). So He said to it: "Go back!" and it went back. Then He said, "Come forth!" and it came forth. Then He said, "I have created you as a magnificent creation, and have honored you over the entirety of my creation."
>
> Then He created Anti-Consciousness from a murky, brackish sea. So He said to it: "Go back!" and it went back. Then He said, "Come forth!" and it did not come forth. So he said to it, "Are you conceited?" and cursed it.

---

52 In addition to the situation in Aristotelianism, the bifurcation of faith and works in Pauline Christianity and within what was to become Ashʿarī theology are also cases in point.

53 Aristotelian cognitivism involves a bifurcation between learning and knowing (i.e., induction and deductive demonstration), in sharp contrast to the method of Socrates, whose approach is closer in spirit to the Islamic methodology.

54 It must be remembered that, in the Islamic sources, there is no opposition between spiritual and material per se. A spiritual entity is non-physical, but *not* immaterial.

Then He gave Nexal-Consciousness seventy-five troops. When Anti-Consciousness saw that with which God had honored Nexal-Consciousness and what He had given it, Anti-Consciousness developed an enmity to Nexal-Consciousness, and said, "O my Cherisher-Lord! This [Nexal-Consciousness] is a creation like me. You have created it, honored it, and strengthened it, while I am its opposite and have no strength against it. So give me troops like those you have given Nexal Consciousness!" God said, "Yes [I will do so]. But if you disobey again after that I will remove you and your troops from my Mercy." Anti-Consciousness replied, "I am well pleased!" So God gave Anti-Consciousness seventy-five troops.

And so came to be, from among the seventy-five troops that God gave Nexal-Consciousness [along with their opposites from the troops of Anti-Consciousness], the following:

Good, which is the chief of staff of Nexal-Consciousness; He made bad its opposite, and it is the chief of staff of Anti-Consciousness.

Īmān, and its opposite is *kufr*.[55]

Affirming [the truth], and its opposite is rejection.

Hope, and its opposite is despair.

Justice, and its opposite is tyranny.

[For the rest of the troops of ʿAql and Jahl see Table 1.1]

So these dispositions of Nexal-Consciousness do not all *cohere* (*ijtimāʿ*) except in a prophet, the *heir* (*waṣī*) of a prophet, or a *muʾmin*[56] whose heart has been tested for īmān. As for the rest of those who move in the orbit of our *dynamic loving* (*walayah*), any one of them will have at least some of these troops until he is cleansed of the troops of Anti-Consciousness: When that happens, he comes to be in the highest rank among the prophets and heirs. And that can only be perceived by cognizing Nexal-Consciousness and its troops, and by avoiding Anti-Consciousness and its troops.

Current research also reveals that '*jahl*' is another name for '*nafs*' in the Qur'anic sense that may be translated by 'ego':

> Surely the Ego does command to evil, except that for which my Cherisher-Lord has mercy.
> (Qur'an 12:53)

55 These two words are ubiquitous throughout the Qur'an and Sunnah, but difficult to translate; they have been subject to severe misunderstandings over the centuries. 'Secure and dynamic belief and action'comes close to a reasonable translation of '*īmān*'.

56 '*Muʾmin*' is the active participle, i.e., the doer, of *īmān*.

Table 1.1: Troops of Nexal-Consciousness and Anti-Consciousness.

The Troops of Nexal-Consciousness	The Troops of Anti-Consciousness	The Troops of Nexal-Consciousness	The Troops of Anti-Consciousness
good	bad	faithfulness	treachery
īmān	*kufr*	sincerity	insincerity
belief	rejection	vigor	lethargy
hope	despair	intelligence	stupidity
justice	tyranny	cognizance	denial
well pleased-ness	displeasure	tolerance/graciousness	open enmity
thankfulness	ingratitude	trustworthiness	beguiling
striving	giving up	discretion	indiscretion
reliance	avarice	communion	neglect (communion)
compassion	cruelty	fasting	breaking fast
mercy	anger	*jihād*	cowardice
knowledge	ignorance	pilgrimage (Mecca)	dissolving the pact
understanding	foolishness	prudence	backbiting
decency	indecency	goodness to parents	refractoriness
detachment	longing	genuineness	showing off
gentleness	roughness	right	wrong
wariness	recklessness	covering (oneself)	self-display
humility	pride	precaution	exposing (oneself)
deliberation	haste	pure impartiality	fanatic bias
forbearance	foolhardiness	rectifying	factiousness
deep silence	incoherence	cleanliness	filthiness
yielding (to truth)	arrogance	modesty	immodesty
full assent	doubt	resolution (conflict)	enmity
patience	impatience	rest	tiredness
forgiveness	revenge	ease	difficulty
richness	poverty	giving blessing	denying blessing
remembrance	negligence	health and security	affliction
memory	forgetfulness	economy	extravagance
cordiality	cutting off of ties	wisdom	inclination
contentment	covetousness	solemnness	flippancy
munificence	stinginess	felicity	misery
affection	hostility	turning (to repent)	persistence (in bad)
fulfillment	betrayal	seeking forgiveness	heedlessness
obedience	disobedience	discipline	indulgence
meekness	insolence	supplication	haughtiness
safety	tribulation	energetic-ness	laziness
love	hatred	joy	grief
truthfulness	lying	friendship	separation
the true	the false	generosity	miserliness

Source: Authors' own.

> Indeed! I swear by the self-accusing ego! (Qur'an 75:2)

> O Tranquil Ego! Return to your Cherisher-Lord, well pleased with Him and He well pleased with you. So enter among my adorer-servants! And enter my Garden! (Qur'an 89:27–30)

Allah (swt) thus commands ignorance (= ego) to return. At first it *ignores* the command,[57] but then it is given a choice: "*If* you disobey again after that I will remove you and your troops from my Mercy." How does the ego obey? By submitting itself and its troops to nexal-consciousness and the latter's troops. But what is the engine of that process of development? The engine is the first dialectical lynchpin, that of *prehending* (*ʿaql*) and *wise practicing* (*ḥikmah*). Together, both dialectical lynchpins constitute a concrete, dynamic objective-logical system.

5 Two Approaches to Objective Logic: Informal and Formal

In contemporary philosophy and science, two approaches to a systematization of objective logic may be identified: one more informal, the other more formal. Lack of space precludes extensive discussion; for greater development and technical detail, see the authors' forthcoming book, *The Logical Foundations of Islamic Economics: Objective Logic and Phenomenology of Consciousness and Action*. What follows is a summary account of each approach.

5.1 Informal Objective Logic: Scale of Forms

The informal approach is well-illustrated by examples from the primary sources. There are countless traditions and *āyāt* of the Qur'an that articulate various stages and processes of self-transcendence in Islam. A comprehensive example is articulated in the following Hadith narrated by Muḥammad ibn ʿAlī al-Bāqir (ʿa):

> *Īmān* (dynamic security in belief and action) is above *islām* (initial acknowledgment and submission) by a degree. And *taqwā* (dynamic awareness) is above *īmān* by a degree. And *yaqīn* (dynamic certainty) is above *taqwā* by a degree. And nothing has been so little-apportioned amongst the adoring-servants as *yaqīn*.[58]

57 The semantic field of 'ignorance' and its cognates, such as 'ignore', provide a happy instance of near identity between the semantic field of an English word with that of a corresponding Qur'anic Arabic word.

58 In some *aḥādīth* three degrees are mentioned: *Islam*, *īmān*, and *iḥsān* (*beautiful action*). In these traditions, '*iḥsān*' is used to encompass the highest stage of *taqwā* plus *yaqīn*. See Hamid (2011b, pp. 71–72).

The crucial thing to notice here is that each higher degree absorbs and develops its predecessor. These stages, constitute differences of both kind and degree. Here is an example found in a number of aḥādīth. To paraphrase: Consider the courtyard of the Forbidden Mosque (al-Masjid al-Ḥarām) and the Kaʿbah which lies at its center. The courtyard of the mosque is not nearly as precious as the Kaʿbah itself, although it remains a sacred place of safety and security, where it is forbidden to harm or kill anyone. The Forbidden Mosque symbolizes Islam. Now if you see a man in the courtyard, you can say that he is in the Forbidden Mosque, but you cannot say that he is in the Kaʿbah. On the other hand, if you see a man in the Kaʿbah, you can say that he is in the Forbidden Mosque. So being in the Kaʿbah absorbs being in the Forbidden Mosque, but being in the Forbidden Mosque does not absorb being in the Kaʿbah. Thus, one may enter *islām* without entering *īmān*, but one cannot enter *īmān* without entering and remaining within *islām*.[59]

Here is an example from the Qur'an, illustrating the scale of self-transcendence within *taqwā*:

> There is no blame on those who are dynamically believing and do deeds of righteousness regarding what they consume as long as they are dynamically aware, are dynamically believing, and do deeds of righteousness. Then they are dynamically aware and dynamically believing. Then they are dynamically aware and act beautifully. And Allah loves those who act beautifully. (Qur'an 5:93)

The scale of self-transcendence from *islām* through *yaqīn* thus constitutes what R. G. Collingwood calls a *scale of forms*.[60] A scale of forms involves an *overlap of classes* (i.e., of categories, universes of discourse, genera) in which a difference in kind is combined with a difference in degree. The genus animal is different in *kind* from that of plant, yet animal also involves a higher *degree* of developedness of the characteristic feature of plant, viz, biological growth.[61]

Yaqīn is different in kind from *taqwā*, *taqwā* from *īmān*, and *īmān* from *islām*. Yet *īmān* is also a higher degree of Islam, *taqwā* of *īmān*, and *yaqīn* of *taqwā*. One of the difficulties involved in establishing a genuine taxonomy of Islamic science lies

---

59 See Hamid (2011b, pp. 39–43). The relevant *aḥādīth* are paraphrased on p. 40.

60 See Collingwood (2005, Ch. 3).

61 A version of this scale of forms was discovered by Aristotle, and articulated by him into a system of metaphysics. The next stage in the Aristotelian scale of forms is that of the human being, followed by the celestial intellects, followed by the Prime Mover (= God). But Aristotle's scale is one of fixed genera (= universe of discourse) with no way to connect its objective-logical structure with the first principles of demonstration posited for each genus. Put another way: Aristotle was unable to connect the *intraconnective* demonstrative logic *within* any given genus with the *inter-connective* objective logic *between* the genera That is, objective logic is bifurcated from subjective logic. See our forthcoming book for details as well as Chapter 4 of Mure (1959).

in precisely articulating, as a coherent scale of forms, the structure of overlap of kind and degree between the subdisciplines of the Islamic sciences. This is a matter that deserves further study and research.[62]

5.2 Formal Objective Logic: Functors and Natural Transformations

In the 20th century, in the context of category and topos theory, mathematicians discovered powerful, formal tools for making objective logic precise: *functors* and *natural transformations*. Again, space precludes detailed development; readers are referred to the aforementioned, forthcoming book. We restrict ourselves to two examples.

For the first, we consider Benedetto Croce's dialectic of distincts and opposites. This is important for economics in general, and Islamic Economics in particular, because i) it provides a phenomenological treatment of the economic and the moral as terms of a scale of forms; and ii) it does so against an *original, primordial* dialectic involving the theoretical and the practical. That original dialectic is *preserved* or *realized* in the dialectic of the aesthetic and the economic, where 'economic' is used in some contemporary Western sense. But this dialectic takes place at a level of abstraction: It does not capture the fullness of the human being, who is something more than an economic animal that seeks mere aesthetic fulfillment. According to Croce, the aesthetic is succeeded and absorbed by the conceptual, and the economic is succeeded and absorbed by the moral. That is, the economic is absorbed by the moral and is a necessary condition of the moral. But the moral is more than the economic. As Croce's commentator Mure emphasizes, the mistaken belief in a bifurcation between the economic and the moral has resulted in a "great deal of bad ethical theory".[63]

In formal objective logic, the absorption of one category (= universe of discourse) into a higher category, with precise specification of difference and/or residue, is articulated by a *functor*, a special kind of objective mapping. Loosely speaking, a *functor category* is constituted by i) some categories; ii) the functors that specify the transcendence, development, or decay of one category into another; which are organized as a systematic sequence of *realizations* or *preservations* – the corresponding Qur'anic expression is *āthār* (*imprints*) – of iii) some original dialectic of categories. Unpacking and expanding this description is beyond the current scope, but the Figures 1.1 and 1.2 will give some flavor of the formalism.

62 A perusal of Hamid (2011b), e.g., Chapter 2, will illustrate some of the difficulties involved in articulating a proper Islamic taxonomy of self-transcendence. At the time of writing that book, the author was unaware of Collingwood's framework of a scale of forms, in terms of which the earlier attempt to outline a taxonomy could possibly have been better articulated.
63 See Mure (1958, p. 22).

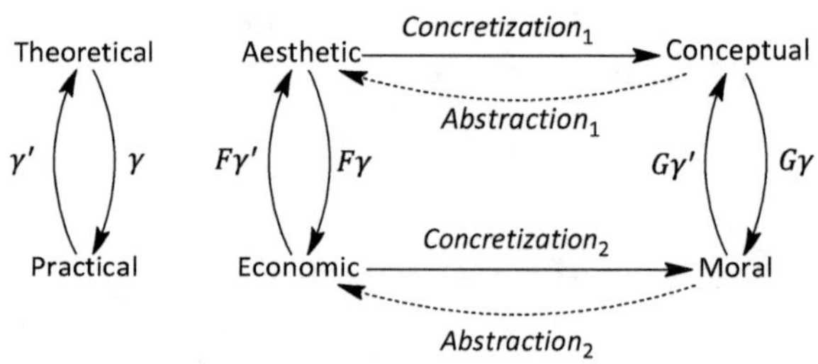

Figure 1.1: A Representation of the Croce Topos.
Source: Authors' own.

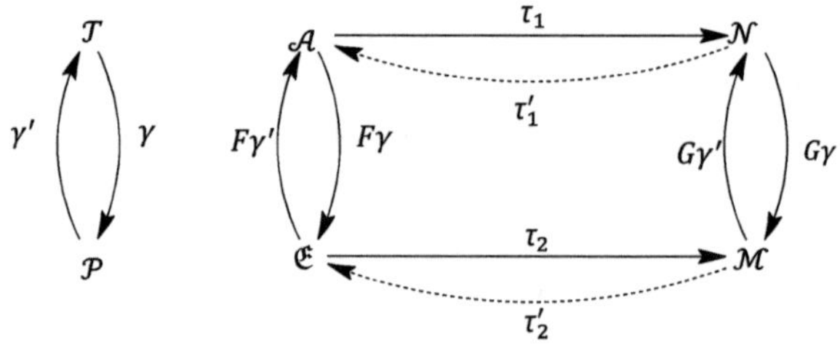

Figure 1.2: A Formal Representation of the Croce Topos.
Source: Authors' own.

The original dialectic of the theoretical and the practical is imprinted on the phenomenological background of four modes of human experience as two realizations (= preservations): a dialectic of the aesthetic and the economic, and a dialectic of the conceptual and the moral. These two imprinted dialectics are related by two natural transformations τ and τ': one of concretization (= development, self-transcendence) and one of abstraction (= decay, self-corruption). τ_1 and τ_2 are components of τ; τ_1' and τ_2' are *components* of τ', (see Figure 1.2)

These diagrams illustrate what may be called the *Croce topos*, a functor category constituted as described above. There are two dialectical lynchpins: The original and the natural transformations. These two lynchpins are *orthogonal* to one another. We may say that it takes at least two mutually orthogonal and dialectical lynchpins to constitute a concrete objective-logical system.

The Islamic phenomenology is far richer, and much more concrete, than that of Croce. If we restrict ourselves to the two lynchpins of the Islamic phenomenology of consciousness and action discussed earlier, we find that they are also orthogonal. The original *topos* – loosely speaking, a topos is a naturally closed or complete category – is that of the nexus and the ego: The *ego* (*nafs*) seeks to develop towards submission to and harmony with the *nexus* (*ʿaql*). The engine of that development also works towards mutual *coherence* (*ijtimāʿ*) of the troops of the nexus. Thus, it involves natural transformations between the 75 troops of intrinsic value, orthogonal to the upward movement of the ego.

Let our original topos of consciousness be designated as $\mathcal{A}_0$. It is constituted by i) nexus (= consciousness proper), designated by $\mathfrak{C}_0$; ii) ego/ignorance (= anti-consciousness, ego-consciousness), designated by $\mathfrak{C}_0^{nt}$; and iii) ego-consciousness' upwards movement (= functor) of development (= self-transcendence) towards nexal-consciousness, designated by ψ_0^{nt}; and iv) ego-consciousness' downwards movement of decay (= self-corruption) away from nexal-consciousness, designated by ψ_0. The abbreviation 'nt' is short for 'anti'.

The 75-plus-75 troops of consciousness and anti-consciousness form a background of modalities of human experience. Given a pair constituted by one modality (= "troop") of nexal-consciousness and its opposite anti-modality, the original topos of consciousness is preserved in that pair: The anti-modality may grow to submit to its opposite or it may decay to ultimate removal from the mercy of Allah (swt). At the same time, that growth ultimately depends on *coherence* (*ijtimāʿ*): Thus, the engine constituted by the dialectic of prehending and wise practicing also entails natural transformations between the modalities. A general illustration of the resultant objective-logical system is provided by Figure 1.3.

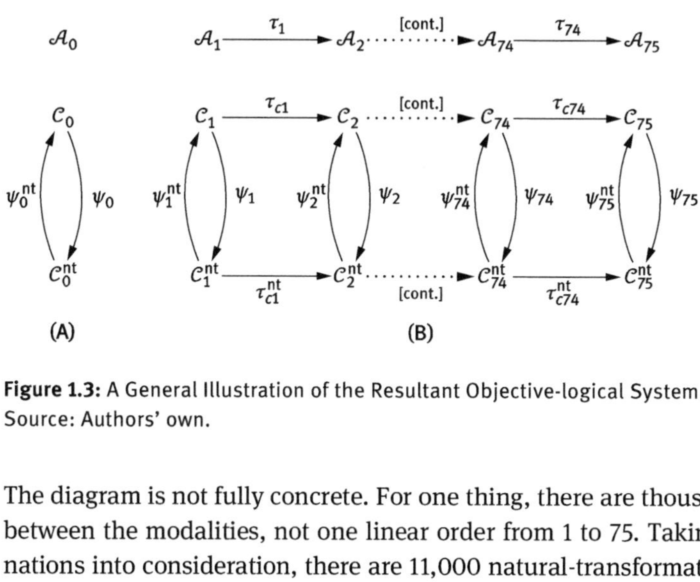

Figure 1.3: A General Illustration of the Resultant Objective-logical System.
Source: Authors' own.

The diagram is not fully concrete. For one thing, there are thousands of combinations between the modalities, not one linear order from 1 to 75. Taking all possible combinations into consideration, there are 11,000 natural-transformation pairs in the background of modalities of consciousness, each of which takes the form of Figure 1.4. The minimal unit of concrete human consciousness is not any particular modality, but a natural transformation unit, for every modality is definable and exists only in terms of at least one other. We can say that, from the perspective of the Hadith of the Troops of ʿAql and Jahl, the Islamic phenomenology of consciousness and action thus involves 11,000 units or dimensions of human consciousness. Development of

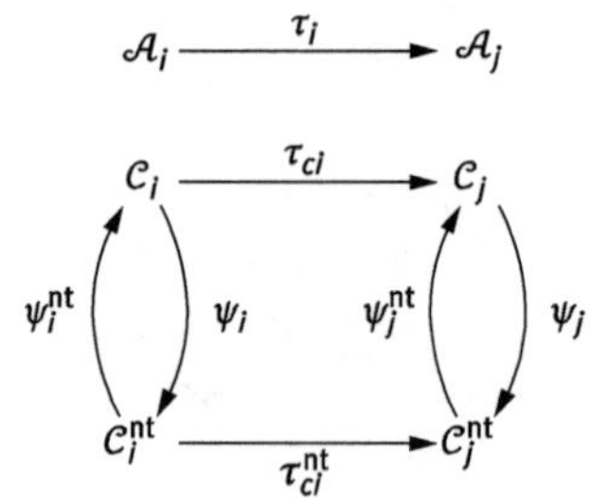

Figure 1.4: Natural-transformation Pairs in the Background of Modalities of Consciousness.
Source: Authors' own.

the implications of this discovery for Islamic phenomenology and Islamic Economics constitutes an important avenue for further, extensive scientific research for researchers in these fields.

Furthermore, there is at least one other lynchpin that has not been taken into account in the above discussion. The dialectic of *adoration-service* (*ʿubūdiyyah*) and *cherishing lordship* (*rubūbiyyah*) constitutes another original topos, one just as important as that of nexus and ego.

6 Transcending Cartesian Dualism: The Monism of the Qur'an

One weakness found in some of the current research in Islamic Economics is that, despite the criticism of scientism on the part of many of its advocates, it rarely advances beyond a Cartesian dualism of a personal consciousness which confronts an impersonal object; this leads to a practical dualism of fideism and scientism (to be discussed further down. Consider, for example, the following statement of Asad Zaman (2018):

> For reasons detailed elsewhere, European conceptions about the nature of knowledge were distorted by a battle between Science and Religion which lasted for centuries, and was eventually won by Science. Because of this battle, the West came to the false and misleading view that Science is the only reliable source of knowledge. *This is certainly true about the external world, but completely false about our internal personal lives, which cannot be explored by standard scientific techniques.* [Our emphasis.]

Two of Zaman's results are of interest here. The first, that "the West came to the false and misleading view that Science [in some accepted, narrow sense] is the only reliable source of knowledge" agrees with our own conclusion, even if arrived at from a different route. The trouble begins with the second conclusion:

> This is certainly true about the external world, but completely false about our internal personal lives, which cannot be explored by standard scientific techniques."

Although Zaman rightly rejects scientism, he does so at the cost of maintaining the wholly untenable Cartesian dualism between an "external" world, governed by the impersonal physical sciences, and an "internal personal" world, inaccessible to science and governed by another set of laws that have no effect on the external world. This leads to metaphysical commitments such as i) a dualism maintained in commerce by God (original Cartesianism), ii) reduction of the world to physical matter (physicalist materialism), or iii) reduction of the world to personal mind (subjective idealism). The first scenario is as inexplicable and untenable as the atomism of the Kalām, and presages the contemporary dualism of scientism and fideism (as we will discuss further on); the second takes us towards scientism, which has already been rejected; and the third takes us down one route towards solipsism. More generally, the realist view that the world consists of utterly separate personal minds which confront an independent, external world governed by quantitative science is, in the words of Mure, an "economic observer's" view which, by another route, leads inescapably to solipsism and skepticism.[64]

But even from the Islamic vantage point, Cartesian dualism is untenable. For the Qur'anic position is that the world is ultimately one, featuring no fundamental discordance:

> You will not see in the creation of Al-Raḥmān any mutual incongruity or discord.
> (Qur'an 67:3)
>
> The Fashioning of Allah who made everything as an intricate whole. (Qur'an 27:68)

Cartesian dualism is in direct conflict with this principle of monism. It is significant that the Qur'an, emphatically, does not ask one to take this matter on mere faith, but to directly and deeply observe:

> So return your vision again [and observe]! Do you see any cleavage? Then return your vision again and again [and look]; your vision will come back to you bedazzled and weary as well.
> (Qur'an 67:3)

Cosmological pluralism (inclusive of dualism) is ultimately unthinkable by reason or by any stage of consciousness that transcends its periphery. Cartesian dualism, in its original form or that of any of its many descendants, has always been *phenomenologically found* (*mawjūd*) unsatisfactory by the human spirit; hence the common motivation to embrace some form of reductionism to a single abstract principle – even if misguided, as in some variety of physicalist materialism or subjective idealism – or concrete dialectic (such as objective idealism). The core *wijdān* (*existential experience*)

---

64 See, e.g., Mure (1958), pp. 166–167.

of the human being resists any ultimate, absolute bifurcation of the world, as forcefully pointed out in Qur'an 67:3 above.

One result towards which our investigations lead is this: Any *genuine* science must be able to account for the characteristics of the "internal personal" world; at the same time, any genuine system of intrinsic value must be able to account for the characteristics of the "external" world.[65] Any genuine science must ultimately involve intrinsic value, and any system of intrinsic value must ultimately involve science. (Current civilizational consciousness is currently very far from appreciating this noble goal, let alone achieving it.)

The thesis of the current project may be stated as follows: *The importance and relevance of Islamic Economics lies, in large measure, in the struggle to determine and articulate a type of (scientific) system that integrates the categories of human economic, as well as moral, self-transcending (= spiritual) experience into an (objective-logical) intricate, coherent whole.* The informal and formal objective-logical examples provided earlier illustrate the thesis and, at minimum, provide a proof-of-concept on the basis of which further research may be conducted.

7 Towards a Science of Iqtiṣād

The thesis outlined in the preceding paragraph is rich enough to encompass, and general enough to extend, a particular consensus which is largely shared by a subset of specialists in the field that includes figures such as Abdel–Rahman Yosri Ahmed, Zaman Asad, Ali Khan, Abbas Mirakhor, and Mohammad Nejatullah Siddiqi.[66] Implicit within Islam is a concrete, systematic framework and methodology, based on certain philosophical considerations, for organizing and developing economics institutions, which i) is distinctive and unique vis-à-vis secular European ideologies; ii) is communicable to mainstream economists; and iii) yields empirically testable results.

Our objective is to extend this consensus by placing it in the context of a more general system of science, in an appropriately broad sense of 'science', one that is consistent with and flows from the Prophetic, Islamic, sources. In the absence of such an integrated approach, it will be difficult, perhaps impossible, to avoid the

---

65 The concrete nature of consciousness discussed earlier entails that every thought (= act of conscious prehending on the part) of a given thinker has a real object; there is an intimate nexus between thinking and its object that negates any absolute bifurcation between knowing and that which is known. Even when (pseudo-) thinking (such as fantasy) fails to shadow some material extension, its object is not merely abstract or personal to that thinker. Thus any absolute distinction between an internal, personal world and an external, impersonal world is negated. Rather there is a dialectical contrast between any individual locus of consciousness (subjective) and that which is prehended by consciousness (objective) that transcends the personal contours of that individual.
66 See Mirakhor (2006, pp. 22–24).

ultimately non-Islamic dualism of fideism and scientism. Such a system of Islamic Economics will integrate the economic (in the narrow, contemporary sense) with intrinsic value in an integrated science of development and self-transcendence. For Islamic Economics, i.e., iqtiṣād, is inseparable from self-transcendence. Consider the following scale of forms mentioned in the Qur'an:

> Then we made to inherit the Decree those whom we have chosen from amongst our servants. Among them is one [type] who does injustice due to one's ego, and among them is one [type] who acts in a balanced and efficient manner (*muqtaṣid*). And amongst them is one [type] who outstrips the rest in acts of goodness by the permission of God; that is the great virtue! (35:32)

In the commentary of Imām Ṣādiq (ʿa):

> The one who is unjust is the one who hovers about his ego. The one who is balanced and efficient (*muqtaṣid*) is the one who hovers about his center. And the one who outstrips the rest is the one who hovers about his Lord.

Contemporary economic science by and large focuses on ego consciousness combined with peripheral consciousness (= economic rationality) and some system of associated rules. *Iqtiṣād*, on the other hand, is truly operative only when central consciousness is activated. Yet a necessary condition of *iqtiṣād* is a system of economic rules. In addition, *iqtiṣād* is a *bridge* between ego-consciousness and Allah-consciousness – perhaps it is even appropriate to associate *iqtiṣād* with the *sirāṭ* (*overpass*) everyone in the next life has to cross in order to finally reach felicity. Hence the need for an integrated science that overcomes any bifurcation. An objective-logical approach to the matter appears inescapable.

Zaman is correct in his identification and criticism of the philosophical error of scientism. However, in order to escape scientism and solipsism one has to abandon the economic observer's vantage point. This Zaman does not do: Instead he sets up and develops a strong bifurcation between the Islamic and the economic.[67] Zaman is also correct in his contention that a genuinely Islamic framework and methodology is in fundamental conflict with those of secular ideologies with respect to certain principles. However, with respect to the core issue of the category (= universe of discourse) involved in the discipline of contemporary economics (with its associated objects and mappings), the solution does not lie in yet more Cartesian-style bifurcation and dualism. Rather, an objective-logical approach is needed to exhibit that economic category as a dialectical phase in the human development and self-transcendence that is core to an Islamic framework and methodology. And an Islamic framework and methodology, as we will show, exhibits itself as a phenomenology of consciousness and action. One of the aims of an Islamic system built on that phenomenology is to transcend and supersede the dualisms that dominate Western thinking, such as those of theory

67 See, e.g., his "Islam vs. Economics" (Zaman 2015, p. 48)

and practice (Aristotelianism), learning and knowing (Aristotelianism), personal and impersonal worlds (Cartesianism), scientism and fideism (the current zeitgeist). In place of these abstractions, an Islamic system seeks to show a progressive, *efficient* (*mustaqīm*) path to *knowledge* (*ʿilm*), followed by *objective certainty* (*yaqīn*),[68] then followed by *cognizance* (*maʿrifah*) of the whole, each in intimate conjunction with the stage of experience and practice of intrinsic value specific to it.

The available scientific formalism for objective logic is developed within the context of mathematical category and topos theory. Although they constitute a conceptual tool of the highest order, the philosophical and scientific potential of categories and toposes has hardly been tapped; the range of their possible application to Islamic Economics is virtually unlimited. Without using the expression 'objective logic', one can find aspects of its sense expressed by many philosophers and scientists, from ancient to contemporary, as well as important applications. After all, it did not take Aristotle's discovery of formal deductive logic for thinkers to engage in cogent deduction. Similarly, one can find countless exemplifications of objective-logical struggle in the history of human thought: It is an ubiquitous endeavor, indispensable in any effort to discover and explicate a coherent *system* of science in any of the senses we have considered. Looking at it the other way around, it should be noted that the mathematical theory of categories and toposes constitutes one *particular* paradigm for a sufficiently *general* theory of formal objective logic; at the moment it is also the only *formal* paradigm that we have.

It may be the case that the crises facing the "*ummah*" of Muslims are, as Zaman puts it, "of types never before seen in [Muslim] history".[69] This is on the right track, but it does not go far enough. For these crises are rooted in severe errors of commission

68 *Certainty* is to be distinguished from mere *certitude*: The former is a state of knowing the truth, the latter a state of surety that may or may not shadow the true or the real.

69 An *ummah* is a community whose members share a common, self-transcending *objective* (*umm*) under the leadership of a righteous *imām*. This is the paradigm of the original, archetypal ummah that existed under the leadership of the Messenger (ṣ). An ummah is also the concrete, organic reality of an objective-logical system, one that consists of two sub-categories and the mappings between them: The *imām* (*leader*), the *ma'mūm* (*someone who is led*), and the mutual exchange of *dynamic loving* (*walayah*) between them in the form of i) guidance and *purification* (*tazkiyah*) from the *imām*, and ii) *becoming purified* (*tazakkiyy*) and guided on the part of the *ma'mūm* – through following the *imām*.

> Say! If you have come to especially love Allah, then follow me and Allah will especially love you. (3:31)
> He [the Messenger] purifies them and teaches them the Decree and Wisdom. (62:2)
> Surely whosoever receives the purification is successful. (87:14)
> The Propheth as more walayah with the dynamic believers thant hey have with themselves. (33:6)

In the final analysis, an *ummah* without a loving, guided, guiding, and beloved *imām* is an abstraction.

This point deserves to be further elaborated and fathomed deeply.

and judgment made by the earliest generation of Muslim history. Progressive thinkers and liberation theologians of the near-contemporary Muslim world, from the generation of Allama Iqbal and Muhammad Abduh to that of Sayyid Maududi, Sayyid Qutb, Shariati, and Imām Khomeini, have all recognized and emphasized this fact in one manner or other. For workers in the field of Islamic Economics, that insight has to be developed and more deeply fathomed. Despite their impressive historical accomplishments, neither the immediate post-Prophetic generations nor the classical age of Muslim civilization adequately developed, except in disparate pieces here and there, the framework and methodology, the *system*, of science implicit within the Qur'an and authentic Sunnah. Before that system could mature in an organic manner, severe errors were made which spawned the three negative aberrations personified in the famous cults of the *religious elites in service to unjust wealth distribution and class superiority* (*nākithīn*), *tyrants* (*qāsiṭīn*), and *fanatics* (*māriqīn*). The revolving *mill-stone* (*raḥā*) of Islam came, in short order, to a complete stop, as the Messenger (ṣ) had famously predicted. Then, where simplistic norms and formulas of piety were transcended, the trappings of the *meta-categorical* contours of Christian theology, Aristotelianism, and Neoplatonic philosophy took over the Muslim mind, with disastrous consequence. This was then followed by the absorption of the Muslim mind into the meta-categorical context of contemporary Western civilization. At the end of this trajectory lies the current cauldron of crises.

It is far beyond the scope of the present note to outline that critical history in detail or in brief, although it is a task that remains in urgent need of accomplishment. Critical, yet productive and dynamic, awareness is one of the sides of '*taqwā*'. A concrete concept of *taqwā*, in turn, is a necessary ingredient in the formulation of any definition of "Islamic Economics".[70] And one of the *raisons d'être* of Islamic Economics is to play a crucial role in proffering effective solutions to these crises:

> If only the people of the communities had dynamically believed [stage of consciousness and action] and then became dynamically aware [next stage of consciousness and action], we would have opened upon them blessings from the heaven and the earth. But they belied [the Messenger], so We chastised and restrained them on account of what, and the manner in which, they earned.
>
> (Qur'an 7:96)

Acknowledgements: Thanks first and foremost belong to the Inventor (Badīʿ) of the world, which He made as a firm, intricate whole. The authors owe a debt of gratitude to Hossein Askari, John Corcoran, Ali Y. Al-Hamad, William Lawvere, Bilal Muhammad, Thierry Vanroy, and others.

70 An extensive discussion and development of the scale of forms involved in *taqwa* and *iḥsān* is provided in Chapters 2 and 3 of Hamid (2011b). Certain aspects of that effort are developed more formally and technically in the authors' aforementioned, forthcoming book.

References

Barber, Benjamin R. 2007. *Consumed: How Markets Corrupt Children, Infantilize Adults, and Swallow Citizens Whole*. New York: W. W. Norton.

Collingwood, Robin G. 2005. *An Essay on Philosophical Method*." Oxford: Oxford University Press.

Dalton, George. 1971. *Primitive, Archaic, and Modern Economics: Essays of Karl Polanyi*. Boston: Beacon Press.

Gowdy, John. 1998. *Limited Wants, Unlimited Means*. Washington, DC: Island Press.

Hamid, Idris S. 2011a. *Islam, Sign and Creation: The Spirituality of Walayah*. New York: Global Scholarly Publications.

Hamid, Idris S. 2011b. *Islam, Station and Process: The Spirituality of Walayah*. New York: Global Scholarly Publications.

Hasanuzzaman, S. M. 1984. "Definitions of Islamic Economics." *Journal of Research in Islamic Economics* 1 (2): 56–60.

Khan, M. A. (2000). "Globalization of Financial Markets and Islamic Financial Institutions." *Islamic Economic Studies* 8 (1): 19–66.

Lawvere, F. William. and Robert Rosebrugh. 2003. *Sets for Mathematics*. Cambridge: Cambridge University Press.

Mirakhor, Abbas. 2006. "A Note On Islamic Economics." *International Journal of Shīʿī Studies 4*(1): 11–78.

Mirakhor, Abbas, and Hossein Askari. 2017. *Ideal Islamic Economy*. New York: Palgrave Macmillan.

Mullainathan, Sendhil, and Eldar Shafir. 2013. *Scarcity: why having too little means so much*. New York: Penguin Books.

Mure, Geoffrey R. G. 1958. *Retreat From Truth*. New York: Oxford, Basil Blackwell.

Mure, Geoffrey R. G. 1959. *Introduction to Hegel*. Oxford: Oxford University Press. (First published in 1940.)

Rehman, Scheherazade S., and Hossein Askari. 2010. "An Economic IslamicityIndex (EI^2)" *Global Economy Journal* 10(3): 1–37.

Siddiqi, M. N. (2004). Current State of Knowledge and the Development of the Discipline. (Keynote Address to the Round Table on Islamic Economics, Islamic Development Bank, Jeddah, May 26–27.)

Skidelsky, Edward, and Robert, Skidelsky. 2012. *How Much is Enough: Money and the Good Life*. New York: Other Press LLC.

Zaman, Asad. 2015. Islam Versus Economics. In K. Hassan & M. Lewis (Eds.) *Handbook on Islam and Economic Life*. Cheltenham: Edward Elgar Press.

Zaman, Asad. 2017. "Reviving the Promise of Islamic Economics." *International Journal of Economics, Management and Accounting*, *5*(2), 205–225.

Zaman, Asad. 2018. The Search for Knowledge. The Nation, (March 12). Retrieved from https://nation.com.pk/12-Mar-2018/the-search-for-knowledge

Masudul Alam Choudhury, Mahfuzul Alam Taifur

Chapter 2: Consilience as Islamic Methodology of Tawhid: The General Socio-Scientific Framework

1 Introduction

The permanently parting divide between religion and science has been ingrained by the heteronomous perspective of the a priori and a posteriori separated domains of socio-scientific reasoning. Unity of knowledge has been abandoned in the face of the problem of heteronomy. The philosophy of science comprising the ontological, epistemological, phenomenological, and sustained inter-causal nature of the recursive continuity of organic relations has never been possible in the Islamic socio-scientific world-system. Deductive reasoning and inductive reasoning as noumenon and phenomenon, respectively, remain apart from each other, as in Kantian ontological and epistemological socio-scientific construction of rationalist reasoning.

The ensuing erroneous character of the great methodological problematique as the existing heteronomous nature of socio-scientific thought, methodology, application, and their divided properties between a priori and a posteriori reasoning carried in continuity is the essential nature of God-dissension of the modern socio-scientific age. Likewise, sheer invoking of the metaphysics of religion is a disabling mental construct. It has no methodological analytics, and thereby no potentiality for socio-scientific reasoning and application. The age is now as it has always been, to establish the analytical methodology of organic unity of reasoning, organization, application, and the recursive continuity of inter-causal relations between entities in the generality and particulars of the world-system that ensue along sustainability of historical consciousness of being and becoming of 'everything'. True socio-scientific worldview is based on endogenous embedding of morality and ethics from its derived methodology and the ensuing formalism and empirical applications. Thereby, the nature of the meta-socio-scientific world-system that ensues and sustains the emergent abstracto-empirical worldview of knowledge and thought defines the field of consilience, unity of knowledge (Wilson, 1998) – of monotheism in the truly Islamic case.

The principal objective of this chapter is to derive a sustainable and overarching methodological worldview of consilience, organic unity of knowledge as learning symbiosis between religion and science. Consilience is thereby derived and formalized as the core of true socio-scientific reality of Islamic inquiry. Such a derivation has its farthest extant of symbiotic unity of being and becoming in every detail in 'everything'. A particularity of such a *Tawhidi* consilience study is found in a reconstructed understanding of Islamic economics within the fold of transdisciplinarity.

https://doi.org/10.1515/9783110587920-002

Throughout this chapter the uniqueness and universality of the *Tawhidi* methodological worldview in meta-science, characterized by the specificity of Islamic economics, is sufficiently explained and formalized by consilience, meaning organic unity of knowledge in the monotheistic sense. Therefore, while this study is expounding a theory of consilience, unity of knowledge at work in a theory of meta-science of inter-causality between multivariates for establishing a wellbeing criterion amongst all, this is also the coterminous theory of *Tawhidi* worldview in 'everything'. A theological and metaphysical approach to the study of *Tawhid* is thereby supplanted by the phenomenological methodology derived from the Qur'anic foundation of the monotheistic worldview of organic unity of knowledge as symbiotic pairing in 'everything' (Qur'an, 36:36).[71] No theocratic inhibition thereby exists in the derivation, formalism, and application of consilience as unity of knowledge derived from the *Tawhidi* primal ontological origin of the Qur'an. The order of consilience is mapped onto the mind and matter unison of the world-system of unity of knowledge by *Sunnah* (teachings of the Prophet Muhammad (sawa)).

2 The *Tawhidi* Methodological Groundwork Reflective of Consilience, Unity of Monotheistic Knowledge

In the study of consilience, the unity of knowledge according to *Tawhid* as the primal ontology of Islamic methodological worldview in 'everything', the following stages of the methodology and the derived method arising from formalism and analysis are permanently upheld. Firstly, the primal ontology of *Tawhid* is explained by the supercardinality[72] of *Qur'anic* meaning of organic unity of knowledge and its appearance

---

71 Qur'an (36:36): "Exalted is He who created all pairs – from what the earth grows and from themselves and from that which they do not know."

72 Supercardinality (Ω) is the abstract mathematical topology (non-dimensional mathematical function) that establishes the following continuous functionals: (i) $S\subset\Omega$ by way of the reversible relational functional, $\Omega \leftrightarrow S$. (ii) Likewise the functionals, $S \leftrightarrow X$; and thus, $\Omega \leftrightarrow S \leftrightarrow X$. (iii) Therefore, the example of the organically unified domains of *a priori* and *a posteriori* multi-causal reversible relations are defined by knowledge-flows according to unity of knowledge and denoted by $\{\theta\} \subset \{X\} \in (\Omega,S)$ by the relationship $(\Omega,S) \leftrightarrow \{X\} \leftrightarrow \{\theta\}$. In the example of mathematical operation, $\{X\} \leftrightarrow \{\theta\} \Leftrightarrow \{\mathbf{X}(\theta)\}$; (Ω,S) as the epistemology; thereby say, $(2+2) \leftrightarrow 2^{\theta}.2^{\theta} = 2^{2\theta}$ and higher analytic forms of 2^{θ}. In the end, since $\{\theta\} \in (\Omega,S)$; therefore, the functional, $\{2^{\theta}, 2^{2\theta},....\} \equiv$ divine law in one case (*sunnat Allah*) $\in(\Omega,S)$, the totality mapped by the advancing understanding and application of *Sunnah* as ontological mapping of the supercardinal domain of *sunnat Allah*, denoted by S. Hence a numerical equivalence is established between the supercardinal domain of *sunnat Allah* through *Sunnah* and the experimental world-system. All functions are interrelations ($\leftrightarrow$). Such interrelations are inter-convertible by reversibility of knowledge production and continuity in the form of togetherness (complementarities and participation) as invoked by the *Qur'an* and transmitted to the creative understanding by *Sunnah* of the Prophet Muhammad (sawa). The transmission by *Sunnah* is essential to connect the divine with the creative order.

This first stage of the primal ontological order of knowledge in its being leading to becoming is further discoursed by the most learned authorities of Islam. They form the Qur'anic role models of *ulul-amr*. *Ulul-amr* as individuals and institutional collectivity participate in the consultative and discursive stages of articulating on the rules and meanings of specific issues arising in the process of deriving worldly understanding of the derived rules of the *Qur'an*. This initiating ontology is explicated and transmitted by the medium of Prophetic *Sunnah* (teachings and practices). Independent and rationalist opinion must be avoided unless such discursively derived knowledge is strictly in concert with the *Tawhidi* worldview of the Qur'an and Sunnah.

The latter days' corruption by the human concocted secularization of *Shariah*-compliance (Islamic law) at this stage of the epistemology of deriving rules and guidance for explicating the unravelling world-system must be avoided. Along with this, jurisprudence (*fiqh*) and opinion (*fatwa*) must be turned into re-visiting the *Qur'an* and *Sunnah* and the recasting of investigation by discursive practices of the participating learned ones (*ulul-amr*). Contrary to this practice, the history of *Shariah* had fallen into divisions and dissensions between sects, clergies, and theologies in Islam. Thereby, the immanence of secularization of and by '*Shariah*-compliance' has proved to be the rise of sects (madhabs) and groupings like *Sunni* and *Shiite* in the corrupted body framework of the Islamic worldview of *Tawhid*.

The third stage of progression of the knowledge-flows derived by the ontological and epistemological reference is utilized to evaluate the generality and specifics of the issues and problems of the world-system under study for the purposes of estimating the actual ('as is') and the reconstructive possibilities of these ('as it ought to be'). This evaluative approach (estimation and simulation) leads to the quantification of the wellbeing criterion in respect of the endogenous inter-variable system of causal relations that implicate degrees of participation and complementarities between variables representing *Maqasid al–Shariah* recommended choices in consonance with the *Qur'an* and *Sunnah*. The evaluation of the wellbeing function (*maslahah*), subject to the circular causation relations between the selected variables in respect of the 'as is' leading to simulation of 'as it ought to be' reconstructive nature of the desired state of the world-system and its inter-variable relational dynamics for a holistic interpretation

involving simply the corporeal function and extension of the reading, understanding, and applying of the monotheistic law (unity of knowledge) in the order of world-system in all shapes and forms (extendibility across systems and their organically relations, meaning complementary multi-causal reversible relations). The property of multi-causal reversibility by the organic interrelations is that of continuity in knowledge, space, and time.

of results and recommendations for change. This is the stage of phenomenological inquiry that combines the ontological and epistemological groundwork to establish the empirical derivation of quantitative forms.

In the fourth stage, the evaluation (estimation followed by simulation) of the wellbeing function (*maslahah*), subject to the inter-variable circular causation relations, results in intra-system and inter-system evaluations across multi-dimensional intra-system combined with inter-system cybernetic kind of analytical investigation. Such a process of evaluation of the wellbeing criterion, subject to systems of circular causation between variables, is a continuous phenomenon that occurs in continuums of knowledge-flows as methodologically derived in stage 1. The originary methodology of consilience of *Tawhid* is then induced in the use of phenomenology of evaluation of wellbeing, subject to circular causation between the entire set of endogenous variables. This mode of inter-variable circular causation represents the inter-variable consilience of *Tawhid* as endogenous multivariates.

In the fifth stage, the subsequent emanation of evolutionary learning across intra-system linked with inter-system evolutionary learning processes marks the property of sustainability across the continuums of knowledge and knowledge-induced space and time. The holism of the above-mentioned processes marking every point of history as events of evolutionary processes is a coordinate in the continuum of historical consciousness (Lucaks, 1968; Maritain, 1973; Burstein, 1991). It describes the unity between abstraction and empirical application in the unified ontological, epistemological, and phenomenological design of the abstracto-empirical, equivalently moral-material unison of the *Tawhidi* worldview of consilience, the organic unity of entities and their extended inter-relations by knowledge-induction.

The formal depiction of the five stages of the full methodology for a single system and cybernetic view of multiverse is formally shown in Figure 2.1.

3 Background and Review of Traditional Literature

Joseph Schumpeter writing on the emergence of metaphysical basis of science and the religion of the Schoolmen of their time established the fact that, modern science benefited from its isolation from the holistic concept of unity of the world-system that was embedded in the earlier socio-scientific conception. The path towards such growing dichotomy between religion and science was blazed by the great Occidental thinkers, Immanuel Kant, David Hume, Charles Darwin, carrying on the modern age to Edmund Husserl, Bertrand Russell, Rudolph Carnap, Karl Popper, Steven Weinberg, Richard Dawkins, and many others (Dampier, 1961). On the side of Economics and Epistemology there are the key thinkers of a contesting world of religion and science like Karl Marx, the rationalist dialectician Frederick Hegel, Jurgens Habermas, Immanuel Wallerstein, and others (Mahomedy, 2017).

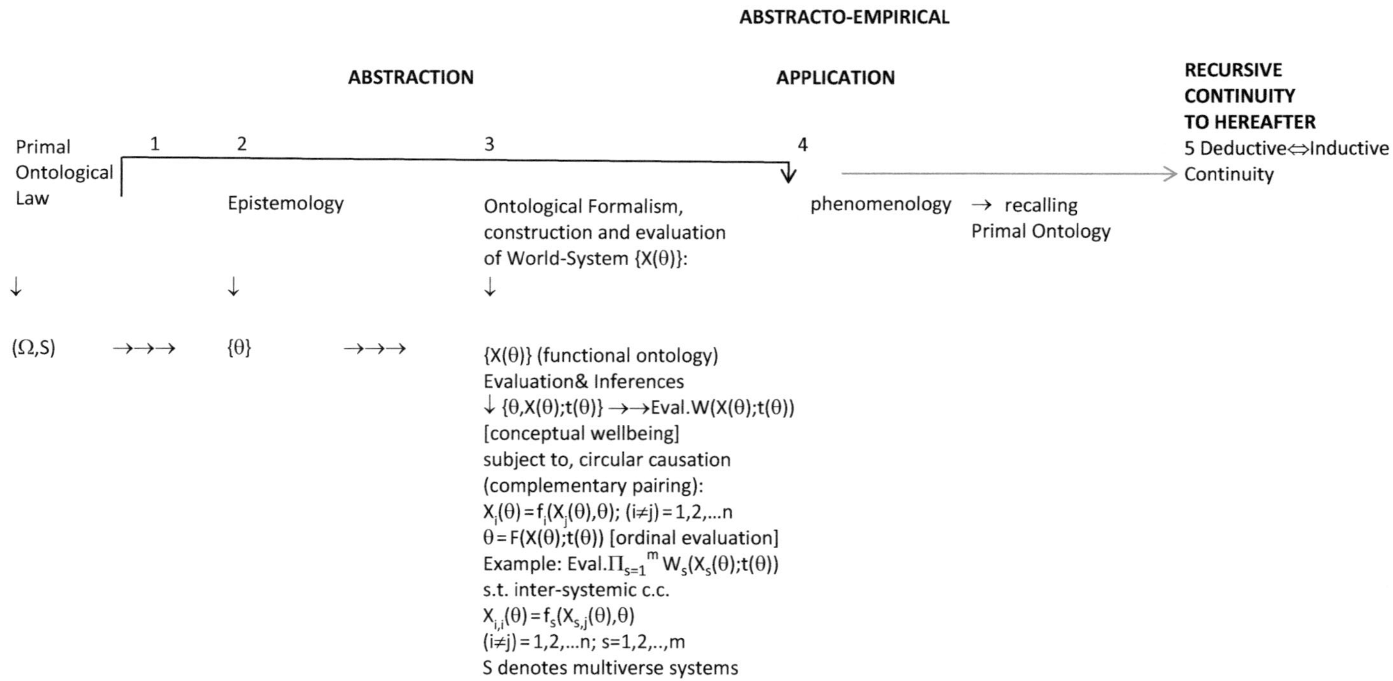

Figure 2.1: Universal Model of Consilience: Religion and Science and Beyond.

What was the reason for the denial of religion in science of the God-dissenting thinkers of the social and natural sciences? Several reasons can be pointed out. We consider those analytical reasons of critical divide, away from true realism of the holistic methodological worldview beyond the intellectual self-conceiving psychology. The central analytical consequence of a methodological problematic way of inherent perception- yet not true reality – of a dichotomous socio-scientific world-system in the mind-matter universe of ontological, epistemological, and phenomenological design of reasoning under rationalism, has given rise to the belief of irrelevance of the holistic universe of unity of 'everything' (Barrow, 1991). The resulting socio-scientific pattern of heteronomous thought in an otherwise holistic realism of intrinsic unity and methodological harmony has paved the way of rationalistic thinking. This attribute grounded the way of dichotomous reasoning. Such reasoning caused the emergence of thought, such as the irrelevance of God, and thereby the denial in God-dissension (Dawkins, 2008). The neutrality perception of the analytic way of explaining the creative dynamics of the divine law at work can be read off Hawking's (1988, pp. 15–16) words respecting natural science:

> The eventual goal of science is to provide a single theory that describes the whole universe. However, the approach most scientists actually follow is to separate the problem into parts. First, there are the laws that tell us how the universe changes with time [...] Second, there is the question of the initial state of the universe. Some people feel that science should be concerned with only the first part; they regard the question of the initial situation as a matter for metaphysics or religion. They say that God, being omnipotent, could have started the universe off any way he wanted. That may be so, but in that case he also could have made it develop in a completely arbitrary way. Yet it appears that he chose to make it evolve in a very regular way according to certain laws. It therefore seems equally reasonable to suppose that there are also laws governing the initial state.

Although the web-search characterizes some great thinkers as God-dissenters, they cannot be characterized as such if they have rejected the heteronomous pattern of rationalistic thinking for the benefit of the episteme of unity of knowledge. The episteme of unity of knowledge is termed Consilience. Edward O. Wilson as the writer of the book entitled, *Consilience: The Unity of Knowledge* (Wilson, 1998 op cit) therefore, cannot be taken as God-dissenter. Wilson in fact raised the possibility of the holistic way of reasoning between religion and science in his following words (Wilson, 1998 op cit, p. 264): "Looked at in proper perspective, God subsumes science, science does not subsume God. [...] Scientific research is not designed to explore all of the wondrous varieties of human experience. The idea of God in contrast, has the capacity to explain everything, not just measurable phenomena, but phenomena personally felt and sublimely sensed, including revelation that can be communicated solely through spiritual channels."

4 God-Dissension Caused by the Heteronomy of Reasoning

There are other two reasons underlying the socio-scientific problematique of heteronomy leading to God-dissenting thinking: The Kantian divide (Kant, trans. Friedrich, 1949) between a priori (pure reason) and a posteriori (practical reason); and thereby the dichotomy between deductive and inductive reasoning, that is entrenched as a permanent divide between how science argued against the Schoolmen of the European Enlightenment regarding the irrelevance of heteronomous God (a priori = moral imperative) in science. Metaphysics ceased to be characterized as an elect of science. The same was the problematique of rationalist reasoning in Hume's (1988) sensate world of causal relations and forms of the solely a posteriori world-system and of its inductive nature.

The further cause of the consequences that heteronomy has left behind as a socio-scientific problematique is the absence of analytical socio-scientific theoretical and practical methodology that would logically delineate the world-system of consilience and lead into relevant application and sustained continuity of the unitary worldview. The harmful effect of heteronomy in further developing the sciences towards unity of knowledge by interactively integrating and activating evolutionary learning systems is mentioned by Bhaskar (2002, p. 146): "So long as there is any element of heteronomy, any unfulfilled intentionality, any attachment, any fixation within you, your freedom will be to that extent restricted". Indeed, the meta-reality we are looking for as the consilience between religion and science in the framework of analytic methodological issues is the threshold of meta-science. This is beyond metaphysics and the narrow perspective of abstracto-empirical physicalism and non-physicalism (Hawking and Penrose, 2010).

Figure 2.2 explains the problem of heteronomy as of Kant and Hume's followed by its permanence as socio-scientific problematique in reasoning. Contrary to heteronomy is the phenomenology of consilience in meta-science of unity of being and becoming caused by endogenous learning processes of moral-material concrescence. This is the same as the establishment of historical consciousness in knowledge, and knowledge-induced space, and time dimensions.

In Kantian theory of knowledge with heteronomy in Figure 2.2, there is no continuity between a priori (deductive) reasoning domain 'A' and a posteriori (inductive) reasoning domain 'C'. Thereby, $A \cap C = \varnothing$A. Thus consilience does not exist between the reasoning domains and the entities of A and C due to the gap of the otherwise continuous correspondence that ought to exist by $A \cap C \neq \varnothing$ A. This means that, continuous correspondence would exist giving continuity to the interrelated correspondences between deductive and inductive reasoning, and thereby, between a priori domain and a posteriori domain.

The a priori domain indeed comprises the moral imperative of Kant's pure reason. Kant indeed wanted consilience between A and C. Thereby, the continuity of correspondence between these ought to exist. This unity of knowledge would then be shown by the mappings T1 and T2 recursively in their continuous interrelations. But there was no explainable model to explain such continuity to exist. Thus the dysfunction of rationalism was caused by human choice that was random in nature. This result is standardized for all of science by the derived axiom of rationality. Thereby, rationality derived from rationalism did not allow for the existence and presence of the determining a priori place of religion in an axiomatic originality existing recursively in organic relationship with a posteriori domain. This possibility would otherwise then be shown by inter-causality, T1 $\leftrightarrow$ T2.

Consilience would then be actualized by unity of knowledge in being and becoming of the world-system taken in its various diversities along with their variables and their relations. All continuous organic interrelations like {T1,T2} imply the incontrovertible recursive relations of inter-causality between the primal ontological law replacing rationalism and its derived axiom of rationality.[73]

The ultimate result was then the discontinuity between two distinct correspondences in the ruptured theory of knowledge. These are namely, T2′ from A to B in the domain of absence of continuity between A and C; and T1′ from C to B, showing that there is no relevance of any consilience type continuity in rationalism and rationality axiom. The moral imperative of Kant thus became a randomly determined rationalist project.

We then write as follows:

$$\{T1'\} \to \{H1\} \subset H;\ \{T2'\} \to \{H2\} \subset H,\ \textit{such that}\ \{H1\} \cap \{H2\} = \varnothing$$

thereby,

$$\left[\{T1'\} \to \{H1\} \subset H\right] \cap \left[\{T2'\} \to \{H2\} \subset H\right] = \varnothing \tag{1}$$

This property is true for every point of rationalist transformation, and hence for similar T-preserving mappings. Consilience is thereby ruptured everywhere in H.

The 'ϕ' space between the two rationalist heteronomous spaces would be annulled by the existence of the continuous mappings like,

$$T1'\textit{and}\ T2',\ \textit{thus}\ T1' \cup T2' \subset T;\ T1' \cap T2' \neq \varnothing \subset T;\ \textit{thereby}\ T1' \cup \cap T2' \neq \varnothing \subset T \tag{2}$$

73 Rationality derived from rationalism is an epistemic philosophy of methodological individualism, which acquires the properties of transitivity of pre-ordered preferences; assertion of full information causing steady-state equilibrium, and a necessary existence of optimality caused by the postulate of scarcity, and thereby, competition for scarce resources by self-interest.

Every positive monotonic transformation of these relations would belong to a similar form of transformation of T, say the family, $\mathfrak{I}(T)$. Thus the operations between A and C in the form of their annulment of heteronomy in B establishes a manifold topology (Maddox, 1970) of unity of knowledge.

Hume's a posteriori reasoning based on the assertion of the causality assumption of sensate properties of materiality existing in interrelationships between things, can be explained by Figure 2.2 as well. Now the mappings like {T1′} go from B to H and end in H2 as explained above. The rest of the continuity and the part of H1 as explained in Figure 2.2 remain absent. A posteriori reasoning is thereby dissociated from a priori reasoning. This also marks the heteronomous disjoint nature between noumenon and phenomenon; and between deductive and inductive reasoning.

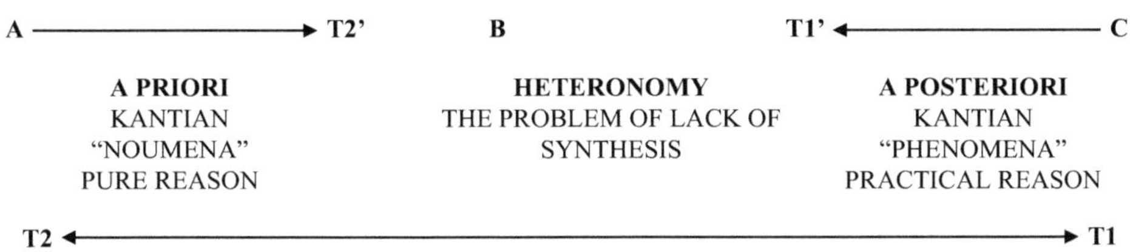

Figure 2.2: Consilience Versus the Problem of Kantian Heteronomy.
Source: Authors' own.

The contrary is the case for the analytical property of such attributes in consilience as the unity of being and becoming between religion and science. We thereby write for the case of consilience: (i) a priori (religion) ⇔ a posteriori (science). (ii) deductive ⇔ inductive. The symbol "⇔" means recursive circular causality of organic inter-relations existing in continuity by consilience between the two sides across every event occurring in knowledge, space, and time dimensions.

5 Explaining Inter-Causality between Religion, Science, and the Development of Meta-Science

The dynamics of inter-causality is of the nature of recursive continuity of cause and effect. The inherent dynamics do not end up with simply one affecting the other representative variables and their relations. The example is of the set of variables and their formal relations appearing as points in A causally affecting points in B. That is, circular causation here means, $A \rightarrow B$; and thereby, $\{xA\} \rightarrow \{xB\}$; and $\{fA(xA)\} \rightarrow \{fB(xB)\}$;

and simultaneously the causal relations B→A, etc. When such two recursive mappings exist, but in their separable (i.e. econometrically structural relations) continuous and differential analytic forms, there may still exist the condition of heteronomy continuously and analytically, as explained by expressions (1) and (2) and Figure 2.1. Consequently, cause and effect causality can exist continuously in the dialectical heteronomous states by causing,

$$[\{xA\} \to \{xB\}] \cap [\{xB\} \to \{xA\}] = \varnothing \subset H;\ and$$

$$[\{fA(xA)\} \to \{fB(xB)\}] \cap [\{fB(xB)\} \to \{fA(xA)\}] = \varnothing \subset H;\ and\ so\ on \qquad (3)$$

occurring all over the heteronomous topological space of all dichotomous mappings denoted by the family ℑ(H).

Furthermore, H1∩H2 = ф (expressions 1 and 2) implies the possibility of some inclinations that are left out of the God-dissenting nature of heteronomy in morality and consilience. For instance, Kant's moral imperative; Wilson's consilience between religion and science (biology); and Tawney's good society contrary to his moral explanation of the Acquisitive Society (Tawney, 1948) leave out the formulation of God-world-continuity relations in the morally conscious world-system (Choudhury, 2014).

The conversion from the heteronomous universe to the morally conscious world-system of the causally unified nature necessarily implies that, unity of knowledge embeds all complementing entities, variables, and their relations. Let such denominations of unity of knowledge measured parametrically either by algorithms ('functional' ontologies) or by questionnaire survey be denoted by quantitative ordinals {θ}. These parameters are discursively determined by the dynamics of interaction leading to integration (consensus), and thereby to the learning processes of knowledge in the evolutionary world-system as it attains higher levels of unity in inter-systemic and intra-systemic processes of being and becoming. The evolutionary learning processes are continuous, recursive, and sustained in both the unified world-system of inter-causality and in the oppositely poised dissociative causality as of Kant's a priori rationalism and Hume's a posteriori reasoning. In the contrasting cases, namely of co-evolutionary dialectical convergences in the presence of unity of knowledge (Expression 2); and in the case of heteronomous relations, knowledge-flows and 'de-knowledge'-flows (i.e. falsehood signified by inner differentiation and methodological individualism) assume numerical values for {θ} and {θ'}, respectively.

Thereby, all variables and their functional relations and transformations are embedded by the knowledge and 'de-knowledge' values, as the case may be. For the case of moral (religious) choices let the θ-embedded vector be denoted by X(θ). For the case of rationalism and the rationality of methodological individualism of the heteronomous relations, let the vector be denoted by X'(θ'). All respective functional relations and their monotonic positive transformations in the two cases are determined by their distinctly interactive, integrative, and evolutionary determinations of {(θ,θ'), (X(θ),X'(θ'))} values and their 'functionals', {(f(θ,X(θ)), f'(θ',X'(θ'))}.

6 Consilience Contra Heteronomy in Meta-Socio-Scientific Reasoning

Figure 2.3 shows the flux between the heteronomous world-system and the unified world-system in consilience. The box shown is pervasive in non-Cartesian coordinates such as (a priori $x(\theta)$; a posteriori $y(\theta)$), $\theta = \text{plim} \cup \text{IInteractions} \cap \text{IIntegration}\{\theta\text{II}\}$; $\{x(\theta)\} \Leftrightarrow \{y(\theta)\}$; $d\theta/dI > 0$ for all discursive interaction and integration along the evolutionary learning processes of unity of knowledge. Although every resulting point along the evolutionary learning process trajectories represents topological events in the sustained continuity of knowledge (θ), knowledge-induced space ($x(\theta)$), and time $t(\theta)$, the element of time acts simply as a momentary recorder of the continuous state of events. But this role of time does not bestow it with the dynamics of relational causality, input and output continuity, and complexity in development and change.

Figure 2.3 can be adapted to the case of those episteme that marginally, yet unsuccessfully, voice the importance of the moral imperative in historical consciousness (Lucaks, 1968; Kant, see Infeld, 1963; Bhaskar, op cit; Aquinas, see Torrell, 2005).[74] The dividing H-line between religion (a priori) and science (a posteriori) represents non-symbiotic thinking as the rejection of probability limit in attaining unity of knowledge. The shifting of the H-line represents the depth of the 'marginalist' heteronomous thinking. This allows for some degree of thinking along the methodology of consilience. Yet this allowance remains distanced from the evolutionary learning effect of IIE-processes on gaining unity of knowledge; thus, bringing religion and science to advancing levels of evolutionary convergence.[75]

74 Torrell (2005) explains: The circular plan, as of circular causation, remained a worldly process in the *Summa*. The divine law, just as in Kantian heteronomy, remained numinous for the world-system. On the circular plan of religion and the world-system, Thomas Aquinas' idea of circular causation in *Summa* is explained by Torrell (op cit, p. 27–36): "The work (*Summa*) is in fact constructed according to a circular plan that draws the reader into the 'going-out-from-returning-to' (*exitus-reditus*) movement, which is that of the entire universe coming from God to creation and returning to him as its final end."

75 Evolutionary convergence (Choudhury, 2011) is the property of never-ending and random movements around sequences of evolutionary equilibriums in the following way: Let $\{\theta_p\}$ denote analytic learning values in process 'p' around the specific evolutionary equilibrium value of 'θ_p*'. An evolutionary convergent equilibrium of $\{\theta_p\}$-value is defined by, $\theta_p - \theta_p^* > \varepsilon_1(\theta_p)$, for an arbitrary positive numerical value of $\varepsilon_1(\theta_p) > 0$. This implies the evolutionary convergence in $x(\theta)$-values as, $x_p(\theta_p) - x_p^*(\theta_p^*) > \varepsilon_2(x_p(\theta_p))$; for an arbitrary positive numerical value of $\varepsilon_2(x_p(\theta_p)) > 0$. Evolutionary convergences over learning processes are never attained, because they are continuously subjected to estimation and simulation across simulacra of evolutionary learning possibilities for analytic values of $\{\theta_p, x_p(\theta_p)\}$. Note the difference in the definition of limit in real functional analysis.

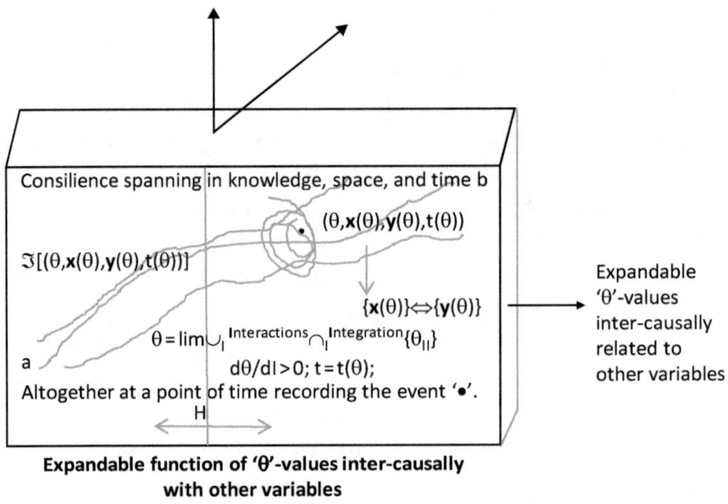

Figure 2.3: Consilience of Religion and Science Embedding the Entirety of Knowledge, Space, and Time Dimensions.
Source: Authors' own.

Heteronomy remained permanent in socio-scientific reasoning despite the voice of morality, religion, and truth of the ultimate reality. There was no discovery of the universally generalized methodological abstracto-empirical worldview towards explaining the imminent nature of meta-science in the generality and particulars of the diversely unified world-system.

7 Systemic Extensions

In regards to the formalism of Figures 2.2 and 2.3, consilience versus heteronomy being extendible in all of the non-Cartesian topology as manifold of $\{\theta, X(\theta), t(\theta)\}$, implies widely inter-systemic interaction, integration, evolutionary (IIE) and learning continuums of the same type according to the episteme of unity of knowledge. This episteme of consilience embeds all the details of consequential intra-system and inter-system knowledge-induced unification dynamics over knowledge, and knowledge-induced space and time dimensions.

Extending the explanation of Figure 2.3 to the case of multi-system and multiverse unity of being and becoming by virtue of transformations in the form of families of functionals, $\Im[(\theta, x(\theta), y(\theta), t(\theta))]$, yields the following formalism:

$$\Im[\theta, x(\theta), y(\theta), t(\theta)] = \prod s\Im s[\theta, x(\theta), y(\theta), t(\theta)] \quad (4)$$

where 's' denotes enumerated systems.

This functional is evaluated subject to inter-causal relations between the variables of the vector, $\{x(\theta), y(\theta), t(\theta)\}$s across intra- and inter- systems(s). The inter-variable and systemic circular causality exists as, $x(\theta) \Leftrightarrow y(\theta)$.

That is inter-causality relations are,

$$x_i(\theta) = f_i\left[x_j(\theta), y(\theta), t(\theta)\right]; \text{ where, } \left(x_i(\theta), x_j(\theta)\right) = x(\theta);\ i,j = 1,\ 2,\ \ldots n1$$

$$y_i(\theta) = g_i\left[x(\theta), y_i(\theta), y_j(\theta), t(\theta)\right]; \text{where, } (y_i(\theta), y_j(\theta)) = y(\theta); i,j = 1,\ 2,\ \ldots n2$$

$\theta = F\left(x(\theta), y(\theta), t(\theta)\right)\theta$ as quantitative wellbeing measure to evaluate the degrees of complementarities that exist or ought to exist between the variables by the θ-embedding effect of moral-material endogeneity.

The above equations are estimated and simulated for degrees of inter-variable complementarities and for quantifying the degree of unity of knowledge formed via the evaluation of inter-causal relations between the variables and evolutionary learning signified by estimated followed by simulated values of '$\{\theta, x(\theta), y(\theta)\}$' for the problem under study.

$\theta = \text{plim} \cup^{\text{I=Interactions}} \cap^{\text{I=Integration}} \{\theta\text{II}\}$, which by the implicit function theorem of inversion of continuously differentiable analytic functions can be written as,

$$\theta = \text{plim} \cup^{\text{I = Interactions}} \cap^{\text{I = Integration}} \{\theta_{\text{II}}\} = \prod{}_{\text{s}} F_{\text{s}}(x(\theta), y(\theta), t(\theta))_{\text{s}}$$

$$d\theta/dI > 0 \Rightarrow d\theta/dx(\theta)s > 0; d\theta/dy(\theta)_{\text{s}}.$$

The above multi-system relations uphold in the continuum of all observations across time in the non-Cartesian topological manifold (Kupka and Peixoto, 1993) as described in Figure 2.3.

Figure 2.3 further proves the fact that, as long as the constraint of resource scarcity is upheld in all of socio-scientific arguments, the competition signified by mainstream socio-scientific marginal substitution between religion and science will abide, even though this can be along the marginal heteronomy surface mentioned earlier. We find the axiom of resource scarcity to prevail in all of science as process (Hull, 1988) and in economy and finance by their core postulate of resource scarcity; and in society by social Darwinism of relationship as between society and climate change (Urry, 2015, pp. 45–59).

On the other hand, if resources can be continuously regenerated, this can extend the two-dimensional box of Figure 2.3 within enlarged elastic multi-dimensional boxes of the knowledge, and knowledge-induced space, and time dimensions, as shown in Figure 2.3. The postulate of scarcity then falls apart and 'marginal substitution' is replaced by pervasive complementarities in evolutionary learning everywhere within the multi-dimensional (three-dimensional) box(es) of Figure 2.3.

Thus, the central property of consilience as a socio-scientific analytic with continuously recursive ontological, epistemological and phenomenological functions in evolutionary learning is resource regeneration governed by consciousness. This property establishes the principle of universal complementarities between the good things of life (Daly, 1992). This property of evolutionary learning and continuous resource regeneration replaces the fictive permanent property of marginalism on smooth and convex (concave) optimal surfaces. Such surfaces fail to continue learning at the optimal and steady-state points. Shackle (1972) characterizes such steady-state equilibrating optimal states of resource allocation as the end of novelty by finite learning.

Attained points in such 'marginalist' states can be expanded only by exogenous injection of resources. Endogenous role of consciousness and self-governing evolutionary and punctuated equilibriums have failed to exist in economic thought by and large, except for some special cases (Robinson in Burstein, 1991; Georgescu-Roegen, 1981; Boulding, 1981). Unity of knowledge between religion and science cannot occur. Pervasive complementarities between the good things of life (e.g. life-fulfillment possibilities) herald the possibility of consilience between religion – representing the good things enunciated by the primal ontological law as of monotheism – and science as analytic formalism of universal complementarities as the functional design of the ontological law of unity of knowledge.

One more property among several other analytical ones in relation to evolutionary learning non-convex surfaces in the context of unity of knowledge should be noted. Along the tortuous trajectory 'ab' in Figure 2.3, any 'bit' of it, say $[a \rightarrow fab](\theta)]$, the recursive nature of inter-causality between the points 'a' and 'b', yields the following reversibility result of circular causation: $[a \rightarrow fab](\theta) \otimes [b \rightarrow fba](\theta) = fb \otimes fa = \alpha(\theta).I$.I is the identity function. $\alpha(\theta)$ denotes the deflection function of reverse circular causation between the functions fb and fa (Choudhury, 2013).

In the case of intra-system and inter-system multidimensional circular causations the above relations are extended to the form,

$$\Pi_s \Pi_i [a_i \rightarrow fa_i b_i]_s(\theta_s) x [b_i \rightarrow fb_i a_i]_s(\theta_s) = fbxfa = \alpha_{is}(\theta_s).I = \alpha_i(\theta).I, i = 1, 2, \ldots n; \quad s = 1, 2, \ldots S.$$

This expression means that, all the intra-systemic and inter-systemic variables are finally comprised in a vector (also matrixes, tensors) space of all the emergent sequence of variables across evolutionary learning systems.

Application, example 1: Complementarities between Religion and Science – inter-systemic causality between the primal ontological law of monotheism and the scientific materiality of world-system

An example of such a case in consilience theory of religion and science is this: Monotheism as the primal ontological law of religion stands as the premise for understanding religion-to-science unity of knowledge between all good things of life (e.g. worldly affairs and cosmological resources – religion-science.[76] This is simultaneously followed by the reproduction of resources in the scientific world by adopting the principle of universal complementarities to regenerate resources. The most important of such resources as input and output in sustaining wellbeing is knowledge. Thus, science responds to the principle of universal complementarities between the good things of life as the sure sign of the monotheistic primal ontological law of unity of being and becoming.

Thus, the two circular causations compounded together are of the nature of 'a'⇔'b'. The result is the analytic evaluation of the 'as is' followed by the simulacra of 'as it ought to be' evaluations of the wellbeing criterion of inter-variables. The circular causation relations yield the evolutionary levels of wellbeing by the processes of learning and sustainability through pervasive complementarities caused by $\{\theta\}$ along IIE-learning processes. The primal ontological law of *Tawhidi* unity of knowledge is thus inter-connected with the evolutionary learning possibility of wellbeing in worldly experience.

Application, example 2: *Tawhidi* complementarities between Religion and Science – intra-systemic causality between the primal ontological law of monotheism and the scientific materiality of world-system

Figure 2.4 shows the transformation of social preferences along lines of IIE-learning processes as cases of knowledge-induced dynamic preferences. In this figure, we have avoided many of the details of three dimensional preference curves that would exist everywhere within the Edgeworth-Bowley type box of knowledge-induced vectors like $(B,M,I,\theta)[\theta]$. Hence by knowledge-induction of the variables, the point 'a' is able to include the points like (A,c,B) of Figure 2.2 by the elastic space provided by the evolutionary learning neighborhood of a point like 'a' and all points of similar kind that fill up Figure 2.4 by 'θ'-induction. The result is an ever-enlarging IIE-learning box of peaceful coexistence by inter-causality among all the variables of the vector $(B,M,I,\theta)[\theta]$.[77] Such is the characterization of the political economy of conflict resolution in the multidimensional world of IIE-learning processes of the vector.

76 Kant (trans Friedrich, op cit) wrote: "Two things fill the mind with ever new and increasing awe and admiration the more frequently and continuously reflection is occupied with them; the starred heaven above me and the moral law within me. I ought not to seek either outside my field of vision, as though they were either shrouded in obscurity or were visionary. I see them confronting me and link them immediately with the consciousness of my existence."

77 Each of these vectors of variables would have its own multivariate composition. B: benevolent preferences (peace); I: integrative preferences (conflict resolution); M: malevolent preferences (conflict).

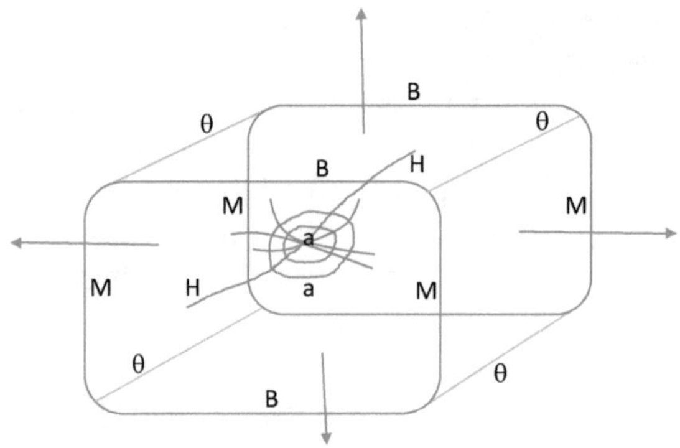

Figure 2.4: Multi-dimensional (3-dimensional) θ-induced Edgeworth-Bowley Box of Learning in (B,M,θ).
Source: Authors' own.

Application, example 3: Derivation of political economy of peace (*Tawhidi* ontological law) in complementary multidimensional event systems (socio-scientific order)[78]

In the broadened understanding of consilience between religion and science we take the political economy of intra-system understanding of complementarities between peace (B), conflict resolution (I), wellbeing, and the variables within these categories of the ontological law of moral worth. We treat them within the analytic model of complementarities as science. The IIE-learning properties are thereby invoked, and unity of knowledge for the common good as wellbeing is explained. The structure of the IIE-learning event systems spanning over knowledge, and knowledge-induced space and time surrounds the multidimensional neighborhoods of 'a' in Figure 2.4.

Figure 2.4 shows how Table 2.1 in respect of peace as the multidimensional meaning of political economy of conflict (M) and conflict resolution (I) concerning vectors of the type X(θ) span across ever-increasing fields of human possibilities by peace (B). Every one of the resulting such IIE-learning trajectories is a feasible path of political economy of conflict resolution. By contrariness such paths follow the same explanatory methodology but apply to the political economy of conflict.[79]

78 Extracted from Mahfuzul A. Taifur's submission of a paper to *International Journal of Ethics and Systems* (IJOES).

79 The completeness of the methodological worldview explaining the entire meaning of political economy of peace as the study of organic relations of inter-causality between diverse systems is a mathematical topological concept (Maddox, 1970). The following definition forms the topological meaning: If T denotes truth (political economy of conflict resolution) and F denotes falsehood (political economy of conflict) then $T \cup F = \Omega$; $T \cap F = \phi \epsilon \Omega$. These are open spaces. On them a class of continuous mappings say $\mathfrak{I}$ on the open space of Ω preserves the above-mentioned properties.

Table 2.1: Elements of Inter-variable Relations between Human Rights (Law), Socioeconomic Development, and Peace in the Theme of Political Economy of Peace.

Elements of Human Rights	Human Development	Peace
x(θ): denotes enactment of United Nations peace- making; peace-building, equality in political freedom, and access to legal defence	y(θ): human freedoms of life, liberty, thought, equality, political freedom, speech, belief, practice of religion, property rights, wellbeing and health, human resource development, cultural freedom, community life, social security, poverty alleviation, and freedom	z(θ): global discourse for establishing common wellbeing; peacemaking; peace building; respect of national and group differences of belief, religion; tolerance and respect, conflict resolution

Source: Authors' own.

Figure 2.4 explains the interconnected IIE-learning processes at every event point of the ever-widening gyrations along the path of the political economy of peace as conflict resolution dynamics or the path of the time-dynamics of conflict-based (dialectical) study of political economy. While all the paths within IIE-learning systems show pluralistic evolution arising from the ontological origin of unity of knowledge, the points in such learning fields disperse because of their increasingly greater degrees of diversities. Peace as inter-causal balance of organic unity of relations between entities and variables could expand from the level mentioned in Table 2.1 into ecological issues, intergenerational issues, and socio-ethical issues of finance, business, and technology, and so on (Inglott, 1990). Consequently, convergence to the unique path of truth and goodness of the good society remains always possible; yet greater discursive learning efforts of integration arising out of interaction and leading to integration and evolution are required. The unique and universal IIE-path of truth and goodness in certainty is shown by the expanding evolutionary paths in Figure 2.4.

In reference to the characterization of political economy of peace as convergence towards conflict resolution across multivariate topology, as explained in reference to Table 2.1, we explain the following scenarios in Figure 2.4: For every event point along the IIE-learning trajectory HH there exist points like 'a' in the domain of intersection of the three sets of vectors (matrices, tensors etc.) (Gel'fand, 1961). These entities are denoted by $x(\theta)$, $y(\theta)$, $z(\theta)$.

In Figure 2.4, the conflict resolution domain of political economy of peace is denoted by,

$$X(\theta) = \cup^{I=\text{interaction}} \cap^{I=\text{integration}} [\{x(\theta)\} \cap y(\theta) \cap z(\theta)]; \quad \text{with } dv(\theta)/d\theta > 0 \Leftrightarrow dW(v(\theta))/d\theta > 0 \tag{5}$$

$$v(\theta) = (x(\theta), y(\theta), z(\theta)).$$

The IIE-learning processes experienced in the conflict resolution domain in the presence of its learning dynamics enlarge the extant of political economy of the mutually convergent domains. Thus, outlying points are intercepted in the probability limits of $(\theta,X(\theta))$ of the evolutionary learning points. Such intercepted points by progressive learning expand the entire domain of conflict resolution perspective of political economy of peace as we have explained this in terms of its epistemic relational concept of unity of knowledge. Boulding type of conflicting and independent social preferences are now transformed into conflict resolution by the socially inclusive and rehabilitating 'θ'-effect (Boulding, 1971).

8 Impossibility for Consilience in Modern Scientific Marginalist Methodology

A reference to Dasgupta (1987) points out the permanent entrenchment of 'marginalism' in all of economic science. The explanation given above respecting the shifting nature of the conflicting domains of religion (a priori, noumenon, deductive) and science (a posteriori, phenomenon, inductive) under condition of scarcity of resources and the absence of the continuous sustainability of consciousness by evolutionary learning in self and the other, is the permanent feature of 'marginalism' vis-a-vis competition, rationalism and rationality, self-interest, and methodological individualism (Buchanan, 1999). The assumptions for problem solving under conditions of steady-state equilibrium, optimality, and specified smooth and convex (concave) forms of problem-solving surfaces with 'marginalist' concepts of price, value, opportunity cost, and exogenous independence of morality and ethics, are fictions not reality in the experiential world-system.

Thereby, religion is treated as a group of leisure activities and science as a group of creative activities. Time is the scarce resource to be spent between the religious and scientific human activities. Then the well-known concave to the origin individual indifference curve (welfare surface), and convex to the origin production possibilities surface become convenient tools of problem-solving. Such analytical results of the methodology of liberalism remain contrary to the meta-scientific nature of evolutionary learning in its continuous search for the phenomenology of meta-reality of unity of knowledge.

Examples of such two groups of intra-system and inter-system choices are firstly, entitlement and empowerment (ethical goods). Both of these ends when governed by the axiom of resource scarcity and competition. The end result is competing groups within the ethical order. Secondly, there are choices like the welfare of the rich (capitalism i.e. science) and of the poor (charity i.e. morality). The rich and the poor are known to be the two most irreconcilable social groups (Nitzan and Bichler, 2000). Thus in every case, the axioms of resource scarcity and competition lead into social contracts that prevail in the presence of 'marginal' rates of substitution between the competing choices made intra-system and inter-systems.

Thus, two opposite natures of the world-systems emerge according to methodological individualism. Firstly, there is the steady-state equilibrium and optimal nature of the non-learning world-system. It is moved only by exogenous injection of resources and technology. The second kind of the world-system is the dialectical one. Its nature on the other hand is without convergence but is interrupted by conflict and individualism of optimal self-interest behaviour along its evolutionary trajectory like 'HH' of Figure 2.3 (Sztompka, 1991; Rawls, 1971).

9 Conclusion: The Generalized Model of Consilience between Religion and Science, and Beyond

In conclusion to the project on consilience for religion and science and beyond in regards to the episteme of unity of knowledge, we conclude with the generalized model of the emerging meta-science. This model encompasses the abstraction and the applied domains in their continuity by recursion across the knowledge, space, and time dimensions. From the generalized system model of consilience, particular problem solving abstracto-empirical inquiries arise in compliance with the universal and unique ontological nature of the general theory of consilience. The end of the pursuit of generalized system is the mathematical continuity by meta-scientific discursive recursion of evolutionary learning processes of ontology, epistemology, and phenomenology in knowledge, space, and time dimensions.

The generalized system model takes its axiomatic origin in the Primal Ontological Law of Monotheism (religion), Tawhid. The structure of this supercardinal[80] domain of knowledge and Being is unbounded continuity. Its Final Closure is in the very

80 Let Ω denotes the denumerable 'complete' space with a well-defined function, 'f', which is mathematically defined as, $\lim_\theta[f(\theta)] \subset \Omega$, for every element of abstraction existing as entities, variables, and complex relations in the multi-dimensions of knowledge, space, and time. Thus Ω being denumerable is not numinous. Ω is 'unbounded' by the property that, if there exists an open domain $\Omega' \supset \Omega$, then there exists the supremum property. Supremum means the maximum of the least open-ended denumerable bounds. The supremum makes the generalized Ω to be the unbounded supremum. This satisfies the property: $\lim_\theta[\sup(f(\theta),f'(\theta')...] \subset \Omega \subset \Omega' \subset .... \subset \sup\{\Omega, \Omega', ...\}$. Thus $\sup\{\Omega, \Omega',....\} = \Omega$ by notation, is the abstract yet denumerably open space of completeness and unboundedness. Ω is therefore superspace or supercardinal in nature. In other words, Ω defines and generates all relations concerning things. Such relations as derived from the ontological law are denoted by the set $\{\theta\}$. $\{\theta\}$ are thereby indefinitely many, and hence open in multi-dimensions of knowledge, space, and time. Ω contains $\{\theta\}$ openly and indefinitely extended. Ω causes $\{\theta\}$ to arise in the first place. $\{\theta\}$ subsequently reflects its relationship with Ω through abstraction and evolutionary learning. Ω is therefore all encompassing and thus supercardinal.

large-scale end of the multiverses governed by the monotheistic unity of knowledge (Tawhid reflected in religion-science complementarity). This is the meaning of the Beginning and the End in the Qur'an. That is, the Beginning is the Monotheistic Ontological Law and the End is the cumulative knowledge evolution of unity of the world-system at the great event of the Hereafter (Qur'an 78:1–5).

The countless inter-causal relational multiverses start from the mathematically complete but unbounded totality of knowledge comprising Truth, the differentiating Falsehood, and the temporarily indeterminate state between Truth and Falsehood. Such a mixed state is interpreted as science as process. The indeterminate is well-determined as the learnt unity of knowledge evolves to higher levels of certainty, being premised in the Primal Ontology of unity of knowledge (religion).

We denote the supercardinal Monotheistic Primal Ontology of Being by Ω. Ω is mapped by the primal endowed correspondence, denoted by 'S', onto the existential multiverse world-systems, by the mediation of derived knowledge. This universal ontological mapping is denoted by $\{\theta\} \leftarrow S(\Omega) = (\Omega,S)$, and all possible combinations and compounding of $\{\theta\}$ so derived.

Likewise, there is the contrary to $\{\theta\}$, denoted by $\{\theta'\}$, that also arises by the same type of mapping but as mathematical opposites. Thus, $\{\theta\}\cup\{\theta'\} \subset (\Omega,S)$; $\{\theta\}\cap\{\theta'\} = \phi \subset (\Omega,S)$; therefore, $\{\theta\}\cup\cap\{\theta'\} \subset (\Omega,S)$. All real-valued transformations of the various θ-functions are contained in (Ω,S). Finally, the monotheistic universality and uniqueness properties are established by the identity, (Ω,S). This means that the Beginning is actualized by the End of the consciously evolutionary learning multiverses of true reality by the function of the Primal Ontology of unity of knowledge and at the banishment of rationalism in every shape, form, and explanation.

(Ω,S) is therefore the supercardinal knowledge-induced topology of manifold (Dewitt, 1992). $\{\theta\}$ and $\{\theta'\}$ denote the derived knowledge from the Ontological Law of Monotheism as unity of knowledge in the good things of life (Truth); and the differentiated aggregation of knowledge in the choices contrary to Truth, that is Falsehood, and the disappearing temporarily indeterminate perceptions (Bergson noted on perception, see Bertrand Russell, 1990).[81] The two opposite θ-type values form distinct epistemological premises in Truth (unity of knowledge by participatory complementarities between the good things of life determined by the Primal Ontological Law), and Falsehood (differentiation of knowledge by rationalism and the postulate of rationality).

From the Primal Ontological Law and the derivation of the Epistemological premise of consilience in $\{\theta\}$ (thereby, $\{\theta'\}$ in rationalism and rationality) there simultaneously arises the 'functional' ontological nature (Gruber, 1993) of the world-system $\{\theta,X(\theta),t(\theta)\}$ in generality and its particulars. It is likewise for $\{\theta',X'(\theta'),t(\theta')\}$.

81 Bergson remarked as noted by Bertrand Russell, "Perception is the lowest state of mind; it is like mind without memory".

We denote the multiverse manifold of world-system by functionals, $\Im\{\theta,X(\theta),t(\theta)\}$, with $\{\theta\}$ derived by epistemological compliance as explained above. Since both $\{\theta\}$ and $\Im\{\theta,X(\theta),t(\theta)\}$ belong to human experience, they are configured interactions leading to consensus (integration), and thereafter continuously evolving by learning processes (IIE-learning processes) across the knowledge, space, and time dimensions. Such functional ontologies described by the dimensional spanning of $\{\theta,X(\theta),t(\theta)\}$ carry with them all the ontological and epistemological attributes. Thereby, the circular causation expression is invoked to quantify, simulate, and analyze the wellbeing in the world-system under study by way of pervasive complementarities between the requisite variables. The resulting value of $\{\theta\}$ corresponding to the various selected variables, and as ontologically expressed in its functional form, yields the meaning of wellbeing evaluated by inter-causal relations of degrees of complementarities. The functional ontological model so derived is the generalized system model.

The explanation by abstraction and the quantitative evaluation of the corresponding 'functional' ontological model together establish the meaning of phenomenology (systemic consciousness) and its empirical possibility of valuation. The structure of phenomenological abstraction is carried through from the primal ontological and epistemological foundations. Its empirical context in any socio-scientific inquiry is given by evaluation and analysis of the functional ontological form that is formalized in accordance with the methodological and pertinent ontological algorithm (i.e. 'functional' ontologies). One level of the IIE-learning process is thus completed.

Next, the end of any learning process is carried forward continuously in evolutionary form over time by recalling the Primal Ontological Monotheistic Law. Thereby, the deductive beginning (Ω,S) once again starts up the new process from the end of the inductive state of the previous process; and so on. Consequently, Deductive $\Leftrightarrow$ Inductive (e.g. a priori $\Leftrightarrow$ a posteriori).

Time as mechanism for recording evolutionary events is determined by the level of knowledge and the socio-scientific valuation of the system by variables and relations that time records. Consequently, evaluative trajectories of evolutionary learning events are determined for continuous progress of classes of events signified by $\Im\{\theta,X(\theta),t(\theta)\}$.

References

Barrow, John D. 1991. *Theories of Everything, the Quest for Ultimate Explanation*. Oxford: Oxford University Press.

Bhaskar, Roy. 2002. *Reflections on Meta-Reality, Transcendence, Emancipation and Everyday Life*. New Delhi: Sage Foundation.

Boulding, Kenneth E. 1981. *Evolutionary Economics*. New York: Russell Sage.

Boulding, Kenneth E. 1971. "Economics as a moral science." In *Humanistic Society*, edited by Glass J.F.and Staude J.R. Pacific Palisades: Goodyear Publishing Co. Inc.

Burstein, Meyer. 1991. "History versus Equilibrium: Joan Robinson and Time in Economics." In *The Joan Robinson Legacy*, edited by Ingrid H. Rima, 49–61. Armonk: M.E. Sharpe Inc.

Buchanan, James M. 1999. "The domain of constitutional economics." In his *The Logical Foundations of Constitutional Liberty*. Indianapolis: Liberty Fund.

Choudhury, Masudul A. 2014. *The Socio-Cybernetic Study of God and the World-System*. Philadelphia: IdeasGroup Inc.

Choudhury, Masudul A. 2013. "Complexity and endogeneity in economic modelling." *Kybernetes, International Journal of Systems, Cybernetics, and Management Studies* 42(2): 226–240.

Choudhury, Masudul A. 2011. "On the existence of evolutionary learning equilibriums." *SQU Journal for Science* 16:68–81.

Daly, Herman E. 1992. "From empty-world to full-world economics: Recognizing an historical turning point ineconomic development." In *Environmentally Sustainable Economic Development: Building on Brundtland*, edited by R. Goodland, H.E. Daly, S. el-Serafy and B. von Droste, 29–40. Paris: UNESCO.

Dampier, William C. 1961. *A History of Science and Its Relations with Philosophy and Religion*. Cambridge:Cambridge University Press.

Dasgupta, Ajit K. 1987. *Epochs of Economic Theory*. Oxford: Basil Blackwell.

Dawkins, Richard. 2008. *The God Delusion*. Boston: Houghton Mifflin Co.

Dewitt, Bryce. 1992. *Supermanifolds*. Cambridge: Cambridge University Press.

Gel'fand, Izrail M. 1961. *Lectures on Linear Algebra*. New York: Interscience Publishers Inc.

Georgescu-Roegen, Nicholas. 1981. *The Entropy Law and the Economic Process*. Cambridge: Harvard University Press.

Gruber, Thomas R. 1993. "A translation approach to portable ontologies." *Knowledge Acquisition* 5(2): 199–200.

Hawking, StephenW. 1988. *A Brief History of Time: From the Big Bang to Black Holes*. New York: BantamBooks.

Hawking, Stephen W., and Roger Penrose. 2010. *The Nature of Space and Time*. Princeton: Princeton University Press.

Hull, David. 1988. "Science as a selection process." In his *Science as a Process: An Evolutionary Account of the Social and Conceptual Development of Science*. Chicago: The University of Chicago Press.

Husserl, Edmund. 1964. *The Idea of Phenomenology*. Translated by W.P. Alston, and G. Nakhnikian. Hague: MartinusNijhoff.

Hume, David. 1988. *An Enquiry Concerning Human Understanding*. Buffalo: Prometheus Books.

Inglott, Peter S. 1990. "The rights of future generations: Some socio-philosophical considerations." In *Our Responsibilities Towards Future Generations*, edited by S. Busuttil, E. Agius, P.S. Inglott, and T.Macelli, 17–27. Malta: Foundation for International Studies and UNESCO.

Kant, Immanuel and Carl J. Friedrich. 1949. *The philosophy of Kant: Immanuel Kant's moral and political writings*.New York: Modern Library.

Kant, Immanuel. 1963. "The general principle of morality". In *Kant's Lectures on Ethics*. Translated by Louis Infield. Indianapolis: Hackett Publishing Co.

Kupka, Ivan A.K. and M.M. Peixoto. 1993. "On the enumerative geometry of geodesics." In *From Topology to Computation: Proceedings of the Smalefest*, edited by M.W. Hirsch, J.E. Marsden, and M. Shub, 243–253. New York: Springer-Verlag.

Lukacs, John. 1968. *Historical Consciousness*. New York: Harper & Row Publishers.

Maddox, I. J. 1970. *Elements of Functional Analysis*. Cambridge: Cambridge University Press.

Mahomedy, Abdulkader C. 2017. "Why the Rationalist Foundations of Modern Science are unsuitable for Islamic Economics." Ph.D. thesis in Economics, Department of School of

Accounting, Economics, and Finance, College of Law and Management Studies, University of Kwazulu-Natal, South Africa.

Maritain, Jacques. 1973. *On the Philosophy of History*, edited by J.W. Evans. Clifton: Augustus M. Kelley Publishers.

Nitzan, Jonathen and Shimshon Bichler. 2000. "Capital accumulation: Breaking the dualism of 'economics' and 'politics'." In *Global Political Economy, Contemporary Issues*, edited by Ronen Palan, 67–88. London: Routledge.

Popper, Karl. 2004. *The Logic of Scientific Discovery*. London: Routledge.

Rawls, John. 1971. *A Theory of Justice*. Cambridge: Harvard University Press.

Russell, Bertrand. 1990. "Bergson." In his *A History of Western Philosophy*, 756–65. London: UnwinPaperbacks.

Sen, Amartya. 1988. "Conduct, ethics and economics." In *On Ethics & Economics*, 88–89. Oxford: Basil Blackwell.

Shackle, George L.S. 1972. *Epistemics & Economics: A Critique of Economic Theory*. Cambridge: CambridgeUniversity Press.

Sztompka, Piotr. 1991. *Society in Action: The Theory of Social Becoming*. Chicago: The University of Chicago Press.

Tawney, Richard H. 1948. *The Acquisitive Society*. New York: Harcourt, Brace & Co.

Torrell, Jean-Pierre. 2005. "A circular plan", in *Aquinas' SUMMA, Background, Structure, and Reception*, 27–36. Translated by Benedict M. Gueven. Washington D.C.: The Catholic University of America Press.

Urry, John. 2015. "Climate change and society." In *Why the Social Sciences Matter*, edited by J. Michie and C.L. Cooper, 45–59. Houndmills: Palgrave Macmillan.

Wilson, Edward O. 1998. *Consilience: The Unity of Knowledge*. New York: Vantage Books.

Sami Al-Suwailem

Chapter 3: Economics for a Better Future

1 Introduction

Scarcity is the cornerstone of economics, or at least that's what we get from reading economics textbooks (e.g. Samuelson and Nordhaus, 2010, p. xix; Sowell, 2015, p. 2). But, scarcity implies some obvious consequences that are at odds with the teachings and practice of mainstream economics. For example:

- Scarcity requires conservation of natural resources. Mainstream economics is still suspicious of climate change and environmental threats. Textbooks pay little attention to the scarcity of natural resources and how does this impact economic analysis.
- Scarcity implies frugality and prudence in spending and consumption. Yet, little in mainstream economics tells us to be prudent or frugal. In fact, we are instructed to set the level of consumption to "maximize" utility and pleasure. Extravagancy and conspicuous consumption are not an exception; they are mainstream.
- Scarcity implies limited capital, but the standard assumption of a perfect capital market is the ability to borrow or lend "unlimited" amount of capital at the "risk-free" rate.
- Scarcity entails a few bubbles as they end up in the destruction of scarce wealth. Yet, mainstream economics failed in warning against, let alone preventing, the largest bubble in history, which precipitated the Global Financial Crisis.

The internal inconsistency of economic theory, together with its failures to predict and explain major economic events, cast serious doubts over its status as a "science." These doubts led econo-physicist Jean-Philippe Bouchaud (2008) to write in Nature: "Economics Needs a Scientific Revolution." It also led UCLA economist Roger A. Farmer (2016, p. x) to write: "economics must change." Naturally, the revolution and the change we are looking for does not dispense with the remarkable achievements of the economics profession. Rather, it aims to identify the source of inconsistency and, accordingly, find the missing link between the theory and the real world. This chapter is an attempt towards this objective.

2 Growth Unlimited

According to Neoclassical theory, diminishing marginal returns imply that the economy should converge to steady-state growth, whereby all economic variables

https://doi.org/10.1515/9783110587920-003

(consumption, investment, etc.) grow at constant rates, which need not be zero (see e.g. Barro and Sala-i-Martin, 2003, ch. 1). Even at the steady-state, the economy could have positive growth rates. But for how long? The theory puts no limits on how long economic growth can last. In principle, it could go on forever. There is "no long-run limit to the growth of output" (Sowell, 2008, p. 290). "Market prices give no reason to believe that natural resources are a limit to economic growth," writes Harvard economist George Mankiw (2014, p. 532). There is always a demand for new goods and services because people have "infinite desires" for more material goods (Buchholz, 2007, p. 88). In the words of Harvard economist Benjamin Friedman (2005), "insatiable material wants drove the economic machine" (p. 40).

J.M. Keynes wrote his General Theory to refute some basic premises of the Classical theory, and to show that supply can, in principle, be limited by effective demand. But there is no mention by Keynes of an upper limit of demand or the economy in general (see Keynes, 1930, and Skidelsky, 2010, pp. 143–144).

The result is that scarcity has been eliminated from the roots of economic thinking. Economics is no more about "economizing;" instead, it is about allocation and efficiency. If there is scarcity, it is only local or relative. In the aggregate, there is no such thing as scarcity.

With this worldview, we can easily understand the odd consequences:

- There is no reason to worry about the limits of resources and the environment. With unlimited resources comes unlimited capital and "risk-free" rate of return.
- With "infinite desires" or "insatiable preferences," there is little room for frugality or prudence.[82]
- Bubbles are no more seen as pathological: if the economy can grow forever, why not some prices grow forever as well?[83]

It is not difficult to see why "rational bubbles" and "rational Ponzi games" are perfectly consistent with this view. If there is no aggregate scarcity, then an agent may simply shift the cost or burden of a transaction to the next one, who in turn shifts it to the next, etc. For how long this Ponzi game can go on? For as long as the economy can grow. And for how long the economy can grow? For as long as the sun shines (Murphy, 2012)! Thus, Ponzi games, in principle, are not pathological. They follow naturally from the assumption of unlimited growth.

Not only this is destructive to the economy, it negates even relative scarcity. Agents can get "something-for-nothing" because each is able to shift losses to another, and the other to another, for as long as the economy is growing. If there is no

82 Unlike Keynes, classical economists stressed thrift and frugality (Skousen, 2016, pp. 38, 345). These virtues, however, almost disappeared from mainstream economics.

83 The fact that neoclassical theory permits "rational bubbles" and "Ponzi games" is detailed in Al-Suwailem (2017).

aggregate scarcity, then there should be no relative scarcity. Ponzi schemes bridge the gap between the two. To get something-for-nothing negates the basic principle of scarcity. And without scarcity, there is no economics.

But why economists gave up on the raison d'être of their discipline? The reason is another, more sacred, principle: free markets. Whenever scarcity implies some restrictions on the freedom of markets, e.g. environmental controls, freedom supersedes scarcity. This is strange given that markets exist because of scarcity! This makes us wonder if economics is actually a science.

3 Criterion of Science

In 1687, Isaac Newton (1642–1726) published his famous *Philosophia Naturalis Principia Mathematica* (Mathematical Principles of Natural Philosophy). The book became a gold standard for scientific inquiry. Adam Smith (1723–1790) read Newton's Principia and was particularly impressed with what he calls the "Newtonian method" (Skinner, 2008, p. 541). Economists, since then, were trying hard to follow the path of physics. For example, they talk about "laws of motion" (e.g. Leijonhufvud, 2006); "the law of gravity" (Samuelson, 1957, p. 184), "quantum theory of economics," (Samuelson, 1977; Mirowiski, 1989, pp. 382–383), etc.

But despite the "physics envy," economics lacks the most fundamental criterion of science: Conservation Principles. These principles govern all-natural phenomena, as Nobel laureate Richard Feynman (2015, p. 33) points out. The most famous of these principles is the conservation of energy. This law states that, in an isolated system, total energy is constant. The system cannot generate energy from nothing, and thus the total amount of energy in the isolated system must be conserved. But what is energy?

3.1 Formulating the Conservation Law

Defining energy has been a tricky question. As Feynman explains, there are many forms of energy, and we cannot tell in advance all of these forms. Hence, "we have no knowledge of what energy is," notes Feynman (p. 34). As mathematician and physicist Ian Stewart (2012, p. 49) points out, "energy, as a concept, is not so much a physical thing as a convenient fiction that helps to balance the mechanical books." This shows that "energy" essentially is an economic (or accounting) concept: It is defined in a manner so as to preserve the balance of natural forces. Without this balance, the numbers describing the system will not add up, and we end up with 1 = 0.

According to physicist and philosopher Ernst Mach (1911, p. 19), there are two ways to characterize the conservation of energy:

- Total energy = potential energy + kinetic energy.
- The impossibility of perpetual motion.

The first criterion is usually specific to mechanical systems. It requires knowing in advance the exact formulas for both potential and kinetic energy. As Feynman points out, energy has so many forms that we do not know in advance. If some forms of energy are not known, we will not be able to tell if total energy was conserved or not. In contrast, the second approach does not require the advanced knowledge of the various forms of energy. All it requires is that the physical system cannot produce more energy than it starts with. So, if we know the starting kind of energy, we can tell if the system can produce perpetual motion or not.

According to Mach (1911, pp. 19–20), the postulate of the impossibility of perpetual motion "served as the foundation of the most important extensions of the physical sciences" since the time of Galileo. "Science has grown almost more by what it has learned to ignore than by what it has had to take into account" notes Mach (p. 64).

More precisely, suppose an isolated system S at time $t = 0$ has a total measurable energy E. Suppose we are able to convert E at time $t = 1$ to a different form of energy, X. As discussed earlier, the precise nature of X may not be always fully known in advance. But one thing we are sure of: If we convert X at time $t = 2$ back to the same form of energy we started with, then the resulting energy cannot exceed E. That is, $E \rightarrow X \rightarrow E' \leq E$. Perpetual motion results when we have $E' > E$. The latter means that we are able to make something out of nothing, which is impossible. In an isolated system, we will never be able to produce more energy than we started with, no matter how ingenious the technologies we are able to use.

3.2 Alchemy vs. Chemistry

The impossibility of perpetual motion, or something-from-nothing, is the criterion that identifies science from superstition. The difference between alchemy and chemistry lies in acknowledging the conservation laws. For centuries, the ultimate dream of alchemy was to discover the "philosopher's stone," which allows the creation of precious metals (gold) from non-precious ones. As this was impossible due to the conservation of mass, alchemists frequently resorted to fraudulently counterfeiting gold.[84]

It was not until Antoine-Laurent de Lavoisier (1743–1794) formulated the law of conservation of mass, that chemistry as a science became independent of alchemy

84 William Brock (1992, p. 34) reports that in 1317, the Pope John XXII ordered all alchemists to leave France for making counterfeit money.

(see Brock, 1992, ch. 3). The same criterion identifies astronomy from astrology. Despite the heavy use of mathematics in astrology (Levinovitz, 2016), it is not a science. The reason is that astrology endorses a framework that allows for something-from-nothing.

It is not difficult to see that a bubble is a system based on something-for-nothing. Each player in a bubble or a Ponzi game is making money at the expense of the other, and the other of the other, etc. But the economy obviously is finite, and growth cannot go on forever. Yet, neoclassical theory permits "rational Ponzi games" (Blanchard and Weil, 2001). To describe a bubble or a Ponzi game as "rational" is equivalent to describing a perpetual motion plan as scientific – it is an oxymoron. Mainstream economics today seems to be trapped in the age of alchemy, as witnessed by the global investor George Soros in his Alchemy of Finance, and former governor of Bank of England, Marvin King in The End of Alchemy, among others.

This is not to say that economics made no successes whatsoever. As Noah Smith (2014) points out, there are many successes: auctions theory, BART models, gravity models, are examples. But alchemy and astrology also had some successes as well; they were not completely fraud. The successes of economics, however, are barely visible in comparison to the massive failures leading to the worst two crises in the history of mankind: the Global Financial Crisis and the Environmental Crisis.

The core problem with mainstream economics is that it is unable to distinguish "alchemy" from "chemistry." The theory as it stands has no room for conservation principles. Perpetual motion, whether in bubbles or perpetual growth, is perfectly admissible in neoclassical theory. Chemistry became a science only when it endorsed conservation principles and denounced the something-for-nothing doctrine of alchemy. For economics to become a science proper, there is no other alternative to denouncing perpetual motion. This is not an impossible mission. Below we discuss how to develop "conservation principles" of the economy based on the accumulated wealth of economic reasoning.

4 Economic Conservation Laws

There have been many attempts to formulate conservation laws in economics (e.g. Sato and Ramachandran, 1990; Yakovenko, 2013). These attempts adopt a narrow approach and focus on specific variables (e.g. money or value) or ratios (e.g. capital-output ratio or income-wealth ratio) as being conserved. But, as we have seen earlier, to determine what is to be conserved in science proved to be elusive and fragile. In economics, the problem is even worse, as the variables thought to be conserved are model-dependent, not to mention the lack of empirical support.

4.1 Impossibility of Economic Perpetual Motion

The alternative, and more fruitful, approach, is to define conservation based on the impossibility of perpetual motion, as discussed earlier. In the economy, it is not difficult to identify perpetual motion: Bubbles and Ponzi or Pyramid schemes. These phenomena necessarily involve something-for-nothing for the collective group of players. These games emerge from 2-person zero-sum games, whereby one player wins if, and only if, the other loses. Since an exchange is supposed to be fair to both parties, ex ante payoffs of the two players should be equal, so that $\pi_A^e = \pi_B^e$, where π_A^e and π_B^e are the ex ante (expected) payoffs for players A and B, respectively. But, for zero-sum games, ex post payoffs will always be such that, if one player gets π, where π is a real number, then the other will get $-\pi$. If the equality is still maintained, this implies the absurdity 1 = −1, or, equivalently, 1 = 0. By definition, therefore, a zero-sum game is a game that systematically results in something-for-nothing.

A 2-person zero-sum game can easily transform into an n-person game when the loser seeks to shift the loss to another player, who will shift it to another, etc. Ponzi or Pyramid schemes are simply *n*-person zero-sum games. Because a Ponzi scheme or a bubble involves many players, each player believes that he or she is not playing a zero-sum game, since in case of loss he is able to shift the loss to a third player. But the scheme cannot go on forever, and the last player (the "greater fool") will definitely be a loser. By backward induction, it follows that each transaction is actually a zero-sum game.

4.2 Pareto Optimality

Formulated in this manner, the economic conservation law is consistent with the well-known principle of Pareto optimality. A transaction is Pareto optimal or superior if, after completing the transaction, no party is worse off, and at least one party is better off. A zero-sum game is obviously inconsistent with the Pareto criterion.

In presence of uncertainty, a trade might result in a win-win or a win-lose outcome. The Pareto criterion is still valid in this case as long as the win-win outcome is the dominant outcome.[85]

Such is the case in normal trade. Zero-sum games differ from Pareto-superior trade under uncertainty, in two respects:

- If ex ante uncertainty is removed from the game, the zero-sum game will not be acceptable to both players – the potential loser will definitely refuse to play. In

85 More specifically, as long as the likelihood of win-win exceeds that of win-lose, and the payoff for each party at the win-win outcome is no less than that of the win-lose.

a normal trade, in contrast, if uncertainty were removed, the transaction with the win-win outcome will be Pareto-improving.
- The losing party in a zero-sum game will seek to recover the losses in the same manner they occurred, i.e. by playing another zero-sum game with another party, resulting in a Ponzi game.[86] In the normal course of business, in contrast, recovering the losses in the same manner in which they occurred will result in another normal trade, but not in a Ponzi game or any other wealth-destructing scheme. This will become clearer when we discuss the Law of Markets below.

4.3 Value of Trade

Is trade a zero-sum game? This seems a strange question given the well-known gains from trade. Trade makes both parties better off, so it cannot be a zero-sum game. The fact that, in the absence of uncertainty, the two parties agree voluntarily to trade, is sufficient to prove that normal trade is not a zero-sum game. It is in principle a win-win transaction.

Some economists believed that value from trade must be conserved given that commodities are traded at their fair value (Mirowski, 1989, p. 121; Keen, 2011, pp. 215–218). But this view ignores the critical role of emergence. Trade rearranges resources between the two parties so that each will be more productive than before. Thus, trade produces gains even when the trade is conducted at the market price without exploitation of any sort. Reallocation of goods and services can release untapped resources and thus create surplus value.

Historical discussions of surplus value were predominantly reductionist: the value of a commodity is reduced to the sum of the values of its inputs (e.g. Keen, 2011, p. 153). But this approach ignores emergent properties arising from the rearrangement of resources. The ways in which a particular commodity can be combined with other commodities to create new goods and services cannot be systematically predictable. Sellers, in general, cannot foresee all the potential uses of their products in order to incorporate them into their prices.

Thus, the value of the commodity is not always the sum of the values of the inputs – the whole is greater than the sum. In fact, this might be a major function of a free market: To allow for novel and unforeseeable uses of commodities, which is a driving force of growth. If a commodity were completely reducible to its inputs, then there would be no point in producing the commodity in the first place; in a free market, it would be completely redundant. A commodity produced in a free

86 If the game is played again with the same party, the result will be akin to the Dollar Auction game. See: Colman (1999), pp. 196–199.

market, therefore, must have value beyond its inputs. This added value, however, cannot be systematically quantified in advance.

The above discussion shows that value is not conserved in trade. The relationship between conservation and emergence can be elaborated using the metaphor provided by philosopher Emily Meyerson (1930, pp. 92–93). Meyerson points out that we might have a set of fixed elements, but the arrangements of these elements can create different manifolds, "just as with the aid of the same letters one can compose a tragedy or a comedy." The number of alphabets is fixed, but the number of words and sentences that can be generated from it is virtually unlimited. By fixing the number of alphabets, words will cluster in families and trees, generating meanings of higher dimensions with more powerful expressive powers. Conservation induces us to move to higher dimensions where creativity has no limits.

5 The Law of Markets

Classical economists were able to develop an important concept that is now an essential part of economic theory. It is called Law of Markets or Say's Law (Baumol, 1999). The basic idea is simple, but the insight is deep and helps in understanding a wide range of economic phenomena. The Law is a direct application of the conservation law, as we shall see.

Let us start with a simple trade of two commodities. The trade is a simultaneous purchase and sale: purchase of one commodity and sale of the other. For each purchase, there is a sale, and for each sale, there is a purchase.[87] This is a very simple idea, but it has a deep insight. It implies that for each demand there is supply and vice versa. It follows that if there is an excess demand for one commodity, there must be an excess supply of the other. There cannot be an excess demand for both commodities simultaneously. To extend the concept to multiple commodities is straightforward. If there are more buyers than sellers in one market, there should be more sellers than buyers in other market(s).

The Classical economists conclude that there should be no aggregate over-production or "general glut," i.e. too much supply. They reason that, whatever the amount of goods produced, its production must have been supported by a corresponding demand for other goods and services. So, if too much was produced for one market, it must be the case that too much was purchased in other markets. Accordingly, on the aggregate, there should be no imbalances, i.e. no aggregate excess supply or excess demand. Such imbalances are conceived for individual markets, but cannot apply to the whole. To think so is to commit the fallacy of composition.

87 This reminds of Newton's Third Law: For each action there is a reaction equal in magnitude and opposite in direction. See below.

Thus, the entire economy of markets is interconnected. This connection is valuable because it allows supply and demand in different markets to react to each other, and by adjusting prices, markets can be balanced. An aggregate imbalance is obviously not sustainable and there has to be a correction. Hence, Classical economists held the view that such imbalances are not possible in the long run (Robbins, 1998, Lecture 21).

5.1 Enter Money

The markets so far operate based on a barter system. Let us introduce money. Money plays the role of an intermediary between purchase and sale, or between supply and demand. It also connects various markets across a larger range of participants and regions (Muller, 2002, p. 246). As long as money works to connect supply with demand, markets should operate smoothly. But in some cases, money fails to perform this function.

One important case is hoarding. If for any reason, people keep money and refuse to spend it, then markets fail to connect. In this case, we would have an aggregate imbalance. Markets will not be able to achieve equilibrium. But why people would hoard money if it is only a means to obtain goods and services?

The answer was provided by J.M. Keynes (1936) in his *General Theory*. The book is a response to the Great Depression, whereby economies in the West suffered persistent high unemployment (i.e. excess supply of labor) without a corresponding excess demand in other markets of goods and services, resulting in a prolonged aggregate imbalance. The Classics believed that money is only a means to possess goods and services, so hoarding could rarely happen, and if it ever does, it is only temporary (Baumol, 1999). They also believed that with flexible prices, all goods can be sold (Kates, 1998, p. 106), so there should be no aggregate imbalance. The Great Depression proved this was not the case.

Keynes emphasized, inter alia, the important role of expectations and radical uncertainty in the economy. In normal circumstances, investors invest in the hope that the investment will pay back. Producers produce in the hope that their products will be sold. Buyers buy and consume assuming their income will cover their expenses. Markets operate based on expectations. It is basically a coordination game (Leijonhufvud, 1968; Skidelsky, 2010). If agents expect others will spend, they will spend. But if they expect others to abstain, they will also abstain.

In normal circumstances, economic needs are sufficient to stimulate people to spend. But in the aftermath of a huge crash like that of 1929, the confidence of investors, and most agents, was deeply shaken. In such an environment, there are few reasons to expect others to spend, but many more reasons to expect them to abstain and thus to hoard. With hoarding, the real value of money starts to rise as prices of assets decline. This positive return on money induces people to hoard even more and for a longer period to benefit from the appreciation of the value of money. It becomes a vicious circle: the initial shock-initiated hoarding, which caused the real value of money to rise, leading to more hoarding, etc.

5.2 Bubbles and Ponzi Games

The mirror image of hoarding is bubbles and Ponzi games. In a bubble, speculation generates its own returns, just as hoarding generates its own returns. In both cases, a positive feedback loop creates a self-generating return. While both cases are forms of vicious circles, hoarding is a downward spiral, while speculation is an upward spiral. Hoarding affects the saving side, while speculation affects the investment side.

In Ponzi debt games, the borrower repays the due debt by additional borrowing. With many players in the debt market, borrowers may borrow from one lender to pay the other. In this manner, money will be essentially circulating in a closed loop. Moreover, as debt grows, debt services and interest compounds, so that lenders have no incentive to stop playing the game. Borrowers, on the other hand, have no incentive to settle the debt and they will be better off to roll it over or to refinance. Debt Ponzi games, therefore, break the Law of Markets and lead to aggregate imbalances.

Don Patinkin, in *Money, Interest, and Prices*, points out how rollover of debt leads to an imbalance of markets and, thus, the violation of Say's law. He writes:

> Before describing the properties of the demand function for bonds, we must first add restrictions which will keep it finite. In the absence of such restrictions, each individual would choose to borrow indefinitely large amounts [...] and to provide for the payment of principal and interest on them by borrowing still larger amounts [...] In this way he could continue interminably to refund his debt no matter what its magnitude. This, in turn, would enable him to demand unlimited amounts of commodities [...]. (Patinkin, 1989, p. 68)

The way out, notes Patinkin, is either to assume a kind of market imperfection that prevents an agent "from borrowing all he wants to at the going rate of interest." Alternatively, it might be assumed that an agent must pay off his or her debt on a particular date (Patinkin, 1989, p. 68).

Modern formulations assume "No Ponzi Game" condition (NPG). NPG requires that the present discounted value of the debt of an agent shall be asymptotically zero (Blanchard and Fischer, 1989, pp. 49–50). However, in overlapping-generations models, NPG fails to be satisfied for the aggregate economy, even though it might be satisfied with respect to each individual lender. A borrower may borrow from the young then pay him when he becomes old by borrowing from another young agent, and keep doing so forever (O'Connell, S. and S. Zeldes, 1988).

In general, any scheme for self-generating returns will make money fail to perform its function in linking markets for goods and services. This causes the breakdown of the Law of Markets, resulting in unsustainable imbalances. The Classics undermined the possibilities of such pathologies, arguing that, since they are not sustainable, they must be short-lived, and market, therefore, must correct itself.

There are two problems with this reasoning:

- Being unsustainable does not necessarily imply that the pathologies are short-lived. Cancer is not sustainable, but it may take a long while before its full implications are actualized.
- These pathologies need not be self-correcting. When a gigantic bubble crashes, it might take a generation or two before the economy goes back to its normal trajectory. As already noted, the market requires coordination between players. Coordination, in turn, is based on trust, which is exogenous to the market. Once a bubble crashes, trust is lost or severely inflicted, and the market will be irreversibly impaired. Only when trust is restored that the economy can go back to normal. Restoration of trust, however, is not trivial – it requires a change of regime to be rebuilt. This process is exogenous to the market; the market is unable to restore trust by itself.

5.3 Saving and Investment: Walras vs. Keynes

If markets are perfectly connected, and Say's Law holds, then saving and investment are (almost) always equal to each other. Every saving decision is an investment decision. This is the view of Classical and neoclassical economists. But how saving is actually connected to investment is not very obvious in general equilibrium theory. According to Michio Morishima (1977, ch. 12), Walras thought that savers might either lend money to businesses, who then use the money to purchase capital goods. Alternatively, savers might purchase capital goods and then lease them to businesses. For Walras, the two alternatives, in theory, are essentially equivalent.

As Morishima elaborates, these two channels between saving and investment can be equivalent only if Say's Law holds perfectly well. In this case, aggregate investment is always smoothly and quickly adjusted and equated to aggregate saving (p. 187). But if this is not the case, as Keynes argues, then the two channels (lending money and leasing capital goods) are no more equivalent. If savings are channeled through lending money, the link between saving and investment might break down when money falls into a vicious circle trap. Keynes realized that the Great Depression resulted from a persistent disconnection between saving and investment due to hoarding. Markets will be able to correct themselves only if they are properly connected. But there is no guarantee that they are. Hence, Keynes described his theory as "The General Theory," whereby the Classical case of self-correcting markets is only a special case.

Aggregate investment may not necessarily respond smoothly and quickly to aggregate saving. But this does not necessarily break the basic connection between markets as envisaged the Law of Markets. What does are the pathological cases discussed above, whereby vicious circles lead eventually to a breakdown of the system, as was the case in the Great Depression and the Global Financial Crisis.

5.4 Back to Scarcity

The two pathological phenomena, hoarding and Ponzi games, are clear cases of something-for-nothing, and thus the violation of the principle of scarcity or the conservation law. Since these pathologies contravene the Law of Markets, it follows that the Law can be viewed as a conservation law.[88] If the Law of Markets is formulated as "for each supply there is demand, so that aggregate supply must equal aggregate demand," it will have a noticeable resemblance to Newton's third law: "For each action there is a reaction equal in magnitude and opposite in direction." Put differently, the failure of money to connect markets for goods and services arises primarily from vicious circles with self-generating returns. These vicious circles are clear examples of perpetual economic motion, which contradicts conservation laws.

Consequently, to the extent that the Law of Markets aims to prevent such vicious circles, it reflects a conservation principle for markets. Since agents, in general, are free to transact or to hoard, the Law is viewed more of a normative principle, not a positive description of reality. From this perspective, economics is like medicine: it attempts to understand the normal behavior or the system, but also to identify the possible pathologies. The failure of the Law of Markets, in reality, does not invalidate its prescriptive value. Policies and regulations that help to curb vicious circles can improve the efficiency and productivity of markets.

6 The Role of Finance

Trade contributes to wealth creation, and therefore growth, as discussed earlier. But there is another important means to support growth: Debt.

6.1 Good Debt vs. Bad Debt

Debt allows markets to expand beyond the currently available means. If debt is created through bonds or interest-based lending, then we might end up with a structural disconnection between markets. As Patinkin points out, there is no reason in this case for not financing debt repayment using additional borrowing, ending up

88 The Law of Markets has a noticeable resemblance to Newton's third law, which implies the conservation of momentum. See Feynman (2015, ch. 10).

in a Ponzi debt game. So how to utilize debt without breaking the connection between markets?

The answer to this question takes us back to the relationship between saving and investment, discussed earlier (Section 5.3). As pointed out above, Walras thought there was no material difference between lending money and leasing capital goods. But, as Morishima objected, there is, in fact, a substantial one. Leasing involves harmony between saving and investment, while lending does not. This allows us to formulate the following distinction between two forms of debt, or financing in general:

If debt is created as an integral part of a trade transaction, e.g. markup sale or leasing, the connection between markets will be, in principle, intact. However, once debt is disconnected from trade, we end up with a pure interchange of money for money, in which case there is no reliable mechanism to prevent vicious circles from developing. Vicious circles lead to imbalances and, eventually, to the breakdown of the market.

This criterion allows us to differentiate between good debt and bad debt. Whenever debt breaks away from real economic activities, it starts growing on its own, creating self-generating returns, as in hoarding or Ponzi debt games. Since debt, in general, is required for growth and expansion of economic activities, the alternative is to integrate financing with trade of goods and services, as it is the case in markup sale and leasing, and similar arrangements.[89]

In this manner, markets are connected, in principle, so that they are able to adjust and rebalance to allocate available resources to the most productive uses. This is not to say that markets will necessarily achieve full-employment equilibrium. They may never do. But the market mechanism will become fruitful if markets are properly connected and no "loose joints" threaten its resilience.

6.2 Money and Debt

We are accustomed to thinking that money was invented to avoid the costs of barter. While this is a helpful metaphor, historically the evidence points to a different story. Communities were able to solve the problem of double wants through deferred payment or credit system (Graeber, 2014, p. 36). A buyer will take the desired good and become indebted to the seller for the equivalent value. Subsequently, the buyer will settle the debt using tokens or any other good considered suitable. Thus, currency or coins evolved as a means to settle debt (Ingham, 2004, p. 46). Historically, the credit system preceded the issuance of coinage by thousands of years (Graeber, 2014, p. 38). While mainstream economics emphasizes transactional

89 For an alternative criterion for distinguishing good debt from bad debt, see Bezemer (2018).

money over debt, the above approach shows that the emphasis should be the other way around.[90]

What concerns us here is that, according to this view, money evolved in a manner whereby debt was fully integrated with markets. Debt is created as a deferred payment of a good or service, after which it is settled using coins or any other good. From this perspective, financing historically preceded currency and was from the start playing the role of linking markets. Accordingly, the idea of good debt is not only consistent with economic reasoning, but also with the natural history of money and credit.

This can be linked to the value of trade credit versus banking credit. Mike Burkart and Tore Ellingsen (2004) argue that trade credit provides in-kind financing of inputs that cannot be easily diverted to less productive activities. The close relationship between the supplier and the firm makes the financing less prone to credit rationing and allows for better monitoring and disciplined utilization of resources, compared to banking credit. Moreover, it can provide a cushion against cyclical market movements.

6.3 Financial Intermediation

If we think of the economy as a system of markets for goods and services, then it is natural to think of the "joints" or links between these markets as entities that facilitate the flow of information and resources across the economy. This is supposed to the function of the financial sector.

But when the financial sector becomes disentangled from the real economy, this will hinder the normal functioning of markets. Based on data on 20 countries over 3 decades, Cecchetti and Kharroubi (2015) show that, beyond a certain point, debt growth reduces the growth of real GDP. Moreover, the growth of the financial sector can become a drag on productivity growth. The empirical study of Arcand et al. (2015) confirms the overall conclusion: There is a limit to the size of the financial sector, beyond which it becomes a burden on the real economy.

Furthermore, financial markets will become more unstable as they become disconnected from the real economy. Lux and Marchesi (1999) show how financial markets become volatile and unstable when they are dominated by "chartists," i.e. players who base their trading decisions on predicting the behavior of other players. In contrast, when the market is dominated by "fundamentalists," those who base their decisions on the fundamentals of the underlying asset, the market becomes stable.

---

90 Joseph Stiglitz and Bruce Greenwald (2003) argue that the emphasis on transactional demand for money is "seriously flawed" (p. 2). Instead, they emphasize the role of credit (loanable funds) in economic activities.

Because of the critical role of financial intermediation in connecting various sectors of the economy, their impairment causes more damage to the economy than that arising from the impairment of goods' markets. This has been established in several studies at the international level. Carmen Reinhard and Kenneth Rogoff (2009), and the International Monetary Fund (2008, 2009), conducted studies covering a large number of countries over several decades. These studies show that, overall, economic downturns preceded by financial stress or crises cost the economy on average 3 times that of downturns originating purely from the real sector. The cumulative loss in real GDP in presence of financial crises is about 14% of GDP at the peak prior to the downturn. The loss is only 5% without financial crises. Moreover, the downturn lasts on average 20–48 months in presence of financial crises, but 9–12 months year in their absence.

The above studies, among others, confirm the critical role of financial intermediation in the normal operations of markets. The financial sector facilitates the flow of information and resources among markets. It cannot, therefore, itself become just another set of markets. This leads in theory to infinite regress, and in reality, makes the financial sector more volatile and unstable. A crisis in the financial sector, moreover, has a long-lasting impact on the real economy as it directly affects confidence and expectations.

6.4 Islamic Finance

Principles of Islamic finance aim to balance market and non-market activities. Precepts governing market activities revolve around the balanced relationship between risk and return. When it comes to finance, it holds that finance must be anchored in the real economy. In this regard, two main precepts of Islamic finance regulate financial contracting:

- Prohibition of usury or interest-based lending, and
- Prohibition of gambling.

These two precepts are hardly peculiar to Islamic teachings. They are shared with all faiths of divine origin. From an economic point of view, however, the two precepts allow for smooth interconnection of markets of goods and services, and prevent the development of vicious circles that cause the failure of normal functioning of markets. These principles can be viewed as "conservation laws" that prevent perpetual economic motion.

Scarcity is implicitly acknowledged in the Qur'an in the many phrases instructing believers to avoid *israf* or extravagant spending. To economize (*iqtisad*) is viewed as a character of prophets. Some writers thought that scarcity is inconsistent with "blessing" (*barakah*) offered to believers. But the Qur'an (7:96) makes it clear that blessing is a result of responsible behavior: "Had the people of villages believed and been cautious, We would have opened to them blessings from heaven and earth." To be cautious (*taqwa*) means to be responsible and prudent, which implies conserving and economizing on resources. This will bring in the blessings.

Despite the appealing rationale of Islamic finance, implementation of its principles is by no means trivial. There is a long way to go to establish efficient structures and systems that achieve these objectives. Nonetheless, it is an area ripe for innovation and creativity that could add value to economic progress.

7 Science, Economics, and Morality

There is no science without conservation laws. And there is no economics without scarcity. Mainstream economics has somehow lost both. The price we are paying is no less than the worst two crises in the history of mankind: the Global Financial Crisis and the imminent Environmental Crisis. If we are to seek a better future, we certainly need to reform the field to prevent such crises from happening in the future.

Since economics is a social science, it is obvious that the conservation laws are normative in nature. It is not difficult to see that, in the economic sphere, conservation laws and moral values are effectively two sides of the same coin. The Golden Rule, love for your brother what you love for yourself, guards against zero-sum games, where one can win only at the expense of the other. Frugality and modesty serve to conserve resources and protect the environment.

Economics, from Adam Smith until J.M. Keynes, was understood to be a moral science (Staveren and Peil, 2009). In addition to being the founder of modern economics, Adam Smith was also a scholar of morality, as clearly reflected in his Theory of Moral Sentiments. Despite receiving considerable income from multiple resources, Smith lived modestly and humbly. Upon his death in 1790, his estate was minimal, as he gave away most of his income in acts of charity, which he took care to conceal (Muller, 2002, p. 54). The view that economics is "value-free" itself is value-laden. But more important, to ignore core values of economic behavior means to ignore the main criteria of modern science.

8 Conclusion

For economics to serve a better future, we need to formulate its core principles within a scientific framework. This framework has proved to be exceptionally valuable in the progress of science over the last 400 years. There is no reason why economics cannot adopt the same principles. The same principles, it turns out, encapsulates the core moral values that guide economic behavior. Core moral values, like the Golden

Rule, prudence, and modesty, are universal in nature. They are shared across most faiths and cultures.

The revolution that Bouchaud (2008) calls for might not be as radical as it might appear. The progress made in economics in the past decades will not be lost if we build economic theory on principles of conservation laws and the corresponding moral values. As we have seen, the economic conservation laws are derived from principles that are accepted, in general, by the profession over the past 200 years. There will be no loss of rigor if we build economic theory on principles of conservation and the corresponding moral values. The two go hand in hand. The better future we are looking for might be closer than we might think.

References

Al-Suwailem, Sami. 2017. "Is Economics a Science?," In *The Limits of Mathematical Modeling in the Social Sciences*, edited by F. Doria, 207–265. World Scientific.

Arcand, Jean-Louis, Enrico Berkes, and Ugo Panizza. 2015. "Too Much Finance?" *Journal of Economic Growth* 20: 105–148.

Barro, Robert and X. Sala-i-Martin. 2003. *Economic Growth*. Cambridge: MIT Press.

Baumol, William J. 1999. "Say's Law," *Journal of Economic Perspectives* 13: 195–204.

Bezemer, Dirk. 2018. "Unproductive Debt Causes Crisis: Connecting the History of Money to the Current Crisis," In *Money, Currency and Crisis: In Search of Trust, 2000 BC to AD 2000*, edited by in by R.J. van der Spek and Bas van Leeuwen, ch. 3. London: Routledge.

Blanchard, Olivier and Stanley Fischer. 1989. *Lectures on Macroeconomics*. Cambridge: MIT Press.

Blanchard, Olivier and Philippe Weil. 2001. "Dynamic Effciency, the Riskless Rate, and Debt Ponzi Games under Uncertainty," *Advances in Macroeconomics* 1: 1–23.

Bouchaud, Jean-Philippe. 2008. "Economics Needs a Scientific Revolution," *Nature* 455: 1181.

Brock, William. 1992. *The Fontana History of Chemistry*. London: Fontana.

Buchholz, Todd. 2007. *New Ideas from Dead Economists: An Introduction to Modern Economic Thought*. NY: Penguin Putnam Inc.

Burkart, Mike and Tore Ellingsen. 2004. "In-Kind Finance: A Theory of Trade Credit," *American Economic Review* 94: 569–590.

Cecchetti, Stephen G. and Enisse Kharroubi. 2015. "Why Does Financial Sector Growth Crowd Out Real Economic Growth?" *Center for Economic Policy Research, Discussion Paper no. DP10642*.

Colman, Anrew M. 1999. *Game Theory & Its Applications in the Social and Biological Sciences*. London: Routledge.

Farmer, Roger E.A. 2016. *Prosperity for All*. NY: Oxford University Press.

Feynman, Richard. 2015. *The Feynman Lectures on Physics, New Millennium Edition, vol. 1*. NY: Basic Books.

Friedman, Benjamin M. 2005. *The Moral Consequences of Economic Growth*. New York: Alfred A. Knopf.

Graeber, David. 2014. *Debt: The First 5000 Years*. New York: Melville House.

IMF. 2009. *World Economic Report*. International Monetary Fund, October.

IMF. 2008. *World Economic Report*. International Monetary Fund, October.

Ingham, Geoffrey. 2004. *The Nature of Money*. Cambridge, UK: Polity Press.

Kates, Steven. 1998. *Say's Law and The Keynesian Revolution: How Macroeconomic Theory Lost its Way*. UK: Edward Elgar Publishing.

Keen, S. 2011. Debunking Economics: The Naked Emperor Dethroned?, Zed Books.
Keynes, John M. 1930. "Economic Possibilities for our Grandchildren," in his *Essays in Persuasion*, 358–373. W. W. Norton & Co.
Keynes, John M. 1936. *The General Theory of Employment, Interest, and Money*. London: Macmillan.
King, Mervin. 2016. *The End of Alchemy: Money, Banking, and the Future of the Global Economy*. London: W. W. Norton & Company.
Leijonhufvud, A. 2006. "Keynes as a Marshallian," In *The Cambridge Companian to Keynes*, edited by R. Backhouse and B. Bateman, Cambridge University Press.
Leijonhufvud, Axel. 1968. *On Keynesian Economics and the Economics of Keynes: A Study in Monetary Theory*. New York and London: Oxford University Press.
Levinovitz, Alan J. 2016. "The New Astrology: By Fetishising Mathematical Models, Economists Turned Economics into a Highly Paid Pseudoscience," *Aeon*, April 6, aeon.com.
Lux, Thomas and Michele Marchesi. 1999. "Scaling and Criticality in a Stochastic Multi-agent Model of a Financial Market," *Nature* 397: 498–500.
Mach, Ernst. 1911. *History and Root of the Principle of the Conservation of Energy*. Chicago: Open Court Publishing.
Mankiw, Gregory. 2014. *Principles of Economics*, 7th ed., Cengage Learning.
Meyerson, E. 1930. Identity and Reality, Routledge.
Mirowski, Philip. 1989. *More Heat than Light: Economics as Social Physics, Physics as Nature's Economics*. Cambridge: Cambridge University Press.
Morishima, Michio. 1977. *Walras' Economics: A Pure Theory of Capital and Money*. Cambridge: Cambridge University Press.
Muller, Jerry Z. 2002. *The Mind and The Market: Capitalism in Modern European Thought*. New York: Knopf.
Murphy, Tom. 2012. "Exponential Economist Meets Finite Physicist," *Do the Math*, dothemath.ucsd.edu (visited 10 August 2018).
O'Connell, Stephen and Stephen Zeldes. 1988. "Rational Ponzi Games," *International Economic Review* 29, no. 3: 431–50.
Patinkin, Don. 1989. *Money, Interest, and Prices*, second edition abridged. Cambridge: MIT Press.
Reinhart, Carmen and Kenneth Rogoff. 2009. *This Time is Different: Eight Centuries of Financial Folly*. New Jersey: Princeton University Press.
Robbins, Lionel. 1998. *A History of Economic Thought*, edited by S. Medema and W. Samuels. New Jersey: Princeton University Press.
Samuelson, Paul. 1957. "Intertemporal Price Equilibrium: A Prologue to the Theory of Speculation," *Weltwirtschaftliches Archiv* 79: 181–221.
Samuelson, Paul. 1977. "A Quantum Theory Model of Economics," *The Collected Scientific Papers* 4, edited by H. Nagatani and K. Crowley. Cambridge: MIT Press: 104–110.
Samuelson, Paul and William D. Nordhaus. 2010. *Economics*, 19th edition. New York: McGraw-Hill.
Sato, Ryuzo, and Rama V. Ramachandran. 1990. *Conservation Laws and Symmetry: Applications to Economics and Finance*. Boston: Kluwer Academic Publishers.
Skidelsky, Robert. 2010. *Keynes: The Return of the Master*. New York: PublicAffairs.
Skinner, Andrew S. 2008. "Adam Smith" In *The New Palgrave Dictionary of Economics*, edited by Steven Durlauf and L. Blume, 537–567. Palgrave Macmillan UK.
Skousen, Mark. 2016. *The Making of Modern Economics*. New York: Routledge.
Smith, N. 2014. "Here's What Economics Gets Right," Bloomberg View, Dec. 31.
Soros, George. 2003. *Alchemy of Finance*. Wiley.
Sowell, Thomas. 1972. *Say's Law: An Historical Analysis*. New Jersey: Princeton University Press.
Sowell, Thomas. 2008. "Say's Law," In *The New Palgrave Dictionary of Economics*, edited by Steven Durlauf and L. Blume, 289–292. Palgrave Macmillan UK.

Sowell, Thomas. 2015. *Basic Economics*. 5th edition. Basic Books.
Staveren, Irene, and Jan Peil. 2009. "Introduction," In *Handbook of Economics and Ethics*, edited by Irene Staveren, xvi–xviii. Edward Elgar Publishing.
Stewart, Ian. 2012. *In Pursuit of the Unknown: 17 Equations that Changed the World*. London: Basic Books.
Stiglitz, Joseph and Bruce Greenwald. 2003. *Towards a New Paradigm in Monetary Economics*. Cambridge: Cambridge University Press.
Wattles, Jeffrey. 1996. *The Golden Rule*. New York: Oxford University Press.
Yakovenko, Victor. 2013. "Application of Statistical Mechanics to Economics," In *Social Fairness and Economics*, edited by L. Taylor, A. Rezai and T. Michl. London: Routledge.

Hazik Mohamed, Abbas Mirakhor, Nuri Erbaş

Chapter 4: Game-Theoretic Investigation into Economic Behavior

1 Introduction

The neo-classical model in economics envisages humans as compassionless and only self-concerning. Under such assumptions, maximizing one's own utility can easily erode trust and deplete resources, leading to the "tragedy of the commons" and free-rider problem, which can be attributed to ill-defined property rights and imperfect information. Well-known examples that can arise out of poorly-defined property rights are over-farming and overfishing. Free-riding, such as tax evasion, stems mostly from imperfect information. On the other hand, environmental pollution and global warming seem to be a combination of the tragedy-of-the-commons and free-rider problems. Weakly enforced property rights can also result in the tragedy-of-the-commons such as poorly policed territorial waters, leading to overfishing and piracy. The breakdown of trust and cooperation as well as the failure of institutions to govern effectively can be seen as one of the critical causes of the global financial meltdown (de Larosière, 2009). As such, in order to achieve the vision of prosperity and progress, proper mechanisms for ensuring trust, honesty and cooperation are required. Trust and cooperation are important in reducing inefficiencies and waste of shared exhaustible resources. Social norms, including religious rules like Islamic tenets on property rights and preferred behavior in uncertainty provide a core to build around and self-enforce such mechanisms.

Modern economics, however, in its attempt to instill ethics into economics as preferences or constraints relies on its own conceptions of reason and rationality and removes revelation as an authentic source for consideration. This part is missing in contemporary economics, where all economic goals are directed to the happiness of human beings in this world. A rational individual is free to maximize his utility as much as possible without any moral, social or religious commitment that involves a "hereafter" reward and punishment of the consequences of economic choices and decisions made. Those aspects, instead, are constraints that will morally restrict an individual to maximize his utility. Hence, the Islamic economics system utilizes and integrates both reason with revelation in choice selection and economic value application.

Acknowledgements: The authors acknowledge the financial support from the Ministry of Higher Education Malaysia (MOHE) (FRGS/1/2015/SS08/INCEIF/01/1) and the University Malaya-INCEIF research grant.

https://doi.org/10.1515/9783110587920-004

The failure to understand the causes for the repeated cycles of financial crashes and debt crises continues to haunt the global conventional financial system. Reinhart and Rogoff (2011) contend that the rocky road to defaults (and in most nations, serial defaults) lies in the human nature that makes flawed decisions, putting financial institutions, central banks and sovereign nations into an economic spiral through over-leveraging. Reinhart and Rogoff (2011) find that across time, place, cultures, institutions and political systems, financial crises still happen, regardless of the monetary system (viz. gold standard, Bretton-Woods and current floating-rate system). As such, the root cause of these issues seems to be buried deeply in the human psyche and social behaviors. It would be invaluable to know specifics for countries and regions to really understand the mechanics of the processes behind their individual crises. Like Keynes, Akerlof and Shiller (2009) know that managing these "animal spirits" requires the steady hand of governance – simply allowing markets to work is not enough. Conventional economic theories and models may be insufficient to the task of dive into an in-depth analysis of default cycles and financial crises. It would require the opening of the proverbial Pandora's box – these animal spirits and psychological fallibilities that are behind the thought processes that drive all decisions – the mysterious internal workings of human cognition and motivation that have been locked up in a 'black box' until recently. The neo-classical *homo-economicus* model can no longer be relied upon as it is not consistent with the real world and empirical evidence. Its continued use to predict human economic behavior would be imprudent and destructive.

Thus, the objective of this chapter is to extend the behavioral investigation into testing the level of adherence towards the rules of behavior in the society. It presents a comparative analysis of the behavior of Muslims and non-Muslims by employing a selection of experimental games. The game-theoretical examination is performed with participants from Malaysia and Singapore with diverse backgrounds in terms of age, education, income and profession.

2 Rules of Economic Behavior According to Qur'an and Sunnah

Mirakhor (2009) argues that central among the rules that constitute the institutional structure of the ideal economy are the rules governing property, production, exchange, distribution and redistribution, and market conduct. From an institutional perspective,

> the ideal economy is composed of a collection of institutions – rules of conduct and their enforcement characteristics – designed by the Law Giver, prescribed in the Meta-framework

> (specified in the Qur'an) and operationalized by the Archetype Model (the way the Messenger understood and implemented the rules) to deal with allocation of resources, production and exchange of goods and services, and distribution-redistribution of resulting income and wealth. (Mirakhor 2009, p. 59)

Mirakhor and Askari (2010) note that Adam Smith (in the Theory of Moral Sentiments) concisely and clearly shares some of the foundational scaffolding of Islam: belief in the One and Only Creator; belief in the accountability of the Day of Judgment; belief in the necessity of compliance with the rules prescribed by the Creator; and belief that justice is achieved with full compliance with rules. The foundational scaffolding of Islam underlines the productive role that religion can play in markets. The Islamic market principles derived from the Qur'an and the Sunnah are a perfect example of the role that the foundational scaffolding can play. It is clear that Smith considers the internalization of the rules, being consciously aware of the ever-presence of the Creator and acting accordingly, as crucial to all productive human conduct, including economic transactions. Mirakhor and Askari (2010) also stress that the rules reduce uncertainty and transaction costs, and that these rules promote coordination and make collective action possible. In addition, Mirakhor and Askari (2010) believe that rule-compliance promotes social solidarity. Social cohesion can enhance growth by reducing transaction costs, that is, the costs incurred in making economic exchanges, such as information gathering, communications, and contract enforcement (Coase, 1960). Since Williamson (1998), the concept of transaction cost has also been applied to the effects of informal institutions, including trust and non-discrimination. In societies where norms of trust or cooperation between differing ethnic, sectarian, or other identity groups are low, the costs of economic cooperation will be higher, thereby inhibiting economic activity. Empirical studies have also shown generalized social trust to be predictor of future rates of economic growth (Knack and Keefer, 1997).

This chapter examines the behaviors prescribed according to Islamic tenets that can strengthen the case for guidance in addressing market failures, such as negative externalities from narrow decision-making and their eradication through ethical, social and legal means. It draws upon these rules of behavior from the Qur'an and Sunnah to test the level of more adherence via experimental games using sample of social groups of Muslims and non-Muslims.

2.1 Promoting Rule-compliance and Discouraging Non-compliance (Capstone Rule)

The duty of commanding the good and forbidding evil, incumbent on individuals as well as the whole community, is the most important means of enforcement of rules prescribed in the Meta-framework. The absence of this is also an effective promoter of social solidarity and preserver of social order. The existence of oppression, corruption, massive inequality and poverty in a society is *prima facie* evidence of non-compliance and outright shirking of this duty. No one is absolved from the necessity of performing the duty of commanding rule-compliance and forbidding rule-violation. This is particularly binding *visa-à-vis* the rulers. Even though there is particular emphasis both in the Qur'an and in the Sunnah of the Messenger on just political authority, the individual members of the society are not absolved from the duty of commanding the authorities, at all levels, to righteous conduct and forbidding them from rule violations whenever the individuals recognize the necessity of doing so.

In addition, the rules governing the markets are related to appropriate behavior of all market participants. The Qur'an acknowledges the need for markets and affirms their crucial existence as well as places emphasis on contracts of exchange (*al-bay'*) and trade (*tijarah*). As a rule, the Qur'an recognizes the validity of market transactions based on mutual consent, and this conditional freedom of choice and freedom of contract. This, in turn, requires the acknowledgement and affirmation of private property rights. Also, the proper structure of institutions and adherence to rule compliance are crucial in achieving the objectives of institutions. Mirakhor (2009, p. 47) also adds that:

> The Messenger (sawa) specified operational rules of conduct in the market place, appointed a market supervisor to ensure rule compliance, and encouraged internalization of these rules by participants before their entrance into the market. Compliance with the rules of market behavior ensures the emergence of prices that are fair and just. So long as market participants are rule compliant, no direct interference with the price mechanism is permitted, even though the legitimate authority has the power and the responsibility of supervision of market operations.

2.2 Cooperation

In order to enact regulations and secure compliance and accountability, there has to be cooperation among the institutions involving the regulators, agents and market-players. The Qur'anic verse that underlines this behavior is: "Help (cooperate) one another in *Al-Birr* and *Al-Taqwa* (virtue, righteousness and piety); but do not help (cooperate) one another in sin and transgression" (Qur'an, 5:2). The fulfilment of Allah's (swt) trust (*amanah*) is the collective prerogative and responsibility of the whole community and the individual is just an active partner in the process. It is difficult for any individual to survive alone; the personal needs necessitate human interaction and cooperation in society. The community as a whole becomes responsible for the accomplishment of this trust. However, no meaningful, extensive and long-lasting cooperation is possible without effective good understanding of the ultimate goals of existence and proper rules of governance. The more people participate in the process of cooperation, the more effective the outcome are.

2.3 Contract

In general, Islam secures all worldly activities, including economic transactions, on contracts. The Primordial Covenant between the Creator and humans (*mithaq*) is basically a contractual agreement between creation and the Creator, which imposes the obligation on humans to recognize the Creator as their Provider and Sustainer (*Rabb*). From an operational standpoint, that cognizance is an affirmation that in their conduct on the earth, they will comply with the rules prescribed by their Cherisher Lord. Faithfulness to the terms of all contracts entered into, establishing justice, reward for rule compliance and punishment for rule violation on the Day of Accountability are linked to the fulfilment of obligations incurred under the stipulation of terms and conditions of the Primordial Covenant. This proposition links humans directly to their Creator and to one another.

In a direct, clear, and unambiguous verse, the Qur'an commands: "fulfill the Covenant of Allah," (Qur'an, 6:152). In an equally clear verse it generalizes this imperative to all contracts: "fulfill all contracts," (Qur'an, 5:1). Thus, faithfulness to the terms of every covenant, contract, or oath to carry out obligations one has committed to become a reflection of the Primordial Covenant.

2.4 Property Rights

In Islam, Allah's (swt) ultimate ownership of property supersedes that of the individual. The Qur'an and the Sunnah, clearly and explicitly indicates that Allah (swt) is the sole owner of wealth and that people, as vicegerents, are merely trustees or custodians. In practice, the individual claims to *al-mal,* which denotes all the resources made subservient to man are recognized and safeguarded by law. The sanctity of private property rights has been affirmed by Prophet Muhammad (sawa) when he delivered his last sermon, known as *khutbat-hajjatilwadaa*: "O people! Verily your blood, your property and your honor are as sacred and inviolable as the sacred inviolability of this day of yours, this month of yours and this very town (of yours)."

The property rights are not, however, absolute as the use of property owned is restricted, by the prohibition of *riba* (interest) and the obligation to give *zakah* (alms). The Qur'an (57:7) explicitly ordains Muslims to: "Believe in Allah (swt) and His Messenger, and spend of that whereof He made you successors (trustee)" By implication, the ownership of *al-mal* is understood to be a trust and its disposal is considered to be a test of faith since the owner has to use it in accordance with God's revealed wisdom. The Qur'an (6:165) further states that: "It is He who hath made you (His) vicegerents (or stewards), successors of the earth. He hath raised some of you above others in degrees [of rank] that He may try you through what He has given you" Hence, a person entrusted with wealth can achieve the highest degree of virtue (*falah*) by spending out of his wealth within the boundaries prescribed by *Shariah*.

Interestingly, economists have recognized that market trading is essential in reconciling private desires with public purposes. One central component of the legal foundations of markets relates to property rights over objects and circumstances. An effective system of properly defined property rights provides the foundations for economic growth. In so doing, *Shariah* explicitly specifies a complete system of rules and principles that regulates the legitimate sources of acquiring *al-mal* (property), its growth, and its disposal. These moral limits, which will be discussed in further detail below, are meant to achieve two vital objectives: preserving *al-adl* (socio-economic justice) and promoting *al-ihsan* (mutual benevolence) (Qur'an 16:90). *Al-adl* and *al-ihsan* are meant to articulate the notion that people should have equal opportunities, not necessarily equal riches.

More specifically, by emphasizing *al-adl*, the *Shariah* intends to eliminate all forms of economic inequality, injustice, exploitation, oppression, and wrongdoing, where a person either deprives others of their rights or does not fulfill his own obligations toward them. The concept of *al-adl* does not permit the existence of systematic inequalities in the distribution of income that the ownership of wealth has not only economic dimensions but also social implications.

Al-ihsan, on the other hand, is a reassurance that *al-mal* (property) is to be used to protect the welfare of the community (ummah). Restoring both *al-adl* and *al-ihsan* are necessary and sufficient conditions for an equitable distribution of income. Other precepts specified by *Shariah*, to restore *al-adl* and *al-ihsan*, include the prohibition of both avarice and wasteful spending (Qur'an, 17:27). Overspending (*israf*), waste (*itlaf*), ostentatious and opulent spending (*itraf*) are also prohibited because they entail consumption beyond the average standard for society and, therefore, violate the principle of responsibility. Hence, people are encouraged to be modest and utilize the available resources to attain both the mundane and the spiritual objectives of *Shariah*. Another important injunction required for the restoration of *al-adl* and *al-ihsan*, is the proscription of hoarding (e.g. commodities and *kanz*). Hoarding is prohibited due to its negative externality on wealth and income distribution. In today's economic thinking, hoarding can be harmful because it limits the productive capacity of resources and leads to the concentration of wealth in the hands of few. Chapra (1985) writes, "Islam provides an economic system that makes it absolutely imperative to use God-given resources for fulfilling the essential needs of all human beings and providing them with decent living conditions."

In addition, Ibn Abbas reported that the Messenger of Allah (sawa) said: "The people (i.e. humanity) are partners in three things – in water, herbage and fire". Water, trees, pastures and fire, being things of natural resource and common use are considered public property in Islamic thought. This does not mean, however, that humans are given free rein to use (and abuse) the resources Allah (swt) has provided us either on individual or collective basis. Humankind is urged to harness responsibly the various resources (public property) that Allah (swt) has made available on this earth. Humans are encouraged to enjoy the good things that God has created, but to do so within the boundaries that He has given. Doing so is not regarded as sinful as long as it follows His path and does not transgress His limits. Allah (swt) says: "It is He Who produces gardens, with trellises and without, and dates, and tilth with produce of all kinds, and olives and pomegranates, similar (in kind) and different (in variety): eat of their fruit in their season, but render the dues that are proper on the day that the harvest is gathered. But waste not by excess: for Allah (swt) loves not those who waste" (Qur'an, 6:141).

In line with previous arguments, the fundamentals of Islamic Law lay the legal foundations for internalization. Private property must be used and disposed of in favor of public good and should not cause public harm. Here, the Islamic principles exhort justice and benevolence in the name of the Creator, the ultimate owner of all property in perpetuum. Thus, an ethical and legal basis is provided to overcome the barriers of transactions costs for a fair and ethical solution that internalizes externalities arising from the existence of property rights.

2.5 Reciprocity

The concept of reciprocity revolves around in-kind responses for the actions of others, which are in relation to justice, including gratitude, mutuality, and the Golden Rule. This concept describes "reciprocal" or "two-way", relationship between one's self and others that involves both sides acting equally, and in a mutual fashion. The Messenger of Allah advises Muslims that whoever passes his night satiated and restful in his home with his family, while poor neighbours pass the night hungry, has no true belief.

From the macro-view of markets, the rule of reciprocity can be similarly applied to many economic activities such as trade concessions, where governments make mutually beneficial trade arrangements to reduce tariffs. The principle of reciprocity, therefore, promotes fair trade as concessions from one country are equaled by similar concessions from trading partners. It can also address market failures stemming from mistrust, and asymmetric information as parties interact cooperatively and maintain trade relations, even without explicit incentives and assurances.

2.6 Right not to be Harmed, and the Obligation not to Harm (Golden Rule)

This is essentially known as the Golden Rule. It is a maxim, ethical code or a universal morality that fundamentally states that one should treat others as one would like others to treat oneself (Positive form). Alternatively, the Silver Rule implies that one should not treat others in ways that one would not like to be treated

Blackburn (2001, p. 101) also states that the Golden Rule can be "found in some form in almost every ethical tradition". Not surprisingly, this rule of no harm is also reflected by generally accepted principles underlying the regulation of Patents, the United Nations Watercourses Convention (UNWC), and the Three Laws of Robotics. All belief systems, including Islam, emphasize the importance of protecting people from harm. The Prophet (sawa) is reported to have said: "to cause harm to others is not allowed in Islam.", "Whoever wishes to be delivered from the fire and to enter paradise should treat other people as they wish to be treated themselves" (reported by Sahih Muslim), "Do unto all men as you would wish to have done unto you; and reject for others what you would reject for yourself" (reported by Abu Dawud).

Arguably, the world may be a better place if we treated each other as the Golden Rule suggests. The Golden Rule simply states that all of us are to treat other people as we would wish other people to treat us in return. Almost all organized religions, philosophical systems, and secular systems of morality include these essential ethics. It is a universal rule that applies to all humanity irrespective of religion, race, and ethnicity. The application of these rules requires greater empathy for others and the ability to imagine themselves, vividly and accurately, in the other person's position and conditions. It also requires a good understanding of the impact of our actions on the lives of others. And for many centuries the idea has been influential among people of very diverse cultures which suggest that the golden rule has an important moral value. In addition, it is arguably the most essential basis for the modern concept of human rights, in which each individual has a right to just treatment, and a reciprocal responsibility to ensure justice for others. There has been research published arguing that some 'sense' of fair play and the Golden Rule may be stated and rooted in terms of neuro-scientific and neuro-ethical principles. Also, markets thrive where there is justice, equality and fairness.

Gensler (2013) notes that Islamic Golden Rule formulas deal with people's desires toward others (what one wishes, loves, or prefers) over and above actions (what one does), as in the examples from the *Qur'an* and *Sunnah*. Thus, this tradition has both Golden Rule forms: about desires and about actions. Indeed, Gensler (2013) also observes that the forms about desires are more distinctive, and that very few other traditions have Golden Rule forms about desires.

2.7 Trust

Arguably, economies and societies with lower levels of trust tend to be less productive and have more stifling levels of regulation – Higher barriers to entry, lower levels of freedoms in price-setting, more formalistic legal systems, and reduced product and labor market flexibility are reflective of the serious implications of the lack of trust (Aghion et al., 2010).

With respect to trust, it is important to note that the foundations of human behavior in Islam lie in the purpose of creations. Allah (swt) expressed His Will to the angels about creating on earth a new being who would be the best of all His creations and would be assigned the status of His vicegerent (*khalifah*). The angels expressed reservation, fearing that the new being would create chaos and disorder, shed blood, and bring suffering to his own species. In response, God only said to the angels that they did not know what He knew. God then breathed into Adam (a.s.) His Own Spirit (Qur'an 15:29; 32:9; 38:72). Thus, Adam was created not only with such faculties of hearing, seeing, and understanding; he also received the potential to develop advanced qualities such as being caring, responsible, kind, just, wise, forgiving, etc. Human beings, therefore, are unique and privileged as compared to other kinds of creation. The Qur'an also speaks of a covenant between man and Allah (swt) (Qur'an 7:172) in which man recognizes Allah (swt)'s as his Creator. In other words, the ability to perceive the existence of the Supreme Being is inborn in human nature.

Thus, the role of *khalifah* (God's vicegerent) is essentially based on the concept of trust (*amanah*). Allah (swt) has invested man His trust – a trust which the heavens, earth, and mountains refused to accept because they were afraid of its heavy burden (Surah al-Ahzab, Qur'an 33:72) – a trust which defines the rights and responsibilities in relation to humans, the environment and the rest of God's creation. As a *khalifah*, man is entrusted with an *amanah* to establish justice on earth by means of the virtues, initiative, creativity and labor (*isti'mar*) and infinite bounties endowed to him by Allah (swt) that "He brought You forth from the earth and settled You therein" (Surah Hud, Qur'an 11:61) to fulfill God's creative work in the universe. Nature has been created for the settlement of human beings but man is also required to establish a moral social order. The concept of *amanah* determines the individual's relationship with the society, and humanity at large. Man is attached to these institutions both procedurally and spiritually. The individual has a weighty contract with his society, with the animal world, with the plant and mineral worlds, and with the universe. The concept of *amanah* implies that in all his actions, man should choose to prosper the earth (*islah*) by making the best use of resources and to fully utilize the virtues inherent in him to *isti'mar* the earth. *Ifsad* (*fasad*) or adversity or corruption, is to be avoided in managing one's role as a *khalifah*. Being a *khalifah*, man has also been granted authority to freely manage nature / universe and to cooperate with his fellow beings to complete the task of *khalifah*. This part, Izutsu (2004) says, is in the realm of "human ethics" which should be guided by those "divine ethics." *Amanah* makes human life meaningful because it makes him squarely responsible for creating a moral social order. It provides him with the opportunity to demonstrate his ability to be God's vicegerent on earth. In other words, the Qur'an, like the Old Testament, gives the human being dignity; it presents unity and nobility of purpose. Similarly, the Prophet (sawa) said: "One who is dishonest in this world and does not return the trust to its owner and dies in this state has left the world being out of my ummah (nation) and is not considered as my follower and he will meet Allah making Him angry and furious, that is, he will meet with Divine chastisement."

Thus, this set of seven rules (Capstone Rule, Cooperation, Contract, Property Rights, Reciprocity, Golden Rule and Trust) can be extracted from the *Qur'an* and *Sunnah*. These rules underpin the very behaviors prescribed by Islamic principles and they strengthen the argument that the Islamic ideology provides clear guidance in addressing many issues of social and economic life, including market failures and negative externalities stemming from narrow decision-making.

3 Methodology

3.1 A Primer on Game Theory

Game theory provides the conceptual and procedural tools for studying social interaction, including the characteristics of players, rules of the game, informational structure, and payoffs associated with particular strategic interactions (Camerer, 2003). Game theory is the study of mathematical models of strategic interaction between rational decision-makers. It has applications in all fields of social science, as well as in logic and computer science. At its most basic level, game theory is the study of how people, companies or nations (referred to as agents or players) determine strategies in different situations in the face of competing strategies acted out by other agents or players. It facilitates cross-disciplinary information exchange and provides a unified analytical framework (Davis and Holt, 1993). The game theoretical approach can be useful in examination of the significance of Islamic rules of behavior across people, and in our case, regardless of age, education, gender and income.

This analytical study uses game-theoretical experiments to test the significance of normative rules of behaviour. Since people tend to view themselves as rather well-behaved and profess to be so, it is possible to directly observe the individual behavior in order to assess more objectively the significance of character and attitudes. Also, the experimental tests can provide insights into how people behave in real-life problems as opposed to theoretical economic conditions. These tests can shed light also on how Muslims behave in real-life situations as opposed to what Islam prescribes as normative rules of conduct. It is with the social experimental games that it may be possible to gain a better understanding of the psychological biases that influence the behavior of human beings, Muslim and otherwise. and have a significant aggregate impact on the social and economic system.

Table 4.1 describes the appropriate games selected to test for the relevant rules of behavior. Participants act out the scenarios defined by the different games and their behavioral outcomes are recorded in order to test the adherence to the rules of behavior defined by ... via sentence-unscrambling tasks.

Table 4.1: Institutional Rules and Theoretical Games.

Institutional Rules (Formal Rules)	Game Theory (Games to Test Compliance of Rules)
Affirming Rule-compliance and Discouraging Non-compliance (Capstone Rule)	Rowing Game *(original variant of Stag Hunt)*
Cooperation	Prisoner's Dilemma Game
Contract	Ultimatum Game
Property Rights	Cake-cutting Game
Right not to be Harmed, and the Obligation not to Harm (Golden Rule)	Volunteer's Dilemma
Trust and Reciprocity	Trust Game

Source: Authors' own.

3.2 Games Description

The methodology of this study aims to assess the behavior of the subject pool, which are players consisting of Muslim and non-Muslim groups) in six different scenarios (games). The same games are played by these two groups. For the purpose of this chapter, all of these six games consist of the following properties: There is a set of participants, whom we call the players. There will be two players in each game, except for the Volunteer's Dilemma game which will have an incremental number of players.

- Each player has a set of options for how to behave, which are the player's possible strategies.
- For each strategic choice, each player receives a payoff that depends on the strategies selected by other participants. The payoffs represent generally incentives for participation in the game, with the plausible assumption that each player prefers larger payoffs to smaller ones.

In implementing the game to Muslim and non-Muslim groups, the instructions are read to participants gradually in each session. Neutral terminologies should be used to avoid any potential bias. The test subjects do not know what is being tested for in each game to ensure neutrality and objectiveness in our outcomes. This allows to extract actual behavioral responses as they would behave naturally in real life. The test subjects only know the boundaries of the scenarios that are predefined from the outset, not the end of each scenario, data observations are collected to examine the decisions made under different conditions. It should also be noted here that the focus of this study is placed on simple, one-off games, in which players simultaneously and independently choose their individual actions, and do so only once. The six games implemented for the purposes of this analysis are given in the following subsections.

3.2.1 Rowing Game (Test for Capstone Rule)

The rowing game is created to test for the Capstone Rule which is 'to enjoin good and forbid evil'. It is derived from the original Stag Hunt Dilemma presented by Jean-Jacque Rousseau in 'A Discourse on Inequality' to illustrate how 'mutual undertakings' create a tension between individual rationality and group benefit. The rowing game is an original game which is a variant of the documented Stag Hunt game. The game is a prototype of a social contract where the hunters have the choice of hunting hare or hunting deer. The chances of getting a hare are independent of what others do. There is no chance of bagging a deer by oneself, but the chances of a successful deer hunt go up sharply with the number of hunters. A deer is much more valuable than a hare.

Similarly, David Hume (1978) provides the example where two individuals who must row a boat. If both choose to row, they can successfully move the boat and get to where they want to go (social utopia as described by *Qur'an* and *Sunnah*). However, if one rower does not, the other wastes his effort and they go around in circles, not getting anywhere. In order to achieve maximum mutual benefit, both rowers are required to match their efforts so that the boat travels straight to the destination or goal, but the results from Stag Hunt games show that although payoff levels do not affect strategic decisions, monetary pay-offs can affect behavior (Feltovich et al., 2008).

In this study, the game is played with cash to indicate effort of rowing – S$10/RM10 for maximum rowing effort, S$5/RM7 medium effort and S$2/RM5 for low effort. In reality, the rowers only get to where they want to go if their efforts match; any mismatch however slight will result in straying off. A matching bonus is paid out to both players if their premiums match; S$10/RM10 is paid for matching maximum premiums, S$5/RM7 is paid for matching medium premiums, etc. Results are tabulated based on premium placed and difference in their contributions.

3.2.2 Prisoner's Dilemma Game (Test for Rule of Cooperation)

In the Prisoner's Dilemma Game, the two players are suspects supposedly apprehended by the police and are being interrogated in separate rooms. Each of the suspects is presented with the following options:

- Confess, and if your partner does not confess, then you will get a reduced sentence and your partner will be charged with the crime. Your confession will be sufficient to convict the other player of robbery and imprisoned for 5 years.
- If both players confess, then both would be convicted of robbery, but the sentence would be shorter, 2 years due to the guilty plea.
- If neither confesses, then no conviction can be made and both suspects would be released.
- Both players are offered the same deal.

In the classical version of the game, the suspects are interrogated in separate rooms. Each can either confess, thereby implicating the other, or keep silent. No matter what the other suspect does, each can improve his own position (self-interest) by confessing. If the other confesses, then one had better do the same to avoid a poorer outcome by holding out. If the other keeps silent, then one can obtain the favorable treatment accorded a state's witness by confessing. However, the best outcome if both do not confess (cooperate), as there would be no crime to charge them with.

The prisoner's dilemma is a typical example in game theory that shows why two purely "rational" individuals might not cooperate, even if it appears that it is in their best interests. The interesting part of this result is that pursuing individual reward logically leads both of the prisoners to betray, when they would get a better reward if they both cooperated.

3.2.3 Ultimatum Game (Test for Rule of Contract)

The ultimatum game is played between two parties and the first player is referred to as the "offerer" and the second player will be called "responder". He game is played with a deck of cards (red - diamonds & hearts while black - club & spades). The players indicate their choice through the red or black cards (Holt and Capra, 2000). The payoff for red is S$5/RM5, and black indicate no change but the player's partner earns S$10/RM10. The two parties will be playing for S$20/RM20. Player 1 (offerer) makes an offer to player 2 (responder) of S$/RMxx from a total of S$/RM20. If the responder accepts the offer, then offerer is paid S$/RM(20 – xx) and responder receives S$/RMxx. If responder rejects the offer, the game ends with both players getting nothing.

Under a strictly utilitarian view of economics, player 1 would give player 2 the lowest possible amount. In this case of 20 dollar/ringgit bills, an offer of a dollar would suffice. Since money is to be gained effortlessly, player 2 should accept the offer. It may appear that player 1 is acting irrationally is departing with the money, but a strictly utilitarian view may not necessarily reflect how people actually behave when faced with such decisions. In experiments based on the ultimatum game, test subjects on the receiving end routinely reject offers they find too low, and subjects who must choose how much to give often offer more than the lowest amount. This unlikely behavior provides unique insights into the human mind and how social interactions take place.

The ultimatum game is also important from a sociological perspective, because it illustrates the human unwillingness to accept injustice. Faithfulness to the terms of agreements and promises, commitment to justice, and reward for rule compliance, are part of the fulfillment of moral and legal obligations. Also, the tendency to refuse small offers may also be seen as relevant to the concept of honour.

3.2.4 Cake-cutting Game (Test for Rule of Property Rights)

The cake-cutting game is a kind of fair division game. The problem involves a divisible and heterogeneous resource, in this case, an actual cake to be divided between 2 players so that each of them feels they got a fair share. For this study, one person would cut the cake into two pieces, after which the other person gets to choose which piece he/she wants. This obviously gives the first person great incentive to carefully cut the cake into equal halves, otherwise he/she will get stuck with the smaller one. However, the resource has to be divided among partners who have different preferences over different parts of the cake, i.e., some people prefer the chocolate toppings, some prefer the cherries, some just want as large a piece as possible, etc. The division should be subjectively fair, i.e., each person should receive a piece that he/she believes to be a fair share. This game tests for the respect of property rights and just allocation based on objective valuation.

In this research, envy-freeness and proportionality are used to tabulate agreeableness on equitability. Envy-freeness and proportionality are equivalent when there are only two players – that is, the existence of one property implies the existence of the other (Brams et al., 2006). Thus, if each player receives what he or she thinks is at least half the cake (proportionality), neither thinks the other player would receive more (envy-freeness). After 'cut and choose', player 2 (chooser) indicates fairness by rewarding player 1 (cutter) with S$10/RM20. Similarly, player 1 (cutter) indicates fairness by rewarding player 2 (chooser) with S$10/RM20. The existence of envy-free feelings allows the players to exchange the money and is an indication of fair division. No exchange of cash or one-sided exchange indicates unfairness.

3.2.5 Volunteer's Dilemma (Test for Golden Rule)

The rule of the 'Right not to be Harmed, and the Obligation not to Harm' is known as the Golden Rule as it is akin to 'do unto others as you would have them do unto you'. The game is a multiplayer version of the chicken game, where "volunteering" is akin to swerving. If no one volunteers, the worst possible outcome is obtained. If any one person elects to volunteer, the rest benefit by not doing so. In this research, the game is played in a symmetric-payoff design, the benefit to every member of the group if at least one person volunteered was S$2/RM2 and the individual cost of volunteering was S$1/RM1. If there were no volunteers in the group, each participant earned nothing. The game will be played with 2, 4, 6, 8, 10 players where everyone starts with S$2/RM2.

A public good is only produced if at least one person volunteers. In this game, bystanders decide independently on whether to sacrifice something for the benefit of the group. Because it will cost the volunteer to ensure mutual benefit, there is a greater incentive for free-riding. The social phenomena of the bystander effect and diffusion of responsibility heavily relate to the volunteer's dilemma (Poundstone, 1993).

The story of Kitty Genovese is often used as a classic example of the volunteer's dilemma. Genovese was stabbed to death in an alley where various residential apartments overlooked the assault. Although many people were aware of the assault at the time (even though they may not have been aware of the exact scope and nature of the assault), only one person contacted the police. It was assumed that people did not get involved because they thought others would contact the police, and people did not want to incur the costs of getting involved in the dispute (Takooshian, 2014). The apparent lack of reaction by numerous neighbors purported to have watched the scene or to have heard Genovese's cries for help, although erroneously reported, prompted research into diffusion of responsibility and the bystander effect. Social psychologists John M. Darley and Bibb Latané started this line of research, showing that contrary to common expectations, larger numbers of bystanders decrease the likelihood that someone will step forward and help a victim (Zimbardo, 2014). The reasons may have to do with the notion that onlookers see that others are not helping either, that onlookers believe others will know better how to help, and that onlookers feel uncertain about helping while others are watching. The Kitty Genovese case thus became a classic feature of social psychology textbooks.

3.2.6 Trust Game (Test for the Rules of Trust & Reciprocity)

In the trust game, the first player (investor) decides how much money he is given (S$40/RM40) to keep and how much to give to player 2 (trustee) as an investment. This first stage of the game is a test of trust (of player 1) and trustworthiness (of player 2). The amount invested earns a certain return (triple of the amount invested). Player 2 must now decide how much to give back to player 1. Ultimately, both players are better off with the investment but player 1 takes a risk with investing in player 2 and counting on that he/she is trustworthy. This game underscores the value of trust as a social capital that makes social interactions more efficient.

The Trust Game was designed by Berg and McCabe (1995) and is also called as the “investment game”. It is an experiment in decision-making to measure trust in economic decisions and to demonstrate that trust is as basic to economic transactions as self-interest. As “trust is not intrinsically part of mainstream economics”, the success of this experiment in demonstrating the primacy of trust is problematic for basic assumptions of standard economics, which tend to ignore trust. Under standard economic assumptions of rational self-interest, the predicted actions of the first player in the trust game will be that he will choose to invest nothing. However, in the original Berg et al. experiment, thirty out of thirty-two game trials resulted in a violation of the results predicted by standard economic theory. In these thirty cases, first players sent money that averaged slightly over fifty percent of their original endowment.

Given the above discussion, Table 4.2 provides a summary of the decision rules, payoffs and sample sizes for each of the six games described previously.

3.3 Priming Instrument

The experimental results are tested for significance, in particular, for the significance of possible differences between Muslim and non-Muslim subjects. In order to statistically control for religious effects, priming instrument is used following Shariff and Norenzyan (2007) to segregate Islamic-salient subjects within the Muslim group as well as the religious-salient subjects within the non-Muslim group through sentence-unscrambling tasks. The sentences vary depending on whether the subject is in the Islamic-salient condition or the control condition. Five of the sentences unscrambled by Islamic-salient subjects contain religious content. None of the control subjects’ sentences contain religious content. An advantage of this priming instrument is that it is subtle; compared with blatant primes, subtle primes more reliably cause behavior to conform to norms (Wheeler and Petty, 2001), which aids in interpreting our results within our theoretical framework of self-categorization. The basic idea is that priming a social category temporarily increases the strength of affiliation with that category. Stronger affiliation with a category causes behavior to shift towards that category’s norms, so comparing primed and unprimed behavior allows us to infer something about what the category’s norms are and how they affect steady-state behavior.

Table 4.2: Summary of Games' Decision Rules, Payoffs and Sample Sizes.

Game	Decision Rules	Payoffs	SG Size	MY Size	Total Size
Game 1 – Test for Capstone Rule (Rowing Game)	Player 1 & Player 2 decide how fast they want to row	If rowing effort matches, a matching premium is paid accordingly	18 Non-Muslim (11 primed) 12 Muslim (7 primed)	20 Non-Muslim (11 primed) 20 Muslim (9 primed)	38 Non-Muslim (22 primed) 32 Muslim (16 primed)
Game 2 – Test for Cooperation (Prisoner's Dilemma)	Player 1 & Player 2 indicate their choices with red or black cards	Payoff for a red card is S$5/RM5 but a black card get the other player S$10/RM10	18 Non-Muslim (11 primed) 12 Muslim (7 primed)	20 Non-Muslim (11 primed) 20 Muslim (9 primed)	38 Non-Muslim (22 primed) 32 Muslim (16 primed)
Game 3 – Test for Contract Rule (Ultimatum Game)	Player 1 makes and offer which Player 2 can decide to accept or reject	If Player 2 accepts the offer, both players keep the money. If Player 2 rejects, then both players lose all the money	18 Non-Muslim (11 primed) – 8 Offerers (6 primed) – 10 Responders (5 primed) 12 Muslim (7 primed) – 7 Offerers (3 primed) – 5 Responders (4 primed)	20 Non-Muslim (11 primed) – 11 Offerers (5 primed) – 9 Responders (6 primed) 20 Muslim (9 primed) – 9 Offerers (4 primed) – 11 Responders (5 primed)	38 Non-Muslim (22 primed) – 19 Offerers (11 primed) – 19 Responders (11 primed) 32 Muslim (16 primed) – 16 Offerers (7 primed) – 16 Responders (9 primed)
Game 4 – Test for Property Rights Rule (Cake-cutting Game)	Player 1 cuts a piece of cake then Player 2 chooses which piece for himself/herself	Player 1 and Player 2 indicate fairness of 'cutting' and 'choosing' through rewarding S$10/RM20	18 Non-Muslim (11 primed) – 8 Cutters (4 primed) – 10 Choosers (7 primed) 12 Muslim (7 primed) – 6 Cutters (3 primed) – 6 Choosers (4 primed)	20 Non-Muslim (11 primed) – 10 Cutters (6 primed) – 10 Choosers (5 primed) 20 Muslim (9 primed) – 10 Cutters (4 primed) – 10 Choosers (5 primed)	38 Non-Muslim (22 primed) – 18 Cutters (10 primed) – 20 Choosers (12 primed) 32 Muslim (16 primed) – 16 Cutters (7 primed) – 16 Choosers (9 primed)

(continued)

Table 4.2 (continued)

Game	Decision Rules	Payoffs	SG Size	MY Size	Total Size
Game 4 – Test for Property Rights Rule (Cake-cutting Game)	Player 1 cuts a piece of cake then Player 2 chooses which piece for himself/herself	Player 1 and Player 2 indicate fairness of 'cutting' and 'choosing' through rewarding S$10/RM20	18 Non-Muslim (11 primed) – 8 Cutters (4 primed) – 10 Choosers (7 primed) 12 Muslim (7 primed) – 6 Cutters (3 primed) – 6 Choosers (4 primed)	20 Non-Muslim (11 primed) – 10 Cutters (6 primed) – 10 Choosers (5 primed) 20 Muslim (9 primed) – 10 Cutters (4 primed) – 10 Choosers (5 primed)	38 Non-Muslim (22 primed) – 18 Cutters (10 primed) – 20 Choosers (12 primed) 32 Muslim (16 primed) – 16 Cutters (7 primed) – 16 Choosers (9 primed)
Game 5 – Test for Golden Rule (Volunteer's Dilemma)	Starts with pairs then progressively increased by pairs to 10 players. Player volunteers but loses S$1/RM1 in the process.	As long as 1 player volunteers, everyone in the group gets S$2/RM2. If there are no volunteers, the group gets nothing.	18 Non-Muslim (11 primed) 12 Muslim (7 primed)	20 Non-Muslim (11 primed) 20 Muslim (9 primed)	38 Non-Muslim (22 primed) 32 Muslim (16 primed)
Game 6 – Test for Trust & Reciprocity (Trust Game)	Player 1 starts with S$40/RM40 and decides how much to invest in Player 2. Moderator decides that investment has tripled. Player 2 now decides how much to give back to Player 1.	Player 1 retains uninvested amount plus what Player 2 returns. Player 2 keeps what is not returned.	18 Non-Muslim (11 primed) – 9 Investors (5 primed) – 9 Trustees (6 primed) 12 Muslim (7 primed) – 6 Investors (4 primed) – 6 Trustees (3 primed)	20 Non-Muslim (11 primed) – 8 Investors (4 primed) – 12 Trustees (7 primed) 20 Muslim (9 primed) – 12 Investors (6 primed) – 8 Trustees (3 primed)	38 Non-Muslim (22 primed) – 17 Investors (9 primed) – 21 Trustees (13 primed) 32 Muslim (16 primed) – 18 Investors (10 primed) – 14 Trustees (6 primed)

Source: Authors' own.

Friedman and Cassar (2004) find that undergraduate students are a good choice for the subject pool for several reasons. Firstly, if the experiment is done at a university facility, the subject pool is readily accessible, making it convenient to recruit. Secondly, most students have a low opportunity cost. Thirdly, students tend to have a steep learning curve and could be easily taught on how to follow the instructions of the game, and lastly, they seldom know much about the hypotheses of the study. It may be argued that graduate student and faculty members can potentially be unreliable subjects that tend to become interested in the experiment itself and to respond based on their own understanding of the issues rather than according to the incentives embedded in the game.

In light of these arguments, the present experiment is based on participants with relatively equal gender representation and different age groupings and educational backgrounds. The sample includes 40 participants from Malaysia and 30 from Singapore, reflecting variations in the proportions of Muslims within these countries.

4 Results and Discussion

Due to the small sample sizes, non-parametric tests were carried out to adequately analyze the data. Mann-Whitney U tests are used for their versatility to conduct the two-sided test of significance. There are three main reasons for selecting the Mann-Whitney U method to test for differences among groups based on religion and priming with regards to rule-compliance:

- Level of measurement of the dependent variable: The measurement level of “rule-compliance” is determined as an interval, which allows the calculation of the median (not mean) of each group, and tests for differences between means.
- Number of groups based on independent variable: For each independent variable (games), there are 2 main groups and 4 sub-groups (i.e. Main Group 1 – Religion: sub-groups of Muslim and non-Muslim; Main Group 2 – Priming: sub-groups of Primed and Unprimed). The non-parametric Mann-Whitney U test is used to evaluate differences between groups. The Wilconson signed-rank test may not be appropriate for the purposes of the present experiment. It is also noted that other test that deal with more than two groups such as the Kruskal-Wallis and Friedman test is not required either.
- Relation between groups: As noted above, the Mann-Whitney U test is used to assess differences between independent groups. Independent measures involve using two separate groups of participants, each containing different individuals, where each participant only takes part in each condition once. In Wilcoxon Signed-rank test, the comparison is made among related groups, matched samples, or repeated measurements on a single sample.

In Table 4.3, the evidence from the statistical tests suggests that the null hypothesis is usually accepted. This implies that there are no significant differences between the groups with respect to the mean values of adherence to the Capstone rule, Cooperation, Contract, Property Rights, Golden rule, Trust and Reciprocity.

Table 4.3: Mann-Whitney U Tests for Religion (Muslim or non-Muslim).

Game	Rules	N	Mann-Whitney U	Standard Error	t-statistics (2-sided test)
1	Capstone Rule	70	600.5	68.112	0.912
2	Cooperation	70	554	73.435	0.462
3	Contract	35	158.5	14.649	0.832
4	Property Rights	35	135	12.186	0.944
5	Golden Rule	70	656.5	83.481	0.561
6	Trust	35	171.5	16.703	0.546
7	Reciprocity	34	139	13.689	0.568

Source: Authors' calculations.

The results of the statistical analysis based on the Mann-Whitney U non-parametric tests indicate that the null hypothesis of positive relation between religious behavior and rule compliance is rejected. Similarly, there is no evidence of a significant positive relation between rule compliance and priming effects.[91]

In Table 4.4, under Game 5, it is noted that the significance for priming data-set for the Golden Rule is 0.071 < 0.100, the only marginally significant data point in all the data-sets. This corresponds to the large difference in performance where primed subjects volunteered 61% versus 31% of unprimed subjects. The statistics reported for this game are found to be significant except for the Golden Rule game with priming.

91 The test was initially designed in 1945 by Wilcoxon for two samples of the same size and was further developed in 1947 by Mann and Whitney to cover different sample sizes. Thus, the test is also called Mann-Whitney-Wilcoxon (MWW), Wilcoxon rank-sum test, Wilcoxon-Mann-Whitney test, or Wilcoxon two-sample test. The U test is a non-parametric test, in contrast to the t-test; it does not compare mean scores but median scores of two samples. Thus, it is much more robust against outliers and heavy tail distributions. Because the Mann-Whitney U test is a non-parametric test, it does not require a special distribution of the dependent variable in the analysis. Therefore, it is an appropriate test to compare groups when the dependent variable is not normally distributed and at least of ordinal scale.

Table 4.4: Mann-Whitney U Tests for Priming (Primed or Unprimed).

Game	Rules	N	Mann-Whitney U	Standard Error	t-statistics (2-sided test)
1	Capstone Rule	70	599	68.112	0.895
2	Cooperation	70	592	73.435	0.828
3	Contract	35	145.5	14.649	0.832
4	Property Rights	35	136	12.186	0.59
5	Golden Rule	70	758.5	83.481	0.071
6	Trust	35	155	16.649	0.935
7	Reciprocity	34	137	14.17	0.864

Source: Authors' calculations.

On aggregate, it may be concluded that there is no statistically significant evidence that rule compliance is different between Muslim and non-Musliim participants, and between primed and unprimed groups. Subtle nuances are observed when primary data are analyzed in percentage terms in Table 4.5, which summarizes the result of experimental games based on primary percentage rules. The evidence suggests also that religious identity and convictions can affect the economic behavior of individuals. It appears that Muslims tend to outperform in four game experiments, namely, tests based on cooperation, Golden Rule, trust, and reciprocity. The priming in Muslims is associated with an increase in the adherence to the rule of contract and Golden Rule against unprimed Muslim counterparts, who tend to perform better for tests on property rights and trust.

Table 4.5 summarizes the result of experimental games based on primary percentage rules. On aggregate, the evidence suggests that religious identity and convictions affect the economic behavior of individuals. It appears that Muslims tend to outperform in four of the game experiments, namely, tests based on cooperation, Golden Rule, trust, and reciprocity.

Since the statistical analyses could not detect any significance, we refer to our primary percentage values. The investigations revealed that religious identity salience resulted in Muslims outperforming non-Muslims in four of the seven experiments – Cooperation, Golden Rule, Trust and Reciprocity. The priming in Muslims caused increased adherence to Rule of Contract and Golden Rule against their unprimed Muslim counterparts, who performed better for the tests on Property Rights and Trust. However, there is no evidence that Islamic identity affects the adherence to the capstone rule, cooperation and reciprocity as both primed and unprimed Muslim segments in Singapore and Malaysia tend to have similar performances. Among the group of non-Muslim participants, religious identity is found to be associated with stronger adherence to capstone rule, property rights,

Table 4.5: Summary of Game Results based on Primary Percentage Values.

	Game 1	**Game 2**	**Game 3**	**Game 4**	**Game 5**	**Game 6**	
	Capstone Rule	**Rule of Cooperation**	**Rule of Contract**	**Property Rights**	**Golden Rule**	**Rule of Trust**	**Rule of Reciprocity**
Muslim Priming Effects	P < unP	P = unP	P > unP	P < unP	P > unP	P < unP	P = unP
Non-Muslim Priming Effects	P > unP	P < unP	P < unP	P > unP	P > unP	P > unP	P < unP
Combined (M & nM) Priming Effects	P > unP	P < unP	P < unP	P < unP	P > unP	P = unP	P < unP
Muslim vs non-Muslim	M = nonM	M > nonM	M < nonM	M < nonM	M > nonM	M > nonM	M > nonM

Source: Authors' calculations.
Note: P = primed; UnP = unprimed subjects and M = Muslim and nonM = non-Muslim participants and > means performs better and < means conversely according to the primary criteria of the experimental game.

Golden Rule and trust with negative effects on the rules of cooperation, contract and reciprocity.

The results indicate that priming is likely to affect only five out of the seven game outcomes in the Muslim group, as compared to non-Muslims, where priming exerts a significant influence on the outcome of all games. It may be argued that Islamic values captured in the rules of cooperation and reciprocity are already significantly embedded in the life of Muslims to the extent that even priming has no significant impact on behavioral outcomes. Interestingly, where positive effects of religious identity are expected in both groups, there are rather significant negative effects from triggering the religious identity with respect to the rules of Cooperation and Reciprocity. This may indicate a reactionary behavior towards religious identity. For instance, poorer performance by both primed groups of Muslims and non-Muslims with respect to Cooperation and Reciprocity may indicate perceptions of irrelevant reference to religious identity and the rather poorer performance. The negative effect of primes in both groups for the respective tests may have triggered an adversarial view of others and that their game partners were outside of their social network (particularly shared values) based on religious identity.

5 Conclusion

There is an increasing interest in behavioral economics and behavioral finance, which hold the potential of exploring how people make morally acceptable financial decisions, how emotions can affect markets, and how to enhance constructive behavioral norms. The focus in behavioral finance is placed on the impact of emotions, and framing, heuristics and market forces on investments, firm behavior, market, regulation and education.

The experimental games on rule-compliance can be useful in understanding the determinants of human behavior. Behavioral norms can be derived from divine revelation as Qur'an provides general guidelines for good behavior.

> Recite to them [O Muḥammad!] the news of him whom We had given our signs, but he abandoned them and the devil pursued him so that he became one of the deviants; if We had willed, We would have exalted him through those signs, but he gravitated down to the earth and followed his own desires. (Qur'an 7:175–176)

As "(man) gravitate(s) down to the earth," his conscience becomes dull. Such people cannot effectively listen to the voice of their true, higher nature "[as though] these people are being called from a distant place" (Qur'an 41:44). For to draw near to God is to obey Him, and to be rule-compliant is to comply to His Rules at every decision point in life. Hence, one becomes *muttaqqin* only when one is fully rule compliant all the time. Here, there is a leap from *fitri* consciousness (iman) to the status of *taqwa* and *al-ihsan*, where the believers behave with all conscience for Allah (swt). The argument is about constancy and consistency in adherence to Allah's (swt) commands through the course of a day and through time as it is in the nature of Man to tire, to forget, to be overcome by emotions, to be influenced by the social environment and to be attracted to material wealth and power.

> Verily, man was created impatient, irritable when evil touches him and niggardly when good touches him. Except for those devoted to prayer those who remain constant in their prayers. (Qur'an 70:19–23)

Man's cognitive faculties are immense, but the sense of morality and responsibility depend on individual choice and decision-making that are in turn, subject to emotional factors. Hence, an individual's blessings including leaps in spiritual consciousness as well as worldly economic gains are conditional upon making the right choices under constraints. The compliance to such rules of behavior does not only improve economic performance and social welfare but helps individuals in achieving their higher potential. The adherence to the rules-based system has the potential of reducing cognitive and psychological biases. Thus, it is possible to conceive behavioral policies that encourage people to seek innovative solutions to social dilemmas. The alternative approach is useful in improving ways of thinking and developing role models that expand mental concepts and frames, thereby overcoming stereotypes, improve trust, encourage collective action and increase risk-sharing transactions.

References

Aghion, Philippe, Yann Algan, Pierre Cahuc, Andrei Shleifer. 2010. "Distrust and Regulation." *Quarterly Journal of Economics*, 125(3): 1015–1049.

Akerlof, George. and Robert Shiller. 2009. *Animal Spirits: How Human Psychology Drives the Economy, and Why It Matters for Global Capitalism*. Princeton: Princeton University Press.

Berg, J., Dickhaut, J., and McCabe, K. 1995. *Trust, Reciprocity, and Social History*, Games and Economic Behaviour, 10, 122–42.

Blackburn, Simon. 2001. *Ethics: A Very Short Introduction*. Oxford: Oxford University Press.

Brams, Steven, Michael Jones, and Christian Klamler. 2006. *Better Ways to Cut a Cake*. Stony Brook Center for Game Theory, NY.

Camerer, Colin F. 2003. *Behavioral Game Theory: Experiments in Strategic Interaction*, Princeton: Princeton University Press.

Chapra, M. Umer. 1985. *Towards a Just Monetary System*, (Vol. 8). International Institute of Islamic Thought (IIIT).

Coase, Ronald. 1960. "The Problem of Social Cost." *Journal of Law and Economics*, 3(1),1–44.

Davis, Douglas D. and Charles A. Holt. 1993. *Experimental Economics*. Princeton, NJ: Princeton University Press.

de Larosière Group 2009. *The High-Level Group of Financial Supervision in the EU*, Brussels.

Feltovich, Nick, Atsushi Iwasaki, and Sobei H. Oda 2008. *Payoff Levels, Loss Avoidance, and Equilibrium Selection in the Stag Hunt: An Experimental Study*, Working Paper, University of Aberdeen.

Friedman, Daniel, and Alessandra Cassar. 2004. *Economics Lab: An Intensive Course in Experimental Economics*, London: Routledge.

Gensler, Harry J. 2013. *Ethics and the Golden Rule*. New York: Routledge Press.

Holt, Charles A., and Monica Capra. 2000. *Classroom Games: Prisoner's Dilemma*, Unpublished. Partially funded by National Science Foundation (SBR-9617784 and SBR-9818683).

Hume, David. 1978. *A Treatise of Human Nature* (Second Edition). Clarendon Press, Oxford. Edited by L. A. Selby-Bigge. Revised by P. Nidditch. First published 1739.

Izutsu, Toshihiko. 2004. *Ethico-Religious Concepts in the Qur´an*, Kuala Lumpur: Islamic Book Trust.

Knack, Stephen, and Philip Keefer. 1997. "Does Social Capital Have an Economic Payoff? A Cross-Country Investigation." *Quarterly Journal of Economics* 112(4): 1251–1288

Mirakhor, Abbas. 2009. Islamic Economics and Finance: An Institutional Perspective. *IIUM Journal of Economics and Management* 17(1): 31–72.

Mirakhor, Abbas, and Hossein Askari. 2010. *Islam and the Path to Human and Economic Development*. New York: Palgrave Macmillan.

Poundstone, William. 1993. *Prisoner's Dilemma: John von Neumann, Game Theory, and the Puzzle of the Bomb*. New York: Anchor Books.

Reinhart, Carmen. and Kenneth Rogoff. 2011. "From Financial Crash to Debt Crises." *American Economic Review* 101(5): 1676–1706.

Shariff, Azim F. and Ara Norenzayan. 2007. "God Is Watching You: Priming God Concepts Increases Prosocial Behavior in an Anonymous Economic Game." *Psychological Science* 18: 803–809.

Takooshian, Harold. 2014. "Not Just a Bystander: The 1964 Kitty Genovese Tragedy: What Have We Learned?" *Psychology Today*, March 24, 2014.
Wheeler, S. Christian, and Richard E. Petty. 2001. "The Effects of Stereotype Activation on Behavior: A Review of Possible Mechanisms." *Psychological Bulletin* 127(6): 797–826.
Williamson, Oliver E. 2000. "The New Institutional Economics: Taking Stock, Looking Ahead." *Journal of Economic Literature*, 38(3): 595–613.
Williamson, Oliver E. 1998. "The Transaction Cost Economics: How It Works; Where It Is Headed." *De Economist* 146(1).
Zimbardo, Philip. 2014. Dr. Philip Zimbardo on the Bystander Effect and the Murder of Kitty Genovese. www.bystanderrevolution.org. *Bystander Revolution*. Retrieved 18 June 2015.

Part II: **Interest Rates, Economic Uncertainty and Macroeconomic Policies**

Nabil ElMaghrebi

Chapter 5: Interest Rates, Unconventional Monetary Policies and Market Volatility Expectations

1 Introduction

An important question that arises with respect to the relation between monetary policy and financial markets is whether changes and shifts in monetary policy, anticipated or otherwise, have adverse effects on asset pricing and the determination of risk premia. From the perspective of Islamic finance and economics, the issue is important not least because of the distinct paradigm of conducting monetary policy without interest rates. Arguably, the mechanics of monetary policy are intrinsically different from the conventional and non-traditional measures that recently pursued to create inflationary environment and stimulate the economy. Given the prohibition of *riba*, there is no room for positive, zero, or negative interest rates. The contents and analytics of these separate mechanics are important in their own right, but they fall beyond the scope of the present study. The issues addressed here concern the relation between the conduct of monetary policy and the formation of volatility expectations in financial markets. Based on the model-free volatility index that measures forward-looking volatility expectations, it is possible to examine the question of whether the setting of interest rates by monetary authorities is bound to generate unwarranted levels of uncertainty in financial markets. The additional issue arises also as to whether policy announcements are sufficient to absorb these levels of excess volatility, and whether forward guidance can moderate the anticipated price fluctuations.

Forward guidance by central banks is part of the communication strategies aimed at providing greater clarity about the future course of monetary policies. Not just for the sake of transparent policy-making, forward guidance can be also pursued for its potential ability to entrench expectations about inflation rates and shape anticipations about real interest rates. It is associated with unconventional monetary policies that address low rates of economic growth and inflation with zero interest rates and quantitative easing. There are concerns about the distortive effects of non-traditional policies on price discovery in asset markets and about the role of central banks in financial markets. But the question remains also as to whether forward guidance is useful in attenuating market volatility associated with uncertainty ahead of monetary policy meetings. Thus, the focus in the present study is made on expectations about price volatility around monetary policy meetings, which represent a form of feedback from financial markets and commodities exchanges. In addition to the levels of asset prices, volatility feedbacks are important for the expectations channels of monetary policy transmission during periods of financial instability.

https://doi.org/10.1515/9783110587920-005

It is also noted that forward guidance is pursued in the presence of *purdah* rules, which represent unofficial guidelines for prudent silence by central banks around policy meetings. Given these self-imposed limits on communication and transparency, it may be argued that the interaction between policymaking and price discovery during financial crises grows in complexity in the absence of forward guidance. The arrival of new macroeconomic information may alter attitudes toward risk, increase asset price volatility, and precipitate changes in monetary policy that may be otherwise unwarranted. As much as current levels of market volatility can be conducive to changes in policy, market expectations about future levels of volatility can also affect future policy. The formation of volatility expectations in financial markets can thus differ under forward guidance from policymakers, or lack thereof. Forward guidance may not be useful only in conveying monetary policy by entrenching inflation expectations, but also in absorbing part of the uncertainty surrounding policy meetings. The present study examines the impact of forward guidance on the formation of volatility expectations around monetary policy meetings.

It is noted that forward guidance is a distinctive feature of monetary policies at the zero-lower bound of interest rates. Following the Japanese asset bubble's burst, the Bank of Japan's recourse to zero-interest rate policy, untraditional methods of quantitative easing and forward guidance set a unique precedent for other central banks, including the Federal Reserve, Bank of England and European Central Bank to implement similar measures in response to the U.S. credit crisis and euro-area sovereign debt problems. As a means of central bank communication, forward guidance is aimed at resolving uncertainty about future policy, which is conducive to financial stability. The forms of policy-rate forward guidance and balance sheet forward guidance can improve the effectiveness of monetary policy by shaping expectations in financial markets. Filardo and Hofmann (2014) argue that forward guidance on policy rates can affect financial markets through three main conduits: changes in the levels of future expected short-term yields as well as long-term bond yields, changes in volatility of market expectations about future policy rates, and asymmetric responses of market participants to specific economic indicators relative to other releases of new macroeconomic information that are deemed less relevant to expected changes in monetary policy.

As noted by Bernanke and Reinhart (2004), policy measures near the zero-lower bound on nominal interest rates may take the form of changes in the composition of the central bank's balance sheet or expansion of its size beyond that required for zero-policy rate through quantitative easing programs. Policy may be also pursued through forward guidance that provides assurances to financial markets that policy rates will be maintained at lower levels than currently expected. Because forward guidance is primarily aimed at shaping forward-looking expectations about interest rates, the focus is typically made on the response of short- and long-term bond yields. With the exception of bond markets, the literature on the reaction of financial markets to forward guidance is rather limited.

The behavior of volatility implicit in options prices on equity indices can provide, however, useful additional insights on the effects of forward guidance on the formation of expectations about stock market volatility. This particular aspect of the relation between forward guidance and expectations about asset volatility is also important because, as noted by Fawley and Neely (2013), changes in real interest rates are conducive to changes in asset prices through their potential impact on firm decisions to invest, bank decisions to lend, and household decisions to consume, or to invest in housing markets. To the extent that monetary policy can influence the short-term and long-term economic decisions, forward guidance does not affect solely the volatility of future policy rates. It is also bound to affect the expected levels of volatility for other financial assets including equity prices. Significant effects on the formation of market expectations have in turn some important bearing on risk premia.

Thus, the natural question arises as to what extent forward guidance affects the formation of market expectations about fluctuations in equity prices. One way to address this issue is to examine the behavior of implied volatility around monetary policy meetings. The level of volatility expectations is likely to increase in anticipation of monetary policy meetings, reflecting thereby differences in investors' beliefs and uncertainty about the outcome of meetings. In contrast, post-meeting announcements have the opposite effect of whittling the anticipated levels of volatility down. As far as forward guidance is concerned, the issue is whether it can be useful in shifting the foci of market participants away from the announcements following policy meetings toward the release of economic information. The main proposition is that insofar that forward guidance is effective in affecting market expectations, market perceptions of lower uncertainty about the outcome of meetings would translate into a decrease in the anticipated levels of volatility in the equity market before meetings.

If forward guidance is aimed at reinforcing inflation expectations, then market expectations about future levels of asset prices should be taken into consideration as well. Mishkin (2009) identifies valuation risk and macroeconomic risk as important elements of financial instability, and argues that spillovers from financial markets can have adverse implications for output and employment. Monetary policy can thus be more potent during financial crises because aggressiveness of monetary easing can decreases the likelihood of adverse feedback loops. The tests of forward-looking Taylor rule for the Federal Reserve by Jovanovic and Zimmermann (2010) provide evidence that for given levels of inflation and output, policy rates are inversely related to measures of stock market uncertainty such as implied volatility.

In order to test for the effects of forward guidance on market expectations about short-term volatility, the present study examines the behavior of anticipated levels of market volatility around monetary policy meetings using the event-study methodology. Given its earlier adoption of zero-interest rate policy and forward guidance practice, it is on the Bank of Japan policy board meetings that the focus is made.[92] Changes in the level of volatility expectations in Japanese financial markets are measured by the model-free volatility index based on the Nikkei 225 index options. Because this volatility benchmark is reflective of the consensus among options market participants about forward-looking expectations, it can be regarded as an empirical proxy for uncertainty as argued by Bloom (2009), among others. Because of its negative correlation with market returns, it is also considered as a gauge of investors' fear and market sentiment, which can be useful in assessing the impact of forward guidance on financial markets.

To the best of the authors' knowledge, this is the first study that examines the relation between forward guidance about monetary policy and forward-looking volatility expectations in financial markets. The behavior of volatility expectations is important for a better understanding of market sentiment, financial crises and financial stability. The potential contributions of this study to the existing literature are three-fold. Whereas the focus is typically made on the impact of forward guidance on inflation expectations and interest rates, the present study explores the feedback from financial markets in terms of volatility expectations. Second, the significance of the short-term relation between forward guidance and forward-looking volatility is assessed around policy meetings using the event-study analysis. Third, the important distinction is made between open-ended and state-contingent forward guidance. The empirical evidence suggests that different rounds of forward guidance have indeed different effects on the formation of volatility expectations. Judging from the significance of forecast errors, which reflect departures of volatility expectations from realized volatility, state-contingent forward guidance may be more effective than open-ended guidance in managing expectations around monetary policy meetings. Furthermore, the absence of forward guidance during periods of financial instability is associated with anticipations of increased volatility and significant forecast errors around policy meetings.

The remainder of this chapteris organized as follows. The next section discusses the different rounds of forward guidance adopted by the Bank of Japan as a monetary transmission mechanism. Section 3 introduces the model-free volatility index and event-study methodology. Section 4 discusses the empirical evidence about the dynamics of implied volatility around monetary policy meetings under different rounds of forward guidance. Section 5 examines the behavior of forecast errors, which represent deviations of volatility expectations from realized volatility, with respect to forward guidance and financial instability. Section 6 concludes the chapter.

---

92 The Bank of Japan introduced forward guidance under the zero-interest rate policy as early as April 1999. As noted by Filardo and Hofmann (2014) indicates that forward guidance on policy rates was adopted also by the Federal Reserve in December 2003, and new forward guidance policies were introduced by the Bank of England and the European Central Bank in mid-2013.

2 The Bank of Japan's Forward Guidance About Monetary Policy

The earliest indication of forward guidance by the Bank of Japan was its explicit commitment in April 1999 to zero-interest rate policy (ZIRP), almost a decade after the burst of the Japanese asset bubble and nearly two decades before the onset of the U.S. credit crisis. The ZIRP inception and commitment to its continuation "until deflation concerns are dispelled." are part of the Bank's efforts to entrench inflationary expectations. As argued by Shirai (2013), the statement by the Bank of Japan governor in this respect can be regarded as an open-ended forward guidance. This first round of forward guidance was rather short-lived as the uncollateralized overnight call rate was raised in August 2000 despite the elusive evidence of inflation expectations. This rate increase signaled also the end of the zero-interest rate policy.

The second round of forward guidance is associated with a commitment to pursue monetary easing until "the inflation rate becomes stably above zero." This state-contingent forward guidance is accompanied with the lowering of the policy rate, which signaled the reintroduction of the ZIRP in March 2001 in an implicit recognition that its termination in August 2000 was rather premature.[93] A target for bank reserves held at the Bank of Japan became the main instrument for money market operations in replacement of the uncollateralized overnight call rate. Quantitative easing was pursued through the expansion of asset purchases to a wider range of securities including essentially long-term Japanese government bonds. These measures were aimed at providing banks with ample liquidity, with excess reserves beyond the required levels for zero overnight call rates.

To add further clarity in the implementation of forward guidance, it was stated in October 2003 that exit from ZIRP unconventional measures would be subject to a set of requirements, as noted by Ito and Mishkin (2006). The necessary conditions include he latest figure of core consumer price index, measured on a year-on-year basis, taking zero or positive value, with the additional requirement that the observed tendency is confirmed for subsequent months. It was further required that core CPI forecasts by most board members are not indicative of a drift and reversion to deflation over the foreseeable future. These conditions were deemed to be fully satisfied by the core CPI, and overall CPI as well, and the uncollateralized overnight call rate was reinstated as the target for money market operations in March 2006. Given the significant downward revisions of the core CPI figures in August of the

93 As argued by Cargill, Hutchison, and Ito (2000), the early exit may be explained by the "independence trap", as concerns about the establishment of credibility and independence take precedence over policy, resulting in monetary measures becoming conservative, timid, and tentative.

same year, the exit from expansionary monetary policy and forward guidance can be regarded, in retrospect again, as rather precipitated.[94]

A third round of forward guidance can be identified, as argued again by Shirai (2013), as starting from October 2010 with a commitment to a comprehensive monetary easing policy through ZIRP and a second round of quantitative easing with asset purchase programs extending to securities other than long-tern government bonds. This monetary easing policy was to be maintained until price stability was in sight, conditional on the absence of serious risk factors, and based on an "understanding" of medium to long-term price stability. This state-contingent forward guidance relied on the policy board's "understanding" of price stability as the core CPI ranging from zero to two percent, with one percent as the central tendency of the distribution. The commitment to monetary expansion was further clarified in February 2012 as conditional on the Bank's judgment that the one percent "goal", rather than "understanding", is in sight. The inflation "goal" is distinguished from inflation "target" as the emphasis is made on inflation expectation rather than outcome.

As noted by Humpage (2012), the setting of an inflation goal rather than inflation target leaves room for flexibility given the economic uncertainties, but because monetary policy is function of inflation expectations, flexibility may inhibit its effectiveness. There is also forward guidance in January 2013 through a commitment to achieve the two-percent target as long as the Bank judges it appropriate to continue the ZIRP and asset purchase programs. With the introduction of quantitative and qualitative easing (QQE) in April 2013, forward guidance evolved into assurances to achieve the same target "as long as it is necessary for maintaining that target in a stable manner." Also, this commitment leaves room for appropriate adjustments in response to perceived risks to economic activity and asset prices.

With the focus being made mainly on the effects of asset purchase programs, the literature on the unconventional monetary policy instrument of forward guidance is rather scant.[95] The empirical tests by Moessner and Nelson (2008) provide no evidence that financial markets systematically overweigh policy rate guidance. This suggests that forward guidance from central bankers is not associated with the risk of impairing the functioning of financial markets. Campbell et al. (2012) examine the macroeconomic effects of forward guidance, and whether it constitutes, at the zero bound, a substitute for lower interest rates. The results indicate that it is the surprise element in the FOMC policy announcements that exerts significant influence on treasury

94 As far as the effectiveness of the QE program from March 2001 to March 2006 is concerned, there is evidence from Honda (2014), based on a partial equilibrium model of asset markets that does not incorporate expectations, that the produced the anticipated stimulating effects on investment and production through the Tobin's Q channel.

95 A useful review of the theoretical and empirical literature on the effects of central bank communication on financial markets is provided by Blinder et al. (2008).

yields, corporate borrowing costs and private macroeconomic forecasts.[96] The evidence from Moessner (2013) indicates also that the FOMC policy rate guidance has the effect of flattening the yield curve, and reducing the implied interest rates, particularly at medium-term horizons. The results are significant even in the presence of asset purchase announcements. Also, Filardo and Hofmann (2014) suggest that forward guidance is conducive to lower volatility of expectations about future interest rates.

As far as forward guidance by the Bank of Japan is concerned, there is also evidence from Filardo and Hofmann (2014) that the Bank of Japan's announcement of comprehensive monetary easing policy in October 2010 had only limited effects on three-month Euro/Yen futures rates. This may be explained by deep-rooted expectations that an increase in policy rate would take place only in the distant future. In contrast, the QQE announcement in April 2013 of a shift from policy-rate forward guidance to balance sheet forward guidance affected the term premia in the bond markets, but with no significant impact on futures rates. Also, Ueda (2012b) provides a classification of nontraditional monetary policy measures by the Bank of Japan, and evidence that efforts through pure quantitative easing to inflate central bank's balance sheet and to generate portfolio rebalancing were not effective. In contrast, forward guidance to manage expectations about future policy rates as well as targeted asset purchases to restrict fluctuations in interest rates were rather more effective. Starting from February 2016, the Bank of Japan shifted its mechanisms for monetary operations toward the implementation of negative interest rates. The unconventional measures of quantitative and qualitative monetary easing and negative interest rates are deemed to be effective for yield curve control. Thus, the new framework for monetary policy is aimed at enhancing the transmission channels.

There may be mixed evidence on the short-term and long-run effectiveness of nontraditional monetary policy, but the four rounds of forward guidance explained above, constitute unprecedented exercises in managing expectations in financial markets under persistent deflationary pressures, and expansionary monetary policies characterized by zero or negative interest rates and asset purchase programs. As suggested by Ueda (2005), the ZIRP can be regarded as an attempt to affect market expectations about future monetary policy rather than changing the prevailing policy instruments. It is further argued that the inception of quantitative easing as incremental monetary stimulus is another attempt to alter expectations about policy rates when nominal interest rates cannot be further depressed given the zero-lower bound. The reintroduction of quantitative easing and further monetary expansion through

---

96 Campbell et al. (2012) make the important distinction between two types of FOMC forward guidance based either on an explicit commitment to future policy action or on a likely policy action conditional on macroeconomic forecasts. It is also suggested that the risks of undermining the Federal Reserve's price stability mandate, which are associated with explicit forward guidance, can be managed by conditional forward guidance.

both quantitative and qualitative easing are consistent with the notion that these measures are not solely aimed at reinforcing the monetary transmission channels but also at shaping expectations in financial markets.

3 Model-Free Volatility Index and Event-Study Analysis

The impact of macroeconomic information and monetary policy on financial markets is usually assessed using the first moment of asset return distribution. However, as argued by Carr and Wu (2009), investors are not only exposed to uncertainty about the level of returns, but to uncertainty about the variance of returns as well. Given the importance of the stochastic properties of return variance, there is a growing literature on ex ante volatility expectations derived from short-term volatility implicit in options prices. Despite early evidence of upward bias in the implied volatility from S&P 100 from early studies by Christensen and Prabhala (1998) and Fleming (1998), more recent results suggest that forward-looking volatility expectations contain additional information about future volatility beyond that conveyed by historical returns. For instance, Busch et al. (2011) provide evidence of incremental information from the stock, bond and foreign exchange markets upon distinguishing between the continuous component and jump components of market volatility. Although the results from Becker, Clements, and White (2006) indicate that the model-free VIX index is not efficient with respect to all elements of past-information set, it is shown by Becker, Clements, and McClelland (2009) to subsume nevertheless information in past jumps in volatility and provide additional information about future jumps. As with ex post measures of market volatility, there is also strong evidence of the tendency for implied volatility to increase in association with falling prices and decrease in bullish markets, as suggested by Whaley (2000) and Bollerslev and Zhou (2006), inter alia.[97]

Thus, the empirical literature suggests that forward-looking volatility indices can be useful for forecasting market volatility, and estimating volatility risk premium. They can aid also in understanding the relation between macroeconomic information and financial markets. There is early evidence from Ederington and Lee (1996) that implied volatility tends to increase before the release of macroeconomic information. The persistence of higher volatility expectations is associated with unscheduled, and thus unanticipated, releases, as these ex ante expectations are more likely to decline after scheduled announcements as the uncertainty about the anticipated impact is resolved. Further tests by Fornari (2004) suggest

97 It is also possible to use vector autoregression analysis of implied volatility indices as in Nikkinen and Sahlström (2004), to examine the relation between the anticipated levels of uncertainty across markets, which is reflective of the degree of market integration.

that estimates of implied volatility from swaption markets tend to fall in association with the release of U.S. macroeconomic variables. The observed decrease on announcement dates is consistent with the behavior of realized volatility, and with the dissipation of the induced uncertainty over the average life of options following the releases. The results from Füss et al. (2011), based on tests of the reaction of VIX and VDAX indices to the arrival of macroeconomic information, suggest also a tendency for both volatility benchmarks to decline on announcement dates. Judging from the impact of announcements of macroeconomic information during the US financial crisis, these effects seem to be more significant during periods of increased financial instability.

As with the release of macroeconomic information, there is also evidence of the sensitivity of market volatility to monetary policy announcements. For instance, the results from Carr and Wu (2006) suggest that higher uncertainty about the Federal Reserve Fund Rate is reflected by the behavior of the new VIX index. There is also evidence from Maghrebi (2007), based on estimates of volatility implicit in the Nikkei 225 index options, of increased uncertainty before the Bank of Japan's monetary policy meetings. Post-meeting announcements have the effect of reducing the perceived levels of uncertainty, but the results seem to be sensitive also to the prevailing market conditions. Also, Vähämaa and Äijö (2010) provide evidence that implied volatility decreases after the Federal Open Market Committee meetings, and that the impact of policy decisions on implied volatility is more significant during periods of monetary expansion. In light of this empirical literature, this section reviews in brief the construction of model-free volatility index before discussing the event-study analysis of the impact of forward guidance on the dynamics of volatility expectations around policy meetings.

3.1 Model-Free Volatility Index

The construction of the model-free volatility index derived from Nikkei 225 options traded on the Osaka Exchange does not depend on a particular option valuation model such as the Black-Scholes option pricing model. It is based on the concept of the fair value of future variance developed by Demeterfi et al. (1999).

$$V = (2/T)\left[rT - \{(S_0/S_*)e^{rT} - 1\} - ln(S_*/S_0) + e^{rT}\int_0^{S_*} \{P(T,K)/K^2\}dK + e^{rT}\int_{S_*}^{\infty} \{C(T,K)/K^2\}dK \right] \quad (1)$$

where T is the time remaining to expiration, r is the risk-free rate, K is the exercise price, whereas C and P represent the call and put option premia, respectively. The current price of the underlying asset is denoted by S_0 whereas S_* is a reference price that approximates at-the-money forward level. This reference price delimits the boundary between liquid put and liquid call options. It is demonstrated by Jiang and Tian (2007) that Equation (1) is also theoretically consistent with the concept of model-free implied variance introduced by Britten-Jones and Neuberger (2000).

$$v^2 = 2e^{rT}\left[\int_0^{F_0}\{P(T,K)/K^2\}dK + \int_{F_0}^{\infty}\{C(T,K)/K^2\}dK\right], \tag{2}$$

where F_0 represents the forward price level. It is the model-free approach described by Equation (2) that underlies the methodology followed by the Chicago Board Options Exchange to develop the new VIX index. This volatility index provides an estimate of short-term volatility using the spectrum of exercise prices rather than just at-the-money options.

$$v^2 = 2/T\left[e^{rT}\sum_i(\Delta K_i/K_i^2)Q(T,K) - (1/2)\{(F_0/K_0)-1\}^2\right] \tag{3}$$

where K_0 identifies the exercise price immediately below the estimated forward level F_0, and $Q(T,K)$ represents the bid-ask quotes for put and call options with exercise prices $K_i < F_0$ and $K_i > F_0$, respectively. The numerical approach is similar to the fitting of interest rate processes to bond prices, as it extracts information from the relation of option premia with exercise prices.[98] The options with near-term and next-term maturities are used to compute the respective implied variances, and the interpolation process is applied for the hypothetical options with fixed one-month expirations that underlie the volatility index calculations.

The model-free volatility index constructed according to Equation (3) provides an aggregate estimate of forward-looking expectations about short-term volatility in financial markets. The formation of volatility expectations depends on market beliefs and perceptions about economic uncertainty. The results from Masset and Wallmeir (2010) based on DAX index options indicate that returns

98 The forward level is determined using the put-call parity relation and the exercise price K_0 is associated with the minimum call-put spread. As demonstrated also by Jiang and Tian (2007), the implementation of the CBOE procedure can be associated with various approximation errors related to the truncation, discretization, Taylor expansion and interpolation processes. Fukasawa, Ishida, Maghrebi, Oya, Ubukata and Yamazaki (2011) propose a new approach to the approximation of the expected quadratic variations of asset prices based on options premia, and an interpolation scheme for the volatility surface that is consistent with arbitrage bounds.

Granger-cause changes in implied volatility.[99] The evidence from Markov-regime switching models by Maghrebi, Holmes and Oya (2014) indicates that volatility expectations are function of the dynamics of market returns, and the realignment process following forecast errors. It is also shown that financial instability has the potential of increasing the likelihood of regimes of volatility expectations governed solely by the asymmetric relationship with market returns. There is thus evidence that financial instability has the potential of impairing the error-correction mechanism that underlies the formation of volatility expectations. This implies also that insofar that forward guidance provides some clarity about monetary policy, it can be also useful in consolidating market beliefs about future fluctuations in asset prices.

It is also important to note that the model-free volatility index described by Equation (3) reflects short-term expectations about price fluctuations over periods of time inclusive of monthly policy meetings. An increase in uncertainty about the outcome of policy meetings can be reflected by higher levels of model-free volatility index. Consistent with the study by Ederington and Lee (1996), post-meeting announcements may have the effect of decreasing the expected level of volatility as the uncertainty associated with policy meetings is resolved. To the extent that forward guidance provides some clarity about the future course of monetary policy, it has the potential of limiting the tendency for volatility index to surge before meetings. Also, the empirical findings by Ehrmann and Fratzscher (2008) suggest that statements during *purdah* periods prior to the Federal Open Market Committee meetings have the potential of altering the levels of short-term interest rates more significantly than during other periods. Given the sensitivity of market expectations to pre-meeting statements, the rationale for *purdah* restrictions may lie therefore in the avoidance of excessive volatility. But the results indicate also that immediate post-meeting statements are likely to lower uncertainty. The effectiveness of post-meeting statements as policy tool is consistent with the objectives of forward guidance as communication strategy under zero interest-rate policy.

It is possible to test the empirical proposition that the impact of forward guidance on the feedback process from financial markets can be captured by volatility expectations around policy meetings. Under forward guidance, the focus may shift away from policy meetings toward the release of macroeconomic information upon which future monetary policy actions are conditioned. Thus, forward guidance may have the effect of lowering the levels of uncertainty, and thus volatility expectations, before policy meetings. It can also diminish the significance of post-meeting announcement effects on volatility expectations.

---

99 This is consistent with earlier evidence of high correlation between volatility indices in the European financial markets from Äijö (2008), who suggests also that Granger-causality runs from the VDAX index to other volatility indices.

3.2 Event-Study Analysis of Volatility Expectations Around Policy Meetings

The impact of policy announcements on financial markets is traditionally assessed using regression models with dummy variables representing the announcement dates, as in the empirical studies by Ederington and Lee (1996), Fornari (2004), and Moessner (2013). There is also evidence from Vähämaa and Äijö (2010) on the behavior of implied volatility around the FOMC meetings, but these studies do not rely on the event-study methodology. Another strand of this empirical literature however uses event studies such as Ait-Sahalia et al. (2012) who examine the impact of policy announcements on interbank credit and liquidity risk premia during the U.S. financial crisis. Also, Gagnon, Raskin, Remache, and Sack (2010) and Krishnamurthy and Vissing-Jorgensen (2011) use the same methodology to test the significance of the relation between quantitative easing and interest rates.

The essence of event studies is to aggregate the observed changes in the variables of interest across similar events and assess their statistical significance. But, as rightly argued by Filardo and Hofmann (2014), caution should be made against drawing strong conclusions from event studies of policy rate forward guidance given the failure to take into consideration prior market expectations or the impact of simultaneous news such as asset purchase announcements. While recognizing the importance of these caveats, the present study provides some evidence about the behavior of volatility expectations around policy meetings and the potential effects of announcements and forward guidance. As in Gagnon, Raskin, Remache, and Sack (2010), the event-study assumes that volatility expectations are not affected by other economic events, that markets are efficient in the sense that market expectations reflect the arrival of new information on instantaneous basis, and that the event windows are sufficiently wide to capture the short-term effects of announcements. Given the argument by Filardo and Hofmann (2014), it is further assumed that prior market expectations are reflected by the distribution of ex ante levels of implied volatility outside the event windows.

Thus, the event-study methodology used to test the proposition that forward guidance lowers volatility expectations before monetary policy meetings, and reducing the post-meeting announcements effects can be implemented as follows. To assess the behavior of volatility expectations around policy meetings, it is possible to the event-window W containing a fixed number of days surrounding each meeting. There is a tradeoff between the widening of the window to measure the reaction of volatility expectations over an extended period, and its narrowing to avoid the contamination from subsequent meetings and related information. With the implementation of the new Bank of Japan Law in April 1998, the monetary policy meetings are held in principle twice a month, around the 10th and 25th of the month. Following the regulatory guidelines adopted in April 2001, the first meeting of the month is expected to extend over two consecutive days. Based on presentations of reports on economic and financial developments made on the first day, discussions of monetary policy and voting on proposals are made in the morning of the second day. It is thus expected that decisions reached at the end of the two-day meetings can be made public with immediate releases allowing financial markets some time to digest the informational content of policy decisions within the same day.[100]

There are no a priori conditions regarding the optimal number of days in the event windows. For instance, Gagnon, Raskin, Remache, and Sack (2010) set narrow windows of one trading day, whereas Aït-Sahalia et al. (2012) use five-day event-windows. Given the above guidelines for the scheduling of regular meetings by the Bank of Japan, there are in principle two weeks separating policy meetings within the same month. Over the sample period, there are many months in which only one meeting was scheduled, whereas three meetings were held in the months of September and October 2008 in response to the U.S. financial crisis.[101] Given these conditions and consistent with the approach by Aït-Sahalia et al. (2012), the event-window is inclusive of five trading days before and five days after the policy meetings.[102]

Given the scheduling of one-day and two-day monetary policy meetings, events are identified with the dates in which policy meetings are concluded and policy announcements are made. For any day $\tau \in W = [-w, \ldots, -1, 0, +1, \ldots, +w]$ in the event window L_m with the policy meeting being held at $\tau = 0$, it is possible to estimate the average implied volatility as $\bar{v}_\tau = \sum_m v_{\tau,m}/M$, where $v_{\tau,m}$ represents the expected volatility for day τ with respect to a given policy meeting m, and M denotes the number of policy meetings in the sample period. If the levels of volatility expectations within the event windows are found to be statistically different from averages of observations outside these windows, then monetary policy meetings may be regarded as significant events that affect the formation of volatility expectations. It is also possible to define the abnormal differences for each event day τ relative to pre-event observations from each estimation window as follows,

$$ad_{\tau,m} = v_{\tau,m} - \bar{v}_{Lm} \tag{4}$$

100 This implies that uncertainty about policy decisions remains over the first meeting day and it cannot be resolved until the announcement is made at the end of the second day. Given the absence of official announcement on the first business day of meeting, market perceptions of economic uncertainty can be plausibly assumed to be unaltered.

101 There were also unscheduled monetary policy meetings, which were held in December 2008, December 2009, May and August 2010, and November 2011 in consideration of economic and financial developments.

102 Robustness tests were also conducted on the basis of event windows spanning three and four days surrounding the policy meetings. The results from these robustness tests are qualitatively similar to those reported here.

where $\bar{v}_{Lm}$ represents the average volatility over the estimation window L_m preceding a given policy meeting m. Thus, the average abnormal differences over the total number of meetings can be derived from Equation (4) as $\overline{ad}_\tau = \frac{1}{M}\sum_m ad_{\tau,m}$. Also, cumulative abnormal differences across time within each event window can be measured as $cad_{\tau,m} = \sum_\tau ad_{\tau,m}$. The average cumulative abnormal differences can be computed as $acad_\tau = \frac{1}{M}\sum_m \sum_\tau ad_{\tau,m}$ to measure the aggregate impact of policy meeting announcements across all event windows. Following the parametric testing approach by Aït-Sahalia et al. (2012), the t-statistics for average cumulative abnormal differences can be computed on the basis of the standard deviation of abnormal differences over the pre-event estimation windows.

$$\sigma_\tau(acad) = \left\{\frac{1}{(M-1)}\sum_m \sum_l (v_{l,m} - \bar{v}_{Lm})^2 / L_m\right\}^{1/2} \tag{5}$$

This measure of variation in abnormal differences is, as argued by Aït-Sahalia et al. (2012), more balanced than that based on squared differences. It is assumed that the t-statistics $tacad_\tau = acad_\tau/\sigma_\tau(acad)$ converge asymptotically toward the normal distribution.[103] Alternatively, the cross-sectional *t*-statistics for average cumulative abnormal differences can be computed using the standard deviation of cumulative abnormal differences.

$$\sigma_{\tau,cross} = \left\{\frac{1}{(M-1)}\sum_m (cad_{\tau,m} - acad_\tau)^2\right\}^{1/2} \tag{6}$$

In contrast to the *t*-statistics derived from standard deviations of abnormal differences over the estimation windows according to Equation (5), the sectional t-tests based on Equation (6) are robust to an increase in variance induced by the event itself.

The behavior of market returns and daily changes in implied volatility can be similarly assessed for each day in the event windows using the averages $\overline{\Delta v}_t = \sum_m \Delta v_{t,m}/M$ and $\bar{r}_t = \sum_m r_{t,m}/M$, respectively. It can be assumed, following Merton (1973) and Hull and White (1987), that implied variance $v_t^2 = \int_t^{Te} v^2(s)ds$ represents the mean anticipated daily volatility over the life of the option until expiration at T_e, with $v^2(s)$ denoting the instantaneous variance at time s. The implied variance can thus, be approximated in discrete time as $v_t^2 = T_t^{-1}\sum_{u=t+1}^{Te} v_{u,t}^2$, where T_t denotes

103 An alternative approach to the assessment of statistical significance is to use the standard errors of implied volatility based on the remaining observations falling outside the event-windows W. The set Ω of observations from non-event periods is thus inclusive of all estimation windows L_m as well. The average implied volatilities from the N observations included in Ω can be expressed as $\bar{v}_N = \frac{1}{N}\sum_{i\in\Omega} v_i$, and the standard deviation can be computed as $\sigma_N = \{\frac{1}{(N-1)}\sum_{i\in\Omega}(v_i - \bar{v}_N)^2\}^{1/2}$. Thus, the average volatility expectations during event windows can be compared to the long-term drift derived from the remaining sample period in which no policy announcements are anticipated and no announcement effects are considered.

the time remaining from t until expiration at T_e. Ederington and Lee (1996) show that, the daily change in implied variance is due to the removal of day t from the remaining period until expiration and the revision of expectations regarding volatilities from $t+1$ until maturity. This is true with respect to any given maturity date T_e for which the time remaining to expiration is bound to decrease. However, since the hypothetical options underlying the model-free volatility index are associated with a rolling time-to-expiration fixed at one month, changes in implied variance would be reflective not only of the removal of day t and revisions of expectations from $t+1$ until T_e, but also of the incremental expectations about volatility for the additional date T_e+1. Thus, perceptions of higher uncertainty in anticipation of announcements on policy meeting days may be reflected by implied variance until the removal of the meeting day t from the period covered by market expectations. As argued by Ederington and Lee (1996), rational expectations imply that the mean revision of expected volatilities across announcements should be approximately equal to zero because upward and downward revisions are equally likely.

4 Forward Guidance and The Dynamics of Volatility Expectations Around Policy Meetings

In light of the above theoretical discussion of model-free volatility index and event-study methodology, this section examines the dynamics of volatility expectations in association with the Bank of Japan's monetary policy meetings. It considers first the relation between the volatility index and policy rates during different rounds of forward guidance. Next, it tests for the significance of market perceptions of uncertainty and significance of market returns around policy meetings. It addresses then the impact of different rounds of forward guidance on volatility expectations around policy meetings. Of particular import is the distinction between the effects of various rounds of open-ended and state-contingent forward guidance on feedback from financial markets. The evidence sheds light on the formation of volatility expectations, the dynamics of forecast errors, and the impact of forward guidance during periods of financial instability.

4.1 Policy Rates and Volatility Expectations

It is possible at this point to examine the relation between volatility expectations and policy rates in consideration of the different rounds of forward guidance. Figure 5.1 describes the time-series of the uncollateralized overnight call rate disseminated by the Bank of Japan and the behavior of the model-free volatility index computed using the closing prices of the Nikkei225 options. The sample observations cover a total

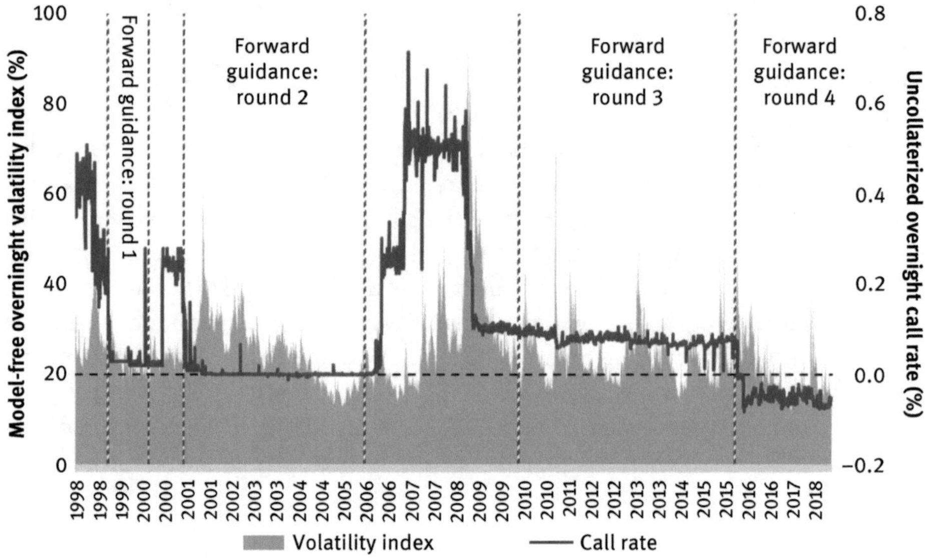

Figure 5.1: The Behavior of Model-free Volatility index and Uncollateralized Overnight Call Rates.
Source: The Bank of Japan statistics, Author's calculations.
Notes: The four rounds of forward guidance about the Bank of Japan's monetary policy run from April 1999 to August 2000, from March 2001 to March 2006, from October 2010 to January 2016, and from February 2016 to August 2018, respectively.

period of more than two decades, starting from April 1998, the date in which the new Act of the Bank of Japan became effective, and ending in August 2018. It is clear that the expected level of market volatility is itself volatile. There are sharp increases in association with the onset of financial crises such as the U.S. credit crisis and the euro-area sovereign debt problems. There is a tendency for jumps in volatility expectations to be followed by monotonous decreases toward historical levels. In this respect, Maghrebi, Holmes and Oya (2014) examine the short-term dynamics of volatility expectations using Markov-regime models, and provide evidence that regimes are governed by different degrees of mean reversion and correlation with market returns. The insignificance of the adjustment process to forecast errors during periods of financial instability suggests that past information may not provide useful guidance about future levels of uncertainty. Forward guidance about monetary policy at the zero lower bound may thus provide some guidance during periods of financial instability and influence the formation of market expectations.

These volatility dynamics can be examined in relation to the observed changes in the uncollateralized overnight call rates. The first round of forward guidance followed the introduction of the zero-interest rate policy and it was conditional on the dissipation of deflation concerns. There are no clear patterns in volatility expectations during this period, the termination of which was rather precipitated despite the lack of evidence of receding deflationary pressures. During the second round of forward guidance associated with the ZIRP reintroduction, the implied volatility index exhibits a tendency to decrease towards historically low levels. This second round covers also the period from April 2004 to March 2006, which is identified by Panetta et al. (2006) as associated with lower volatility across various financial markets in industrialized and emerging economies. The overnight call rate was replaced by a target for bank reserves as the main instrument for money market operations. It is clear that the uncollateralized call rate, which represents a weighted average rate for each trading day, approached the zero-lower bound, but it also took negative values during this period. As noted by Ueda (2012a), some bank borrowing was based on negative overnight rates on certain trading days, and this may be conducive to easing effects. The termination of this second round of forward guidance in March 2006 was followed by the reinstatement of the overnight call rate as the target for money market operations. But the conclusion of this round of guidance took place under an environment characterized by a renewed tendency for the anticipated levels of market volatility to increase. The fourth round of forward guidance with QE and negative interest rates, which started in February 2016, is also accompanied by lower volatility expectations.

The policy decisions to maintain overnight call rates near 0.25 percent and 0.50 percent were announced in July 2006 and in February 2007, respectively. It is clear from Figure 5.1 that there are wider fluctuations in the overnight call rates and an increase in volatility expectations in association with the second target. It is in response to the onset of the U.S. financial crisis that the target policy rate was then decreased to 0.3 and 0.1 percent in October and December 2008, respectively. It can be, plausibly, argued that the lowering of the call rate was made, in part, in response to market perceptions of higher levels of financial uncertainty, and given the subsequent fall in implied volatility, the shift in monetary policy seems to have immediate effects on the formation of market expectations. The pursuance of monetary policy under the zero lower bound continued into the third round of forward guidance, which coincides with development of the euro-area sovereign debt problems in October 2010. There is indeed a decrease in market volatility expectations since the inception of forward guidance, and lowering of call rates in response to the jump in volatility expectations in March 2011.

Thus, judging from Figure 5.1, the relation between fluctuations in the policy rate and volatility expectations seems to be dependent on the prevailing degree of financial instability. In this respect, the different rounds of forward guidance were pursued under the conditions of interest rates approaching the zero lower bound, and have the potential of affecting the forward-looking expectations about market volatility. Panels A, B, and C of Table 5.1 present, respectively, the distributional properties of the expected volatility levels and differences as well as market returns during these different rounds and the interceding period between the second and third rounds. It is clear from Panel A that the average level of implied volatility over

Table 5.1: Distributional Moments of Model-free Volatility Index and Market Returns.

Sample Period	Mean	Max.	Min.	St. Dev.	Skewness	Kurtosis	Jarque-Bera
Panel A- Levels of volatility expectations							
Full Period Apr. 1998–Aug. 2018	0.2529	0.9145	0.1153	0.0862	2.473	13.899	31805.66
No forward guidance period							
NFG Apr. 2006–Sep. 2010	0.2940	0.9145	0.1364	0.1308	2.028	7.686	1878.88
Forward guidance rounds							
FG1 Apr. 1999–Aug. 2000	0.2280	0.2971	0.1846	0.0232	0.503	3.028	15.66
FG2 Mar. 2001–Mar. 2006	0.2558	0.6373	0.1153	0.0720	0.611	4.026	140.63
FG3 Oct. 2010–Jan. 2016	0.2400	0.7008	0.1399	0.0595	1.941	11.019	4600.46
FG4 Feb. 2016–Aug. 2018	0.2046	0.4974	0.1221	0.0614	1.213	4.306	213.58
Panel B- Differences in volatility expectations							
Full Period Apr. 1998–Aug. 2018	−0.0001	0.2909	−0.1766	0.0187	1.836	31.730	186227.68
No forward guidance period							
NFG Apr. 2006–Sep. 2010	0.0001	0.1767	−0.1078	0.0224	1.150	12.347	4531.85
Forward guidance rounds							
FG1 Apr. 1999–Aug. 2000	−0.0001	0.1005	−0.0291	0.0104	2.493	26.020	8575.84
FG2 Mar. 2001–Mar. 2006	−0.0000	0.1918	−0.1571	0.0163	1.394	40.812	79484.36
FG3 Oct. 2010–Jan. 2016	0.0000	0.2909	−0.1766	0.0208	2.878	46.273	110450.41
FG4 Feb. 2016–Aug. 2018	−0.0002	0.1253	−0.0935	0.0184	1.214	12.810	2872.34

Panel C- Market returns							
Full Period Apr. 1998–Aug. 2018	0.0001	0.1323	−0.1211	0.0146	−0.366	9.526	9573.77
No forward guidance period							
NFG Apr. 2006–Sep. 2010	−0.0005	0.1323	−0.1211	0.0180	−0.387	10.978	3142.98
Forward guidance rounds							
FG1 Apr. 1999–Aug. 2000	0.0002	0.0355	−0.0723	0.0127	−0.604	6.044	165.76
FG2 Mar. 2001–Mar. 2006	0.0002	0.0722	−0.0686	0.0140	−0.074	4.760	172.52
FG3 Oct. 2010–Jan. 2016	0.0004	0.0743	−0.1115	0.0135	−0.623	8.925	2124.48
FG4 Feb. 2016–Aug. 2018	0.0004	0.0691	−0.0825	0.0117	−0.582	12.142	2388.80

Notes: The full sample period extends from April 1998 throughout August 2018, and includes 5328 observations. The four rounds of forward guidance are defined over the subperiods from April 1999 to August 2000 (FG1 with 371 observations), from March 2001 to March 2006 (FG2 with 1327 observations), from October 2010 to January 2016 (FG3 with 1391 observations), and from February 2016 to August 2018 (FG4 with 675 observations), respectively. The period of no forward guidance extends from April 2006 to September 2010 with 1174 observations.

the full sample period is closer to that prevailing during the second round of forward guidance than other periods. Apart from the mid-period, it is this second round that is associated with the highest estimates of mean and standard deviation.

The results in Panel B suggest that daily changes in volatility expectations tend to be insignificant, given the zero mean differences, over the full period as well as the different rounds of forward guidance. The evidence from Panel C indicates that the opposite signs associated with average market returns and volatility differences are indicative of the inverse relation between market returns and the model-free volatility index as a gauge of investors' fear and market sentiment. The likelihood for these series to follow the normal distribution is rather low, as they tend to exhibit higher skewness and leptokurtic properties. Whereas the distribution of returns seems to be negatively skewed, that of volatility expectations, either in the levels or differences, tends to be rather positively skewed.

4.2 Volatility Expectations and Monetary Policy Announcements

The behavior of the model-free volatility index around the Bank of Japan's monetary policy meetings can be described by Figure 5.2, based on five-day event windows.[104] There is a tendency for the average levels of expected volatility to increase despite the observed fall three days before meetings. Judging from the decrease on meeting days, there is also evidence of announcement effects on the average levels of uncertainty perceived by market participants. The announcement effects seem to be short-lived as volatility expectations continue to rise after meeting days, and decrease only over the last three days of the event window. The overall decline in volatility expectations after the Bank of Japan's monetary policy meetings is consistent with the results by Vähämaa and Äijö (2010) which suggest a tendency for implied volatility to decrease after the FOMC meetings. These patterns are also reflected by the daily changes in implied volatility, which tend to be negatively correlated with market returns. Thus, the dynamics of volatility expectations are, to some extent, reflective of the changing levels of uncertainty around monetary policy meetings.

It is possible to test for significant changes in volatility expectations around the Bank of Japan's monetary policy meetings using various measures of abnormal differences, cumulative averages and standard errors. In particular, the question is whether the observed averages of implied volatility in Figure 5.2 are significantly higher than averages prevailing during periods not associated with policy meetings. The results reported in Table 5.2 are based on event windows of five days, and estimation periods of seven days preceding the event windows for the full sample period including 301

104 The robustness tests based on three- and four-day event windows are associated with estimation results that are qualitatively similar to those based on five-day windows reported here.

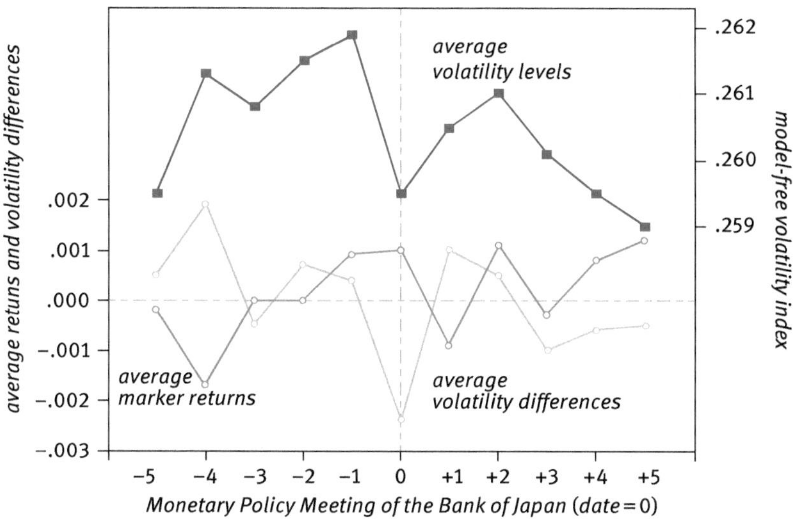

Figure 5.2: Volatility Expectations and Market Returns around Monetary Policy Meetings.
Source: Author's own.
Note: The sample period extends from Apr. 1998 to Aug. 2018, including daily observations of market returns and volatility index levels.

policy meetings. Judging from the average abnormal differences in the level of volatility expectations reported in Panel A of Table 5.2, it appears that implied volatility around policy meetings tends to rise significantly to levels that are no consistent with those observed outside event windows. Also, the abnormal differences in the levels of implied volatility are on average positive prior to meetings. These abnormal differences are found to be statistically insignificant based on standard errors from estimation periods according to Equation (5) as well as from standard errors within event windows. Thus, the evidence suggests that volatility expectations tend to rise above the levels observed over the estimation periods, but this increase remains marginal before policy meetings. Judging from the negative sign for the estimate of differences on the meeting date, any significance seems to be whittled down by announcement effects.

With respect to daily changes in implied volatility reported in Panel B, it appears that abnormal differences tend to alternate signs and remain insignificant. The fluctuations in expected volatility are thus consistent, in magnitude, with those prevailing during pre-event estimation periods. They are also in line with the asymmetric dynamic relation between changes in volatility expectations and market returns, as suggested by Panel C. The only statistically significant changes in market returns are associated with abnormal differences in expected volatility taking the opposite signs. The evidence from abnormal differences is in line with the patterns observed in Figure 5.2 with respect to the levels of implied volatility, changes in volatility expectations and market returns. It lends support to the proposition that uncertainty about monetary

Table 5.2: The Behavior of Abnormal Differences in Volatility Expectations and Market Returns around Monetary Policy Meetings.

−5	−4	−3	−2	−1	Date of Meeting ($\tau = 0$)	+1	+2	+3	+4	+5
Panel A- Average abnormal differences in the level of expected volatility										
0.0001	0.0020 [b]	0.0015	0.0021 [a]	0.0025 [a]	0.0002	0.0012	0.0017 [c]	0.0007	0.0001	−0.0004
[0.1404]	[2.2575]	[1.6459]	[2.3909]	[2.8397]	[0.1744]	[1.3421]	[1.9306]	[0.8384]	[0.1681]	[−0.3991]
(0.0932)	(1.0841)	(0.7964)	(1.0217)	(1.0918)	(0.0641)	(0.3791)	(0.5226)	(0.2401)	(0.0524)	(−0.1206)
Panel B- Average abnormal differences in daily changes of expected volatility										
0.0005	0.0019 [c]	−0.0005	0.0007	0.0004	−0.0024 [b]	0.0011	0.0005	−0.0010	−0.0006	−0.0005
[0.5284]	[1.8936]	[−0.5227]	[0.6787]	[0.4163]	[−2.3412]	[1.0529]	[0.5400]	[−0.9482]	[−0.5747]	[−0.4833]
(0.4978)	(1.5670)	(−0.5137)	(0.6636)	(0.4200)	(−1.9446)	(0.6378)	(0.4451)	(−0.7985)	(−0.4586)	(−0.4682)
Panel C- Average abnormal differences in market returns										
−0.0001	−0.0015 [c]	0.0002	0.0002	0.0010	0.0011	−0.0007	0.0012	−0.0002	0.0010	0.0014 [c]
[−0.1078]	[−1.9735]	[0.2020]	[0.2326]	[1.3291]	[1.4244]	[−0.9529]	[1.5907]	[−0.2518]	[1.2249]	[1.7814]
(−0.0863)	(−1.5724)	(0.1848)	(0.1913)	(0.9868)	(1.0873)	(−0.7358)	(1.2213)	(−0.2128)	(1.0993)	(1.4499)

Notes: The averages implied volatility and market returns are estimated with respect to all scheduled monetary policy meetings. The sample period extends from April 1998 to August 2018, and includes 301 policy meetings. Figures in square brackets refer to t-statistics based on standard errors calculated from observations within estimation windows, according to Equation [5]. Figures in parentheses refer to t-statistics based on standard errors calculated from observations within event windows. Significance at the 1, 5, and 10 percent levels indicated by the superscripts [a, b, c], respectively, refers to tests based on standard errors from estimation windows.

policy can be dissipated by immediate announcements, as suggested by the results of Fornari (2004) and Nikkinen and Sahlström (2004). The announcement effects can be however short-lived and of limited significance. Thus, the natural question arises as to whether forward guidance can be useful in managing market expectations of excessive volatility in association with monetary policy meetings. As argued above, the issue is important insofar that expectations channels are crucial for the conduct of monetary policies and inflation targeting. Managing expectations is an important part of the attempts by central banks to enhance the effectiveness of the signaling effects and the impact of money market operations.

4.3 Forward Guidance and The Dynamics of Volatility Expectations

The event-study methodology is applied to tests for different patterns of volatility expectations during different rounds of forward guidance by the Bank of Japan. As with the previous Table 5.2, the abnormal differences in the expected levels of market volatility reported in Panel A of Table 5.3 are estimated with respect to the four rounds of forward guidance (FG1 guidance from April 1999 to August 2000, FG2 from March 2001 to March 2006, FG3 from October 2010 to January 2016, and FG4 from February 2016 until the end of the sample period in August 2018) as well as the period of no forward guidance separating NFG from April 2006 to September 2010, which separates the former round from the latter. In contrast to the results obtained for the full sample period, it is clear that the first round of forward guidance is associated with significantly negative abnormal differences in the levels of volatility expectations. The average levels of volatility expectations during the event windows remain lower than those associated with estimation periods. The duration of this first round was rather short, but the behavior of volatility expectations seems to be repeated during the fourth round, albeit at lower levels of statistical significance.

The second round of forward guidance is also associated with a distinct pattern of volatility expectations. Indeed, the abnormal differences are found to be associated with opposite signs and statistically insignificant. This evidence suggests that forward guidance may have had the desirable effect of maintaining volatility expectations around policy meetings at the same levels as those observed before these events. The third round of forward guidance is also associated with insignificant abnormal differences prior to policy meetings, a pattern that is similar to the second round. But, the abnormal differences during the post-meeting days tend to be positive and significant. It may be argued that forward guidance was effective in suppressing surges in volatility expectations ahead of policy meetings, but not renewed perceptions of rising uncertainty following policy announcements.

In addition to these clear differences in the reaction of volatility expectations to various rounds of forward guidance, it is noted that the period of no forward guidance

Table 5.3: Forward Guidance and the Volatility Expectations.

Sample Period	**−5**	**−4**	**−3**	**−2**	**−1**	**Meeting date=0**	**+1**	**+2**	**+3**	**+4**	**+5**
					Panel A- Average abnormal differences in the levels of implied volatility						
No guidance (NFG)	0.0085 [a]	0.0119 [a]	0.0054 [b]	0.0102 [a]	0.0133 [a]	0.0125 [a]	0.0138 [a]	0.0142 [a]	0.0092 [a]	0.0096 [a]	0.0078 [a]
(Apr. 2006~Sep. 2010)	[3.6486]	[5.1014]	[2.2953]	[4.3600]	[5.6791]	[5.3249]	[5.8953]	[6.0847]	[3.9197]	[4.1145]	[3.3493]
First round (FG1)	−0.0050 [c]	−0.0079 [a]	−0.0066 [b]	−0.0073 [a]	−0.0088 [a]	−0.0096 [a]	−0.0089 [a]	−0.0098 [a]	−0.0080 [a]	−0.0088 [a]	−0.0054 [c]
(Apr. 1999~Aug. 2000)	[−1.8125]	[−2.8780]	[−2.3957]	[−2.6438]	[−3.2172]	[−3.5060]	[−3.2313]	[−3.5775]	[−2.9186]	[−3.2243]	[−1.9639]
Second round (FG2)	−0.0016	0.0020	0.0027 [c]	0.0021	0.0027 [c]	0.0007	−0.0019	−0.0014	−0.0033 [b]	−0.0009	−0.0027 [c]
(Mar. 2001~Mar. 2006)	[−1.0037]	[1.2489]	[1.7233]	[1.3241]	[1.7065]	[0.4402]	[−1.2453]	[−0.8797]	[−2.1164]	[−0.5589]	[−1.7348]
Third round (FG3)	−0.0012	0.0002	0.0036 [b]	0.0023	0.0000	−0.0036 [b]	0.0023	0.0020	0.0034 [b]	−0.0009	−0.0002
(Oct. 2010~Jan. 2016)	[−0.7655]	[0.1148]	[2.2437]	[1.4044]	[−0.0236]	[−2.2328]	[1.4069]	[1.2685]	[2.1455]	[−0.5813]	[−0.1481]
Fourth round (FG4)	−0.0043	−0.0058	−0.0084 [b]	−0.0085 [b]	−0.0070 [c]	−0.0164 [a]	−0.0169 [a]	−0.0137 [a]	−0.0074 [c]	−0.0101 [a]	−0.0112 [a]
(Feb. 2016~Aug. 2018)	[−1.1356]	[−1.5432]	[−2.2332]	[−2.2758]	[−1.8722]	[−4.3617]	[−4.5069]	[−3.6397]	[−1.9734]	[−2.6967]	[−2.9738]
					Panel B- Average abnormal differences in daily changes of implied volatility						
No guidance (NFG)	0.0040	0.0023	−0.0077 [a]	0.0037	0.0020	−0.0019	0.0002	−0.0006	−0.0062 [b]	−0.0006	−0.0029
(Apr. 2006~Sep. 2010)	[1.4952]	[0.8629]	[−2.8646]	[1.3984]	[0.7458]	[−0.7186]	[0.0906]	[−0.2430]	[−2.3034]	[−0.2381]	[−1.0783]
First round (FG1)	−0.0064 [a]	−0.0033	0.0010	−0.0010	−0.0019	−0.0012	0.0004	−0.0013	0.0014	−0.0012	0.0031
(Apr. 1999~Aug. 2000)	[−2.8685]	[−1.4843]	[0.4307]	[−0.4730]	[−0.8755]	[−0.5233]	[0.1740]	[−0.5945]	[0.6492]	[−0.5442]	[1.3934]
Second round (FG2)	−0.0023	0.0033 [c]	0.0005	−0.0008	0.0004	−0.0022	−0.0028	0.0004	−0.0021	0.0022	−0.0020
(Mar. 2001~Mar. 2006)	[−1.2638]	[1.7867]	[0.2861]	[−0.4510]	[0.2085]	[−1.1828]	[−1.5365]	[0.1943]	[−1.1578]	[1.2001]	[−1.1065]
Third round (FG3)	0.0015	0.0020	0.0040 [b]	−0.0008	−0.0017	−0.0030	0.0064 [a]	0.0003	0.0020	−0.0038 [c]	0.0012
(Oct. 2010~Jan. 2016)	[0.7804]	[1.0170]	[2.0569]	[−0.4149]	[−0.9051]	[−1.5556]	[3.3149]	[0.1688]	[1.0143]	[−1.9865]	[0.6447]
Fourth round (FG4)	0.0068 [c]	0.0009	−0.0002	0.0022	0.0039	−0.0070 [c]	0.0018	0.0056	0.0086 [b]	−0.0003	0.0013
(Feb. 2016~Aug. 2018)	[1.8676]	[0.2354]	[−0.0574]	[0.6137]	[1.0763]	[−1.9231]	[0.5074]	[1.5569]	[2.3855]	[−0.0919]	[0.3707]

Panel C- Average abnormal differences in market returns

No guidance (NFG)	−0.0034 [c]	−0.0033 [c]	0.0053 [a]	−0.0023	−0.0002	0.0008	−0.0022	0.0033	0.0024	0.0013	0.0039 [c]
(Apr. 2006~Sep. 2010)	[−1.7231]	[−1.6920]	[2.7024]	[−1.1662]	[−0.0989]	[0.4045]	[−1.1197]	[1.6695]	[1.2508]	[0.6591]	[1.9762]
First round (FG1)	0.0032	0.0005	−0.0024	0.0010	0.0010	0.0017	−0.0015	0.0001	−0.0019	−0.0025	−0.0013
(Apr. 1999~Aug. 2000)	[1.2857]	[0.1887]	[−0.9622]	[0.3861]	[0.3787]	[0.6853]	[−0.5842]	[0.0566]	[−0.7415]	[−0.9820]	[−0.5045]
Second round (FG2)	0.0005	−0.0039 [a]	−0.0014	−0.0015	0.0023	0.0009	0.0016	0.0025	−0.0009	0.0013	0.0011
(Mar. 2001~Mar. 2006)	[0.3512]	[−2.6131]	[−0.9658]	[−0.9662]	[1.5290]	[0.5671]	[1.0660]	[1.6505]	[−0.6023]	[0.8452]	[0.7323]
Third round (FG3)	0.0017	0.0000	−0.0019	0.0029 [b]	0.0028 [b]	0.0022	−0.0019	0.0014	−0.0008	0.0020	−0.0005
(Oct. 2010~Jan. 2016)	[1.2362]	[−0.0109]	[−1.3868]	[2.0831]	[2.0313]	[1.6090]	[−1.3687]	[0.9757]	[−0.5749]	[1.4679]	[−0.3661]
Fourth round (FG4)	−0.0026	−0.0014	−0.0004	0.0008	−0.0020	−0.0031	−0.0012	−0.0047 [b]	−0.0046 [b]	−0.0012	−0.0014
(Feb. 2016~Aug. 2018)	[−1.1807]	[−0.6304]	[−0.1873]	[0.3623]	[−0.9292]	[−1.3888]	[−0.5623]	[−2.1457]	[−2.0906]	[−0.5627]	[−0.6355]

Notes: The averages and cumulative averages of changes in implied volatility and market returns are estimated for the three rounds of forward guidance extending from April 1999 to August 2000 (Period FG1), from March 2001 to March 2006 (Period FG2), from October 2010 to January 2016 (Period FG3), and from February 2016 to August 2018 (Period FG4), respectively. These rounds are inclusive of 26, 80, 76 and 20 meetings, respectively. The period of no-forward guidance separating the last two rounds (Period NFG) runs from April 2006 to September 2010, and it is inclusive of 70 policy meetings. Figures in square brackets refer to t-statistics based on standard errors calculated from observations within estimation windows. Significance at the 1, 5, and 10 percent levels is indicated by the Significance at the 1, 5, and 10 percent levels is indicated by the superscripts [a], [b], [c], respectively.

is the only one associated with positive and significant abnormal differences in volatility expectations both before and after policy meetings. The positive sign is indicative of the elevation of volatility expectations above pre-event estimation levels in the absence of forward guidance. This stands in sharp contrast to the patterns obtained with respect to the first round of forward guidance associated with negative abnormal differences, and in particular, the second round characterized by insignificant differentials. Thus, the lack of commitment to particular measures of monetary policy is conducive to a reversal of market perceptions toward higher uncertainty ahead of monetary policy meetings and announcements. This evidence is consistent with the earlier results by Ederington and Lee (1996) that implied volatility tends to increase in anticipation of the release of macroeconomic information, and by Füss et al. (2011) that it tends to decrease on the announcement dates.

At this juncture, it is recalled that, as argued by Shirai (2013), the first round can be characterized as an open-ended forward guidance given the commitment to continue the zero-interest rate policy until deflation concerns are dispelled. The second and third rounds were rather regarded as state-contingent forward guidance, with commitments to pursue monetary policy until the inflation rate become stably above zero for the former round, and until an "understanding" of medium to long-term price stability and inflation goal is achieved for the latter round. Albeit the duration of the first round was short and its termination premature, it can still be argued that state-contingent forward guidance can be more effective in moderating market expectations than open-ended forward guidance. Forward guidance is conducive to market perceptions of lower uncertainty levels around policy meetings, and in particular the prevention of excessive volatility in anticipation of policy announcements. Forward guidance seems to eliminate the element of surprise in policy announcements, which as suggested by Campbel et al. (2012), affects market forecasts, borrowing costs and bond yields.

This is also consistent with the empirical results by Filardo and Hofmann (2014), which indicate that forward guidance leads to lower volatility in market expectations about future interest rates. Thus, the new evidence suggests that forward guidance under the zero-lower bound, either in open-ended or state-contingent form, can be an effective instrument of monetary policy transmission.

It is also important to note from Panel B that abnormal differences in daily changes of volatility expectations remain statistically insignificant. This tendency is particularly evident with respect to the first and second rounds of forward guidance, and extends to the period of no guidance. The results from Panel C suggest that forward guidance does not significantly affect the return-generating process either. Abnormal differences in market returns are generally found to significant only once for the second round, and twice for the third and fourth rounds of forward guidance. Thus, as with changes in volatility expectations, average abnormal differences in market returns remain generally insignificant over the event windows days. Thus, though the different rounds of forward guidance have significant implications for the levels of volatility expectations, there is no evidence from the behavior of market returns that forward guidance weakens the feedback process involving financial markets.

In light of the above results, it is possible at this point, to examine the behavior of cumulative abnormal differences in volatility expectations. With reference to Figure 5.3, there is clear evidence of a tendency for abnormal differences to cumulate to higher levels in the absence of forward guidance. The first round of open-ended forward guidance is associated with the lowest cumulative levels of abnormal volatility differences. In contrast, the second and third rounds exhibit a tendency for volatility differences to increase prior to policy meetings and decrease in association with policy announcements. There is a subsequent rebound in cumulative abnormal differences after announcement with respect to the third round. The observed pattern for the fourth round indicates a tendency for cumulative differences to decrease most significantly in association with policy announcements. Thus, the different patterns of cumulative averages of abnormal volatility differences suggest that forward guidance affects the dynamics of volatility expectations around monetary policy meetings.

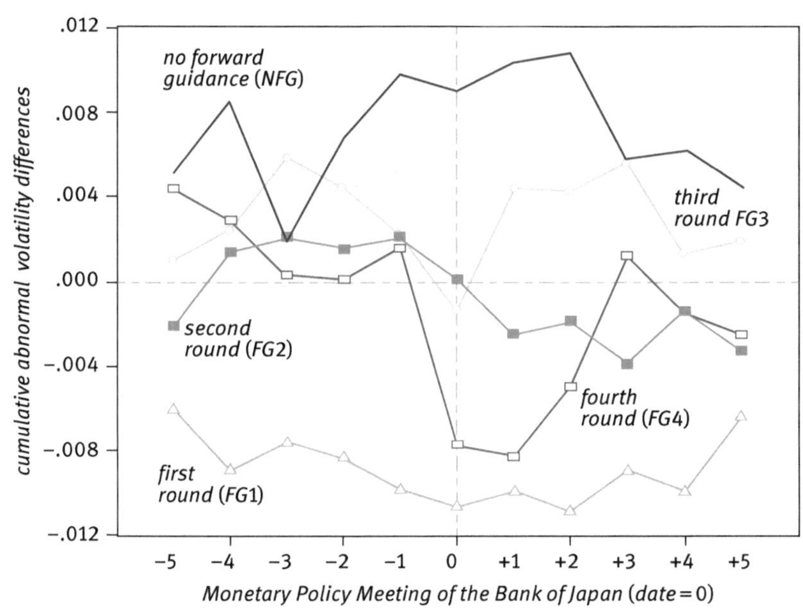

Figure 5.3: The Behavior of Cumulative Abnormal Differences in Volatility Expectations around Monetary Policy Meetings.
Source: Author's own.

5 Forecast Errors Around Monetary Policy Meetings and The Impact of Financial Crises

To assess whether the behavior of volatility expectations around monetary policy meetings is justified on ex post basis, it is possible to test for the significance of forecast errors. The issue is whether the increase in volatility expectations prior to policy announcements relative to estimation windows and the behavior of abnormal differences are consistent with the behavior of realized volatility. The prediction errors are defined as the spread between implied volatility and the realized volatility as follows

$$\varphi_t = v_t - rv_t \tag{7}$$

where rv_t is the estimate of realized volatility based on squared returns $rv_t = \left(n^{-1}\sum_{k=t+1}^{t+\delta} r_k^2\right)^{1/2}$ and n denotes the number of return observations from $t+1$ to $t+\delta$. The estimation of realized variances from the observed returns over the rolling period of $\delta = 30$ is consistent with the fixed one-month expiration of the hypothetical option underling the model-free volatility index. The derivation of realized volatility proceeds with the same process of annualization, which allows for a comparative analysis with implied volatility. The *ex post* estimates of forecast errors φ in Equation (7) are also consistent with the definition of variance risk premium in Bollerslev, Tauchen and Zhou (2009), among others.

In contrast to the previous discussion, the focus is made here on the behavior of average forecast errors rather than on abnormal differences or averages cumulative differences. The significance of average forecast errors around policy meetings is reported in Panel A of Table 5.4, with respect to policy meetings during the full period as well as the different rounds of forward guidance. The forecast errors around policy meetings held during the full sample period are found to be on average negative and significant. This strong evidence indicates a tendency to underestimate the future levels of market volatility. The forecast errors are persistently significant irrespective of the duration of time preceding or following policy meetings. It is important to note also that this pattern applies to the period of no forward guidance.

It is clear however that there are discrepancies in the behavior of forecast errors with reference to the different rounds of forward guidance. The forecast errors remain significant for policy meetings during the first round FG1, but this significance tends to fade away during the subsequent rounds of state-contingent guidance FG2, FG3 and FG4, except for the policy meeting dates and immediately preceding dates. The insignificance of prediction errors during these rounds suggests that forward guidance about the future course of monetary policy can be helpful in partially reducing the uncertainty associated with policy meetings. In contrast to other rounds, it is forward guidance FG2 that seems to be more effective in realigning the levels of

Table 5.4: The Behaviour of Forecast Errors around Monetary Policy Meetings.

	Panel A– Average levels of forecast errors						Panel B– Average differences in forecast errors					
			Forward guidance periods						Forward guidance periods			
Event window	Full period	No guidance (NFG)	First round (FG1)	Second round (FG2)	Third round (FG3)	Fourth round (FG4)	Full period	No guidance (NFG)	First round (FG1)	Second round (FG2)	Third round (FG3)	Fourth round (FG4)
−5	−0.0139 [a]	−0.0361 [a]	−0.0063	−0.0002	−0.0051	−0.0014	0.0005	0.0023 [b]	−0.0039 [c]	0.0003	0.0006	0.0051 [a]
	[−8.0530]	[−9.4885]	[−1.3714]	[−0.0583]	[−1.2111]	[−0.4125]	[0.8919]	[2.1692]	[−2.0470]	[0.4022]	[0.4491]	[3.8617]
−4	−0.0126	−0.0335 [a]	−0.0152 [a]	0.0017	−0.0026	−0.0021	0.0013 [a]	0.0026 [a]	−0.0089 [a]	0.0019 [b]	0.0025 [c]	−0.0007
	[−7.3062]	[−8.8005]	[−3.3208]	[0.5682]	[−0.6244]	[−0.6321]	[2.3651]	[2.4711]	[−4.6868]	[2.2567]	[1.9802]	[−0.5587]
−3	−0.0115 [a]	−0.0367 [a]	−0.0108 [b]	0.0038	0.0009	−0.0061 [c]	0.0012 [b]	−0.0032 [a]	0.0044 [b]	0.0020 [a]	0.0035 [a]	−0.0040 [a]
	[−6.6265]	[−9.6442]	[−2.3553]	[1.2374]	[0.2189]	[−1.8147]	[2.1529]	[−3.0306]	[2.3212]	[2.4105]	[2.8457]	[−3.0086]
−2	−0.0124 [a]	−0.0362 [a]	−0.0124 [a]	0.0035	−0.0034	−0.0053	−0.0009	0.0005	−0.0016	−0.0003	−0.0043 [a]	0.0008
	[−7.1448]	[−9.5147]	[−2.7093]	[1.1385]	[−0.8144]	[−1.5639]	[−1.6416]	[0.4651]	[−0.8511]	[−0.3564]	[−3.4871]	[0.6380]
−1	−0.0127 [a]	−0.0333 [a]	−0.0151 [a]	0.0054 [c]	−0.0093 [b]	−0.0018	−0.0003	0.0030 [a]	−0.0027	0.0019 [b]	−0.0059 [a]	0.0035 [a]
	[−7.3135]	[−8.7378]	[−3.2964]	[1.7584]	[−2.2159]	[−0.5371]	[−0.5344]	[2.7906]	[−1.4117]	[2.2330]	[−4.7297]	[2.6122]
Policy meeting (date=0)	−0.0148 [a]	−0.0340 [a]	−0.0163 [a]	0.0054 [c]	−0.0135 [a]	−0.0137 [a]	−0.0022 [a]	−0.0008	−0.0012	0.0001	−0.0042 [a]	−0.0119 [a]
	[−8.5701]	[−8.9424]	[−3.5489]	[1.7871]	[−3.2107]	[−4.0597]	[−3.9799]	[−0.7347]	[−0.6070]	[0.1035]	[−3.3571]	[−8.9615]
+1	−0.0137 [a]	−0.0318 [a]	−0.0160 [a]	0.0000	−0.0036	−0.0125 [a]	0.0011 [b]	0.0022 [b]	0.0003	−0.0054 [a]	0.0099 [a]	0.0012
	[−7.9244]	[−8.3565]	[−3.4927]	[0.0004]	[−0.8608]	[−3.7006]	[2.0453]	[2.1044]	[0.1351]	[−6.4358]	[7.9305]	[0.9135]
+2	−0.0125 [a]	−0.0305 [a]	−0.0169 [a]	0.0006	−0.0010	−0.0085 [b]	0.0012 [b]	0.0013	−0.0009	0.0006	0.0026 [b]	0.0040 [a]
	[−7.2225]	[−8.0120]	[−3.6873]	[0.1971]	[−0.2449]	[−2.5254]	[2.2228]	[1.2376]	[−0.4679]	[0.7083]	[2.0785]	[2.9897]

(continued)

Table 5.4 (continued)

	Panel A– Average levels of forecast errors						Panel B– Average differences in forecast errors					
			Forward guidance periods						Forward guidance periods			
Event window	Full period	No guidance (NFG)	First round (FG1)	Second round (FG2)	Third round (FG3)	Fourth round (FG4)	Full period	No guidance (NFG)	First round (FG1)	Second round (FG2)	Third round (FG3)	Fourth round (FG4)
+3	−0.0128 [a]	−0.0352 [a]	−0.0152 [a]	−0.0002	0.0018	0.0002	−0.0003	−0.0047 [a]	0.0017	−0.0008	0.0028 [b]	0.0087 [a]
	[−7.3922]	[−9.2558]	[−3.3115]	[−0.0579]	[0.4258]	[0.0504]	[−0.5375]	[−4.4677]	[0.9035]	[−0.9183]	[2.2634]	[6.5532]
+4	−0.0130 [a]	−0.0337 [a]	−0.0122 [a]	0.0015	−0.0024	−0.0048	−0.0002	0.0015	0.0029	0.0017 [b]	−0.0042 [a]	−0.0050 [a]
	[−7.4830]	[−8.8583]	[−2.6715]	[0.5074]	[−0.5636]	[−1.4244]	[−0.2876]	[1.4277]	[1.5388]	[2.0363]	[−3.3391]	[−3.7522]
+5	−0.0141 [a]	−0.0349 [a]	−0.0121 [a]	−0.0007	−0.0043 [c]	−0.0086 [a]	−0.0011 [b]	−0.0012	0.0002	−0.0022 [a]	−0.0019 [a]	−0.0038
	[−8.1250]	[−9.1676]	[−2.6296]	[−0.2262]	[−1.0248]	[−2.5551]	[−2.0331]	[−1.1109]	[0.1008]	[−2.6426]	[−1.5565]	[−2.8764]

Notes: The averages and cumulative averages of changes in implied volatility and market returns are estimated for the three rounds of forward guidance extending from April 1999 to August 2000 (Period FG1), from March 2001 to March 2006 (Period FG2), from October 2010 to January 2016 (Period FG3), and from February 2016 to August 2018 (Period FG4), respectively. These rounds are inclusive of 26, 80, 76 and 20 meetings, respectively. The period of no-forward guidance separating the last two rounds (Period NFG) runs from April 2006 to September 2010, and it is inclusive of 70 policy meetings. Figures in square brackets refer to t-statistics based on standard errors calculated from observations within estimation windows. Significance at the 1, 5, and 10 percent levels is indicated by the Significance at the 1, 5, and 10 percent levels is indicated by the superscripts [a, b, c,] respectively.

volatility expectations with realized volatility. The evidence indicates indeed that it is only at the 10 percent level that forecast errors are significant around policy meetings during this second round.

It is important to consider again the significance of forecast errors around policy meetings in the absence of forward guidance. The asymmetric behavior of forecast errors constitutes clear evidence that forward guidance has the potential of affecting the formation of volatility expectations in financial markets in different ways. The event-study tests are not designed to measure the direct impact in terms of entrenching expectations about inflation, but it can be argued following Filardo and Hofmann (2014) again, that forward guidance can affect financial markets through the reduction of fluctuations in market expectations about the future path of policy rates in particular. Thus, the clarification of policy stance can lower the expected volatility of asset prices due to unanticipated changes in policy rates.

It is clear from Figure 5.4 that different patterns of average forecast errors can be discerned for different rounds of forward guidance. The evidence suggests that for the first round of open-ended forward guidance, average forecast errors remain negative, and show little variations around monetary policy meetings. This pattern is also exhibited by the dynamics of forecast errors during the first round of open-

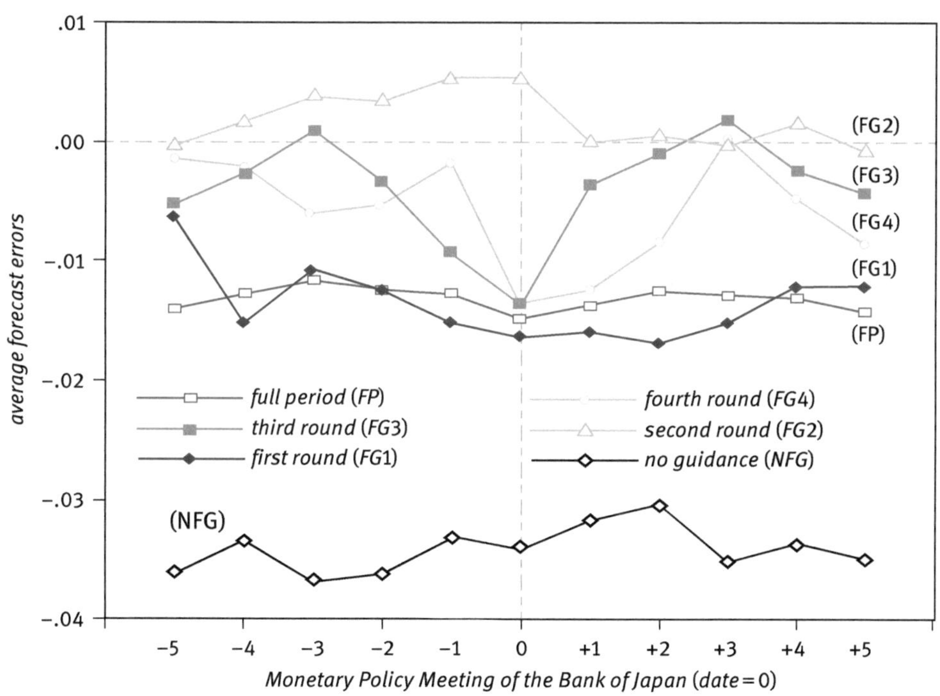

Figure 5.4: The Behavior of Average Forecast Errors around Monetary Policy Meetings.
Source: Author's own.

ended forward guidance, characterized with the underestimation of market volatility. In contrast, the third and fourth rounds, which are defined as state-contingent guidance, are associated with rebounds following policy announcements. This increase reflects the realignment of volatility expectations with realized volatility. It is the second round that seems to present some level of consistency between expectations and realized volatility, with forecast errors remaining closer to the zero-critical line than for other rounds. It is clear also that in the absence of forward guidance, forecast errors remain clearly detached from other alternative patterns. The negative and significant errors reflect a tendency to underestimate future market volatility. Since this period is inclusive of the U.S. financial crisis, the sharp fall in asset prices and increase in realized volatility are also reflective of the financial instability and concerns about the Japanese economy. The evidence suggests that market participants did not anticipate the onset of the financial crisis, but the increase in uncertainty was not mitigated by forward guidance about future policy rates.

It is possible to examine also the realignment process of volatility expectations following forecast errors in terms of the momentum for upward or downward bias. With reference to Panel-B of Table 5.4, which describes the daily differences in forecast errors rather than the levels, it is clear that the error dynamics differ also across the various rounds of forward guidance. There is weaker evidence of statistically significant changes in forecast errors during the open-ended forward guidance FG1, which implies that there remains a tendency for underestimating market volatility around policy meetings. In contrast, daily differences in forecast errors are found to be significant at either the 1 or 5 percent levels for other rounds of state-contingent guidance, including FG2, and in particular FG3 and FG4. The estimates are statistically significant but not persistently associated with the negative or positive sign, and this suggests the absence of upward or downward bias in relation to policy meetings. There are also significant changes in forecast errors for policy meetings during the interceding period NFG, but they seem to have no substantial impact on the overall tendency to underestimate market volatility in the absence of forward guidance.

Thus, forward guidance has the potential of affecting future asset prices in financial markets and the formation of expectations about market volatility. It may be argued that the behavior of volatility expectations during the financial crisis may have been different under another round of forward guidance. But a possible counter-argument is that forward guidance constitutes just another instrument of unconventional monetary policy, and minimizing valuation risk is not the principal aim of monetary policy during periods of financial instability. For instance, Mishkin (2009) argues in this regard that the rationale behind lower interest rates and non-conventional monetary policy measures is to mitigate macroeconomic risk defined in terms of the adverse effects of financial disruptions on aggregate economic activity. Nevertheless, forward guidance can be effective in the stabilization of financial markets insofar that higher volatility expectations reflecting uncertainty ahead of monetary policy meetings are concerned.

On aggregate, the evidence from Tables 5.3 and 5.4 as well as Figure 5.4 suggest that different rounds of forward guidance have different effects on the formation of volatility expectations and the dynamics of forecast errors. The open-ended forward guidance FG1 is associated with a downward bias in the estimation of market volatility that is significant irrespective of the locus of trading around policy meetings. In contrast, rounds of state-contingent forward guidance seem to have the desirable effects of restraining volatility expectations from rising in anticipation of policy announcements. In particular, the second round FG2 seems to be more effective in absorbing the observed increase of volatility expectations before policy meetings due to perceived uncertainty about future policy rates. The evidence suggests that insofar that forecast errors remain insignificant, forward guidance can be useful also in shaping the beliefs in consistency with rational expectations. A similar impact on volatility expectations is associated with the last rounds of state-contingent guidance FG3 and FG4 with QQE under zero and negative interest rates, respectively. But the effects on forecast errors are not as pronounced as under the previous round FG2.

In the absence of forward guidance however, the evidence suggests that cumulative average differences in volatility expectations increase and forecast errors remain negative and significant over the event window. As argued above, part of the explanation is that this period separates two rounds of state-contingent guidance and coincides with the onset of the U.S. financial crisis. As noted by Maghrebi, Holmes and Oya (2014), financial instability has the potential of altering the formation of volatility expectations in financial markets, and render the realignment process following forecast errors rather insignificant. Under these conditions, past information may not provide useful guidance during financial crises as market expectations become more sensitive to forward-looking macroeconomic information and contemporaneous price movements. Thus, the absence of forward guidance precisely at times of financial instability may have exacerbated its impact on financial markets, as far as market expectations about the future path of policy rates and the anticipated levels of fluctuations in asset prices are concerned.

6 Conclusion

The debate about the effectiveness of unconventional monetary policy by the Bank of Japan in promoting the fiancial system stability and in stimulating the real economy, proceeds on the basis of little or no empirical evidence, as argued by Honda (2014). An important aspect of this relation is the impact of forward guidance, as a non-traditional instrument of monetary policy communication, on the expectations channels and feedback from financial markets in terms of volatility expectations. Since forward guidance, in either of its open-ended or state-contingent forms, provides some clarity about the conduct of future monetary policy, the issue is whether it can be also useful in absorbing the incremental uncertainty usually perceived by market participants ahead of policy meetings. To the best of our knowledge, this is the first study that contributes to this debate by examining the effect of forward guidance about monetary policy on forward-looking volatility expectations in financial markets.

The empirical evidence from the event-study analysis indicates that various rounds of forward guidance are indeed conducive to different patterns of volatility expectations around policy meetings. In the absence of forward guidance, implied volatility around policy meetings tends to rise above average levels observed in pre-event estimation periods. Judging from its potential of absorbing uncertainty prior to policy announcements, forward guidance has some moderating effects on volatility expectations. This lends support to the proposition that forward guidance aimed at entrenching inflation expectations can be useful in shaping volatility expectations in financial markets. This adds to the important evidence from Filardo and Hofmann (2014) that forward guidance has been effective in reducing the volatility of near-term expectations about policy rates. Thus, forward guidance is conducive to a shift of foci away from monetary policy announcements toward the arrival of new macroeconomic information. The evidence suggests also that state-contingent forward guidance is conducive to lower volatility expectations around policy meetings and generally insignificant forecast errors. It is state-contingent rather than open-ended forward guidance that may be more effective in managing the expectations feedback from financial markets.

It is difficult, however, to draw strong conclusions about the effectiveness of forward guidance in reinforcing the expectations channels of monetary policy in terms of inflation expectations and interest rates. Indeed, this event-study is not designed to provide empirical evidence about the impact of forward guidance on inflation expectations or the feedback transmission mechanism based on interest rate expectations. The results lend, nevertheless, support to the empirical proposition that volatility expectations in financial markets can be lowered through forward guidance about future monetary policy. Thus, further empirical studies are needed to shed light on the effectiveness of state-contingent guidance in entrenching inflation expectations and stimulating the Japanese economy. In this respect, Honda (2014) argues that quantitative easing in combination with the initial round of state-contingent forward guidance by the Bank of Japan had a stimulating effect on investment and production through Tobin's Q. The empirical tests of nonlinearities in the relation between Tobin's Q and production under different regimes of forward guidance present an interesting avenue for future research. Further studies can also shed light on the usefulness of the model-free volatility index for monetary policy, given its ability to capture changes in forward-looking expectations about asset prices, which constitute feedback from financial markets.

The empirical evidence suggests also that forward guidance constitutes an instrument of communication strategy that may be more useful precisely at times of financial instability. The implications of these results should be understood in light of self-imposed *purdah* rules, which explain the absence of central bank communication around policy meetings. As argued by Ehrman and Fratzscher (2008), *purdah* rules may be conducive to higher volatility and unnecessary speculative activities. The potential for counterproductive effects reinforces the rationale behind forward guidance during periods of financial instability. As noted by Maghrebi, Holmes and Oya (2014), the error-correction process underlying the formation of volatility expectations can be impaired by the onset of financial crises. As with the abstinence from communication, the absence of forward guidance changes the complexion of financial decisions as market participants seek guidance, not so much from historical information, as from forward-looking volatility indices and forward-looking monetary policy.

From the perspective of Islamic finance and economy, neither positive nor negative, and not even zero interest rates are allowed. There is no room for conventional monetary policies based on raising or lowering of positive interest rates. There is no place either for unconventional monetary policies based on forward guidance coupled with zero or negative interest rates. But there is room for central banks to influence market conditions and to transmit the signal effects of monetary policy through Islamic banks. The scope and effectiveness of monetary operations may naturally differ from the conditions underlying he conventional system, but the objectives of price stability and monetary base are not dissimilar. The challenges tasks of design and implementation of policy measures are even more complex for central banks presented with dual financial systems. Part of the problem with the conduct of monetary policies based on interest rates has to do with a failure to recognize the importance of the natural rate of return in the real economy.

Part of the problems associated with the limited room for maneuver in monetary policy stems from the anchoring of the entire financial system on predetermined rates of return, interest rates that are independent of the states of nature of the real economy. In the absence of risk sharing and equity financing, the system is inherently biased toward the accumulation of debt, and the formation of asset bubbles leads inevitably to the perpetuation of financial crises. With the advent of quantitative and qualitative easing, there are also legitimate concerns about the controversial role of central banks in financial markets and their growing balance sheets. It is important to address the above issues from both the theoretical and empirical perspectives. But from the perspective of Islamic finance and economics where interest rates are not permitted, independent of their sign and magnitude, there is compelling evidence that policy uncertainty affects the formation of volatility expectations. This analytical evidence suggests that no amount of forward guidance can eliminate the excessive amount of policy uncertainty leading to unwarranted price fluctuations in financial assets, and shifting risk premia in the real economy.

References

Äijö, Janne. 2008. "Implied volatility term structure linkages between VDAX, VSMI and VSTOXX volatility indices." *Global Finance Journal* 18(3): 290–302.

Aït-Sahalia, Yacine, Jochen Andritzky, Andreas Jobst, Sylwia Nowak, and Natalia Tamirisa. 2012. "Market response to policy initiatives during the global financial crisis." *Journal of International Economics* 87(1): 162–177.

Becker, Ralf, Adam E. Clements, and Smith I. White. 2006. "On the informational efficiency of S&P 500 implied volatility." *The North American Journal of Economics and Finance* 17(2): 139–153.

Becker, Ralf, Adam E. Clements, and Andrew McClelland. 2009. "The jump component of S&P 500 volatility and the VIX index." *Journal of Banking and Finance* 33(3): 1033–1038.

Bernanke, Ben S., and Vincert R. Reinhart. 2004. "Conducting monetary policy at very low short-term interest rates." *American Economic Review* 94(2): 85–90.

Blinder, Alan, Michael Ehrmann, Marcel Fratzscher, Jakob De Haan, and David-Jan Jansen. 2008. "Central bank communication and monetary policy: a survey of theory and evidence." *Journal of Economic Literature* 46(4): 910–945.

Bloom, N. 2009. "The impact of uncertainty shocks." *Econometrica* 77(3): 623–685.

Bollerslev, Tim, and Hao Zhou. 2006. "Volatility puzzles: a simple framework for gauging return-volatility regressions." *Journal of Econometrics* 131(1–2): 123–150.

Bollerslev, Tim, George Tauchen, and Hao Zhou. 2009. "Expected stock returns and variance risk premia." *The Review of Financial Studies* 22(11): 4463–4492.

Britten-Jones, Mark, and Anthony Neuberger. 2000. "Option prices, implied price processes and stochastic volatility." *Journal of Finance* 55(2): 839–866.

Busch, Thomas, Bent Jesper Christensen, and Morten Nielsen. 2011. "The role of implied volatility in forecasting future realized volatility and jumps in foreign exchange, stock, and bond markets." *Journal of Econometrics* 160(1): 48–57.

Campbell, Jeffrey R., Charles L. Evans, Jonas Fisher, and Alejandro Justiniano. 2012. "Macroeconomic effects of Federal Reserve forward guidance." *Brookings Papers on Economic Activity* 43(1): 1–80.

Cargill, Thomas F., Michael M. Hutchison, and Takatoshi Ito. 2000. *Financial policy and central banking in Japan*. Cambridge: MIT Press.

Carr, Peter, and Liuren Wu. 2006. "A tale of two indices." *The Journal of Derivatives* 13(3): 13–29.

Carr, Peter, and Liuren Wu. 2009. "Variance risk premia." *Review of Financial Studies* 22(3): 1311–1341.

Christensen, B.J., and N.R. Prabhala. 1998. "The relation between implied and realized volatility." *Journal of Financial Economics* 50(1998): 125–50.

Demeterfi, Krevsimir, Emanuel Derman, Madeeha M. Kamal, Joseph Zou. 1999. "More than you ever wanted to know about volatility swaps." Quantitative Strategies Research Notes, Goldman Sacks.

Ederington, Louis H., and Jae Ha Lee. 1996. "The creation and resolution of market uncertainty: the impact of information releases on implied volatility." *Journal of Financial and Quantitative Analysis* 31(4): 513–539.

Ehrmann, Michael, and Marcel Fratzscher. 2008. "Purdah: On the rationale for central bank silence around policy meetings." European Central Bank Working Paper Series, No. 848.

Fawley, Brett W., and Christopher Neely. 2013. "Four stories of quantitative easing," *Federal Reserve Bank of St. Louis Review*, January/February 2013: 51–88.

Filardo, Andrew, and Boris Hofmann 2014, "Forward guidance at the zero-lower bound," *BIS Quarterly Review, Bank for International Settlements, March*: 38–53.

Fleming, Jeff 1998, "The quality of market volatility forecasts implied by S&P 100 index option prices." *Journal of Empirical Finance* 5(4): 317–345.

Fornari, Fabio. 2004, "Macroeconomic announcements and implied volatility in swaption markets," *BIS Quarterly Review, Bank for International Settlements, March*: 79–86.

Fukasawa, Masaaki, Isao Ishida, Nabil Maghrebi, Kosuke Oya, Masato Ubukata, and Kazutoshi Yamazaki. 2011. "Model-free implied volatility: from surface to index." *International Journal of Theoretical and Applied Finance* 14(4): 433–463.

Füss, Roland, Ferdinand Mager, Holger Wohlenberg, and Lu Zhao. 2011. "The impact of macroeconomic announcements on implied volatility." *Applied Financial Economics* 21(21): 1571–1580.

Gagnon, J., Matthew Raskin, Julie Remache, and Brian P. Sack. 2010. "Large-scale asset purchases by the Federal Reserve: Did they work?" Federal Reserve Bank of New York Staff Reports, no. 441.

Honda, Yuzo. 2014. "The effectiveness of non-traditional monetary policy: The case of Japan." *The Japanese Economic Review* 65(1): 1–23.

Hull, John, and Alan White. 1987. "The pricing of options on assets with stochastic volatilities," *Journal of Finance* 42(2): 281–300.

Humpage, Owen F. 2012. "Communication, credibility and price stability: Lessons learned from Japan." Federal Reserve Bank of Cleveland Economic Commentary No. 2012–09.

Ito, Takatoshi, and Frederic S. Mishkin. 2006. "Two decades of Japanese monetary policy and the deflation problem." In *Monetary policy under very low inflation in the Pacific Rim*, edited by Takatoshi Ito, and Andrew K. Rose. Chicago: University of Chicago Press.

Jiang, George, and Yisong Sam Tian. 2007. "Extracting model-free volatility from option prices: an examination of the VIX index." *The Journal of Derivatives* 14(3): 35–60.

Jovanovic, Mario, and Tobias Zimmermann. 2010. "Stock market uncertainty and monetary policy reaction functions of the Federal Reserve Bank," *The B.E. Journal of Macroeconomics* 10(1): 1935–1690.

Krishnamurthy, Arvind, and Annette Vissing-Jorgensen. 2011. "The effects of quantitative easing on interest rates: channels and implications for policy." *Brookings Papers on Economic Activity*, Fall 2011: 215–280.

Maghrebi, Nabil. 2007. "The Bank of Japan monetary policy meetings and the behaviour of the Nikkei225 implied volatility index", *Osaka Economic Papers* 57(4): 84–99.

Maghrebi, Nabil, Mark J. Holmes, and Kosuke Oya. 2014. "Financial instability and the short-term dynamics of volatility expectations." *Applied Financial Economics* 24(6): 377–395.

Masset, Philippe, and Martin A. Wallmeier. 2010. "A high-frequency investigation of the interaction between volatility and DAX returns." *European Financial Management* 16(3): 327–344.

Merton, Robert C. 1973. "Theory of rational option pricing," *Bell Journal of Economics and Management Science* 4(1): 141–183.

Mishkin, Frederic S. 2009. "Is monetary policy effective during financial crises?." *American Economic Review* 99(2): 573–577.

Moessner Richhild.2013, "Effects of explicit FOMC policy rate guidance on interest rate expectations," *Economics Letters* 121(2): 170–173.

Moessner, Richhild, and William Richard Nelson. 2008. "Central bank policy rate guidance and financial market functioning." *International Journal of Central Banking* 4(4): 193–226.

Nikkinen, Jussi, and Petri Sahlström. 2004. "Impact of the federal open market committee's meetings and scheduled macroeconomic news on stock market uncertainty." *International Review of Financial Analysis* 13: 1–12.

Panetta, Fabio, Paolo Angelini, Giuseppe Grande, Aviram Levy, Roberto Perli, Pinar Yesin, Stefan Gerlach, Srichander Ramaswamy, and Michela Scatigna. 2006. "The recent behaviour of financial market volatility," BIS Paper No. 29, Basel: Bank for International Settlements, Monetary and Economic Department.

Shirai, Sayuri. 2013. "Monetary policy and forward guidance in Japan," *Speech at the International Monetary Fund*, Washington DC, September 19, 2013.

Ueda, Kazuo. 2005. "The Bank of Japan's struggle with the zero lower bound on nominal interest rates: Exercises in expectations management." *International Finance* 8(2): 329–350.
Ueda, Kazuo. 2012a. "The effectiveness of non-traditional monetary policy measures: the case of the Bank of Japan." *The Japanese Economic Review* 63(1): 1–22.
Ueda, Kazuo. 2012b. "Japan's deflation and the Bank of Japan's experience with nontraditional monetary policy." *Journal of Money, Credit and Banking* 44(1): 175–190.
Vähämaa, Sami, and Janne Jaakko Äijö. 2010. "The Fed's policy decisions and implied volatility." *Journal of Futures Markets* 31(10): 995–1010.
Whaley, Robert E. 2000. "The Investor Fear Gauge." *Journal of Portfolio Management* 26(3): 12–17.

Seyid F. Mahmud, Kaoru Yamaguchi, Murat A. Yülek

Chapter 6: Beyond DSGE: An Accounting System Dynamics Modelling Approach

1 Introduction

The advent of the global financial crisis that started in 2007–2008 took a host of economists, policy makers, regulators and international institutions by surprise. It was evident that reliance on the Standard Macroeconomic Model (SMM) simply led to failure to predict the crisis. The crises followed a long period of 'great moderation' (Stock and Watson 2002) characterized by a significant decline in macroeconomic volatility and stable inflation. Many economists believed that the history ended. For example, Olivier Blanchard (2008), the director of Research at the International Monetary Fund, concluded that the "state of macro was good", and a "broad convergence of vision" was now achieved. Similarly, Robert Lucas (2003), a Nobel laureate now believed that the "things were under control" and "central problem of depression-prevention has been solved". Another former Chairman of the Fed, Ben Bernanke attributed the success of economic performance during Great Moderation to improved policy making (Bernanke, 2004).

Following the emergence of the crises, however, Alan Greenspan, another former Chairman of the Governors of the Federal Reserve Bank (Fed), admitted, in 2008, that the mainstream approaches to the workings of the financial markets have been flawed.[105] Nobel laureate Joseph Stiglitz (2011) pointed out that the SMM not only failed in predicting the current crisis but they were also modest in understanding the severity and the ensuing recession that followed the crisis.

The "Great Moderation" also came under the scrutiny, under post-crisis analysis, that had earlier led many to believe that all is well with the current state of macroeconomics. As Blanchard (2014) acknowledged: "The main lesson of the crisis is that we were too close to those dark corners than we thought. The Great Moderation had fooled not only macroeconomists. Financial institutions and regulators also underestimated the risks. The result was a financial structure that was increasingly exposed to potential shocks."

Lawrence Summers suggested another explanation in this post crisis debate, in his speech to the IMF (Summers, 2014). While commenting on the great recession that followed the crisis, he referred it as an era of "secular stagnation," and in his view it had been with us for a long before the crisis. Summers, in fact, was suggesting that the recession was there long before, but its visibility had been masked by

105 Alan Greenspan admitted this in his testimony to the House Committee on Oversight and Government Reform of USA House of Representatives, on October 23, 2008.

https://doi.org/10.1515/9783110587920-006

the subprime bubble and once that the bubble busted it became evident (Keen, 2014). Similarly, Paul Krugman, another Nobel laureate, concluded that the 'secular stagnation' may have started as early as 1985, masked by the rise in household debt (Krugman, 2009).

In short, the crisis generated important anomalies for the conventional economic theory. First, it failed to foresee the crisis forthcoming. Second, the downturn has persisted for a long period of time since the crisis. Third, the period of great moderation had been reinterpreted in the light of secular stagnation argument casting doubt over the success of new consensus macroeconomic models.

There was yet another important anomaly in the post-1980s related to one of the key theoretical pillars linking the monetary and the real sectors of the economy, namely, the quantity theory of money which linked monetary variables to nominal GDP. With velocity of money stable, the implication of the quantity theory of money is that changes in the stock of money have predictable consequences on nominal GDP. Therefore, having control over the stock of money has implications for inflation. In other words, the stability of the money-price link depends on stable velocity of money.

This relationship simply collapsed in the 1980s when a consistent and persistent trend of declining velocity was observed in most of developed and emerging economies as given in Figure 6.1. Given the importance of stable velocity in policy making, considerable efforts have been made to resolve the puzzle. But the results were not conclusive (Stone and Thornton 1987).[106] That led to some rightly to argue that the quantity theory of money "is now [...] one of the weakest stones in the foundation" (Boughton 1991).

From the above discussion, two conclusions may emerge. Firstly, the crisis is not a simple 'tail' event; and it is not a simple accident that the Standard Macroeconomic Model failed to foresee it. Secondly, from an initial response of having no need for any major overhauling of the standard model, about ten years after the crises, economists are starting to recognize the need to incorporate the ways financial systems work in the right fashion in the macroeconomic theory.

Thus, better models are needed to explain how macroeconomics really work accounting for the complexities of the financial system. Accounting System Dynamics (ASD) approach is an attempt in that direction. The ASD approach is in the stock-flow consistent category of modelling and reflects the complexities of the money-creation ability of the financial system. There are different views on the latter; how money is created by the banking system has been a continuing debate with significant policy

106 The authors have argued that one possible explanation may be related to the specification problem, according to one of the arguments in the report. In the standard calculation of velocity, it is being assumed that -all money transactions are for the final goods and services produced in the economy. However, if these transactions also include intermediate and financial transactions, the velocity measure could vary according to the proportions of transactions in the real sector of the economy.

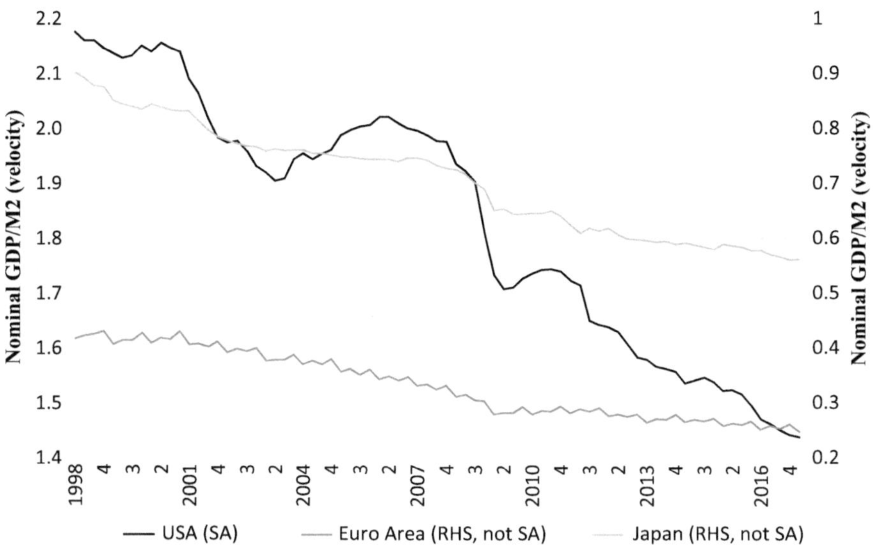

Figure 6.1: Recent Trends in Velocity of Money.
Source: Federal Reserve Bank of St. Louis (FRED).

implications. In the Fractional Reserve Banking (FRB) and Intermediation of Loanable Funds (ILF) theories, the causality runs from fiat money to bank created money. In the endogenous view of money (also called financing-through-money-creation: FMC), causality is reversed. The ASD approach can incorporate the complexities of money creation into macroeconomic modeling. By that, it can be used to assess the outcomes of different money creation and financial intermediation models as enumerated above.

In this chapter, the SMM and its shortcomings are reviewed and then the framework of the ASD approach is proposed as an alternative approach to macroeconomic modelling. Some of simulation-based results of the ASD approach are also discussed and the outcomes of different money creation models are assessed with reference to the stability of the monetary system. The chapter also introduces the notion of Public Money System, which is primarily based on the notion of 100% reserve banking. Section 2 starts with a critical review of the Standard Macroeconomic Model and highlights some of the anomalies generated the conventional approach and their probable explanations. Section 3 then presents the analytical framework of the Accounting System Dynamic (ASD) approach to macroeconomic modelling and contrasts it with the SMM. Section 4 delves into the ASD to identify the inherent instability of the current money creation mechanism and proposes an alternative monetary system, the public money system, which is inherently stable. Section 5 concludes the chapter.

2 The Standard Macroeconomic Model: A Critical Review

The theoretical background of the mainstream macroeconomic modelling that culminated in the 'New Consensus' in macroeconomics in the 1980s, reflected in the development of Dynamic Stochastic General Equilibrium (DSGE) family of standard models that became the main tool of the New Consensus. Mahmud, Yamaguchi and Yülek (2017) call that duo the Standard Macro Model. Preventing the models to explain the real world sufficiently, these shortcomings played a key role in the DSGE models' failure to predict the global financial crises. The DSGE models are basically short run models. They profoundly rely on the process of market adjustments and are believed that these adjustments will finally restore equilibrium in the short run. This conviction is founded on four simple 'key' assumptions. First, consumers maximize their utility under a budget constraint. Second, firms maximize profits under a resource constraint. Third, markets have the built-in dynamics to restore equilibrium in response to some external shocks. Finally, the representative agents are being guided by rational expectations.

The DSGE models do allow for short-run deviations from the steady state equilibrium due to presence of sticky wages and prices, adjustment costs and other exogenous shocks. However, by assuming 'rational' behavior of market participants and the inherent ability of the markets to clear, DSGE models always produce the intertemporal trend towards equilibrium.

Tovar (2008) notes that one of the crucial shortcomings of DSGE model is their inability to incorporate the financial sector properly. This exclusion is justified on the basis of the so-called 'efficient market hypothesis' where financial markets always clear (Krugman, 2009). The hypothesis rests on the belief that market prices of financial assets follow the fundamentals of the markets. Consequently, aggregate financial wealth does not have any consequence to the behavior of agents and/or to the dynamics of the economy. Cechetti and Kharroubi (2012) also argue that while constructing a theoretical structure of the economy as a whole, debt is trivial as the liabilities of all borrowers are being cancelled out by the assets of all lenders and therefore money does not have any active role in these models.

The monetary side of the economy is therefore fully constrained by the real side of the economy; money in these models is treated as 'veil', a mere unit of account that facilitates transactions of goods and services. In fact, the DSGE models incorporate the entire financial system in the form of a simple money multiplier mechanism.

Thus, the following are the key features of DSGE models, (i) They are based on the micro-underpinning of individuals' and firms' optimization framework; (ii) They assume that the economy is either in equilibrium or it will return to equilibrium soon if disturbed by unanticipated external shocks; (iii) Uncertainty is dealt by the proposition that a rational individual can accurately foresee the future (Rational Expectations);

On the other hand, the shortcomings of the DSGE models from the point of view of our discussion at this stage are: (i) They treat a complex monetary market economy as a barter system; (ii) Money supply is explained through a simple 'money multiplier' model; (iii) Failing to incorporate the complexity of the financial sector including the roles of credit and debt in the macro economy.

3 Endogenous Money: Resolving Puzzles of Anomalies

The financial crisis of 2007 brought an abrupt end to the "Great Moderation", a long period of economic stability (Bernanke 2004; Davis and Kahn, 2008; Gali and Gambetti, 2009) since mid-1980s. The Great Moderation not only saw unusual macroeconomic stability but also a rise in assets prices and strong growth in credit in relation to output. Importantly, there was a marked shift of credit flows to the financial sector compared to the real sector. Significant shifts in credits, during a credit boom, from relatively low risk, low-return investments in the real sector to high risk, high return ones in the financial sectors (real estate and financial assets) can increase the financial fragility of the system (Beck et al., 2012).

The SMM, by not taking into account the central role of credit and the process of its creation has failed to predict and explain both the long-standing recession and financial crises. It simply ignored the role of money and complex process of its creation. The paradigm rests on treating money as a unit of account, linking money to the transactions of goods and services only, and ignoring the 'endogenous view' of money, where money is also a form of credit.

1.1 The Creation of Bank Money: A Brief Survey of Earlier Discussion

The role of banks as financial intermediaries has been a contentious issue during different times in the 20th century. One of the oldest views supported 'the credit creation theory' (or, endogenous view of money; also known as financing-through-money-creation: FMC), where banks are considered to individually create money through accounting operations when they extend a loan.[107] The theory was dominant until about mid-to late 1920s (Werner, 2015). It was later replaced by the fractional reserve banking/money

107 Macleod (1894), Withers (1916, 1921), Schumpeter (1934), Wicksell (1898) and Hahn (1924).

multiplier model (FRB). In this model, banks needed excess reserves before they could lend money to the borrowers. The excess reserves are created, initially, through an injection of government created 'fiat money'. The recipients of the fiat money can lend a fraction it, ultimately creating credit money in the magnitude of a multiple of the initial deposit of fiat money. In this process 'only' the banking system as whole can collectively contribute to the expansion of money.[108]

The FRB view had a considerable influence until about 1960s (Werner, 2015). It gave way to the most dominant theory today, the 'Intermediation of loanable fund theory' (ILF) which argues that banks are 'financial intermediaries' that simply collect savings (deposits) of savers and lending them to borrowers, in the process acting as any non-bank financial institution.[109] In this view of banking, neither an individual bank nor the banking sector as whole can expand/contract money supply. ILF has therefore two broad implications for the mainstream theoretical models. First, by confining the role of banks as intermediaries, any active role of banks can simply be ignored in the modelling. Second, the level of private debt across the economy can also be ignored because a 'loan' is regarded as a transfer of spending power from one individual to another. As one person's spending power goes down and another's going up, the aggregate debt level has only distributional consequences.

1.2 The Endogenous View of Money: Can It Solve the Puzzles?

Endogenous view of money or 'credit creation theory' (FMC) basically rests on the idea that when a bank makes an initial loan to a borrower, it simultaneously creates an equivalent deposit. Thus, credit and money are created endogenously, independent of prior cash deposits. The bank can obtain the reserves later to meet the reserve requirements or withdrawals as needed (Fullwiler, 2013).

Hence, according to the endogenous view of money, the direction of the causality is precisely the reverse of that is being maintained by the ILF as well as the FRB views. Importantly, many practitioners today support the causality proposed by the endogenous view; many central bank heads and practitioners have been supporting the endogenous view of money in the past.

The senior Vice-President of the New York Federal Reserve, Alan Holmes (Holmes, 1969), stated that treating banks as mere intermediaries between savers and lenders was erroneous. He argued that the view "that the banking system only

108 Aschheim (1959), Smith (1966), Guttentag and Lindsay (1968), Samuelson (1948) and others. Fractional reserve banking system is mostly discussed in the undergraduate textbooks, at the graduate level and theoretical macro modeling where the 'financial intermediary' role of the banking system is being entertained.

109 Gurley and Shaw (1955), Gutteng and Lindsay (1968), Tobin (1963), and many others. For detailed review of literature on this subject see Werner (2014, 2015), and Vivian and Spearman (2015).

expands loans after the [Federal Reserve] System (or market factors) has put reserves in the banking system" was based on "a naive assumption" and that "In the real world, banks extend credit, creating deposits in the process, and look for the reserves later" (Holmes, 1969). So, according to Holmes, banks do not need deposits in order lend and banks can create spending power by issuing loans.[110] In one of the recent Bundesbank (2009) reports about the banking system in the Euro-zone, it is suggested that "In the Eurosystem, money is primarily created through the extension of bank credit ... The commercial banks can create money themselves, the so-called giro money". Another recently published article by the Bank of England (Jakab et al. 2015), argued "the creation of gross positions with zero net principle value, but of course with a positive net interest rate flow to the bank over time, is precisely the meaning of bank financing, the very rationale for the existence of banks" (Jakab and Kumhof 2015). In another article published in Bank of England's quarterly review (McLeay et al., 2014), the ILF is discredited by the endorsement of the view that commercial banks are actually creators of deposit money which is what endogenous money view suggests. By lending money that banks do not possess, commercial banks are in effect creating new money (McLeay et al. 2014).

1.3 The Anomaly of 'declining velocity of money': Can Endogenous View of Money Solve the Puzzle?

In light of the discussion above, it is now presented some of the explanations of anomalies discussed earlier, based on the endogenous view of money. The section starts with the anomaly of 'declining velocity of money', as it has had severe implications for the stability of money-price link central to the SMM approach. Subsequently, other explanations are added to other anomalies such as protracted recession that followed the crisis, inefficacy of traditional monetary measures and gross failure of DSGE models in foreseeing the crisis.

Referring back to the macroeconomic relationship between money, GDP and prices, the equation of exchange or what is known as 'quantity theory of money' runs as:

$$M.v = P.Y \tag{1}$$

In the typical empirical work, some aggregate of 'private sector deposits', such as *M1, M2, M3* are being employed to represent M, the money stock. P.Y represents the nominal value of national income and v is the velocity of money.

110 Fullwiler (2013) describes in detail the banking model in actual practice and the endogenous money perspective on the interactions between central bank operations and banks. The study shows that interest on reserve balance does not obstruct the transmission of monetary policy and quantitative easing may not necessarily increase it.

Invoking the equilibrium condition in the money market, M, in effect, also represents demand for money. This fundamental relationship captures some of the key aspects of the SMM theoretical framework and underlying assumptions. With the loanable fund theory of intermediation (ILF) theory, M is taken as an exogenous variable, managed by different monetary tools of the central bank, such as open market operations and reserve requirements. Furthermore, money exists in equilibrium in strict proportion of the transactions in goods and services in the real sector of the economy.

A stable relationship, implied by this equation, has appeared to hold stably until the 1970s. However, it broke down completely during 1980s. The drop in the velocity was more consistent and profound in the developed economies (Figure 6.1). This had broad implications for the monetary policy as it implied an unstable demand for money hence posing challenges in implementing an effective monetary policy. Given the significance of the issue, it prompted considerable efforts in search for solving this 'puzzle'.

Recently, Werner (2005) has presented an alternative account of the anomaly by employing the endogenous money view and credit flows to the financial and non-financial sectors into his analyses. Werner (2005) develops what he refers to as 'quantity theory of credit'. The quantity theory of credit is noteworthy as it offers simple explanation of the puzzle. Thus, it is worth expounding on the basic features of Werner's theory and present some of his empirical findings in support of his theory.

Werner (2005) starts with the observation that use of some deposit aggregate in Equation (1) may not be appropriate because only the purchasing power that is actually used for transactions should matter in the equation. The traditional monetary aggregates, such as M1, M2, M3, refer to money deposited with the banks reflecting the potential, and not the effective purchasing power; it is only actual spending that is expected to affect GDP in Equation (1).

By defining money as private sector assets, such as deposits, it may not be clear where to draw the line among wide spectrum of private assets. Werner proposes that this issue can be resolved by changing the focus from traditional use of monetary aggregates to a measure of 'credit creation'. Total bank credit as a measure of money supply M in Equation (1) should represent the effective purchasing power as money is being borrowed with specific intent to be used in transactions. Another advantage of using credit aggregates is that these are available by economic sectors, providing additional information the direction of flows. Friedman (1987) had also made a similar suggestion of the feasibility of dividing the money flows into different sectors of the economy:

That decomposition was not possible with the deposit aggregates, such as M1, M2 and M3. Contrary to the traditional interpretation of Equation (1), where all money is tied to the transactions in the real sector of the economy, by using total credit based on the 'credit creation' view of money, it is possible to distinguish between flows to the real and financial sectors of the economy.

Werner starts with a dichotomous credit-money circulation as:

$$C = C_R + C_F \tag{2}$$

where C represents total loans by the deposit taking financial institutions, C_R represents credit flows for real transaction (such as investment and consumption), and C_F for the financial transactions (such as real estate purchases, which are not part of GDP). PR represents the prices in the real side of the economy. So for the real economy, Equation (1) can be redefined as:

$$C_R.v_R = P_R.Y \tag{3}$$

In this re-interpretation of the equation of exchange, the stock of credit money that flows into the real economy determines the nominal value of goods and services. v_R represents the stable 'real' velocity of credit money. Likewise, credit to financial transactions can be written as an independent exchange equation.

Werner (1993, 1997) shows that the widely observed velocity decline in case of Japan is not necessarily linked to financial innovations or deregulations directly, but can be explained simply by noting the increase in money used for transactions that are not part of the real sector, i.e. asset transactions.

From Equation (3) it follows that bank credit creation should boost nominal growth in GDP corroborated by Figure 6.2a which shows the close association of nominal GDP (P.Y) and credit to the real economy (C_R). Similarly, the close association between credit flows to financial transactions (C_F), in this case credit to real estate transactions) and the price of land is also shown in Figure 6.2b.

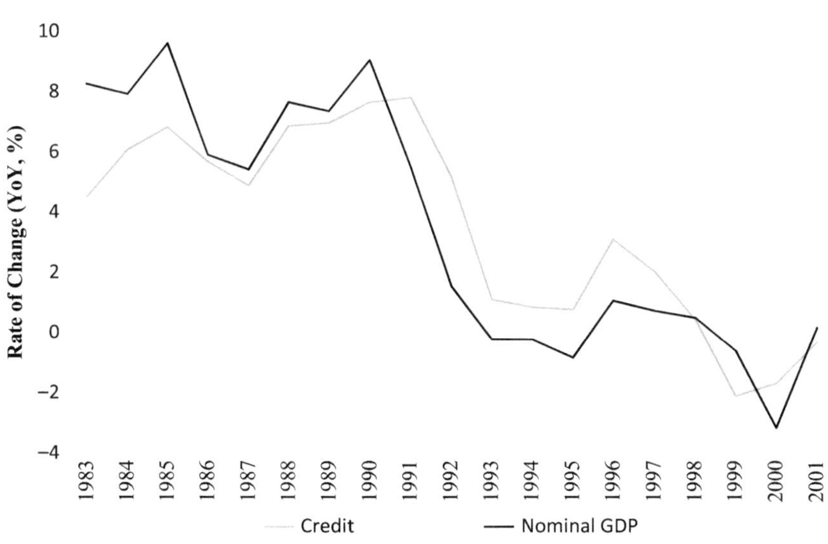

Figure 6.2a: Growth Driven by Credit Creation for GDP Transactions (CR), Japan.
Source: Federal Reserve Bank of St. Louis (FRED).

Figure 6.2b: Credit Used for Real Estate Transactions and Land Prices (Japan).
Source: Federal Reserve Bank of St. Louis (FRED).

Similar observations have been made for the US economy (Figures 6.3a and 6.3b). Again, the close correspondence between growth of credit to the real sector and nominal growth in GDP shows that growth in all final goods-and-services transactions

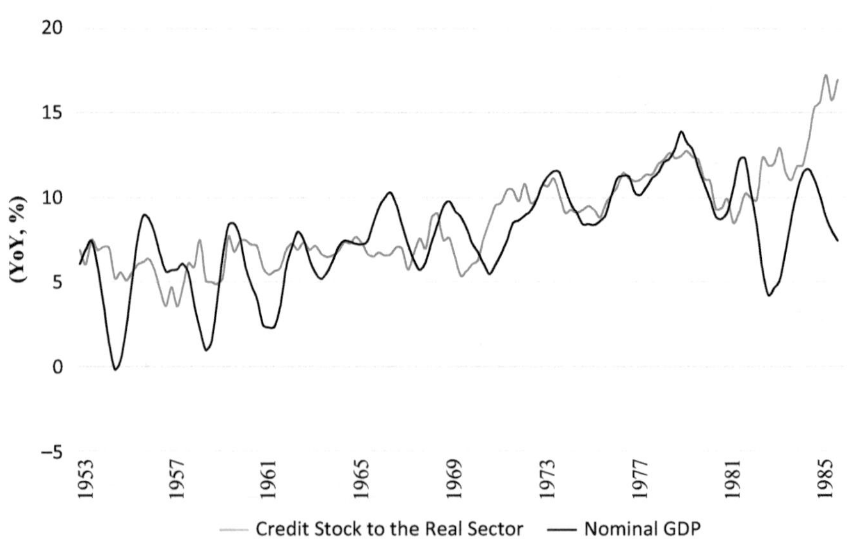

Figure 6.3a: Credit to the Real Sector in the USA.
Source: Federal Reserve Bank of St. Louis (FRED).

Figure 6.3b: Credit to the Property Sector in the USA.
Source: Federal Reserve Bank of St. Louis (FRED) and Bank for International Settlements (BIS) database.

requires additional money. The close correspondence with GDP, however, does not hold for the growth of total bank credit stock. Again, this highlights the fact that we may need to make distinction between different categories of credit, performing different economic functions (LSE Report, 2011). Just as credit flows to the real sector facilitates liquidity in the real sector of the economy, credit flows to the financial sector provides liquidity for the assets markets. This is why credits to financial sector do not follow any close track to GDP as financial transactions do not contribute to GDP. Thus, the endogenous view of money coupled with the decomposition of credit flows into the real and financial sectors provide one possible explanation that resolves the puzzle of unstable, declining velocity.

1.4 Balance Sheet Recession: An explanation of Protracted Downturn

Koo (2011), among others, warns that the Western economies might be heading towards a Japanese-style lost decades. He presents remarkable similarities between recent movements the house prices in the Western economies and those in Japan 15 years ago, as given in Figure 6.4. He argues that the post 2007–08 recession, is not an ordinary recession, instead he draws a distinction between a normal recession and one driven due to the deleveraging process of the post-crisis by the private

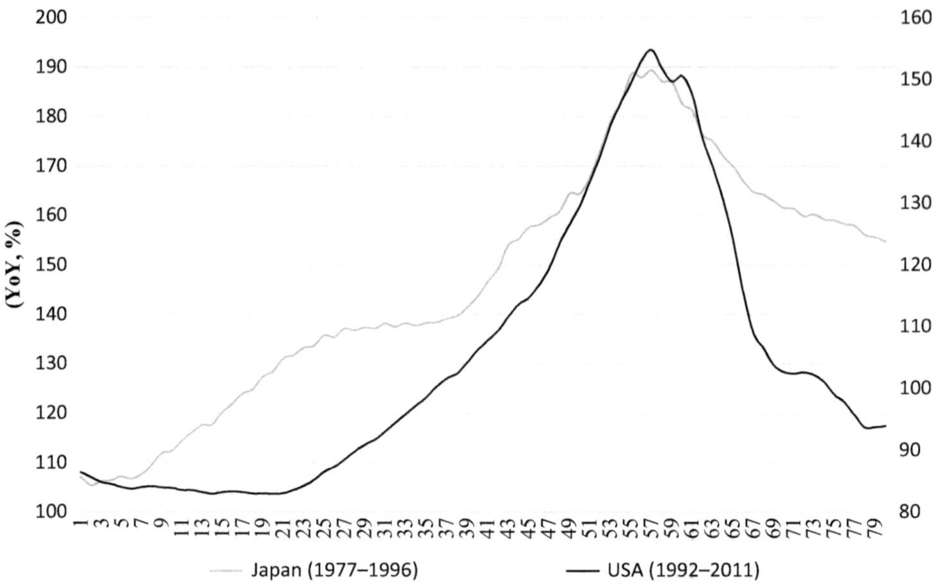

Figure 6.4: Comparison of US Housing Prices with Japanese Experience.
Source: Federal Reserve Bank of St. Louis (FRED).

sector. It is being contended that after the sudden and significant collapse of asset prices, the net worth of the private sector also encountered huge drop. In order to restore the financial health, households and firms are being forced to repair their balance sheets by increasing savings and repaying their debt. This process of deleveraging took the economy into deep recession as aggregate demand starts falling.

As noted earlier, under the endogenous view of money, it is the creation of bank credit that injects liquidity into the system. As the private sector begins saving and paying down their debt in aggregate, it can lead to decrease in money supply, regardless of how much of base money is supplied by the central bank. The money supply (which is defined mostly as bank deposits) starts contracting as private sector collectively draws down on these deposits by repaying the debt. In the extreme case, when nobody borrows money from the banks the money multiplier hit zero or negative value at margin.

In the absence of the endogenous view of money and exclusion of financial markets in SMM approach such behavior may not be anticipated or visualized and may lead to prescribing policies that are not helpful in dealing with the situation.

The traditional prescriptions of monetary policy to reduce interest rates and some unusual measures like quantitative easing by the Federal Reserve have not been effective in increasing the aggregate demand. Massive injections of liquidity by Federal Reserve in the US and Bank of England in UK not only failed but had hardly any impact on the money supply (Figures 6.5a and 6.5b).

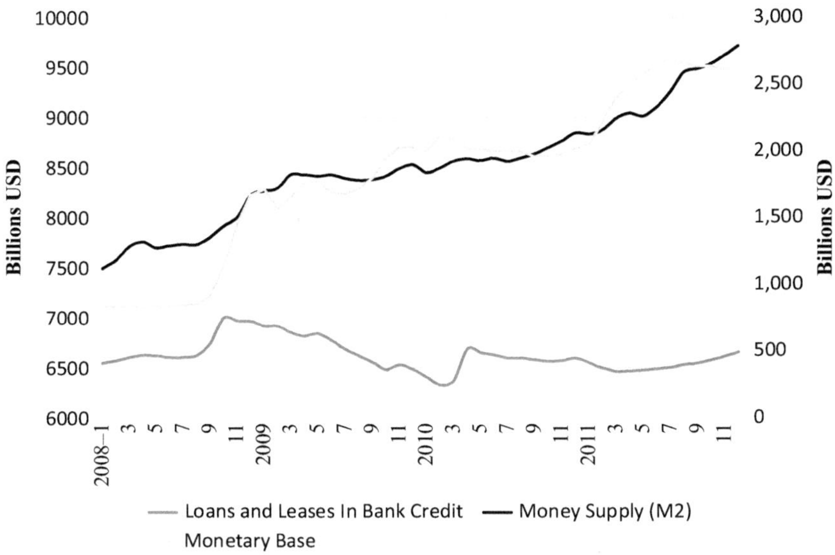

Figure 6.5a: Failure of Liquidity Injection to Increase Money Supply (US).
Source: Federal Reserve Bank of St. Louis (FRED).

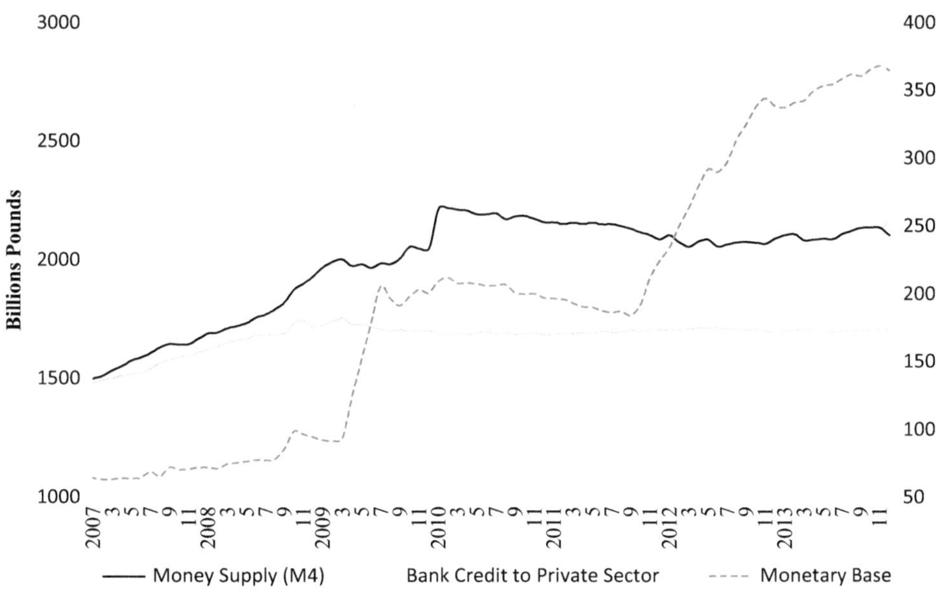

Figure 6.5b: Failure of Liquidity Injection to Increase Money Supply (UK).
Source: Federal Reserve Bank of St. Louis (FRED).

Koo (2016) further explains that mainstream economics assumes that private sector is forward-looking and therefore there will always be someone who will be willing to borrow money to invest when real interest rates are low enough. Until 2008, the private sector borrowers in US and Europe responded to changes in interest rates. However, when debt-financed bubble collapsed, the debt remained on the balance sheets while asset prices plunged. It required businesses and households to focus on paying down their debt despite significant drop in the interest rates (Balance sheet recession).[111]

One of the implications drawn by Koo (2016) is that under balance sheet recessionary conditions, instead of prescribing to fiscal consolidation, fiscal stimulus is needed until the private sector has finished deleveraging and ready to borrow and spend savings.

4 The Alternative: The Accounting System Dynamics Models

On the periphery of the current mainstream, several non-neoclassical economists have been working on the 'Stock-Flow-Consistent' (SFC) models. The Accounting System Dynamics (ASD) models is one such type of SFC models that have the potential to overcome the shortcomings of the SMM discussed in the previous section.

The SFC models incorporate all financial flows into the model endogenously and solve complex differential equations numerically which enable them to overcome the key deficiency of the DSGE models cited above. It is worthwhile to note that SFC models are still in the process of development and may need some time to get both acknowledged and to find ways to be integrated into the mainstream approach.

The SFC models are primarily types of macro models that comprehensibly integrate all stocks and flows of an economy (Caverzasi and Godin, 2013). The SFC approach starts with the 'circular flow' view of the monetary economy, in which, every transaction of goods and services finds its counterpart in a flow of credit/debt instrument, each flow comes from somewhere and goes somewhere (Bezemer, 2010). These models represent the economy in terms of a balance sheet, where, by definition liabilities and assets are balanced.

The historical roots of these models can be traced back to the works of Copeland (1949) who sought to find answers to fundamental economic questions such as "when do total purchases of our national product increase?", "where does the money come from to finance them?", "when do purchases of our national product decline?" and "what becomes of the money that is not spent?" (Copeland 1949). Those questions led

111 A balance sheet recession is a type of economic recession when individuals or companies to collectively focus on paying down debt rather than spending or investing, causing economic growth to slow or decline.

him to lay the foundation of an approach that enabled him to integrate real and financial flows of an economy (Caverzasi and Godin 2013). Copeland introduced the quadruple-entry system, which has become one of the crucial elements in the contemporary SFC models, in which someone's inflow is someone else's outflow, based on double-entry system of accounting.

The contemporary non-orthodox economists who have been following the SFC approach include Godley, Baker, Hudson, Keen, Yamaguchi and others.[112] Some of them have been successful in predicting the crisis and have also been contributing to the development of a theoretical framework based of the SFC approach. For example, Wynne Godley and others (Godley and Lavoie, 2007) made, in April 2007, their predictions of slowdown of output growth to almost zero 'sometime between 2007 and 2008. In November 2007, Godley and Zezza again forecasted a significant drop in borrowing and private expenditures with severe consequences for growth and unemployment in coming quarters (Godley and Zezza, 2006). Hudson (2006) had warned about the record mortgage debt and rising debt-service payments that will divert income from the consumer spending and this may push the economy into Japan-style stagnation.

Thus, SFC models may bring in benefits that are not possessed by the SMM. In the next section introduction to Accounting System Dynamic (ASD) macroeconomic modelling approach is presented as an alternative to SMM.

1.5 SFC Approach of System Dynamics

The criticism levied against the SMM cannot be effective unless providing its alternative model. Most of SMM could be said to originate from the general equilibrium model, so-called Arrow-Debreu model (Arrow and Debreu, 1954), and "Theory of Value" by Debreu (1959), which has dominated the mindset in economics. However, Yamaguchi (1988) recognizes that Debreu's Theory of Value is built on several fictions to accomplish its rigorous mathematical formulation; that is, (i) timeless and static, (ii) classless such as workers and shareholders, and (iii) moneyless, which had led him to conclude that "these fictions present logical inconsistencies, and accordingly they cannot be acceptable (Yamaguchi, p.48, 1988)".[113] According to Yamaguchi and his colleagues, system dynamics modeling can indeed overcome logical inconsistencies of SMM. However, Yamaguchi also recognizes that the system dynamics modeling has to be integrated with double-entry bookkeeping principle of accounting system.

112 For the theoretical literature outlining SFC approach, see Baker et al. (2005), Keen (1995, 2009), Hudson (2006b), Godley and Wray (2000), Godley and Zezza (2006), Godley and Lavoie (2007), Yamaguchi (2013).

113 See Yamaguchi (pp. 41–48, 1988) for detailed seven critiques of Prof. Debreu's "Theory of Value".

System Dynamics is designed to capture dynamic behaviors of state variables (so called in differential equations) in terms of stock-flow relation. In Figure 6.6, a state variable is represented in a stock box labeled Commodity (which has a commodity unit), while the level of stock can only be changed by the amount of flows such as Sales and Purchases (which have a time unit such as unit/month).[114]

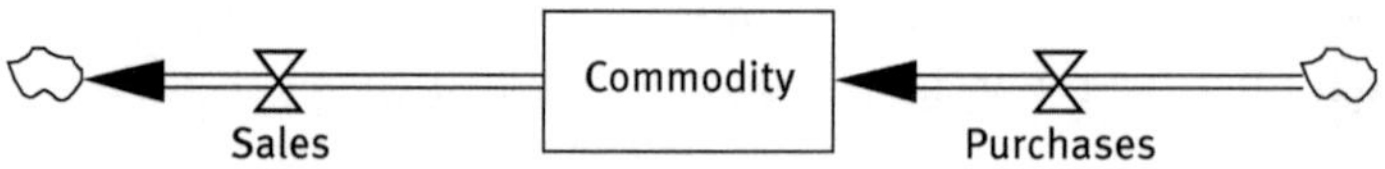

Figure 6.6: Stock-flow Relation of Dynamics.
Source: Own figure.

Commodity can be interpreted as inventory. In this simple dynamic modeling, equilibrium is attained when "Purchases = Sales", so that net charge in commodity inventory becomes zero. If Sales are not equal to Purchases, inventory increases or decreases. In either case, we can easily model both states of equilibrium and off-equilibrium in this stock-flow presentation.

On the other hand, in textbook macroeconomic models in which Sales are interpreted as GDP and Purchases as consisting of $C + I + G$, equilibrium can only be formalized as equation such that

$$GDP = C + I + G \ (equilibrium\ equation) \tag{4}$$

Furthermore, off-equilibrium state could only be described as identity such that

$$GDP = C + I^{*} + G \ (off-equilibrium\ equation) \tag{5}$$

where I^{*} includes inventory investment. Hence, under the analytical framework of SMM modeling, off-equilibrium state is hard to be modeled as equation, compared with the stock-flow modeling approach. This is the reason why SMM has to be constrained to the equilibrium analysis.[115]

4.1.1 Co-flows of Money and Commodity

Even kids are fully aware that they cannot buy commodity without money; that is, all economic transactions have to be performed with money that plays a role as a medium of exchanges. In Figure 6.7, money is represented as another stock (whose

114 The interested reader is referred to Chapter 1 of Yamaguchi (2013) for more comprehensive presentation of system dynamics modelling.

115 The interested reader is referred to Chapter 2 of Yamaguchi (2013) for further discussions.

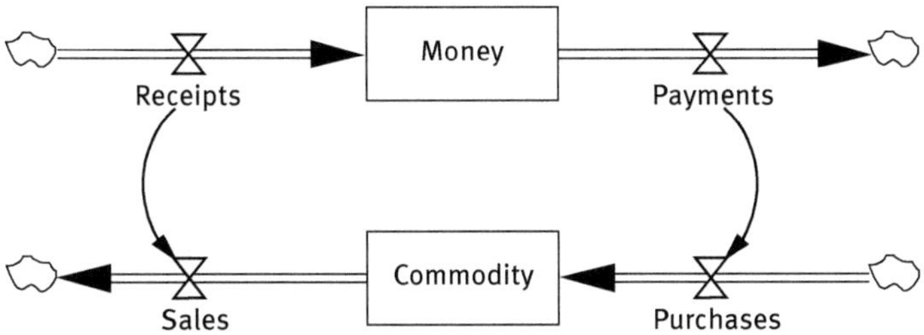

Figure 6.7: Co-flows of Commodity and Money.
Source: Own figure.

unit is dollar), while receipts and payments are illustrated as flows (whose units are dollar/month). To introduce money as a stock-flow relation, at least the following three pieces of information on money have to be identified; that is, money as stock, a unit to measure its amount, and volumes of its flows as a medium of exchange for goods and services.

From these modeling requirements, three essential functions of money, as explained in standard textbooks, are derived:
- Unit of account (unit of money stock has to be determined before modeling);
- Medium of exchange (flow amount of money stock has to be determined in relation to co-flow commodity);
- Store of value (money has to be modeled as the amount of stock).

The co-flow relation of money and commodity is the prerequisite of economic modeling of any transaction. Commodity cannot be traded without payment of money! If sufficient amount of money does not exist or payments by debt obligation are not accepted, transactions cannot be performed at all.[116] This monetary constraint has been entirely overlooked by economic dynamics researchers of Goodwin Growth Cycle Model (Goodwin, 1967). This one example exemplifies how money is needed to claim that an economic model is rational.

In general equilibrium framework of SMM, an auctioneer of the economy is assumed to quote prices p until equilibrium is attained such that Purchases (p^*) = Sales (p^*). What Arrow-Debreu model has demonstrated is the existence proof of such equilibrium prices p^* in all markets, except money. Once such equilibrium prices p^* are attained, all economic agents are allowed to trade at the equilibrium prices without money. Hence, money has been considered as a veil of real economy. It is now clear that such moneyless SMM is logically inconsistent as a real economic model.

116 The reader may easily confirm how monetary constraint affects behaviors of business cycle in a monetary Goodwin model in Chapter 4 (Macroeconomic System Overview) of Yamaguchi (2013).

4.1.2 Accounting System Dynamics

Under the co-flow transactions of money and commodity, buyers have to give up their money assets to increase their commodity assets, while sellers have to give up commodity assets to increase their money assets. In short, commodity transactions with money are always booked as an increase and decrease of assets simultaneously. According to the double-entry bookkeeping rule of accounting, commodity transactions with money as illustrated in Figure 6.7 can be described as in Table 6.1.

Table 6.1: Journal Entries of Transactions with Money.

Buyers		Sellers	
Debit (Assets)	Credit (Assets)	Debit (Assets)	Credit (Assets)
Commodity (+)	Money (–)	Money (+)	Commodity (–)

Source: Authors' own table.

In this way System Dynamics (SD) approach is integrated with double-entry principles of accounting system. This integrated modeling method is called Accounting System Dynamics (ASD) by Yamaguchi (2003).

4.1.3 Creation of Debt Money out of Nothing

As discussed above, the root cause of the failures of the SMM (whether neoclassical, Keynesian or monetarist) lies in the failure of properly incorporating roles of money and finance in their models. ASD economic models try to fix this failure with the introduction of money. What is money, then? According to Table 6.2 (Yamaguchi and Yamaguchi, 2017), money is first of all classified into two categories; public money and debt money.

Public money has historically been issued by the public sector such as government (legislative or executive branch) and sovereign powers such as king, queen and emperors at interest-free. Public money issuers can only obtain seigniorage once at a time of money issuance. On the other hand, debt money is issued by private banks at interest. It consists of legal tender and functional-money.

Debt money issued by (private) central banks is called base money which is legal tender, while debt money issued by private banks mainly consists of bank deposits which function as money; that is, functional-money. What is legal tender, then? Zarlenga quotes Aristotle's (384–322 BC) articulation on money as follows: "It has the name nomisma – because it exists not by nature, but by law (nomos) and it is in our power to change it and make it useless." (Zarlenga, 2002)

Table 6.2: Classification of Money: Public Money Vs Debt Money.

	Public money	Debt money	
Media	**Money as legal tender**		**Functional money**
Non-metal commodities	Shell, cloth (silk), woods, stones, etc.		
Metal coinage	Non-precious metal coins, gold, silver and copper coins		Metal ingots such as gold
Paper notes	Public money notes by PMI admin.	Goldsmith certificates Central bank notes	
Digital cards and accounts	Digital public money (PM)	Digital cash Central bank digital currency	Bank deposits (Credits by loans)

Source: Authors' own table.

Following Aristotle, it is plausible to define money as legal tender in the sense that people cannot refuse to accept it in exchange for commodity. In other words, money always co-flows as legal tender along with commodity inseparably as illustrated in Figure 6.8.

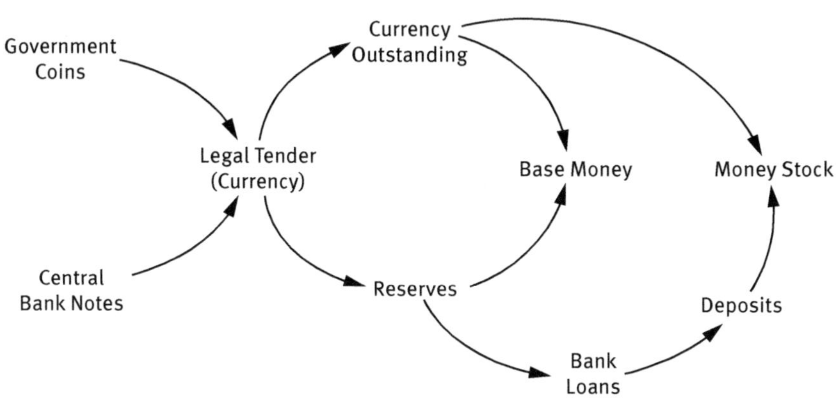

Figure 6.8: Base Money as Legal Tender.
Source: Own figure.

In order to define money as legal tender, there must be specific laws that stipulate the legal issuance of money. In Japan, for example, the Currency Unit and Money Issuance Act (revised in 1987) and the Bank of Japan Act (revised in 1997) enable both the government and the Bank of Japan to issue coins and banknotes, respectively. Consequently, in Japan, currency, consisting of government coins and Bank of Japan notes, is specifically defined by law as legal tender, such that it cannot be refused as a means of payment; that is why it is alternatively called fiat money. Figure 6.8 illustrates the state of currency (coins and banknotes) as legal tender.

Under the current debt money system, once currency is put into circulation as legal tender, it begins to split into two parts: currency outstanding and reserves with the central bank. The sum of these parts is called base money. Hence, base money is by definition legal tender.

$$Base\ Money = Currency\ Outstanding + Reserves \tag{6}$$

Although central banks are legally allowed to issue base money, it can issue base money only when someone comes to borrow at interest. Those who come to borrow from the central bank are mainly commercial banks and government. Base money is issued against various lending facilities or asset purchases using the double-entry accounting rule. Base money is thus booked as liabilities on the balance sheet of the central bank, and backed by various types of assets, such as gold, discount loans to commercial banks and loans to the government (securities) as illustrated in Figure 6.9.

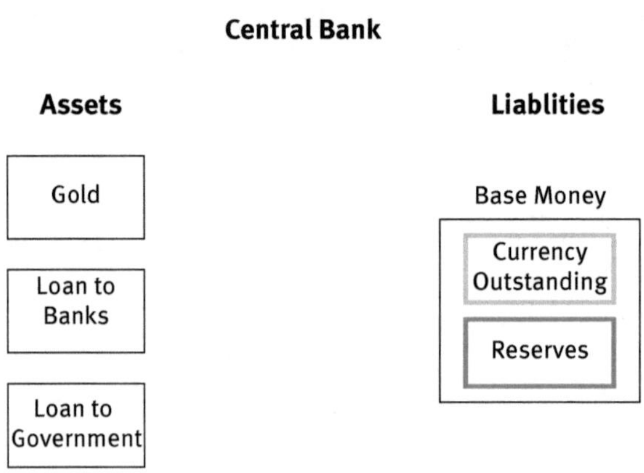

Figure 6.9: Issuance of Base Money Backed by Various Types of Assets.
Source: Own figure.

On the other hand, under the debt money system, banks can create deposits out of nothing by merely granting loans, collectively, to the non-banking economic sectors. Deposits thus created are used for transaction payments as if they are money as illustrated in Figure 6.10.

Using double-entry accounting principle, this transaction is booked as in Table 6.3. Hence, all transactions are booked within the account of assets. Does this mean that deposits, created by banks, become legal tender, similar to money, such that no one can refuse to accept? According to Masaaki Shirakawa, former governor of the Bank of Japan, the answer is negative:

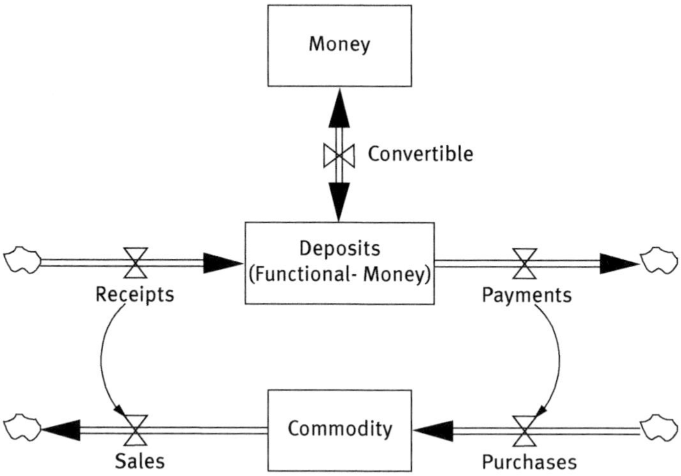

Figure 6.10: Deposits as Functional-money.
Source: Authors' own figure.

Table 6.3: Journal Entries of Transactions with Deposits.

Buyers		**Sellers**	
Debit (Assets)	Credit (Assets)	Debit (Assets)	Credit (Assets)
Commodity (+)	Deposits (–)	Deposits (+)	Commodity (–)

Source: Authors' own table.

Contrary to the central bank notes, creditors can refuse to accept bank deposits as the payments of debt obligations because of credit risks associated with bankruptcies of debtors' banks. However, in normal times, bank deposits function as money because of creditors' confidence that bank deposits can be converted to central bank notes (Shirakawa, 2008; emphasis added by the authors).

What is meant here is that deposits are accepted for commodity transactions in Figure 6.10 only when their convertibility to money is presumed by their recipients. In this sense, they are not legal tender. Henceforth, we may regard deposits as functional-money, technically different from legal tender. Based on the assumption that deposits function as money, standard textbooks define another concept of monetary aggregate in addition to money as

$$Money\ Stock = Currency\ in\ Circulation + Deposits \tag{7}$$

Money stock thus defined is the total amount of money available in the economy as a medium of exchange for transactions and economic activities.

4.1.4 System Design Failures of Debt Money

Once ASD modeling method is established, it has not been a hard work to construct generic macroeconomic models, consisting of five sectors of the economy such as central bank, commercial banks, consumers, producers and government (and foreign sector), as alternative macroeconomic models to SMM (Yamaguchi, 2013). Throughout these model constructions, it is demonstrated that the current debt money system is poorly designed such that monetary instability is inescapable, causing booms and busts, economic recessions and unemployment, income inequalities, inter alia. This is mainly because money stock as defined above is endogenously created and destroyed, so that central banks cannot control its amount, contrary to the standard Keynesian view that it can be controlled by central banks through monetary policies such as open market operations.

To demonstrate monetary instability, Yamaguchi and Yamaguchi (2016) have built a simple stock approach model of debt money creation that is equivalent to the above FMC theory of money creation, and obtained the simulation results as in Figure 6.11. In the figure, base money is kept stable, though its composite part of currency in circulation (or outstanding) fluctuates cyclically. This stable base money, however, surprisingly yields cyclical fluctuations of money stock as well as bank loans.

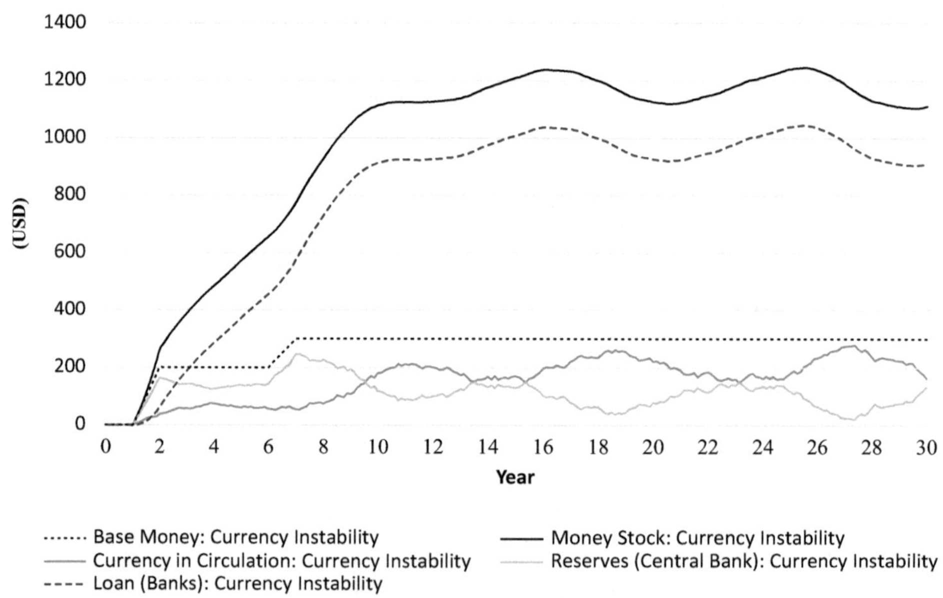

Figure 6.11: Stable Base Money and Money Stock Instability.
Source: Own figure.

The foremost conclusion of this simulation result is evident. Under the debt money system, even stable base money (stable monetary policy) creates unstable money stock. In other words, central banks cannot wholly control the amount of money stock. This explains why the quantitative easing (QE) policies recently introduced in Japan, USA and EU countries have all failed.

These failures are not caused by misconducts of policy-makers, but by the debt money system itself. Another negative outcome of the system design failures is the accumulated national debts of these countries. It is now obvious that debt crises cannot be solved within the current debt money system that has caused them. Hence, a new design of the macroeconomic system is needed.

4.1.5 Public Money System

If airplane crashes occur repeatedly, engineers will try to figure out whether these are caused by human errors or system design failures. When crashes are identified as the faults in the system design, engineers will be forced to draw new designs for the planes. Thanks to their repeated efforts at re-design, we have now safer airplanes than before.

In a similar fashion, monetary instabilities discussed above are due to failures in the design of the fractional reserve banking system. Faced with the ongoing financial crises and accumulating government debts triggered by the instability of the current debt money system, economists are now, like engineers of airplanes, obliged to re-design our failing monetary and economic system.

Can they re-design it? Yamaguchi (2013) attempts to answer that question by a new design, the public money system. It is based on the monetary reform of the Chicago Plan which was proposed in 1930's to attain monetary and financial stabilities as well as debt liquidation of government.

The Great Depression in 1929 was the first major economic disaster caused by the system design failures of the debt money. Faced with these design failures, eight economists at the University of Chicago proposed an alternative system design which was later named "The Chicago Plan for Banking Reform" in 1933.[117] The plan was, then, vehemently advocated by Irving Fisher (1935) of Yale University, and a group of five

117 They were: G.V. Cox, Aaron Director, Paul Douglas, A.G. Hart, F.H. Knight, L.W. Mints, Henry Schulz, and H.C. Simons. Their proposal was handed over, through Henry A. Wallace, Secretary of Agriculture, to the President Franklin D. Roosevelt on March 16, 1933. Unfortunately it failed to be implemented. Instead, less restrictive Banking Act of 1933 to bankers, known as Glass-Steagal Act was legalized on June 16, 1933 (Phillips, 1995). The Act was, alas, repealed in 1999 by the president Bill Clinton.

economists[118] under the name "A Program for Monetary reform" (Douglas et al., 1939). Their proposal was to introduce a reserve requirement of 100% for demand deposits.

The same idea was followed through by Zarlenga (2002). ASD macroeconomic models by Yamaguchi (2013) featuring public money system is also its continuation. Fundamentals of the public money system in a nutshell are the following;

- Public money administration under legislative branch of government issues public money,
- Required reserve ratio of 100% is attained among all banks, and
- Public money is put into circulation constantly to sustain economic growth and welfare.

The simulation results of ASD model developed by Mahmud, Yamaguchi, and Yülek (2017) under the public money system are illustrated in Figure 6.12. Whenever a 100% reserve ratio is applied to an unstable monetary behavior of the above Figure 6.12 at t = 10, they get, all of sudden, transformed into the stable ones. More specifically, instability of the money stock under a fractional (not 100%) reserve ratio (line 2) is perfectly subdued by the introduction of the 100% reserve ratio, so that base money becomes identical to money stock. Theoretically, money stock is shown to become equal to base money under 100% reserve ratio. That is to say, functional-money disappears completely from the circulation and money stock becomes equal to legal tender (that is, base money). Accordingly, monetary stability is completely restored and money stock never gets affected by loanable behaviors of banks.

Furthermore, to increase the amount of public money in circulation to recover the original level, it is assumed that $200 of public money is newly issued at t = 18 for 5 years. In this way, the original level of money stock is restored in Figure 6.12. If more money stock is needed for sustaining economic growth and welfare, public money will be further put into circulation.

4.1.6 Banks as Genuine Intermediaries and Islamic Finance

Under the public money system, banks can no longer create money out of nothing by making loans at interest. Banks are obliged to make loans with the existing money at hand and share their investment risks with borrowers.

To be more specific, banks under the public money system become genuine intermediaries in the following sense. First, banks would be obliged to hold full

118 They are Paul H. Douglas, University of Chicago; Frank D. Graham, Princeton University; Earl J. Hamilton, Duke University; Willford I. King, New York University; and Charles R. Whittlesey, Princeton University.

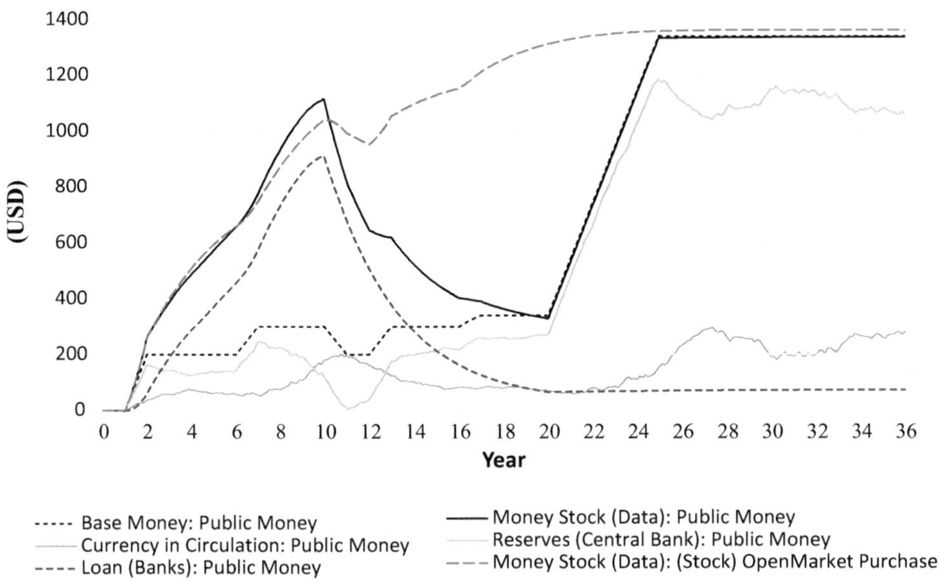

Figure 6.12: 100% Reserve Requirement Rule Introduced at t = 10 and Public Money Put into Circulation at t = 18 for 5 Years.
Source: Own figure.

amount of customers' deposits. In consequence, the non-banking economic sectors can safely use their deposits anytime as legal tender for their transactions and economic activities. On the other hand, depositors have to pay service charges to the banks in exchange for these transaction services, like the present-day ATM service charges. These service charges in turn become a stable source of earned income for banks. In this way, robust and stable banking and financial management will be established.

Second, as by-product, banks no longer need to borrow or lend in the inter-bank money market. The inter-bank interest rate for borrowing or lending excess reserves will no longer be applicable to one another.

Third, loanable funds for banks come from three sources: their own capital, repaid loans, and time deposits. Among these, time deposits will be a main source of loanable funds. Time deposits are nothing but the surplus deposits that are not needed for daily and short-term transactions, so that they are saved to the time deposits account. Accordingly, banks become efficient by offering higher interest rates for saving and lower interest for loans. Bubbles and bursts created by debt money out of nothing can no longer occur, and existing financial markets are constrained to real zero-sum games; that is, losers and winners coexist. This implies that existing financial bonds and securities are no longer attractive to the banks as a whole. And loanable funds tend to be invested in real economy from which positive interest revenues are obtained for banks as a whole, so long as the economy continues to grow.

In this way interest rates are competitively determined in the public money market, according to the available amount of saving and investment in the economy. They are no longer the instruments of monetary policies by central banks. Interest revenues thus obtained through arbitrage or spread of lending and borrowing truly become banks' earned income for their efforts in providing investment banking services. Interest revenues, in this sense, are no longer unearned income out of nothing.

It is true that investment, whether real or financial, has been a risky economic activity through history. Accordingly, to avoid investment risks, earned interest income (or losses) by banks from investment must be shared among banks, time deposits savers and borrower-investors under the public money system.

Islamic finance has been based on interest -free banking, and profits generated by means of loans have been shared with all creditors or stakeholders. In consequence, risk-sharing system under the public money system as explained above turns out to be very similar to the one that has been historically practiced as "participatory banking" system under Islamic banking and finance.[119] In Japan, a similar "mutual social financing" system known as Tanomoshi-kou has been practiced since the 12th century. These risk-sharing managerial practices might have evolved into the modern cooperative banking in countries such as Germany, Japan and USA. In sum, banking and financial practices under the public money system discussed above turn out to be perfectly compatible with Islamic finance and cooperative banking.

5 Conclusion

This chapter reviews the shortcomings of SMM in explaining the actual economic conditions and processes. The chapter also proposes the notion of ASD as an alternative approach to macroeconomic modelling. The SMM, by not incorporating the complexities of the banking system, carries a number of shortcomings that reduce benefits from its use such as not being able to explain why some anomalies occur or when financial crises approach. Thus, the SMM has limited use for economic policy and reform purposes. The stock-flow consistent ASD model is better positioned to explain how the real-world economics work. Its use can be better assessed as more models are developed in the future.

The ASD enables the simulation and assessment of the outcomes of money creation process by the banks. In this regard, the chapter provides the simulation results which point out that the fractional reserve banking system inherently causes

119 For instance, see the report: Participation Banks 2016 by TKBB (Participation Banks Association of Turkey), established in 2002.

monetary instabilities even when the base money (monetary policy) is stable. In other words, under the fractional reserve banking system, central banks simply cannot wholly control the amount of money stock, explaining why (i) the quantitative easing (QE) policies recently introduced in Japan, USA and EU countries have all failed; and (ii) why debt is continuously mounting in these countries.

The conclusion that these failures are policy- proof and are due to the design of the debt money system itself, suggests that they can be remedied by a re-design of the macroeconomic and financial system. It is proposed in this chapter that the public money system is a prospective solution to the problems caused the debt-based financial system. It is also noted that the main tenets of Islamic finance, including the notion of risk-sharing and prohibition of interest, is fully compliant with the principles of banking and financial practices under the public money system.

References

Arrow, Kenneth J. and Gerard Debreu. 1954. "Existence of an Equilibrium for a Competitive Economy." *Econometrica* 22(3): 265–290.

Aschheim, Joseph. 1959. "Commercial Banks and Financial Intermediaries: Fallacies and Policy Implications." *Journal of Political Economy* 67(1): 59–71.

Baker, Dean, Bradford Delong, and Paul Krugman. 2005. "Asset Returns and Economic Growth." *Brookings Papers on Economic Activity* 36(1): 289–330.

Beck, Thorsten, Tao Chen, Chen Lin, and Frank M. Song. 2012. "Financial Innovation: The Bright and the Dark Sides." Working Papers 052012, Hong Kong Institute for Monetary Research.

Bernanke, Ben. 2000. *Essays on the Great Depression*. Princeton: Princeton University Press.

Bernanke, Ben. "The Great Moderation." At the meeting of the Eastern Economic Association, Washington, D.C., February 20, 2004.

Bezemer, D. J. 2010. "Understanding financial crisis through accounting models". *Accounting, Organizations and Society* 35(7): 676–688.

Blanchard, Olivier. 2008. *The State of Macro*. National Bureau of Economic Research (NBER); Peter G. Peterson Institute for International Economics.

Blanchard, Olivier. 2014. "How the crisis changed macroeconomics." World Economic Forum. Accessed 06 October, 2014.

Boughton, J. M. 1991. "Long-run money demand in large industrial countries. " *IMF Staff Papers* 38(1): 1–32.

Brown, J. 2015. "Chart o' the Day: The (non) Velocity of Money. " CSLA, Accessed October 8, 2015. https://thereformedbroker.com/2015/10/08/chart-o-the-day-the-non-velocity-of-money/

Bundesbank. 2009. *Geld und Geldpolitik*. Frankfurt: Deutsche Bundesbank.

Caverzasi, E. and Godin, A. 2013. "Stock flow: consistent modelling through the ages." Working Paper Series 745, The Levy Economics Institute of Bard College.

Cecchetti, S. and Kharroubi, E. 2012. "Reassessing the impact of finance on growth." BIS Working Papers 381.

Copeland, M. 1949. "Social accounting for money flows." *The Accounting Review* 24(3): 254–264.

Davis, J. and Kahn, James. 2008. "Interpreting the Great Moderation: changes in the volatility of economic activity at the macro and micro levels." Staff Report no. 334, Federal Reserve Bank of New York.

Debreu, G. 1959. *Theory of Value*. Yale University Press.

Douglas, P. H., *et al.* 1939. "A program for monetary reform."

Eggertsson, G. B. & Krugman, P. 2012. "Debt, deleveraging, and the liquidity trap: a Fisher-Minsky-Koo approach." *The Quarterly Journal of Economics* 127(3): 1469–1513.

Fisher, I. 1945. *100% Money: Designed to keep checking banks 100% liquid; to prevent inflation and deflation; largely to cure or prevent depressions: and to wipe out much of the national debt*. 3th ed. New Haven: The City Printing Company.

Forrester, J. 1961. *Industrial Dynamics*. Waltham: Pegasus Communications.

Friedman, M. 1987. "Monetary Policy: Tactics versus Strategy." In *The Search for Stable Money: Essays on Monetary reform*, 361–82. Chicago/London: University of Chicago Press.

Fullwiler, S. T. 2013. "An endogenous money perspective on the post-crisis monetary policy debate." *Review of Keynesian Economics* 1(2):171–194.

Gali, J. and Gambetti, L. 2009. "On the sources of the Great Moderation." *American Economic Journal: Macroeconomics* 1(1): 26–57.

Godley, W. and Lavoie, M. 2007. *Monetary Economics: An Integrated Approach to Credit, Money, Income, Production and Wealth*. Palgrave Macmillan, New York, xliii.

Godley, W. and Wray, L. R. 2000. "Is Goldilocks doomed?" *Journal of Economic Issues* 34(1): 201–206.

Godley, W. & Zezza, G. 2006. "Debt and lending: a cri de coeur." Levy Institute at Bard College Policy Notes: April.

Goodwin, R. 1967. "A Growth Cycle" In *Socialism, Capitalism and Economic Growth*, edited by C.H. Feinstein, 54–58. Cambridge University Press, UK.

Gurley, J. G. and Shaw, E.S. 1955. "Financial aspects of economic development." *American Economic Review* 45: 515–528.

Guttentag, J. M. & Lindsay, R. 1968. "The uniqueness of commercial banks. " *Journal of Political Economy*, 76(5): 991–1014.

Hahn, L. A. 1924. *Volkswirtschaftliche Theorie des Bankkredits*. 2nd ed. Tübingen: Mohr.

Hudson, M. 2006. "The road to serfdom: an illustrated guide to the coming real estate collapse." *Harper's Magazine*.

Holmes, A. 1969. "Controlling Monetary Aggregates." In *Proceedings of the Monetary Conference held on Nantucket Island, June, 2006*. The Federal Reserve Bank of Boston.

Hudson, M. 2006. "Saving, Asset-Price Inflation, and Debt-Induced Deflation" In *Money, Financial Instability and Stabilization Policy*, edited by L. Randall Wray and Matthew Forstater (Edward Elgar, 2006):104–24.

Goodwin, R. 1967. "A Growth Cycle" In *Socialism, Capitalism and Economic Growth*, edited by C.H. Feinstein, 54–58. Cambridge University Press, UK.

Jakab Z. and Kumhof, M. 2015. "Banks are not intermediaries of loanable funds and why this matters." Working Paper 529, Bank of England.

Keen, S. 1995. "Finance and economic breakdown: model-ling Minsky's Financial Instability Hypothesis." *Journal of Post Keynesian Economics*, 17(4)4: 607–635.

Keen, S. 2009. "The dynamics of the monetary circuit." In *The political economy of monetary circuits*, 161–187. Palgrave Macmillan UK.

Keen, S. 2014. "Secular stagnation and endogenous money" *Real-World Economics Review* 66: 2–11.

Koo, R. 2011. "The world in balance sheet recession: causes, cure, and politics." *Real-World Economics Review* 58(12): 19–37.

Koo, R. 2016. "Authorities and markets continue to ignore real economy and act on textbook assumptions." Tokyo: Nomura Research Institute.

Krugman, Paul. 2009. "How did economists get it so wrong?" *New York Times*, September.

Macleod, H. D. 1894. *The theory of credit*. Volume2. London: Longmans, Green.

Mahmud, S. F., Yamaguchi, K. and Yülek, M. A. 2017. *Money Matters: Some Puzzles, Anomalies and Crises in the Standard Macroeconomic Model*. Peter Lang.
McLeay, M., Radia, A. and Thomas, R. 2014. "Money creation in the modern economy." *Bank of England Quarterly Bulletin*, First Quarter.
Phillips, R. J. 1995. "The Chicago Plan and New Deal Banking Reform (Armonk, NY, ME Sharpe)." *The economic contributions of Hyman Minsky, 61*.
LSE. 2011. "Getting in shape: leveraging our assets, developing opportunities." *Annual Report*. London, Stock Exchange Group.
Lucas, Robert E. Jr. 2003. "Macroeconomic priorities." *American Economic Review 93*: 1–14.
Samuelson, P. 1948. *Economics*. New York: McGraw- Hill.
Schumpeter, J. 1934. *The theory of economic development*. Cambridge: Harvard University Press.
Shirakawa, M. 2008. *Modern monetary policy in theory and practice*. Tokyo: Nihon Keizai.
Smith, P. F. 1966. "The concepts of money and commercial banks." *Journal of Finance* 21(4): 635–648.
Sterman, J.D. 2000. *Business Dynamics – Systems Thinking and Modeling for a Complex World*. New York: The McGraw-Hill Companies.
Stiglitz, Joseph E. 2011. "Rethinking macroeconomics: what failed, and how to repair it." *Journal of European Economic Association* 9(4): 591–645.
Stock, J. H. and Watson W. 2002. "Has the Business Cycle Changed and Why", NBER Macroeconomics Annual 2000, National Bureau of Economic Research, 159–230.
Stone, C. and Thornton D. L. 1987. "Solving the 1980s' velocity puzzle: a progress report" Federal Reserve Bank of St. Louis, August – September.
Tobin, J. 1963. "Commercial Banks as Creators of 'Money'", Published in Dean Carson, ed., *Banking and Monetary Studies*, for the Comptroller of the Currency, U.S. Treasury, Richard D. Irwin, 408–419.
Tobin, J. 1984. "On the efficiency of the financial system." Lloyds Bank Annual Review 153: 1–15.
Summers, L. 2014 "U.S. Economic Prospects: Secular Stagnation, Hysteresis, and the Zero Lower Bound." *Business Economics* Vol. 49, No. 2.
Tovar, C. 2008. "DSGE models and central banks." Bank of International Settlements, Monetary and Economic Department Working Paper 28. Basel: BIS.
Turner, A. 2013. "Debt, Money, and Mephistopheles – How do we get out of this mess?" Group of Thirty, Occasional paper, No. 87(Washington, D.C.), May.
Vivian, R. W. and Spearman, N. 2015. "Some clarity on banks as financial intermediaries and money "creators"." Working paper No. 523, Johannesburg, South Africa: School of Economic and Business Services, University of the Witwatersrand.
Werner, R. A. 1993. "Japanese capital flows: did the world suffer from yen illusion? Toward a quantity theory of disaggregated credit." In *the Proceedings of the Annual Conference of the Royal Economic Society*, London.
Werner, R. A. 1997. "Towards a new monetary paradigm: a quantity theorem of disaggregated credit, with evidence from Japan" *Kredit und Kapital*, 30(2): 276–309.
Werner, R. A. 2005. *New Paradigm in Macroeconomics*. Basingstoke: Palgrave Macmillan, Vol. 213.
Werner, R. A. 2014. "How do banks create money, and why can other firms not do the same? An explanation for the coexistence of lending and deposit-taking. " *International Review of Financial Analysis*, No. 36:71–77.
Werner, R. A. 2015 "A lost century in economics: three theories of banking and the conclusive evidence." *International Review of Financial Analysis*.
Wicksell, K. 1898. *Geldzins und Güterpreise. Eine Untersuchung über die den Tauschwert des Geldes bestimmenden Ursachen*. Jena: Gustav Fischer (tr., 1936. *Interest and prices: a study of the causes regulating the value of money*. London: Macmillan).

Withers, H. 1916. *Business of finance*. London: Smith, El-det & Co.
Xu Hailiang. 2011. "Macroeconomics after the great recession: consensus or conflict?" *Electronic thesis, and Dissertations*, 720. Graduate Studies, University of Denver, USA.
Withers, H. 1921. *The meaning of money*. New York: EP Dutton and Company, Vol. 2.
Yamaguchi, K. 1988. *Beyond Walras, Keynes and Marx – Synthesis in Economic Theory Toward a New Social Design*. American University Studies Series XVI, Economics; Vol. 3, Peter Lang Publishing Inc., New York.
Yamaguchi, K. 2003. "Principle of Accounting System Dynamics – Modeling Corporate Financial Statements." In *Proceedings of the 21st International Conference of the System Dynamics Society*, New York City, USA. (ISBN 0-9672914-9-6).
Yamaguchi, K. 2013. *Money and Macroeconomic Dynamics – Accounting System Dynamics approach*. (ISBN 978-4-907291-01-3). Available at http://www.muratopia.org/Yamaguchi/MacroBook.html.
Yamaguchi, K., and Yamaguchi, Y. 2015. "ASD Macroeconomic Model of Japan on the Flow of Funds and National Accounts – Report on its Early Stage Development." In *Proceedings of the 33rd International Conference of the System Dynamics Society*, Cambridge, Massachusetts, USA.
Yamaguchi, K., and Yamaguchi, Y. 2016. "Head and Tail of Money Creation and its System Design Failures – Toward the Alternative System Design." In *Proceedings of the 34th International Conference of the System Dynamics Society*, Delft, the Netherlands.
Yamaguchi, K., and Yamaguchi, Y. 2017. "Public Money, Debt Money and Blockchain-based Money Classified – EPM as Money of the Futures." Working Paper No.1. Japan Futures Research Center. www.muratopia.net.
Zarlenga, S. 2002. *The lost science of money: the mythology of money, the story of power*. Valatie. New York: American Monetary Institute.

Azura Othman

Chapter 7: Equity-based Macroeconomic Policies: An Alternative Solution to Economic Stability and Development

1 Introduction

Achieving stable growth and development is often stated as the ultimate goal of economic policies. Whilst economic stability is unequivocally understood in terms of fairly steady constant output growth and consistently low inflation, these are diverging views about the meaning of economic development. Economic development has been traditionally regarded as the achievement of material growth. In the pursuit of economic growth, the focus is placed on sustainability, and inclusiveness, as well as, the ethical and environmental aspects of commerce. These broader perspectives are reflected in the United Nations Sustainable Development Goals, which include good health and well-being, gender equality, affordable and clean energy, and reduced inequalities, inter alia.

Since economic growth does not always translate into better well-being and widely shared gains, policy choices that promote shared opportunity in the accumulation of productive assets is essential for meaningful economic and social change. There is a need for efficient and accountable government actions and policies that promote inclusive growth and cooperation with the non-government sector. In order to achieve inclusive growth, benefits should not persistently and disproportionately accrue to a small and exclusive segment of the society. Greater inclusiveness requires more equitable distributions of income and economic opportunities irrespective of ethnicity, gender and religion. High levels of inequality are often associated with social unrest and volatile economic performance. Therefore, growth and social inclusion have to be pursued together. Policy measures should reflect a system of incentives that promotes social development and sustainable economic growth.

It is noted that some economists such as Keynes argue that free market economies do not have the capacity of self-correction without state intervention. Totally free markets tend to serve the narrow interests of parties vested with sufficient economic power to accumulate and direct resources. The recourse to government intervention has become more relevant today in the wake of the recent global financial crises and euro-debt problem. The high levels of world poverty and income inequality constitute further justification for government interference. The role of the state is to ensure that access to resources is efficiently distributed, that equal opportunities for means of livelihood are guaranteed, and that markets are properly supervised to ensure orderly and just practice. The state must actively complement market forces to

https://doi.org/10.1515/9783110587920-007

ensure that individual action and private interest do not systematically diverge from public interest. This function is exercised through policy-making and supervision.

With the greater emphasis on the connection between economic, social and environmental perspectives, there is a paradigm shift in conventional economics, in which the moral dimension of development becomes more prominent. The policies and inducements put in place must elicit the desired responses to achieve the needed outcomes and it is important to note that the behavioral element that contributes to the desired responses. Naturally, this behavior is shaped by the worldview adopted by economic agents. The worldview determines the values and preferences that define actions and decisions in all endeavors. In the context of conventional economics, this worldview is motivated by rationality, pursuit of personal gain, and promotion of self-interest, and it focuses on material interests and benefits alone. The incentive structures or sanctions put in place to guide human behavior in the economy are based on man-made rules and are subject to discretionary changes and individual influence (Othman et al., 2017). There is, however, a distinctive worldview that includes the additional dimension based on moral and spiritual values.

The Islamic worldview places, indeed, greater emphasis on the development of individual active and moral consciousness in all social interactions. The interest of the society at large, those of individual human beings and those of all other creatures are imbedded in the various actions of economic agents. In the context of Islamic worldview, every person is accountable for all of his/her actions and the rules of behavior to achieve material and non-material progress are grounded in the injunctions contained in the *Qur'an*. Unlike the conventional economic system, the system of reward and retributions for rule compliance and rule violation is based on a set of rules that are divine and absolute.

The examination of economic activities from the Islamic perspective does not differ significantly from conventional economics with respect to profit motivation, private ownership and market forces. However, rather than being granted absolute discretion to make decisions within the realm of man-made rules and regulations, economic agents are bound by the divine rules prescribed in the *Qur'an* in performing economic transactions. This is because Islam is a complete way of life, and it regulates the behavior of man in religious duties as well as in social interactions and economic relations.

One of the main principles of the Islamic economic system is the prohibition of interest (or *riba*). Islam ordains fair and equitable dealings and the prohibition is based on the argument that interest-bearing contracts shift significantly the risks of financial transactions to borrowers. The loan transaction itself violates the basic principle of protecting property rights, as the right of ownership of money lent is not fully transferred. The lender retains property rights to the principal, in addition to collateral, as well as claims on the property of the borrower in the form of the principal plus interest.

Instead of interest-based transactions, Islam promotes equitable exchange and encourages the sharing of both the risk and rewards associated with transactions. Equity finance is an example of financing that is not based on interest and the return is closely tied to the performance of the underlying asset in the real sector. Thus, the risk and any future rewards or losses are shared between financiers and entrepreneurs. In order to promote social and economic justice, Islam defines the scope and limits of commercial transactions and promotes the development of the real sector and the success of ventures that benefit the society without detrimental effects to the environment. It also requires from the rich class in the society to redeem the rights of the poorer class through distribution and redistribution rules such as Islamic levies, charity and inheritance redistribution channels.

The desired economic outcomes include social justice and equity where the interests of individual economic agents are aligned with public interest and income is fairly shared among all members of the society. The set of desired outcomes includes also trust and transparency where transactions are anchored through legally-binding contracts with clear and secure property rights. It is trust among people – and trust-governed cooperation and coordination can be also achieved through risk-sharing, which promotes stronger human interactions and lower income disparity. A more equitable distribution of income and better circulation of wealth in the society can pave the way toward continued economic development. It is also important that finance remains grounded in the real economy. This economic outcome can be achieved with the development of non-interest based financial instruments, where economic risks are spread among parties according to their levels of risk tolerance and the rates of return are tied to the performance of the real sector. Hence a closer relationship between the financial and real sectors can be developed and financial stability can be achieved.

2 The Limits of Standard Macroeconomic Policies

The economic policy tools advocated in this chapter are oriented towards the above desired economic outcomes. Growth-enhancing activities to achieve sustainable economic development have to focus more on the real sector of the economy rather than the financial sector. The recurrence of debt crises continues to generate arguments about the fundamental stability of conventional financial system and the effectiveness of macroeconomic policies. The inherent instability of the financial system can be explained by policies and practices that encourage the accumulation of debt and give little importance to the social and ethical dimensions. The existence of "rentiers", who thrive on such policies further widens the divergence between the financial and real sector of the economy (Othman and Mirakhor, 2013).

It is noted that economic downturns are usually preceded by periods of strong credit growth and house price inflation. Therefore, it is the interest-based financial system that is at the core of debt crises, and subsequent economic recessions (Othman et al., 2017). (Keynes 1936) expressed doubts about the sustainability of a system based on interest-bearing debt, arguing that market capitalism, left to itself, would create "two evils", namely, unemployment and poor income and wealth distribution. The failure to address these problem then increases systematic risk (Mirakhor and Krichene, 2009).

The tax structure also constitutes an important aspect of the fiscal policy, as the revenues generated by fair and effective tax systems have the potential to sustain government spending. Many countries adopt progressive tax systems, where the amount of tax-imposed increases with the income level. At the same time, consumption tax, including value added tax (VAT) and goods and services tax (GST) may constitute a significant source of government revenues but they are regarded as regressive affecting the rich and the poor alike. Complex tax systems require high administrative resources and might also discourage compliance. This complexity may give rise to differing interpretations and create loopholes and opportunities for shrewd taxpayers to avoid or reduce tax payments.

Standard fiscal management practices include the issuance of interest-bearing debt that is often used to finance budget deficits. As these debt-instruments are usually sold wholesale and in large denominations, participation is limited to economically able segments of the society such as banks and financial institutions and high net-worth individuals. This tends to exacerbate the bias in income distribution towards higher income strata. There are also adverse distributional effects arising from the shifting of debt burden from present to future generations. The middle- and lower-income classes carry the burden of taxes needed to service government debt, held by higher income groups and foreign creditors.

Similarly, monetary policy relies on the relationship between interest-rates and money supply to influence economic growth, inflation, exchange rates and unemployment. However, success of monetary policy depends on the effectiveness of transmission mechanisms and independence of the central bank. The problem of transmission reflects the divergence between the objectives of policy makers and the private banking sector. The failure of the banking sector in transmitting the increased liquidity to the real economy affects the course and effectiveness of the monetary policy.

3 Fiscal and Monetary Policies in Islamic Economics

To address the problems underlying the current policy dilemma, it is possible to propose a two-pronged solution based on the reform of the tax system, and fundamental changes in the way governments finance spending and operate monetary policy. The distinctive feature of this alternative solution is that it is based on the concept of risk sharing. The management of fiscal deficits and funding of economic activities are achieved through the issuance of interest-free policy instruments to the general public at low denominations. These risk-sharing financing modes can then serve as instruments for interest-free monetary policy operations. Simplest taxation systems are easier to administer and comply with. The fairness of the system derives from the notion that the tax amount levied is proportional to the taxpayer's ability to contribute. The need for tax simplification is justified also by the necessity to induce voluntary declaration from taxpayers. Tax policy should not overburden contributors and should be conducive to income redistribution from the rich to the poor.

With respect to monetary policy, it is important to devise financial instruments based on the concept of risk-sharing with equity finance ensuring that money supply is altered through asset-based activities. Monetary policy influences portfolio adjustments of the private sector through the expansion and contraction of money supply through capital market rather than money markets. Thus, an expansion in money supply is bound to be accompanied with an increase in real production. Financing instruments issued by the government can be used by monetary authorities to affect portfolio adjustments by the private sector. These transmission channels can be used to achieve the objectives of monetary policy while promoting greater resilience to economic shocks.

The interest-free instruments based on a risk-sharing concept are represented by equity participation shares (EPS). Its risk is fairly spread among a large number of participants through an efficient stock market, closer coordination between the financial and real sectors can be promoted and benefits of economic growth and financial system stability can be shared. In contrast, the practice of issuing debt-based instruments has its own limitations, confidence amongst debt investors reaches a turning point leading to significant risk premium and higher cost of borrowing. Therefore, rather than borrowing to finance fiscal adjustments, the government can issue EPS to fund development programs. Furthermore, the EPS can be also used as monetary policy instruments. The papers must have low denominations and be traded in secondary markets so that a large class of investors, not just institutional investors, can take advantage of investment opportunities. By allowing the papers to be openly traded in the secondary market, the EPS holders can redeem or liquidate holding positions and institutional investors to pay the prevailing market prices in managing their asset portfolios. In this way, economic opportunities would be equally available to all segments of the society avoiding thereby the concentration among the more financially able. In order to contract the money supply, EPS papers can be issued directly to the market to mop up excess liquidity in the financial markets. The contraction effects can be immediate and leakages arising from financial intermediation can be reduced. It is also possible for monetary authority to increase money supply by purchasing these papers from the private sector.

The rate of return on these papers should be referenced to the rate of return of the real sector of the economy. The rate can be benchmarked against the average rate of return in the equity markets, which are generally higher than the pre-determined rates of interest. This mechanism presents investors with better expected returns on their savings. These fiscal and monetary policy instruments have also the potential to enhance governance and transparency, as the government is held more accountable to the general public with regard to the effective implementation of risk-sharing instruments.

4 Simulation of Equity-based Macroeconomic Policy Effects

The previous sections focused on the inherent contingencies and limits of standard macroeconomic policies and the potential merits of alternative fiscal and monetary policies based on risk-sharing financing. The present section describes the simulation method and empirical dataset used to exercise the impact of such policies. The empirical variables are based on the historical performance of the Malaysian economy, which enjoyed strong economic growth rates averaging 7.5% until the 1997–1998 Asian currency crisis. The average post-crisis growth rate of 5% remains high compared to neighboring countries. Despite the higher economic growth, Malaysia sustained large fiscal deficits. The introduction of fiscal stimulus to circumvent the adverse effects of the U.S. credit and financial crisis was made in the midst of tight fiscal conditions. The debt to GDP ratio temporarily approached the self-imposed debt-ceiling threshold of 55% of GDP. These are also important issues related to the 'hidden' debts in the form of contingent liabilities such as government guarantees on private debt and 'off balance sheet' borrowings not reported as Federal Government debt. The implementation of GST in 2015 generated government revenues that contributed to the reduction of the fiscal deficit. However, this is achieved at the expense of rising cost of living.

With respect to monetary policy, the focus is made on ensuring the stability of prices and the financial system. Various measures related to exchange rate regimes, capital controls and policy transition channels are introduced over the past five decades in order to improve macroeconomic management and maintain monetary stability. For instance, there was a shift from monetary targeting to interest rate targeting with floating exchange rate, and a framework for interest rate setting was introduced by Bank Negara Malaysia (BNM). The overnight policy rate replaced the 3-month intervention rate as the indicator of monetary policy stance as the first step in the transmission of monetary impulses. During the global financial crisis of 2007–2009, BNM made attempts to stabilize financial markets with monetary policy expansion meant to mitigate the selling pressures and capital outflows (Othman et al., 2017). Policy communication has been strengthened in recent years through the regular release of policy announcements. As Malaysia has successfully created a vibrant Islamic financial system over the last three decades, the framework for monetary operations and liquidity management is inclusive of instruments adapted for conventional and Islamic financial markets.

With respect to fiscal policy, it is noted that the proposal for fiscal reform includes a financing structure that is based on risk-sharing instruments. The equity participation shares (EPS), discussed above, replace government debt in the course of financing fiscal deficit and development expenditures. The EPS are backed by government development projects, and the rate of return is thus tagged to the rate of return in the real sector.[120]

The current tax structure will be reformed into a flat rate tax on income, which is regarded as presumably easier to administer and more difficult to manipulate. Low-income groups are not liable to tax based on a minimum threshold for tax and those in the low tax bracket under the current tax structure as opposed to the one proposed may benefit from a direct monetary compensation. Additionally, a wealth tax on high income groups would also be levied.

4.1 Simulation Model

The effectiveness of the proposed equity based fiscal policy can be reflected by the sustainability of fiscal positions. Fiscal sustainability can be assessed either by using sustainability indicators or sustainability tests, which involve econometric analysis. It is possible to examine the stationarity of various fiscal variables with non-stationarity implying unsustainable fiscal positions. It is also possible to use cointegration tests and explore the existence of long-run equilibrium relationships between the fiscal variables of interest (Escario, Gadea, and Sabaté, 2012; Bajo-Rubio, Díaz-Roldán, and Esteve, 2010; Baharumshah and Lau, 2007; Arghyrou and Luintel, 2007; Goyal, Khundrakpam, and Ray, 2004; Hakkio and Rush, 1991). Abdullah, Mustafa, and Dahalan (2012) for example, used VAR and cointegration analysis to study Malaysian fiscal sustainability. The regression analysis based on the Dynamic Ordinary Least Squares (DOLS) can also be used to examine the viability of the proposed fiscal policy framework relative to the existing framework.

The analysis of fiscal conditions in Malaysia is based on sample observations obtained from the World Bank database (World Bank website), monthly statistical bulletin of the BNM (Bank Negara Malaysia, 2013), and the annual report of the Government of Malaysia Department of Statistics ("Annual Report", 2014), and

120 The rate of return used in this study is based on the benchmark pricing rate derived by Omar, Noor, and Meera (2010).

Valuation and Property Services Department ("Property Market Report", 2014). The sample period extends from 1970 to 2013. Based on these observations, it is possible to simulate new tax revenue stream and federal government liability positions under the proposed policy framework. The two variables of interest are represented by government expenditures and revenues. The simulation exercise results in the generation of tax revenues under the assumption of new flat rates for income and wealth taxes. The tax revenues are simulated using actual data on income and wealth and optimal combinations of flat tax rates that generate tax revenues higher than under the existing structure is determined. The simulated stream of government expenditures is also generated using the EPS alternative for the financing of fiscal deficit and development expenditures. The EPS substitutes the debt-based borrowing, progressively reducing government borrowing thereby the debt service. The generated series from both simulation exercises are then used in calculating the fiscal sustainability indicator and in empirically assessing fiscal sustainability using appropriate econometric methods.

4.2 Simulation of Tax Revenues

The simulated tax revenues based on the flat tax rates on income (y) and wealth (w) can be represented as follows:

$$T_t = yY_t + wW_t \tag{1}$$

where T_t represents the total tax revenue at time t, y is the flat tax rate on income and w is the flat tax rate on wealth, satisfying the conditions $15\% \ll y \ll 30\%$ and $2\% \ll w \ll 10\%$. Y_t represents total income of individuals above exemption threshold level and total income of companies, and W_t refers to the sum of financial assets and private liabilities, respectively.[121] The new government revenues can be derived as follows:

$$NR_t = yY_t + wW_t + OR \tag{2}$$

where OR represents other non-tax revenues of the government.

The simulation of tax revenues is based on the assessment of different combinations of the flat rates of y and w within the ranges associated within Equation (1). The benchmark rates are based on the injunctions contained in Surah 8 Al Anfal, Verse 41 of the *Qur'an*, indicating a tax rate of 20% on income, and 2.5% on wealth, which is the rate of *zakah*. Additionally, the lowest tax rate in the Asia Pacific region (17%)

121 With reference to previous studies on wealth inequality in Malaysia by Khalid (2011, 2014). The total wealth is inclusive of financial assets (savings and investments) and physical assets (real properties and fixed assets) net of liabilities.

and the 2014 income tax rate in Malaysia (25%) are used as the lower and upper boundaries for y. The tax rate on wealth ranges between the rate of *zakah* (2.5%) and the lowest property tax in the region, 10% for Singapore.[122] It is noted that the wealth tax rates suggested by the recent study on wealth inequality by (Piketty, 2014) is between 5% to 6%. Based on the income and wealth tax boundaries explained above, it is possible to determine the optimal combination of income and wealth tax rates that generates more revenues than the actual tax collections, which includes direct and indirect tax and stamp duties.

It is noted also that the proposed tax structure provides for a threshold of minimum income, above which tax payment becomes compulsory. This is similar to the concept of *nisab* in *zakah*.[123] The definition of this minimum threshold is based on various benchmarks including the United Nation's absolute poverty line and the revised estimates of the poverty line income (PLI) by the Malaysia Economic Planning Unit and the Malaysia Human Development Report (2013).[124]

4.3 Simulation of Government Expenditures Based on Risk-Sharing Financing Modes

The proposed tax structure allows for deficits to be financed by the EPS, which are backed by government development projects instead of interest-bearing bonds. The interest payments and hence government spending can be therefore adjusted to the extent of the reduced amounts of borrowing. Since the return on EPS investment depends on the return on the portfolio of government development projects, no costs accrue to the government out of the EPS issuances. The following equations represent the functions of government expenditures and EPS issuance, respectively:

$$G_t = G_{Dv} + G_{Op} \tag{3}$$

$$EPS = G_{Dv} + (G_{Op} - T) \tag{4}$$

122 With reference to the Inland Revenue Authority of Singapore, it is noted that the 10% tax rate is the general property tax rate in Singapore. The property tax is also applied on owner occupied residential property but at a progressive rate that ranges from 0% to 16% depending on the annual value of the property.

123 *Nisab* means the minimum amount of property or wealth that must be owned by a Muslim before he/she is obligated for *zakah*. It is also defined as a measurement that determines the obligation for paying *zakah*.

124 The PLI is defined as the income necessary to buy a group of foods necessary to meet the nutritional needs of household. The income is also sufficient to meet other basic necessities such as clothing, rent, fuel and utilities, transport and communications, medical expenses, education and recreation.

where G_{Dv} denotes government development expenditures, G_{Op} its operating expenditures excluding interest payments with $G_{Op} > T$. Therefore, the new government expenditures can be derived as follows:

$$NGG_t = G_t - EPS + r_t\, D_{t-1} \tag{5}$$

where $r_t\, D_{t-1}$ is the interest on government debts, D.

The empirical tests of fiscal sustainability can be conducted under different scenarios, where the existing fiscal conditions are reflected by R and GG (Scenario 1), a reformed tax structure based on a flat tax system, represented by NR and GG (Scenario 2), government financing policy based on interest-free financing, represented by R and NGG (Scenario 3), and flat rate system and interest-free government financing policy, represented by NR and NGG (Scenario 4), where R and NR are the actual and simulated government revenues, respectively. G is government expenditure (excluding interest payments), and GG (NGG) represent the actual (simulated) government expenditures including interest payments ($G_t + r_t D_{t-1}$).

4.4 Econometric Analysis of Fiscal Sustainability

For the purpose of the present empirical tests, fiscal sustainability is defined in terms of the government's ability to raise enough revenues to meet current and future financial obligations in the absence of debt-default and major modifications in current taxation and spending policies.

Fiscal sustainability is assessed by using the sustainability index and simulated data based on the proposed fiscal framework. It is possible to corroborate the results of the above tests using unit-root tests. These tests are followed by the examination of cointegration relationships between R and GG, to test for the sustainability of existing fiscal conditions; between NR and NGG, to test the sustainability of a proposed fiscal framework based on a flat tax system and an interest-free government financing; between R and NGG, to test for the effects of the proposed government financing policy on fiscal sustainability; and between GG and NR, to test for the effect of the proposed tax structure on fiscal sustainability. The dynamic OLS modelling is applied to determine the long-run relationship between the above variables. It is also possible to address the question of whether the proposed fiscal framework is associated with larger impact on the economy by comparing the results of the dynamic regression model under R and GG framework with the model estimation for NR and NGG under the proposed fiscal framework. Thus, the analysis allows for the assessment of the merits of the fiscal sustainability under the reformed fiscal framework (scenario 4) against the existing fiscal framework (scenario 1), thereby providing some evidence on the potential impact of fiscal and monetary policies devised for Islamic economics.

The Engle-Granger regression equation can be expressed as follows:

$$R_t = \alpha + \beta_1 GG_t + \mu_t \tag{6}$$

Previous studies including Quintos (1995) and Martin (2000) examine the necessary and sufficient conditions for deficit sustainability by testing whether GG_t and R_t in Equation (6) are cointegrated with $\beta = 1$. In line with the existing literature including (Quintos, 1995; Martin, 2000; Baharumshah and Lau, 2007), strong sustainability is reflected by the constraints of the process and the cointegration between R and GG and between NR and NGG, with the cointegration coefficient $\beta = 1$; weak sustainability is indicated by the cointegration coefficient of $0 < \beta < 1$; there is evidence of unsustainable fiscal position with $\beta \leq 0$. It is noted finally that estimate of $\beta > 1$ is not consistent with fiscal deficit, as it implies that government revenues are growing faster than government expenditure.

The Dynamic Ordinary Least Squares (DOLS) with structural break is used as it derives a more efficient estimates of the cointegration vector than Ordinary Least Squares (OLS) (Stock and Watson 1993). It addresses the possible endogeneity of regressors and small sample bias. Thus, it is to include the dummy variables representing structural breaks and Equation (6) is adjusted as follows:

$$R_t = \alpha + D_f + \beta_1 GG_t + \beta_2 (D_f{}^* GG_t) + \sum_{j=-p} \gamma_j GG_{t-j} + \sum_{j=-p} \delta_j \ (D_f{}^* GG_{t-j}) + \mu_t \tag{7}$$

where D_f is a dummy variable representing structural break and j is the number of leads and lags in the DOLS equation. The Wald procedure is used to test for any restriction on the model following (Miyazaki, 2014). The above tests are applied on the pairs of variables (GG and R), (GG and NR), (NGG and R), as well as, (NGG and NR) with respect to the various scenarios 1 to 4 explained above.

5 Analyzing Evidence

The results of the simulation exercise suggest the tax rates of 21% for income and 5.5% for wealth leading to optimal tax revenues under the proposed fiscal structure. Figure 7.1 describes the new tax revenue stream (NR) under the proposed tax structure against the actual tax revenue (R).

It is clear that that R and NR follow approximately the same trend. However, from the year 2003 onwards, NR increases at a faster rate than R. In the earlier years with lower GDP, less wealth tax could be collected in comparison to the periods with real GDP growth rates between 7% to 10%. The behavior of the new government expenditure (NGG) in relation to the existing government expenditures (GG) is described by Figure 7.2.

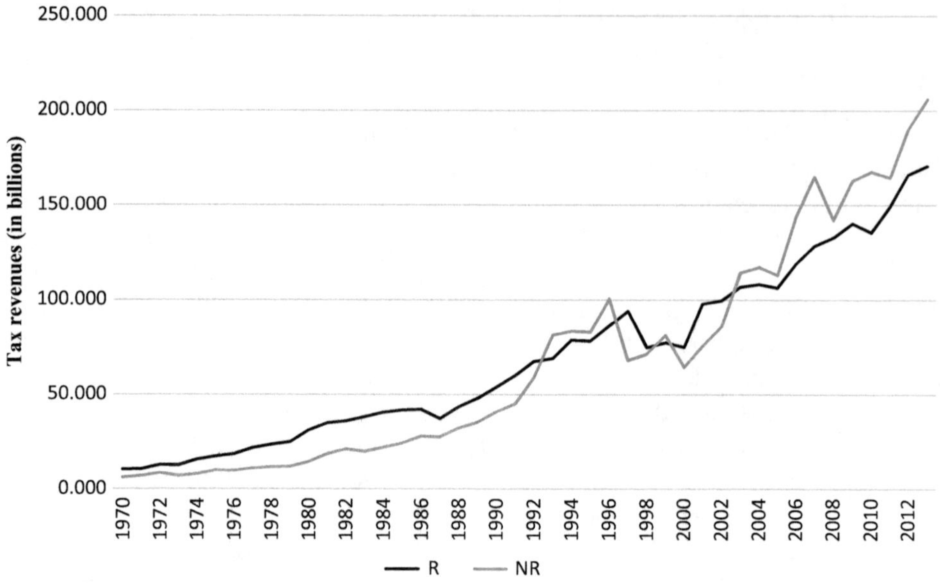

Figure 7.1: Actual and Simulated Tax Revenues.
Source: Author's calculations.

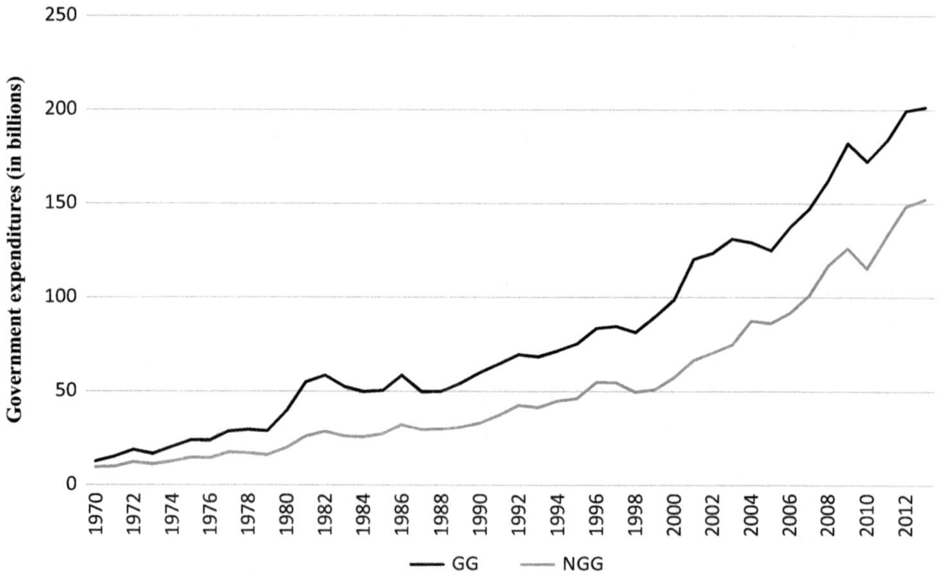

Figure 7.2: Actual and New Government Expenditure.
Source: Author's calculations.

Similar to the government revenues, there is an upward trend for government expenditures under the existing and proposed fiscal framework but it appears that GG is rising at a faster rate than NGG. It seems also that NGG is consistently lower than G. Under the new fiscal structure, the debt burden is progressively reduced as government expenditures are financed through participation from the public and private sectors. It is the financing mechanism based on risk-sharing that explains the lower NGG.

5.1 Index of Fiscal Sustainability

The fiscal sustainability indicator (FSI) can be expressed as follows:

$$FSI_t = (\beta_t - \lambda_t) = \left(\frac{1+r_t}{1+g_t} - \frac{ps_t - ps^*}{d_{t-1} - d^*}\right) \tag{8}$$

where d_t and d^* are the debt-to-GDP ratio and target debt-to-GDP ratio, respectively. The discount factor is represented by β_t and λ_t indicates the intensity of the policy response at time t given the debt-ratio gap in the previous period. The intensity term λ_t is represented by $\frac{ps_t - ps^*}{d_{t-1} - d^*}$, where ps_t is the primary surplus-to-GDP and ps^* is the targeted ratio. The FSI reflects fiscal sustainability when its absolute value is below 1 ($|\beta_t - \lambda_t| < 1$). The FSI is calculated recursively for the period from 1980 to 2013 using the actual and the simulated data.

Table 7.1: Summary of FSI Result and Its Components.

	Existing Fiscal Policy	Proposed Fiscal Policy
	Frequency	
$\beta > \lambda$	41.2%	14.7%
$\lambda < 0$	55.9%	0.09%

Source: Author's calculations.
Note: This table reveals that the instances when the value of β is higher than λ, suggesting a high FSI value, is present in higher frequency under the existing fiscal framework than the proposed framework. A higher λ value indicates an improved fiscal stance, and the instances where the value is lower than 0 (negative figure) thereby increasing the value of FSI is also higher under the existing fiscal framework. In conclusion, the frequency of FSI values greater than unity is higher under the existing fiscal framework.

Figure 7.3 suggests that fiscal policy under the existing fiscal framework is not sustainable. The FSI level moved below unity since 1995 and remained so until the end of the sample period. The bar chart (FSI*) describes the behavior of the FSI on the right side

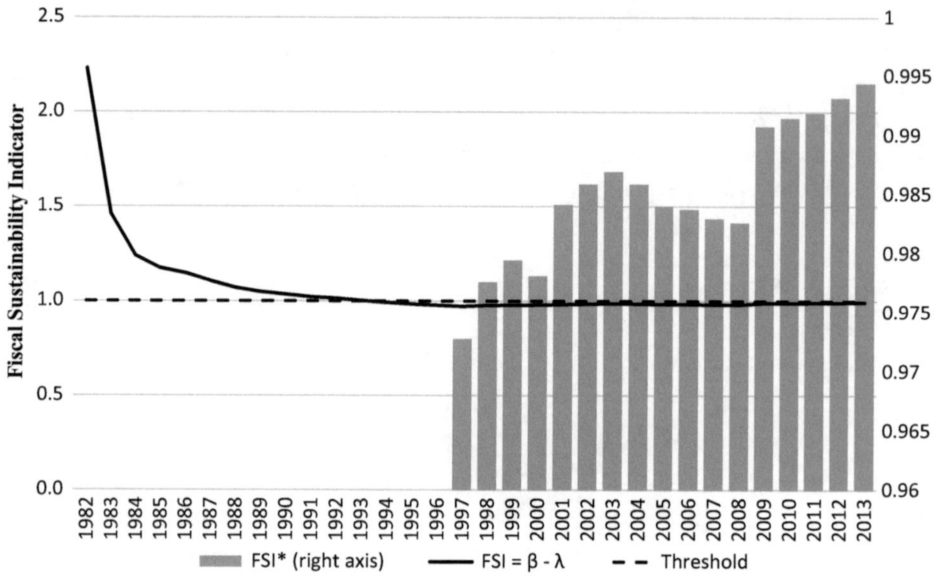

Figure 7.3: Fiscal Sustainability Indicator under Existing Fiscal Policy.
Source: Author's calculations.

from the year 1997 onwards in order to demonstrate that fiscal sustainability is deteriorating as the levels of FSI approach unity. This behavior can be compared to the FSI' under the proposed fiscal framework as shown in Figure 7.4.

It is clear that since 1985, the conditions for fiscal sustainability continue to improve, as shown by the downward trend for FSI values. The comparison of Figures 7.3 and 7.4 indicates that fiscal sustainability position is likely to improve under the proposed fiscal framework rather than the existing one.

5.2 Sustainability Test

The results of stationary tests performed on GG, R, NR and NGG are reported in Table 7.2. Judging from various tests, there is unit root in the levels or evidence of I(0) for the series R, GG, NR and NGG.

According to Hakkio and Rush (1991), if the time series of government expenditures and revenues contain a unit root, then it is possible to look for long-run relationship. Debt would be unsustainable in the absence of long-term relationship. The evidence from Table 7.3 suggests that there is indeed a cointegrating relationship between government expenditures and government revenues in both the actual and simulated data. Therefore, it can be concluded that the fiscal conditions are sustainable under each of the four scenarios mentioned above.

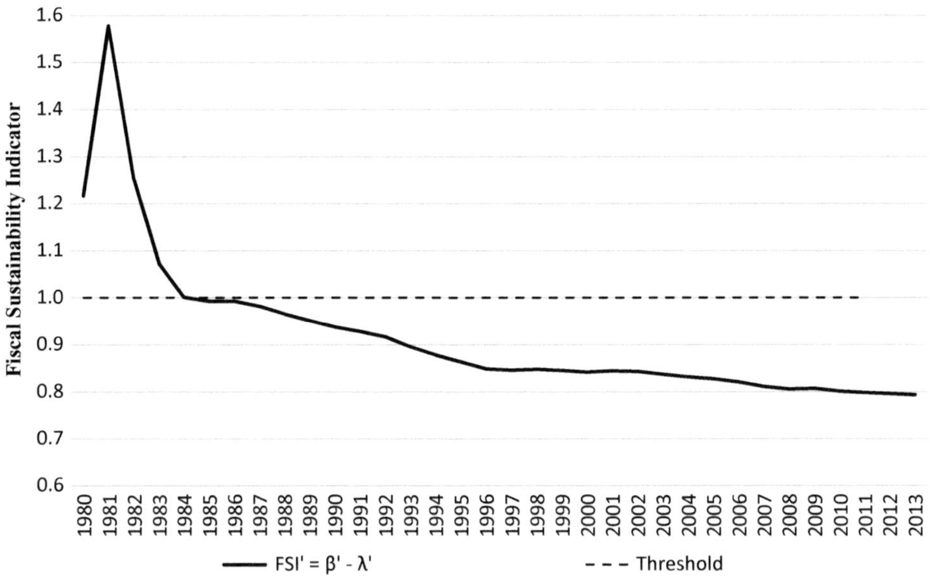

Figure 7.4: Fiscal Sustainability Indicator under Proposed Fiscal Policy.
Source: Author's calculations.

The results presented above are consistent with previous studies by Baharumshah and Lau (2007) and Abdullah, Mustafa, and Dahalan (2012). The sustainability index is indicative of fiscal sustainability under the current framework, but the tendency is weakening. The more recent FSI levels indicate that high debts and persistent deficits may not be sustainable in the long run. There is a rich literature about the effects of debt on the economy including (Arcand, Berkes, and Panizza 2015; Baum, Checherita-Westphal, and Rother 2013; Lima, Gaglianone, and Sampaio 2008; Reinhart and Rogoff 2009), inter alia. The evidence lends support to the proposition that the increasing debt levels in Malaysia affects the primary surplus and debt ratio, and are conducive to the deterioration of the fiscal conditions. (Baum, Checherita-Westphal, and Rother 2013) suggest that there is a positive short-run impact of debt on GDP growth. This positive impact fades away as the debt to GDP ratio increases to around 67%. When the debt to GDP ratio exceed 95%, additional debt has negative effects on economic activities as pressure mounts on long term interest rates. The evidence from (Reinhart and Rogoff 2009, 2010) indicates that when debt rises to above 90% of the GDP, a 'tipping point' is reached and economic starts to slow down.

The results of DOLS regressions reported in Table 7.4 suggest that the proposed fiscal framework is likely to ensure fiscal sustainability. The magnitude of the regression coefficients associated with the independent variables is higher under the proposed framework than the existing framework. The improved government revenues

Table 7.2: Results of Unit Root and Stationarity Test.

	Level			First Difference				
	ADF	ADF-GLS	PP	Z-A	ADF	ADF-GLS	PP	Z-A
GG	−0.812(0)	−0.936(0)	−0.426(6)	−2.538(0) [2006]	−4.755***(3)	−6.318***(0)	−6.829***(12)	−6.155***(3) [1987]
R	−1.399(0)	−1.457(0)	−1.045(7)	−2.939(0) [2006]	−4.944***(3)	−5.094***(3)	−10.344***(18)	−5.917***(3) [1998]
NGG	2.332(9)	−1.218(9)	3.393(42)	−0.147(2) [2006]	−7.413***(1)	−7.435***(1)	−9.518***(33)	−8.809***(1) [2001]
NR	−0.848(3)	−1.237(3)	−1.059(4)	−2.293(3) [2006]	−3.609**(5)	−3.099*(2)	−8.562***(3)	−4.921*(5) [1997]

Source: Author's calculations.

Note: Unit root tests for actual government revenue and expenditure and the simulated government revenue and expenditure. Sample period is from 1970 to 2013. All tests include intercept and linear trend (except Z-A test with only intercept). Asterisks *,**,*** denote level of significance at 10%, 5% and 1% respectively. Figures in ( ) are the lag length and the figures in [ ] are the break point for Z-A test. Except for *NGG*, which uses the Schwarz Information Criterion (SIC), the lag length is chosen using Akaike Information Criterion (AIC) for the ADF and ADF-GLS tests by setting the maximum lag length as nine, and the Newey-West Bandwidth using Bartlett Kernel for the PP test. The maximum lag length for all variables set for the Z-A test is eight with the exception of maximum lag length of two for *NG*. The asymptotic and finite sample critical values for ADF and PP tests is obtained from Mackinnon, (1996) and from Elliot, Rothenberg, & Stock, (1996) for ADF-GLS test.

Table 7.3: Results of Johansen Cointegration Test.

Null	Alternative	Test Statistics			
Hypothesis (*GG* and *R*)		**Critical Value**		**Critical Value**	
H_0	H_1	**Trace**	**5%**	**Max-Eigen**	**5%**
$r=0$	$r\geq1$	23.1108**	20.2618	16.5054**	15.8921
$r\leq1$	$r=2$	6.6055	9.1645	6.6055	9.1645
Hypothesis (*GG* and *NR*)		**Critical Value**		**Critical Value**	
H_0	H_1	**Trace**	**5%**	**Max-Eigen**	**5%**
$r=0$	$r\geq1$	30.2838**	20.26184	22.5271**	15.8921
$r\leq1$	$r=2$	7.7566	9.16455	7.7566	9.16455
Hypothesis (*R* and *NGG*)		**Critical Value**		**Critical Value**	
H_0	H_1	**Trace**	**5%**	**Max-Eigen**	**5%**
$r=0$	$r\geq1$	34.4363**	20.2618	28.8725**	15.8921
$r\leq1$	$r=2$	5.5639	9.1645	5.5639	9.14555
Hypothesis (*NGG* and *NR*)		**Critical Value**		**Critical Value**	
H_0	H_1	**Trace**	**5%**	**Max-Eigen**	**5%**
$r=0$	$r\geq1$	32.5759	20.2618	25.6436**	15.8921
$r\leq1$	$r=2$	6.9324**	9.16455	6.9324	9.16455

Source: Author's calculations.
Note: Cointegration tests for actual government revenue and expenditure and the simulated government revenue and expenditure. Sample period is from 1970 to 2013.
The test assumes no deterministic trend in the data but include an intercept. Asterisks ** indicates rejection of the hypothesis at the 5% significance level. The lag length is one for *GG* and *R*, three for *NGG* and *R* and *NGG* and *NR* based on sequential modified LR test statistics for all cases, and four for *GG* and *NR* based on AIC.

and expenditures under the proposed fiscal framework contributes toward the reduction of budget deficits. Therefore, these are strong economic incentives to reform fiscal policy through changes in the tax structure and risk-sharing finance.

6 Conclusion and Policy Recommendations

The simulation results reported in this study indicate that risk-sharing finance can play a significant role in the conduct of macroeconomic policies. The traditional fiscal policies are conducive to side effects, such as chronic inflation in the financial system and can generate instability. There is indeed clear evidence of increasing total debt

Table 7.4: Results of Dynamic OLS Estimation with Structural Break.

Lags & Leads	Dependent Variable	R				NR			
	Independent Variable	β_1	β_2	**Wald statistics**	$\bar{R}^2$	β_3	β_4	**Wald statistics**	$\bar{R}^2$
1	***GG***	0.7322*** (0.0433)	−0.0068 (0.1579)	157.3189***	0.9812				
2	***GG***	0.7709*** (0.0707)	−0.0473 (0.2473)	53.3410***	0.9776				
3	***GG***	0.8884*** (0.0657)	−0.2713 (2.0959)	74.8976***	0.9822				
1	***NGG***					1.3962*** (0.1708)	0.7099 (0.3556)	48.1492***	0.9570
2	***NGG***					1.0785*** (0.2780)	0.7970 (0.4577)	14.1144***	0.9571
3	***NGG***					0.8864 (0.6952)	0.7999 (0.7532)	14.6294***	0.9739

Source: Author's calculations.

Note: The coefficients for the leading and lagged values of GG_t, $D_{f1}{\star}GG_t$, NGG_t and $D_{f2}{\star}NGG_t$ are not shown for brevity. A constant term and D_{f1} and D_{f2} are included in the regression equation (results not shown as the coefficients are not significant). Figures in brackets represent standard errors. Asterisks *** indicates significance at 1%.

The above shows the results for scenario 1 (R-GG) and scenario 4 (NR-NGG).

relative to global GDP and a decoupling of the financial and real sectors. The decoupling is proceeding unabated and macroeconomic policies are unable to reverse this dichotomy or even to attenuate the impact of adverse economic and financial trends. On the social and environmental aspects, income and wealth distribution across the world are worsening and environmental degradation is rather intensifying. These developments have given rise to regime uncertainty with growing doubts regarding the efficacy and sustainability of the prevailing economic and financial paradigm. There is stronger awareness among many scholars and policy-makers that the interest-based debt system is an important source of economic and financial instability (see for example, (King 2015; Reinhart and Rogoff 2009; Turner 2015). Solutions offered cover the spectrum ranging from the switching of monetary regimes from debt to equity-based policies. (Stiglitz 2015) suggests the renegotiation of social contracts to completely overhaul the system of economic governance. It may be argued that these proposals fall short of addressing the core issue of the interest mechanism, which is regarded by (Keynes 1936) as the "villain of the piece".

The literature suggests that the main factors contributing to the making of financial crises include low interest rates, high liquidity which can incentivize increased default risk, financial innovation and weak regulation. It is this structure of incentives that encourages excessive risk-taking in search of higher yields. This set of incentives is based on the preference for debt over equity. This preference manifests in the tax advantage for debt and in the legal and administrative structures that tend to protect creditors against the violation of debt contracts but offer little protection to equity holders. Thus, debt gives the tendency for risk-shifting to tax payers through bailouts of financial institutions at times of financial crises.

Thus, there is a need for the development of a comprehensive and dynamic regulatory framework based on the risk-sharing principle underlying the Islamic financial system. The incentive system is inclusive of strong restrictions inclusive of prohibited behavior and encouraging desirable conduct. The framework needs to be comprehensive, covering all financial transactions, instruments and institutions without exception. It should have sufficient built-in flexibility and dynamism to allow stay ahead of the innovation curve and minimize the risk of regulatory arbitrage.

Compliance with the prescribed rules of behavior reduces uncertainty and promotes collective action via cooperation. The rules governing transactions should promote trustworthiness, truthfulness, faithfulness to the terms and conditions of agreements and transparency. These conditions create a dynamic and strong economy where information flows are unhindered, and participants engage in transactions confidently. The internalization of the rules of behavior by individuals and institutions also reduces the levels of uncertainty and ambiguity in decision-making, and promotes cooperation and coordination, which reduces transaction costs. The problems of information asymmetry can thus be reduced leading to higher efficiency and stronger economic growth. Given the prevailing deficit in trust, ethics, and morality, the stability of the financial system and well-being of society will hinge on the restoration of trust, rebuilding of social capital, and strengthening of institutions. Risk-sharing has the ability to strengthen social solidarity by enhancing cooperation among economic agents. While the specific financial innovations and failures of regulation that contributed to the credit crunch were new, the underlying macroeconomic warning signs were familiar from many previous crises in the past.

The issuance of equity participation shares (EPS) allows for broader public participation in economic activity with returns closely tied to the real economy. The purpose is to tap on idle funds and generate higher returns than savings rates. This thereby transforms the existing role of financial intermediation where savings are converted into high return instruments with minimum reward for the depositors. The EPS can also be regarded as a financial instrument useful in conduct of monetary policy. The EPS are tradable in secondary market and the level of the liquidity in the economy can thus be adjusted through purchase and selling that can have a more immediate effect than usual interest rate transmission mechanism underlying conventional monetary policies. The expansion in money supply through EPS channels is more likely to lead to increase in real production and thus employment and income. This important feature makes monetary policy far more potent together with a transformed fiscal framework. The use of EPS as a monetary policy instrument provide an interest free alternative to standard macroeconomic policies.

The EPS schemes promote financial inclusion as more equitable opportunities to access the wealth of the nation are provided to all segments of the society regardless of status and income levels. The positive distribution of income to participating stakeholders would in turn reduce the oligopolistic nature of rent seekers and riskless financial intermediation. The real challenge lies in the difficulties to steer off the path dependency resulting from the traditional reliance on the interest-based financial system. It is important to demonstrate the potential benefits of an alternative system that promotes risk-sharing, financial stability, and sustainable economic growth in order to gain acceptance.

References

Abdullah, Hussin, Muszafarshah Mohd Mustafa, and Jauhari Dahalan. 2012. "An Empirical Study on Fiscal Sustainability in Malaysia." *International Journal of Academic Research in Business and Social Sciences* 2(1): 72–90.

Arcand, Jean Louis, Enrico Berkes, and Ugo Panizza. 2015. "Too Much Finance?" *Journal of Economic Growth* 20(2): 105–48.

Arghyrou, Michael G., and Kul B. Luintel. 2007. "Government Solvency: Revisiting Some EMU Countries." *Journal of Macroeconomics* 29(2): 87–410.

Baharumshah, Ahmad Zubaidi, and Evan Lau. 2007. "Regime Changes and the Sustainability of Fiscal Imbalance in East Asian Countries." *Economic Modelling* 24(6): 878–94.

Bajo-Rubio, Oscar, Carmen Díaz-Roldán, and Vicente Esteve. 2010. "On the Sustainability of Government Deficits: Some Long-Term Evidence for Spain, 1850–2000." *Journal of Applied Economics* 13(2): 263–81.
Bank Negara Malaysia. 2013. *Monthly Statistical Report, no. 3*. Kuala Lumpur.
Baum, Anja, C Checherita-Westphal, and Philipp Rother. 2013. "Debt and Growth: New Evidence for the Euro Area." *Journal of International Money and Finance* 32: 809–21.
Department of Statistics Malaysia. 2014. *"Annual Report."* Malaysia.
Elliot, Graham, Thomas J Rothenberg, and James H Stock. 1996. "Efficient Tests for Autoregressive Unit Root." *Econometrica* 64(4): 813–36.
Escario, Regina, María Dolores Gadea, and Marcela Sabaté. 2012. "Multicointegration, Seigniorage and Fiscal Sustainability. Spain 1857–2000." *Journal of Policy Modeling* 34(2): 270–83.
Goyal, Rajan, J.K Khundrakpam, and Partha Ray. 2004. "Is India's Public Finance Unsustainable? Or, Are the Claims Exaggerated?" *Journal of Policy Modeling* 26(3): 401–20.
Hakkio, Craig S, and Mark Rush. 1991. "Is the Budget Deficit 'Too Large'?" *Economic Enquiry* 29: 425–29.
Keynes, John Maynard. 1936. *The General Theory of Employment, Interest and Money. The General Theory of Employment*. London: Macmillan.
Khalid, Muhammed Abdul. 2011. "Household Wealth in Malaysia: Composition and Inequality among Ethnic Groups." *Jurnal Ekonomi Malaysia* 45: 71–80.
Khalid, Muhammed Abdul. 2014. *The Colour of Inequality*. Kuala Lumpur, Malaysia: MPH Group Publishing Sdn Bhd.
King, Mervyn. 2015. *The End of Alchemy – Money, Banking and the Future of the Global Economy*. Little, Borwn.
Lima, Luiz Renato, Wagner Piazza Gaglianone, and R. M B Sampaio. 2008. "Debt Ceiling and Fiscal Sustainability in Brazil: A Quantile Autoregression Approach." *Journal of Development Economics* 86(2): 313–35.
Mackinnon, James G. 1996. "Numerical Distribution Functions for Unit Root and Cointegration Tests." *Journal of Applied Econometrics* 11(6): 601–18.
Martin, Gael M. 2000. "US Deficit Sustainability: A New Approach Based on Multiple Endogenous Breaks." *Journal of Applied Econometrics* 15(1): 83–105.
Mirakhor, Abbas, and Noureddine Krichene. 2009. "The Recent Crisis: Lessons for Islamic Finance." *Journal of Islamic Economics, Banking and Finance* 5(1): 9–58.
Miyazaki, Tomomi. 2014. "Fiscal Reform and Fiscal Sustainability: Evidence from Australia and Sweden." *International Review of Economics and Finance* 33: 141–51.
Omar, Mohd Azmi, Azman Md Noor, and Ahamed Kameel Mydin Meera. 2010. "Islamic Pricing Benchmark." *International Shari'ah Research Academy for Islamic Finance Research Paper* 16: 1–85.
Othman, Azura, Norhanim Mat Sari, Syed Othman Alhabshi, and Abbas Mirakhor. 2017. *Macroeconomic Policy and Islamic Finance in Malaysia*. New York, NY, USA: Palgrave Macmillan.
Othman, Azura, and Abbas Mirakhor. 192013. "Islam and Development: Policy Challenges." In *Economic Development and Islamic Finance*, edited by Zamir Iqbal and Abbas Mirakhor. Washington D.C.: World Bank Group.
Piketty, Thomas. 2014. *Capital in the Twenty-First Century*. Cambridge: Harvard University Press.
Quintos, Carmela E. 1995. "Sustainability of the Deficit Process with Structural Shifts." *Journal of Business and Economic Statistics* 13(4): 409–17.
Reinhart, Carmen M, and Kenneth S. Rogoff. 2009. *This Time Is Different: Eight Centuries of Financial Follies*. Princeton, N.J.: Princeton University Press.

Reinhart, Carmen M, and Kenneth S. Rogoff. 2010. "Growth in a Time of Debt." NBER Working Paper 15639, National Bureau of Economic Research, Cambridge, MA.

Salih, Kamal, Lee Hwok-Aun, and Muhammed Abdul Khalid. 2014. "Malaysian Human Development Report 2013 – Redesigning an Inclusive Future." Malaysia.

Stiglitz, Joseph E. 2015. *The Great Divide: Unequal Societies and What We Can Do About Them*. New York: W.W.Norton & Company, Inc.

Stock, James H, and Mark W Watson. 1993. "A Simple Estimation of Cointegrating Vectors in Higher Order Integrated Systems." *Econometrica* 61: 783–820.

The World Bank. n.d. *"The World Bank Open Data."* available at https://data.worldbank.org/country/malaysia

Turner, Adair. 2015. *Between Debt and the Devil: Money, Credit, and Fixing Global Finance*. Princeton, N.J.: Princeton University Press.

Valuation and Property Services Department Malaysia. 2014. *"Property Market Report."* Malaysia.

Part III: Microeconomic Modelling of Asset Prices and Equity Portfolio Analysis

Belal Ehsan Baaquie, Nabil ElMaghrebi

Chapter 8: Statistical Microeconomic Modelling of Asset Prices: Some Perspectives from Islamic Finance and Economics

1 Statistical Microeconomics

The theory of commodity pricing is one of the foundations of economic theory and applications. A mathematical model is proposed, from first principles and based on the formalism of statistical physics, for describing the prices of commodities. Both spot and futures prices are analyzed. The calibration and predictions of the model, based on market data, provide strong evidence in support of the model.

Consider the behavior of market prices. As can be seen from Figure 8.1, the price of silver and gold appear to have a random time evolution. Furthermore, the two prices seem to be positively correlated; in contrast, the price of gold and oil seem to be negatively correlated. Market data seems to indicate that commodity prices are stochastic variables, and it is this feature of market prices that leads to its statistical modelling. Statistical microeconomics takes the commodity prices as random stochastic processes, and in particular, aims to explain the auto- and cross-correlation of commodity prices.

The price of the commodity for one unit of quantity $\hat{q}_i$ is denoted by $\hat{P}_i$. The market price of a commodity – denoted by p_i – is defined to be independent of the unit of quantity, and given by

$$P_i = \hat{P}_i \hat{q}_i; i = 1,\ 2, \cdots,\ N$$

It is noted that all commodity market prices are positive $P_i > 0,\ i = 1,\ 2,\ \cdots,\ N$ and are postulated to be classical random variables undergoing a continuous stochastic process. All observed prices are random samples of the random prices. All the information about prices, including their dynamics, is contained in an action functional $\mathcal{A}$, that is given, similar to statistical mechanics, by

$$\mathcal{A} = -\int_{-\infty}^{+\infty} dt \mathcal{L}(t) = \int_{-\infty}^{+\infty} dt(\mathcal{T} + \mathcal{V})$$

Acknowledgements: The authors thank Professor Emmanuel Haven and Professor Sandro Sozzo for many stimulating discussions as well as their kind hospitality at the Institute for Quantum Social and Cognitive Science. They would like also to thank Dr Sudip Patra for many useful discussions.

https://doi.org/10.1515/9783110587920-008

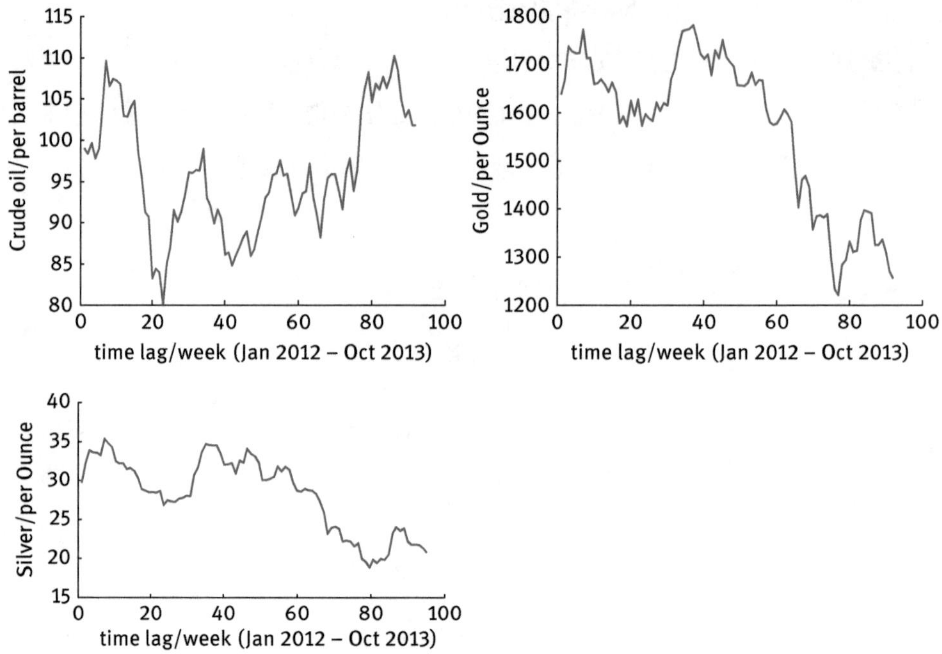

Figure 8.1: Weekly Prices of Oil, Gold and Silver.
Source: Authors' calculations.
Note: The sample periods extends from Jan 8, 2012 to Oct 13, 2013.

where $\mathcal{L}(t)$ is the *Lagrangian* for commodity prices. $\mathcal{T}$, in analogy with mechanics, is the 'kinetic term' determining the time dependence of commodity prices and $\mathcal{V}$ is the 'potential' determining the equilibrium properties.

The action functional determines the probability distribution function of the prices given by the Boltzmann distribution $e^{-\mathcal{A}}$. The statistical theory is defined by the Feynman path integral

$$Z = \int Dx\, exp\{-\mathcal{A}[x]\} = \prod_{-\infty}^{+\infty} \int dx(t) exp\{-\mathcal{A}[x]\}$$

where the commodity price is $P = p_0 e^x$.

The fundamental question is what are $\mathcal{T}$ and $\mathcal{V}$ for commodities.

2 Microeconomic Potential $\mathcal{V}$: Supply and Demand

The demand $\mathcal{D}$ determines consumption and supply function $\mathcal{S}$ determines production. Supply and demand have the same dimension and hence can be unified into a single entity by adding them – to yield the microeconomic potential defined by

$$\mathcal{V} = \mathcal{D} + \mathcal{S}$$

For a single commodity, the microeconomic potential, as shown in Figure 8.2, is postulated to be given by

$$\mathcal{V} = \frac{1}{2}\left[\frac{\tilde{d}}{P^a} + \tilde{s}P^b\right] = \frac{1}{2}\left[de^{-ax} + sde^{bx}\right] \tag{1}$$

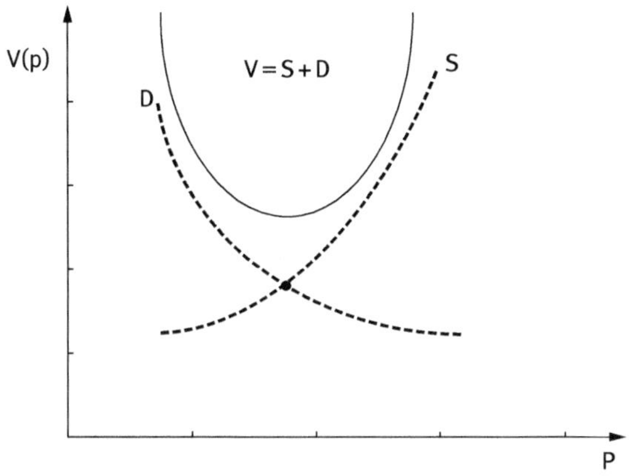

Figure 8.2: Supply and Demand for One Commodity.
Source: Authors' calculations.

It is noted that market prices provide strong support for the assumed form of the microeconomic potential. The limiting behavior of the potential given in Equation 1 is described by

$$\mathcal{V} = \begin{cases} d/P^a, \ P \approx 0: \mathcal{D}: \textit{demand function} \\ sP^b, \ P \gg 1: \mathcal{S}: \textit{supply function} \end{cases}$$

Due to the competing behavior of supply and demand, namely supply rises and demand falls with increasing prices, it is guaranteed that the microeconomic potential $\mathcal{V}$ will always have a minimum.

The microeconomic potential $\mathcal{V}$ can also have multiple minima, as shown in Figure 8.3. This allows one to model the change of price by the tunnelling of the equilibrium price from one minimum to another. For such cases of the microeconomic potential, the break-up of $\mathcal{V}$ into $\mathcal{D}$ and $\mathcal{S}$ is only asymptotic. From Figure 8.3, it is expected that the price will 'tunnel' from p_1 to $p_2 > p_1$.

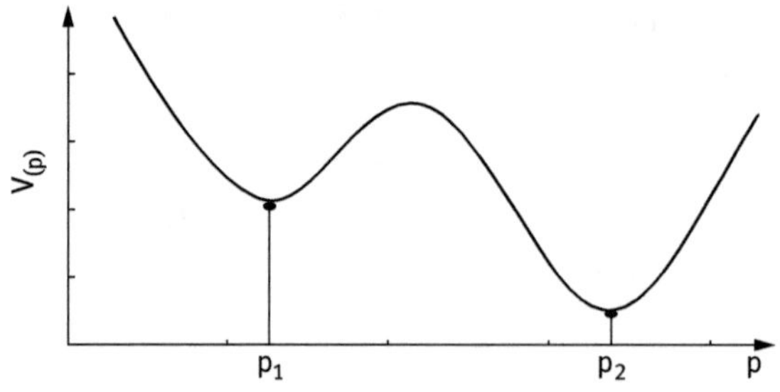

Figure 8.3: Microeconomic Potential with Multiple Minima.
Source: Authors' calculations.

As with Figure 8.2, it is possible to describe the supply and demand functions of price for two commodities as shown in Figure 8.4. The right-side figure presents the intersection line between the supply and demand surfaces shown separately. The microeconomic potential described by the left-side figure reflects the unique minimum for the set of two commodity prices as indicated by the point at the surface bottom.

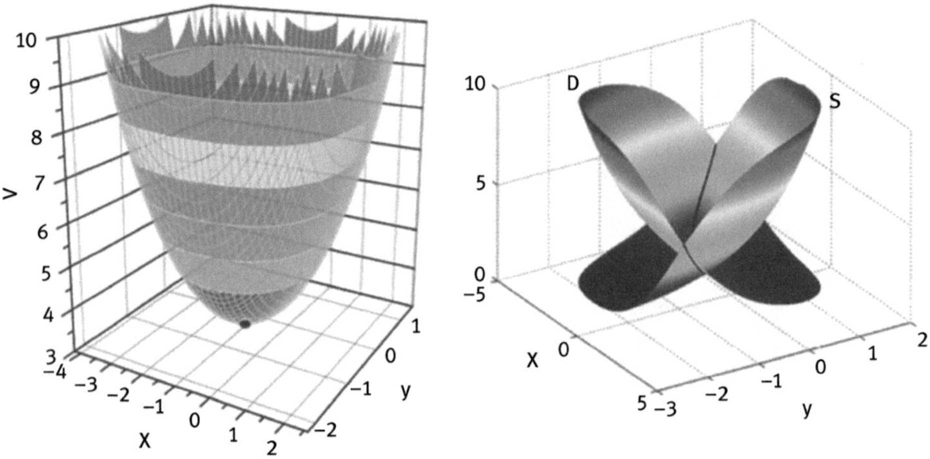

Figure 8.4: Prices for Two Commodities.
Source: Authors' calculations.
Note: Figure on the left shows the microeconomic potential and on the right shows supply and demand surfaces drawn separately for two commodities.

It is noted that since the dynamics of market prices depend on economic information, the microeconomic potential is also conditional on the available set of information. The formation of price expectations is affected by the nature of risk factors such as supply and income shocks, variations in output and employment, and changing inflation expectations. From the perspective of Islamic finance and economics, the focus is made on the distribution of risks and the role of risk-sharing in absorbing shocks and the determination of equilibrium prices according to competitive market forces. Prices should not be governed by risk-transfer relations or predetermined ex ante. Thus, the microeconomic potential should be reflective of the interaction between production and consumption within a competitive exchange economy based on risk-sharing relations.

3 Market Prices: Minimizing Microeconomic Potential

Statistical microeconomics is based on a fundamental change of paradigm from standard microeconomics, as explained in various references including Varian (1992), inter alia. To obtain the equilibrium price, the prices need to be time independent and yield $\partial x/\partial t = 0$. In statistical microeconomics, the equilibrium market price P_0 is determined by the minimum of the microeconomic potential. For N-commodities, minimizing the potential yields the market price P_0 such that

$$\frac{\partial \mathcal{V}(P_0)}{\partial P} = 0 \Rightarrow \frac{\partial \mathcal{D}(P_0)}{\partial P} = -\frac{\partial \mathcal{S}(P_0)}{\partial P}$$

For a single commodity with potential given by Equation (1), minimizing the potential yields

$$\mathcal{D} = \frac{1}{2}\frac{d}{P^a};\ \mathcal{S} = \frac{1}{2}sP^b \Rightarrow P_0 = \left(\frac{ad}{bs}\right)^{1/(a+b)}$$

In contrast, standard microeconomics requires supply equal to demand for the equilibrium price. Hence

$$Supply = Demand \Rightarrow \mathcal{S}(P^*) = \mathcal{D}(P^*) \Rightarrow P^* = \left(\frac{d}{s}\right)^{1/(a+b)} \neq P_0$$

The potential for multiple commodities couples commodities with vastly different prices, such as wheat and gold. Our empirical analysis shows that the market prices cannot be directly coupled for an effective modeling of multiple commodities. Instead, to compare different commodities, one needs to define normalized commodity prices. Let P_i be the prices of commodities; normalized commodity prices y_i are given by

$$P_i = p_{0i}e^{x_i},\ i = 1,\ \cdots, N;\ y_i = \frac{x_i - \bar{x}_i}{\sigma(x_i)}$$

where the average price is $E(x_i) = \bar{x}_i$ and volatility is $E(x_i^2) - \bar{x}_i^2 = \sigma^2(x_i)$.

Our studies show that the correlation of the commodity prices is encoded in a cross-commodity potential term, governed by parameters Δ_{ij}. The cross-correlator term is neither supply nor demand; the full potential for N commodities is given by

$$\mathcal{V} = \frac{1}{2}\sum_{i=1}^{N}\left[d_i e^{-a_i y_i} + s_i e^{b_i y_i}\right] + \frac{1}{2}\sum_{i\neq j=1}^{N} \Delta_{ij} y_i y_j$$

The Slutsky's equation relates the effect of change in the price of one commodity on the price of another. However, there seems to be no apparent connection between the Slutsky's equation and the concept of Δ_{ij}. This is because the Slutsky's equation is derived from the properties of the Marshallian and Hicksian demand curves, which are not related to the microeconomic potential (see Varian, 1992).

Minimizing the microeconomic potential depends on the dynamic properties of the demand and supply functions. Short-selling activities have also implications for the microeconomic potential. It may be argued that short-selling facilitates price discovery and market efficiency. In contrast, short-sales may be regarded as market transactions leading to increased volatility and weaker investor confidence particularly during periods of financial instability.

Short-sales are associated with selling pressures leading to increased supply in the first phase of asset borrowing, and with buying pressures leading to increased demand during the second and final phase of purchasing and returning the asset. It is clear that the selling and buying pressures can affect the microeconomic potential. The minimization of this potential is function of the source of selling and buying pressures and restrictions on short selling.

From the perspective of Islamic finance and economics, it may be argued that short-selling in impermissible on the basis that possession may not be sufficient for exchange relations. This argument is consistent with the rationale behind the Securities and Exchange Commission SEC Rule 201. The circuit-breaker rule restricts short sales and it is based on a clear distinction between short-sellers and long-sellers with ownership of the asset preceding sale. The uptick rule gives precedence to long sellers over short sellers in selling shares once the circuit breaker is triggered. This rule recognizes the ability of long sellers to sell first, and gives priority to exchange relations based on ownership not mere possession.

Thus, short-sales directly affect the supply and demand functions, and restrictions on short-selling may be useful in reducing or eliminating the distortive effects of sales of borrowed assets on the definition of microeconomic potential. It is the minimization of the microeconomic potential that leads to equilibrium prices, and it is important that supply and demand functions are not artificially inflated with borrowed assets. It may be thus, assumed that the microeconomic potential is defined with respect to a competitive economy driven by exchange relations based on risk-sharing and ownership of real assets and financial assets.

4 Microeconomic Kinetic Term $\mathcal{T}$: Circulation

The kinetic part $\mathcal{T}$ represents circulation, exchange and liquidity of the market. Taking the cue from finance, for a single commodity the kinetic term is given by

$$\mathcal{T} = \frac{1}{2}\left[L\left(\frac{\partial^2 x}{\partial t^2}\right)^2 + \tilde{L}\left(\frac{\partial x}{\partial t}\right)^2\right]$$

The acceleration term $(\partial^2 x/\partial t^2)^2$ does not appear in Newtonian or quantum mechanics and makes the system dissimilar to physics.

The kinetic term for multiple commodities is dictated by the fact that most commodities like wheat, copper, gold, oil and so on have their own markets and their prices change only slightly when the prices of other commodities change. In other words, the prices of other commodities appear as perturbations on the price of a single major commodity. For this reason, it is assumed in this model that all the effects of other commodities are encoded by the cross-term in the microeconomic potential given by Δ_{ij}; and furthermore, it is assumed that the kinetic term of the commodities do not contain any cross-terms. Hence, the kinetic term for N commodities is modeled as follows:

$$\mathcal{T} = \frac{1}{2}\sum_{i=1}^{N}\left[L_i\left(\frac{\partial^2 y_i}{\partial t^2}\right)^2 + \tilde{L}_i\left(\frac{\partial y_i}{\partial t}\right)^2\right]$$

As with the microeconomic potential, it may be argued that short selling has a bearing on the kinetic term as well. Since the kinetic term reflects price evolution over time, short selling in its two inter-dependent phases is bound to affect this process. The significance and timing of selling and buying pressures associated with the short selling process should be understood not only in relation with market conditions and the demand and supply functions. They have direct implications for the stochastic properties and correlation structure, and thus the kinetic term as well. The analysis of short-sales is an illustration of the potential effects of speculative activities and risk-transfer relations. In contrast, it is risk-sharing relations that promote exchange relations in the real economy and financial system, and that should, thus, define the microeconomic action functional leading to equilibrium asset prices.

5 Microeconomic Action and Path Integral

The *Lagrangian* encodes the complete economic cycle

$$\begin{aligned}\mathcal{L} &= \mathcal{T} + \mathcal{V} = \mathcal{S} + \mathcal{T} + \mathcal{D}\\ &= \textit{production} + \textit{exchange} + \textit{consumption}\end{aligned}$$

For N commodities, the acceleration *Lagrangian* $\mathcal{L} = \mathcal{T} + \mathcal{V}$ is given by

$$\mathcal{L}(t) = \frac{1}{2}\sum_{i=1}^{N}\left[L_i\left(\frac{\partial^2 y_i}{\partial t^2}\right)^2 + L_i\left(\frac{\partial y_i}{\partial t}\right)^2\right] + \frac{1}{2}\sum_{i=1}^{N}\left[d_i e^{-a_i y_i} + s_i e^{b_i y_i}\right] + \frac{1}{2}\sum_{i \neq j=1}^{N} \Delta_{ij} y_i y_j$$

The correlation of the different commodities is in the potential term and given by *Δij*, with the kinetic term being a sum of single commodities. The choice of the *Lagrangian* reflects the expectation that the correlation of different commodities $|\Delta_{ij}| < 0.1$, and it affects a particular commodity only perturbatively, changing the parameters of individual markets by about 10%. This expectation is supported by price observations.

Feynman Path Integral. The statistical averaging over all the random values of the price is given by the path integral

$$Z = \prod_{i=1}^{N}\prod_{t=-\infty}^{+\infty}\int_{-\infty}^{+\infty} dy_i(t) e^{-A} \equiv \int \mathcal{D}y e^{-A}$$

All correlation functions of commodities are given by

$$E\left[y_i(t_1) y_j(t_2)\cdots y_k(t_L)\right] = \int Dy\, y_i(t_1) y_j(t_2)\cdots y_k(t_L) e^{-A}$$

Expanding the action $\mathcal{A}$ about $y_i \approx 0$ yields

$$\mathcal{L} = \frac{1}{2}\sum_{i}^{N}\left[L_i\left(\frac{\partial^2 y_i}{\partial t^2}\right)^2 + \widetilde{L}_i\left(\frac{\partial y_i}{\partial t}\right)^2 + \gamma_i y_i^2\right] - \sum_{i \neq j=1}^{N} \Delta_{ij}\, y_i\, y_j + O(y^3)$$

It may be argued that the *Lagrangian* encodes the various phases of the economic cycle insofar that different risk factors that shape patterns in production, exchange and consumption are fully embedded in these functions. These risk s can be either shared or transferred between parties, or otherwise shifted to third parties in the aftermath of economic and financial crises. Risk-sharing and risk-transfer relations can affect the microeconomic action functional in asymmetric ways.

The transfer of risk with interest-bearing debt implies state-independent payoffs given the determination of prices ex ante. In contrast, risk-sharing relations are based on state-contingent payoffs, with asset prices depending on the risks inherent to economic activities and factors affecting production, exchange and consumption. It is important that the prices of assets including commodities and financial securities y_i and cross terms in the microeconomic potential Δ_{ij} can be described as random stochastic variables rather than pre-determined ex ante. Thus, it may be understood that the analysis of the microeconomic action function is underpinned by the assumption that prices are driven by risk-sharing relations in a dynamic exchange economy.

6 Correlation Functions

The correlation function is given by

$$E[y(\tau)y(\tau')] = \frac{1}{Z}\int Dy\, y_I(\tau)y_J(\tau')e^{-\mathcal{A}};\; E[y_I^2(\tau)] = 1$$

The action $\mathcal{A}$ is examined about the equilibrium point of $y_i \approx 0$. The Gaussian path integral yields the following auto-correlation function

$$E[y_I(\tau)y_J(\tau')] = G_I(\tau,\tau') + O(\Delta_{IJ}^2)$$

$$G_I(\tau-\tau') = \frac{exp\{-\omega_I|\tau-\tau'|cos(\theta_I)\}}{sin(\theta_I)} sin[\theta_I + \omega_I|\tau-\tau'|sin(\theta_I)]$$

Fitting the data with $G_I(\tau,\tau')$ yields ω_I, θ_I; hence

$$\gamma_I = \frac{\omega_I}{4cos(\theta_I)} : \text{fixes } \gamma_I;\; \omega_I = \left(\frac{\gamma_I}{L_I}\right)^{\frac{1}{4}} : \text{fixes } L_I$$

and

$$\theta_I = \frac{1}{2}cos^{-1}\left(\frac{\tilde{L}_I}{2\sqrt{\gamma_I L_I}}\right) : fixes\, \tilde{L}_I$$

The cross-commodities correlation function G_{ij}, for $I \neq J$, is given by

$$G_{IJ}(\tau) = \Delta_{IJ}\int_{-\infty}^{\infty} G_I(t)G_J(t-\tau)dt \tag{2}$$

where $G_I(t)$ is the single commodity correlation function given by

$$G_I(t) = E[y_I(0)y_J(t)]$$

An analytic expression has been derived for $G_{II}(\tau)$ that makes the calibration viable. The model gives a very specific expression for the cross-correlator since $G_I(t)$ is the single commodities auto-correlator. There is only one adjustable parameter Δ_{IJ} for a pair of commodities for any lag time t.

To evaluate the microeconomic potential and fully calibrate the model, one needs to evaluate $E[y_I^3(\tau)]$ and $E[y_I^4(\tau)]$. The Gaussian approximation cannot yield a potential that has a minimum; hence, by itself, the Gaussian approximation is not sufficient for model the behavior of commodities.

Hence, it can be concluded that the model is essentially nonlinear.

Market time versus calendar time. In quantum mathematical models of financial and economic instruments, calendar time t is replaced by non-linear market time $z(t)$ defined by

$$z = \lambda \left(\frac{t}{\lambda}\right)^{\eta}; \; \eta < 1; \; \eta\text{: index of market time}$$

As shown in Figure 8.5, future time z flows more slowly than calendar time for $t > \lambda$ and faster for $t < \lambda$.

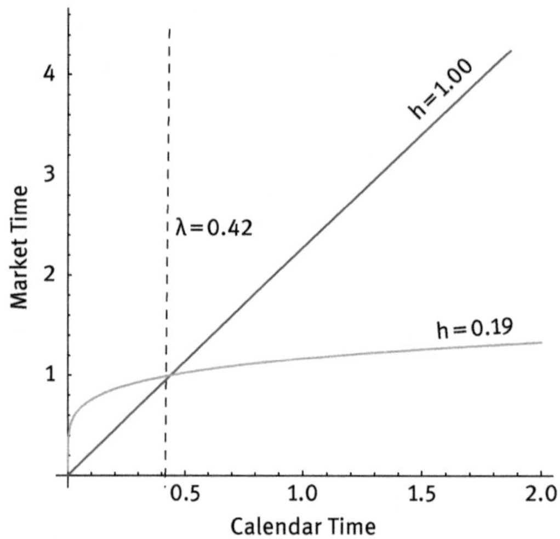

Figure 8.5: Market Future Time $z = \lambda \left(\frac{t}{\lambda}\right)^{\eta}$.
Source: Authors' calculations.
Note: In the figure $\lambda = 0.42$.

7 Empirical Study

The following commodities given in Table 8.1 have been examined in previous work by Baaquie, Yu and Du (2016).

The empirical correlation function $E_{Data}[y_I(0)y_J(\tau)]$ is defined by taking the moving average of data to be equal to the correlation function. More precisely, discretize time so that $= n\in$, $\tau = k\in$ and data is $y_I(t) \to y_I(n)$.

The correlation function $G_{IJ}(\tau) = G_{JI}(\tau)$ in the statistical model for commodity prices is a symmetric function of IJ; to match market data with the model, one needs to explicitly symmetrize the empirical evaluation of the correlation function so as to obtain a symmetric $E_{Data}[y_I(0)y_J(\tau)]$.

Table 8.1: Commodities Examined.

Number	commodity	Type	Number	commodity	Type
1	Crude oil	Energy	10	Cocoa	Food
2	Heating oil		11	Soybeans oil	
3	Brent oil		12	Orange juice	
4	Natural gas		13	Live cattle	
5	Copper	Metal	14	Wheat	Grain
6	Gold		15	Corn	
7	Silver		16	Soybean	
8	Platinum		17	Rough rice	
9	Palladium		18	Cotton	Miscellaneous

Source: Authors' calculations.

Hence, a symmetrized empirical propagator is defined as follows

$$E_{Data}[y_I(0)y_J(\tau)] = \frac{1}{2}\left[\frac{1}{N}\sum_{n=0}^{N-k} y_I(n)y_J(n+k) + \frac{1}{N}\sum_{n=0}^{N-k} y_J(n)y_I(n+k)\right]$$

The model is matched with data as follows

$$E_{Data}[y_I(0)y_J(\tau)] = G_{IJ}(z(\tau));\ z = \lambda\left(\frac{t}{\lambda}\right)^{\eta}$$

Fitting the data with $G_{IJ}(z(\tau))$ yields ω_I, θ_I, Δ_{IJ}, and λ, η, which are independent of I and J.

7.1 Auto-correlators

The empirical and model auto-correlator for oil and copper and natural gas are given in Figure 8.6. The model can accurately fit the data for all single commodities (with $R^2 > 0.95$) for a duration of up to about 300 days. The statistical microeconmics model gives an accurate fit for the oil correlator depending on the regime of the data. For long-duration time lag, there are cases for which the market still shows large fluctuations, as shown for the case of oil in Figure 8.7; these cases cannot be fit by the model's correlation function since the model's correlations become negligible for very long time lag due to exponential damping.

7.2 Microeconomic Potential $\mathcal{V}$ for Oil

The calibration of all the parameters $a, b,\ L$ and γ yields values greater than zero, as expected. The value for $\tilde{L}$ is positive or negative depending on the commodity.

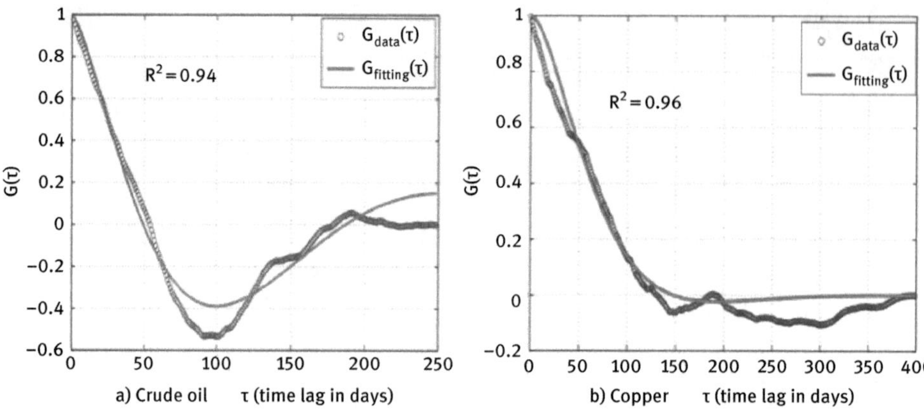

Figure 8.6: Empirical and Model Result for a) oil and b) Copper.
Source: Authors' calculations.

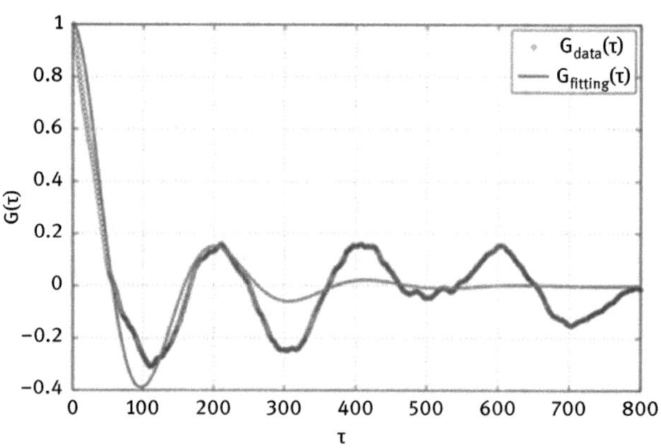

Figure 8.7: Empirical and Model Result, for Oil, for a Time Lag of a Long Duration.
Source: Authors' calculations.

The value of the single commodity parameters is stable when the correlation of other commodities is included since $\Delta_{IJ} < 0.08$ (except for a single cross-correlator).

The shape of the microeconomic potential for crude oil shown in Figure 8.8 is noteworthy. The potential has a wide, deep and almost flat minimum – which is unique – and then a sharp rise of the potential for both very large and very small values of the price. Potential similar to one found for commodities have also been discussed by Haven and Khrennikov (2013). The sharp rise is asymmetric, showing that the buyers, who affect the potential for small values of the price, are driven by considerations different from the potential for high prices – which affects the sellers. One can speculate that the sharp rise in the potential is due to information publicly

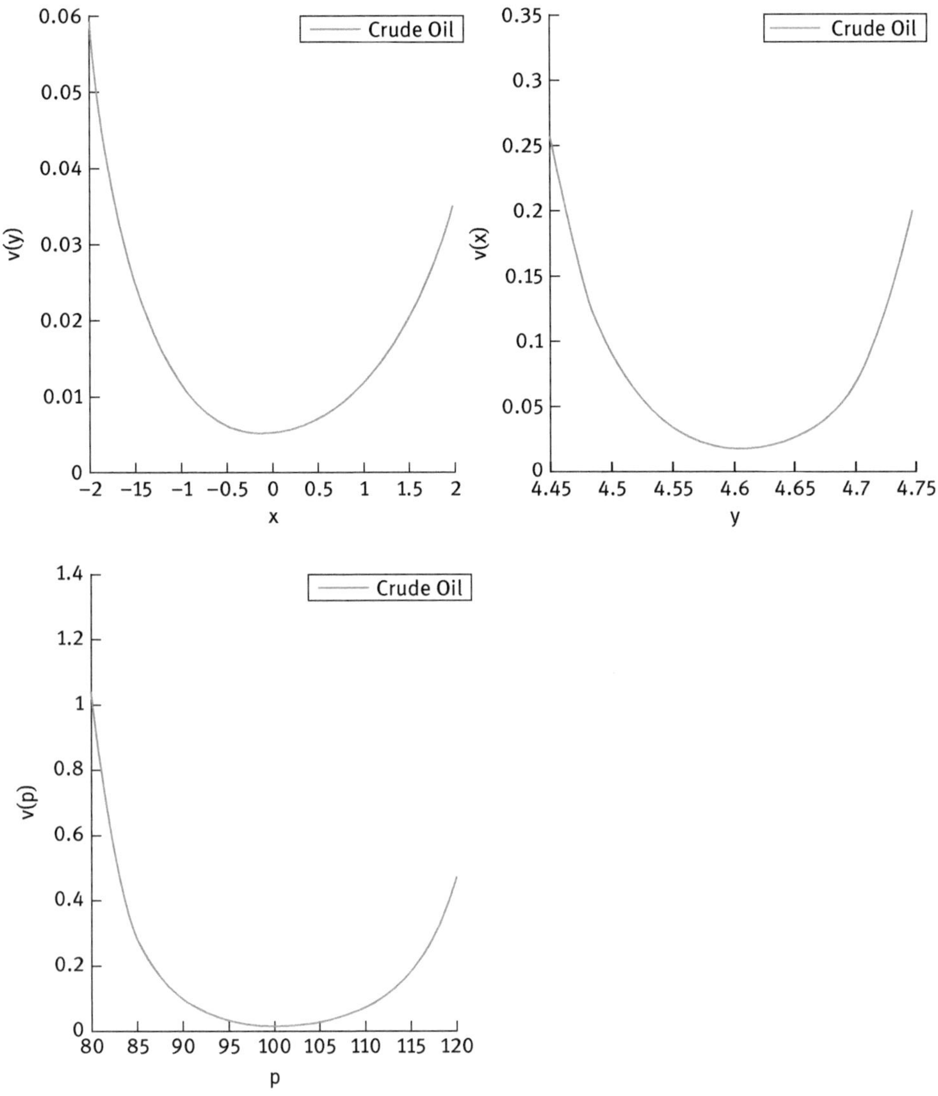

Figure 8.8: Microeconomic Potential of Crude Oil in Terms of $y = (x - \bar{x})/\sigma(x)$, $x = log(p/p_0)$ and Market Price p.
Source: Authors' calculations.

available so that all market players – both buyers and sellers – know the limits of what to expect for the equilibrium price.

The wide and deep valley around the minimum can be attributed to information asymmetry: different market participants are privy to different amounts of information about the price of the commodity and hence are not in agreement as to what should be the equilibrium market price – which determines the minimum of the potential. This leads to wide variations in the price the participants are willing to trade, and reflected in the wide and flat values of the potential around the minimum.

Thus, the dynamics of market prices depend on the set of information available to market participants, and information asymmetries have differential effects on the microeconomic potential and equilibrium prices. As noted earlier with respect to the definition of microeconomic potential, the focus on risk-sharing in Islamic finance and economics is justified on the grounds that it facilitates the absorption of shocks, promotes economic and financial stability, and allows for the determination of equilibrium prices driven by competitive market forces. Thus, the set of available information is important for risk-sharing mechanisms to be effective in the formation of expectations and the optimal distribution of risks in the economy.

7.3 Multiple Commodities Correlation Parameter Δ_{ij}

The values of $|\Delta_{IJ}|$ for 18 commodities is given in Figure 8.9. Since the coupling of two commodities by Δ_{IJ} in the Lagrangian is not a symmetric function of I and J, the evidence from Figure 8.9 is indeed indicative of the expected asymmetry. Commodity prices are mostly positively correlated, with a few being negatively correlated. Note the remarkable fact, that ignoring one value of $|\Delta_{6,17}| = 0.1$, the value of all the $|\Delta_{IJ}| < 0.08$. The fact $|\Delta_{IJ}| < 0.08$ provides strong evidence of the correctness of the approach of considering the multi-commodities model as a perturbation of the single commodities, which requires $|\Delta_{IJ}| \ll 1$.

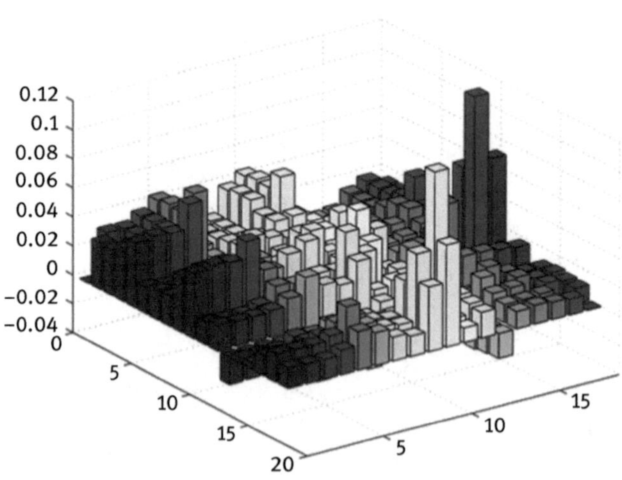

Figure 8.9: Matrix of Δ_{ij} for 18 Commodities $|\Delta_{IJ}| < 0.08$.
Source: Authors' calculations.

7.4 Empirical Results for Cross-correlators

For the model chosen, any two commodities can be fit accurately. The fit for Gold and Silver is given in Figure 8.10. The three correlators for gold and silver are fitted well, with R^2 given by the following

$$R^2 = \begin{pmatrix} R^2_{G_{11}} & R^2_{G_{12}} \\ * & R^2_{G_{22}} \end{pmatrix} = \begin{pmatrix} 0.837 & 0.923 \\ * & 0.863 \end{pmatrix}$$

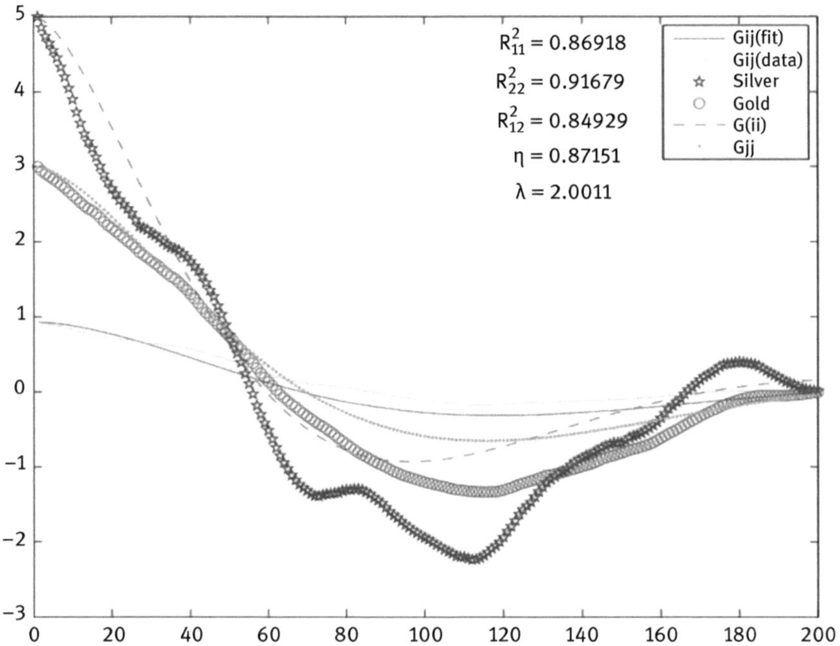

Figure 8.10: Silver and Gold Auto- and Cross-Correlators.
Source: Authors' calculations.

The model works very well for up to three commodities, but fails to simultaneously fit the auto- and cross-correlator of four commodities. To illustrate this point, the error R^2 for this set of commodities is given below (see also Baaquie, Yu and Du, 2016).

$$R^2 = \begin{pmatrix} 0.834 & 0.885 & 0.507 & 0.074 \\ * & 0.827 & 0.725 & 0.435 \\ * & * & 0.749 & 0.809 \\ * & * & * & 0.377 \end{pmatrix}$$

8 Futures Commodity Prices

Market futures prices $p_i(t,\xi)$ of a commodity, labelled by i – for calendar time t and future time ξ – are given by

$$p_i(t,\xi) = p_0\, e^{x_i(t,\xi)}$$

As shown in Figure 8.11, which describes the relation between calendar time and future time, spot commodity prices are given at the boundary of $\xi = t$.

$$P_i(t) = p_i(t,t) = p_0 e^{x_i(t,t)}$$

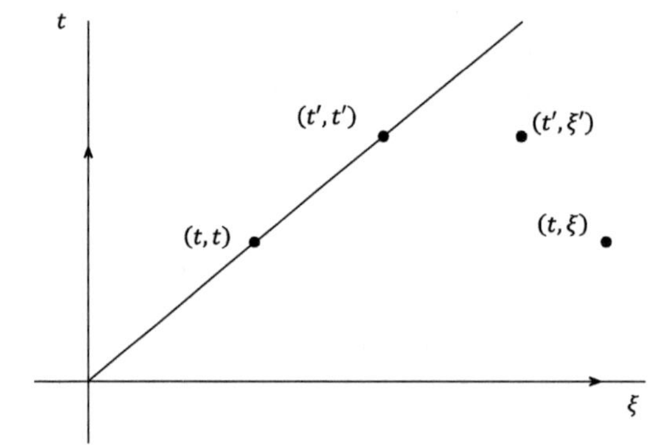

Figure 8.11: Points on the Boundary are Calendar Time (t,t); (t',t') and Points away from Boundary (t,ξ); (t',ξ') are Located in Future Time.
Source: Authors' calculations.

A symmetric generalization of the multiple spot *Lagrangian* yields the *Lagrangian* for futures commodity prices, as proposed by Baaquie and Yu (2018)

$$\mathcal{L}(t,\xi) = \frac{1}{2}\sum_{i}^{N} L_i \left[\left(\frac{\partial^2 y_i}{\partial t^2} + \alpha_i^2 \frac{\partial^2 y_i}{\partial \xi^2} \right)^2 + \frac{\tilde{L}_i}{L_i} \left(\left(\frac{\partial y_i}{\partial t} \right)^2 + \alpha_i^2 \left(\frac{\partial y_i}{\partial \xi} \right)^2 \right) \right]$$
$$+ \sum_{i=1}^{N} \left[d_i e^{-a_i y_i} + s_i e^{b_i y_i} \right] - \frac{1}{2} \sum_{ij;i\neq j}^{N} \Delta_{ij} y_i y_j$$

The futures *Lagrangian* has new terms $\partial^2 y_i/\partial\xi^2$ and $\partial y_i/\partial\xi$ that are purely 'kinetic' in the sense that they attenuate and dampen out fluctuations in the future time ξ direction. The term $y(t,\xi)$ is defined over the semi-infinite domain. The Neumann boundary condition is imposed at $t = \xi$ due to the fact that $y(t,t)$ is a stochastic variable (see Baaquie, 2004). This yields the following Fourier expansion

$$y(t,\xi)=\int_{-\infty}^{\infty}\frac{d\omega}{2\pi}\int_{0}^{\infty}\frac{dk}{\pi/2}e^{i\omega t}cos(k(\xi-t))y(\omega,k);\, y^{*}(\omega,k)=y(-\omega,-k)$$

The Gaussian expansion for the action is given by

$$\mathcal{A}=\frac{1}{2\pi^2}\int_{-\infty}^{\infty}d\omega\int_{0}^{\infty}dky(-\omega,k)\Delta^{-1}(\omega,k)y(\omega,k)+O(y^3)$$

$$\Delta^{-1}(\omega,k)=L(\omega^2+\alpha^2k^2+\gamma_1^2)(\omega^2+\alpha^2k^2+\gamma_2^2)$$

$$\gamma_1^2+\gamma_2^2=\frac{\widetilde{L}}{L};\, \gamma_1^2\gamma_2^2=\alpha^2d+b^2s$$

In order to determine the microeconomic potential for futures, the spot potential is extended into the future to capture the forward-looking expectations underlying futures prices. Since forward and futures prices depend on the formation today of forward-looking expectations about market prices at a future point in time, these prices may be regarded as measures of market expectations about spot prices. The new kinetic terms added to the spot *Lagrangian* contribute toward the attenuation of futures price fluctuations. It is noted that futures prices should converge toward spot prices at maturity. The basis, which is defined as the difference between futures and spot prices, should also converge toward zero at maturity. This convergence reflects a pricing mechanism that attenuates fluctuations until maturity. Thus, the definition of the microeconomic potential can be more complex for futures prices than for spot prices. The projection of the potential for spot prices into the future may capture only part of the complex dynamics of futures contracts.

9 Correlation Function

At this level, it is possible to consider the Gaussian approximation. Using Gaussian path integration, the propagator is given by

$$G(t,\xi;t',\xi')=E[y(t,\xi)y(t',\xi')=\frac{1}{Z}\int Dye^{-S}y(t,\xi)y(t',\xi')$$

$$=\frac{1}{\pi^2}-\int_{-\infty}^{\infty}d\omega\int_{-\infty}^{\infty}dke^{i\omega(t-t')}cos(k(\xi-t))cos(k(\xi'-t'))\Delta(\omega,k)$$

$$=D(t-t';\theta-\theta')+D(t-t';\theta+\theta')$$

A derivation yields

$$D(t,\theta) = \frac{1}{2L\pi\alpha}\frac{1}{\gamma_2^2 - \gamma_1^2}\left[K_0\left(\gamma_1\sqrt{\tau^2 + \left(\frac{\theta}{\alpha}\right)^2}\right) - K_0\left(\gamma_2\sqrt{\tau^2 + \left(\frac{\theta}{\alpha}\right)^2}\right)\right]$$

where K_0 is the modified Bessel function of second kind.

9.1 Empirical Correlators

Commodities lie on the complex branch with

$$\gamma_1 = re^{i\phi} = \gamma_2^*$$

It is possible to define the following elements of the correlation function.

$$z_+^2 = \tau^2 + \left(\frac{\theta + \theta'}{\alpha}\right)^2; \; z_-^2 = \tau^2 + \left(\frac{\theta - \theta'}{\alpha}\right)^2$$

$$\tau = t - t'; \; \theta = \xi - t; \; \theta' = \xi' - t'$$

The correlation function is given by the following expression where $\Im$ is the imaginary part

$$G(t,\xi;t',\xi') = G(z_+;z_-) = -4\phi\Im\left[K_0(\gamma_1 z_+) + K_0(\gamma_1 z_-)\right]: \text{Real}$$

To connect the model's correlation function with the empirical one, denoted by $G_E(t,\xi;t',\xi')$, it is important to consider the following expression

$$G_E(t,\xi;t',\xi') = G(m(z_+);m(z_-)); \; m(z) = \lambda\left(\frac{z}{\lambda}\right)^\eta : \text{market time}$$

Note the crucial reduction of the dependence of the correlation from calendar time and future time to z_+ and z_- expressions

$$t,\xi;t',\xi' \to z_+;z_-$$

in making the transition from the empirical correlation function $G_E(t,\xi;t',\xi')$ to the model's correlation function $G(m(z_+);m(z_-))$.

The following are three distinct cases for the correlation function that are observed in spot and futures markets, and are empirically examined.

(1) Spot-spot price correlation function. The spot-spot rate correlation function $G(t,t;t',t')$ provides a model distinct from the spot rate model. The futures modelling of the spot rate correlator given by $G(t,t;t',t')$ cannot be reduced to the spot

rate correlator. However, both models give excellent fits of the market correlator and both models have their own advantages.

$$G(t,t;t',t') = G(\tau;\tau) = -8\phi\Im\left[K_0(\gamma_1\tau)\right];\ z_+ = \tau = z_-$$

(2) Spot-futures price correlation function.

$$G(t,t;t',\xi') = G(z_+;z_+) = -8\phi\Im\left[K_0(\gamma_1 z_+)\right];\ z_+^2 = \tau^2 + \left(\frac{\theta'}{\alpha}\right)^2 = z_-^2$$

(3) Futures-futures price correlation function.

$$G(t,\xi;t',\xi') = G(z_+;z_-) = -4\phi\Im\left[K_0(\gamma_1 z_+) + K_0(\gamma_1 z_-)\right]$$

9.1.1 Spot-spot prices correlation

All spot rates have excellent fits between model and market correlators. Figure 8.12 shows the fit for gold and soya beans correlation for spot-spot prices having $R^2 = 0.97$

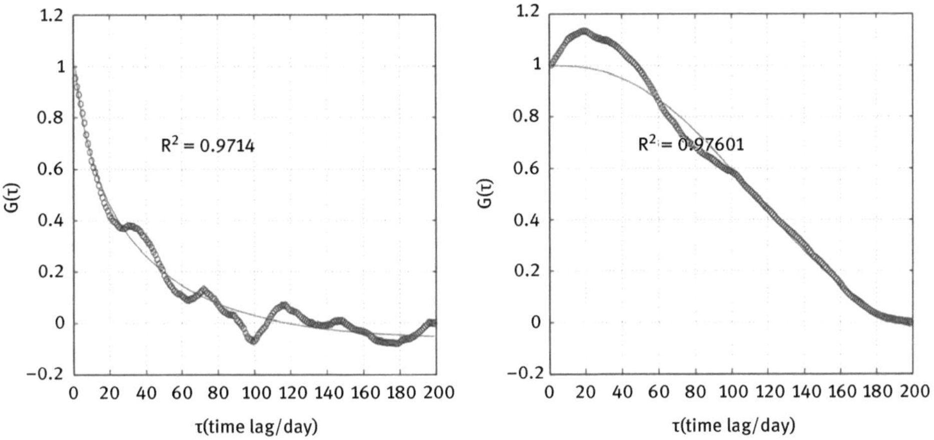

Figure 8.12: Fitting Spot Rates for a) Gold and b) Soybeans.
Source: Authors' calculations.
Note: The smooth curve is the model's best fit to data. (Jan 1 2011- Oct 18 2011)

9.1.2 Spot-futures

The model has excellent fits for all the spot-futures studied. Figure 8.13 describes the empirical results for the correlation between spot and futures crude oil prices, with $R^2 = 0.98$.

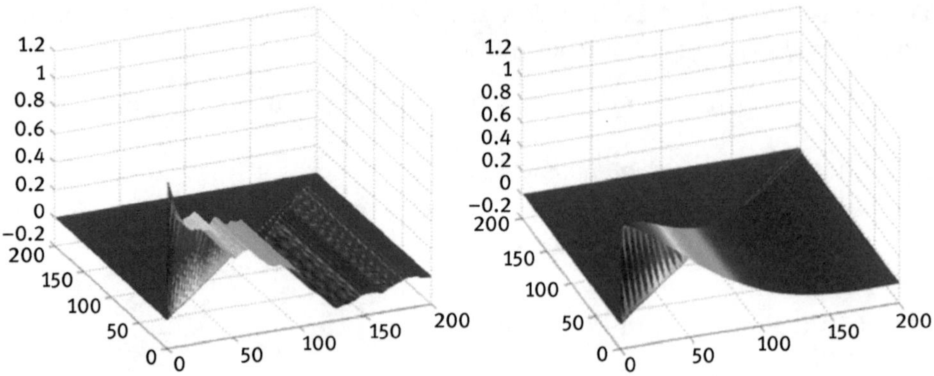

Figure 8.13: $G(t, \xi; 0, 0)$ of Crude Oil Futures Data and Fit.
Source: Authors' calculations.
Note: Sample data covers from Jan 1, 2011 to Oct 18, 2011.

9.2 Reduction of Variables $t, \xi; t', \xi' \rightarrow z_+; z_-$

Note the crucial reduction of the dependence of the correlation is valid only for a specific choice of α. The evidence from Figure 8.14 indicates that the binning of the propagator $D_E^{(k)}(a,b,c)$ for constant $z_\pm$ results in scattered parameter values for alpha $\alpha = 19.98$ – pointing to a possible common value equal to the expected value

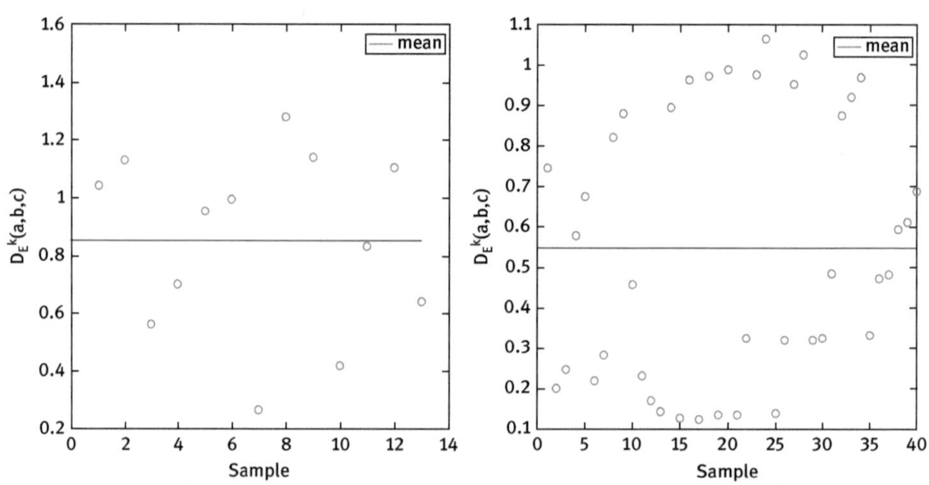

Figure 8.14: Binning of 10 Years Oil Futures Data of $D_E^{(k)}(a,b,c)$.
Source: Authors' calculations.
Note: Figure on the left is drawn with $\alpha = 19.98$ and for 14 sample points. Figure on the right is drawn with $\alpha = 1$ and for 40 sample points. Sample period is from Nov 20, 2015 to Sep 8, 2016.

represented by the mean. For the case of $\alpha = 1$, the data bunches appear around two extremities – ruling out a common value. The existence of α reducing the dependence of correlation to $z_\pm$ is model-independent.

9.2.1 Futures-futures Prices Correlation

Given the unique parameter value of alpha = 19.98 that provides the best fit of the empirical propagator with the model propagator, it is possible to graphically describe also the relation between the model propagator G_M (z+ ; z−) and estimated propagator G_E (z+ ; z−), as shown in Figure 8.15. Thus as argued by Baaquie and Yu (2018), the best fit with R^2 = 0.69 may not be very high but acceptable, and it can be improved with high-performance machines. The obtained value of α is rather high for the futures-futures case. The reason is that the highest contributions to the propagator stem from futures prices, which are far distanced in the future (again see Baaquie and Yu, 2018).

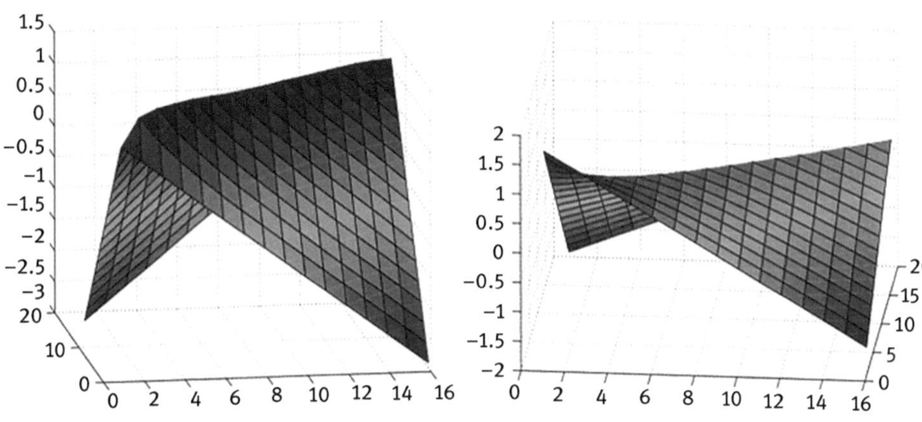

Figure 8.15: a) Empirical $G_E(z_+; z_-)$ and b) Model $G_M(z_+; z_-)$ for Oil Futures Prices.
Source: Authors' calculations.
Note: Sample period is from Nov 20, 2015 to Sep 8, 2016.

The evidence from the model correlation functions and market estimates suggests that, in the absence of discontinuous price changes, the model does not seem to depend significantly on the full range of the potential. Price volatility is an important factor that enters in the definition of normalized prices, and affects potential and kinetic terms as well as correlation functions. Shocks to the production, exchange and consumption functions are bound to affect the microeconomic action functional. The exogenous shocks may be absorbed by risk-sharing relations, which promote price stability and stable financial systems.

In contrast, risk-transfer relations and speculative trading based on margin trading and short selling increase the probability of speculative bubbles and crashes leading to higher volatility and discontinuous price changes. It is price stability that may lessen for instance the need for significant new kinetic terms used to attenuate price fluctuations for the futures *Lagrangian*. Thus, the correlation function may be reflective not only of the impact of systematic risks on asset prices but also of the effects of risk-sharing and risk-transfer mechanisms in the economy.

10 Summary

The model and empirical behavior of the multiple spot as well as futures prices for various commodities has been studied. Market data provides convincing evidence for the microeconomic action functional is given, for both spot and futures price, by the following expression

$$\mathcal{A} = \int dt\mathcal{L} = \int dt(\mathcal{T} + \mathcal{V})$$

The sample includes 18 major commodities in addition to the futures price of oil. All single commodity auto-correlators could be accurately modelled for almost 200–300 days. The pricing of commodities is the result of a) the combination of supply and demand, encoded in the potential $\mathcal{V}$ and of b) the role of exchange and distribution, as in the kinetic term $\mathcal{T}$. The price is not determined by only supply and demand. The model for futures prices is far more complicated than the simpler model for spot prices. The model for futures prices is far more complicated than the simpler model for spot prices, and further analysis is needed to consider its more complex dynamics.

From our empirical studies, it is found that the model is quite insensitive to the full range of the potential. One needs to have a microeconomic potential that has a minimum to ensure an equilibrium price. Only the three terms from the exponential supply and demand enter into the calibration, given by

$$d_i e^{-a_i y_i} + s_i e^{b_i y_i} \simeq \frac{\gamma_i}{2} y_i^2 + \frac{\alpha_i}{3!} y_i^3 + \frac{\beta_i}{4!} y_i^4$$

However, for a discontinuous change of prices, the full range of the potential function becomes important. The price of wheat had a sudden increase, shown in Figure 8.16, and can be interpreted as a tunneling event. The full range of the potential, including the double-well of microeconomic potential with multiple minima as shown in Figure 8.3, is required for the tunneling to have taken place.

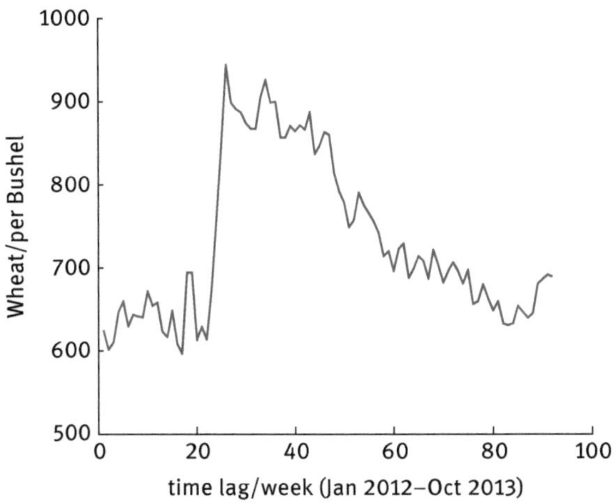

Figure 8.16: Tunneling from a Lower to a Higher Price.
Source: Authors' calculations.
Note: Sample period is from Jan 8, 2012 to Oct 13, 2013.

11 Future Directions

An economic principle is required to explain the modelling of asset prices using the microeconomic potential and the kinetic term. One needs to find, for instance, reasons – grounded on the economic principle – that explain why the microeconomic potential supersedes the independent modelling of supply and demand. There is indeed much more to the concept of microeconomic potential than demand and supply, as it contains more information than the equilibrium price resulting from the intersection of demand and supply functions. The potential combines demand and supply into one function, and it contains more information than the aggregate of these functions.

For the microeconomic kinetic term, one possible explanation is that it models the process of exchange and of circulation. In particular, the parameters L, $\tilde{L}$ could be determined for a commodity by the market liquidity and turnover of the commodity in question. The analysis of the kinetic term is important because it contains the time derivatives of prices. It does not appear in standard microeconomic models, which are usually focused only on the intersection between supply and demand.

A fundamental underlying socio-political-economic principle is required that unifies production, circulation, distribution, exchange and consumption. The principle should provide a theoretical explanation as well as a derivation the microeconomic action functional for both spot and futures prices. From the perspective of Islamic finance and economics, the focus is made on the impact of risk-sharing and short-selling activities on the definition of the microeconomic potential and kinetic terms. It may be argued that the demand and supply functions should not be defined by market forces driven by consumer sovereignty, short sales, margin trading, and scarcity of resources, but by genuine factors related to resource abundance, rational constraints on consumer behavior and asset-redistribution based on risk-sharing. Risk-sharing is regarded as the defining principle of Islamic finance, and future research may shed some light on its role within the unifying system and mechanisms underlying asset pricing and exchange relations in the economy.

References

Baaquie, Belal E and Miao Yu. 2018. "Statistical field theory of futures commodity prices". *Physica A: Statistical Mechanics and its Applications* 492: 250–264.

Baaquie, Belal E, Miao Yu, and Xin Du. 2016. "Multiple commodities in statistical microeconomics: Model and market". *Physica A: Statistical Mechanics and its Applications*, 462: 912–929.

Baaquie, Belal E. 2004. Quantum finance: Path integrals and Hamiltonians for options and interest rates. Cambridge; Cambridge University Press.

Haven, Emmanuel and Andrei Khrennikov. 2013. *Quantum Social Science*. Cambridge; Cambridge University Press.

Varian, Hal R. 1992. *Microeconomic Analysis*. W. W. Norton & Company, USA, 3rd edition.

Seyed Kazem Sadr, Reza Gholami

Chapter 9: Monitoring Strategy in Profit-Loss Sharing Arrangements: Cost or Investment?

1 Introduction

The Islamic banking industry has witnessed robust growth since its inception three decades ago. Total *Shariah* compliant assets rose for the seventh consecutive year from $1,166bn in 2012 to $1,267bn in 2013 according to a survey by the Banker. Growth was slower than in previous years but remained a healthy 8.67% giving an average annual growth rate of 16.02% since 2006. Despite the financial crisis in the *ribawi system* between 2008 and 2010, the Islamic banking industry experienced only a moderate slowdown in its profitability and soon exhibited a resilient growth post crisis period. The expansion of Islamic banking has in the past few years accelerated, with the industry diversifying out of traditional territories into countries with large Muslim populations such as the United Kingdom. Africa in particular, with a Muslim population of more than 400 million, has seen an expansion in recent years (see Moody's, 2008). Islamic finance overall has been expanding gradually in all parts of the world, with the major concentration in the Organization of Islamic Cooperation (OIC) countries.[125]

Despite this remarkable performance, the balance sheet of many Islamic banks exhibits a strong dominance and preference for financial products with fixed rates of return. In a sample of Islamic banks in 2007 the share of profit-loss sharing (PLS) products varied between zero to 24% with a median share of 3% (Sundarajan 2007). At the country level, share of the PLS contracts varied from 3% in Malaysia (Muda & Ismail 2010) to more than 30% in Indonesia 37% in Indonesia (Ascarya and Rokhimah 2008, Ajija et al. 2012). It is argued that these conditions are not optimal. Mirakhor (1987) demonstrates that a concentration on fixed rates of return may lead to lower overall expected returns. Further the risk of bankruptcy can be decreased when participation products are added to the bank's portfolios. Strong criticism can be levied against current practices by Islamic banks, which seem to diverge from the theoretical models of financing initially envisaged by Islamic finance (Rosly, 1999;

125 As reported in OIC Outlook Series in 2012, the largest centers for Islamic finance industry is in Middle East, including Iran, with a share of 35.7% in total Islamic finance assets, Saudi Arabia, 13.9%, United Arab Emirates (UAE), 8.7%, Kuwait, 7.3%, Bahrain, 5.3%, and Qatar, 4.8%. In other OIC member countries in the Middle East and North Africa such as Turkey, Sudan, Egypt, Jordan and Syria, Islamic finance industry is developing very quickly. In South East Asia, Malaysia has a share of 12.3%. Other OIC member countries in Asia such as Indonesia, which has the largest indigenous Muslim population, and Bangladesh each represent around 1% of the global Islamic finance industry.

https://doi.org/10.1515/9783110587920-009

Mirakhor, 2010; Archer et al., 2010; Farook et al., 2012). Such practices are perceived to be very similar to *ribawi* bank loans (Kader & Leong, 2009). Chong & Liu (2009) suggest that the performance of Islamic banks in Malaysia is not very different from interest-based ribawi banking.

There are however indicators that new trends are emerging in the aftermath of the U.S. Financial Crisis. Indeed, the share of participation products has become significant in some banks and also in some countries. With reference to Table 9.1, it is clear that the combined share of *musharakah* and *mudarabah* products, in 2014 exceed 50% of total finance at 23 Islamic banks (Table 9.1). The same share exceeds 25% of total finance in 36 banks and 10% in 47 banks (Table 9.1). Given the sample of 171 Islamic banks under examination, the increasing adoption of risk-sharing financing products is a necessary part of the realignment process toward Islamic banking. Table 9.2 also indicates that Musharakah and Mudarabah financing to total financing ratio is above 50% only in five countries, namely, Iran, South Africa, UK, Indonesia, and Kenya.

Table 9.1: Risk Sharing Financing to Total Financing Ratio for Individual Banks.

Name	2008	2010	2012	2014
International Investment Bank, Bahrain				1.0000
AL_RAYAN_BANK, United Kingdom				0.9984
Islamic Bank of Britain, United Kingdom				0.9984
Bank Khavarmianeh (Middle East Bank), Iran			1.0000	0.9981
Ghavamin Bank, Iran				0.9648
Bank Day, Iran		0.9717	0.9714	0.9588
Sina Bank, Iran	0.6509	0.8735	0.8701	0.9261
Bank Pasargad, Iran	0.8879	0.8622	0.9091	0.9250
EN Bank, Iran	0.6146	0.7678	0.8551	0.9055
Iran Zamin Bank, Iran			1.0002	0.8899
Panin Bank Syariah, Indonesia		0.8170	0.4947	0.8669
Ayandeh Bank, Iran				0.8343
Blue Nile Mashreg Bank, Sudan	0.5203	0.7410	0.7774	0.8286
Karafarin Bank (PJSC), Iran		0.6244	0.7505	0.8257
Parsian Bank, Iran	0.5522	0.7618	0.8381	0.8242
Bank Shahr, Iran	0.9970	0.4925	0.5225	0.7833
Saman Bank, Iran	0.5390	0.6329	0.7292	0.7825
Ansar Bank, Iran		0.3146	0.5072	0.7568
Albaraka Bank, South Africa	0.4664	0.5071	0.5701	0.6987
Burj Bank, Pakistan	0.4506	0.4004	0.3135	0.6063
Bank Hekmat Iranian, Iran			0.1535	0.6020
Tejarat Bank, Iran	0.2470	0.4966	0.5745	0.5856
Gulf African Bank Limited, Kenya	0.2478	0.3884		0.5523
HSBC Amanah Malaysia, Malaysia		0.1164	0.3760	0.4447
Al-Shamal Islamic Bank, Sudan	0.2196	0.5610	0.4603	0.4384

Table 9.1 (continued)

Name	2008	2010	2012	2014
Standard Chartered Saadiq, Malaysia				0.4002
PT Bank Syariah Bukopin, Indonesia		0.3360	0.3170	0.3940
Saderat Bank, Iran	0.1356	0.2768	0.3429	0.3491
Sarmayeh Bank, Iran	0.6160	0.4532	0.5238	0.3345
Al Salam Bank Bahrain, Bahrain		0.1363	0.3542	0.3251
Post Bank, Iran	0.1062	0.4278	0.2744	0.3133
Mellat Bank, Iran	0.1739	0.4358	0.3237	0.2915
AlSalam Bank Sudan, Sudan	0.1364	0.2479	0.3883	0.2627
Meezan Bank, Pakistan	0.2355	0.2584	0.3448	0.2497
Islami Bank Bangladesh, Bangladesh	0.0301	0.0522	0.0625	0.2318
Al Baraka Bank, Pakistan	0.3173	0.2057	0.1876	0.2266
RHB Islamic Bank, Malaysia		0.1298	0.1553	0.2188
Social Islami Bank, Bangladesh		0.0091	0.0098	0.2030
BankIslami, Pakistan	0.3205	0.3593	0.2611	0.1869
Bahrain Islamic Bank, Bahrain	0.2231	0.1669	0.2025	0.1718
Public Islamic Bank, Malaysia			0.0022	0.1652
Ajman Bank, United Arab Emirates		0.0890	0.2406	0.1536
Dubai Islamic Bank, United Arab Emirates	0.2949	0.2099	0.1748	0.1282
First Security Islami Bank, Bangladesh				0.1199
Al Baraka Islamic Bank, Bahrain	0.0603	0.1112	0.1353	0.1157
Faisal Islamic Bank, Sudan	0.0310	0.0185	0.0734	0.1111
Khaleeji Commercial Bank, Bahrain	0.0920	0.1563	0.2162	0.1065

Source: Islamic Banking Intelligence www.islamicbankingintelligence.com

Table 9.2: Musharakah and Mudarabah Financing to Total Financing Ratio (Country Average of the Selected Banks), 2008–2014.

Row Labels	Average of 2008	Average of 2010	Average of 2012	Average of 2014
Iran	0.4727	0.5707	0.6557	0.7290
South Africa	0.4664	0.5071	0.5701	0.6987
United Kingdom	0.0314	0.0159	0.0118	0.6683
Indonesia	0.2872	0.3544	0.2865	0.6305
Kenya	0.2478	0.3884		0.5523
Pakistan	0.4088	0.3607	0.3073	0.3174
Sudan	0.1669	0.2601	0.3100	0.2919
Bahrain	0.1283	0.1453	0.1798	0.2171
Bangladesh	0.0301	0.0307	0.0361	0.1549
Malaysia	0.0018	0.0463	0.0831	0.1435
United Arab Emirates	0.1884	0.1155	0.1143	0.0630
Qatar	0.1182	0.0301	0.0058	0.0574
Saudi Arabia	0.0979	0.0923	0.0805	0.0518

Table 9.2 (continued)

Row Labels	Average of 2008	Average of 2010	Average of 2012	Average of 2014
Palestine	0.0002	0.0002	0.0273	0.0388
NIGERIA				0.0308
Afghanistan				
Brunei Darussalam		0.0005	0.0062	
Egypt	0.1094	0.2558		
Iraq		0.5356	0.9971	
Jordan	0.0109	0.0095	0.0059	
Maldives			0.0916	
Yemen	0.2938	0.2813	0.2022	

Source: Islamic Banking Intelligence www.islamicbankingintelligence.com.

The question arises as to what explains the small share of participation products in the asset portfolios of Islamic banks. Many studies suggest the significance of problems related to asymmetric information (Siddiqui 2006, 2008, Iqbal and Molyneux 2005, Dar and Presley 2000) and unaccommodative regulation (Khan & Bhatti 2008, Yousef 2004). While regulation issues can be addressed through change in public polies, asymmetric information problem should be solved by Islamic banks themselves as suggested by Sadr (2005). Effective measures include bank monitoring of the conduct of clients. The objective of this chapter is to demonstrate that benefits accrued to monitoring activity can exceed the associated cost. Monitoring is in fact an investment for abating the risks related to the shortage of or asymmetric information among partners. The empirical evidence is based on the effects of monitoring on the returns of properties financed by the Agricultural Bank of Iran.

2 Literature Review

It may be argued, as in Ashour (1999), that fixed-income contracts are optimal because they demand less information in comparison to profit-sharing contracts. However, theoretical and empirical literature indicates that this is not true at all times and places. Stiglitz (1974) shows that the attitudes of parties toward risk is a key factor in explaining the continuous application of profit-sharing contracts in agricultural sector. In another study Trester (1998) argues that some financiers prefer equity to debt contracts in particular industries. Under some conditions, debt contracts are not only optimal but are also infeasible, which implies that equity or profit-sharing contracts are dominant. Anwar (1987) concludes that poor small farmers close to the subsistence level are likely to be risk averse and extremely reluctant to go heavily into debt in order to finance investment in capital intensive inputs or adopt new technology, despite very high expected returns. Yazdani (2006) asserts that fear of the serious consequences of crop failure coupled with debt repayment commitments may discourage small farmers from borrowing under the debt mechanism. Also, Samad and Hassan (1999) suggest that equity contracts can be superior to debt contracts in an economy where informational asymmetries resulting from adverse selection and moral hazard are rare. Thus, there are industries and market conditions under which equity contracts are superior to debt contracts.

Many solutions have been suggested to reduce the asymmetric information problems in so far that the agents' efforts and misreporting levels are concerned. Since effort levels are not observable, a system of incentives may induce agents to supply optimal efforts. For instance, the share of agents may be increased when projects terminate successfully. Using analytical methods and game theory techniques, El Fakir and Tkiouat (2015) show that *equity participation* raises the marginal revenues of agents and hence the level of efforts. In addition to equity participation, other solutions including collaterals and warranties are suggested. Also, the staged financing of a project and close monitoring of the partner may reduce information asymmetry (Sahlman, 1990). The evidence suggests that the staging method is thus frequently used by informal investors (Abalkhail and Presley, 2002). The potential loss of financing and risk of failure in the participation venture constitute another incentive mechanism (Karim, 2002).

Abalkhail and Presley (2002) examine a sample of informal PLS investors in Saudi Arabia and find that, *active personal search* can contribute toward resolving agency problems. The characteristics of entrepreneur including reputation and skills, and product markets have also significant effects on partnership ventures. Moreover, in order to reduce the extent of asymmetric information, informal investors can co-invest frequently by adopting staging finance policies that allow for a better control of entrepreneur behavior and contract renegotiation. Therefore, due diligence and close monitoring in different forms are main instruments of investor in informal system. Furthermore, there are many small initiatives that are successful with PLS arrangements as the result of close monitoring. For instance, *Baitul Mal Wat Tamwil* offers both *musharakah* and *mudarabah* financial products, along with close monitoring (Widiyanto et al. 2011).

An earlier study by Khan (1986) examines the information asymmetry problems associated with participation contracts and the monitoring solution. Given the monitoring cost borne by the financier, Ahmed (2002) proposes random auditing of the partner's accounts, in particular when assets are taken as collateral in the partnership contract. According to this monitoring mechanism, random auditing is implemented whenever reported profits are remarkably lower than expectation. These measures may induce entrepreneurs to report the accounts on more timely and accurate basis. Following standard accounting methods may help diminish misreporting problems, as suggested by Khan (1997) regarding Systematic Performance Auditing. Also, due diligence also can be an appropriate policy (Al-Suwailem, 2002). Thus, misreporting problems can be addressed using standard accounting methods and random auditing. However, these measures may be rather costly for financier. Diamond (1986) suggests the delegation of monitoring function to intermediaries.

Ahmed (2008) provides evidence from bank staff at investment departments that efficient follow-up and close supervision significantly improve the performance of PLS projects. According to Karim (2002), the imposition of incentive-compatible contracts on pilot projects is conducive to growth and profitability. However, Muda and Ismail, (2010) suggest that PLS contracts may not create value for the banking system, and there is a supportive evidence from Samad and Hassan (1999), and Mahrt-Smith (2006) either.

3 The Model

Under the assumptions of efficient markets and complete information, the equilibrium rate of return is commensurate to the level of systematic risk. The violation of these assumptions may lead to arbitrage opportunities where assets are priced independent of the degree of risk undertaken. Also, the Markowitz (1952) theorem implies that investors can construct efficient portfolios that optimize the expected return for a given level of risk. However, the benefits of risk diversification can be inhibited by the absence of timely and accurate information. Therefore, information gathering plays an essential role in investment decisions, portfolio rebalancing and proper functioning of markets in exchange economies. Thus, there is strong incentive for banks to gather information and monitoring the conduct of clients and the implementation process of current projects to optimize risk-adjusted returns. Banks which undertake this initiative make in fact a composite investment, jointly for procurement of labor and capital needed for investment projects and also for the information accruing to the performance of the project.

It is assumed that banks attempt to minimize risk for a level of expected return on the portfolio of assets $\left(\bar{R}_p\right)$. Let w_i represent the weight of asset i in the bank portfolio, the supply of funds for contract i and $\left(\delta_p^2\right)$ and $\left(E\left(\bar{R}_p\right)\right)$ represent the variance of portfolio and its expected mean, respectively. It is possible to express the objective function and constraints are as follows;

$$min \quad \sigma_p^2 = \Sigma_i \Sigma_j w_i w_j \sigma_{ij} \quad i,\ j = 1, 2,\ \ldots,\ n. \tag{1}$$

subject to

$$E(\widetilde{R_p}) = \sum\nolimits_i w_i E(\widetilde{r_i}) = \bar{R}_p \tag{2}$$

It can be further assumed that the covariance terms σ_{ij} between different assets and products are statistically insignificant. The first-order conditions are conducive the following optimal relationships:

$$\frac{\frac{r_i}{\sigma_i^2}}{w_i} = \frac{\frac{r_j}{\sigma_j^2}}{w_j} \Rightarrow \frac{w_i^*}{w_j^*} = \frac{\sigma_i^2}{\sigma_j^2} \cdot \frac{E(\widetilde{R}_j)}{E(\widetilde{R}_i)} \tag{3}$$

Equation (3) indicates that funds should be allocated to various assets in financing products as a function of their respective risk-adjusted returns. The optimal weights and optimal allocation of funds depend on the expected return and variance of assets as well as on the expected return on the portfolio. Thus, any changes in the expected returns and risk levels of any assets resulting from monitoring effects are bound to affect the optimal allocation of bank funds. Any restrictions on the expected portfolio returns will also affect the allocation of funds.

4 Analytical Results

This theoretical model can be used to examine the contribution of monitoring effects to the efficient allocation of portfolio assets in the Agricultural Bank of Iran (ABI) during the five-year period from 1990 to 1994 period. The new Interest Free Law has been approved and implemented since 1984, and the sample period is thus useful in demonstrating how the banking industry adjusted itself to the new Banking Law. It is noted that the Agricultural Bank of Iran (ABI) adopted several measures over time to enhance the efficiency of its Islamic banking services and the operation of its *musharakah* financing in particular (Sadr 2005, Sadr and Iqbal 2002). These measures include economic and financial feasibility studies and supervision of project implementation. The bank selects also the most beneficial projects with respect to private interests and environmental conditions. By studying the record and expertise of clients, the bank minimizes the adverse selection problem and eliminates moral hazard issues. Although the allocation of financial and human resources to monitoring activities may burden the bank with additional spending, the gains may exceed the costs.

The bank does not merely select the most profitable projects, but acquires also incremental information about market conditions during the implementation period. For instance, sometimes, the environmental conditions may not be suitable for the production of the agricultural products in specific regions and this information can be useful for the bank in financing decisions for similar products in similar regions. The bank can reduce associated asymmetric information problems, and thus mitigates the risk of non-compliance of partners by monitoring the subsequent stages of project financing. Indeed, the resources and efforts devoted to appraisal and monitoring constitute also another investment in the information system that complements the financing of projects. Therefore, it can be hypothesized that investment in monitoring efforts will increase the probability of success. The return to investment in participation contracts is expected to be more tangible than in fixed-income contracts because of the reduction of risks related to asymmetric information.

Following Sadr (2005), it is possible to use regression analysis with pooled data to estimate the relation between fund allocation and profit-loss sharing contracts including *salam*, *murabahah*, *musharakah* and *joalah* financing, which account for 80% of the ABI's portfolio of assets.

$$q_{ti} = \alpha + \beta_{1i}\hat{r}_{it} + \beta_{2i}OF_{it} + \beta_{3i}R_{it} + \varepsilon_{it} \quad (4)$$

Equation (4) represents the supply of fund to each instrument *i* at each year *t* by the bank branch managers is a function of expected return to each instrument, r_{it}, the outstanding amount of fund, OF_{ti}, and the return to the bank branch portfolio, R_{it}, judging from the results reported in Table 9.3, it is clear that the supply of fund is a positive and significant function of return on *murabahah*, *musharakah* and *joalah* financing, which are all monitored by the bank. In contrast, this relationship is not significant for *salam* products which are not monitored. A one percent increase in the rate of return of *Musharakah* products increases the return to this investment by 4 Billion Iranian rials. The same rate of increase in installment sale and *joalah* products increases the return by IR21.3 and 1.98 Billion, respectively. It is the higher returns on profit-loss sharing financing with effective monitoring that provide the strong incentive for ABI to continue its monitoring practices. Given its focus and interests on the potential benefits of PLS contract monitoring, Iran has achieved the highest proportion of participation products among Muslim countries (Table 9.3). It seems that similar growth patterns are followed by other Islamic banks.

Table 9.3: Regression Equations Estimation.

Product	Constant (C)	Rate of return (r)	Outstanding fund (B)	Income (Y)	F statistics	R square	Number of observations
Mudarabah	−1468	21.43	0.34		96.06	0.62	120
(t value)	(−2.21)	(2.40)	(12.72)				
Musharakah	35.68	4	0.85		556	0.94	72
(t value)	(0.19)	(2.09)	(32.70)				
Salam	−40.65	0.81	0.96		396	0.87	120
(t value)	(−0.64)	(1.09)	(27.93)				
Joalah	137.24	1.98	0.64	−8.24	486	0.95	75
(t value)	(3.25)	(3.28)	(34)	(22)			

Finally, it is noted that *murabahah* contracts have been in use by ABI since the adoption of the new Islamic law in 1984, whereas *joalah* was gradually replaced by *musharakah* contracts because of high transaction costs (Sadr 1999). Thus, the number of observations for *musharakah* and *joalah* contracts are less than other two contracts. The explanatory variable representing outstanding funds is associated with positive and significant coefficients for all regression models. The managers of bank branches are restricted in the supply of funds to each financing product, and the positive relationship indicates the need for limit relaxation.

5 Conclusion

Two major factors seem to explain the slow pace of adoption of participation finance by Islamic banks. The operative banking rules and regulations in dual systems suit the interest-based *ribawi* banking industry, which is based on debt creation. The regulatory environment is not accommodative of Islamic banking, which is essentially equity-based. The second deterring factor is the presence of asymmetric information problems. Fortunately, these impediments can be removed by monitoring the performance of bank partners. Although the monitoring may impose some constraints, the benefits are likely to offset the costs.

This chapter argues that monitoring per se constitutes an investment in the collection and analysis of information. The investment in information systems enables banks to learn about market conditions and seek similarly profitable investment opportunities elsewhere. It allows bank to learn about the expertise and moral characteristics of partners, and achieve over time the optimal allocation of capital resources based on risk-sharing.

References

Abalkhail, Mohammad, John R. Presley. 2002. "How informal risk capital investors manage asymmetric information in profit and loss sharing contracts." In *Islamic Banking and Finance, New Perspectives On Profit-Sharing And Risk*, 120–138. Cheltenham UK:Edward Elgar Publishing.

Abdalla Ahmed, Gaffar. 2008. "The implication of using profit and loss sharing modes of finance in the banking system, with a particular reference to equity participation (partnership) method in Sudan." *Humanomics* 24(3): 182–206.

Abdul Kader, Radiah., and Kok Leong Yap. April 2009. "The Impact of Interest Rate Changes on Islamic Bank Financing." International Review of Business Research Papers 5(3): 189–201.

Ahmed, Habib. 2002. "Incentive compatible profit-sharing contracts: a theoretical treatment." In *Islamic Banking and Finance, New Perspectives On Profit-Sharing And Risk*, 40–54. Cheltenham UK:Edward Elgar Publishing.

Ajija, S. R., Annisa, E., & Hudaifah, A. 2012. "How Do Islamic Banks Optimize Profit and Loss Sharing Arrangements?" *Economics and Management 16*(2): 118–124.

Al-Suwailem, Sami. 2002. "Decision-making under uncertainty: an Islamic perspective." In *Islamic Banking and Finance, New Perspectives On Profit-Sharing And Risk*, 15–30. Cheltenham UK: Edward Elgar Publishing.

Anwar, Muhammad. 1987. *Modelling Interest-Free Economy; A study in Macro- economics and Development.* US: International Institute of Islamic Thought (IIIT).

Ascarya, D. Y., and G. S. Rokhimah. 2008. "Efficiency Analysis of Conventional and Islamic Banks in Indonesia using Data Envelopment Analysis." Seminar and Sysposium on Implementations of Islamic economics to Positive Economics in the World as Alternative of Conventional Economics System-. Toward Development in the New Era of the Holostic Economics. Universitas Airlangga Surabaya (pp. 1–3).

Ashour, Yousif. 1999. "The Importance of" Murabaha in Long-Term Finance Programs in the Banking Industry." *American Journal of Islamic Social Sciences* 16(4): 87–102.

Askari, Hossein, and Abbas Mirakhor. 2014. "Risk sharing, public policy and the contribution of Banking Industry." *PSL Quarterly Review* 67(271): 345–379.

Chong, Beng Soon., and Ming-Hua Liu. 2009. "Islamic banking: interest-free or interest-based?." Pacific-Basin finance journal 17(1): 125–144.

Dang, Viet. 2010. "Optimal financial contracts with hidden effort, unobservable profits and endogenous costs of effort." *The Quarterly Review of Economics and Finance 50*(1): 75–89.

Dar, Humayon A., and John R. Presley. 2000. "Lack of profit loss sharing in Islamic banking: Management and control imbalances." *International Journal of Islamic Financial Services 2*(2): 3–18.

Diamond, Douglas W. 1984. "Financial intermediation and delegated monitoring." *The Review of Economic Studies* 51(3): 393–414.

El Fakir, Adil, and Mohamed Tkiouat. 2015. "An incentive game theory approach to musharakah contracts." *Asian Journal Of Applied Sciences* 3(4): 736–752.

Fama, Eugene F., and Michael C. Jensen. 1983. "Separation of ownership and control." *The Journal of Law and Economics* 26(2): 301–325.

Iqbal, Munawar, and David T. Llewellyn. 2002. *Islamic banking and finance: new perspectives on profit sharing and risk.* Cheltenham, UK: Edward Elgar Publishing.

Iqbal, Munawar., and Philip Molyneux. 2005. "Efficiency in Islamic banking." In Thirty Years of Islamic Banking, History, Performance and Prospects, 88–104. London UK: Palgrave Macmillan Publishing.

Khalil, Abdel-Fattah A.A., Colin Rickwood, Victor Murinde. 2002. "Evidence on agency-contractual problems in mudarabah financing operations by Islamic banks. In *Islamic Banking and Finance: New Perspectives on Profit-Sharing and Risk*, edited by Munawar Iqbal and David T. Llewellyn, 57–94. Cheltenham, UK: Edward Elgar Publishing.

Khan, M. Mansoor, and M. Ishaq Bhatti. 2008. "Development in Islamic banking: a financial risk-allocation approach." *The Journal of Risk Finance* 9(1): 40–51.

Jensen, Michael C., and William H. Meckling. 1976. "Theory of the firm: Managerial behavior, agency costs and ownership structure." *Journal of Financial Economics* 3(4): 305–360.

Karim, Adiwarman A. 2002. "Incentive-compatible constraints for Islamic banking: some lessons from Bank Muamalat." In *Islamic Banking and Finance: New Perspectives on Profit-Sharing and Risk*, edited by Munawar Iqbal and David T. Llewellyn, 95–108. Cheltenham, UK: Edward Elgar Publishing.

Khan, K., and Manzoor Memon. 2012. "The Testing of Hall's Permanent Income Hypothesis: A Case Study of Pakistan." *Asian Economic and Financial Review 2*(4): 518–522.

Khan, Muhammad Akram. 1997. “Performance auditing for Islamic banks.” *Islamic Economic Studies* 5(1): 23–36.

Khan, Mohsin S. 1986. “Islamic Interest-free Banking: A Theoretical Analysis.” *Staff Papers (International Monetary Fund)* 33(1): 1–27.

Mahrt-Smith, Jan. 2006. “Should Banks Own Equity Stakes in their Borrowers? A Contractual Solution to Hold-Up Problems.” *Journal of Banking & Finance* 30(10): 2911–2929.

Markowitz, Harry. 1952. “Portfolio selection.” *The journal of finance* 7(1): 77–91.

Muda, Ruhaini, and Abdul Ghafar Ismail. 2010. “Profit-loss sharing and value creation in Islamic banks.” *J. Bus. Policy Res* 5(2): 262–281.

Sadr, Seyed Kazem. 1999. “The Role of Musharaka Financing in the Agricultural Bank of Iran.” *Arab Law Quarterly* 14(3): 245–256.

Sadr, Seyed Kazem, and Zamir Iqbal. 2002. “Choice Between Debt and Equity Contracts and Asymmetric Information: Some Empirical Evidence” In *Islamic Banking and Finance: New Perspectives on Profit-Sharing and Risk*, edited by Munawar Iqbal and David T. Llewellyn, 152–154. Cheltenham, UK: Edward Elgar Publishing.

Sadr, Seyed Kazem. 2005. “Choice of Efficient Islamic Financial Instruments and Asymmetric Information.” *Nameh-ye Mofid* 11(48).

Sahlman, William A. 1990. “The structure and governance of venture-capital organizations”. *Journal of Financial Economics* 27(2): 473–521.

Samad, Abdus, and M. Kabir Hassan. 1999. “The performance of Malaysian Islamic banks during 1984–1997: An exploratory study.” *International Journal of Islamic Financial Services* 1(3): 1–14.

Looney, Robert E. 1996 “Financial Innovation in an Islamic Settings: The Case of Pakistan.” *Journal of South Asian and Middle Eastern Studies* 19(4): 1–30.

Siddiqi, Mohammad Nejatullah. 2006. “Islamic Banking and Finance in Theory and Practice: a Survey of State of the Art.” *Islamic Economic Studies* 13(2): 1–48.

Siddiqui, Anjum. 2008. “Financial contracts, risk and performance of Islamic banking.” *Managerial Finance* 34(10): 680–694.

Stiglitz, Joseph E. 1974. “Incentives and risk sharing in sharecropping.” *The Review of Economic Studies* 41(2): 219–255.

Sultan Abou-Ali. 2002. “Comments on Abalkhail and Presley.” In *Islamic Banking and Finance: New Perspectives on Profit-Sharing and Risk*, edited by Munawar Iqbal and David T. Llewellyn, 135–138. Cheltenham, UK: Edward Elgar Publishing.

Sundararajan, Vijay. 2007. “Risk measurement and disclosure in Islamic finance and the implications of profit sharing investment accounts.” In *Advances in Islamic economics and finance: proceedings of 6th International Conference on Islamic Economics and Finance*, edited by Munawar Iqbal, Salman Syed Ali, and Dadang Muljawan. 121–152. Jeddah: Islamic Development Bank.

Trester, Jeffrey J. 1998. “Venture capital contracting under asymmetric information.” *Journal of Banking and Finance* 22(6):675–699.

Widiyanto, Widiyanto, Siti Mutamimah, and Hendar Hendar. 2011. “Effectiveness of Qard al-hasan financing as a poverty alleviation model.” *Economic Journal of Emerging Markets* 3(1): 27–42.

Yazdani, Saeed. 2006. “Analyzing the Impact of Structural Change in Iranian Agricultural Credit System.” *Agricultural Economics Review* 7(2): 1–10.

Yousef, Tarik M. 2004. “The Murabaha Syndrome in Islamic Finance: Laws, Institutions and Politics.” In *The Politics of Islamic Finance*, edited by Clemens Henry and Rodney Wilson: 63–80. Edinburgh: Edinburgh University Press.

Muhammad Wajid Raza, Barbara L'Huillier, Dawood Ashraf

Chapter 10: The Effect of Market Regimes on the Performance of Market Capitalization-Weighted and Smart-Beta *Shariah*-Compliant Equity Portfolios

1 Introduction

A *Shariah*-compliant equity portfolio (SCEP) consists only of stocks that adhere to *Shariah*-compliant investment guidelines. Like any other equity portfolio, the SCEP is implemented by following two-steps – stock selection and a weighting scheme for asset allocation. The stocks are selected by implementing *Shariah*-compliant equity screening criteria usually consisting of two levels of screening: qualitative and quantitative (Ashraf, 2012; Ashraf, 2016; Arslan-Ayaydin et al., 2018).[126] The selection of securities and rebalancing of funds to comply with Islamic screening standards may result in superior returns as compared with an unscreened portfolio (Mohammad and Ashraf, 2015). Although *Shariah*-compliant investment guidelines are explicit on the selection criteria, no guiding principles are available for the weighting of portfolios (Boudt et al., 2019).

Given the silence of *Shariah*-compliant investment guidelines on 'weighting' methods, a recent study by Boudt et al., (2019) highlights the importance of weighting methods in SCEP construction. It is argued that weighting methods have implications for *Shariah*-compliant investors both in terms of the primary objective of adhering to *Shariah* principles, and the secondary objective related to financial performance (traditional risk-return optimization). The evidence suggests that characteristics-based SCEPs, such as market capitalization-weighted, fundamental value-weighted, equal-weighted, and low-risk weighted strategies exhibit different risk and return characteristics.[127] Boudt et al., (2019) also find that the construction style of SCEPs matters as it affects the relative performance of these portfolios.

Recent studies, including Ashraf and Khawaja (2016), Raza and Ashraf (2019) among others, highlight the performance of market capitalization and smart beta

126 For further information we refer readers to the studies by Ashraf (2016) and Raza (2020) which provide a detailed discussion on these screening guidelines.

127 These findings are tested in different geographical markets by Raza and Ashraf (2019).

Note: The views expressed in this paper are those of the author(s) and do not necessarily reflect the views of the Islamic Research and Training Institute or the Islamic Development Bank Group. All the remaining errors are the responsibility of the authors.

https://doi.org/10.1515/9783110587920-010

SCEPs in the long run. This chapter describes SCEPs and argues that the choice of weighting characteristic used for portfolio allocation not only affects the performance of SCEPs, but also results in significantly different financial performances, especially during market downturns. This argument is based on the studies conducted by Barberis and Shleifer (2003), Amenc et al., (2009), and Ardia et al., (2016), where it was shown that the performance of characteristics-based portfolios is time-varying. This chapter contributes to the existing literature on *Shariah*-compliant investment by providing evidence on the behavior of characteristics-based SCEPs during market downturns. More specifically, an attempt is made to answer the question of how characteristics-based (smart beta) SCEPs react to changing market conditions and whether they provide any hedging opportunities during market downturns as often claimed in the popular press.

Data from S&P 500 is used to estimate the investment universe and to obtain *Shariah*-compliant stocks, which are needed to build four characteristics-based portfolios. In order to examine changes in market returns, it is possible to categorize historical observations about market returns for the period 1986–2016 into two market regimes: high market regimes and low market regimes. High and low market regimes are identified using the Markov-regime switching model proposed by Hamilton (1989, 2005). The performance of each characteristics-based SCEP can then be analyzed under each market regime.

The empirical evidence suggests that smart beta SCEPs perform differently during high and low market regimes. Market capitalization SCEPs perform better under high market regimes while the low-risk strategy outperforms other SCEPs during low market regimes. It is also found that market capitalization and fundamental value-weighted SCEPs are tilted toward large stocks and are more pronounced during high market regimes. This is rather intuitive because growth firms tend to perform better when overall market returns are increasing. In addition, equal-weighted SCEPs are found to depend on the size premium in the sense that the tilt towards small stocks is more significant during high market regimes as compared to low market regimes.

The empirical findings also suggest that SCEPs based on a low-risk strategy exhibit superior performance under a low market regime. The superior performance of low risk SCEPs is mainly attributed to the existence of value premium. Finally, the analytical evidence suggests that SCEPs returns and risk characteristics are affected by market regimes. However, under a low market regime, a low-risk strategy constitutes a better hedge as it successfully reduces the maximum drawdown and shows relatively lower value-at-risk and expected shortfall as compared to the remaining three SCEP strategies.

The findings of this study have implications for both individual and institutional investors. It is possible to monitor investment decisions during market recoveries and market downturns. For instance, investors can benefit from these empirical findings and achieve stability in financial performance by designing dynamic allocation strategies that can exploit the time variation in characteristics-based portfolios. The findings of this analytical study are limited to the investment universe of *Shariah*-compliant equity portfolios in the U.S. market for the period 1986–2016. Further studies are thus needed to assess the robustness of these findings in other geographical locations with different time spans.

The rest of this chapter is organized as follows: Section 2 introduces *Shariah*-compliant equity portfolios and smart beta strategies. Section 3 presents the data and methodology that underpins this empirical study while Section 4 summarizes the main findings. Section 5 provides concluding comments.

2 *Shariah*-Compliant Equity Portfolios (SCEPs)

Shariah-compliant equity portfolios are designed to adhere to Islamic jurisprudence principles (*Shariah*) especially designed for *Shariah*-compliant equity investments based on the guidance of *Shariah* scholars (Ashraf, 2016; Ashraf and Khawaja, 2016). These principles are mainly concerned with three areas: being free from *riba* (interest), ethical concerns, and fairness of contract (free of *gharar*, *maysir*, and *mujazafah*). This implies that *Shariah*-compliant investors have additional obligations and preferences as compared to conventional investors when making investment decisions to achieve the primary objective of adhering to *Shariah* principles, and the secondary objective of pursuing higher financial performance (traditional risk-return optimization) (Arslan-Ayaydin et al., 2018).

As noted above, like conventional equity portfolios, SCEPs are implemented in two steps, namely the selection of stocks and their weighting criteria. In the selection step, a *Shariah*-compliant investor selects only those stocks that respect *Shariah*-compliant investment principles (Raza, 2020). This selection is performed according to *Shariah* screens, which are described in Ashraf and Mohammad (2014) and Ashraf (2016) among others. These stock screens are negative exclusionary in nature and are implemented in practice following two stages, namely qualitative screens (sectoral screens) and quantitative screens (financial screens).

Qualitative screens exclude all firms from the investment universe whose core operations are not *Shariah*-compliant. For example, firms producing or distributing alcohol, tobacco, pork or pork-related products, all media agencies (except news agencies), firms providing adult entertainment services, firms engaged in weapons production, and all interest-based financial institutions (conventional banks, conventional insurance) are systematically excluded. These qualitative screens reduce the investment universe significantly (Derigs and Marzban 2008; Ashraf and Khawaja 2016; Boudt et al., 2019). However, the remaining firms may still generate interest-based revenues or pay interest on financial leverage in the course of addressing issues related to working capital requirements and trade financing (Arslan-Ayaydin et al., 2018). Therefore, a second round of screens, known as quantitative screens, are used to further 'clean' the investment universe. These screens mainly focus on three financial indicators of firms: financial leverage, liquid assets, and interest revenues.

The above discussion shows that the selection criteria in *Shariah*-compliance are rather explicit. However, *Shariah*-compliant investment guidelines are silent on the weighting criteria in portfolio management. Most of the world's leading indices are implemented using a market capitalization-weighted strategy. However, studies conducted by Arnott et al., (2005) and Hsu (2006), in the case of conventional portfolios, show that market capitalization may not be an efficient strategy. While Boudt et al., (2019) and Raza and Ashraf (2019) show that *Shariah*-compliant investors should consider alternative weighting strategies for the construction of equity portfolios. The next section discusses why the market capitalization-weighted strategy may not be an optimal choice for the construction of equity portfolios.

2.1 Weighting Allocation Strategies for *Shariah*-Compliant Equity Portfolios

As noted above, current *Shariah*-compliant investment guidelines provided by leading index providers and financial institutions are silent on the weighting methods to be used in SCEP construction. Most of the prominent *Shariah* indices are implemented using the market capitalization-weighted strategy. The possible reasons for this preference are explained next followed by a description of how a SCEP is constructed using this strategy. The main arguments for and against the market capitalization-weighted strategy are then summarized before discussing alternative weighting methods.

2.1.1 Market Capitalization-Weighted Strategy

A market capitalization-based market portfolio holds an important place in the equity investment community as most mutual funds, unit trusts, and exchange-traded funds track the performance of indices constructed using a market capitalization-weighted strategy (Raza and Ashraf, 2019). This approach has a number of advantages. First, it offers opportunities for broader risk diversification. Second, as this weighting strategy mimics the broader market index, it has the ability to automatically rebalance (Perold, 2007). Third, this systematic rebalancing has the potential to reduce the number of transactions in the rebalancing process and thus leads to relatively less turnover as compared to alternative weighted portfolios (Zhang, 2006). Fourth, if the capital asset pricing model (CAPM) of Sharpe (1964) and Lintner (1965) holds, then the market capitalization-weighted portfolio is a mean-variance efficient portfolio. Fifth, as discussed by Perold (2007), the market capitalization-weighted portfolio has, by definition, the ability to aggregate the overall market portfolio, and this explains why it is the only strategy that all investors can theoretically follow. Finally, this strategy has the potential to identify young growth firms, which may not be strong enough in terms of fundamental indicators, but may receive more weight in a market capitalization-weighted index that takes upward price trends for growth stocks into consideration (Arnott et al., 2005).

In a market capitalization-weighted portfolio, the weights of each stock are computed as a function of its market value. The market value is determined as the product of share price and the number of common shares outstanding. In the case of a *Shariah*-compliant equity portfolio, it is possible to:

$$w_{i,t}^{MC} = \frac{P_{i,t}.n_{i,t}.I_{i,t}.S_{i,t}}{\sum_{i=1}^{N} P_{i,t}.n_{i,t}.I_{i,t}.S_{i,t}}, \tag{1}$$

where $S_{i,t}$ is the dummy for *Shariah*-compliance, and it ensures that only *Shariah*-compliant stocks are included in the market capitalization-weighted SCEP at each rebalancing date t. $I_{i,t}$ is the dummy which ensures that firm i belongs to the S&P 500 active constituents at each rebalancing date t.

2.2 Suggested Improvements in Weighting Strategies

As mentioned earlier, the market capitalization-weighted strategy currently holds a prominent position in the investment industry. However, some researchers such as Hsu (2006) among others, criticize the assumption regarding market efficiency that underpins this strategy. The literature on the CAPM rejects the mean-variance efficiency of market capitalization equity indices (Arnott et al., 2005). Hsu (2006) also argues that, based on plausible assumptions regarding stock prices, the market capitalization strategy can be relatively sub-optimal as compared to alternative strategies based on criteria other than market capitalization.

Perold (2007) argues that there are fundamental flaws in the construction of market capitalization-weighted portfolios. The weights assigned to individual firms within the overall equity portfolio are indeed a function of market capitalization. Thus, firms with higher share prices receive larger weights as compared to firms with relatively lower share prices. This often leads to the concentration of portfolios in larger firms (Arnott et al., 2005). This strategy can also lead to performance drag as it tends to overweight overpriced stocks and underweight underpriced stocks. In the case of market reversals, stocks with positive pricing errors can be conducive indeed to severe future losses.

The issue of market capitalization weighting is equally important for *Shariah*-compliant equity investors. As mentioned in Section 2, *Shariah*-compliant investment guidelines mainly focus on negative screening based on the core operations of firms but, they are silent on the weighting methods to be used for the construction of equity portfolios. This indicates that current *Shariah* investment guidelines assume that *Shariah*-compliance can only be violated at the selection stage where many investors provide funds to non-compliant equities. This may be true in the case of an individual investor who contemplates investing in the equity of a single firm. At the level of portfolio investment however, there is no guidance about portfolio weighting for *Shariah*-compliant investors. To address this issue, Derigs and Marzban (2008) advocate a new portfolio framework whereby *Shariah*-compliance should be judged at both the individual stock and portfolio levels.

A recent study by Boudt et al., (2019) suggest that *Shariah*-compliant investors should seriously reassess the use of market capitalization-weighted strategies in the construction of equity portfolios, as they may lead to a clear violation of one of the basic assumptions of the CAPM, namely that investors can invest in all available stocks (Sharpe, 1964; Lintner, 1965). For example, *Shariah* investment guidelines prohibit investment in firms generating interest-based revenues, thus excluding investment in all conventional banks and insurance firms. Because of the restricted investment universe, the CAPM prediction that market equilibrium outcome should lead to investment weighting according to a mean-variance efficient portfolio may not be applicable for *Shariah*-compliant investors.

Another argument against the use of the market capitalization strategy in the construction of SCEPs is put forward by Treynor (2005). It is argued that if stock prices are not efficient, in the sense that prices do not reflect all available information, then the market capitalization strategy can result in two possibly detrimental outcomes. First, underpriced stocks may result in lower capitalization relative to their fair value. Second, overpriced stocks may find higher representation in the form of portfolio weights due to their size. If pricing errors are not persistent, then mean reversion implies that the market capitalization strategy would be conducive to losses due to measurement errors – the determinant of optimal portfolio weight will result in additional losses due to additional investment in stocks with positive investment errors (Hsu, 2006; Treynor, 2005). Finally, Boudt et al., (2019) argue that if the mispricing is significant and the SCEP gains from speculation based on short-run momentum effects in the equity market, then such speculative gains could possibly violate the *Shariah* principles of *gharar* and *mujazafah*.

It is possible to argue however, that mispricing can be defined in terms of temporary deviations by market prices from intrinsic values, and that it is a sign of market inefficiency. Under these conditions, profits may be derived from trading aimed at eliminating arbitrage opportunities. Arbitrage trading is intrinsically different from speculative activities based on margin trading and short sales. Thus, it may be difficult to argue that SCEP gains from mispricing are necessarily made in violation of *Shariah* investment rules.

2.3 Smart Beta Strategies

Smart beta strategies are passive management strategies that use alternative weighting methods in equity portfolio management (Roncalli, 2013) and that are transparent in their application (Hsu et al., 2015). The goal of smart beta strategies is to achieve superior portfolio performance by (a) reducing the overall risk of the portfolio and/or (b) improving risk diversification opportunities across equities. In a broad sense, these strategies refer to the systematic selection and weighting of individual stocks in a portfolio based on factors other than market capitalization (Amenc et al., 2009). The most common stock characteristics that are used to construct smart beta strategies are based on either: the number of stocks in the portfolio, risk characteristics of individual stocks, relative valuation, profitability, or other strong fundamentals of the firm.

Constructing equity portfolios based on characteristics other than market capitalization allows for various smart beta strategies to exploit different opportunities for risk premia by tilting portfolio weights towards equity factors such as size, value, growth, momentum, and profitability, inter alia.[128] In recent years the popularity of characteristics-based strategies has increased significantly, and many new indices and funds have been introduced based on these smart beta strategies. Hsu et al., (2015) note that there are currently more than 250 equity factors.[129] This provides the foundation for the construction of single factor smart beta strategies as well as multi-factor smart beta strategies.

In this study, three types of characteristics-based portfolios are considered, namely the fundamental value-weighted strategy, equal-weighted strategy, and low-risk weighted strategy. Based on a review of the literature on alternative weighting strategies, it is found that these strategies have the three main attributes recommended by Hsu et al., (2015) for the success of smart beta strategies. First, there is theoretical justification and performance persistence underpinning these three strategies. Second, there is strong empirical evidence regarding superior performance across time and different geographical locations. Third, performance is robust to different measures used to identify different risk premia. In addition, Obaidullah (2005) critiques the market capitalization strategy for SCEPs and suggests the use of other measures based on firms' fundamentals such as company size and profitability. Obaidullah (2005) also stresses the benefit of using different strategies under different market conditions.

128 For a detailed discussion about the performance of equity factors, we refer the readers to Barberis and Shleifer (2003).

129 A factor is the combination of securities that have the same risk and return characteristics based on attributes such as size, value, growth, quality, and momentum (Hsu et al., 2015; Bender et al., 2013; Fama and French, 1992, 2015a).

2.3.1 Fundamental Value-weighted Strategy

The market capitalization strategy depends on weighing decisions about the market evaluation of the firm (Hsu, 2006). In contrast, the fundamental value-weighted strategy uses the fundamental strength of the firm, which is assessed using accounting-based financial variables. In practice, these weights can either be implemented as a function of a single accounting-based indicator or as a function of a composite index. In the former case, the weighting decision is based on a single financial indicator such as firm size (total assets or market value), profitability, or liquidity. However, this weighting decision may result in weight concentration in firms with higher book value (Arnott et al., 2005). To overcome this measurement problem a composite index is used instead. It does not focus on only one financial indicator; rather it takes into consideration multiple factors such as book value of equity, sales, dividends, and cash flow. To avoid volatility, fundamental weights are estimated with four years of rolling averages. If there are missing observations for some fundamental indicators, the weights are implemented as a composite index of the remaining three financial indicators.

It can be argued that the fundamental value-weighted strategy also favors large firms but, it also considers liquidity, turnover, and the profitability of firms. Studies conducted by Arnott et al., (2005), Blitz and Swinkels (2008), and Chow et al., (2011) demonstrate that fundamental value-weighted portfolios either outperform or exhibit a similar performance in comparison to market capitalization-weighted portfolios. The outperformance of the fundamental value-weighted strategy also persists in the case of SCEPs (Boudt et al., 2019; Raza and Ashraf, 2019). In the case of SCEPs, the weights of individual firms based on the fundamental value-weighted strategy can be estimated as follows:

$$w_{i,t}^{FW} = \frac{1}{4}\sum_{k=1}^{4}\left(\frac{\max\{x_{k,1},0\}.I_{i,t}.S_{i,t}}{\sum_{j=1}^{N}\max\{x_{k,j},0\}.I_{i,t}.S_{j,t}},\ldots,\frac{\max\{x_{k,N},0\}.I_{i,t}.S_{j,t}}{\sum_{j=1}^{N}\max\{x_{k,j},0\}.I_{i,t}.S_{j,t}}\right) \tag{2}$$

where $x_{1,i}$ is the size of firm i measured as the book value of common equity, and $x_{2,i}$, $x_{3,i}$ and $x_{4,i}$ are four years of rolling averages of annual dividends, net operating cash flows, and sales, respectively. We follow Boudt et al., (2019) and Raza and Ashraf (2019) and implement the fundamental value weights of *Shariah*-compliant portfolios as a function of four financial indicators: size, dividends, cash flow, and sales based on a four year rolling window. These observations are then normalized to estimate the individual weight for each variable. Finally, a composite index is estimated from individual weight's matrices, and the weights are re-normalized to achieve a fully invested portfolio. In the case of missing data for dividends, the fundamental-weight is estimated from the remaining three indicators.

2.3.2 Equal-weighted Strategy

The main benefit of the equal-weighted strategy is that it ignores firm characteristics such as market value or firm size, in the weight allocation decision. Instead, it assigns equal weights to each firm in the portfolio (Benartzi and Thaler, 2001; Windcliff and Phelim, 2004). This strategy is also referred to as the contrarian investment strategy because, and in contrast to the market capitalization strategy, it buys low and sells high, and it allows perfect diversification across the investment universe. Due to its contrarian nature the equal-weighted portfolio performs better in market reversals.

DeMiguel et al., (2007) compared the performance of various weighting strategies using a mean-variance model and other model extensions. They found that none of the 14 models can outperform equal-weighted portfolios in terms of the Sharpe ratio, equivalent returns, and turnover. However, the performance of mean-variance optimized portfolios improves when the estimation window is increased to incorporate a longer time period (DeMiguel et al., 2007). There are, however, studies that criticize these findings including Kritzman et al., (2010) who suggest that the apparent out-performance of the equal-weighted strategy is not due to the optimization process, rather it is the result of the rolling short-term samples used to predict expected returns. Despite this evidence, the equal-weighted strategy still holds a prominent position in the literature on smart beta strategies as numerous studies have shown that the equal-weighted strategy does result in superior returns e.g., Hsu (2006), Hsu et al., (2015), and Bertrand and Lapointe (2015).

Studies conducted by Boudt et al., (2019) and Raza and Ashraf (2019) add to the literature on equal-weighted portfolios by testing the performance of this strategy in the context of the *Shariah*-compliant investment universe, and find evidence that confirms its superior performance. However, a major issue with the equal-weighted strategy is that it results in relatively high risk and high turnover in comparison to the market capitalization-weighted strategy (Boudt et al., 2019). In addition, the equal-weighted portfolio strategy is heuristic, and it can be very simple for investors to use as the weights assigned to each stock are dictated only by the investment universe of stocks to which equal-weights are applied (Chow et al., 2011). But, it should be noted also that this strategy ignores the risk and return characteristics of individual portfolio components.

In this analytical study the equal-weighted strategy for *Shariah*-compliant stocks is implemented with the following formula:

$$w_{i,t}^{EW} = \frac{I_{i,t}.S_{i,t}}{\sum_{j=1}^{N} I_{i,t}.S_{j,t}}, \tag{3}$$

where N represents the number of stocks in the *Shariah*-compliant investment universe.

2.3.3 Low-risk Weighted Strategy

Portfolio construction methodologies based on predicted risk, such as the low-risk portfolio strategy, are gaining more interest (Clarke et al., 2013).[130] The low-risk weighted strategy is motivated, in part, by the seminal work of Ang et al., (2006) on cross-sectional equity risk anomaly.

The low-risk portfolio strategy assigns weights to individual components of a portfolio in such a way that it reduces the overall risk of the portfolio. A low-risk portfolio can be structured by following a heuristic approach (Boudt and Peeters, 2013; Alighanbari et al., 2016; Boudt et al., 2019; Raza and Ashraf, 2019) or by minimum-variance optimization (Chow et al., 2011; Bertrand and Lapointe, 2015).

The heuristic approach first ranks the investment universe based on the relative riskiness of individual stocks and selects less risky stocks to include in the portfolio. The number of low-risk stocks to be included is arbitrary and can vary between funds and indices.[131] Weights are then assigned to each stock based on its risk characteristics such as volatility (Chow et al., 2011). The weights of each portfolio component are inversely proportional to its risk characteristics such that stocks with the lowest risk receive the highest weight and so on. It is important to mention here that the risk of each stock can be calculated as the volatility in stock returns (Boudt et al., 2019), or CAPM beta estimate (Lee, 2011), or semi deviation of stock returns as a measure of downside risk. While the heuristic approach is rather straight forward in its application, it can lead to a value trap.[132]

The optimization-based technique considers both the individual risk component and the effect of correlation between stocks (Baker and Haugen, 2012; Alighanbari et al., 2016). Optimization-based low-risk portfolios can be implemented in many ways, with differences in application primarily stemming from the method of variance-covariance matrix estimation and the nature of constraints introduced, such as budget constraints, maximum weights constraints, short sales, diversification, and turnover (Clarke et al., 2006). Optimization-based weights are flexible, but may face complex computational and tractability problems especially, the estimation of the variance-covariance matrix.[133]

---

130 Studies show risk can be forecasted with relatively higher accuracy as compared to returns which are noisy and exposed to the nature of data.

131 For example, the S&P 500 low volatility index selects the top 100 stocks with the lowest volatility.

132 Low volatility can be the result of less liquidity. To deal with this limitation constraints are often imposed to ensure liquidity, stability, and diversification across sectors and exposure to different geographical markets.

133 The simplest way to estimate the variance-covariance matrix is based on the returns of individual stocks but this method is very sensitive to returns' forecasts and the number of assets within a portfolio. As the number of stocks in a portfolio increases, it increases the size of the variance-covariance matrix, and thus requires more parameters to be estimated. Furthermore, the instability

The popularity of low-risk portfolios is consistent with the empirical evidence lending support to the so-called 'low-risk anomaly' suggesting investors can achieve superior returns by focusing on low-risk portfolios as compared with market capitalization portfolios. The superior performance of low-risk strategies has been documented by a number of studies in different geographical locations. For example, Clarke et al. (2006) suggest that, based on the 1,000 largest U.S. stocks between 1968 and 2005, minimum-variance portfolios achieve a volatility reduction of about 25 percent while delivering comparable or even higher average returns than market capitalization-weighted portfolios. Likewise, Baker and Haugen (2012) provide evidence that the low-risk strategy outperforms the market capitalization-weighted strategy for the sample period from 1971 to 2012. The superior performance of the low-risk strategy is not limited to U.S. markets as shown by Ang et al. (2006). The evidence extends to many developing and emerging markets (Ang et al., 2009; Baker and Haugen 2012). In addition, Blitz et al. (2013) indicate that the superior performance of the low-risk strategy persists even after controlling for value and momentum factors.

There is a considerable body of literature that refers to the higher performance of low-risk portfolios as a 'puzzle'. It is considered to be at odds with one of the most fundamental principles of finance – the trade-off between risk and return. According to this principle the higher the risk associated with an investment, the higher its expected return. The CAPM suggests that investors should not expect superior risk premia from holding assets with risk levels considerably lower than market risk (Alighanbari et al., 2016). None-the-less, the low-risk anomaly is often explained with arguments drawn from behavioural finance literature.[134]

The low-risk strategy is also analyzed in the context of *Shariah*-compliant stocks. In a recent study, Ashraf et al. (2017) demonstrate that *Shariah*-compliant portfolios exhibit higher returns than minimum-variance portfolios and suggest that better performance can be attributed to less risky stocks in such portfolios. Boudt et al. (2019) find that a low-risk strategy when implemented with *Shariah* restrictions outperforms market capitalization *Shariah*-compliant portfolios in the U.S. for the period 1986–2014. Their study is extended by Raza and Ashraf (2019) who find superior performance for low-risk SCEPs in Europe, the GCC, Australia, Canada, Malaysia, and Indonesia.

---

of individual stock volatility and correlation can result in poor estimates (Bouchey and Nimtchinov, 2010). However, recent studies address these issues and more practical and robust techniques have been introduced to estimate the variance-covariance matrix, see for example Ledoit and Wolf (2003), Ledoit and Wolf (2004), Fan et al. (2008), and Boudt et al. (2012).

134 Some of the key reasons for the superior performance of low-risk portfolios suggested from a behavioural finance perspective are: the lottery effect, representativeness, overconfidence, agency issues, and asymmetric issues. For a detail discussion on each of these factors we refer the readers to Alighanbari et al. (2016). Apart from these factors the gain-loss asymmetry also plays a key role in the long run outperformance of the low-risk strategy as compare to the market capitalization strategy.

The present analysis follows Boudt et al. (2019) and Raza and Ashraf (2019) in implementing a low-risk strategy with a heuristic approach that selects a group of 100 stocks with the lowest volatility estimated from two-years rolling windows of stock returns. This methodology is also followed by the S&P 500 low volatility index. The weights in the case of a *Shariah*-compliant portfolio under this low-risk strategy are computed as follows:

$$w_{i,t}^{LR} = \frac{\frac{1}{\sigma_{i,t}}.I_{i,t}.S_{i,t}.L_{i,t}}{\sum_{i=1}^{N}\frac{1}{\sigma_{i,t}}.I_{i,t}.S_{i,t}.L_{i,\ t}}, \tag{4}$$

where $\sigma_{i,t}$ is the return volatility for stock i at time t estimated over a 24-months rolling window and $L_{i,t}$ is the dummy variable indicating whether a stock is included among the 100 least volatile *Shariah* stocks. The dummy $S_{i.t}$ is absent in the case of unrestricted portfolios.

2.4 Time Variation in the Performance of Market Capitalization and Alternative Weighted Portfolios

A detailed review of three well-known smart beta strategies was presented in Section 2.3. The literature mostly highlights the performance of smart beta strategies in comparison with the market capitalization-weighted strategy. As smart beta strategies represent alternative weight allocation strategies based on different risk premia, it is unlikely that one smart beta strategy will consistently perform better than the others and lead to mean-variance efficiency (Ardia et al. 2016). It is argued in this chapter that the performance of each smart beta strategy is time-varying. The intuition behind this argument is founded on the rules-based weight allocation algorithms of each smart beta strategy.

Each smart beta strategy utilizes a unique risk premium associated with different equity factors such as size, growth, value, momentum, and quality factors. The difference lies in the 'factor loadings' which result in heterogeneous weight allocations and sector exposures that subsequently lead to time variations in the performance of each respective portfolio strategy. For example, the market capitalization and fundamental value-weighted strategies are mostly tilted towards stocks of larger firms. Therefore, these two strategies tend to show high exposure to growth stocks (Boudt et al. 2019) and it is expected that these two strategies will perform better in market rallies but underperform during market drawdowns. The equal-weighted strategy is contrarian in nature and by design it invests more in small stocks, thus benefiting from size premium. It is expected that small stocks will perform better in association with market reversals (Barberis and Shleifer, 2003). The low-risk strategy invests in less risky stocks and, therefore, may result in higher tracking errors. The systematic risk of a low-risk strategy (CAPM beta) is significantly different from unity. It is expected that the low-risk strategy will slightly underperform in comparison to market capitalization and fundamental value-weighted strategies in association with market rallies, but show resilience to market drawdowns, as suggested by the earlier findings of Ardia et al. (2016) and Boudt et al. (2019).

The time-varying performance of smart beta strategies is highlighted by a number of studies. Reference can be made to Barberis and Shleifer (2003), Ardia et al. (2016), and Boudt et al. (2019). This study represents an attempt to test the relative performance of *Shariah*-compliant smart beta strategies depending on the Markov regimes vs. equity market regimes.

2.5 The Markov Regime Switching Model and Abrupt Changes in Market Returns

The empirical evidence suggests that economic time series tend to exhibit occasional breaks associated with either the onset of financial crises (Jeanne and Masson, 2000; Hamilton, 2005) or changes in government policies (Hamilton 1989; Sims and Zha 2006) among other significant events. Financial time series can also react to abrupt changes in macroeconomic conditions. For example, the S&P 500 shows a steady upward trend until the onset of the dot-com crisis and then exhibits a downward trend. The same observation applies to the recent U.S. financial crisis.

Abrupt changes in the overall market can affect asset prices (Ang and Bekaert 2002; Guidolin and Timmermann 2008). The related literature refers to such price changes as 'regime shifts' i.e. the overall market often oscillates between a state of lower volatility and a state of higher volatility. There is evidence that the low-volatility state is characterized by steady economic growth while the high-volatility state shows economic contraction (Kritzman et al. 2012). The literature also provides ample evidence for the presence of such regimes during periods of market turbulence, economic growth, inflation, and fluctuations in interest rates (Ang and Bekaert 2002; Kritzman et al. 2012; Boudt et al. 2019).

The econometric question that needs to be addressed is how to identify such regimes in financial time series data? The leading choices to estimate financial regimes are linear models, such as simple autoregressive models (AR), threshold models, moving average models (MA), or even the more advanced mixed autoregressive moving average models (ARMA).

Although linear models are more common and have numerous applications, they are not very successful in capturing non-linear patterns in financial time series data such as volatility asymmetry or volatility clusters in stock market returns. For example, it is evident from the historical prices of S&P 500 for the period 1986–2016 as shown in Figure 10.1, that index prices typically fluctuate around a higher level and are more persistent during market rallies such as upward price events in the 1990s and after the burst of the dot-com bubble. The price index remains at a relatively lower level and is less persistent during periods of market downturns such as during the period 2000–2001 and 2008–2009.

Figure 10.1: Historical Price Movements of S&P 500 over the Period 1986–2016.
Source: S&P 500.

Thus, the literature suggests the use of non-linear models in order to capture non-linear dynamics. Non-linear models include threshold autoregressive models, artificial neural network models, random switching models, and Markov regime switching models, inter alia.[135] However, while non-linear models have the potential to capture

135 The simple use of the autoregressive threshold model comes at a cost as this model suffers from two major limitations. First, the choice of threshold level to decide the cut-off level between high and low regimes may be arbitrary. Second, as the order of lag is subjective it is difficult to generalize it to all financial time series data. The artificial neural network suffers from identification problems and the random switching model is very noisy as it reacts to even minor macroeconomic shocks. Finally, it is noted that threshold autoregressive models can be regarded as part of the family of state-dependent or regime-switching models. The Self-Exciting Threshold Autoregressive (SETAR) model proposed by Chan and Tong (1986) allows for the variable that determines the prevailing state to be represented by the lagged response. In contrast, the Smooth-Transition Autoregressive (STAR) model developed by Terasvirta and Anderson (1992) provides a remedy for the potential of abrupt switches in parameter values by imposing a smoother transition in the regime-switching process.

complex dynamics in the underlying variables they are no panacea and have some limitations including the failure to convergence following local optimum points in the parameter space (Kuan 2002). These models are mostly designed for a specific data pattern and cannot be generalized to diverse data sets with varying data dynamics. In addition, these non-linear models may require demanding mathematical estimation methods.

This study follows Ang and Bekaert (2002) and Kritzman et al. (2012) and estimates the high and low regimes in S&P 500 returns with the Markov regime-switching model. This approach can permit switching behavior among different states governed by transition probabilities. The switching mechanism in Markov regime-switching models is controlled by a latent variable that follows a first order Markov chain. It is important to note that the prevailing state reflected by the latent variable is inferred from available information (Hamilton, 1989). The Markov model assumes that the current state depends on the most recent observation, the first lag which may persist for a specific time. The current state may be subsequently replaced by another state following macroeconomic shocks or some other significant event that has the potential to trigger regime shifts.

3 Data and Methodology

3.1 Data

To evaluate the time-varying performance of market capitalization-weighted portfolios and smart beta SCEPs, the active constituents of S&P 500 are used as the reference investment universe for the sample period 1986–2016. For the purpose of return calculations, monthly observations of adjusted closing prices for all S&P 500 stocks are obtained from the COMPUSTAT database. The estimation of market capitalization is based on quarterly prices and the number of common shares outstanding. The 24-months trailing average of market capitalization is used as the denominator in the calculation of financial ratios.

For *Shariah* screening, data on the fundamental values of all firms is used with quantitative screens based on cash, short-term investments, account receivables, and total debt, with data available on a quarterly basis from the COMPUSTAT database. Qualitative screens are applied using the Global Industrial Classification Standards (GICS) codes for each equity-issuing firm. The GICS codes provide details about related sectors and sub-sectors. To implement fundamental weights, quarterly data for four financial variables namely book value of common equity, dividends, sales, and net operating cash flows are also used. Net operating cash flows are calculated as the difference between operating income before depreciation and total accruals.

3.2 Methodology

It is noted again that the principal objective of this analytical study is to examine the time-varying regime-switching performance of market capitalization and smart beta strategies for *Shariah*-compliant portfolios. The following subsections provide the detailed methodology used for portfolio construction, econometric approach used to identify market regimes, and analysis of the time-varying performance in the presence of market regimes.

3.2.1 Market Capitalization and Smart Beta SCEPs

As noted earlier, *Shariah*-compliant equity portfolios invest only in stocks that meet *Shariah*-compliant investment guidelines. Like conventional portfolios a *Shariah*-compliant equity portfolio is also implemented by first selecting stocks from among the available universe of assets and then assigning weights to each stock within the portfolio. The *Shariah*-compliant asset universe is obtained as a subset of the overall investment universe, which is all stocks in the S&P 500 index. The qualitative and quantitative screening guidelines provided in the fact sheet of the Dow Jones Islamic Market Indices (DJIMI) are applied to screen this investment universe. The qualitative screening rules exclude all firms from the investment universe with core operations based on any of the following non-compliant activities: production and distribution of alcohol, tobacco, pork, adult entertainment services, media agencies (except news), gambling, conventional banks, and conventional insurance. The qualitative screens further exclude from the investment universe all firms with cash and short-term investments exceeding 33% of market capitalization or, with total debt exceeding 33% of market capitalization or, with account receivables exceeding 33% of market capitalization.

The next step is to construct market capitalization-weighted SCEPs and smart-beta SCEPs. Each firm in the investment universe from S&P 500 active constituents is denoted as i where $i = 1, \ldots, N_t$. The portfolios are rebalanced with monthly frequency at time $t = 1, \ldots, T$. To ensure investment is only in the active constituents of S&P 500, the dummy $I_{i,t}$ is introduced with the value of 1 assigned if stock i belongs to S&P 500 at time t, and zero otherwise. To obtain the *Shariah*-compliant investment universe according to the DJIMI *Shariah* investment guidelines, another dummy $S_{i,t}$ is introduced taking the value of 1 if stock i respects both the quantitative and qualitative screening guidelines at each rebalancing time t, and zero otherwise.

Finally, the portfolio weights of market capitalization, fundamental value-weighted, equal-weighted, and low-risk weighted portfolios are also determined according to Equations (1), (2), (3), and (4) respectively. It is important to note that all portfolios are fully invested such that the weights aggregate to 1 and short-selling is not allowed given its prohibition in Islamic finance.

3.2.2 Methodology to Identify Market Regimes

To identify a break in market returns, it is assumed that at time t there is a macroeconomic shock and that the market reacts with an abrupt change in prices. A switch from one regime to another is reflected by a change in market returns, which is not a deterministic event in the sense that the change is not known a priori at time t_0 ahead of the time period t. The change from one state to another is rather stochastic and is caused by some imperfectly predictable underlying variables. However, the persistence in the current state and the switching behavior can be explained with probabilistic models. The Markov regime switching model[136] that encompasses the later states can be expressed as follows:

$$y_t = c_{s_t} + \varnothing y_{t-1} + \varepsilon_t, \tag{5}$$

where s_t is the random variable which takes the value of $s_t = 1$ for the first regime over the period $t = 1, 2 \ldots, t_0$, and the value $s_t = 2$ is for the second regime over the period $t = t_0 + 1, t_0 + 2, \ldots, t_0 + n$. The switching behavior is governed by a transition matrix, denoted by T_p. The elements of the transition probabilities can be written in the following matrix form as:

$$T_p = \begin{bmatrix} P_{ii} & P_{ij} \\ P_{ji} & P_{jj} \end{bmatrix} \tag{6}$$

where P_{ii} is the probability that the state variable will remain in state i, and indicates the likelihood P_{ij} shows that the state will switch from regime i to regime j. In the above transition probability matrix, P_{ij} is estimated as:

$$p_i^j = (X_t = j | X_{t-1} = i) \tag{7}$$

In order to highlight the change from a given state to the other, such as from $s_t = 1$, to $s_t = 2$, a probabilistic model is needed to explain the transition. According to Hamilton (1989), s_t is the realization of a two-state Markov chain governed by the transition probability function:

$$\Pr(s_{tj} = j | s_{t-1} = i,\ s_{t-2} = k, \ldots, y_{t-1},\ y_{t-1}, y_{t-2}, \ldots) = \Pr(s_t = j | s_{t-1} = i) = p_{ij} \tag{8}$$

The specification in Equation (7) shows that the probability of the current state depends only on the most recent observation. As mentioned earlier, the Markov regime-switching model assumes that the current state of the variable s_t is not directly observable, however, its behavior can be inferred from the most recent observation y_t. This inference is expressed in the form of two transition probabilities as:

136 See Laverty et al. (2002) for a simple explanation of the Markov regime switching model.

$$\xi_{jt} = \Pr(s_t = j|\Omega_t;\ \theta) \tag{9}$$

where j represents the probabilities of low and high regimes at time t and these two probabilities add to 1 by construction. Ω_t represents the observations of the variable of interest $y_t,\ y_{t-1}, \ldots, y_t, y_0$ at time t. θ represents the set of parameters included in the estimation of the probabilities of the state variable at each iteration.

Following Hamilton (2010), the set of parameters include the mean and standard deviation values and intercepts $(c_1,\ c_2)$ for high and low regimes respectively, as well as the autoregressive term $\varnothing$, and the transition probabilities to stay in the current regime (P_{11} *and* P_{22}). Thus, these parameters are also useful in estimating the probability density function for both regimes as follows:

$$\eta_{jt} = f(y_t|s_t = j,\ \Omega_{t-1};\ \theta) = \frac{1}{\sqrt{2\pi\sigma}} \exp\left[-\frac{\left(y_t - c_j - \varphi y_{t-1}\right)^2}{2\sigma^2}\right]^2, \tag{10}$$

Based on the conditional density of each observation, it is possible to estimate the final probability of the remaining variable in a specific regime as follows:

$$\Xi_{jt} = \frac{\sum_{i=1}^{2} P_{ij}\xi_{it-1}\eta_{jt}}{f(y_t|\Omega_{t-1};\theta)}, \tag{11}$$

where ξ_{it-1} are probabilities estimated with respect to the most recent period. It is important to note that the observations follow a normal distribution and that the parameters for each iteration are optimized using maximum likelihood estimation as shown is Equation (12).

$$\log f(y_{1,2}, \ldots, y_t|y_0;\ \theta) = \sum_{i=1}^{T} \log\ f(y_t|\Omega_{t-1}{:}\theta), \tag{12}$$

3.2.3 Performance Evaluation

Performance is measured, in terms of risk and return, by analyzing monthly data on an annual basis. To estimate the level of risk for each portfolio, the annualized volatility is computed as the standard deviation of monthly returns, which is annualized with the square-root-of-time rule. The maximum value of drawdowns, value-at-risk, and expected shortfall are also used for risk purposes. The drawdowns are measured using the percentage loss from peak to trough whereas value-at-risk is measured 95% historical value-at-risk, computed as the 5% quantile of the monthly returns. The returns of all SCEPs are assessed relative to the level of risk incurred. For this purpose, we estimate the Sharpe ratio and Jensen's alpha obtained from the five-factor model of Fama and French (2015b).

In order to evaluate the time-varying performance of SCEPs following different weighting strategies with different market regimes, it is possible to carry out the analysis in two steps. The performance of all SCEPs is first evaluated with respect to the full sample period (1984–2016). The full sample period is divided into two periods based on high and low regimes of market returns. This type of analysis enables us to observe clearly the behavior of each SCEP during market rallies as well as times of economic turmoil.

4 Empirical Results and Discussion

In light of the above discussion, the empirical results shed light on two important issues. First, do smart beta strategies perform better than a market capitalization-based strategy when implemented with *Shariah*-compliant stocks? Second, how do smart-beta SCEPs and market capitalization-based portfolios respond to market regimes especially the downturns?

4.1 Performance Using the Full Sample

The performance of the market capitalization-weighted market portfolio and SCEPs for the full sample period is presented in Table 10.1. In terms of overall performance, the SCEPs implemented with market capitalization and smart-beta strategies performed better than market portfolios. Equal-weighted SCEPs achieve the highest annualized returns and outperform both market-capitalization and other smart-beta SCEPs. Fundamental value-weighted SCEPs are found to have similar performance characteristics as market-capitalization SCEPs. Thus, the results presented in Panel A lend support to the earlier work of Arnott et al., (2005) and Boudt et al., (2019).

In term of risk characteristics, the results in Panel B of Table 10.1 indicate that the superior performance of equal-weighted SCEPs, reflected by higher annualized returns, comes at the cost of higher volatility. However, the low-risk strategy results in the lowest risk in terms of volatility whereas market-capitalization SCEPs are associated with maximum losses from peak to trough over the sample period 1986–2016. The low-risk strategy shows resistance to market drawdowns and reduces the maximum drawdown of the market-capitalization strategy by 14.52%. To further assess risk, reference is also made to estimates of value-at-risk and expected shortfall. Equal-weighted SCEPs have the worst losses in terms of value-at-risk and expected shortfall, whereas fundamental value-weighted SCEPs are associated with the lowest expected shortfall as compare to the remaining SCEPs.

Table 10.1: Performance Analysis of Market Capitalization SCEPs and Smart-Beta SCEPs in the Full Sample Period 1986–2016.

	Mkt port	**MC SCEPs**	**FW SCEPs**	**EW SCEPs**	**LR SCEPs**
Panel A: Performance analysis					
Mean (%)	8.25	8.51	8.78	10.37	10.15
Alpha	0.00	0.00	0.01	0.02	0.01
Sharpe Ratio	0.55	0.57	0.62	0.61	0.78
Skewness	−0.81	−0.61	−0.56	−0.47	−0.76
Kurtosis	2.63	2.38	2.34	3.07	4.03
Panel B: Risk analysis					
St. deviation (%)	14.78	14.73	13.97	17.08	12.86
SemiDev	3.26	3.19	3.00	3.61	2.80
MDD	52.56	50.66	40.28	47.28	36.14
VaR	−6.65	−0.06	−0.06	−0.07	−0.05
ES	−11.71	−0.11	−0.10	−0.13	−0.11

Source: Authors' own calculations.
Note: Mkt port, MC, FW, EW, and LR represents the market portfolio which is all stocks in S&P 500, market capitalization, fundamental value-weighted, equal-weighted, and low-risk weighted portfolios, respectively. In panel B Vol, SemiDev, MDD, VaR, and ES represents volatility (standard deviation), semi deviation, maximum drawdowns, value-at-risk, and expected shortfall, respectively.

To check the robustness of these results, the alpha estimates of the market portfolio, market capitalization SCEPs and different smart-beta SCEPs are also reported in Table 10.1. The conclusion drawn from the Sharpe ratio holds true even after controlling for differences in portfolio exposure to the systematic risk factors derived from the estimates of Fama and French's (2015) five factor model. The abnormal returns of market capitalization SCEPs are not significantly different from zero which is consistent with Raza and Ashraf (2019). It is interesting to note also that even after controlling for the five risk factors, abnormal returns associated with smart-beta SCEPs remain positive and statistically significant suggesting the superiority of alternative weighting strategies over the market capitalization strategy.

4.2 Identification of Regimes in Market Returns based on the Regime-Switching Model

The results of estimating the Markov regime-switching model are reported in Table 10.2. An analysis reveals the presence of two regimes of market returns, which can be classified into high regimes (rising returns) and low regimes (diminishing returns). The high regime is associated with increasing returns observed during market rallies while the low regime is reflected by decreasing returns observed during the burst of the dot-com bubble and the onset of the U.S. financial crisis.

Table 10.2: High and Low Regimes in Market Returns.

	High Regime			Low Regime		
	Mean	**SD**	**Persistence**	**Mean**	**SD**	**Persistence**
Market returns	1.10	2.25	96.97	0.64	4.83	98.15

Source: Authors' own calculations.
Note: SD represents standard deviation.

The Markov regimes are governed by different mean values and standard deviations. The high regime is associated with a larger mean value (1.10 vs. 0.64) and considerably lower standard deviation (2.25 vs. 4.83) in comparison with the low regime. This suggests that the low regime is more volatile than the high regime. Persistence values for both regimes are greater than 95% which indicates that both regimes are estimated with high persistence.

The evidence of high persistence suggests that the time series has a long-memory process, which means that shocks are not likely to decay within a short period and that once the return series switches to the alternative regime, the new latent state is also likely to prevail for some period of time. The in-sample historical probability of being in the high regime is presented in Figure 10.2. It is clear that three major events

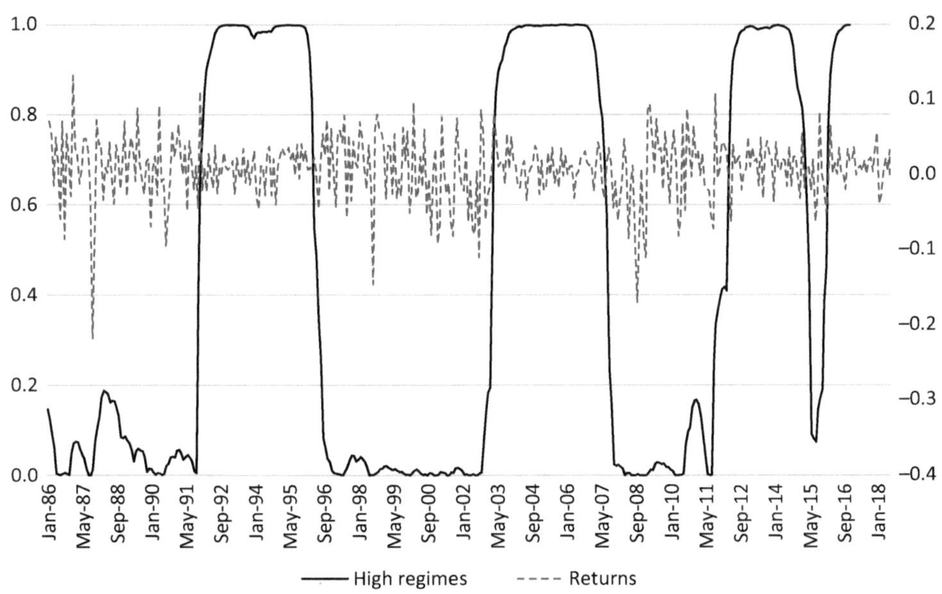

Figure 10.2: Transition Probabilities of Market Returns (Probability of a High Regime).
Source: S&P 500.
Note: This figure shows the historical probabilities of being in a high regime over time (left axis). The dotted line shows the monthly returns of the S&P 500 market index for the sample period 1986–2016 (right axis).

associated with Black Monday (October 1987), the burst of the dot-com bubble (March 2000), and the onset of the recent U.S. financial crisis (September 2008), are accurately identified as triggers for the presence of low market regimes.

4.3 Regime-dependent Performance of Market Capitalization and Smart-beta SCEPs

4.3.1 Raw and Risk Adjusted Performance

Table 10.3 presents the performance of the market portfolio (all stock S&P 500), market capitalization, and three smart beta SCEPs under both high and low regimes suggesting that market regimes significantly affect the performance of SCEPs. The left panel of Table 10.3 shows that all four SCEPs exhibited lower returns and higher volatility resulting in a lower Sharpe ratio under high regimes as compared with the market portfolio of an unrestricted S&P 500. Market-capitalization SCEPs and equal-weighted SCEPs perform better than fundamental value-weighted and low-risk SCEPs under high market regimes. However, the superior performance of equal-weighted SCEPs vanishes after adjusting for risk. This can be explained by the fact that market-capitalization SCEPs tend to mimic overall market movements with relatively lower tracking errors and yield higher returns during bullish market regimes.

Table 10.3: Performance of Market Capitalization and Smart-Beta SCEPs in High and Low Regimes.

	High regime			Low regime		
	Mean (%)	**SD (%)**	**SR**	**Mean (%)**	**SD (%)**	**SR**
Market portfolio	13.77	5.98	2.30	3.91	13.92	0.28
Market capitalization	12.25	8.73	1.40	6.77	17.92	0.37
Fundamental value-weighted	11.91	8.62	1.38	6.79	16.86	0.40
Equal-weighted	13.50	9.98	1.35	8.41	20.83	0.41
Low-risk	10.59	7.93	1.33	8.73	15.6	0.55

Source: S&P 500.
Note: Mean represents annualize average returns, SD represents annualized volatility (standard deviation) and SR represents the Sharpe ratio of *Shariah*-compliant equity portfolios.

As discussed in Section 4.1, a low regime is characterized by lower returns and higher volatility, and is often associated with economic shocks. Therefore, most equity portfolios are expected to underperform during low market regimes. The results reported in the right panel of Table 10.3 suggest that SCEPs outperformed the market portfolio. The market-capitalization, fundamental value-weighted and equal-weighted SCEPs are associated with higher annualized returns under low regimes. Low-risk SCEPs are found to perform best under low market regimes. This result is also intuitive because under a low-risk strategy the focus of investment is made on stocks with low risk profiles, which strengthen the potential of outperforming other portfolios during market downturns.

4.3.2 Regime-specific Risk Characteristics

Table 10.4 presents risk characteristics of the market portfolio and SCEPs depending on the regimes. The analysis of regime-specific risk is based on the estimation of maximum drawdown, value-at-risk, and expected shortfalls for all SCEPs under different market regimes. The major finding is that all SCEPs are invariably riskier when the market is in a low market regime. From Table 10.4 it is clear that the maximum amount of losses a single portfolio category suffered in the low regime for the period 1986–2016 was market capitalization as it recorded the highest maximum drawdown of 66.10%. In contrast, smart-beta SCEPs exhibit some degree of resilience to drawdowns, resulting in relatively lower losses. The fundamental value-weighted, equal-weighted, and low-risk portfolios successfully reduce the overall drawdowns of market capitalization by 8.91%, 7.63%, and 22.86%, respectively suggesting that SCEPs provide hedging benefits during the contraction of capital markets phase.

4.3.3 Performance Comparison of Market Portfolios and *Shariah*-compliant Portfolios Under Market Regimes

Results in Table 10.4 also compare the performance of the unrestricted market portfolio with SCEPs in high and low market regimes. We can see that the unrestricted market portfolio results in higher returns in market rallies as compare to all SCEPs. An interesting finding is that in market downturns SCEPs can be used as a hedge against market drawdowns. This can be seen in the right panel of Table 10.4 where the SCEPs show significantly higher performance as compared to the market portfolio in low market regimes.

The SCEPs outperform the market portfolio not only in terms of returns but also provide resistance to huge losses in low market regimes. The market portfolio suffers 66.10% drawdowns in declining market turmoil. In comparison SCEPs provide hedging benefits and reduce the drawdown of the market portfolio up to 43.24% (low risk SCEP).

Table 10.4: Regime-specific Risk Characteristics of Market Capitalization and Smart-Beta SCEPs.

	High regime			Low regime		
	MDD	**VaR**	**ES**	**MDD**	**VaR**	**ES**
Market portfolio	10.41	−1.58	−1.51	72.13	−7.01	−12.30
Market capitalization	7.84	−3.14	−4.21	66.10	−7.52	−11.09
Fundamental value-weighted	7.08	−2.86	−4.00	57.19	−7.09	−10.59
Equal-weighted	10.75	−3.59	−4.66	58.47	−9.25	−12.88
Low-risk	6.48	−2.77	−3.79	43.24	−6.32	−10.30

Source: Authors' own.
Note: MDD, VaR, and ES represents maximum drawdowns, value-at-risk, and expected shortfall, respectively.

4.4 Performance-attribution Under Market Regimes

Judging from the results reported in Tables 10.3 and 10.4, it is clear that the performance and risk characteristics of market capitalization and smart-beta SCEPs vary significantly under different market regimes. Consequently, the question arises as to what are the key factors governing the performance of SCEPs in market regimes? It is possible to seek some answers to this question from the performance-attribution analysis, which can be applied to each SCEP under each regime. This analysis allows for the classification of SCEP performances according to their respective different risk premia.

The performance-attribution analysis is based on the four-factor model proposed by Carhart (1997). The premia associated with factor mimicking portfolios reflects the proportion of mean returns on each SCEP that is attributable to the four investment strategies. The results of the model estimates are presented in Table 10.5.

The evidence suggests that all SCEPs show relatively high exposure to market risk under the high market regime. The beta estimates of these portfolios tend to differ from unity under the low regime. It is under the high regime that the beta estimates of market-capitalization, fundamental value-weighted, and equal-weighted portfolios are found to be close to unity, indicating that returns associated with these portfolio strategies tend to move together. However, low-risk SCEPs behave differently from the rest of the SCEPs showing relatively less exposure to market risk under both regimes, and specifically so under the low market regime, where the beta coefficient amounts to 0.75. This suggests that low-risk SCEPs tend to underperform during market rallies but perform better during times of economic turmoil. These findings corroborate the evidence from Tables 10.3 and 10.4, where low-risk SCEPs are found to earn higher risk-adjusted returns and have less risk under low market regimes. These returns are also consistent with the findings of Ashraf and Mohammad (2014), Boudt et al., (2019), and Raza and Ashraf (2019).

Table 10.5: Performance-attribution Following the Four-factor Model.

	Alpha	Beta	SMB	HML	MOM
Panel A: High regime					
Market capitalization	0.006	0.96	−0.21	−0.21	−0.01
Fundamental value-weighted	0.009	0.95	−0.25	−0.08	−0.01
Equal-weighted	0.029	1.01	0.20	−0.02	−0.16
Low-risk weighted	0.021	0.82	−0.32	0.08	−0.07
Panel B: Low regime					
Market capitalization	−0.002	0.89	−0.19	−0.16	−0.04
Fundamental value-weighted	−0.002	0.81	−0.20	−0.02	−0.07
Equal-weighted	0.000	0.97	0.01	−0.07	−0.08
Low-risk weighted	0.003	0.75	−0.24	0.25	−0.03

Source: Carhart (1997).
Note: SMB and HML represent returns on value-weighted, zero-investment, factor-mimicking portfolios for size and book-to-market equity. MOM is the momentum factor of Carhart (1997).

In terms of exposure to different risk premia under different market regimes, it is noted that market-capitalization, fundamental value-weighted, and low-risk weighted portfolios show negative loadings on the size factor under the high regime. This means that during periods of increasing returns, these three portfolio strategies are bound to invest more heavily in large capitalization stocks. This result is intuitive because both market-capitalization and fundamental value-weighted strategies assign higher weights to larger market capitalization or stocks with stronger fundamentals in terms of larger size and higher profitability. The low-risk strategy also favors value firms as compared to new or growth firms, and this behavior is more prominent under the high regime. It is also noted that the equal-weighted strategy shows positive loadings on SMB. This confirms the finding that the weights assigned by the equal-weighted strategy are tilted more toward small stocks, albeit the tilt is more discernible under the high market regime.

Finally, there is evidence of negative loadings on value (HML) for market-capitalization, fundamental value-weighted, and equal-weighted strategies. This suggests that these three strategies depend on growth premium and allocate more funds to young firms. The market-capitalization and fundamental value-weighted strategies invest more in growth stocks under the high regime. Conversely, the low-risk strategy has positive HML loadings, suggesting a preference for value firms under the low regime. It is also important to note that all SCEPs show negative loadings on the momentum factor.

5 Conclusion

The increasing literature on the inefficiency of market capitalization strategies and the development of smart-beta strategies in the last decade provide strong motivation for *Shariah*-compliant equity investors to seriously consider alternative weighting methods. Recent studies show that smart-beta strategies perform better than market capitalization when implemented with *Shariah*-compliant stocks.

This chapter addresses the question of whether the performance of *Shariah*-compliant equity portfolios following different asset allocation strategies is any different during various market conditions. This chapter adds further evidence to the literature by evaluating the performance of market-capitalization and smart-beta SCEPs under high and low market regimes. The study is carried out using the constituents of the S&P 500 index for the period 1986–2016. The Markov regime-switching model is used to describe the behavior of portfolio strategies under different market conditions.

The empirical evidence clearly demonstrates that market regimes exert significant differences on the performance of market-capitalization and smart-beta SCEPs. More specifically, market-capitalization and fundamental value-weighted strategies perform better under bullish and less volatile markets, while the low-risk strategy has the potential of serving as a hedge during bearish and more volatile periods.

The findings of this chapter have implications for both individual and institutional investors as they can benefit from these findings by designing a dynamic allocation strategy tilted toward different risk premia under different market regimes. However, it should be noted that the evidence is limited to the asset universe of the U.S. market for the period 1986–2016. Further studies are needed to determine the robustness of these results with respect to other geographical locations and over different time spans. Nevertheless, the overriding evidence is that the existence of different regimes governing the behavior of economic and financial variables in the realm of Islamic finance cannot be ignored. It is possible to use the large family of regime-switching models to constantly monitor the dynamics of Islamic capital markets and their dependence on latent states. This would allow investors to rebalance *Shariah*-compliant equity portfolios and allow regulators to understand evolving markets and complex dynamics in ways that promote rational decisions based on risk-sharing and risk-hedging principles.

References

Alighanbari, Mehdi, Stuart Doole, and Durga Shankar. 2016. "Designing Low-Volatility Strategies." *The Journal of Index Investing* 7 (3): 21–33.

Amenc, Noel, Felix Goltz, and Veronique Le Sourd. 2009. "The Performance of Characteristics-based Indices." *European Financial Management* 15 (2): 241–278.

Ang, Andrew, and Geert Bekaert. 2002. “International asset allocation with regime shifts.” *The Review of Financial Studies* 15 (4): 1137–1187.
Ang, Andrew, Hodrick J Robert, Xing Yuhang, and Zhang Xiaoyan. 2009. “High idiosyncratic volatility and low returns: International and further US evidence.” *High idiosyncratiJournal of Financial Economics* 91 (9): 1–23.
Ang, Andrew, Robert J Hordrick, Yuhang Xing, and Xiaoyan Zhang. 2006. “The cross-section of volatility and expected returns.” *The Journal of Finance* 61 (1): 259–299.
Ardia, David, Kris Boudt, and Marjan Wauters. 2016. “The economic benefits of market timing the style allocation of characteristic-based portfolios.” *The North American Journal of Economics and Finance* 37: 38–62.
Arnott, Robert D, and J M West. 2006. “Fundamental Indexes: Current and future applications.” *Institutional Investor’s A guide to Exchange Traded Funds and Indexing Innovations.*
Arnott, Robert D, Jason Hsu, and Philip Moore. 2005. “Fundamental indexation.” *Financial Analysts Journal* 61 (2): 83–99.
Arslan-Ayaydin, Özgür, Kris Boudt, and Muhammad Wajid Raza. 2018. “Avoiding interest-based revenues while constructing *Shariah*-compliant portfolios: false negatives and false positives.” *The Journal of Portfolio Management* 44(5): 136–143.
Ashraf, Dawood. 2012. “Performance evaluation of Islamic mutual funds relative to conventional funds: Empirical evidence from Saudi Arabia.” *International Journal of Islamic and Middle Eastern Finance and Management* 6(2): 105–121.
Ashraf, Dawood. 2016. “Does Shari’ah Screening Cause Abnormal Return? Empirical Evidence from Islamic Equity Indices.” *Journal of Business Ethics* 134(2): 209–228.
Ashraf, Dawood, and Mohsin Khawaja. 2016 “Does the *Shariah* screening process matter? Evidence from *Shariah* compliant portfolios.” *Journal of Economic Behavior & Organization* 132: 77–92.
Ashraf, Dawood, and Nazeeruddin Mohammad. 2014. “Matching perception with the reality – Performance of Islamic equity investments.” *Pacific-Basin Finance Journal* 28: 175–189.
Ashraf, Dawood, Karl Felixson, Mohsin Khawaja, and Syed Mujahid Hussain. 2017 “Do constraints on financial and operating leverage affect the performance of Islamic equity portfolios?.” *Pacific-Basin Finance Journal* 42: 171–182.
Baker, Malcolm, Brendan Bradley, and Jeffrey Wurgl. 2011. “Benchmarks as limits to arbitrage: Understanding the low-volatility anomaly.” *Financial Analysts Journal* 67 (1): 40–54.
Baker, Nardin L, and Robert A Haugen. 2012. “Low risk stocks outperform within all observable markets of the world.” *SSRN, working paper.*
Barberis, Nicholas, and Andrei Shleifer. 2003. “Style investing.” *Journal of financial Economics* 68 (2): 161–199.
Benartzi, Shlomo, and Richard H Thaler. 2001. “Naive diversification strategies in defined contribution saving plans.” *American Economic Review* 91 (1): 79–98.
Bender, Jennifer, Briand Remy, Melas Dimitris, and Subramanian Raman. 2013. “Foundations of factor investing.” *Working paper, SSRN.*
Bertrand, Philippe, and Vincent Lapointe. 2015. “How performance of risk-based strategies is modified by socially responsible investment universe?” *International Review of Financial Analysis* 38: 175–190.
Blitz, David, and Laurens Swinkels. 2008. “Fundamental indexation: An active value strategy in disguise.” *Journal of Asset Management* 9 (4): 264–269.
Blitz, David, Juan Pang, and Pim Van Vliet. 2013. “The volatility effect in emerging markets.” *Emerging Markets Review* 16: 31–45.

Bouchey, Paul, and Vissilii Nimtchinov. 2010. "Paul Bouchey, C. F. A., & Nemtchinov, V. (2010). Minimum-Variance Strategies. europe, 3, 18-8." *Investment management consultants association, Europe. Working paper* 20–25.

Boudt, Kris, and B Peeters. 2013. "Smart harvesting of equity style premia." *Finvex fourth white paper. Finvex Group.*

Boudt, Kris, Jonathan Cornelissen, and Christophe Croux. 2012. "The Gaussian rank correlation estimator: robustness properties." *Statistics and Computing* 22 (2): 471–483.

Boudt, Kris, Muhammad Wajid Raza, and Dawood Ashraf. 2019. "Macro-financial regimes and performance of *Shariah*-compliant equity portfolios". *Journal of International Financial Markets, Institutions and Money*, 60, 252–266.

Boudt, Kris, Muhammad Wajid Raza, and Marjan Wauters. 2019. "Evaluating the *Shariah*-compliance of equity portfolios: The weighting method matters". *International Review of Financial Analysis*, 63, 406–417.

Carhart, Mark M. 1997. "On persistence in mutual fund performance." *The Journal of finance* 52 (1): 57–82.

Chan, Kung Sik, and Howell Tong. (1986). On estimating thresholds in autoregressive models. *Journal of time series analysis* 7(3): 179–190.

Chow, Tzee-man, Hsu Jason, Vitali Kalesnik, and Little Bry. 2011. "A survey of alternative equity index strategies." *Financial Analysts Journal* 67 (5): 37–57.

Clarke, Roger, Harindra de Silva, and Steven Thorley. 2013. "Risk parity, maximum diversification, and minimum variance: An analytic perspective." *The Journal of Portfolio Management* 39 (3): 39–53.

Clarke, Roger, Harindra De Silva, and Steven Thorley. 2011. "Minimum-variance portfolio composition." *Journal of Portfolio Management* 37 (2): 31–45.

Clarke, Roger, Harindra De Silva, and Steven Thorley. 2006. "Minimum-variance portfolios in the US equity market." *Journal of Portfolio Management* 33 (1): 1–14.

DeMiguel, Victor, Lorenzo Garlappi, and Raman Uppal. 2007. "Optimal versus naive diversification: How inefficient is the 1/N portfolio strategy?" *The review of Financial studies* 22 (5): 1915–1953.

Derigs, Ulrich, and Shehab Marzban. 2008. "Review and analysis of current *Shariah*-compliant equity screening practices." *International Journal of Islamic and Middle Eastern Finance and Management* 1 (4): 285–303.

Fama, Eugene F, and Kenneth R French. 2015. "A five-factor asset pricing model." *Journal of Financial Economics* 116: 1–22.

Fama, Eugene F, and Kenneth R French. 2015. "Incremental variables and the investment opportunity set." *Journal of Financial Economics* 117 (3): 470–488.

Fama, Eugene F, and Kenneth, R French. 1992. "The cross-section of expected stock returns" *The Journal of Finance* 47(2): 427–465.

Fan, Jianqing, Yingying Fan, and Jinchi Lv. 2008. "High dimensional covariance matrix estimation using a factor modeL." *Journal of Econometrics* 147 (1): 186–197.

Guidolin, Massimo, and Allan Timmermann. 2008. "International asset allocation under regime switching, skew, and kurtosis preferences." *The Review of Financial Studies* 21 (2): 889–935.

Hamilton, James D. 2005. "What's real about the business cycle?" *National Bureau of Economic Research, NBER Working Paper No. 11161.*

Hamilton, James D. 1989. "A new approach to the economic analysis of nonstationary time series and the business cycle." *Journal of the Econometric Society* 57 (2): 357–384.

Hamilton, James D. 2010. "Regime switching models." *In Macroeconometrics and time series analysis, Palgrave Macmillan, London* 202–209.

Hsu, Jason, Kalesnik Vitali, and Viswanathan Vivek. 2015. "A framework for assessing factors and implementing smart beta strategies." *The Journal of Index Investing* 6 (1): 89.

Hsu, Jason C. 2006. "Cap-weighted portfolios are sub-optimal portfolios1." *Journal of Investment Management* 4 (3): 1–10.
ISRA, Securities Commission Malaysia and Khazanah Nasional. 2017. *Sukuk. Principles & Practices.* Kuala Lumpur: ISRA and Securities Commission Malaysia.
ISRA, Securities Commission Malaysia, Khazanah Nasional. 2015. *Islamic Capital Market. Principles & Practices.* Kuala Lumpur: ISRA and Securities Commission Malaysia.
Jeanne, Olivier, and Paul Masson. 2000. "Currency crises, sunspots and Markov-switching regimes." *Journal of international economics* 50 (2): 327–350.
Kritzman, Mark, Sebastien Page, and David Turkingtn. 2012. "Regime shifts: Implications for dynamic strategies (corrected)." *Financial Analysts Journal* 68 (3): 22–39.
Kritzman, Mark, Sébastien Page, and David Turkington. 2010. "In defense of optimization: the fallacy of 1/N." *Financial Analysts Journal* 66 (2): 31–39.
Kuan, Chung-Ming. 2002. "Lecture on the Markov switching model." *Institute of Economics Academia Sinica, working paper series* 1–30.
Laverty, W H, M J Miket, and I W Kelly. 2002. "Simulation of hidden Markov models with EXCEL." *Journal of the Royal Statistical Society: Series D (The Statistician)* 51 (1): 31–40.
Ledoit, Olivier, and Michael Wolf. 2003. "Honey, I shrunk the sample covariance matrix." *SSRN, working paper.*
Lee, W. 2011. "Risk based asset allocation; A new answer to an old question." *Journal of portfolio managment* 37 (4): 11–28.
Lintner, John. 1965. "Security prices, risk, and maximal gains from diversification." *The journal of finance* 20 (4): 587–615.
Mohammad, N., & Ashraf, D. 2015. The market timing ability and return performance of Islamic equities: An empirical study. *Pacific-Basin Finance Journa*, 34, 169–183. https://doi.org/10.1016/j.pacfin.2015.07.001.
Mohammad, Nazeeruddin, and Dawood Ashraf. 2015. The market timing ability and return performance of Islamic equities: An empirical study. *Pacific-Basin Finance Journal*, 34, 169–183.
Obaidullah, Mohammed. 2005. "Islamic financial services".
Perold, Andre F. 2007. "Fundamentally flawed indexing." *Financial Analysts Journal* 63 (6): 31–37.
Raza, Muhammad Wajid. 2020. "Does the Choice of Stock Selection Criteria Matter for *Shariah*-Compliant Investors?" Available at SSRN 3299238.
Raza, Muhammad Wajid, and Dawood Ashraf. 2019. "Does the application of smart beta strategies enhance portfolio performance? The case of Islamic equity investments." *International Review of Economics & Finance*, 60, 46–61.
Sharpe, William F. 1964. "Capital asset prices: A theory of market equilibrium under conditions of risk." *The Journal of Finance* 19 (3): 425–442.
Sims, Christopher A., and Tao Zha. 2006. "Were there regime switches in US monetary policy?" *American Economic Review* 96 (1): 54–81.
Terasvirta, Timo, and Heather M. Anderson. 1992. "Characterizing nonlinearities in business cycles using smooth transition autoregressive models." *Journal of applied econometrics* 7(1): 119–136.
Vangelisti, Marco. 1992. "Minimum-Variance Strategies: Do they work." *Barra Newsletter.*
Windcliff, Health, and Boyle P Phelim. 2004. "The 1/n pension investment puzzle." *North American Actuarial Journal* 8 (3): 31–45.
Zhang, X Frank. 2006. "Information uncertainty and stock returns." *The Journal of Finance* 61 (1): 105–137.

Siti Raihana Hamzah

Chapter 11: Analysis of the Risk of Failure in Sukuk Portfolios

1 Introduction

The rapid growth of Islamic capital markets intrinsically related to inception of *sukuk*. These Islamic bonds differ from conventional ones in two main aspects: They abide by the principle of *riba* prohibition and offer risk-sharing modes to issuers and sovereigns alike. *Sukuk* transactions prioritize the ownership stake of the underlying asset and require the income to be generated from the underlying asset rather than pro-rata ownership of assets for a pre-defined period during which the risk and return of cash flows generated by the underlying assets are passed to the sukuk holders (Iqbal and Mirakhor, 2013). It can be argued that this rule promotes transparency, fairness and just investment mechanisms that have the potential to reduce income inequality and economic vulnerability (Askari et al. 2012; Farook 2009; Mirakhor and Iqbal 2013).

Sukuk can be used to raise funds for governments and corporations seeking large-scale *Shariah*-compliant financing. It also provides Islamic banks, takaful companies and other Islamic financial institutions offering Islamic financial services opportunities for long-term investments. The issuance of *sukuk* in smaller denominations enables a large pool of investors to provide financing (ISRA, Securities Commission Malaysia and Khazanah Nasional 2017). It can be argued that many definitions from international standard-setting bodies, the *sukuk* represents universal *Shariah* principles reflected by the existence of special-purpose company, asset ownership and the basis of real assets as well as usufructs (Ariff, Iqbal and Mohamad 2012). Thus, *sukuk* is an asset-based security with the underlying asset being necessarily *Shariah*-compliant in both nature and form of usage. In addition, *sukuk* eligibility lies in the recordability of asset ownership in some form, and it is transferable among contractual parties. In light of these conditions, *sukuk* ensures that return on investment is justified by pro rata ownership and commensurate rate exposure ownership (Godlewski, Turki-Asiss and Weill 2011; Nazar 2011).[137,138,139]

---

137 According to the Accounting and Auditing Organization for Islamic Financial Institutions (AAOIFI), *sukuk* is a "certificate of equal value representing undivided shares in ownership of tangible assets, usufructs and services, assets of particular projects or special investment activity".

138 Reference can be made to the Islamic Financial Service Board (IFSB), where *sukuk* is defined as a "certificate with each *sakk* representing a proportional undivided ownership right in tangible asset, or a pool of predominantly tangible asset, or a business venture (such as *mudarabah*). These assets may in specific project or investment activity be in accordance with *Shariah* rules and principles".

139 International Islamic Financial Market defines *sukuk* as a "commercial paper that provides an investor with ownership in an underlying asset".

https://doi.org/10.1515/9783110587920-011

The various definitions of *sukuk* reflect the diverging opinions held on the nature of the underlying assets used for issuance. For example, AAOIFI and the IFSB only permit tangible assets such as property, plant, equipment and similar assets with physical substance, as well as a mixture of tangible and intangible assets, with the predominance of tangible portions. It appears that these two international bodies do not permit *sukuk* with intangible assets such as intellectual property rights and similar assets with no physical substance. They do not permit either portfolios consisting of predominantly intangible assets and financial assets. Portfolios consisting of only financial assets, such as liabilities, receivables and debts, are not allowed according to the Securities Commission Malaysia (SC). Furthermore, the SC Malaysia Shariah Advisory Committee (SAC) recognizes financial assets, such as receivables and debt, arising from Shariah-compliant activities created from sale-based transactions, such as commodity *murabahah*, as permissible underlying assets for the issuance and trading of sukuk. It also allows for trading of *sukuk* with 100% receivables at par, premium or discount. Meanwhile, most scholars outside Malaysia allow for the trading of *sukuk* if the majority of underlying assets are physical, but the portion of financial asset in the portfolio cannot be exchanged except at par value (ISRA, Securities Commission Malaysia, Khazanah Nasional, 2015).

Development of *sukuk* markets as a new investment instrument, the global volume of *sukuk* issuance and trading remains high despite the 2007–2008 financial crisis.[140] The global market for *sukuk* has developed into a significant source for fund-raising in international capital markets through *Shariah*-acceptable structures (IIFM 2010; Godlewski et al. 2011; Diaw 2011; Alam, Hassan and Haque 2013). *Sukuk* were considered as financial instrument that could be marketed to small regional markets such as Malaysia. However, becoming an international product with the potential to tap a broad international base of institutional investors, *sukuk* is now casting a wider net in terms of acceptance and is open to both Muslim and non-Muslim investors (Linklaters 2012). During the first half of 2014, the global *sukuk* market remained resilient and outperformed volatile global conventional bonds. The surge in sukuk issuances in the traditional Islamic finance hubs of the Gulf Cooperation Council (GCC) and Malaysia, together with significant deals in other countries including Turkey, Pakistan and the United Kingdom have also contributed to the global emergence of *sukuk* markets in the global financial landscape (Farook 2009; Bintawim and Saud 2011; Samad and Hassan 1999).

There is high demand from international investors for foreign currency-denominated sukuk and Malaysia continues to dominate the *sukuk* market, with two-thirds of the outstanding sukuk issued globally. The pick-up in the sukuk

140 Even though, in 2008, volume fell dramatically, it was merely a slowdown effect of the global financial crisis as compared to conventional bonds. The decline was caused by investors losing their confidence in investments and being hesitant to take any further risk.

market in Malaysia is mostly because of infrastructure funding needs due to the ETP by the sovereign as well as by Islamic banks as a result of the Basel III. Malaysia, which pioneered Islamic finance three decades ago, remains the world's biggest sukuk market. The popularity of *sukuk* highlights as excessive demand for it but supply remains strictly constrained, causing some degree of volatility (Mohammed 2012).

Judging from Table 11.1, it is clear that *sukuk* markets continue to develop. However, there are two main concerns about the potential for sustainable development, which center around *sukuk*'s ability to represent a unique *Shariah* instrument capable of simultaneously upholding *Shariah* norms and preserving its distinct features from conventional instruments.

Through its remarkable growth, *sukuk* has become a promising instrument that offers numerous advantages to the increasing number of Muslims who insist on the compliance of asset holdings to Islamic law (Wilson 2008; Ahmad and Radzi 2011; Zaid et al. 2011). For instance, in Malaysia, MIFC[141] expects a huge sukuk expansion because 61.4% of the population is Muslim (Wilson 2008; Nazar 2011; ISRA 2011). Furthermore, Malaysia has a long-term strategy for *sukuk* development, as outlined in the Capital Market Masterplan (CMP), launched in October 2001, and the Capital Market Masterplan 2 (CMP2), launched in April 2011. Nonetheless, despite incrementally higher issuances, the demand continues to outgrow.

Together with the persistent deficit in supply of *sukuk*, there are concerns about the issue of replication. Major issuers of conventional bonds question the rationale behind switching to sukuk (Mohammed 2012). Howladar (2009) argues that despite their Arabic nomenclature names such as *ijarah* and *murabahah*, most existing sukuk structures are, in reality, unsecured securities that do not represent actual asset ownership.[142] *Sukuk* operations are analogous to that of conventional bonds, except investors own part of the underlying assets, which collateralizes debtor repayments (Jobst 2007). This argument is further justified by Haneef (2009), who claims that holders of replication *sukuk* contract are on the same level as unsecured creditors. From a structural perspective, Ali (2008) argues that despite attempts to abide by *Shariah* principles, the resulting contracts are complex legal structures and are hard to comprehend. The similarities between the replication *sukuk* and conventional bonds seem obvious also from the perspectives of pricing and calculation of fields (Rohmatunnisa 2008).

In its very first issuance, *Bai Bithaman Ajil* contract was used to issue *sukuk* by Shell MDS Sdn Bhd in 1990. According to Muhamed and Radzi (2011) the bulk of *sukuk* issued in Malaysia were structured to emulate conventional bonds (*Murabahah, Bai Bithaman Ajil* and *Ijarah sukuk*) until the onset of the U.S. Credit Crisis of 2007. Despite

141 Bank Negara Malaysia, Fully Automated System for Tendering/Issuance (FAST).
142 In Jobst (2007).

Table 11.1: Main Phases of the *Sukuk* Market.

Period	Key Developments
Pre-1990s	**Initial attempts at developing *sukuk*** – Muqaradah bonds issued in Jordan as early as 1978 – Issuance of participation term certificates in Pakistan since 1980 – First Government Investment Issues (GII) in 1983 by the Government of Malaysia (GOM) – Issuance of revenue sharing certificates in Turkey in 1984 – Period of ad-hoc development. No active market emerged
1990–2000	**Early *sukuk* issuances** – First corporate *sukuk* issued by Shell MDS Malaysia in 1990 – Followed by small local issuances, mainly in Malaysia – Period of theory and model building. No active market developed
2001–2015	**The emergence of the *sukuk* market** – Market emerged with the Government of Bahrain's first sovereign *sukuk* issue (in the form of *Ijarah sukuk*) in the domestic market in 2001. Investors had recourse to the asset and were thus ranked pari pasu with secured creditors – The issue of the first rated international asset-based *ijarah sukuk* by the Government of Malaysia, which gave a boost to market development – The issue of other *sukuk* in Malaysia such as the world's first exchangeable *sukuk* by Khazanah Nasional Berhad (Khazanah), Malaysia in 2006 – Followed by several local and international issuances – Rise in issuances until the effects of the global financial crisis in 2008 were felt – *Shariah* compliance issues raised by the Accounting and Auditing Organisation for Islamic Financial Institutions (AAOIFI) in 2008 regarding partnership-based *sukuk* – After a slump in 2008, the market registered a rising trend once again – *Shariah* compliance issues raised by the International Islamic Fiqh Academy of the Organisation of Islamic Cooperation (IFA-OIC) in 2012 regarding repurchase undertaking in *Ijarah sukuk* – Recently, innovative product developments have been seen, such as retail *sukuk*, perpetual *sukuk*, subordinated *sukuk*, SRI *sukuk* and *sukuk* for developing waqf assets
2016–future	**Expansion of *sukuk* market** – Strong investor appetite for *sukuk* will lead to demand exceeding supply – The expectation is that fully-fledged *Shariah*-compliant institutions will allocate more of their assets to *sukuk* based on the limited availability of Islamic instruments – Predictions are that *Shariah*-compliant windows and conventional investors will allocate more of their Islamic assets to *sukuk*, perceiving it to be the most secure and easiest *Shariah* investment option currently available – Strong growth of Islamic finance and the halal industry – More jurisdictions joining the bandwagon as issuers – Further innovation expected

Source: ISRA, Securities Commission Malaysia and Khazanah Nasional (2017).

issuance with underlying permissible assets and partnership-based contracts, most of the criticism about sukuk tend to center around the ownership structure. Bacha and Mirakhor (2013) argues that eight sukuk contracts dominated the Malaysian market in the early years of its inception: *Bai Bithaman Ajil* (BBA; lump-sum deferred sale), *Bay Inah* (sale with immediate purchase), *Bay Salam* (forward sale), *Ijarah* (lease-based transaction), *Murabahah* (profit markup sale), *Mudarabah* (profit- and loss-sharing arrangement), *Musharakah* (partnership, with both partners providing labour and capital) and *Istisna* (progress-based arrangement – manufacturing). The tendency to replicate conventional bonds continues to dominate global sukuk markets. According to the Securities Commission of Malaysia (Bacha and Mirakhor 2013), there is sharp criticism from *Shariah* scholars in the GCC and the Middle East, especially for the regular income-generating process. It is possible to argue their regular issuance should not be considered as fixed issuance, but criticism raises, nonetheless, about non-*Shariah* compliance and economic inefficiency (Nazar 2011).

The sukuk market has been also tested with defaults of at least three sukuk in the Middle East and 26 in Malaysia (Hafizi et al. 2014). These defaults reflect the discrepancies that may exist between the implications of the underlying concept used to structure the *sukuk* and the implementation (Adam and Thomas 2004). Regulatory measures were taken by the Securities Commission of Malaysia, which provided Guidelines on the Offering of Islamic Securities in 2004. These guidelines refer to *sukuk musharakah* and *mudarabah* while omitting the controversial *ijarah, murabahah* and *Bai Bithaman Ajil*. Kamil (2013) argues that the sukuk issuance should be based only on *musharakah* and *mudarabah* contracts.

It is noted that Ahmad and Radzi (2011) and Rohmatunnisa (2008) rejected the criticism levied against replication arguing that *sukuk* do not amount to conventional debt because it is the underlying *Shariah*-compliant assets that render *sukuk* tradable. The *sukuk* structure relies on the transfer of asset ownership between issuers and investors. Hence, the periodic income of sukuk is generated from the underlying asset itself, while bonds use interest rates as reference for the rate of return (Godlewski et al. 2011). Thus, while bonds represent a real debt obligation relationship, *sukuk* reflects ownership of stakes in the underlying asset. Moreover, the sale of bonds constitutes the sale of debt, whereas sukuk represents the sale of a share in the underlying asset. As such, it can be argued that *sukuk* prices depend on the market value of the underlying asset (Bidabad and Allahyarifard 2008; Khalil 2011). It may be better to describe *sukuk* as Islamic investment certificates, because they may have the same objective as conventional bonds, but they should not be deemed as instruments for debt financing and should be considered with different operational, legal and regulatory frameworks than conventional bonds (Bacha and Mirakhor 2013).

In light of the above arguments, the issue of replication remains the object of controversy of opinions. Nazar (2011), Wilson (2008) and Zaid et al. (2011) claim that *sukuk* innovations do not always yield positive results if they are designed to imitate conventional bonds. Meanwhile, Diaw (2011) argues that taking beneficial values from conventional bonds does not harm *sukuk* as long as *Shariah* requirements can be satisfied. For example, to design a pricing model for *Ijarah* sukuk, Rohmatunnisa (2008) refers to two types of conventional models of leasing, as illustrated by Schallheim (1994). The conventional models are represented by the formal mortgage system, as illustrated by Ebrahim and Ahmed (2008), and the cost of capital in a non-interest economy, as described by Mirakhor (1996). Furthermore, Jobst (2007) and Maurer (2010) suggest that Islamic finance can synthesize close equivalent to equity, mortgages and derivatives used in conventional finance. The synthesized securities can still be governed by the *Shariah*, which bans interest and speculation, under that income is derived from profits of a shared business. The above models justify valuation models for sukuk using the put-call parity concept, where *sukuk* arrangements are modelled using the concept of present value. The only way in which *sukuk* diverges from bonds is the reliance on the use of underlying assets rather than pre-determined interest rates.

The objective of this chapter is to analytically determine that *sukuk* can represent investment instrument if it is appropriately structured, following *Shariah* principles. It is noted that the basic rule in *Shariah* is to ensure justice and fairness in all dealings, which explains the laying down of prohibitions against certain transactions, albeit concluded by mutual consent, *riba*, *gharar* and *maysir*, and those involving illicit goods (Diaw 2011). It is also shown that efficient portfolios can be built even in the absence of debt instruments and risk-free assets (Mirakhor 1987). The Modern Portfolio Theory proposed by Markowitz (1952) assumes the existence of risk-free asset that allows for the definition of a unique capital market line (CML) that represents the allocations of capital between risk-free and risky assets. The optimal portfolio is the point at which the CML is tangent to the frontier, and this market portfolio can be held by all market participant, leading to the deviation of the equilibrium capital and pricing model (Ryland, 2009).

The level of risk-free rate is bound to affect that of portfolio risk. The risk-free asset has zero covariation with risky assets, but the level of risk-free rate affects the slope of the CML line and thus the level of the portfolio risk, which depends also on the risk tolerance of individuals (Bishop 2009). In the real investment world, the risk is typically associated with an uncertain return (high risk offers high return) on investment, meaning that a risk-free asset is a non-existent concept. Although government bonds usually assumed to represent the risk-free asset because of the low probability of default, these assets do still contain elements of risk such as inflation and income risk (Hubbard 2012). The analysis of an efficient portfolio in the absence of risk-free assets can be used to examine Islamic capital markets with tradable *Shariah* products (Nasir 2008). The rejection of risk-free assets is in line with the findings of the previous chapter, which showed that gaining, without taking any related risk, can harm the overall financial system. Theoretically, restrictions of Islamic finance do not represent a serious impediment to optimal and well-diversified portfolios (Mirakhor 1987).

This analytical approach involves the two steps of portfolio construction and the identification of the probability of default for portfolios on the efficient frontier. In the first step, an efficient portfolio is constructed in the absence of risk-free assets with four types of *sukuk*, issued by listed firms in Malaysia: sukuk *mudarabah*, *musharakah*, *ijarah* and *murabahah*, with no risk-free assets. *Sukuk Ijarah* is defined as certificates of ownership in leased assets where investors own shares of the asset and its related income. *Sukuk murabahah* represents certificates. The proceeds of which are used to acquire certain goods or commodities for future sale, under a *murabahah* agreement. The *sukuk* holders own the underlying goods or commodities and are entitled to the realised sales price of the same. *Sukuk musharakah* provide the possibility to raise funds for capital participation or project financing where shareholders share both the associated risks and returns. business may seek capital participation in its corporate capital or for a specific project. The *sukuk* holders share in the risks and rewards of the business at the general or specified sub-business or project level. *Sukuk mudarabah* provide an entrepreneur (*mudarib*) access to funds from capital providers for business project financing where *sukuk* holders share the related in the risk and rewards.

The analysis is based on the treatment of all financial assets as contingent claims, with no interest rate-based debt contracts allowed. The returns are determined in the real sector, where economic activities take place. Profit is derived after payments for labor and capital are made and prior to its sharing between managers and equity-holders. Because the financial economy and real economy are considered in a one-to-one mapping, equity financing is stable and adjustable to shocks and it is, thereby, immune to banking crises (Mirakhor 1993).

In the second step, the Chebyshev theorem is applied to determine the probability of default for the efficient portfolio. This theorem is generally used for estimating the probability of a dreaded event, such as default or insolvency, by evaluating the degree of significance with which a random variable is likely to deviate from its expected value (Grechuket al. 2010). The central principle of safety first in actuarial science is based on the objective of reducing the probability of default, with other significant applications in engineering, safety and quality control (Rockafellar et al. 2006). Thus, this analysis is applied to examine the asymmetric effects of debt financing, which may increase the default risk as the leverage ratio increases in the firm's capital structure.

2 Efficient Portfolios of Nth Sukuk Assets

As noted earlier, *sukuk* are financial certificates that put the issuer under the obligation to pay income to *sukuk* holders in the form of profit-sharing, margins or fees, and to reimburse *sukuk* funds as they mature (Tariq 2004). The performance of sukuk portfolios can be measured with the mean-variance analysis (Lee et al. 2010). The demand for assets is determined by factors that affect the present value of the income stream as derived from the holding of these assets. When formulating their demand for assets, investors compare the expected rate of return from each asset individually, whether in the form of dividends or of price changes that entail capital gains or losses. It is important also to consider the associated risks under inflationary conditions, financial assets may incur the risk of depreciation, while physical assets may appreciate significantly. Financial assets denominated in the local currency may thus become less attractive than those denominated in foreign currency (Mangram 2013).

Markowitz Portfolio Theory implies that the portfolio variance is function not only of the variances of each individual assets but also of the covariance arise (Mangram 2013). The mean-variance analysis is an invaluable tool for allocating capital among assets. It determines how the combination of not perfectly positive correlated assets can reduce the portfolio's variance (Lee et al. 2010a). In the mean-variance analysis, efficient portfolios can be constructed, depending on risk-aversion levels. The efficient frontier allows investors to maintain stock portfolios in the same proportions under the proviso that they are sure of future expectations. Therefore, investment portfolios differ only in the relative proportions of stocks and bonds, regardless of their risk tolerance (Chiu and Wong 2011; Mangram 2013).

3 *Sukuk* Portfolio Modelling

The mean-variance analysis presents a coherent approach to the modelling of optimal *sukuk* portfolio based on the trade-off between risk and return. This section briefly describes the Markowitz' theory of portfolio selection and its application to *sukuk*.

3.1 Portfolio with N-th *Sukuk* Assets

Consider *sukuk* assets $S_1, S_2, S_3, .., S_n$ with random returns denoted as $\hat{K}_i$ for each *sukuk i*. Let E_i and σ_i denote expected return and the standard deviation. For $i \neq j$, ρ_{ij} denotes the correlation coefficient for returns on *sukuk* S_i and S_j. Let $E = \left[E(\bar{R}_1), E(\bar{R}_2) ... E(\bar{R}_n)\right]^T$ denote the vector of expected returns and $\Sigma = \sigma_{ij}$ be the n x n symmetric covariance matrix with $\sigma_{ii} = \sigma_i^2$ and $\sigma_{ij} = \rho_{ij}\sigma_i\sigma_j$ for $i \neq j$. The proportion of total funds invested in *sukuk* i is represented by w_i with $\Sigma w_i = 1$. The expected return portfolio vector $E(\tilde{R}_p)$ can be expressed as the sum of the weighted expected returns on individual *sukuk* $E(\tilde{R}_1)$.

$$E(\tilde{R}_p) = w_1 E(\tilde{R}_1) + w_2 E(\tilde{R}_2) + ... + w_n E(\tilde{R}_n) \tag{1}$$

or

$$E(\tilde{R}_p) = \sum_{i=1}^{n} w_i E(\tilde{R}_i) \tag{2}$$

Similarly, the variance of *sukuk* portfolio $Var(\tilde{R}_p)$ or σ_p^2 can be expressed as:

$$\sigma_p^2 = \sum_{i,j} \rho_{ij}\sigma_i\sigma_j w_i w_j \tag{3}$$

or

$$\sigma_p^2 = \sum_{i=1}^{n}\sum_{j=1}^{n} \sigma_{ij} w_i w_j \tag{4}$$

Where the correlation coefficient $\rho_{ij} = \sigma_{ij}/\sigma_i\sigma_j$ is function of the covariance term σ_{ij}, which describes the interaction between *sukuk* returns. The sign of the correlation coefficient depends on that of the covariance and negative correlations have the potential to reduce the *sukuk* portfolio risk.

Sukuk portfolios are selected from the efficient portfolio frontier which represents dominant portfolios with higher expected returns for a given level of risk and with low variance for a given level of expected return. Thus, the minimum variance portfolio can be mathematically determined as follows:

$$min\ \sigma_p^2 = \sum_{i=1}^{n}\sum_{j=1}^{n} \sigma_{ij} w_i w_j \tag{5}$$

$$subject\ to \sum_{i=1}^{n} w_i E(\tilde{R}_i) = \mu_p$$

$$\sum_{i=1}^{n} w_i = 1 \text{ and } w_i \geq 0$$

The minimum variance is determined by the constraint that the expected return on the sukuk portfolio amounts to $E^*(\tilde{R}_p)$. The optimization problem is solved given the constraints that weighted average of the expected returns is equal to pre-determined rate of return, sum of the weights is equal to one and all of the weights are non-negative. The *Lagrangian* function can thus be expressed as:

$$min\ \sigma_p^2 = \sum_{i=1}^{n}\sum_{j=1}^{n} \sigma_{ij} w_i w_j + \lambda_1\left(1 - \sum_{i=1}^{n} w_i\right) + \lambda_1\left(\mu_p - \sum_{i=1}^{n} w_i E(\tilde{R}_i)\right) \tag{6}$$

where λ_1 and λ_2 are the Lagrange multipliers.

The partial derivatives with respect to each of the variables: w_1, w_2, w_3, w_4, λ_1 *and* λ_2 are set to zero following system of equations in expressed matrix form ***CX*** = ***K*** as follows:

$$\begin{bmatrix} 2\sigma_{11} & \cdots & 2\sigma_{1n} & E(\tilde{R}_1) & 1 \\ \vdots & \ddots & \vdots & \vdots & \vdots \\ 2\sigma_{n1} & \cdots & 2\sigma_{nn} & E(\tilde{R}_n) & 1 \\ E(\tilde{R}_1) & \cdots & E(\tilde{R}_n) & 0 & 0 \\ 1 & \cdots & 1 & 0 & 0 \end{bmatrix} \begin{bmatrix} w_1 \\ \vdots \\ w_n \\ \gamma_1 \\ \gamma_2 \end{bmatrix} = \begin{bmatrix} 0 \\ \vdots \\ 0 \\ \mu_p \\ 1 \end{bmatrix}$$

where **C** is the matrix including expected returns as well as variance terms, **X** is the vector of portfolio weights and *Lagrange* multipliers, and **K** is the vector including the level of expected portfolio returns.

This optimization matrix can be solved using the Jacobian matrix rearrangement, which transfers ***CX*** = ***K*** into $\boldsymbol{X}=\boldsymbol{C}^{-1}\boldsymbol{K}$, where $\boldsymbol{C}^{-1}$ is the inverse matrix.[143]

3.2 Portfolio with Four Sukuk Assets

The present analysis focuses on the construction of an efficient portfolio *sukuk* including *murabahah, ijarah, musharakah and mudarabah* assets. Given the vector of expected returns (μ_i) and the variance-covariance matrix (Σ), it is possible to determine the minimum sukuk portfolios solving the constrained minimization problem:

$$min\ \sigma_p^2 = w'\Sigma w \tag{7}$$

subject to

$$\mu_p = w'\mu$$

$$w'1 = 1$$

The *Lagrangian* function can be expressed as:

$$L(w,\ \lambda_1,\ \lambda_2) = w'\Sigma x + \lambda_1\left(w'\mu - \mu_p\right) + \lambda_2(w'1 - 1) \tag{8}$$

143 It is noted that $\boldsymbol{CX}=\boldsymbol{K}$ can be expressed as $\boldsymbol{C}^{-1}\boldsymbol{CX}=\boldsymbol{C}^{-1}\boldsymbol{K}$, and $\boldsymbol{IX}=\boldsymbol{C}^{-1}\boldsymbol{K}$ where ***I*** is the identity matrix.

The first-order conditions for portfolio variance minimization lead to the following linear equations:

$$\frac{\partial L(w,\lambda_1,\lambda_2)}{\partial w} = 2\Sigma x + \lambda_1 \mu + \lambda_2 1 = 0 \tag{9}$$

$$\frac{\partial L(w,\lambda_1,\lambda_2)}{\partial \lambda_1} = x'\mu - \mu_p = 0 \tag{10}$$

$$\frac{\partial L(w,\lambda_1,\lambda_2)}{\partial \lambda_2} = x'1 - 1 = 0 \tag{11}$$

Thus, the solution for the matrix $\boldsymbol{CX} = \boldsymbol{K}$ can be derived as

$$\boldsymbol{X} = \boldsymbol{C}^{-1}\boldsymbol{K} \tag{12}$$

$$= \frac{1}{\det(M)} M^T \begin{pmatrix} 0 \\ \mu_p^* \\ 1 \end{pmatrix} \tag{13}$$

where

$$M = \begin{pmatrix} 2\Sigma & \boldsymbol{\mu} & \mathbf{1} \\ \boldsymbol{\mu}' & 0 & 0 \\ \mathbf{1}' & 0 & 0 \end{pmatrix} \tag{14}$$

The first four elements of **X** are the portfolio weights $(w_1, w_2, w_3, w_4)'$ for the minimum variance portfolio with expected return μ_p. Efficient portfolios are constrained with expected returns higher or equal to the expected return on the global minimum variance portfolio.

3.3 Probability of Default

The failure of the *sukuk* portfolio can be defined as the realization of losses exceeding the amount of assessment. This depends on the degree of leverage $(k \geq 0)$ in the sukuk portfolio where $\sum w_i = 1/k$. As noted earlier, portfolio weights are not allowed to be negative. The random variable $(\tilde{R}_p)$can deviate from the mean (μ_p) at least by the parameter *d*. Using the concept of Chebyshev Inequality, the probability of failure (P_f) can be defined as:

$$P_f = prob\left(\left|\tilde{R}_p - \mu_p\right| \geq d\right) \leq \frac{\sigma_p^2}{d^2} \tag{15}$$

Where d is any positive number.[144] Assuming that d can be defined as $(d = \mu_p - r^*)$, the probability of negative deviation from the mean can be bounded as follows:

$$P_f = prob(\tilde{R}_p < r^*) \leq \frac{\sigma_p^2}{(\mu_p - r^*)^2} \tag{16}$$

If the loss threshold is set, for instance, at –1, it is possible to redefine the probability of failure as:

$$P_f = prob(\tilde{R}_p < -1) \leq \frac{\sigma_p^2}{(\mu_p + 1)^2} \tag{17}$$

This inequality suggests that the risk of failure increases with higher variance and lower expected return. Thus, in consideration of the probability of failure, the random returns on *sukuk* portfolio are governed by the level of portfolio risk and expected returns on *sukuk murabahah* (μ_1), *sukuk ijarah* (μ_2), *sukuk musharakah* (μ_3) and *sukuk mudarabah* (μ_4) as follows:

$$prob(\tilde{R}_p < -1) \leq \frac{\sigma_p^2}{(\mu_p + 1)^2} = \frac{\sigma_p^2}{(w_1\mu_1 + w_2\mu_2 + w_3\mu_3 + w_4\mu_4 + 1)^2} \tag{18}$$

3.4 Probability of Default on Debt-based and Equity-based Sukuk

The empirical question arises as to whether debt-based *sukuk*, including *murabahah, BBA, ijarah sukuk*, contribute to the risk of failure given the similarities with conventional bonds and associated probabilities of default. The argument is that the higher the proportion of debt-based sukuk in portfolio, the higher the probability of default is. Early work by Mirakhor (1987) examined the role of Islamic financial constraints in decreasing the default probability for investment portfolios. Despite evidence that efficient portfolios can be constructed without risk-free assets, the focus here is on the variance of debt-based contracts as opposed to equity-based contracts. Thus, in this section it is demonstrated that concentration given on debt-based assets rather than equity-based assets upon constructing an efficient portfolio may expose the portfolio to a higher probability of default.

As demonstrated above, the objective of the process is to minimize the variance of the sukuk portfolio returns. The first-order conditions lead the optimal values of

144 Readers can refer to the early work by Roy (1952) for mathematical derivation and discussions of the concept of safety-first.

portfolio weights for on *sukuk murabahah, sukuk ijarah, sukuk musharakah* and *sukuk mudarabah*, respectively.

$$\frac{\delta\sigma^2}{\delta w_1} = 2w_1\sigma_1^2 + 2w_2\sigma_{12} + 2w_3\sigma_{13} + 2w_4\sigma_{14} = 0 \tag{19}$$

$$\frac{\delta\sigma^2}{\delta w_2} = 2w_2\sigma_2^2 + 2w_1\sigma_{12} + 2w_3\sigma_{23} + 2w_4\sigma_{24} = 0 \tag{20}$$

$$\frac{\delta\sigma^2}{\delta w_3} = 2w_3\sigma_3^2 + 2w_1\sigma_{23} + 2w_1\sigma_{13} = 0 \tag{21}$$

$$\frac{\delta\sigma^2}{\delta w_4} = 2w_1\sigma_4^2 + 2w_2\sigma_{24} + 2w_1\sigma_{14} = 0 \tag{22}$$

The objective is to compare the probability of default associated with debt-based *sukuk* (*sukuk murabahah* and *sukuk ijarah*) with the likelihood of default related to equity-based *sukuk* (*sukuk musharakah* and *sukuk mudarabah*). Thus, the expected returns on the aggregate for debt-based *sukuk* $(E(\tilde{R}_d))$and on the aggregate equity-based *sukuk* $(E(\tilde{R}_e))$can be expressed as:

$$E(\tilde{R}_p) = w_d E(\tilde{R}_d) + w_e E(\tilde{R}_e) \tag{23}$$

where $(E(\tilde{R}_p))$ is the expected portfolio return, $w_d = w_1 + w_2$ and $w_e = w_3 + w_4$ are the weights of debt-based sukuk and equity-based sukuk, respectively. The expected returns $(E(\tilde{R}_d))$ and $(E(\tilde{R}_e))$ are associated with debt-based sukuk and equity-based sukuk, respectively. As noted earlier, the sum of w_d and w_e represents the degree of leverage or asset ratio (k) such that:

$$w_d + w_e = \frac{1}{k} \tag{24}$$

The sukuk portfolio variance depends on the variance (σ_d^2) and (σ_e^2) for debt-based and equity-based sukuk and the covariance term is:

$$\sigma_p^2 = w_d^2\sigma_d^2 + w_e^2\sigma_e^2 + 2w_d w_e \sigma_{de} \tag{25}$$

Thus, the probability of default is

$$prob(\tilde{R}_p < -1) \leq \frac{\sigma_p^2}{(\mu_p + 1)^2} = \frac{w_d^2\sigma_d^2 + w_e^2\sigma_e^2 + 2w_d w_e \sigma_{de}}{(w_d E(\tilde{R}_d) + w_e E(\tilde{R}_e) + 1)^2} \tag{26}$$

It is clear that the probability of failure depends not only on the individual levels of risk for debt-based and equity-based *sukuk* but also on the covariance between these assets. Thus, as noted by Mirakhor (1987), the probability of default for Islamic banks is not just change of equity risk but of the correlation with debt-based assets and expected returns as well.

The first-order condition:

$$\frac{\delta\sigma_p^2}{\delta w_d} = 2w_d\sigma_d^2 + 2w_e\sigma_{de} = 0 \tag{27}$$

$$\frac{\delta\sigma_p^2}{\delta w_e} = 2w_e\sigma_e^2 + 2w_d\sigma_{de} = 0 \tag{28}$$

Noting that $w_d = 1/k - w_e$, the optimal weights for debt-based and equity-based *sukuk* that minimize the *sukuk* portfolio variance are such that:

$$w_d^* = \frac{\sigma_e^2 - \sigma_{de}}{k(\sigma_d^2 + \sigma_e^2 - 2\sigma_{de})} \tag{29}$$

$$w_e^* = \frac{\sigma_d^2 - \sigma_{de}}{k(\sigma_d^2 + \sigma_e^2 - 2\sigma_{de})} \tag{30}$$

These optimal weights satisfy the constraint on the capital to asset ratio (k). It is also noted that the probability of failure depends on the levels of expected returns and variance terms. The minimum variance *sukuk* portfolio can be derived with the optimal weights (w_d^*) and (w_e^*).

Again, following Mirakhor (1987), it is noted that the existence of global minimum depends on the sufficient condition that $\sigma_d^{*2} > \sigma_{de}^2$ and $\sigma_e^{*2} > \sigma_{de}^2$. That allows for w_d^* and w_e^* to represent an interior point. Variance minimization can, however, be conducive to higher risk of failure as suggested by the expression of the probability of failure as a feature not only of the variance-covariance terms but also on the expected returns, as well. Thus, the minimization of the different probability functions can provide different perspectives on optimal weights. The portfolio is made on debt-based assets but the mathematical derivation can be similarly applied to equity-based assets.

The first-order condition for the default probability implies that

$$w_d^* = \frac{\sigma_e^2(E(\tilde{R}_d) + k) - \sigma_{de}(E(\tilde{R}_e) + k)}{k[\sigma_d^2(E(\tilde{R}_e) + k) + \sigma_e^2(E(\tilde{R}_d) + k) - 2\sigma_{de}(E(\tilde{R}_d) - E(\tilde{R}_e) + 2k)]} \tag{31}$$

It is clear that w_d^* is an increasing function of σ_e^2 and $E(\tilde{R}_d)$ and decreasing function of σ_d^2 and $E(\tilde{R}_e)$. It is an increasing function of the covariance term only if $\sigma_{de} < \sigma_e^2(E(\tilde{R}_d) + k)/(E(\tilde{R}_d) + k/E)$. The ratio of expected return on debt-based sukuk and equity-based sukuk plays therefore a crucial role on determination of optimal weights.

The optimal weights w_d^* and $w_e^* = 1/k - w_d^*$ that minimize the risk failure depend not only on the variance-covariance terms but also on the expected returns, as well. It is also clear from Equations (31) and (32) that

$$
\begin{aligned}
w_d^{**} &= w_d^{*} \ if \ E(\tilde{R}_d) = E(\tilde{R}_e) \\
w_d^{**} &> w_d^{*} \ if \ E(\tilde{R}_d) > E(\tilde{R}_e) \\
w_d^{**} &< w_d^{*} \ if \ E(\tilde{R}_d) < E(\tilde{R}_e)
\end{aligned}
\tag{32}
$$

Equation (32) implies that concentration on debt-based *sukuk* in order to reduce the portfolio's variance may reduce the probability of default if the expected return of debt-based *sukuk* is more than the expected return of equity-based *sukuk* i.e. $R_e < R_d$. On the other hand, concentration on debt-based *sukuk* also may increase the probability of default if the expected return from equity-based *sukuk* exceed the expected return from debt-based *sukuk* i.e. $R_d < R_e$; assuming that the variances are the same. This is explained in (33) that if $R_d < R_e$ then $w_d^{**} < w_d^{*}$ which indicates if expected return of the equity will be more than debt, then portion of the debt-based *sukuk* in the portfolio is not minimal in order to minimize the right hand side of the probability function $\frac{\sigma^2}{(\bar{R}+1)^2}$. Thus, w_d^{**} is not a global minimum point and w_d^{*} is not an interior point.

4 Empirical Evidence

It is possible to construct portfolios with the four types of including *sukuk murabahah, sukuk ijarah, sukuk musharakah* and *sukuk mudarabah* with price observations over the monthly period from 2010 to 2014 for sukuk issuances for four distinct firms in Malaysia: 1 Malaysia Development Berhad (1MDB), representing *sukuk murabahah*; Syarikat Prasarana Negara Berhad, representing *sukuk ijarah*; Sarawak Power Berhad, representing *sukuk musharakah*; and Mukah Power Generation Berhad, representing *sukuk mudarabah*. The monthly data were gathered from the Thomson Reuters, Bondstream and Datastream databases. Tables 11.2 and 11.3 show the average returns, standard deviations and correlation matrix for the rates of return on the assets in this study.

Table 11.2: Average Annualized Return and Standard Deviation of Sukuk Assets.

Contract	Average annualized return (%)	Risk (%)
Sukuk murabahah	19.173	3.891
Sukuk ijarah	9.751	2.184
Sukuk musharakah	9.344	2.245
Sukuk mudarabah	9.210	2.556

Source: Author's calculations.

Table 11.2 shows that, in terms of annualized mean returns, *sukuk murabahah* have the highest returns followed by *sukuk ijarah, sukuk musharakah* and *sukuk mudarabah.*

Table 11.3: Correlation Between Sukuk Assets.

Contract	Sukuk murabahah	Sukuk ijarah	Sukuk musharakah	Sukuk mudarabah
Sukuk murabahah	1.000			
Sukuk ijarah	0.545	1.000		
Sukuk musharakah	0.358	0.420	1.000	
Sukuk mudarabah	0.165	0.456	0.607	1.000

Source: Author's calculations.

Judging from the estimates, *sukuk murabahah* is also associated with the higher level of risk followed by *sukuk mudarabah, sukuk musharakah,* and *sukuk ijarah.* Theoretically, *murabahah* (a debt-based *sukuk*) should reflect lower level of risk because investors are entitled to fixed income relative to the uncertain income concomitant to equity-based *sukuk.* The literature suggests that the higher risk of *sukuk murabahah* may be reflective of the state-independent fixed claims that cannot be adjusted to variations in the performance of the underlying assets. The higher risk may be attributed also to potential liquidity problem as far as non-tradable *sukuk* are concerned (Kamaluddin et al. 2012).

Table 11.3 shows the estimates of coefficients for the different *sukuk.* Following the threshold for correlation values suggested by Hinkle et al. (2003), there is evidence of high correlation. The relationship is found between *mudarabah* and *musharakah sukuk,* followed by the correlation between *ijarah* and *murabahah. Sukuk ijarah* are weakly correlated with *mudarabah* and *musharakah.* However, the weakest correlation is found between *murabahah* and *mudarabah sukuk.*

The strong correlation between *sukuk ijarah* and *sukuk murabahah* may be reflective of the shared propensity of being debt-based. Similarly, *sukuk Musharakah* and *sukuk Mudarabah* may stem from the fact that they are debt-based securities.

Sukuk portfolios on the efficient frontier can be generated under the reflection of no short-selling allowed. Given a larger expected portfolio of 18%, the possible portfolio contributions are reported in Table 11.4, which indicates that the portfolio weights of 88% and 12% would be allocated to *murababah* and *musharakah sukuk,* respectively.

Thus, in order to achieve the target level of expected returns, the portfolios on the efficient frontier described by Figure 11.1, are now inclusive of *ijarah* and *murababah sukuk.*

With reference to Table 11.5, it appears that correlation is lower for portfolios exclusive of both *ijarah* and *musharakah* or exclusive of both *ijarah* and *mudarabah sukuk.* The focus on those portfolios is that lower correlation is indicative of higher diversifications. The exclusion of *ijarah* and *mudarabah* has the additional merit of being conducive to lower coefficient variation.

Table 11.4: Restricted Efficient Frontier (No Short-selling).

Portfolio Number	Return (%)	St. Dev. (%)	Sukuk Murabahah (%)	Sukuk Ijarah (%)	Sukuk Musharakah (%)	Sukuk Mudarabah (%)
A	16.711	1.554	75	0	25	0
B	17.000	1.594	78	0	22	0
C	17.500	1.665	83	0	17	0
D	18.000	1.738	88	0	12	0
E	18.500	1.813	93	0	7	0
F	19.000	1.889	98	0	2	0

Source: Author's calculations.

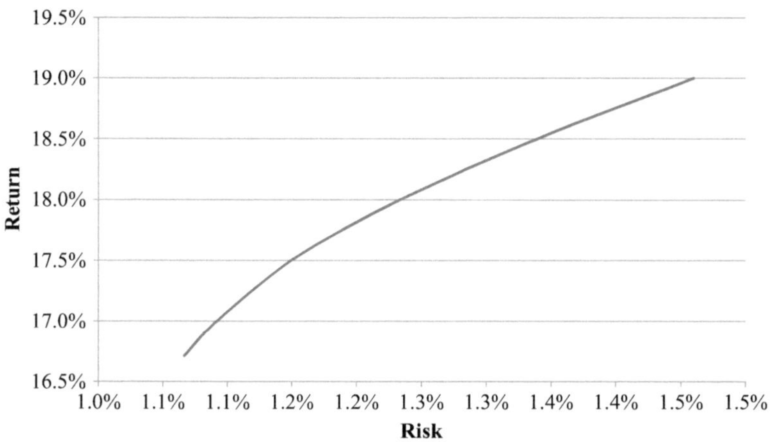

Figure 11.1: Efficient Frontier of Four Sukuk Assets.
Source: Authors' calculations.

Finally, it is possible to examine the probability of defaultassociated with different efficient portfolios. As reported in Table 11.6, the probability of default expressed as

$$prob\left(\tilde{R}_p < -1\right) = \frac{\sigma_p^2}{\left(\mu_p + 1\right)^2} = \frac{(0.01554)^2}{(0.1671+1)^2} = 0.018\% \tag{33}$$

This expression is lowest for the minimum variance portfolio. The portfolio risk is minimized by holding three assets as such debt-based sukuk and equity-based sukuk.

As shown in Figure 11.2, there is evidence that the probability of default increases monotonically from portfolio A to F as the proportion of debt-based *sukuk* increases and that of equity-based *sukuk* decreases.

Table 11.5: Average Correlation and Correlation of Covariance.

Sukuk Portfolio	Average Correlation	Average Coefficient of Variation
All *Sukuk* Assets	0.43	23.62
Portfolio excluding Murabahah	0.50	24.73
Portfolio excluding Ijarah	0.38	24.02
Portfolio excluding Musharakah	0.39	23.48
Portfolio excluding Mudarabah	0.44	22.24
Portfolio excluding Murabahah and Ijarah	0.61	25.89
Portfolio excluding Murabahah and Musharakah	0.46	25.08
Portfolio excluding Murabahah and Mudarabah	0.42	23.22
Portfolio excluding Ijarah and Musharakah	**0.16**	**24.02**
Portfolio excluding Ijarah and Mudarabah	**0.36**	**22.16**
Portfolio excluding Musharakah and Mudarabah	0.56	21.35

Source: Author's calculations.

Table 11.6: Probability of Default of the Efficient Portfolios.

Portfolio number	Return (%)	Risk (%)	Debt-based *sukuk* (%)	Equity-based *sukuk* (%)	Probability of default (%)
A	16.711	1.5544	75	25	0.018
B	17.000	1.5940	78	22	0.019
C	17.500	1.6650	83	17	0.020
D	18.000	1.7380	88	12	0.022
E	18.500	1.8130	93	7	0.023
F	19.000	1.8890	98	2	0.025

Source: Author's calculations.

5 Conclusion

In Islamic finance, investment in risk-free assets is prohibited because *riba* as interest accruals represents a pre-determined income that should be derived rather on ex-post basis from the return on entrepreneurial investment (Mirakhor, 1987). Even in the absence of risk-free assets, the recourse to optimization techniques is still warranted because they can shed light on issues such as efficient allocation of resources, maximization of profits and utility functions, exploitation of price arbitrage opportunities, and enhancement of economic growth (Mirakhor and Krichene, 2014).

The optimal portfolio selection is also important in Islamic finance as it facilitates risk diversification. The mathematical analysis demonstrates that the portfolio

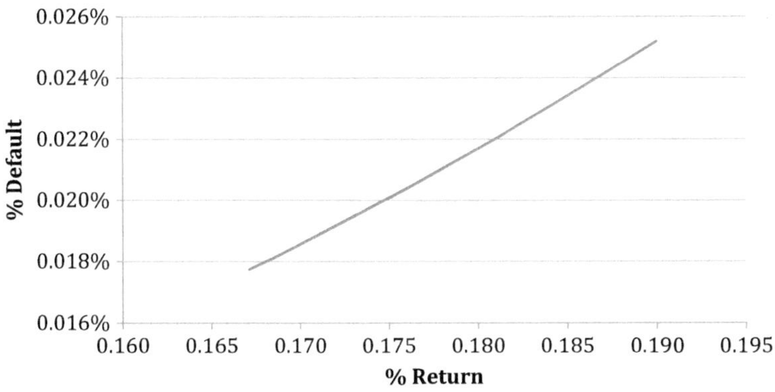

Figure 11.2: Efficient Portfolios with the Probability of Default.
Source: Authors' calculations.

variance leads to optimal weights on debt-based and equity-based *sukuk*. The relation between the optimal weights derived from these alternative exercises may differ indeed, depending on the sign and significance of the difference between the expected returns and debt-based and equity-based *sukuk*.

As with conventional bonds, there may be strong preference for debt portfolio by the variance of returns on equity as opposed to the fixed-income nature of debt-based sukuk. However, the reliance of Islamic bonds on debt and the minimized portfolio variance may not amount to optimal decisions in the sense that the probability of failure is not minimized. Thus, there is a need to reconsider the guiding principles and position risk-sharing at the heart of efficient portfolio analysis in Islamic finance and banking.

References

Adam, Nathif J. and Thomas, Abdulkader. 2004. *Islamic Bonds: Your Guide to Issuing, Structuring and Investing in Sukuk*. London: Euromoney Books.

Ahmad, Wahida and Rafisah Mat Radzi. 2011. "Sustainability of *Sukuk* and Conventional Bonds during Financial Crisis: Malaysia's Capital Market". *Global Economy and Finance Journal* 4(2): 33–45.

Alam, Nafis, M. Kabir Hassan, and Mohammad Aminul Haque. 2013. "Are Islamic Bonds Different from Conventional Bonds? International Evidence from Capital Market Tests." *Borsa Istanbul Review* 13(3): 22–29.

Ali, Salman Syed. 2008. "Islamic Capital Markets. Products, Regulation and Development". *Proceeding of International Conference*. Saudi Arabia: Islamic Development Bank.

Andrew Donald, Roy. 1952. "Safety First and the Holding of Assets" *Econometrica* 20(3): 431–449.

Ariff, Mohamed, Munawar Iqbal, and Shamsher Mohamad. 2012. *Islamic Debt Market for Sukuk Securities: The Theory and Practice of Profit-Sharing Investment (Foundation of Islamic Finance Series)*. UK: Edward Elgar Pub.

Askari, Hossein. 2012. "Islamic Finance, Risk-Sharing, and International Financial Stability." *Yale Journal of International Affairs* 7(1): 1–8.

Askari, Hossein, Zamir Iqbal, and Abbas Mirakhor. 2014. *Challenges in Economic and Financial Policy Formulation: An Islamic Perspective*. New York: Palgrave Macmillan.

Bacha, Obiyathulla I. and Abbas Mirakhor. 2013. *Islamic Capital Markets: A Comparative Approach*. Singapore: John Wiley & Sons Singapore Pte Ltd.

Bacha, Obiyathulla I. and Abbas Mirakhor. 2014. "Risk-sharing in Corporate and Public Finance". Inceif, KL.

Bidabad, Bijan and Mahmoud Allahyarifard. 2008. "Assets and Liabilities Management in Islamic Banking." *Paper presented at the 3rd International Conference on Islamic Banking and Finance, Karachi, 24–25 March.*

Bintawim, Samar Saud S. 2011. "Performance analysis of Islamic banking: Some evidence from Saudi Arabian banking sector". Japan: Ritsumeikan Asia Pacific University.

Bishop, Steven. 2009. "A Conservative and Consistent Approach to WACC Estimation by Valuers". Value Advisor Associates.

Ching, Ooi Tee. 2019. "SC cautiously optimistic of higher sukuk issuance in 2019". Accessed 31 May 2019. https://www.nst.com.my/business/2019/04/484031/sc-cautiously-optimistic-higher-sukuk-issuance-2019

Chiu, Mei Choi and Hoi Ying Wong. 2011. "Mean-variance Portfolio Selection of Conintegrated Assets." *Journal of Economic Dynamics and Control* 35(8): 1369–1385.

Diaw, Abdou. 2011. *Performance/Commodity-Linked Sukuk for Private and Public Sector Funding: Some Proposed Models* (Doctoral Dissertation). International Centre for Education in Islamic Finance (INCEIF).

Ebrahim, M.Shahid. 2008, "Can an Asian Home Financing Model Elevate the Economic Status of the Underprivileged?", 2008 International Conference on Business and Finance, Hyderabad, India.

Farook, Sayd. 2009. *Islamic Capital Markets and Investment Banking: The Definitive Guide*. UK: Thomson Reuters.

Godlewski, Christopher J., Rima Turk-Ariss and Laurent Weill. 2011. "Do Markets Perceive Sukuk and Conventional Bonds as Different Financing Instruments". [BOFIT Discussion Papers 6]. Finland: Institute for Economies in Transition.

Grechuk, Bogdan, Anton Molyboha, and Michael Zabarankin. 2010. "Chebyshev Inequalities with Law Invariant Deviation Measures." *Probability in the Engineering and Informational Sciences* 24(1): 145–170.

Hafizi, A.M, Shahida Shahimi, Mohd Hafizuddin Syah Bangaan Abdullah, M. Badrul Hakimi Daud. 2015. "Road to default: Tracoma holding Berhad Bai Bithaman Ajil Debt securities (BaIDS)." Emerald Emerging Markets Case Studies.

Haneef, Rafe. 2009. "From "Asset-backed" to "Asset-light": The Intricate History of *Sukuk*". *ISRA International Journal of Islamic Finance* 1(1): 103–126.

Haneef, Rafe and Abbas Mirakhor. 2011. "Islamic Finance: Legal and Institutional Challenges." *Practitioner's Article of Journal (English)* 6(1).

Hinkle, Dennis E, William Wiersma, and Stephen G Jurs. 2003. *Applied statistics for the behavioral sciences*. Boston, Mass: Houghton Mifflin.

Howladar, Khalid. 2009. "The Future of Sukuk: Substance over Form? Understanding Islamic Securitisation, Asset-Backed and AAOIFI principles", Moody's Investor Service, 6 May 2009.

Hubbard, Glenn. 2012. "Consequences of government deficits and debt." *International Journal of Central Banking* 1: 203–234.
International *Shariah* Research Academy (ISRA). 2011. *Islamic Financial Systems: Principles & Operations*. Kuala Lumpur.
International Islamic Financial Market (IIFM). 2014. *A Comprehensive study of the Global Sukuk Market. IIFM Sukuk Report 4th Edition*. Bahrain.
Iqbal, Zamir and Abbas Mirakhor. 2013. *Economic Development and Islamic Finance*. Washington DC: International Bank for Reconstruction and Development/The World Bank.
Jobst, Andreas A. 2007. "The Economics of Islamic Finance and Securitisation." *The Journal of Structured Finance* 13(1): 6–27.
Kamaluddin, N., Ab. Manan, S. K., Sufian, F. and Htay, S. N. N., 2012. "Shariah Principles of Sukuk Structure in Malaysia Islamic Capital Market". 3rd Terengganu International Business and Economic Conference (TIBEC III). UiTM Terengganu.
Kamil, W.A.R, 2013. *Malaysian Sukuk Market Handbook*. Kuala Lumpur: RAM Rating Services Berhad.
Khalil, K. M., 2011. "Sukuk: Definition, Structure, And Accounting Issues." MPRA Paper No. 33675: Islamic Science University of Malaysia (USIM). Malaysia.
Lee, Cheng-Few, Alice C. Lee, and John Lee. 2010a. *Foundation of Portfolio Theory*. In Lee, Cheng-Few, Alice C. Lee, and John Lee. *Handbook of Quantitative Finance and Risk Management (Volume 1)*. Springer Science+Business Media. New York, USA.
Lee, Cheng-Few, Alice C. Lee, and John Lee. 2010b. *Risk-Aversion, Capital Asset Allocation, and Markowitz Portfolio-Selection Model*. In Lee, Cheng-Few, Alice C. Lee, and John Lee. *Handbook of Quantitative Finance and Risk Management (Volume 2)*. Springer Science+Business Media. New York, USA.
Linklaters LLP. 2012. "Shari'a-compliant Securities." Accessed June 10, 2019. content.linklaters.com/pdfs/mkt/london/161211_Sharia_Compliant_Securities_*Sukuk*_Flyer.pdf
Mangram, Myles. 2013. "A Simplified Perspective of the Markowitz Portfolio Theory". *Global Journal of Business Research* 7(1): 59–70.
Markowitz, Harry. 1952. "Portfolio Selection". *The Journal of Finance* 7(1):77–91.
Maurer, Bill. 2010. "Form versus substance: AAOIFI projects and Islamic fundamentals in the case of *sukuk*." *Journal of Islamic Accounting and Business Research*, 1(1): 32–41.
Mirakhor, Abbas. 1987. "Analysis of Short-Term Asset Concentration in Islamic Banking". IMF Working Paper WP/87/67.
Mirakhor, Abbas. 1993. "Equilibrium in Non-Interest Open Economy." *JKAU: Islamic Econ* 5: 3–23.
Mirakhor, Abbas. 1996. "Cost of Capital and Investment In A Non-interest Economy." *Islamic Economics Studies* 4(1).
Mirakhor, Abbas. 2011a. "Epistemological Foundation of Finance: Islamic and Conventional". Foundations of Islamic Finance Conference Series.
Mirakhor, Abbas. 2011b. "Risk Sharing and Public Policy". 5th International Islamic Capital Market Forum, Securities Commission Malaysia. KL.
Mirakhor, Abbas and Zamir Iqbal. 2013. *Economic Development and Islamic Finance*. Washington, DC: The World Bank: Series on Directions in Development.
Mirakhor, Abbas and Noureddin Krichene. 2014. *Introductory Mathematics and Statistics for Islamic Finance*. Wiley Finance Series.
Mohammed, Anzal. 2012. "The Sukuk supply squeeze: Too much cash chasing too few deals." *Islamic Finance News* 9(39).
Muhamed, Nurul Aini and Rafisah Mat Radzi. 2011. "Implication of Sukuk Structuring: The Comparison on The Structure of Asset Based and Asset Backed." In 2nd International Conference on Business and Economic Research (2nd ICBER 2011).

Nasir, bin Mohd Yatim. 2008. "*Sukuk* (Islamic Bond): A Crucial Financial Instrument for Securitisation of Debt for the Debt-holders in Shari 'ah-compliant Capital Market." *International Journal of Biometrics* 4(10): 166–172.

Nazar, Jhordy Kashoogie. 2011. "Regulatory and Financial Implications of *Sukuk*'s Legal Challenges for Sustainable *Sukuk* Development in Islamic Capital Market". 8th International Conference on Islamic Economics and Finance (pp1–16). Qatar: Centre for Islamic Economics and Finance, Qatar Faculty of Islamic Studies, Qatar Foundation.

Rockafellar, R. Tyrrell, Stan Uryasev, and Michael Zabarankin. 2006. "Optimality Conditions in Portfolio Analysis with General Deviation Measures." *Mathematical Programming* 108(2): 515–540.

Rohmatunnisa, Dinna. 2008. *Design of ijarah sukuk* [Master Dissertation]. Nottingham University.

Ryland, Philip. 2009. *Investment: An A-Z Guide*.UK: Profile Books.

Samad, Abdus and M. Kabir Hassan. 1999. "The Performance of Malaysian Islamic Bank during 1984–1997: An Exploratory Study." *International Journal of Islamic Financial Services* 1(3): 1–14.

Securities Commission Malaysia. 2009. *The Islamic Securities (Sukuk) Market*. KL.

Schallheim, James S. 1994. *Lease or buy? Principles for sound decision making*. Boston: Harvard Business School Press.

Tariq, Ali Arsalan. 2004. *Managing Financial Risks of Sukuk Structures*. Master Dissertation. Loughborough, UK.

Wilson, Rodney. 2008. "Innovation in the Structuring of Islamic *Sukuk* Securities." *Humanomics* 24(3): 170–181.

Zin, Mohamad Zaid Mohd, Nadiyah Hashim, NK Khalid, Hajar Opir, and Rohaya Sulaiman. 2011. "The Implementation of *Sukuk* in Islamic Finance." In *International Poceedinfs of Economic Development and Research* 10: 455–460.

Seyed Kazem Sadr

Chapter 12: A Portfolio of Islamic Private and Social Financial Instruments

1 Introduction

The principal aim of this chapter is twofold. First, it represents an attempt to demonstrate that the set of commercial and social financial instruments sanctioned by the Islamic Shariah as permissible are indeed complementary with respect to their respective risk-return profiles and can be used to contrast a balanced portfolio of financial assets. It is further argued that the same complementary relationship exists between social altruistic modes of finance and those used for pure private purposes. This allows households and institutional investors to select portfolios composed of different assets such that financial and non-financial returns can be maximized on the basis of the risk–return attributes of each asset. The composition of mixed portfolios can be altered to account for the different levels of household income and savings rates. At lower levels of income, portfolios may be tilted toward private and commercial financial instruments. At higher levels of income however, the proportion of social instruments may become more dominant. The choice of diversified portfolios with varying compositions of private and philanthropic assets is consistent with the rules of Shariah that give precedence to personal and communal spending.

The second objective of this analytical study is to demonstrate that the implementation of Islamic property rights and the rules of exchange create an economic system in which financial and real sectors are strongly integrated, and where the generation of any flows of income in the former sector is intrinsically linked to the creation of real assets in the latter sector. Consequently, the two sectors are bound to move and grow in tandem as the nominal sector cannot expand without the concurrent creation of value in the real sector. No speculative activity and excessive risk-taking is permissible and therefore all investment and business incomes are earned when they are associated with new developments in the real sector. Thus, it is argued, in the second part of this chapter, that the Islamic economy promotes growth with a stable flow of national income.

Some emphasis will be made on the prohibition of interest or *riba*, which has a major impact on the structure and performance of the financial sector of the economy. It is conducive to the elimination of the loans market (Toutounchian 2009), and the widening and deepening of capital markets. Consequently, the financial status and functions of banks and other participants in the money market would change as they become new participants in the capital market. Due to this process of legal and financial transformation, theres is stronger consistency and harmony in the growth of the financial and real sectors. The abolition of interest-based securities fosters

https://doi.org/10.1515/9783110587920-012

equity-inancing, which in turn can promote investment in the real sector, and subsequently the sustainable growth of aggregate output. Therefore, the optimal selection of portfolios from the available set of *Shariah*-compliant financial instruments in an Islamic economy has the potential of promoting economic growth and social welfare.

2 The Risk-Return Profile of Commercial and Social Financial Instruments

All members of society are entitled to opportunities for earning decent living for self-sufficiency and family wellbeing. To balance the rights with obligations, each member has to make reasonable efforts to earn sufficient income and invest the savings to promote better living standards. living status. Members are also invited by the Islamic code of behavior to take care of neighbors and positively contribute to the large community. A spectrum of commercial and philanthropic financial instruments is made available by the *Shariah* for the purposes of investment in ventures that would benefit both private and social interests (Çizakça 2011). The commercial instruments reflect assets with fixed or variable rates of return and with varying risk profiles (Table 12.1). It is possible to demonstrate that the philanthropic or social financial investment vehicles are complementary to the private or commercial investments. Given the dual private and social responsibilities of members of an Islamic society, it is incumbent on each member to fulfill these duties simultaneously according to the priorities defined by *Shariah* (Sadr 2015). Members have to choose among the set of available options those that serve best their personal and social missions. Given the risk-return profile of private or commercial modes and the longer maturity time span of the social types of investment, agents are bound to select the optimal combination or portfolio of assets that maximizes the sum of expected private and social benefits. It is noted that the two types of assets are not perfect substitutes with respect to the priorities defined by *Shariah* for self-sufficiency, family wellbeing, and the limits levied on private consumption expenditure.

The decision to form a portfolio will be determined by the pool and diversity of instruments available for an investor in financial markets, attitude towards risk, opportunities for risk diversification, and preference for liquidity (Markowitz 1952, Iqbal 2002). In an Islamic economy, investors have access to large sets of assets with different risk and return characteristics to choose from and to construct a diversified portfolio (Sadr and Iqbal 2002). When faced with decisions under uncertainty in Islamic capital markets, investors can weigh the trade-off between expected return and variance and fully benefit from portfolio risk diversification to match individual needs and social obligations (Iqbal 2002).

Table 12.1: The List of Commercial and Social Financial Instruments.

	Category	Instrument	Return	Risk
Commercial Instruments	1	Qard	None	Nill
		Murabahah	Positive (+)	Minor
	2	Nesiah sale	Positive (+)	Minor
		Salaf	Positive (+)	Minor
		Instalment sale	Positive (++)	Minor
		Ijarah	Positive (++)	Minor
	3	Ijarah wa al-tamweel	Positive (++)	Minor
		Istisna	Positive (++)	Minor
		Joalah	Positive (++)	Minor
	4	Mudarabah	Major	Major
		Musharakah	Major	Major
Social Financial Instruments		Qard-hasan	Very high	Non
		Zakah and khoms	Very high	None
		Infaq	Very high	None
		Waqf	Very high	None

Source: Author's own calculations.

Table 12.1 reposts a list of commercial and philanthropic investment vehicles with varying returns commensurate with the measures of risk in an Islamic economy. The commercial instruments can be grouped into four classes. The first class includes *Qard* contracts that differ from *Qard-Hasan*, which results from benevolent behavior and belongs to the social category. *Qard* or debt financing entails neither return nor risk as *Shariah* rules prohibit lenders from demanding incremental pecuniary or non-pecuniary benefits from borrowers beyond the total amount of the loan. Yet, it entitles the lender to call for repayment of the loan at any time, if the period of repayment is not predetermined. This privilege makes the *Qard* financial instrument, in a sense, a risk-free contract. If the borrower fails to pay back the loan on time, the lender has the right to take over the collateral, if provided before, or to be compensated by other assets from the borrower.

The second category is composed of four different instruments whose rate of return is determined in advance, when the terms of the contract are negotiated. The purpose and duration of the contract have to be specified, too. The terms of the contract for *murabahah*, *nesiah* sale and *salaf* agreements guarantee the return for the investor and minimize the probability of default by the entrepreneur. These instruments are predominantly applied for short-term financial activities by Islamic banks. Market conditions rarely change during this period, lowering thereby the significance of market risk. The overall risks of these modes of financing are negligible and the rates of profit are expected to be represented by the average rate of return.

The profit rate associated with the financing modes listed in the third group are also agreed upon at the outset of the contract negotiations. The installment sale, *ijarah, ijarah wa al-tamweel, istisna and joalah* and are mostly used by Islamic banks for long-term investments. Subsequently, the risk involved is higher than short-term modes, but the return agreed upon may be higher than market rates.

Musharakah and *mudarabah* contracts constitute the fourth group, whose rate of return may be expected by parties but it is not determined in advance. Instead, the respective shares from the total returns should be agreed upon by the investors and entrepreneurs. Although all financial agreements listed in Table 12.1 can be used for both short-term and long-term investments, in practice *mudarabah* is used for short term commercial enterprises and *musharakah* mostly for long term financing by Islamic banks. The rate of return of either financial contract is expected to be higher than the market rate and that of other listed instruments. The respective risk of default by agents is also higher.

It is possible in the private sector of an Islamic economy that risk-avert investors opt for lower risk and lower return instruments, listed in the first three classes, and that risk-lovers choose the risk-sharing instruments listed in the fifth category. Risk-neutral investors may choose a portfolio of both latter groups. The significance of the tools listed in Table 12.1 derives from the fact that there is a variety of financial instruments to choose from by investors with different preferences for risk sharing (Udovitch 1970). The implementation of *riba-free* rule in an economy does not, in fact, deprive savers with high risk aversion from earning safer income by selecting lo-risk portfolios composed of assets listed in the second and third category. Thus, the incentives for saving and investment are not suppressed in an interest-free economy. There is an opportunity for innovators to invest in new technologies and high payoff-ventures by resorting to the risk-sharing financing modes listed in the fourth category.

3 Social Financial Instruments

The implementation of Islamic ethical precepts has important implications for sustainable economic growth in Muslim countries. At recession periods, the benevolent contributions have provided food security, clothing, fuel and shelter services for the poor and vulnerable income families (Çizakça 2000, Abdel Mohsin 2016). Under normal economic conditions, philanthropic funds can be invested in building schools, higher education centers, hospitals, roads, water saving houses, and also in the construction of mosques and religious congregation courts (Çizakça 2000, Abdel Mohsin 2016). The enhancement of altruistic giving will provide social protection for vulnerable and low-income families and further contributes to financing of public investment projects (Çizakça 2000). It will save government expenditures, contribute to efficient allocation of economic resources, and promote aggregate demand and supply in the economy.

In Islam, a set of economic activities are proposed and made partly obligatory and partly optional so that individuals with varying degrees of wealth can contribute to the economic wellbeing of the Islamic community. The required financial transfers include *zakah* and *khums*, which are types of perpetual annual income and wealth transfers from individuals with excess holding to those short of sustenance means (Kahf 2004, Shirazi 2014). Shirazi 2014). The highly recommended practices include *waqf*, alms *giving* and *qard-hasan* (Farooq 2011, Najeeb and Lahsanah 2013) among other voluntary transfers (Table 12.1). Individuals who have invested their excess funds in the socially desirable projects like schools, hospitals and roads have also a strong incentive to donate assets to the public. Endowment activities are the most significant form of private to public wealth transfer in Islam (Abdel Mohsin 2016). For voluntary income transfers, alms giving can be considered as an optimal economic undertaking (Sadr et.al. 2014). In cases where shortage of individuals' budget does not permit donation, *bona fide* loaning of the precautionary saving is foreseen (Sadr 2014 and 2015). It is remarkable that moral incentives for all kinds of voluntary contributions from wealth, income and savings are provided by the *Shariah*. It seems as if a diversified and spiritually rewarding portfolio can be designed for devout wealth holders by combining short, medium and long-term assets with safer returns and minimum risk. In fact, the construction of portfolios of altruistic assets was exemplified by the Prophet's (sawa) progeny and companions at the early periods of Islam (Sadr 2016a) and followed by devoted Muslims thereafter (Abdel Mohsin et al. 2016). By stipulating the legal forms of alternative optional giving, the Shariah has motivated the altruistic human motives for financial donations to the needy fellow human beings.

As mentioned earlier, the two sets of commercial and philanthropic financial instruments are complementary in the sense that investment weights can be reflective of the priorities of the Islamic community. At lower levels of income, financing for wellbeing of the nuclear family has the highest priority. At higher income levels, the consumption expenditure of the extended family and relatives has the second priority. As the family income increases, further, the living standard of the whole family members could be enhanced, if it would not surpass the *kafaf* level whence the *israf* prohibition or no extravagancy rule may be violated. Since the rewards to philanthropic investments are guaranteed by the *Holy Qur'an*, rational Muslim believers should choose a portfolio of commercial and social tools, which maximizes the total pecuniary and non-pecuniary benefits. This choice explains the prolific investment ventures undertaken by the benevolent believers for the charity and *waqf* activities. These philanthropic financial instruments are presented in the category five of Table 12.1.

4 Characteristics of a Riba-free Economy

In an Islamic economy, no debt-based product such as bond or derivatives will be issued by either the government or private firms, thanks to the prohibition of *riba*. The permissible products are shares or *sukuk* of either public or private companies, which have fixed or variable rates of return. Therefore, all financial assets in the respective markets represent an entitlement to the property rights of real properties, capital goods, commodities and services, which renders them real-asset-linked securities.

In fact, no debt financing through loans will be performed in the financial sector. If, for example, the value of a financial asset would increase in the financial markets, because of increased demand for it, this price signal will be transferred to the real sector, and the price of respective equipment or building would increase, too, and naturally, the producers will increase their supplies to benefit from the gained opportunity.

On the other hand, if due to achievement of efficiency in the operation or construction of a plant, its expected future return would increase, the price of the corresponding asset would go up, too, in a perfect competitive financial sector. It is, consequently, conceivable that there exists a direct relationship between the prices of assets in the real and financial sector. It is evident further that additional income could be gained in the financial sector only if value is created in the real sector beforehand.

For example, a deferred payment sale of capital equipment such as a tractor through *nesiah sale* is possible only when that tractor would be used in the farming sector for production of crops. Without this value creation in the real sector, the *nesiah sale* of tractor and earning of additional income at the end of the sale period are not achievable. Therefore, the flow of additional money income in the financial sector of the economy is always in tandem with the additional value created in the real sector.

In fact, the *Shariah* principles of transactions prohibit *riba* and leave no opportunity for gaining income in the financial sector without generating comparative surplus in the real sector. This is why the circular flow of nominal income is always parallel and equivalent to that of real income. Output growth will then be promoted in the real sector of the economy and the employment rate is enhanced. Due to this balanced income flows in both the financial and real sectors, both sectors are bound to grow together and converge, increasing thereby the likelihood that the economy remains in a stable equilibrium (Askari et.al. 2010 and 2014).

5 The Role of Money and Capital in the Financial Sector

The implementation of the Islamic principles of finance does not only change the structure of financial markets by eliminating the loan market from the economy. It also affects the performance, the width and depth of capital markets. The role that money plays in the economy can be more efficient. The potentially crucial changes in the money and capital markets will be examined hereafter, and the implications for the adoption of monetary l policies by central banks will also be discussed.

It is often argued that money is a unit of account, medium of exchange and store of value. In an Islamic economy, the demand for money by economic agents can indeed by justified by the need for transactions and precautionary measures. The rules governing markets such as the prohibition of *riba*, ambiguity in the terms of contract, cheating, harming other parties directly or indirectly and illegitimate methods of income earning, leave little room for what is known as speculative demand for money (Askari, Iqbal and Mirakhor 2014, Sadr 2016). Absence of loan market in an Islamic economy leaves no room for this type of activities in financial markets. What is perceivable is speculation over the price of commodities and real assets. The effective implementation of rules governing market transaction would foster the dissemination of accurate market information and prohibit the hoarding of goods and services. Furthermore, effective monitoring and supervision have the potential of reducing the speculative activities of market participants.

Economists have defined money by its functions, which are mentioned above, and not by the type of property right that dictates its use. It is the property rights of holding a liquid asset which distinguishes money from the capital (Toutounchian 2009). According to legal definition of the sale contract (*al-bay'*), a commodity (*mabeea*) is exchanged by the capital (*Ras al-mal* or *thaman*) in this contract. That is, when a sale contract is concluded, the service or commodity that is offered by the seller is exchanged by cash or real capital, paid by the buyer. The sale contracts are irrevocable; they cannot be annulled after conclusion. Therefore, it can be argued that a liquid asset that is not assigned for payment in legitimate contracts, and that can be freely allocated represents money. But when the asset is entangled in a contract, it is deemed as capital, and it is subject to the set of rules applicable to respective contracts. This asset can no longer be used for purposes other than those specified in the contractual agreements.

This legal distinction helps to understand why a liquid asset can be the subject of payment, trading, investment and income generation when it is transferred through a legitimate contract. The contractual arrangement changes the legal status of the asset from a monetary into capital asset. Money is not bounded by a contract and thus cannot earn any return. It, of course, can be loaned without interest, but even then, it has to be the subject of a contractual agreement (Sadr 2016b).

The above distinction also helps to differentiate monetary policy from financial policy. The former is carried out in *ribawi* economies and it is not implementable in an Islamic economic system. The latter is absolutely permissible, however. The main difference reflects the notion that a financial sector independent from the real sector cannot be formed in an Islamic economy. The two sectors are bound to move and grow together, but it is the real sector that takes precedence and leadership over the financial sector.

The distinctions made above are also useful in understanding the type of policies that central banks can adopt for the purposes of managing inflation and coping with economic recessions. Open market operations can be performed with the buying and selling of securities such as *Sukuk*, shares or other permissible financial assets. Clearly, the essence of financial policy is centered on the promotion of sustainable and equitable growth as every activity in the financial sector is linked to a value-creating activity in the real sector. Indeed, by promoting or controlling aggregate demand and supply in both the financial and real sectors, the objective of financial policy is not only to stimulate growth and control inflation, but to secure stability for the entire economic system as well.

6 The Growth Promotion Attribute of Islamic Finance

To examine the growth-promoting hypothesis put forth by many Islamic economists (Iqbal and Mirakhor 1999, Khan 1987), it was possible to conduct research in Iran on the effects of a shift from a *ribawi* financial system into an interest-free system (Sadr, Kafaei and Haidari 2007). The objective of the study is two fold. On one hand, the aim is to build a model for the estimation of the impact of financial services on the agricultural sector in terms of the significanc of its added value. The broader objective is to examine the macroeconomic effects of the transformation from the *ribawi* to interest-free banking system. The contribution of Islamic finance to the added-value from the agricultural sector is considered in light of the implementation of the Interest Free Banking Law in 1984.

To pursue these two objectives, a system of simultaneous equations consisting of three investment, capital accumulation and production functions is formulated. The volume of real investment in the first equation is assumed to be function of value added, flow of funds, and historical levels of capital stock in the agricultural sector. The second function consists of a capital accumulation identity, and the third function represents the value added depending on the capital stock and labor force in the agricultural sector. The data observations for this analytical study are obtained from the related time-series published by the Central Bank of Iran, the Statistical Center of Iran, and the Management and Planning Organization for the years 1961–1996 (1340 to 1375 Iranian calendar).

The system of simultaneous equations is using the co-integration analysis, including the required preliminary tests (Sadr, Kafaei and Haidari 2007). The long-run and short-run estimation of coefficients for agricultural finance are found to exhibit positive and significant effects on both the capital stock and output levels in the sector. Further, to test for the effects of introducing an Islamic financial system on economic growth in the agricultural sector, the reduced-form of structural functions model is re-estimated, using the same co-integration methodology, except for the use of a dummy variable for the calendar year 1984, which refers to the commencement of Islamic Banking operations.

It is found that the allocation of one billion Rials of financing to the agricultural sector has the potential of generating an added value of 41.1 million Rials. These empirical findings suggest the implementation of Islamic Free Banking Law can be conducive to positive and significant effects on the value added by the agricultural sector. The transformation of the financial system increases the aggregate added-value from the agricultural sector by 0.26 percent, after controlling for contributions from capital stock, labor force and short and long-run credit. This percentage represents almost the total contribution of the labor force. Despite the environmental damage from various natural disasters including drought, flood, and frost, and despite the economic shocks such as wars and sanctions, agricultural finance continues to exert stable and significant influence on the output from the crucial agricultural sector.

7 Conclusion

The main objective of this study is to demonstrate that the risk-return attributes of Islamic commercial and social financial instruments present participants in an Islamic economy with good opportunities for the construction of optimal portfolios. Furthermore, the commercial and social instruments are complementary and augment the risk-return profile of each other. Varying compositions of both sets of instruments can be selected by households in an Islamic economy as income levels increase. This study aims also at examining the issue of how the implementation of Islamic principles of finance can restructure financial markets in ways that allow the financial and real sectors to be integrated, promoting thereby sustainable economic growth.

The ability of participants in an Islamic economy to select portfolios of commercial and social assets is governed by the principles of Islamic finance. Priority is given to one's own family in providing good living standards and then to offering good care to relatives and other community members. The growth-promoting attributes of different financial instruments depend however on the system of property rights, rules of commodity markets and asset exchanges prescribed by the *Shariah*. Insofar as savings and investments activities are concerned, the prohibition of *riba* renders the earning of revenues without the production of goods and services in the real economy rather impermissible. Thus, the risk-sharing principle ensures harmony between the circulation of money and value addition in the financial and real sectors of the economy, and consequently promotes sustainable growth in both sectors. A full-fledged shift from interest-bearing to interest-free economic system contributes significantly to equitable economic growth of the economy, and in particular to the development of the agricultural sector.

References

Abdel Mohsin, Magda Ismail, Hisham Dafterdar, Murat Çizakça, Syed Othman Alhabshi, Shaikh Hamzah Abdul Razak, Seyed Kazem Sadr, Thamina Anwar, Mohammed Obaidullah. 2016. *Financing the Development of Old Waqf Properties*. New York: Palgrave–Macmillan.

Askari, Hossein, Noureddin Krichene and Abbas Mirakhor. 2014. "On Stability of an Islamic Financial System." *PSL Quarterly Review* 67(269): 131–167.

Askari, Hossein, Zamir Iqbal, Noureddin Krichene and Abbas Mirakhor. 2010. *The Stability of Islamic Finance*. Singapore: John Wiley&Sons.

Askari, Hossein, Zamir Iqbal and Abbas Mirakhor. 2014. Challenges in Economic and Financial Policy Formulation. New York: Palgrave–Macmillan.

Çizakça, Murat. 2000. *A History of Philanthropic Foundations: The Islamic World from Seventh Century to the Present*. Istanbul: Bogazici University Press.

Çizakça, Murat. 2011. *Islamic Capitalism and Finance*. Cheltenham: Edward Elgar.

Farooq, Mohammad O. 2011. "Qard Hasan, Wadiah/Amanah and Bank Deposits: Applications and Misapplications of Some Concepts in Islamic Banking." *Arab Law Quarterly* 25(2): 115–146.

Iqbal, Zamir. 2002. *Portfolio Choices and Asset Pricing in Islamic Framework Theoretical Foundations of Islamic Economics* In Theoretical Foundations of Islamic Economics, edited by Habib Ahmed. Jeddah: Islamic Development Bank.

Iqbal, Zamir and Abbas Mirakhor. 1999. "Progress and challenges of Islamic Banking", *Thunderbird Business Review* 41(4/5): 381–405.

Khan, S. R. 1987. *An Economic Analysis of a PLS Model for the Financial Sector* in Khan, M. and Mirakhor, A. (Ed.). The Theoretical Studies in Islamic Banking and Finance, The Institute for Research and Islamic Studies, US, Texas.

Kahf, Monzer (2004). "Shariah and Historical Aspects of Zakat and Waqaf." Paper presented for Islamic Research and Training institute, Islamic Development Bank.

Markowitz, Harry 1952. "Portfolio Selection." *Journal of Finance* 7(1): 77–91.

Najeeb, Syed and Ahcene Lahsana. 2013. "Qard Hasan: Its Shari'ah Rules and Applications in Islamic Finance." *Journal of Islamic Business and Management* 3(1): 15–34.

Sadr, Seyed Kazem. 2016a. *The Economic System of the Early Islamic Period*. New York: Palgrave-Macmillan.

Sadr, Seyed Kazem and Zamir Iqbal. 2002. "Choice Between Debt and Equity Contracts and Asymmetric Information", In Islamic Banking and Finance, ed. by M. Iqbal and D. Liweffyn, Edward Elgar Publishing Limited, Cheleren, UK

Sadr, Seyed Kazem, Mohammad-Ali Kafaie and Bahram Haidari. 2007. "Islamic Agricultural Finance and Growth." *Iranian Economic Review* 12(18): 143–159.

Sadr, Seyed Kazem. 2014. "Qard Hasan financing in Islamic Banks." *ISRA International Journal of Islamic Finance* 6(2): 7–20.

Sadr, Seyed Kazem. 2016b. "Money, Capital and the Islamic Property Rights Paradigm." *Journal of Islamic Economics, Banking and Finance* 12(1): 13–32.

Sadr, Seyed Kazem and Omid Torabi. 2015. "Qard Hasan and Microfinance" in State of Islamic Finance: A Retrospective Assessment and Looking Forward eds: Zamir Iqbal and Zurina Shafi.

Sadr, Seyed Kazem, Syed Othman Alhabshi and Timur Rustemov. 2014. *A Comparative Study of Islamic Microfinance Institutions in Iran*, Pakistan, *Bangladesh*, Indonesia *and Malaysia*, Research Project: RWC 16:04/2013/007, INCEIF, Kuala Lumpur, June.

Shirazi, Nasim Shah. 2014. "Integrating Zakāt and Waqf into the Poverty Reduction Strategy of the IDB Member Countries." Islamic Economic Studies 22(1): 79–108.

Toutounchian, Iraj. 2009. *Islamic Money and Banking*. Singapore: John Wiley Ltd.

Udovitch, Abraham. 1970. *Partnership and profit in Medieval Islam*. Princeton: Princeton University Press.

Part IV: Risk-sharing Finance and Financial Consumer Protection

Thorsten Beck, Zamir Iqbal, Rasim Mutlu

Chapter 13: Do Islamic Banks Contribute to Risk Sharing?

1 Introduction

Across the globe, Islamic banks, also known as participation or Shariah-compliant banks, have in recent years experienced faster growth rates than the conventional banks. Between 2014 and 2015, the Islamic banking industry, on aggregate, grew by 1.4% in US Dollars term, while the total assets of the largest 1,000 global banks grew by a meager 0.6% on year on year basis by the end of 2014 (IFSB 2016). Total assets of Islamic banks worldwide have reached the size of 1.59 trillion USD as of first half of 2015. Islamic banks have become systematically important in various countries (88% of assets) such as Islamic Republic of Iran, Pakistan, Malaysia, Kingdom of Saudi Arabia and Sudan (IFSB 2016). Growth of Islamic banks has not been confined to countries where the majority of population is Muslim, but also in many Western countries such as the UK and Germany where full-fledged Islamic banks or Islamic windows are offering Shariah-compliant products and services.[145]

The basic features that distinguish Islamic banks from conventional banks are the (i) risk-sharing and asset-based financial instruments on both sides of the balance sheet as opposed to debt-based risk-transfer financial intermediation; (ii) materiality or preference for financing of real economic transactions; and (iii) avoidance of activities with excessive uncertainty such as short selling or trading of financial derivatives.[146] Due to these features, in theory, Islamic banks would pose less systemic risk in the financial sector. Islamic banks can also help increase financial inclusion by offering financial products that comply with the religious beliefs of a certain segment of population which are underbanked. In addition, sukuk (Islamic bonds) have been used as an alternative source for market-based financing to meet the growing demand for long term financing such of infrastructure projects (World Bank 2015).

In this study, we focus on the profit-loss sharing (risk-sharing) aspect of Islamic banks and gauge whether a more prominent role of Islamic banks in a country's banking system is associated with higher intertemporal risk-sharing and consumption smoothing. Maturity mis-matches and heavy reliance on short-term debt funding have been argued to be one of the main contributors to the reoccurring financial crisis during past eight centuries (Reinhart and Rogoff 2008). Shiller (2009), asserts that

145 Islamic Window is called a department of a conventional bank offering Islamic financial services.
146 Iqbal and Mirakhor (2011).

https://doi.org/10.1515/9783110587920-013

a system that enables better risk-sharing offers a more stable economic environment and enhances the welfare of the societies. The vitality of risk-sharing in creating a more stable and efficient financial system is also stressed by the Global Chief Economist of Citigroup William Buiter:

> academic literature, which stressed debt's main advantage as allowing a quiet life for creditors (i.e., no need for costly, ex-post monitoring of borrowers by risk and return-sharing investors), probably contributed to the relaxed attitude many lenders and analysts took toward the serious risks that excessive debt entails.[147]

Theory suggests that Islamic banks can play an important role in strengthening intertemporal risk-sharing, given their focus on profit and loss sharing based intermediation rather than deposits with fixed pre-determined payoffs. Well-functioning financial markets (both conventional and Islamic banks) should increase the risk-sharing opportunities of the individuals through borrowing and lending. Individuals who have savings can invest these through financial intermediaries and accumulate wealth that they could use as buffer against future risks, while households and firms who are in need of credit can borrow from financial intermediaries to smooth their consumption and weather the effects of negative income shocks. Thus, higher risk-sharing should enable agents to diversify against shocks to their income stream which in turn would decrease the correlation between changes to their income and consumption. In this study we address the question of whether Islamic banks are better positioned to support this intertemporal risk-sharing than conventional banks.

We relate the importance of Islamic banks to the degree of consumption smoothing in an economy. Specifically, we regress changes in consumption on changes in income and use the consumption smoothing parameter as our proxy for risk-sharing in a country. Using two different sources, Bankscope and Islamic Banks Information System (hereafter IBIS), to construct measures of the importance of Islamic banks we test whether their importance in a country is indeed related to more intertemporal risk-sharing, as proxied by consumption volatility. To our best knowledge, this is the first study that empirically tests this relationship. We use different balance sheet based measure of the significance of Islamic banks, the importance of specific products offered by these banks and different econometric methodologies to test our hypothesis.

This analytical chapter is related to a growing literature on Islamic finance. Beck et al. (2013) find in a large cross-country sample that Islamic banks are less cost-effective, but have higher intermediation ratios, higher asset quality and are better capitalized, which also explains their better performance during the recent crisis. Similarly, Abedifar et al. (2013) find evidence that Islamic banks have lower credit risk and are more stable than conventional banks and their loan quality is less

147 http://willembuiter.com/if.pdf

responsive to domestic interest rate shocks (see also Čihák and Hesse (2010), Pappas, Izzeldin, Fuertes and Ongena (2013), among others). On the country level, Baele et al. (2014) find lower defaults for Islamic than for conventional loans even among the same borrower and same bank in Pakistan, while Zaheer, Ongena and Wijnbergen (2013) show that since Islamic banks' operations are under interest free arrangements, the credit channel of monetary policy might weaken as the size of Islamic banks in a financial sector increase. Using data from Turkey, Ongena and Şendeniz-Yüncü (2011) find that Islamic banks mainly deal with young, multiple-bank, industry-focused and transparent firms, while Beck et al. (2015) find that customers of Islamic banks are more willing to deal with bank branches farther away from their enterprise, suggesting that distance plays less of a role for these borrowers.

The chapter is also related to the literature on income smoothing. While the permanent income hypothesis states that consumption is determined by permanent income and not by transitory changes to income, empirical work shows that consumption varies with output in an economy. Theory points to a positive impact of household credit on relaxing liquidity constraints on households, thus resulting in lower excess sensitivity of household consumption to business cycle variations (Jappelli and Pagano 1989; Bacchetta and Gerlach 1997; Ludvigson 1999). On a more aggregate level, some studies suggest that a more developed financial system is associated with reduced growth volatility (Easterly et al. 2001; Denizer et al. 2002; Raddatz 2006), while others find no robust relationship between these variables (Beck et al. 2006).

Our results do not provide clear evidence of a significant contribution of Islamic banks in intertemporal risk-sharing. Overall, there is at best elusive and insignificant contribution from Islamic banks towards risk-sharing. However, when we dig deeper and analyze the composition of Islamic banks financing, we observe that *mudarabah* investment accounts on the liabilities side that operate according to profit-loss sharing principles have a stronger relationship with intertemporal risk-sharing. Our results suggest that Islamic banks which in their current state tend to use financing modes that are basically following replication of conventional fixed income financial products ought to put more emphasis on developing the financing modes that are more suitable to the principles of risk-sharing in order to contribute to risk-sharing in a more solid manner. We are not surprised by the findings as their contribution to risk-sharing is not expected if they are not practicing risk-sharing finance in its true sense. Islamic banks seem to shy away from risk-sharing finance due to prevailing financial sector with legal and regulatory environment which is less supportive of risk-sharing finance.

The remainder of the chapter is organized as following. Section 2 provides a brief description of the nature and intermediation model of Islamic banks and the risk-sharing concept. Section 3 provides details about the data and the econometric methodology, while Section 4 presents the results. Section 5 provides policy recommendations.

2 Risk-sharing and Islamic Financial Intermediation

Financial systems are crucial for the efficient allocation of resources in a modern economy (see Levine 2005, for an extensive discussion of the theoretical and empirical literature). Financial intermediaries not only channel resources from capital surplus agents (generally households) to capital-deficit ones (businesses) but also allow intertemporal smoothing of households' consumption and businesses' expenditures, enabling both firms and households to share risks. Although both Islamic and commercial banks are financial institutions performing the basic functions described above, in principle they operate under different set of rules.[148] The core pillars on which Islamic banks operations are structured could be summarized as following (Iqbal and Mirakhor 2011):

- Prohibition of interest, and debt. Pre-determined ex ante return is replaced by payoffs dependent ex post returns.
- Risk-sharing: because interest is prohibited, suppliers of funds become investors instead of creditors. The provider of financial capital and the entrepreneur share risks in return for a share of the profits.
- Asset based/backed transactions: money is treated as "potential" capital and there is close linkages and materiality between the financing and underlying real economic activity.
- Prohibition of speculative behavior discourages hoarding and prohibits transactions featuring extreme uncertainties, gambling, and excessive risks.

In the conventional banking system, which is based on debt contracts, risks and rewards are shared asymmetrically, with the debtor bearing both the upside and downside risk while lenders' stake being limited to the debt payment. Debt contracts are used to overcome the problem of asymmetric information, requiring careful screening and close monitoring, which can be delegated to an institution acting on behalf of the collectivity of depositors and investors. Banks thus act as delegated monitor on behalf of depositors.

For Islamic financial institutions, the nature of financial intermediation, including the function of banking, is different from that of conventional financial institutions. This difference is the key to understanding the difference in the nature of conventional and Islamic banking. The basic concept is that both the mobilization and (in theory) the use of funds is based on some form of profit sharing among the depositors, the bank, and the entrepreneurs (users of funds). A typical Islamic bank performs the functions of financial intermediation by screening profitable projects

148 For historical developments and further details on intermediation models, see Iqbal and Mirakhor (2011).

and monitoring the performance of projects on behalf of the investors who deposit their funds with the bank.

Table 13.1 presents a stylized balance sheet of an Islamic bank, displaying different activities and financial instruments. The table in Appendix 1 provides a glossary of common contracts used by Islamic banks. It serves as a good starting point for understanding the dynamics of the risks inherent in Islamic banks.

Table 13.1: Stylized Balance Sheets of Islamic and Conventional Banks.

Islamic Banks		**Conventional Banks**	
Assets	*Liabilities*	*Assets*	*Liabilities*
Trade Financing, Commodity financing, Leases, *Mudarabah* Financing Securities Investment	Investments by Depositors	Loans (Consumer, Corporate) Securities Investments	Deposits
Fees	Capital	Fees	Capital
Main Characteristics			
– Depositors are investors rather than lenders – Risk-sharing through profit and loss sharing accounts – Assets and liabilities are matched – Banks cannot create leverage – Financing of real assets		– Deposits are loans to the bank as debt – Assets invested in fixed income securities and loans – Bank has fixed obligations on deposits but uncertainty on asset returns – Bank is exposed to asset and liabilities mismatch – Banks can create leverage through borrowing	

Source: Iqbal and van Gruening (2008); Askari, Iqbal, and Mirakhor (2012).

The majority of Islamic banks are structured based on a model where the liabilities side of the balance sheet is based on "two-windows." In addition to equity capital, this model divides the "liability" or funding side of the bank balance sheet into two deposit windows, one for demand deposits (current account) and the other for investment or special investment accounts. The choice of window is left to the depositors. Unlike conventional commercial banking, the investment accounts of an Islamic bank are not liabilities in a strict sense because depositors in a conventional bank create immediate claims on the bank, whereas investors-depositors in Islamic banks are like partners.

Money deposited in investment accounts, in contrast, is placed with the depositors' full knowledge that their deposits will be invested in risk-bearing projects; no guarantee is needed or justified. Investment account holders are investors or depositors who enter into a *mudarabah* contract with the bank, where investors act as the supplier of funds (*rab al-mal*) to be invested by the bank on their behalf, as the agent (*mudarib*). The investors share in the profits accruing to the bank's investments on the assets side. Therefore, such profit-sharing investment deposits are not liabilities. Investors' capital is not guaranteed, and they incur losses if the bank does; the form is closer to that of a limited term, non-voting equity or a trust arrangement. Some Islamic banks also offer special investment accounts developed on the basis of a special-purpose or restricted *mudarabah* or on profit and loss sharing (*musharakah*). These special investment accounts, which are similar to close-end mutual funds, are highly customized and targeted toward high-net-worth individuals.

3 Data and Methodology

This section introduces the different data sources and variables we use and presents our methodology. Appendix 1 provides an overview of the different data sources used in this analysis. Table 13.2 presents descriptive statistics for Islamic banks and Table 13.3 presents correlation coefficients.

3.1 Data and Methodology

Only two countries – Islamic Republic of Iran and Sudan – have banking systems fully following Islamic banking principles, while in the rest of the countries Islamic banks operate parallel to conventional banks. In order to gauge the relationship of Islamic banks with aggregate risk-sharing, we proxy the significance of Islamic banks in a country with their share in the financial system. According to the theory of Islamic banking discussed above, countries with a larger presence of Islamic banks are expected to see higher aggregate risk-sharing. We use two different sources, Bankscope and IBIS, to construct measures of the significance of Islamic banks in a country's banking system. The two databases have their strength and weaknesses, and by conducting our analysis using both data sources we aim at both doing a robustness check to see whether our results are sensitive to the data source we use and, second, to combine the relative strengths of each data set. Although Bankscope is comprehensive in terms of coverage and reliability of data for Islamic banks, it is not an exhaustive representation of the overall size of Islamic banks since Bankscope does not include Islamic windows and in order to standardize balance sheets of commercial and Islamic banks some accounts are included within unclear categories of the balance sheet. Furthermore, the classification of Islamic

Table 13.2: Descriptive Statistics.

	Obs.	Mean	Std. Dev.	Min	Max
λ_{OLS}	151	.4806	.233	.00125	1.1376
λ_{IV}	120	.5254	.237	.00152	1.0291
Islamic Bank Assets IBIS (% of GDP)	32	.147	.289	7.52e-06	1.301
Islamic Bank Loans IBIS (% of GDP)	32	.071	.124	.00002	.537
Islamic Bank Assets Bankscope (% of GDP)	31	.120	.219	.00003	.879
Islamic Bank Loans Bankscope (% of GDP)	31	.063	.116	.00001	.474
Current Account (% of GDP)	31	.017	.032	.00001	.2965
Mudarabah Investment Account (% of GDP)	22	.059	.086	1.35e-06	.296
Mudarabah Savings Account (% of GDP)	20	.0136	.017	.00022	.0816
Mudaraba Assets (% of GDP)	15	.0176	.051	3.86e-06	.201
Musharaka Assets (% of GDP)	19	.005	.0103	4.80e-06	.0383
Murabaha Assets (% of GDP)	31	.0507	.095	.000023	.4800
Qard Hasan Assets (% of GDP)	18	.0008	.002	4.01e-08	.0065
Istisna Assets (% of GDP)	13	.004	.004	.00008	.0163
Ijara Assets (% of GDP)	23	.0081	.012	9.09e-07	.0387
Salam Assets (% of GDP)	9	.0015	.0021	1.45e-07	.0058
Domestic credit to private sector	176	42.958	38.745	1.902	195.11
Stock market total value traded to GDP	108	23.72	38.363	.019	229.87
Government expenditure	175	16.19	5.920	4.930	42.52
Chin-ITO Financial Openness Index	181	.220	1.394	−1.88	2.389
Stock market turnover ratio (%)	108	42.01	43.912	.361	197.489

banks according to Bankscope is problematic, since due to their nature some of the Islamic banks are treated as investment banks. On the other hand, IBIS data for Islamic banks are collected from the respective central banks of the jurisdictions the banks are located. IBIS database enables us to analyze the product composition of Islamic banks and to perform a robustness check using aggregate variables. As can be seen in the correlation Table 13.3, there is a high but not perfect correlation in the importance of Islamic banks across the two data sources for the countries for which we have data from both. Finally, the country coverage using these two databases does not completely overlap, which provides us with another sensitivity test.

We use annual data for the period from 1990 to 2011. Our sample consists of 31 and 32 countries depending on whether we use Bankscope or IBIS data source, respectively. The list of countries in Bankscope and IBIS database is provided in Appendix 2. As one can see, some countries are included only in Bankscope while some countries are peculiar to IBIS database, which reflects the difficulty in identifying which bank is actually a Islamic bank or commercial bank. As can be seen in Table 13.3, the share of Islamic banks' total assets (loans) as a share of GDP ranges from 7.52–06 (.0000239) to 1.301(.537) in IBIS database and from 0.000037 (.00001) to .879(.474) in Bankscope database.

Table 13.3: Correlations between Variables.

Panel A: Cross Country Analysis																				
λ_{OLS}	1																			
λ_{IV}	0.8824*	1																		
Islamic Bank Assets IBIS	0.0778	−0.1110	1																	
Islamic Bank Loans IBIS	−0.0397	−0.1701	0.8617*	1																
Islamic Bank Assets Bankscope	−0.2195	−0.3000	0.6853*	0.8735*	1															
Islamic Bank Loans Bankscope	−0.2272	−0.2876	0.6211*	0.8806*	0.9872*	1														
Current Account	0.0941	−0.0331	0.8361*	0.8983*	0.6365*	0.6554*	1													
Mudarabah Investment Account	−0.2230	−0.3296	0.6051*	0.8624*	0.8875*	0.9159*	0.6215*	1												
Mudarabah Savings Account	0.0645	0.0605	0.4491*	0.7851*	0.5482*	0.6419*	0.7562*	0.6871*	1											
Mudaraba Assets	0.2840	0.0981	0.8102*	0.5449*	0.2294	0.1519	0.6140*	0.2102	0.1640	1										
Musharaka Assets	0.2334	0.0820	0.8901*	0.8596*	0.5487*	0.5313*	0.8813*	0.5306*	0.6269*	0.8335*	1									
Qard Hasan Assets	−0.0982	−0.0663	0.6838*	0.9422*	0.8950*	0.9366*	0.8202*	0.8878*	0.8538*	0.2511	0.6910*	1								
Murabaha Assets	0.0047	−0.1744	0.1872	0.4444*	0.3035	0.3773	0.4070*	0.3307	0.9031*	−0.0103	0.3408	0.5466*	1							
Istisna Assets	−0.3960*	−0.5105*	0.3269	0.3680*	0.3502	0.3515	0.2369	0.5333*	0.1110	0.1929	0.1433	0.2789	−0.1265	1						
Ijara Assets	−0.3558	−0.4358*	0.3049	0.4109*	0.5970*	0.5762*	0.1692	0.5013*	0.0625	−0.0028	0.0772	0.3870*	−0.0494	0.6954*	1					
Salam Assets	0.0815	0.0324	0.4764*	0.7431*	0.5696*	0.6357*	0.6696*	0.5725*	0.7932*	0.2247	0.6530*	0.7557*	0.4874*	0.2125	0.3714*	1				
Domestic credit to private sector	−0.2188*	−0.2009*	−0.2075	−0.1706	−0.0397	−0.0242	−0.1872	−0.1147	−0.1788	−0.1928	−0.2185	−0.1116	−0.1394	−0.0518	0.1116	−0.1284	1			
Stock market total value traded to GDP	−0.2737*	−0.1262	−0.1627	−0.1672	−0.1340	−0.1233	−0.0772	−0.2302	−0.1712	0.2367	−0.2156	−0.1632	−0.1593	0.0965	−0.0494	−0.1959	0.6817*	1		
Government expenditure	−0.0978	−0.1936*	−0.0157	0.0426	0.2344	0.2239	0.0185	0.3645	−0.0779	−0.1782	−0.1983	0.1214	−0.1307	0.3335	0.1442	−0.2313	0.1891*	0.0706	1	
Chin–ITO Financial Openness Index	−0.2021*	−0.1366	0.0302	−0.0070	0.1807	0.1590	−0.0234	0.0291	−0.1166	−0.1418	−0.1627	0.0195	−0.2332	0.3699*	0.4098*	−0.0117	0.4848*	0.3533*	0.1771*	1

Panel B: Panel Data Analysis															
λ_{OLS}	1														
λ_{IV}	0.9561*	1													
Islamic Bank Assets IBIS	0.1798*	0.0421	1												
Islamic Bank Loans IBIS	0.1728*	0.0383	0.8183*	1											
Islamic Bank Assets Bankscope	−0.1005	−0.1201	0.5212*	0.4360*	1										
Islamic Bank Loans Bankscope	−0.1412*	−0.1335	0.3790*	0.3330*	0.9773*	1									
Current Account	−0.0009	−0.0369	0.1587*	0.1579*	0.5920*	0.6731*	1								
Mudarabah Investment Account	−0.2677*	−0.2302*	0.1641*	0.4101*	0.8231*	0.8653*	0.6164*	1							
Mudarabah Savings Account	−0.0493	−0.0581	0.1010	0.3443*	0.5997*	0.7020*	0.7810*	0.7906*	1						
Risk–sharing Assets	0.1843*	0.0883	0.7817*	0.9730*	0.2706*	0.1573*	−0.0122	−0.0009	−0.0233	1					
Fixed Income Assets	0.0077	−0.0885	0.6337*	0.8070*	0.7522*	0.7264*	0.5929*	0.8685*	0.7776*	0.6451*	1				
Domestic credit to private sector	−0.1399	−0.0698*	−0.1823*	−0.1457*	−0.0974	−0.0731	−0.0239	−0.0129	−0.1488*	−0.1213*	−0.0753	1			
Stock market total value traded to GDP	−0.1096*	−0.0738*	−0.1298*	−0.1682*	−0.1507*	−0.1429*	−0.0898	−0.1735*	−0.1385	−0.1770*	−0.1121	0.6387*	1		
Government expenditure	0.0721*	0.0443	−0.1370*	−0.1002	0.0225	0.0612	0.2285*	0.2895*	0.0856	−0.1353*	0.0825	0.1324*	0.0417	1	
Chin–ITO Financial Openness Index	−0.1387*	−0.0344	−0.1048*	−0.1271*	−0.0295	−0.0052	0.1229*	0.0331	0.0049	−0.1163*	0.0295	0.4588*	0.3659*	0.1900*	1

Note: λ_{OLS} and λ_{IV} are estimated by rolling regressions with 10 year rolling window using annual data for the period from 1990 to 2011. Rest of the variables are rolling 10-year averages of the available data for the period used in estimating the risk-sharing estimate. * indicate significance levels at 5%.

In order to single out the contribution of Islamic banks to risk-sharing, we include several proxies for other factors that theory predicts might be associated with better risk-sharing. Specifically, we utilize the Chin-Ito financial openness index to capture the effects of international risk-sharing.[149] In quantifying the contribution of welfare state on risk-sharing, we choose to use the ratio of overall government expenditures over GDP.[150] Finally, we use several proxies such as domestic credit to private sector, stock market turnover and traded value, and gross savings in order to capture the contribution of financial markets to risk-sharing and thus isolate the effect of Islamic banks beyond the effect of overall financial sector development. As can be seen in Table 13.2, there is a large cross-country variation in the control variables.

3.2 Methodology

In order to estimate the risk-sharing parameter (consumption smoothing), we rely on data from the Penn World Tables.[151] In quantifying the consumption smoothing parameter, denoted as λ, we follow the basic approach of Campbell and Mankiw (1989) and estimate the following equation, using annual data from 1990 to 2011:

$$\Delta c_t = \alpha + \lambda \Delta y_t + \varepsilon_{t,} \tag{1}$$

where $\Delta c_t(\Delta y_t)$ are four-year change in private consumption (real GDP). The coefficient λ measures the extent of how movements in private consumption are related to the movements in real income. Once we estimate λ coefficient, we exclude the countries for which the coefficient is not statistically significant.

Furthermore, since Δy_t might be correlated with the disturbance term ε_t we instrument Δy_t with its own lags Δy_{t-2}, Δy_{t-3} and Δy_{t-4}. We use the F-test to test the validity of the instruments and keep only the countries for which the instruments of lagged changes in income are statistically significant predictors of the current change in income. Per our logic, defined in prior sections, the higher is λ the lower is risk-sharing in an economy. Hence λ coefficient becomes our proxy for the risk-sharing in a country.

Since the number of countries with Islamic banking is limited, in order to increase the number of observations in our analysis, we conduct the regressions both

---

149 Using sum of trade and export as the proxy for financial openness produced similar results.
150 The main reason we opt to use general government expenditure as the proxy in measuring the strength of welfare state was to increase the number of observations in our analysis, since data for better measures of welfare state such as Coverage of social safety nets is not available for most of the countries with Islamic banking.
151 Detailed information about each variable and the source is provided in Appendix 2.

with the λ estimated from basic OLS regression and λ estimated from Instrumental Variable (IV) regression. Overall the IV and basic OLS regressions make use of 120 (151) observations respectively and the λ coefficient ranges from .0015 to 1.029 (from .0012 to 1.137) respectively (Table 13.2).

The correlations in Table 13.3 show that consumption smoothing parameter estimated by Instrumental Variable regressions is, though insignificant, negatively correlated with both proxies used for the strength of Islamic Banks in a jurisdiction i.e. total assets and loans as percentage of GDP from both databases. On the other hand, the consumption smoothing parameter estimated via basic OLS is positively correlated with Islamic Bank Assets as percentage of GDP from the IBIS database. When we look at the product composition we see that the importance of *Mudarabah* Investment Accounts and *Qard Hasan*, *Istisna* and *Ijarah* assets are negatively correlated with both of the consumption smoothing estimates. The other variables used to capture the correlation of conventional financial products, welfare state and financial openness are all negatively and most of the time significantly correlated with both measures of consumption smoothing parameter.

In the second step, we use cross-country regressions where the explanatory variables are the averages of their available values for the period from 1990 to 2011, which is the same period we use to estimate the risk-sharing parameter.

$$\lambda_i = aX_i + \beta IB_i + \varepsilon_{t,} \tag{2}$$

where IB stands for the share of Islamic banks in a country's financial system. If Islamic banks contribute to intertemporal risk-sharing more than conventional banks, then the coefficient of Islamic banking proxy should be significant and negative. It is important to note that our coefficient estimates do not imply causality, as our regressions are subject to the usual endogeneity concerns of OLS regressions, including reverse causation and omitted variable bias.

To test the sensitivity of our results, we take advantage of the additional insights panel-data analysis might provide an estimate the risk-sharing parameter using a 10-year rolling-window for the period from 1990 to 2011 with the same methodology described above (both OLS and IV). This gives us 22 risk-sharing parameters for each country. For every risk-sharing lambda the explanatory variables are computed as the averages of the same 10-year period that was used in estimating the risk-sharing parameter.

3.3 Results

We present and discuss our different regression results. We present results both using total assets and total loans of Islamic banks before turning to turning to the importance of specific products.

The results in Table 13.4 do not show a robust and significant relationship between the importance of Islamic banking and the degree of inter- temporal risk-sharing in an economy. Here, we first look at the relationship between overall Islamic bank assets as percentage of GDP and risk-sharing (λ) using cross-country regressions. The regressions in columns 1 to 4 are based on total Islamic bank assets from the IBIS database, while the regressions in columns 5 to 8 are based on the Bankscope database. As discussed above, we include stock market total traded value to GDP and domestic credit to GDP variables to extract the effects of conventional financial markets on risk-sharing. Government expenditure as percentage of GDP and the Chin-Ito financial openness index are used to capture the effect of welfare state and financial globalization on risk-sharing. The explanatory variables are the average of their respective annual values for the period from 1990 to 2011. The values of risk-sharing parameter, λ, estimated by basic OLS and instrumental variable regression methods are denoted with OLS and IV, respectively. Furthermore, we add another variable, for robustness check and to increase the number of observations that includes countries without the presence of Islamic banks, taking on the value zero.

Our findings suggest that the contribution of Islamic banks to risk-sharing is at best, elusive. Even though the coefficient of Islamic bank assets is negative in all regressions, it is significant only for regression (1), (3) and (7) that have been computed using the risk-sharing parameter estimated by OLS. Turning to the control variables, we find some weak evidence that higher government expenditures to GDP and higher openness is associated with higher intertemporal risk-sharing.

The results in Table 13.5 confirm our previous findings for measures of loans rather than total assets of Islamic banks. Here, we substitute the total of Islamic bank assets with total of Islamic bank loans as the proxy for the strength of Islamic banks in the financial sector in the country they are operating. All of the eight coefficients of the Islamic bank loans over GDP have a negative sign. All of the coefficients based on IBIS database are insignificant, implying that the positive contribution from Islamic bank loans to risk-sharing is negligible. Although the coefficients of participatory bank loans based on Bankscope are of a higher magnitude, only one (column 8) is significant.

The results in Table 13.6 provide evidence that a more prominent role for risk-sharing accounts on both assets and liability sides of Islamic banks' balance sheets is significantly associated with higher intertemporal risk-sharing in an economy. Here, we analyze the relationship between the importance of current accounts, *mudarabah* savings accounts and *mudarabah* investment accounts of Islamic banks and intertemporal risk-sharing in an economy. This data is taken from IBIS and the values are the averages for the period between 1990 and 2011. Current accounts of participatory banks are similar to the accounts of commercial banks since they can be withdrawn at any time by deposit holders. On the other hand, the *mudarabah* investment and savings accounts are peculiar to Islamic banks since they are

Table 13.4: Risk-sharing and Islamic Bank Assets: Cross-country Regressions.

Dependent Variable (λ)	IBIS Database				Bankscope Database			
	(1)	(2)	(3)	(4)	(5)	(6)	(7)	(8)
	Not IV	IV	Not IV	IV	Not IV	IV	Not IV	IV
Total Islamic Bank Assets (% of GDP)	−0.235*	−0.225			−0.167	−0.213		
	(0.134)	(0.206)			(0.134)	(0.203)		
Domestic credit to private sector (% of GDP)	0.00339*	0.00371**	−0.000310	−0.000547	0.00261	0.00258	−0.000319	−0.000551
	(0.00163)	(0.00170)	(0.000583)	(0.000523)	(0.00185)	(0.00185)	(0.000582)	(0.000523)
Stock market total value traded to GDP (%)	−0.00271*	−0.00162	−0.000883	0.000199	−0.00202	−0.00104	−0.000877	0.000208
	(0.00138)	(0.00264)	(0.000865)	(0.000812)	(0.00241)	(0.00287)	(0.000864)	(0.000809)
General government final consumption expenditure (% of GDP)	−0.00413	−0.00550	−0.00259	−0.0104**	−0.00175	−0.00292	−0.00233	−0.0102**
	(0.00937)	(0.0139)	(0.00439)	(0.00502)	(0.0105)	(0.0133)	(0.00434)	(0.00496)
Chin-ITO Financial Openness Index	−0.0832*	−0.0744	−0.0372**	−0.0114	−0.0714	−0.0564	−0.0371**	−0.0114
	(0.0443)	(0.0512)	(0.0185)	(0.0217)	(0.0414)	(0.0516)	(0.0185)	(0.0217)
Total Islamic Bank Assets (% of GDP) (With 0 for no Islamic Assets)			−0.280**	−0.235			−0.245**	−0.199
	(0.134)	(0.206)	(0.00369)	(0.00379)			(0.119)	(0.156)
Constant	0.500**	0.516**	0.582***	0.703***	0.445**	0.502**	0.578***	0.700***
	(0.175)	(0.202)	(0.0651)	(0.0795)	(0.179)	(0.203)	(0.0643)	(0.0788)
Observations	22	21	96	77	22	21	96	77
R-squared	0.439	0.356	0.167	0.119	0.293	0.250	0.169	0.119

Note: The dependent variable λ is the consumption smoothing parameter, computed according to the methodology explained in the paper. Not IV stands for basic OLS while IV stands for Instrumental Variable regression. Explanatory variables are the averages of the period from 1990 to 2011. *p*-values calculated from robust standard errors are reported, *, **, ***, indicate significance levels at 10%, 5% and 1% level, respectively

Table 13.5: Risk-sharing and Islamic Bank Loans: Cross-country Regressions.

Dependent Variable (λ)	**IBIS database**				**Bankscope Database**			
	(1)	**(2)**	**(3)**	**(4)**	**(5)**	**(6)**	**(7)**	**(8)**
	IV	**Not IV**	**IV**	**Not IV**	**IV**	**Not IV**	**IV**	**Not IV**
Total Islamic Bank Loans (% of GDP)	−0.239	−0.293			−0.356	−0.289		
	(0.331)	(0.213)			(0.386)	(0.254)		
Domestic credit to private sector (% of GDP)	0.00364**	0.00331*	−0.000528	−0.000298	0.00253	0.00256	−0.000548	−0.000318
	(0.00169)	(0.00163)	(0.000521)	(0.000583)	(0.00184)	(0.00184)	(0.000521)	(0.000580)
Stock market total value traded to GDP (%)	−0.00126	−0.00248*	0.000212	−0.000871	−0.000840	−0.00189	0.000224	−0.000862
	(0.00260)	(0.00135)	(0.000822)	(0.000871)	(0.00283)	(0.00238)	(0.000811)	(0.000863)
General government final consumption expenditure (% of GDP)	−0.00654	−0.00450	−0.0105**	−0.00269	−0.00343	−0.00203	−0.0103**	−0.00240
	(0.0141)	(0.00946)	(0.00503)	(0.00439)	(0.0133)	(0.0105)	(0.00497)	(0.00434)
Chin-ITO Financial Openness Index	−0.0807	−0.0902*	−0.0130	−0.0386**	−0.0598	−0.0739*	−0.0121	−0.0378**
	(0.0505)	(0.0435)	(0.0220)	(0.0187)	(0.0503)	(0.0405)	(0.0218)	(0.0185)
Total Islamic Bank Loans (% of GDP)(With 0 for no Islamic Bank Loans)			−0.278	−0.383			−0.342	−0.441*
			(0.330)	(0.277)			(0.309)	(0.247)
Constant	0.529**	0.489**	0.701***	0.580***	0.506**	0.448**	0.701***	0.579***
	(0.204)	(0.174)	(0.0798)	(0.0655)	(0.203)	(0.179)	(0.0788)	(0.0644)
Observations	21	22	77	96	21	22	77	96
R-squared	0.341	0.425	0.109	0.160	0.245	0.290	0.116	0.167

Note: The dependent variable λ is the consumption smoothing parameter, computed according to the methodology explained in the paper. Not IV stands for basic OLS while IV stands for Instrumental Variable regression. Explanatory variables are the averages of the period from 1990 to 2011.
p-values calculated from robust standard errors are reported, *, **, ***, indicate significance levels at 10%, 5% and 1% level, respectively

Table 13.6: Risk-sharing and Current Account and Mudarabah Accounts: Cross-country Regressions.

Dependent Variable (λ)	**(1)**	**(2)**	**(3)**	**(4)**	**(5)**	**(6)**	**(7)**	**(8)**
	IV	**Not IV**	**IV**	**Not IV**	**IV**	**Not IV**	**IV**	**Not IV**
Current Account (% of GDP)	2.695	3.108			2.562	3.027		
	(1.710)	(2.093)			(1.986)	(2.408)		
Mudarabah Investment Account (% of GDP)	−1.614**	−1.501**						
	(0.633)	(0.682)						
Domestic credit to private sector (% of GDP)	0.00195*	0.000415	0.00157	0.000443	0.00194*	0.000396	0.00149	0.000387
	(0.000973)	(0.00130)	(0.000976)	(0.00119)	(0.000972)	(0.00131)	(0.000992)	(0.00119)
Current Account (% of GDP) (With 0 for no Islamic Assets)			2.652	3.155			2.623	3.180
			(1.620)	(2.045)			(1.868)	(2.330)
Mudarabah Investment Account (% of GDP) (With 0 for no Islamic Assets)			−1.637**	−1.542**				
			(0.600)	(0.643)				
Total of Mudarabah Accounts (Saving+Investment) (% of GDP)					−1.340*	−1.276		
					(0.711)	(0.737)		
Total of Mudarabah Accounts (Saving+Investment) (% of GDP) (With 0 for No Saving or Ivestment Account)							−1.313*	−1.262*
							(0.665)	(0.691)
Constant	0.471***	0.464***	0.493***	0.468***	0.487***	0.481***	0.495***	0.469***
	(0.102)	(0.0954)	(0.0764)	(0.0778)	(0.101)	(0.0956)	(0.0781)	(0.0788)
Observations	19	21	27	29	20	22	27	29
R-squared	0.235	0.155	0.174	0.127	0.200	0.124	0.140	0.103

Note: The dependent variable λ is the consumption smoothing parameter, computed according to the methodology explained in the paper. Not IV stands for basic OLS while IV stands for Instrumental Variable regression. Explanatory variables are the averages of the period from 1990 to 2011. Total of Mudarabah Accounts is the sum of Mudarabah Investment Account and Mudarabah Saving Account. Last explanatory variable, Total of Mudarabah Accounts (with 0's for no Saving or Investment Account) is the sum of Mudarabah Investment Account and Mudarabah Saving Account. It takes the value of 0 if there is Islamic banking presence in a country but no Mudarabah Investment or Saving Accounts *p*-values calculated from robust standard errors are reported, * **, *** indicate significance levels at 10%, 5% and 1% level, respectively.

invested according to profit-loss sharing principles. Neither the return nor the principal is guaranteed in these accounts and returns/losses are determined according to the outcome of the activities of bank operations. Investors in these accounts receive their return in proportion to their investment to the projects.

The results in Table 13.6 show negative and significant coefficients for *mudarabah* investment account in all four regressions. As can be seen in Table 13.2, the correlation between *mudarabah* savings accounts and *mudarabah* investment accounts is significant and high (0.687). For this reason, we drop the *mudarabah* savings account in the regressions but as robustness check include it in the aggregate variable denoted as *mudarabah* accounts, which is the sum of *mudarabah* investment and *mudarabah* savings accounts (columns 5–8). This aggregate measure enters negatively in all four regressions and significant in all but one (column 6).

The results in Table 13.7 show limited evidence for the role of specific products offered by Islamic banks. Here, we present the standardized coefficients different

Table 13.7: Risk-sharing and Different Forms of Islamic Financing: Cross-country Regressions.

Dependent Variable (λ)	**(1)** **Not IV**	**(2)** **IV**	**(3)** **Not IV**	**(4)** **IV**
Musharaka Assets (% of GDP)	−2.769	−3.902		
Mudaraba Assets (% of GDP)	−0.305	−0.140		
Murabaha Assets (% of GDP)	2.359	4.014		
Qard Hasan Assets (% of GDP)	−0.377	−0.467*		
Istisna Assets (% of GDP)	−1.260**	−1.321**		
Ijara Assets (% of GDP)	0.080	−0.515		
Salam Assets (% of GDP)	0.830	0.497		
Domestic credit to private sector (% of GDP)	0.010	0.286	0.248	0.392
Stock market turnover ratio (%)	0.136	0.082	−0.084	−0.142
General government final consumption expenditure (% of GDP)	0.064	−0.203	−0.120	−0.209
Chin-ITO Financial Openness Index	−0.393	−0.233	−0.564*	−0.410
Total of Risk-sharing Products of Islamic Bank Assets (% of GDP)			−0.053	−0.167
Total of Fixed Income of Islamic Bank Assets (% of GDP)			−0.102	0.029
R-squared	0.65	0.72	0.38	0.35
Observations	22	21	22	21

Note: The dependent variable λ is the consumption smoothing parameter, computed according to the methodology explained in the paper. Not IV stands for basic OLS while IV stands for Instrumental Variable regression. Explanatory variables are the averages of the period from 1990 to 2011. Musharaka, Mudaraba, Murabaha, Qard Hasan, Ijara, Istisna and Salam are taken from IBIS database and each of these variables are assumed to have value of 0 if the value is not available. Total of Risk-sharing Products of Islamic Bank Assets (% of GDP) is the sum of Musharaka, Mudaraba Qard Hasan assets. Total of Fixed Income of Islamic Bank Assets is the sum of Murabaha, Istisna, Ijara and Salam assets *p*-values calculated from robust standard errors are reported, *, **, ***, indicate significance levels at 10%, 5% and 1% level, respectively.

financial products offered by Islamic banks i.e, *musharaka, mudaraba, murabaha, qard hasan, ijarah, istisna and salam*. We would like to stress, however, that the data obtained from IBIS, although reliable in terms of aggregate values such as loans and assets, might be less reliable when reporting data for different product category. In addition, cross-country consistency between the same product across countries in different countries might not be perfect. In theory, one would expect that *musharaka* and *mudarabah* to be most conducive towards risk-sharing due to the principles under which these products operate. Meanwhile *murabaha* loans, which are basically mark-up sale, should not contribute to risk-sharing as much as the aforementioned two. Although, as expected by theory, *musharaka* and *mudarabah* loans have negative coefficients and *murabaha* have positive coefficients, when one looks at the results, only the coefficients on i*stisna* are significant and negative simultaneously in both columns.

So far, all results have been based on cross-sectional regressions. As a final robustness test, we use panel data techniques and carry out robustness checks for the results presented above that were based on cross-country analysis. As has been noted before, we construct the risk-sharing parameter (λ) using a 10-year rolling window for the period from 1990 to 2011. The explanatory variables are constructed as the rolling 10-year averages that correspond to the same period for which the risk-sharing estimate is calculated. The risk-sharing estimate (λ) is constructed using both OLS and Instrumental Variable regressions, as was the case in cross-country regressions. For each estimate of λ, calculated under two different methodologies (OLS and IV) we conduct Pooled OLS and Fixed-Random Effect regressions. We choose Fixed or Random effect model based on Hausman test.

The results in Tables 13.8 and 13.9 confirm our previous findings of limited statistical and economic significance of the relationship between the importance of Islamic banking and intertemporal risk-sharing. We use asset and loan shares in these regressions, with Table 13.8 reporting results using IBIS data and Table 13.9 reporting results using Bankscope data. In Table 13.8, although in the majority of regressions the coefficients of proxies used for Islamic banking presence (assets and loans) have negative sign, they are either insignificant and/or are of magnitude that is very close to zero. In Table 13.9, all Islamic bank proxies have negative sign but only two of them (columns 3 and 8) are significant.

The results in Table 13.10 confirm our previous findings of the importance of risk-sharing accounts for intertemporal risk-sharing. Here, we consider the relationship of *mudarabah* investment accounts and current accounts of Islamic banks with intertemporal risk-sharing. Given the significant and large correlation (0.79) depicted in Panel B of Table 13.3, between *mudarabah* investment accounts and *mudarabah* saving accounts, we dropped the latter. All four coefficients of *mudarabah* investment accounts are negative and the coefficient of regression (1) is significant.

Finally, Table 13.11 analyzes the correlation between risk-sharing and different types of financial instruments offered by Islamic banks that are grouped in two

Table 13.8: Risk-sharing and Islamic Banking Assets and Loans from IBIS Database: Panel Regressions.

Dependent Variable (λ)	**(1)**	**(2)**	**(3)**	**(4)**	**(5)**	**(6)**	**(7)**	**(8)**
	IV	**Not IV**	**Not IV**	**IV**	**IV**	**Not IV**	**Not IV**	**IV**
Total Islamic Bank Assets (% of GDP)	−0.166	−0.383*	−0.537***	−0.276				
	(0.269)	(0.184)	(0.180)	(0.346)				
Domestic credit to private	0.00363*	0.00204	0.00264	0.00541***	0.00350*	0.00157	0.000250	0.00401**
sector (% of GDP)	(0.00198)	(0.00211)	(0.00285)	(0.00172)	(0.00181)	(0.00175)	(0.00236)	(0.00202)
Stock market total value traded	−0.00214	−0.00249	−0.000715	−0.00193	−0.00161	−0.00120	0.000163	−0.000860
to GDP (%)	(0.00243)	(0.00243)	(0.00237)	(0.00221)	(0.00231)	(0.00196)	(0.00216)	(0.00246)
General government final consumption	−0.00357	−0.00193	−0.0105	−0.0172	−0.00638	−0.00612	−0.00834	−0.0104
expenditure (% of GDP)	(0.0106)	(0.0103)	(0.0137)	(0.0130)	(0.00920)	(0.00857)	(0.0107)	(0.0128)
Chin-ITO Financial Openness Index	−0.0369	−0.0648	0.0505**	0.0684***	−0.0325	−0.0558	−0.0121	0.0322
	(0.0362)	(0.0412)	(0.0207)	(0.0212)	(0.0354)	(0.0331)	(0.0281)	(0.0310)
Bank lending-deposit spread	0.0353	0.00442	−0.0692	0.0313	0.0466	0.0209	−0.0399	0.0382
	(0.0302)	(0.0309)	(0.0727)	(0.0324)	(0.0288)	(0.0277)	(0.0477)	(0.0273)
Total Islamic Loans (% of GDP)					−0.104	−0.504	−0.976*	−0.358
					(0.438)	(0.420)	(0.520)	(0.669)
Constant	0.291	0.572**	0.907	0.380	0.238	0.502**	0.886**	0.303
	(0.254)	(0.241)	(0.604)	(0.370)	(0.261)	(0.234)	(0.384)	(0.319)
Observations	127	163	163	127	116	148	148	116
R-squared	0.198	0.254	0.158	0.2342	0.202	0.235	0.102	0.078
Number of isocodeencoded			17	16			17	16
FE			YES	–			–	–
RE			–	YES			YES	YES
Hausman Test Pvalue			0.0302	0.0682			0.2874	0.6649

Note: The dependent variable λ is the consumption smoothing parameter, computed using 10 year rolling window period according to the methodology explained in the paper. Not IV stands for pooled OLS while IV stands for Instrumental Variable regression. Explanatory variables are the rolling 10-year averages of the period from 1990 to 2011. *p*-values calculated from robust standard errors are reported, *, **, ***, indicate significance levels at 10%, 5% and 1% level, respectively.

Table 13.9: Risk-sharing and Islamic banking Assets and Loans from Bankscope Database: Panel Regressions.

Dependent Variable (λ)	**(1)**	**(2)**	**(3)**	**(4)**	**(5)**	**(6)**	**(7)**	**(8)**
	Not IV	**IV**	**Not IV**	**IV**	**Not IV**	**IV**	**IV**	**Not IV**
Total Islamic Bank Assets (% of GDP)	−0.272	−0.0765	−0.532***	−0.221				
	(0.206)	(0.289)	(0.132)	(0.322)				
Domestic credit to private sector (% of GDP)	0.00176	0.00214	0.00113	0.00333	0.00170	0.00271	0.00402**	0.00135
	(0.00198)	(0.00206)	(0.00301)	(0.00249)	(0.00199)	(0.00197)	(0.00199)	(0.00305)
Stock market total value traded to GDP (%)	−0.000813	0.000184	−0.00118	−0.000263	−0.000649	-6.88e-05	−0.000715	−0.00117
	(0.00236)	(0.00287)	(0.00210)	(0.00315)	(0.00233)	(0.00283)	(0.00280)	(0.00217)
General government final consumption expenditure	−0.00236	−0.00359	−0.0232**	−0.0163	−0.00302	−0.00542	−0.0156	−0.0214**
(% of GDP)	(0.00921)	(0.0114)	(0.00859)	(0.0131)	(0.00925)	(0.0111)	(0.0130)	(0.00924)
Chin-ITO Financial Openness Index	−0.0509	−0.0250	0.0419	0.0555	−0.0537	−0.0243	0.0574	0.0422
	(0.0468)	(0.0442)	(0.0388)	(0.0377)	(0.0463)	(0.0433)	(0.0349)	(0.0390)
Bank lending-deposit spread	0.0237	0.0433	−0.0493	0.0285	0.0235	0.0465	0.0305	−0.0485
	(0.0242)	(0.0306)	(0.0475)	(0.0260)	(0.0261)	(0.0306)	(0.0277)	(0.0484)
Total Islamic Bank Loans (% of GDP)					−0.436	−0.0180	−0.200	−1.033**
					(0.409)	(0.500)	(0.745)	(0.408)
Constant	0.399	0.216	1.068**	0.405	0.404	0.194	0.349	1.027**
	(0.249)	(0.261)	(0.380)	(0.309)	(0.256)	(0.263)	(0.313)	(0.384)
Observations	155	123	155	123	154	122	122	154
R-squared	0.222	0.146	0.189	0.159	0.208	0.159	0.171	0.169
Number of isocodeencoded			18	17			17	18
FE			YES	–			–	YES
RE			–	YES			YES	–
Hausman Test Pvalue			0.0151	0.2218			0.1699	0.0156

Note: The dependent variable λ is the consumption smoothing parameter, computed using 10 year rolling window period according to the methodology explained in the paper. Not IV stands for pooled OLS while IV stands for Instrumental Variable regression. Explanatory variables are the rolling 10-year averages of the period from 1990 to 2011. *p*-values calculated from robust standard errors are reported, *, **, ***, indicate significance levels at 10%, 5% and 1% level, respectively.

Table 13.10: Risk-sharing and Current Account and Mudarabah Investment Accounts: Panel Regressions.

Dependent Variable (λ)	**(1)**	**(2)**	**(3)**	**(4)**
	IV	**Not IV**	**IV**	**Not IV**
Current Account (% of GDP)	2.726***	1.732***	2.333**	0.509
	(0.437)	(0.544)	(1.180)	(0.498)
Mudarabah Investment Account (% of GDP)	−1.132**	−0.412	−0.823	−0.192
	(0.431)	(0.420)	(1.002)	(0.557)
Domestic credit to private sector (% of GDP)	0.00295***	0.00253***	0.00380***	0.00302***
	(0.000665)	(0.000602)	(0.000670)	(0.000676)
General government final consumption expenditure (% of GDP)	−0.0150	−0.0193**	−0.0225**	−0.0211**
	(0.00866)	(0.00650)	(0.0100)	(0.00934)
Chin-ITO Financial Openness Index	0.0163	0.00107	0.0516***	0.0296
	(0.0236)	(0.0268)	(0.0173)	(0.0287)
Gross domestic savings (% of GDP)	−0.0109***	−0.0114***	−0.00990***	−0.0118***
	(0.00316)	(0.00322)	(0.00224)	(0.00387)
Stock market turnover ratio (%)	−1.87e−05	4.70e−05	0.000578	0.000288
	(0.000489)	(0.000382)	(0.000509)	(0.000400)
Constant	0.805***	0.897***	0.778***	0.898***
	(0.239)	(0.194)	(0.218)	(0.208)
Observations	124	167	124	167
R-squared	0.536	0.546	0.271	0.171
Number of isocodeencoded			15	15
FE			–	–
RE			YES	YES
Hausman Test Pvalue			0.5702	0.3418

Note: The dependent variable λ is the consumption smoothing parameter, computed using 10 year rolling window period according to the methodology explained in the paper.
Not IV stands for pooled OLS while IV stands for Instrumental Variable regression. Explanatory variables are the rolling 10-year averages of the period from 1990 to 2011. *p*-values calculated from robust standard errors are reported, *, **, ***, indicate significance levels at 10%, 5% and 1% level, respectively.

different categories, risk-sharing accounts and fixed income accounts. All the variables are in logarithm in order to smooth the variation. The variable Risk-sharing accounts is the sum of *musharaka, murabaha*, and *qard hasan* assets, which in theory should be more conducive towards risk-sharing while Fixed income accounts is the sum of *murabaha, istisna, ijara* and *salam* assets. When we look at the results, the coefficients of risk-sharing accounts and fixed income accounts are as expected, i.e. negative for risk-sharing and positive for fixed income in all four regressions. However, the coefficients of risk-sharing accounts are not statistically significant.

Table 13.11: Risk-sharing and Different Forms of Islamic Financing: Panel Regressions.

	(1)	(2)	(3)	(4)
Dependent Variable (λ)	**IV**	**Not IV**	**IV**	**Not IV**
Logarithm of Total of Risk-sharing Accounts	−0.00533	−0.00607	−0.000724	−0.00387
from IBIS (% of GDP)	(0.00361)	(0.00376)	(0.00573)	(0.00314)
Logarithm of Total of Fixed Income Accounts	0.0111***	0.0102**	0.00639**	0.00669**
from IBIS (% of GDP)	(0.00369)	(0.00409)	(0.00305)	(0.00270)
Logarithm of Domestic Credit (% of GDP)	−0.0183	−0.0299	−0.0908	−0.0826**
	(0.0324)	(0.0269)	(0.0634)	(0.0393)
Logarithm of General government final	0.0280	0.0632	0.0837	0.0615
consumption expenditure (% of GDP)	(0.0628)	(0.0769)	(0.124)	(0.0698)
Logarithm of Chin-ITO Financial Openness	0.00106	−0.0252	−0.0101	0.00232
Index	(0.0244)	(0.0290)	(0.0289)	(0.0225)
Logarithm of Gross savings (% of GDP)	−0.0989**	−0.0834**	0.0969	0.0320
	(0.0478)	(0.0344)	(0.0686)	(0.0354)
Logarithm of Bank lending-deposit spread	−0.0356	−0.0183	−0.0508	−0.0281
	(0.0317)	(0.0287)	(0.0424)	(0.0343)
Constant	0.920***	0.765***	0.507	0.658***
	(0.252)	(0.267)	(0.540)	(0.248)
Observations	1,211	1,622	1,211	1,622
R-squared	0.057	0.076	0.040	0.0379
Number of isocodeencoded			132	139
FE			YES	–
RE			–	YES
Hausman Test Pvalue			0.0023	0.0626

Note: The dependent variable λ is the consumption smoothing parameter, computed using 10 year rolling window period according to the methodology explained in the paper. Not IV stands for pooled OLS while IV stands for Instrumental Variable regression. Explanatory variables are the rolling 10-year log averages of the period from 1990 to 2011. Risk-sharing Accounts are the sum of Musharaka, Murabaha, Qard Hasan assets while Fixed Income Products represent the sum of Murabaha, Istisna, Ijara and Salam assets. *p*-values calculated from robust standard errors are reported, *, **, ***, indicate significance levels at 10%, 5% and 1% level, respectively.

4 Conclusion

In this chapter, we test empirically whether Islamic banks contribute to risk-sharing more than the commercial financial institutions. In theory, when there is perfect risk-sharing in an economy, this should decrease correlation between the changes in consumption and income. Based on this logic we employ the consumption smoothing parameter as our risk-sharing parameter, as the smoother the consumption, the higher is the aggregate degree of intertemporal risk-sharing in the given jurisdiction. We use various proxies to extract possible contribution of welfare state, financial globalization and conventional financial products to risk-sharing in order to isolate the contribution of Islamic banks to risk-sharing.

Our results based on cross-country regressions suggest that the contribution of Islamic banks, when tested with aggregate variables such as total assets and total loans, is at best elusive. The coefficients of Islamic banks' total assets and total loans are either very close to zero or insignificant. However, when we conduct the same analysis with different products of Islamic banks, we find that products like *mudarabah* investment accounts which operate according to profit loss sharing, are more conducive towards risk-sharing than current accounts of Islamic banks.

Whereas this study is the first of its kind analyzing relationship between Islamic banking and consumption-based risk-sharing, there are other studies which have looked into Islamic banking's contribution to risk-sharing in financial contracts. For example, Alaa, Masih, and Mirakhor (2015) find that the Islamic banks appear to be engaging in risk shifting activities and shying away from financial risk-sharing due to lack of incentives in the present regulatory and supervisory framework. Other studies such as Siddiqi (1999) have criticized current model of Islamic banks and their heavy dependence on trade or sale-based contracts, thus calling them suffering from *murabaha* syndrome. Our research has implication for the policy-makers and the regulators in making decisions on the design of financial sectors in their jurisdictions. Further research and analysis are required to fully understand the impediments and constraints on Islamic banks' practices to avoid fully engaging in risk-sharing.

It may be noted that the theoretical modelling and empirical testing of a risk-sharing financial system may require different analytical framework as compared to the conventional finance. There is arguably a need to consider risk-sharing Islamic finance as a macro-economically differentiated system with its own characteristics. The distinctive features, include among others, a different governance structures that eliminate informational problems as well as principal-agent issues, that increase significantly transaction costs. Future research could shed further light on consumption smoothing under a risk-sharing system.

References

Alaabed, Alaa, Mansur Masih, and Abbas Mirakhor. 2015. "Undermining Shared Prosperity? Risk Shifting and Islamic Banking," paper presented at 2015 Inaugural Symposium on Islamic Finance and Economics titled "Islamic Finance: Catalyst for Shared Prosperity" organized by World Bank, IDB, IRTI and Guidance Financial Group in Istanbul, Sep, 8–9, 2015.

Askari, Hossein, Zamir Iqbal, and Abbas Mirakhor. 2012. *Risk-sharing in Finance: The Islamic Finance Alternative.* Singapore: John Wiley and Sons (Asia).

Abedifar, Pejman, Philip Molyneux, and Amine Tarazi. 2013. "Risk in Islamic banking." *Review of Finance* 17(6): 2035–2096.

Bacchetta, Philippe, and Stefan Gerlach. 1997. "Consumption and credit constraints: International evidence." *Journal of Monetary Economics* 40(2): 207–238.
Baele, Lieven, Moazzam Farooq, and Steven Ongena. 2014. "Of religion and redemption: Evidence from default on Islamic loans." *Journal of Banking & Finance* 44: 141–159.
Beck, Thorsten, Asli Demirgüç-Kunt, and Ouarda Merrouche. 2013. "Islamic vs. conventional banking: Business model, efficiency and stability." *Journal of Banking & Finance* 37(2): 433–447.
Beck, Thorsten, Mattias Lundberg, and Giovanni Majnoni. 2006. "Financial intermediary development and growth volatility: Do intermediaries dampen or magnify shocks?." *Journal of International Money and Finance* 25(7): 1146–1167.
Beck, Thorsten, Steven Ongena, and Ilkay Sendeniz-Yuncu. 2015. "Keep Walking? Geographical Proximity, Religion, and Relationship Banking." *Geographical Proximity, Religion, and Relationship Banking*.
Campbell, John Y., and N. Gregory Mankiw. 1989. "Consumption, income and interest rates: Reinterpreting the time series evidence." NBER Macroeconomics Annual 1989, Volume 4. MIT Press: 185–246.
Čihák, Martin, and Heiko Hesse. 2010. "Islamic banks and financial stability: An empirical analysis." *Journal of Financial Services Research* 38(2–3): 95–113.
Denizer, Cevdet A., Murat F. Iyigun, and Ann Owen. 2002. "Finance and macroeconomic volatility." Contributions in Macroeconomics 2(1): 1–32.
Easterly, William, Roumeen Islam, and Joseph E. Stiglitz. 2001. "Shaken and stirred: explaining growth volatility." Annual World Bank conference on development economics. Vol. 191.
Iqbal, Zamir and Abbas Mirakhor. 2011. *Introduction to Islamic Finance: Theory and Practice*, 2nd ed. Singapore: John Wiley and Sons.
Islamic Financial Services Board (IFSB). 2016. *Stability Report 2016*. Kuala Lumpur: Islamic Financial Services Board.
Jappelli, Tullio, and Marco Pagano. 1989. "Consumption and capital market imperfections: An international comparison." *The American Economic Review* 49(5): 1088–1105.
Kammer, Mr Alfred, et al. 2015. "Islamic Finance: Opportunities, Challenges, and Policy Options." No. 15. International Monetary Fund.
Levine, Ross. 2005. "Finance and growth: theory and evidence." In *Handbook of Economic Growth* Vol, edited by Philippe Aghion and Steven Durlauf: 865–934. Amsterdam: North-Holland Elsevier.
Ludvigson, Sydney. "Consumption and credit: a model of time-varying liquidity constraints." *Review of Economics and Statistics* 81(3): 434–447.
Ongena, Steven and İ. Şendeniz-Yüncü. 2011. "Which Firms Engage Small, Foreign, or State Banks? And Who Goes Islamic? Evidence from Turkey." *Journal of Banking and Finance* 35: 3213–3224.
Pappas, Vasileios, Marwan Abdu Izzeldin, Ana-Maria Fuertes, and Steven Ongena. 2013. *A Survival Analysis of Islamic Bank Failure Risk*. Lancaster: Lancaster University (Mimeo).
Raddatz, Claudio. 2006. "Liquidity needs and vulnerability to financial underdevelopment." *Journal of financial economics* 80(3): 677–722.
Reinhart, Carmen M., and Kenneth S. Rogoff. This time is different: A panoramic view of eight centuries of financial crises. No. w13882. National Bureau of Economic Research, 2008.
Shiller, Robert J. 2009. *The new financial order: Risk in the 21st century*. Princeton: Princeton University Press.
Siddiqi, Nejatullah. 1999. "Islamic Finance and Beyond: Premises and Promises of Islamic Economics," Proceedings of the Third Harvard University Forum on Islamic Finance: Local Challenges, Global Opportunities" Harvard University, Cambridge, Massachusetts, October 1, pp.49–53.

World Bank. 2015. *Global financial development report 2015–2016: Long-term Finance*. Washington, D.C.: World Bank Group.

Van Greuning, Hennie, and Zamir Iqbal. 2008. *Risk analysis for Islamic banks*. World Bank Publications.

Zaheer, Sajjad, Steven Ongena, and Sweder JG van Wijnbergen. 2013. "The Transmission of Monetary Policy Through Conventional and Islamic Banks." *International Journal of Central Banking* 9(4): 175–224.

Appendices

Appendix 1: Data Sources.

Variable	Source
Total Islamic bank assets and loans	Bankscope and IBIS
GDP and private consumption	Penn World Tables 8.1
Total Mudarabah (Savings + Investment) and Current accounts	IBIS
Total of Murabaha, Mudaraba, Musharaka, Qard Hassan, Istisna, Salam	IBIS
Domestic credit to private sector (% of GDP)	WDI
Stock market total value traded to GDP (%)	WDI
General government final consumption expenditure (% of GDP)	WDI
Gross domestic savings (% of GDP)	WDI
Domestic credit to private sector (% of GDP)	WDI
Stock market turnover ratio (%)	WDI
Bank lending-deposit spread	WDI
Chin-ITO Financial Openness Index	http://web.pdx.edu/~ito/Chinn-Ito_website.htm

Appendix 2: List of Countries with Islamic Banking data in two data sources.

Bankscope		IBIS	
Bahrain	Qatar	Albania	Lebanon
Bangladesh	Russian Federation	Algeria	Malaysia
Egypt, Arab Rep.	Saudi Arabia	Australia	Pakistan
Gambia, The	Senegal	Azerbaijan	Philippines
Indonesia	Singapore	Bahrain	Qatar
Iran, Islamic Rep.	South Africa	Bangladesh	Saudi Arabia
Iraq	Sudan	Bosnia and Herzegovina	South Africa
Jordan	Syrian Arab Republic	Egypt, Arab Rep.	Sri Lanka
Kenya	Tanzania	Gambia, The	Sudan
Kuwait	Thailand	Indonesia	Switzerland
Lebanon	Tunisia	Iran, Islamic Rep.	Syrian Arab Republic

Appendix 2 (continued)

Bankscope		**IBIS**	
Malaysia	Turkey	Iraq	Tunisia
Maldives	United Arab Emirates	Jordan	Turkey
Mauritania	United Kingdom	Kazakhstan	United Arab Emirates
Pakistan	Yemen, Rep.	Kenya	United Kingdom
Philippines		Kuwait	Yemen, Rep.

Tarık Akın, Zamir Iqbal

Chapter 14: Catalyst for SMEs' Access to Finance in the OIC: Renting Money or Renting Assets?

1 Introduction

Securing firms' access to finance is an important driver for the firms' diversification of risk, mobilization of external financing, and thrive of entrepreneurship, all of which then buttress investment and economic growth. However, access to finance is still a significant impediment for the firms, especially, in the developing and less-developed countries. Among the firms, convincing evidence indicates that small and medium enterprises (SMEs) are particularly constrained in access to finance, while they are the backbone of economies in terms of employment and economic growth. Even if they can have access to finance, the mode of finance may not be compatible with their capital structure and firm characteristics in the sense that it may not give rise to optimal allocation of resources, effective day-to-day operations, productivity increase, and sustained growth over time.

Availability of finance does not automatically guarantee access to finance, especially for SMEs, due to several reasons such as high cost of available mode of finance, and incompatibility between what is available and what is needed. In many developing and particularly less-developed countries, the financial system is dominated by the banking sector, which is typically the largest supplier of external finance for the firms. Even if the banking sector has ample supply of credit in these countries, institutional, legal and socio-economic impediments and financial structure may not facilitate the firms' access to credit. It is usually the SMEs that are disproportionally inflicted by these impediments. This is mostly because the banks widely consider the SMEs to be too risky to extend credit lines without having collateral and credit history. These impediments of access to credit not only cause a large proportion of the SMEs to resort to alternative sources of finance, if any, but also discourage many SMEs to apply for loans. The SMEs which voluntarily exclude themselves from formal financial sector adjust their production and growth strategies with the result of non-optimal allocation of resources, low productivity and forgone growth opportunities.

In comparison to the larger firms, SMEs are more prone to repercussions of barriers in access to finance, as well as, source of finance incompatible with what they really need. Thus, securing proper access to finance arguably make the SMEs thrive disproportionally compared to their larger counterparts. Although SMEs' access to finance is already an important policy issue all over the world, securing access to finance for the SMEs is particularly important for the Organisation for Islamic Cooperation (OIC) countries because i) the OIC group is mostly composed of developing and less-developed

https://doi.org/10.1515/9783110587920-014

countries; and ii) institutional, socio-economic and governance-related factors put extra pressure against development of effective financial services in the OIC group.

One prospective alternative to bank loans in the developing and less-developed countries in general and the OIC group specifically is leasing or its *Shariah*-compliant alternative, *ijarah*.[152] Leasing is "a contract between two parties where one party (the lessor) provides an asset for usage to another party (the lessee) for a specified period of time, in return for specified payments" (Fletcher et al. 2009). As an asset-based mode of finance, the value of the underlying asset subject to the leasing contract and the lessee's ability to generate sufficient cash flow, rather than the lessee's overall creditworthiness matter in leasing contracts (Cusmano 2015). Although the lessor remains the legal owner of the leased asset throughout the contract period, it is the lessee that harnesses the benefits of the leased asset. This means leasing separates legal ownership of an asset from its beneficial use.

There are two main types of leasing contracts: financial and operational lease. A financial lease contract transfers all the risks and rewards of ownership of the asset to the lessee, whereas the lessor remains the legal owner of the asset throughout the leasing contract. Time coverage of a financial lease contract is usually close to the economic life of the underlying asset. Financial lease contracts are typically accompanied by an option to buy the asset at the end of the contract (Cusmano 2015). An operating lease, on the other hand, allows the lessee to use the asset temporarily or for a period much lesser than the economic life of that asset (Kraemer-Eis and Lang 2012). Financial lease contracts are typically used for long-term financing needs of the firms while operating leases are more suitable for operational expenses. *Ijarah* is usually called as Islamic leasing, though there are pronounced differences between leasing and *ijarah*. According to the AAOIFI's "Shari'ah Standard on Ijarah and Ijarah Muntahia Bittamleek" (2015), *ijarah* is defined as "leasing of property pursuant to a contract under which a specified permissible benefit in the form of a usufruct is obtained for a specified period in return for a specified permissible consideration". *Ijarah* derives its permissibility from the Qur'an, the Sunnah, *Ijma* and *Ijtihad*. As defined by the AAOIFI (2015), *Ijarah Muntahia Bittamleek* is

> a form of leasing contract which includes a promise by the lessor to transfer the ownership in the leased property to the lessee, either at the end of the term of the *ijarah* period or by stages during the term of the contract, such transfer of the ownership being executed through one of the means specified in the Standard.

The transfer of ownership can be executed at the end of the contract or by stages during the term of the contract. The main differences between leasing and *ijarah* are as follows:

---

152 In this chapter, we use the term renting asset as a generic term covering both leasing and *ijarah* since both of these mode of finance are based on renting the underlying asset in essence.

- The ownership responsibilities are the main source of divergence between leasing and *ijarah*. Lessor takes the responsibility of all capital costs such as replacement in case of loss and malfunctioning, repair in case of breakdown of the asset and shipping costs. This is because the lessor is the owner of the asset and should be responsible for ensuring that the asset stays in use during the contract period. However, day-to-day and operating expenses should be borne by the lessee (Al-Amine 2011). On the other hand, division of the responsibilities and rights are more blurred in the leasing contract. It should be noted here that maintenance costs can be transferred to the lessee by a seperate contract and agency agreement.
- The conventional leasing doesn't have direct interest payments. However, there are terms in a leasing contract that contain provisions for interest payments such as late payment of the installments (Al-Amine 2011). An *ijarah* contract must be free from any reference to interest and elements of interest.
- Rent is charged to the lessee after the asset is made available in ijarah whereas the rent is charged once the contract is signed in leasing. Since income is generated in leasing prior to the delivery of the asset, it is a form of interest indeed in the leasing contract (Hanif 2016).
- The lessor in leasing contract is usually free in the selection of the asset that will be the subject of the contract while the lessor in an *ijarah* contract will take responsibility of preserving the asset during the contract period. Moreover, the nature of the asset is permissible and will be used in permissible purposes from the *Shariah* perspective in an *ijarah* contract (Al-Amine 2011).
- Transfer, if any, and lease of the asset to the lessee take place through two separate contracts in an *ijarah* contract. However, a single contract includes both sale and lease contract in a lease contract (Hanif 2016).

Leasing is particularly relevant for the SMEs that lack sufficient collateral or credit history and offers access to finance without existing assets, pledge and third-party guarantee. As concluded by Minici and Dominice (2013),

> Leasing is probably the easiest way to fund small nascent businesses' fixed assets. This type of financing is particularly relevant in emerging markets for small enterprises that lack sufficient collateral or credit history. Leasing offers access to finance without a significant existing asset base, and without any pledge or third-party guarantee. Leasing also prevents any misuse of the contracted financial obligations. Finally, it is the least burdensome source of funding from a tax and accounting perspective.

The *Shariah*-compliant counterpart of leasing, *ijarah*, has a significant potential in the OIC countries as it has all the advantages of the leasing. Given its potential in helping SMEs in access to finance, a subsequent question is whether leasing is compatible with the capital structure, needs and growth prospects of SMEs in the developing and less-developed countries. If not, policies to increase availability of leasing for the firms may only increase overall availability of finance without increasing SMEs' access to finance.

This chapter aims to show that *ijarah* has indeed a significant potential to increase SMEs' access to finance in the OIC group by employing a global firm-level survey data. In this regard, this study has important policy implications. Section 2 explains main advantages of resorting to leasing compared to the bank loans in the developing countries. The section also discusses the main differences between leasing and *ijarah*. Section 3 looks into key patterns and observations on SME finance from the World Bank Enterprise Survey (WBES) dataset in the OIC and non-OIC groups and concludes that SME characteristics and country-level determinants of impediments in access to finance justify focusing on *ijarah* for the SMEs in the OIC group. Section 4 presents an empirical model which quantifies that resorting to the *ijarah* (renting asset) rather than debt financing (renting money) would have pronounced positive effects on firm performance. Finally, Section 5 makes policy recommendations based on the data analysis and the regression outputs.

2 Renting Asset and Access to Finance: A Review

In corporate finance literature, the decision between renting money (debt) and renting asset (leasing or *ijarah*) is typically a topic within the context of Modigliani and Miller theorem (1958), which concludes that capital structure of a firm is irrelevant in a world of perfect capital markets and without any frictions such as taxes, and bankruptcy costs. In such a world, the market value of the firm depends solely on the future cash flows generated by the firms' assets. Extending the Modigliani and Miller theorem to the firms' leasing decision, the rent paid by the lessee reflects the underlying cost of owning the asset, so the choice between renting money and renting asset would then solely depends on the relative cost of renting money and renting asset (Penttinen 2013). Rental rate must be equalized to the interest rate in a perfectly competitive world by rendering the firms indifferent between renting money and renting asset. Moreover, in the perfectly competitive market setting, separating the ownership and use of the asset can give rise to opportunities for specialization and more efficiency. Given the indifference between renting money and renting asset decision, the efficiency and specialization gains, which then allows for faster capacity expansion, can be the decisive factors for firms in resorting to renting asset contracts (Penttinen 2013).

From the Islamic finance perspective, renting asset is a risk-sharing mechanism between financier (lessor) and the entrepreneur (lessee). Although *ijarah* is not a completely risk-sharing contract like *mudarabah* or *musharakah*, the contract has transactions with risk-sharing characteristics because risks and rewards are incidental to ownership. Maghrebi (2017) succinctly shows the risk-sharing features of the *ijarah* contract from options theory. In his demonstration, the value of the *ijarah* contract $(v_{ijh,t})$ is written as the present value of the underlying asset itself minus a claim on the same asset after a predetermined period. Let the value of the underlying asset (v_f), which represents the collateral in the equation, decreases by the value of the installments (v_b) and a call option premium (c) over time as given in Equation (1):

$$v_{ijh,t} = v_f - (v_b + c) \tag{1}$$

Assuming that the asset generates a continuous net flow of income to the lessee at the constant fraction of asset value $(\lambda = \omega / v_f)$, where (ω) is the net flow of income in the equation, then the value of *ijarah* contract at time *t* can be written as:

$$\begin{aligned} v_{ijh,t} = v_{f,t} &- \left[v_{f,t}.e^{-\lambda\tau}.\mathrm{N}\{-h\} + b.e^{-\rho\tau}.\mathrm{N}\{h - \sigma/\sqrt{\tau}\}\right] \\ &- \left[v_{f,t}.e^{-\lambda\tau}.\mathrm{N}\{h\} - b.e^{-\rho\tau}.\mathrm{N}\{h - \sigma/\sqrt{\tau}\}\right] \end{aligned} \tag{2}$$

Equation (2) can be further simplified by canceling out the installment payments and with the identity rule for the cumulative density function $(\mathrm{N}\{h\} + \mathrm{N}\{-h\} = 1)$. Equation (3) then gives the simplified formula as follows:

$$v_{ijh,t} = v_f.\left(1 - e^{-\lambda\tau}\right) \tag{3}$$

According to Equation (3), value of the *ijarah* contract is independent from the financing decisions of the firm (Clifford 1979). Moreover, the equation implies that value of the *ijarah* contract doesn't depend on the value of the installments. Instead, the Equation (3) clearly shows that the total value of *ijarah* contract solely depends on the total value of the underlying asset (v_f) multiplied by the usufruct generated from the same asset until the end of contract (Maghrebi 2017).

Renting asset (leasing and *ijarah*) allows firms to have access to finance without need to pledge existing assets in the form of collateral. This facility is especially important for the start-ups and the young SMEs which typically don't have appropriate existing assets to enter loan contracts. Elimination of the need for collateral in accessing to finance separates cash flow potential of the firm from its current balance sheet. As highlighted by Brown et al. (2010), such a separation is "particularly valuable in many low- and middle-income countries where unsecured loans can be difficult to obtain". Through renting asset, financing by the third party is determined by whether the financed asset contributes to the future cash flows rather than the balance sheet value of the collateral. Another direct effect of renting asset compared to renting money is increase in debt capacity of the firm. This is because repossession of a leased asset is easier than foreclosure of a collateral asset in case of default (Eisfeldt and Rampini 2009). Higher debt capacity is especially important for the financially-constrained firms, such as the SMEs, so that they are more likely to value renting asset more than financially less constrained firms because existing assets which are not used for the renting asset can be directed to renting money as collateral. Furthermore, renting asset allows the firms which change their capital assets frequently access the assets with minimal initial costs (Cusmano 2015).

As indicated in the beginning of Section 2, the choice between renting money and renting asset is a function of their relative costs in a world of perfect capital markets. However, the real world has full of market imperfections, which give rise to more constraints for the SMEs compared to their large counterparts. Arguably, the most important market imperfection for the SMEs is asymmetric information. One type of information asymmetry is adverse selection, which refers to difficulty in choosing good projects *ex-ante* due to lack of information on project quality. Another type is moral hazard, which is inability of the lender to enforce effectively the agreed contract ex-post due to costly monitoring and incomplete contract. In case the SMEs face difficulties in entering debt contracts stemming from market imperfections, Ayyagari et al. conclude that (2017)

> interest rates cannot be used as screening technology because the interest rate a bank charges may itself affect the riskiness of the pool of loans, either by attracting high-risk borrowers (adverse selection effect) or by adversely affecting the incentives of borrowers (moral hazard effect).

As underlined by Beck et al. (2006), asymmetric information makes external sources finance more costly than internal sources finance for the firms and the extra cost of external sources of finance is inversely associated with a firm's net worth. This inverse relationship makes it even harder for the SMEs reaching at external finance because they find it quite costly to get external finance and they don't have enough collateral to be eligible for bank loan, as the most important source of external finance. Information asymmetries can be reduced via three ways: "a firm's ability to signal its credit worthiness (incl. an institutional assessment or rating by an independent agency and the provision of collateral), a strong relationship between lender and borrower, and through due diligence/lenders' examination (screening)" (Kraemer-Eis and Lang 2012). But using each of these ways is quite difficult for the SMEs. Lack of collateral impedes signaling creditworthiness, track record is not available for most of the young firms in order to set up a strong relationship with the lender and screening for the small entities is expensive from the side of the supplier of the finance. These difficulties are particularly relevant for the young start-ups, which have higher capacity and employment growth rates compared to their more mature peers (Banerjee 2014).

Weak institutional structures, such as weak governance framework, non-existent credit information systems and poor insolvency regimes, in the developing and less-developed countries can be a good rationale for resorting to renting assets instead of renting money. One important reason why many SMEs can't have access to bank lending is due to weak institutional structures, while the bank lending is the only source of external finance for many firms. In such an environment, the leasing can play a significant role as a complement, even a substitute, for bank lending. It should be, however, noted here that success of renting money also depends on, to a large extent, appropriate institutional framework. For instance, Brown, Chavis, and Klapper (2010) show that there is a positive association between appropriate institutional environment and increasing share of resorting to leasing.

Credit rationing is another reason for the young SMEs without a credit track record to have problems in access to bank lending. Indeed, financial institutions typically lend based on collateral and track record, which are signals of perceived quality, rather than viability and performance of the firms, which stand for the genuine performance of the firms (BIS 2012). Leasing is prone to less adverse selection, because the leased assets typically are of significant importance to the operations of the lessee and default in leasing would lead to collapse of the entire firms (Kraemer-Eis and Lang 2012). As a result, resorting to leasing may decrease adverse selection problem and resulting credit rationing.

In the literature, renting asset is considered as a substitute for debt for risky firms that can't easily access to debt markets (Lease, McConnell, and Schallheim 1990; Rahman and Sankaran 2016; Yan 2006). However, Ang and Peterson (1984) show that leasing and debt are not substitutes but complements. This empirical finding is also supported by Eisfeldt and Rampini (2009), who conclude that acquiring leasing can also increase debt capacity of the firm. It should also be noted that the degree of resorting to leasing and whether debt and leasing are substitutes can change significantly with respect to the firm characteristics and type of industries. Yan (2002), for instance, argues that degree of asymmetric information has a direct impact on the substitutability between leasing and debt. Slotty (2009) confirms that this choice is more important for the SMEs. Apart from confirming importance of leasing for the SMEs in an information asymmetry environment, Chigurupati and Hegde (2009) indicate that leasing mitigates underinvestment problem by decreasing the link between investment and internal funds.

In case there a severe asymmetric information and agency problems, firms are more likely to resort to leasing instead of debt. Empirical studies also indicate that variation in use of leasing is more pronounced across industries compared to the variation within sectors (Graham and Leary 2011). Furthermore, Graham, Lemmon, and Schallheim (1998) conclude that firms using more fixed assets in the production process lean more towards leasing due to the nature of leasing which is tied to a specific fixed asset. Firm characteristics have an impact on the quality of the firms, as well. As shown by Sharpe and Nguyen (1995) low-rated firms are more prone to leasing compared to high-rated firms as ratings have a direct effect on the premium paid on debt. Another attractiveness of leasing for the firms, especially for the SMEs, is that leasing is associated with lower degree of risk compared to other forms of external financing (De Laurentis and Mattei 2009). As highlighted by Schmit (2005), "empirical results also show that lease exposures are relatively low-risk as compared to other means of financing. The presence of physical collaterals no doubt contributes very largely to this reduced risk profile".

3 Patterns in SMEs' Access to Finance

Section 3 employs the World Bank Enterprise Survey (WBES) to show that key characteristics of SMEs in the OIC group justify renting asset in securing access to finance for the SMEs. The observations delineated in this section then provide a ground for Section 4 in which we look for quantitative answers to the prospective benefits of the renting assets based on econometric analysis.

The domestic and commercial datasets on financing patterns of the SMEs are usually too limited and inconsistent to make a comprehensive analysis of geographically diverse firms across different countries (Ayyagari, Demirgüç-Kunt, and Maksimovic 2017). These problems have been mitigated, to some extent, by The World Bank Enterprise Survey (WBES), which is a firm-level survey of a representative sample of an economy's private sector (Ayyagari, Demirgüç-Kunt, and Maksimovic 2017). The WBES reveals important patterns of financing and barriers in access to finance for firms all over the world.[153] It also allows for analyzing more than sixty firm characteristics ranging from size, age, current legal status, export-orientation to having female manager, share of working capital financing, and perceptions in the court system. Since 2005, the WBES has been conducted in over 100 countries with standardized survey instruments and a uniform sampling methodology. The main goal of the WBES is to capture business perceptions about obstacles to business operations and growth. Sample sizes vary between 150 and 9,200 companies per country and data are collected using either simple random or randomly stratified sampling. The dataset employed in this study has more than 131,000 observations from 136 countries, 67 of which have at least two waves of surveys.

The WBES dataset used in this study covers 37 out of 57 OIC countries.[154] In sub-regional categorization, the World Bank classification is employed.[155] The revised dataset used in this study encompasses only the latest available survey wave for each country so as to present solely post Global Financial Crisis picture all over the world

153 However, the WBES shares the typical weaknesses observed in other survey data such as existence of survival bias (Banerjee 2014).

154 The OIC countries in the dataset are as follows (the numbers in parentheses represent sample sizes): Afghanistan (410), Albania (664), Azerbaijan (770), Bangladesh (2946), Benin (300), Bosnia and Herzegovina (721), Burkina Faso (394), Cameroon (724), Chad (150), Côte d'Ivoire (887), Egypt (4711), Gabon (179), Gambia (174), Guinea (373), Guinea-Bissau (159), Guyana (165), Indonesia (2764), Iraq (756), Jordan (573), Kazakhstan (1144), Kyrgyz Republic (505), Lebanon (561), Mali (1035), Mauritania (387), Morocco (407), Mozambique (479), Niger (301), Nigeria (4567), Pakistan (2182), Senegal (1107), Sierra Leone (150), Sudan (738), Suriname (152), Tajikistan (719), Togo (305), Tunisia (592), Turkey (2496), Uganda (1325), Uzbekistan (756), Palestine (434), Yemen (830).

155 According to the World Bank classification, the regional classification of the countries is as follows: Sub-Saharan Africa (SAFR), East Asia and Pacific (EPAC), Europe and Central Asia (ECCA), Latin America (LATM), Middle East and North Africa (MENA) and South Asia (SASI). As the OIC sample in the LATM region is quite low, we dropped the LATM countries from the sample altogether.

and to have a better insight of cross-county comparisons without confounding results. The dataset also allows for decomposing the firms into small (5–20 employees), medium (20–99 employees) and large firms (100+ employees). Although the WBES does not directly provide information on patterns and use of leasing contracts (there is no question regarding use of leasing in the standard questionnaire) richness of the variables that shed light on many other SME characteristics in the WBES provide a good base to evaluate fit of leasing in the OIC group.

In the light of the literature of Section 2 on leasing, the rest of Section 3 attempts to discuss some observations about the SMEs in the OIC group which, to a large extent, supports our contention that leasing can be an important alternative source of finance for the SMEs as a substitute or complement to bank credit. We discuss five observations from the dataset in the rest of Section 3. The bottom-line of these five observations is that disconnectedness from the banking sector due to lack of collateral and credit history is an important driver of the low SME performance in the OIC group, as well as in the rest of the world.

Observation 1: Access to finance is a more serious problem for the SMEs in the OIC group compared to their counterparts in the non-OIC group.

Firms in the WBES are asked to rank on a scale of 0 (no obstacle) to 4 (very severe obstacle), the extent to which access to finance is an obstacle to their current operations. Higher scale value means more severe obstacle for the firm in accessing to finance. Figure 14.1 reveals two main trends for the firms in the OIC and non-OIC groups. Firstly, on average, firms in the OIC group face with more severe obstacle in accessing to finance compared to their counterparts in the non-OIC group with high regional variation. Especially, both SMEs and large firms in the SAFR, the MENA, and the SASI regions in the OIC group have much higher index values compared to their non-OIC counterparts. On the other hand, the firms in the EPAC and the ECCA regions in the OIC group rank a lower score but the gap between the OIC and

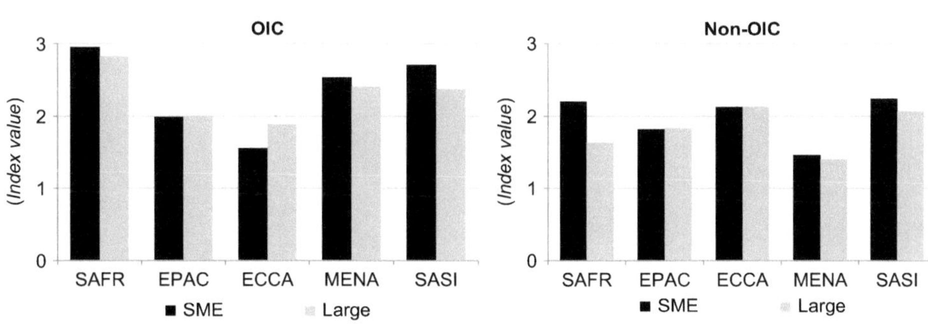

Figure 14.1: Degree of Having Obstacle in Access to Finance.
Source: WB Enterprise Surveys, Authors' calculations. Survey-weighted observations are used through Stata's svy prefix. The WBES dataset used in this study is as of September 2017.

non-OIC group in these regions is not large. Secondly, on average, the difference of the index value between SMEs and large firms is more pronounced in the OIC group. The difference is largest in the SASI region in the OIC group followed by the SAFR and the MENA regions. It is interesting in the figure that larger firms are more constrained in the ECCA regions of the OIC group.

Observation 2: Requirement for collateral and high interest rates combined are the most important reasons for the SMEs in the OIC group not applying for a bank loan.

Firms in the WBES are asked to declare the main reason they don't apply for a loan in the last fiscal year. The responses to this question reveal that, on average, collateral requirements and high interest rates are one of the most important impediments in accessing to finance for the firms in the OIC and the non-OIC groups alike. This observation is an important justification for prospective benefits of resorting to renting asset rather than using bank loan, if possible.

Figure 14.2 reveals two main trends for the firms in the OIC and non-OIC groups. Firstly, on average, firms in the OIC group report that collateral requirements and high interest rates combined is a much more important reason for them not to apply for bank loan compared to their counterparts in the non-OIC group. The percentage of firms indicating that the requirement for collateral requirements and high interest rates combined is the most important reason is highest in the SAFR, the MENA and the SASI regions. Secondly, on average, the gap between SMEs and large firms is much larger within the OIC group compared to the non-OIC group. The difference is largest in the SASI region in the OIC group followed by the SAFR, the EPAC, the MENA, and the ECCA regions. The bottom-line of the Observation 2 is that the share of the SMEs in the OIC group report that collateral requirements and high interest rates combined is the most important reason is much higher than the large firms in the OIC group, as well as, the SMEs in the non-OIC group.

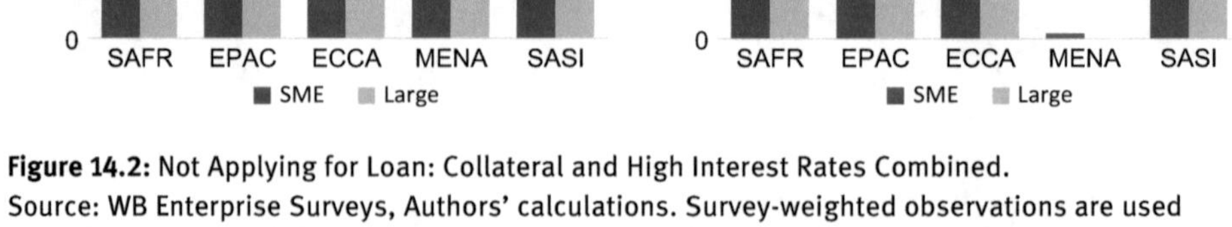

Figure 14.2: Not Applying for Loan: Collateral and High Interest Rates Combined.
Source: WB Enterprise Surveys, Authors' calculations. Survey-weighted observations are used through Stata's svy prefix. The WBES dataset used in this study is as of September 2017.

Observation 3: SMEs in the OIC group are much more credit-constrained than both of their larger counterparts in the region and the SMEs in the non-OIC group.
Since renting asset can help the firms reduce credit constraints and be used as a complement or a substitute to bank loans in certain circumstances, to what extent the SMEs are credit-constrained gives important information about prospective benefits of renting asset instead of renting money. We combine relevant questions on loan applications in the WBES dataset and construct an indicator of the extent of credit-constraints for the firms with the help of the similar studies (EBRD, EIB, and WB 2016; Kuntchev et al. 2013). Set-up of the indicator is illustrated in Appendix 1. The indicator splits the firms into three categories, namely, fully credit-constrained (FCC), partially credit-constrained (PCC), and not credit-constrained (NCC). The FCC firms have difficulty in getting credit; as a result, they don't use external sources of finance. The WBES defines such firms as the ones which are rejected for their loan application and which don't apply for a loan either because of unfavorable terms or conditions of the contracts or they don't think their application would be approved (EBRD et al., 2016). The unfavorable terms and conditions of the contracts include complex application procedures, unfavorable interest rates, high collateral requirements, and insufficient size of loan and maturity. The PCC firms are eligible for accessing to external sources of finance but are discouraged from applying for a loan or their application for a loan that was not fully approved. The NCC firms either have no difficulty in access to external sources of finance or don't apply for a loan as they don't need the loan.

However, these indicators should be taken with caution. As indicated by the EBRD (2016), "the indicator does not incorporate any information on creditworthiness of the firm, and therefore among the credit-constrained firms there may be some that were rationed for good reasons, such as insufficiently productive projects or a bad repayment history". However, reliance on the credit-constraints indicator has several advantages. The literature on SME finance employing the WBES usually focuses solely on use of credit, not access to credit, or analyze self-reported impediments in access to finance based on perceptions rather than objective criteria (Kuntchev et al. 2013). The credit-constraint indicator provides better evaluation of the situation of the firm in access to finance since the indicator is based on objective criteria rather than self-reported perceptions.

By employing the set-up given in Appendix 1, we construct an index of credit-constrained SMEs and large firms over the regions by decomposing the OIC and non-OIC groups separately. Figure 14.3 shows relative share of each type of credit-constrained firms over the firm type, region and country group space. The results indicate that firms are more credit-constrained (FCC or PCC), on average, in the OIC group compared to the non-OIC group. Within the OIC group, SMEs are much more credit-constrained than the large firms. The difference of being-credit constrained is especially pronounced in the SASI, and SAFR regions, followed by the EPAC, the MENA regions. In the ECCA region, as opposed to the general trend, both of the SMEs and the large firms are almost equally credit-constrained. Furthermore, share of the fully credit-constrained (FCC) SMEs in the OIC group is large, especially in the SASI and SAFR regions. Observation 3 clearly indicates that the opportunity to accessing the bank loans is low for the SMEs in the OIC group. One consequence of this observation is that implementing more renting money related policies may not be fully effective in solving SMEs' access to finance problems. In this regard, alternative modes of finance may be more suitable for increasing the SMEs' access to finance in the OIC group.

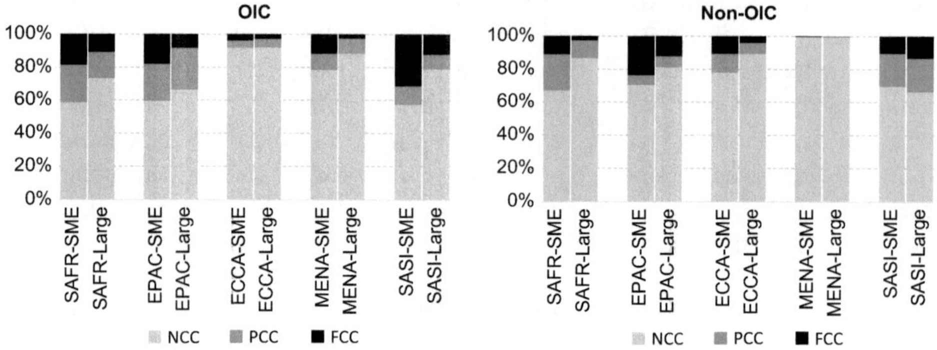

Figure 14.3: Distribution of Credit-Constrained Firms.
Source: WB Enterprise Surveys, Authors' calculations. Survey-weighted observations are used through Stata's svy prefix. The WBES dataset used in this study is as of September 2017.

Observation 4: Disconnectedness of the SMEs from the banking sector in the OIC group is more pronounced.

As delineated in the Observation 3, being credit-constrained is an important impediment for the SMEs in the OIC group for accessing to finance, specifically accessing to bank loans. There is, however, a more serious but implicit impediment for the SMEs in accessing to finance even though they are not within the set of credit-constrained firms. Some of the firms in the survey may declare that they don't need and, subsequently, apply for a loan because they will not invest to expand their business. Their choice of not to invest may be a sign for missed growth opportunities. These firms are called "disconnected" from the bank loans.

To examine whether the disconnected firms may forgo their growth opportunities, we attempt to decompose disconnectedness of the firms into three categories. We define three type of firms with respect to their relationship with the banks: connected, disconnected, and discouraged firms. Connected firms, which consider the banks as a source of finance, are those that apply for loans regardless of whether their loan application is approved or not. Disconnected firms are those that did not apply for any loan as they have sufficient capital. Discouraged firms are those that did not apply for any loans due to terms and conditions. By definition, all disconnected firms are not credit-constrained, but not vice versa. Set-up of the indicator is illustrated in Appendix 2.

In analyzing being disconnected and being discouraged, we exclusively focus on the SMEs rather than comparing the SMEs with their larger peers from here on. Figure 14.4 gives a comparative picture of the disconnected and discouraged SMEs between the OIC and non-OIC groups. The SMEs in the OIC regions are more discouraged than their peers (except ECCA region) in the non-OIC region (figure on the left in Figure 14.4). It means the SMEs in the OIC region face higher impediments in their loan applications due to terms and conditions of the loan contracts. As discussed in Observation 2, high collateral requirements and interest rates are the main obstacles, which are also components of the terms and conditions of the loan contracts, that render an important portion of the SMEs in the OIC group discouraged. On the other hand, as per the figure on the left in Figure 14.4, the SMEs in the OIC group is less disconnected from the banking system (except ECCA region) compared to their peers in the non-OIC group. The two graphs in Figure 14.4 gives a complementary story: The SMEs in the OIC group are less disconnected from the banking system since they don't have sufficient capital in the form of internal capital. However, terms and conditions of the bank loans make them discouraged. Since the most important components of the terms and conditions are collateral requirements and high interest rates, these SMEs can't have easy access to credit because of the two inherent features of the credit mechanism: collateral and interest rate.

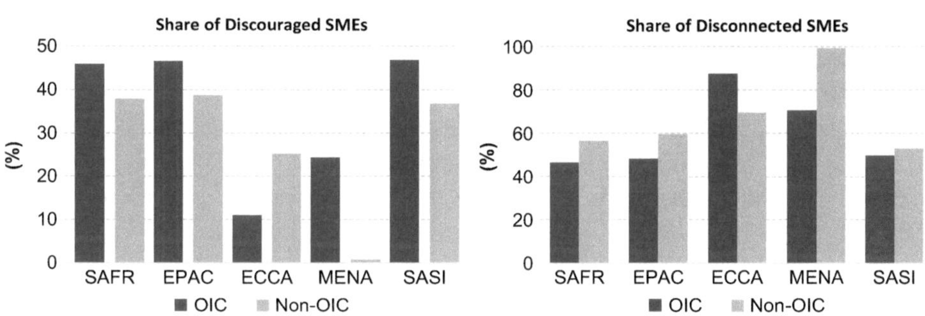

Figure 14.4: Share of Disconnected and Discouraged SMEs.
Source: WB Enterprise Surveys, Authors' calculations. Survey-weighted observations are used through Stata's svy prefix. The WBES dataset used in this study is as of September 2017.

Observation 5: A sizeable share of disconnected SMEs in the OIC group miss growth opportunities.

As discussed in Observation 4, the seemingly reason for being disconnected is having sufficient capital. However, it is also possible that the SMEs disconnect from the banking system due to the fact that they already adjust their production and growth strategies as per the ongoing impediments to access to finance. Thus, they miss their growth potential and work in their second-best optimal operational environment. If these firms have had access to proper financial instruments they can expand their growth boundaries.

Although this is not an easy task to differentiate between the SMEs which already have sufficient capital without any financial impediment for growth and the SMEs which miss their growth opportunities due to impediments in access to finance, we develop a proxy indicator to decompose the total disconnectedness into voluntary and involuntary disconnectedness. To construct the indicator, we use the survey question which asks the firms to sort out the biggest obstacles in their operations. In the WBES, the firms are asked to consider which obstacle (out of a list of 15 prospective obstacles given and access to finance is one of them) is the biggest one to their establishment. If an SME in the survey is classified as disconnected and considers access to finance as the biggest obstacle, we classify this SME as "involuntarily disconnected" because an SME with sufficient capital and optimally allocates its given capital is not expected to consider access to finance as the biggest obstacle. This is an implicit indication that the SME adjusts its production strategy in compliance with the financial constraints. In the light of this observation, we construct an "Involuntary Disconnectedness Ratio (IDR)" which is the ratio of disconnected SMEs which considers access to finance as the biggest obstacle to the all disconnected SMEs. A high level of IDR indicates that the SMEs in a given country group may boost their production if they can surpass their obstacles (mainly collateral) in reaching at bank lending.

Figure 14.5 gives the IDR ratio over the firm size and country groups. On average, IDR seems to be higher in the non-OIC group compared to the OIC group. In addition, the IDR is higher (except the ECCA region) for the SMEs compared to their larger counterparts in the non-OIC group. Regarding the OIC group, the picture changes as per the regions. In the SAFR and the SASI regions, the IDR is quite high for the SMEs whereas the IDR is slightly higher for the large firms in other regions of the OIC group. According to Figure 14.5, around 7 percent of the disconnected SMEs in the OIC group are involuntarily disconnected from the banking system.

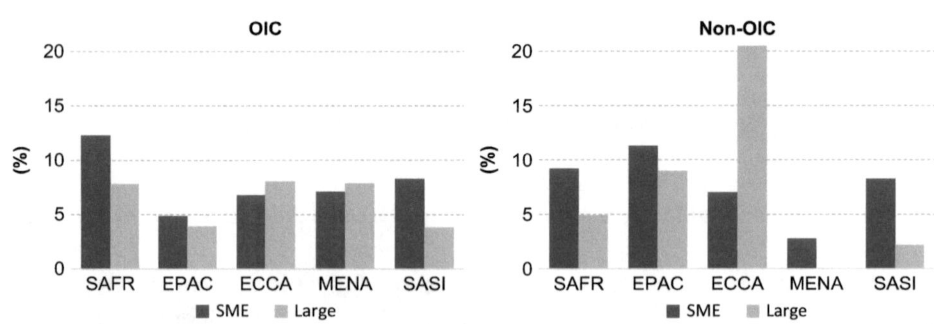

Figure 14.5: Involuntary Disconnectedness Ratio.
Source: WB Enterprise Surveys, Authors' calculations. Survey-weighted observations are used through Stata's svy prefix. The WBES dataset used in this study is as of September 2017.

4 Renting Asset and SME Performance: An Empirical Analysis

In Section 3, we discuss that renting assets as a substitute and/or complement to renting money may increase access to finance for the SMEs in the OIC group through several ways. The policy initiatives targeting the problems in increasing access to finance for the SMEs and then positively affect their performance. Indeed, implementing an alternative mode of finance, renting asset rather than renting money, is justified if it can have a pronounced effect on firm performance. Although, visual representations of the observations support the view that resorting to renting asset rather than renting money may help the SMEs in the OIC group overcome some of their financial constraints, we also need a robust and quantitative framework. In this regard, Section 4 attempts to test whether the variables of the observations have positive outcomes on the firm performance. Although, there are numerous studies investigating role of collateral on firms' access to finance, direct effects of credit-constraints and disconnectedness are still an unchartered water in the empirical studies. This study is an attempt to contribute to the existing literature by empirically analyzing effects of credit-constraints and disconnectedness indicators in the sample of OIC countries.

The empirical analysis is based on two interrelated indicators of firm performance, as the dependent variable, and explanatory variables including firm characteristics, control variable for OIC group, collateral-related exogenous variable(s), disconnectedness and credit-constraint variables. The empirical model can be summarized by the following equation:

$$\begin{aligned} Y_{i,k} = {} & \beta_1 . \textit{Firm characteristics} + \beta_2 . \textit{OIC dummy} + \beta_3 . \textit{SME dummy} \\ & + \beta_4 . \textit{collateral variable} + \beta_5 . \textit{credit constraints} + \beta_6 . \textit{disconnectedness} \end{aligned} \tag{4}$$

where i denotes firm and k denotes the dependent variable. We use standardized beta coefficients in the regression framework instead of regular coefficients. The rationale is that the standardized beta coefficients give the relative impact of each individual explanatory variable on the dependent variable. The higher the absolute value of the beta coefficient, the higher the association between the explanatory variable and the dependent variable. Thus, we can see how important, relatively, each of the explanatory variable on the firm performance indicators.

The firm performance is proxied by employment and sales growth variables, which are calculated as the average growth rate of the sales ($salegrowth_i$) and the employment ($empgrowth_i$) between today and three years before. Following Dimitraki et al. (2013), we calculate these indicators for firm i in Equation (5) and (6) as follows:

$$empgrowth_i = \frac{E_{i,t} - E_{i,t-3}}{((E_{i,t} + E_{i,t-3})/2)} \tag{5}$$

$$salegrowth_i = \frac{S_{i,t} - S_{i,t-3}}{((S_{i,t} + S_{i,t-3})/2)} \tag{6}$$

where $(E_{i,t})$ and $(S_{i,t})$ refer to number of employees and volume of sales, respectively, in firm i at time t. It should be noted here that we look at both of the indicators variables as a proxy for the firm performance because country and firm characteristics may lead to different effects on the employment and sales growth over time. Looking at only one of these indicators may prevent us having a comprehensive view on the effects of the obstacles on the firm performance. We assume that the firm is constrained with respect to the explanatory variable of interest if change in the explanatory variable has a statistically significant effect on these firm performance variables. Our focus is whether the firm is financially constrained. This is because, a firm is defined to be financially constrained if a windfall increase in the supply of funds results in a higher level of employment growth (Beck et al. 2006).

Determination of the relevant firm characteristics, as control variables, is a challenge *per se* because the WBES data includes more than sixty firm characteristics ranging from size, age, current legal status, and export-orientation to having a female manager, share of working capital financing, and perceptions in the court system. Thus, we need to identify the most essential ones and then to end up with the most "parsimonious" structure as much as possible given an ample number of firm characteristics in the dataset. Here we look at the SME finance literature to determine which variables to use in the empirical model.

Abdulsaleh and Worthington (2013) emphasize size, age, ownership type, legal form, location, industry sector, and asset structure as the most important firm characteristics. Batra & Mahmood (2003) analyze the WBES dataset to understand how a variety of firm characteristics affect the firms' experience and perceptions of constraints. In this regard, they conclude that the firms that are private, smaller, younger, devoid of foreign direct investment (FDI), and focus on the domestic market generally tend to face more acute business constraints. Similarly, Kira (2013) find that industrial sector, incorporation, age, and ownership are the basic firm characteristics of SMEs. Wignaraja and Jinjarak (2015) indicate that age, export participation, foreign ownership, managerial experience, financial audit, having ISO certificate and industry determines source of financing and type of collateral.

In line with the literature and relevance to SME financing, we determine age, location, ownership structure, and industry in which an SME operates as the most relevant firm characteristics pertinent to the financing structures of SMEs. Firm age[156] is considered as one of the most important firm characteristics, which has important implications on the firms' access to finance and

156 In the World Bank Enterprise Survey, we don't have direct information on the age of the surveyed firms but the dataset has a variable on the year in which the firm started its operations; subtracting the survey year from this variable gives us the age of the firm.

financing decisions since there is a direct link between age of a firm and its capital structure (Berger and Udell 1995; Bhaird and Lucey 2010). Indeed, sources of financing differ over the life cycle of a firm (age variable is named as *firmage*). By using the sectoral decomposition data in the WBES, we generate a dummy variable (*dummanuf*) which takes 1 if the firm is a manufacturing firm and takes 0 if it is a services firm. Population size and its density are among the important determinants of firms' choice of financing and their access to finance. For instance, proximity to the financial centers or bank branches is an important self-declared reason for not applying for a loan (Demirgüç-Kunt and Klapper 2012). The WBES provides information on the size of the population in which an observation (firm) operates. The so-named population variable is a proxy for the location and rural/urban distinction in the analysis.[157] Ownership structure is assumed to be one of the important factors for private sector development, innovation and economic development. Schumpeter and Elliott (1982) underline that entrepreneur is the prime propeller of economic development. Importance of the ownership structure lies in the fact that the ownership structure as a reflection of corporate governance may substitute for institutional flaws in case institutional structure is not well-developed such as underdeveloped legal system and political rights (Balsmeier and Czarnitzki 2010). In this regard, ownership structure is intimately pertinent to firm's financing choices and degree of impediments in access to finance. In the WBES, we define three types of ownership, shareholding (dummy variable *sharehold*), sole proprietorship (dummy variable *soleprop*), and partnership (dummy variable partnership). We define a firm as export-oriented if its export share in sales is higher than its domestic sales (dummy variable *exporient*). We define an OIC region dummy variable to measure the OIC effect, named as *oic*. In the regressions, we also use OIC regional dummies. Hence, the regional names indicate dummy variables.

To connect firm-specific characteristic and the firm performance to access to finance, we add several access to finance-related variables into the empirical framework. Regarding credit constraints, we introduce dummy variables indicating whether the firm is fully credit constrained (*fcc*), partially credit constrained (*pcc*), and credit constrained (*cconst*). The variable (*accfin*) shows if the firms indicate access to finance as the biggest obstacle to current operations. We also introduce dummy disconnectedness variables (*connected*, *disconnected*, *discouraged*). We also examine the role of the involuntary disconnectedness ratio (*idr*) on firm performance. Appendix 3 reports the

157 In this respect, we classify the location or population variable as follows: Areas with population up to 50,000 is considered as a small city, with population between 50,000 and 1,000,000 are considered as medium sized city and with population over 1,000,000 or capital cities are considered as a large city. Although population decomposition is a bit arbitrary, the main driver of this classification is to have a proxy of location effect in firms' access to finance.

variables used in the empirical model and their summary statistics. Appendix 4 give correlation matrix among the explanatory variables.

In the empirical model, we attempt to test three interrelated hypotheses. Stemming from the observations given in Section 3, the hypotheses are as follows:

Hypothesis 1: Insufficient access to finance has a negative effect on the performance of the SMEs in the OIC group compared to their peers in non-OIC group and large counterparts in the OIC group.

Hypothesis 2: Being credit constrained (fully or partially) is negatively associated with the firm performance indicators.

Hypothesis 3: Disconnected firms have sufficient capital, there is no negative association between disconnectedness and firm performance. However, we expect a negative association between being discouraged from the loan market and firm performance.

Hypothesis 4: Although there is no association between disconnectedness and firm performance overall, involuntary disconnectedness is negatively associated with firm performance.

Appendix 5 and Appendix 6 show regression outputs based on employment growth and sales growth, respectively. We employ the same set of explanatory variables in each of the regression frameworks. There are six regressions for each dependent variable, each of the regressions examines different aspect of the access to finance for the SMEs in the OIC and the non-OIC group comparatively through SME and country group dummies (the models in employment and sales growth regression frameworks are labeled with –e and –s suffixes, respectively.).

Model 1e and Model 1s run the base firm characteristics on firm performance with OIC and the rest of the world combined. Except the *exportshare* variable, all of the firm characteristic variables are significant with expected signs. It is important to note that being an SME in the OIC group is negatively associated with sales growth indicator (*oic*sme* interaction variable), indicating that the SMEs in the OIC group perform worse compared to their peers. The absolute value of the standardized beta coefficient is bigger than other explanatory variables, indicating that being an SME in the OIC is the most important determinant, among the given explanatory variables, on firm performance represented by the sales growth. Model 2e and Model 2s add the *accfin* variable and its interaction with the SME and OIC dummies to the base model. Although having problems in access to finance does not have a statistically significant effect on sales growth, it has an important effect on employment growth specifically for the SMEs in the OIC region (interaction variable *accfin*oic*sme*). The absolute value of the coefficient is as high as other variables of the firm characteristics. Thus, Hypothesis 1 is confirmed in the sense that limited access to finance has a negative effect on the performance of the SMEs in the OIC group.

Model 3e and Model 3s refine access to finance by substituting the *accfin* variable by the credit-constraint indicators and their interactions. The models indicate that only being fully-credit constrained is associated with the firm performance. Fully credit constrained firms (either SMEs or large firms) have worse have lower employment and sales growth. However, there is no SME and OIC group effect with regards to the fully-credit constraint indicator. Thus, we can partly confirm that the Hypothesis 2 is correct given by the dataset. The model outputs underline that only both SMEs and their large counterparts are negatively affected by being fully-credit constrained.

Model 4e and Model 4s empirically test that there is no negative association between disconnectedness and firm performance. As expected, there is an overall positive association between disconnectedness and firm performance (employment and sales growth). However, SME and OIC interactions with the disconnectedness indicator gives a different picture. Although there is no statistically significant association between being an SME in the OIC region and sales growth in Model 4s, Model 4e indicates that the association is negative for the SMEs in the OIC group. This supports the observation that involuntarily disconnected SMEs in the OIC region takes a relatively larger stake in the disconnected firms. We will test this later. Model 5e and Model 5s examines whether there is an association between being a discouraged firm and firm performance. Model 5e shows that there is no such association between employment growth and being discouraged. However, as per Model 5s, sales growth of the all firms (SMEs and large firms) are negatively associated with being discouraged from the loan market. There is no separate SME and OIC effect in the regression. Thus, we confirm Hypothesis 3.

Finally, we focus on involuntary disconnectedness ratio in Model 6e and Model 6s. As we discussed for the Model 4e, the negative association between disconnectedness and firm performance is unexpected and one culprit for it might be the high involuntary disconnectedness for the SMEs in the OIC group. Model 6s shows that there is no association between the IDR and sales growth. On the other hand, both of the IDR variable and its interaction with the SME and OIC dummies are negatively associated with employment growth. Furthermore, absolute value of the beta coefficient of the IDR, SME and OIC interaction term is quite high. It means IDR is an important determinant of the employment growth for the SMEs in the OIC group. Hence, this confirms Hypothesis 4.

5 Conclusion

This chapter highlights several observations about access to finance problems faced by the SMEs in the OIC group. Firstly, access to finance is a more acute problem for the SMEs in the OIC region compared to their peers in the rest of the world. Secondly, collateral and terms and conditions of the loan contracts are the main impediments in access to finance while financial services in the OIC are dominated by the banking sector. This conflict then gives rise to many SMEs in the region to be credit-constrained. Thirdly, even the SMEs which are disconnected from the banking sector may forgo their growth potential as they have already adapted their production strategies and expectations in line with lack of access to finance. Finally, we find that having access to collateral have an impact on SMEs' performance. In this regard, leasing, as well as, *ijarah* (renting assets) can be considered as serious alternatives to the bank lending (renting money).

Bank lending is not only a function of firm characteristics but also a function of macroeconomic context, institutional quality, country risk and information asymmetries. Since many OIC countries have low scores in these variables bank lending widely depends on existence of collateral and credit history. In effect, bank lending will not automatically increase even if the collateral regimes become less stringent. In this picture, switching to the leasing-based options would be easier to increase the SMEs' access to finance in the OIC region. One serious policy option is to set up national and/or regional *ijarah* institutions which can provide *ijarah*-based financing to the SMEs in the OIC group. Although, there are already leasing institutions or bank-based leasing arrangements in these countries, the benefits of national and/or regional *ijarah* institutions will be much more than just securing funding to the SMEs. These institutions can also provide service to guide the SMEs which assets to lease at lower costs by being a hub for connecting the firms that produce the subject matters of the *ijarah* contracts, such as the machinery, and the SMEs that need the subject matters of the *ijarah* contracts. This will have a positive effect on reducing the deadweight losses stemming from searching and seeking the subject matters of the *ijarah* contracts. It is a pre-condition to develop Islamic finance and banking in the OIC group for securing smooth funding in the form of *ijarah*. It can make an argument of encouraging establishment of non-bank financial institutions (NBFIs) to promote *ijarah* or *murabahah* style financing. Such NBFIs should be well-regulated and have good supply of funding to provide services to SMEs.

References

AAOIFI. 2015. *Shari'ah Standards*. Manama, Bahrain: Accounting and Auditing Organization for Islamic Financial Institutions.

Abdulsaleh, Abdulaziz M., and Andrew C. Worthington. 2013. "Small and Medium-Sized Enterprises Financing: A Review of Literature." *International Journal of Business and Management* 8 (14): 36–54.

Al-Amine, Muhammad Al-Bashir Muhammad. 2011. *Global Sukūk and Islamic Securitization Market: Financial Engineering and Product Innovation (Brill's Arab and Islamic Laws)*. Leiden, The Netherlands: Brill – Nijhoff.

Ang, James, and Pamela P. Peterson. 1984. "The Leasing Puzzle." *The Journal of Finance* 39 (4): 1055–65.

Ayyagari, Meghana, Asli Demirgüç-Kunt, and Vojislav Maksimovic. 2017. "SME Finance." *World Bank Policy Research Working Paper*. Vol. 8241. Policy Research Working Papers. The World Bank.

Balsmeier, Benjamin, and Dirk Czarnitzki. 2010. "Ownership Concentration Institutional Development and Firm Performance in Central and Eastern Europe." *ZEW Discussion Paper*. Vol. 10-096.

Banerjee, Ryan. 2014. "SMEs, Financial Constraints and Growth." *BIS Working Papers No 475*.

Batra, Geeta, and Syed Mahmood. 2003. "Direct Support to Private Firms: Evidence on Effectiveness." 3170. *World Bank Policy Research Working Paper*.

Beck, Thorsten, Asli Demirgüç-Kunt, Luc Laeven, and Vojislav Maksimovic. 2006. "The Determinants of Financing Obstacles." *Journal of International Money and Finance* 25 (6): 932–52.

Berger, Allen N., and Gregory F. Udell. 1995. "Relationship Lending and Lines of Credit in Small Firm Finance." *The Journal of Business* 68 (3): 351

Bhaird, Ciaran mac an, and Brian Lucey. 2010. "Determinants of Capital Structure in Irish SMEs." *Small Business Economics* 35 (3): 357–75.

BIS. 2012. "SME Access to External Finance." *BIS Economics Paper* No:16.

Brown, Gregory W., Larry W. Chavis, and Leora F Klapper. 2010. "Institutions, External Financing, and Growth around the World: A New Lease on Life?" *AFA 2008 New Orleans Meetings Paper*. Durham, NC: American Finance Association.

Chigurupati, Vasantharao, and Shantaram P. Hegde. 2009. "Capital Market Frictions, Leasing and Investment." *SSRN Electronic Journal*.

Clifford, Smith. 1979. "Applications of Option Pricing Analysis." In *Handbook of Financial Economics*, 79–121. Amsterdam, The Netherlands: North Holland.

Cusmano, Lucia. 2015. *New Approaches to SME and Entrepreneurial Financing: Broadening the Range of Instruments*. Paris: Organisation for Economic Co-operation and Development.

De Laurentis, Giacomo, and Jacopo Mattei. 2009. "Lessors' Recovery Risk Management Capability." Edited by Giulio Tagliavini. *Managerial Finance* 35 (10): 860–73.

Demirgüç-Kunt, Asli, and Leora Klapper. 2012. "Measuring Financial Inclusion: The Global Findex Database." 6025. Policy Research Working Paper. Washington, D.C.

Dimitraki, Ourania, Leora F Klapper, and Georgios A. Panos. 2013. "Informal Origin, Performance and Conduct in Emerging Markets: Firm-Level Evidence from the Balkans" 44(0).

EBRD, EIB, and WB. 2016. *What's Holding Back the Private Sector in MENA? Lessons from the Enterprise Survey*. Washington, D.C.: The World Bank.

Eisfeldt, Andrea L, and Adriano A Rampini. 2009. "Leasing, Ability to Repossess, and Debt Capacity." *Review of Financial Studies* 22(4): 1621–57.

Fletcher, Matthew, Rachel Freeman, Murat Sultanov, and Umedjan Umarov. 2009. "Leasing in Development: Lessons from Emerging Economies (2nd Edition)." Washington, D.C.

Graham, John R., and Mark T. Leary. 2011. "A Review of Empirical Capital Structure Research and Directions for the Future." *Annual Review of Financial Economics* 3 (1): 309–45.

Graham, John R., Michael L. Lemmon, and James S. Schallheim. 1998. "Debt, Leases, Taxes, and the Endogeneity of Corporate Tax Status." The Journal of Finance 53 (1): 131–62.

Hanif, Muhammad. 2016. "Ijarah Accounting: A Comparison of Conventional IAS-17 and Islamic FAS-8." *Journal of Islamic Economics Banking and Finance* 12(1): 49–62.

Kira, Alex Reuben. 2013. "Determinants of Financing Constraints in East African Countries' SMEs." *International Journal of Business and Management* 8(8): 49–68.

Kraemer-Eis, Helmut, and Frank Lang. 2012. "The Importance of Leasing for SME Financing." *Working Paper 2012/15*. European Investment Fund.

Kuntchev, Veselin, Rita Ramalho, Jorge Rodríguez-Meza, and Judy S Yang. 2013. *What Have We Learned from the Enterprise Surveys Regarding Access to Credit by SMEs?* Policy Research Working Papers. Washington, D.C.: The World Bank.

Lease, Ronald C., John J. McConnell, and James S. Schallheim. 1990. "Realized Returns and the Default and Prepayment Experience of Financial Leasing Contracts." *Financial Management* 19 (2): 11–20.

Maghrebi, Nabil. 2017. "Risk Hedging and Derivatives Markets in Islamic Finance." Industry Talk 10/ 26/2017. Kuala Lumpur, Malaysia: International Centre for Education in Islamic Finance.

Minici, Julia, and Roland Dominice. 2013. *Small Enterprise Impact Investing*. Symbiotics. http:// www.syminvest.com/papers.

Modigliani, Franco, and Merton Howard Miller. 1958. "The Cost of Capital, Corporate Finance and the Theory of Investment." *American Economic Review* 48: 261–97.

Penttinen, Jussi. 2013. "Theory of Financial Lease Contracts: Why All Capital Goods Are Not Leased." University of Helsinki.

Rahman, Shofiqur, and Harikumar Sankaran. 2016. "Are Leases and Debt Substitutes? Evidence From Capital Structure Adjustment." *SSRN Electronic Journal*.

Schmit, Mathias. 2005. "Is Automotive Leasing a Risky Business?" *Finance* 26 (2).

Schumpeter, Joseph A., and John E. Elliott. 1982. *The Theory of Economic Development: An Inquiry into Profits, Capital, Credit, Interest, and the Business Cycle*. Social Science Classics Series (Book 46). Transaction Publishers.

Sharpe, Steven A., and Hien H. Nguyen. 1995. "Capital Market Imperfections and the Incentive to Lease." *Journal of Financial Economics* 39(2–3): 271–94.

Slotty, Constantin F. 2009. "Financial Constraints and the Decision to Lease – Evidence from German SME." *SSRN Electronic Journal*.

Wignaraja, Ganeshan, and Yothin Jinjarak. 2015. "Why Do SMEs Not Borrow More from Banks? Evidence from the People's Republic of China and Southeast Asia." *ADBI Working Paper Series*. Tokyo. http://www.adbi.org/working-paper/2015/01/09/6523.why.do.sme.not.borrow.from.banks/.

Yan, An. 2002. "Leasing and Debt Financing: Substitutes or Complements?" *SSRN Electronic Journal*.

Yan, An. 2006. "Leasing and Debt Financing: Substitutes or Complements?" *Journal of Financial and Quantitative Analysis* 41(03): 709.

Appendices

Appendix 1: Derivation of Credit-Constrained Firms from the WBES Questionnaire.

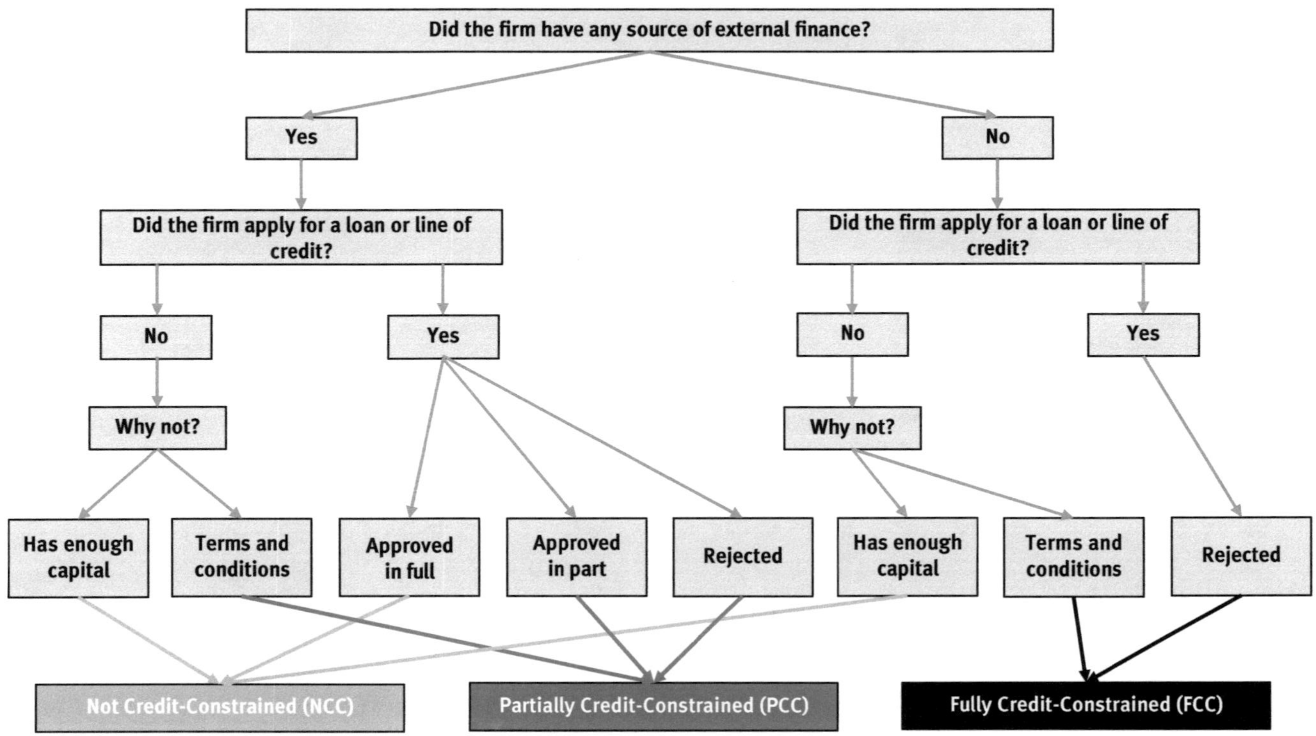

Source: Adapted from EBRD (2016).

Appendix 2: Derivation of Disconnected Firms from the WBES Questionnaire.

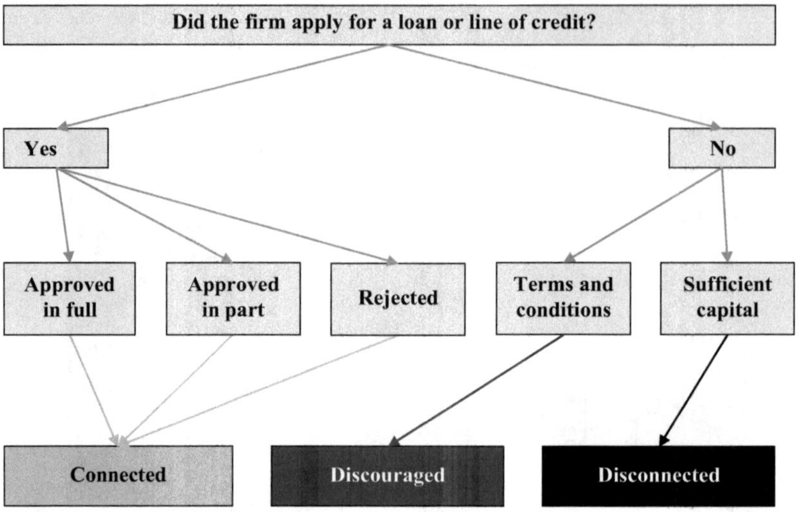

Source: Adapted from EBRD (2016).

Appendix 3: Summary Statistics.

Variable	Explanation	Obs.	Mean	Std. Dev.	Min	Max
smedum	SME dummy	65,981	0.8225	0.3821	0.00	1.00
firmage	Age of firm	64,682	17.1944	14.2115	0.00	214.00
dummanuf	Manufacturing sector dummy	65,981	0.5344	0.4988	0.00	1.00
population	Location of the firm	62,463	2.3086	0.6769	1.00	3.00
sharehold	Shareholding dummy	65,706	0.3698	0.4827	0.00	1.00
soleprop	Sole proprietorship dummy	65,706	0.4026	0.4904	0.00	1.00
exporient	Dummy if export share in sales is higher than its domestic sales	65,821	0.0869	0.2816	0.00	1.00
oic	OIC group dummy	64,765	0.3454	0.4755	0.00	1.00
cconst	Dummy whether the firm is credit-constrained	63,600	0.2638	0.4407	0.00	1.00
accfin	Dummy whether access to finance as the biggest obstacle to current operations	61,504	0.1507	0.3578	0.00	1.00
pcc	Dummy whether the firm is partially credit constrained	49,222	0.5700	0.4951	0.00	1.00
fcc	Dummy whether the firm is fully credit constrained	17,653	0.0000	0.3717	−0.99	0.60
disconnect	Dummy whether the firm is fully disconnected	49,222	0.0742	0.2622	0.00	1.00
discouraged	Dummy whether the firm is fully discouraged	8,659	0.0000	103.3919	−254.91	439.65
idr	Involuntary disconnectedness ratio	25,631	0.0827	0.2754	0.00	1.00

Source: Authors's own calculations.

Appendix 4: Correlation Matrix.

	firmage	dummanuf	population	sharehold	soleprop	exportshare	oic	smedum	accfin	pcc	fcc	disconnect	discouraged
firmage	1.00												
dummanuf	0.14	1.00											
population	0.02	0.02	1.00										
sharehold	0.04	−0.07	−0.23	1.00									
soleprop	−0.09	0.01	0.14	**−0.60**	1.00								
exportshare	0.06	0.15	−0.03	0.08	−0.11	1.00							
oic	0.02	−0.01	0.11	−0.10	0.11	0.05	1.00						
smedum	−0.18	−0.16	−0.05	−0.10	0.19	−0.24	0.03	1.00					
accfin	−0.03	0.00	0.00	−0.07	0.06	−0.04	0.00	0.06	1.00				
pcc	−0.01	0.05	−0.02	−0.06	0.03	0.00	0.01	0.03	0.10	1.00			
fcc	−0.07	−0.01	0.07	−0.04	0.07	−0.07	0.00	0.06	0.10	−0.21	1.00		
disconnect	0.05	−0.05	−0.04	0.13	−0.10	0.07	0.01	−0.08	−0.19	**−0.50**	**−0.51**	1.00	
discouraged	−0.07	0.03	0.05	−0.10	0.09	−0.06	0.02	0.08	0.18	**0.59**	**0.60**	**−0.85**	1.00

Source: Authors's own calculations.

Appendix 5: Regression Outputs – Employment Growth.

	Model 1e	Model 2e	Model 3e	Model 4e	Model 5e	Model 6e
firmage	−0.124***	−0.126***	−0.127***	−0.122***	−0.122***	−0.116***
dummanuf	−0.025***	−0.027***	−0.025***	−0.024***	−0.024***	−0.027***
population	0.019***	0.016***	0.018***	0.021***	0.021***	0.025***
sharehold	−0.013**	−0.011**	−0.009*	−0.015**	−0.013**	0.005
soleprop	0.027***	0.029***	0.030***	0.031***	0.031***	0.025***
exportshare	0	−0.001	−0.001	0.002	0.002	−0.001
oic	0.029***	0.027***	0.030***	0.025**	0.027**	0.005
smedum	−0.058***	−0.058***	−0.057***	−0.049***	−0.050***	−0.054***
oic*sme	−0.007	−0.003	−0.008	0.005	−0.008	0.008
accfin		0.008				
accfin*oic*sme		−0.013**				
fcc			−0.023***			
pcc			−0.005			
fcc*oic*sme			0			
pcc*oic*sme			0.005			
disconnect				0.021***		
disconnect*oic*sme				−0.015*		
discouraged					−0.008	
discouraged*oic*sme					0.005	
idr						0.016*
idr*oic*sme						−0.026***
N	54,511	51,108	53,119	41,084	41,084	21,303
R^2	0.02	0.02	0.02	0.02	0.02	0.02
F	131.69	100.57	90.47	80.09	79.07	36.3

Source: Authors's own calculations.
Standardized beta coefficients
** p<0.10, ** p<0.05, *** p<0.010*

Appendix 6: Regression Outputs – Sales Growthx.

	Model 1e	Model 2e	Model 3e	Model 4e	Model 5e	Model 6e
firmage	−0.048***	−0.048***	−0.050***	−0.045***	−0.045***	−0.035***
dummanuf	0.015***	0.017***	0.015***	0.013**	0.012**	0.005
population	0.003	0.002	0.003	0.012**	0.012**	0.020**
sharehold	0.012**	0.013**	0.011*	0.01	0.012*	0.014
soleprop	−0.017***	−0.017***	−0.017***	−0.015**	−0.016**	−0.024**
exportshare	0.009*	0.004	0.009*	0.011*	0.012*	0.012
oic	0.009	0.007	0.011	0.013	0.013	0.022
smedum	−0.013***	−0.012**	−0.010**	−0.006	−0.006	0.001
oic*sme	−0.091***	−0.096***	−0.096***	−0.102***	−0.097***	−0.107***
accfin		−0.004				
accfin*oic*sme		0.004				
fcc			−0.012**			
pcc			−0.002			
fcc*oic*sme			0.013*			
pcc*oic*sme			−0.011			
disconnect				0.021***		
disconnect*oic*sme				0.009		
discouraged					−0.012**	
discouraged*oic*sme					0.002	
idr						−0.003
idr*oic*sme						0.011
N	44,413	41,894	43,765	33,508	33,508	17,097
R^2	0.01	0.01	0.01	0.01	0.01	0.01
F	48.31	39.83	34.79	28.73	27.56	13.57

Source: Authors's own calculations.
Standardized beta coefficients
** p<0.10, ** p<0.05, *** p<0.010*

Omid Torabi, Abbas Mirakhor

Chapter 15: Fame as an Operational Proxy of "Taqwa": Controlling Asymmetric Information or Gharar in a Game-theoretic Design of Equity-Crowdfunding?

1 Introduction

Islam is a rules-based system where the norms of behavior are principally described in the Quran and Sunnah. Compliance with these rules creates an intense inner awareness of the presence of Allah (swt) in the consciousness of the agents (Iman) that affects their interactions with the creative order. A certain level of awareness creates a positive dynamic feedback process where rule-compliance is conducive to greater awareness. This feedback is bound to continue until no incentive can be powerful enough to non compliance and violation. The state of higher awareness is commonly known as *taqwa*, an intense level of consciousness that provides protection against rule violations leading to the displeasure of Allah (swt). Under this state, each decision or action is undertaken with intending (*niyyah*) to comply with the rules prescribed by the Qur'an. Every action behind which lies such intending is considered a virtuous action (*'amal salih*) and a meritorious action (*hasanah*). An incentive structure in the Qur'an is designed to promote virtuous and meritorious decision-action. This structure involves a systematic, dynamic and nonlinear scalar that multiplies rewards. This multiplier is called *barakah* (blessings) in the Quran, and the magnitude of this scalar ranges between ten and seven hundred.

The Qur'an makes clear that confession of belief in the ideology of Islam (called *millat Ibrahim*) requires actions that externally confirm the inner affirmation of this belief (*'amal salih*, virtuous action). The combination of confession of the belief and its external manifestation through virtuous action constitute active believing (Iman). It is the continuous and persistence of decision-actions, each of which is undertaken in compliance with rules of behavior that paves the way for attainment of strengthened state of consciousness and awareness (*taqwa*). As the repeated actions and decisions of an active believer (agent) are manifested externally, the agent is invested with a reputational capital as a rule-compliant Muslim. For example, two of the most important elements of this accumulated reputation capital are: faithfulness to the terms and conditions of contracts and promises, and trustworthiness. Together these two elements constitute a reputation for the agent as capable of making credible commitments. As such, this reputation for credibility eliminates moral hazard, leading thereby to

https://doi.org/10.1515/9783110587920-015

reduced transactions costs and increased efficiency in contract implementation. The participation of agents with active believing into economic and financial transactions can contribute to the realization of promised multiplied rewards and *barakah*.[158]

There are, to the best knowledge of the authors, no previous analytical studies in the Islamic finance literature, about the impact of credible reputation … and the operation of barakah in financial and economic transactions. This study is an attempt to examine both issues by designing an equity-crowdfunding model involving two games: "with-Fame" and "without-Fame" crowdfunding, and to demonstrate that "with-Fame" game produces better results than "without-Fame" game.

It is noted that crowdfunding is defined as a financing mode offered by a group of individuals rather than through traditional financial intermediaries. Crowdfunding facilitates direct communication between entrepreneurs and investors using an internet platform (Schwienbacher and Larralde 2010). In crowdfunding, each individual in the crowd provides small amounts of funding instead of large amounts supplied by a small group of investors (Voorbraak 2011). Crowdfunding has the potential of increasing entrepreneurship by extending the pool of investors from whom funding can be raised beyond … (Ordanini et al. 2011). Thus, this innovative financing mode can also contribute toward financial inclusion.

Equity-based crowdfunding is a new and different method of fintech to encourage investment in the real sector of economy to increase employment and income. This type of crowdfunding involves an inexpensive way of issuance of shares through the internet where investors can acquire stock in investment projects by providing small amount of funds, with a residual claim over the projects' future cash flow. It has proved to be a viable form of financing, enabling companies to access funding for projects that have failed to mobilize funds from angel investors, government resources, friends or families (Ahlers et al. 2015). Crowd investing facilitates the financing of firm growth and innovation through implementation of projects considered too risky for traditional channels of funding.

---

158 For evidence from the Qur'an supporting the statements in this and the previous paragraph see a few related verses of the Qur'an: Verses 26, 177, 261: Chapter 2; Verses 49, 76: Chapter 3; Verse 1: Chapter 5; Verse 160: 6; Verses 35, 96: Chapter 7; Verses 23, 27, 56: Chapter 8; Verses 4, 119: Chapter 9; Verses 29: 12; 34: Chapter 17; Verse 107: 18; Verse 96: Chapter 19; Verse 56: Chapter 22; Verses 8,14: Chapter 23; Chapter 52: Verse 24; Verses 126, 131, 144, 150, 163, 179: Chapter 26; Verse 84: Chapter 28; Verse 3: Chapter 49; Verse 7: Chapter 59; and Verse 16: Chapter 64. For more detail on rule compliance and its implications for economic and financial transactions see, Ng, et al. (2015); Iqbal and Mirakhor (2017); Mirakhor and Askari (2017). See also Mohamed et al. (2018) for applications of the game-theoretic approach to analyze the impact of rule-compliance behavior.

There are two types of crowdfunding: debt and equity. Heretofore, the former has dominated the latter due to specific and sensitive risks associated with equity crowdfunding. The main risks are fraud where funds are channeled to purposes other than those promised, losses due to project failures and liquidity constraints. These constitute the main drivers of moral hazard and operational risk. There are also problems of information asymmetry where a contractual party possesses incremental information than other parties (Myers and Majluf 1984). Asymmetric information in financial markets are also related to adverse selection and moral hazard, which are conducive to increased transactions costs (Bebczuk 2003). A broad range of approaches to market design are considered in crowdfunding and online market settings in order to reduce information-related market failures. These include signaling, screening, regulatory measures, collateral and guarantees, due diligence, and enhanced reputation or fame monitoring.

One of the innovative methods of addressing the problems of information asymmetry is the reputation mechanism, which allows for more efficient transactions particularly in investment communities with lower levels of compliance with behavioral rules. Gains in efficiency may be also expected in communities where cooperation is inhibited by post-contractual opportunism and information asymmetries. If an investment community enforces punishment rules that prohibit dealing with persons with a track record of adverse behavior, and if the present value of punishment exceeds that of the potential gains from cheating, then the threat of public revelation of cheating behavior provides rational traders with sufficient incentives to cooperate (Dellarocas 2015).

A reputation monitoring mechanism is designed in this analytical study to control for asymmetric information in equity crowdfunding systems. The role of reputation is important in establishing and promoting trust, and reducing the risk of fraud in financial transactions. While there are alternative approaches to deal with fraudulous behavior, fame or reputation may be considered as an effective mechanism where the credibility of a member of the crowdfunding system reflects the extent of commitment and faithfulness to contractual obligations.

Thus, fame constitutes a systematic and metric gauge of reputation, and a clear signaling system for other members of the social network of crowdfunding. This measure of credibility can be developed for all individual users of the system based on their banking credit, social credit, and history of participation and track record of success and failure in previous crowdfunding opportunities. Fame can be deemed as an index that measures and monitors the reputation of individual participants in the social network of crowdfunding. Fame becomes, thus, a reference framework for individual decisions in the areas of investment, third-party guarantees, and other transactions in the financial and economic system. The credibility metrics assigned to each financial transactions can be determined through policies and procedures set by owners and policymakers with the credit-scoring system. Fame is the outcome of the credit-scoring process and it is, thus, function of the properties of each transaction and each individual participant.

Fame is generally considered to be a function of four variables:

$$fame = f(banking\ credit, social\ credit, participation, success)$$

As shown in following sections, "fame" can be designed as an optimal reputation mechanism for equity crowdfunding. For this purpose, this chapter uses the mechanism design, which is a field in economics and game theory that employs an engineering approach to design economic mechanisms, or incentives structures, toward desired objectives in strategic settings in which players act rationally. Since the approach starts at the end of the game then proceeds backwards, reflecting the reverse game theory.

2 Mechanism Design

The mechanism employed in this chapter is the Vickrey–Clarke–Groves mechanism (VCG). Bidders offer bids based on their valuations of the elements of the transaction, without knowing the bids of other people taking part in the auction. The auction system charges each person the damage they cause to other bidders. Moreover, it provides bidders with an incentive structure that ensures that the best strategy for each bidder is to bid their true valuations of the items. It is a generalization of the Vickrey auction for multiple items. Given the assumptions for deriving the utility functions for entrepreneurs and financiers, Section 2.1. gives a mechanism design for the current implementation of the crowdfunding system, which is based on without-fame. Section 2.2. then shows the mechanism design of the proposed framework, which is based on the crowdfunding framework with-fame.

2.1 Utility Functions of Entrepreneur and Financier Without- and With-fame

There are two types of players in the system: entrepreneurs (principals) and financiers (agents). Payoffs of financiers and entrepreneurs in the mechanism is the utility of the project. The main assumptions for both models are as follows:

- The number of potential financiers and entrepreneurs in the equity-crowdfunding system are theoretically unlimited, and there is no limitation in the number and share of financiers to fund a project. $N = \{1, 2, 3, \ldots\ldots, n\}$, where N is the number of financiers in crowdfunding system.
- The entrepreneur presents his/her project in the system in three parts. Firstly, the details of the project including its nature, timeline, the business plan of project and, most importantly, the expected return of the project including forecasting direct yield, indirect awards. Secondly, minimum pledge level of each financier

to participate in the project (p). Third, the targeted level of investment T is equal to the running costs of the project.

- The are two probabilities for project approval for crowdfunding, represented by the social choice function $K = \{0, 1\}$. It takes the value of unity $K = 1$ when the project is expected to start with α probability, and zero $K = 0$ when the project is not anticipated to start with probability $(1 - \alpha)$. The social choice function can be expressed as follows.

$$Project = \begin{cases} K = 1, & P = \alpha \\ K = 0, & P = (1 - \alpha) \end{cases} \tag{1}$$

- Starting the project $(K = 1)$ the entrepreneur needs to collect the funds for the project to target level (T). If n_1 financiers contribute t unit of funds in a project, the necessary condition to start the projects is given by the inequality in Equation (2). T is the minimum amount that the entrepreneur needs to begin the project. If the collected funds are more than T, the entrepreneur has the opportunity to use the extra amount to improve the quality of the project. Therefore, if the mobilized funds for the project are more than T, the quality of project can be better than the initial standard assumption.

$$n_1.t \geq T \tag{2}$$

- Some financiers from an infinite number of financiers agree to take part in the project. The probability of participation is assumed to be binomially distributed as given by Equation (3).

$$prob(n_1 \colon if\ k = 1) = \binom{N}{n_1} \alpha^{n_1} (1 - \alpha)^{N - n_1} \tag{3}$$

  where *prob* is the probability of n_1 financiers agreeing for the project to start.
- The mechanism is a weak balance as $\sum_{i=1}^{n_1} t_i < 0$; and the sum of payoffs is not positive. In addition, it is assumed that there are no alternative external sources of funding. This is a typical assumption about mechanism efficiency.

The utility function of player i is a function of his/her subjective value of the project and his/her contribution to the project. For the sake of simplicity, it is assumed that the strategy of any player is not influenced by those of other players, which implies that each player has a dominant strategy. Furthermore, all players are assumed to rational, and individual rationality implies that negative utility is precluded. This setting is conducive to conditions in which at least one player improves his or her own status. These assumptions allow also for the search of Pareto optimal equilibrium.

2.2 Crowdfunding Mechanism Without-fame

The VCG mechanism is used to design the proposed crowdfunding system. There are two types of players in the system: entrepreneurs (principals) and financiers (agents). The payoffs of financiers are represented by the utility of the project, which depends on the social choice function K. The value and cost of funding of the project for a certain financier i are described by:

$$u_i = U(K, v_i, t_i) \tag{4}$$

The utility function of each financier depends on the individual preferences and payoffs of the project, which can be expressed in terms of equity or goods to be produced during the realization of the project, or in terms of a share of asset ownership. Equation (5) describes this relationship as follows.[159]

$$v_i = v(\theta_i, z) \tag{5}$$

where θ_i indicates the type of the financiers and z stands for the final production after running the project.

The utility function of each financier is given by:

$$u_i = K(v_i - t_i) \tag{6}$$

Therefore, the payoff of all financiers is the sum of utilities of all participant financiers:

$$\sum_{i=1}^{n_1} u_i = K.\rho.N. \sum_{I=1}^{n_1} (v_i - t_i) \tag{7}$$

Since individual rationality is assumed, the utility function of players should not be negative. Hence,

$$u_i > 0 \xrightarrow{yields} \sum_{i=1}^{n_1} u_i > 0 \xrightarrow{yields} v_i > t_i \overset{\text{yields}}{\rightarrow} K = 1 \tag{8}$$

In the case of $K = 1$, the utility of the project for financier i is positive because of the preference for positive payoffs. Accordingly, if $u_i > 0$ then aggregate of u_i is also larger than zero, implying that the collective utility function of all financiers is positive. The explanation is that when a project is funded, it can be shown that subjective value[160] of each financier is more than the cost of funding for that financier, and accumulative utility of the group of financiers increases. Therefore, financiers

159 Players have specific preferences which are actually their private information and is named by "type" here.

160 The subjective value advances the idea that the value of a good is determined by the importance that an acting individual places on a good for the achievement of his desired ends.

vote positively on this project and the minimum target of funds for this project can be mobilized.

On the other side of the game, there exists an entrepreneur whose purpose is to maximize the profit of the project (value maximization):

$$\pi = TR - TC \tag{9}$$

where π, TR, TC indicates profit level, total revenues and total costs of the entrepreneur, respectively.

The return of the project for entrepreneur is from funds which can be equal or more than target level of project (see Equation 10). TC is the announced target amount of funds needed to start the project.

$$\mathrm{TR}(T) \geq TC \tag{10}$$

If the sum of funds allocated for the project is equal to its costs, the net revenue would be zero. If these funds exceed however the project costs, then the net revenues are allowed to increase indefinitely.

$$\pi = K.N.\rho. \sum_{i=1}^{n_1} t_i - TC \tag{11}$$

The net revenue can be also expressed as follows

$$\pi = \begin{cases} \pi = 0, \ if \ K.N.\rho. \sum_{i=1}^{n_1} t_i = TC \\ \pi > 0, \ if \ K.N.\rho. \sum_{i=1}^{n_1} t_i > TC \end{cases} \tag{12}$$

If the payoffs of the entrepreneur are equal to zero, the probability of cheating in the realization of the project increases. Therefore, there is a risk of cheating or fraud under the without-fame mechanism.

2.3 Crowdfunding Mechanism with-fame

Under the fame-augmented mechanism, it is again noted that participants including financiers and entrepreneurs, are rational with positive utility functions as expressed in Equation (4). The subjective value is function of the financier preferences, final payoffs, and fame. Since the perceived level of the project's fame is deemed to be function of the fame of individual entrepreneurs, the subjective value can be expressed as follows.

$$\hat{v} = v(\theta_i, z_i, fame) \tag{13}$$

As fame can be positive, zero or negative, we have:

$$\widehat{v_i} = v_i + f(fame) \begin{cases} a)\ if\ f(fame) = 0 \overset{then}{\rightarrow} \widehat{v_i} = v_i \\ b)\ if\ f(fame) < 0 \overset{then}{\rightarrow} \widehat{v_i} < v_i \\ c)\ if\ f(fame) > 0 \overset{then}{\rightarrow} \widehat{v_i} > v_i \end{cases} \tag{14}$$

As given in Equation (14), three cases are possible:

- At time t_1, entrepreneur enters the crowdfunding system, but he/she has no fame yet. In such circumstances, the financiers' reaction is identical to those in the crowdfunding mechanism without "fame". Hence, payoff and aggregate net surplus are exactly as in the "without- fame" crowdfunding system. However, the difference lies in the entrepreneur's tendency to accumulate fame for himself/herself in the future. As a result, these types of entrepreneurs typically provide better payoffs in their proposal and are also intent on succeeding in projects they undertake in order to collect good feedbacks and enhance their Fame. However, financiers usually do not trust newcomers. Thus, newcomers have to start from small projects to collect fame in the system. Still, there is another alternative for newcomers to enhance their fame by bringing banking or social credit from outside of the system. It can be expected that "with-fame" crowdfunding systems, the risk of cheating, fraud and failure decreases even for newcomers simply because they would be more cautious about their fame. Therefore, the outcome of new projects can be more successful with such mechanism.
- If the fame of any entrepreneur is negative, it is an obvious signal to all players in the system to be alert to potential moral hazard and fraud risks. An entrepreneur with negative fame can be defined as a person who has a poor or unsuccessful track record of activities. Financiers can read details of the history of entrepreneur to know the reasons for their poor fame. The Entrepreneur with poor fame might have cheated or defrauded or had some failure with implementation of earlier projects thereby indicating that he is not to be trusted with the funds needed to finance a proposed project. Another reason to avoid partnering with an entrepreneur with poor Fame is the negative impact of a failed project on financiers' fame. If a financier funds an unsuccessful project, his/her fame will be adversely affected. Hence, very few financiers are interested in investing in a project with an infamous entrepreneur. Hence, the number of failed projects and infamous entrepreneurs will decrease in the system.
- Positive fame for entrepreneurs derives from a history of significant participation with higher rates of success and increased social credit, which can attract stronger interest from financiers to fund the project. Financiers can attribute a certain level of probability of success and lower risk associated with projects on the basis of positive fame. Successful projects can enhance the fame of both entrepreneurs and financiers. Indeed, these synergy effects contribute to the sufficient funding and efficient management of projects. Financiers under

these conditions would be looking for famous entrepreneurs with past experience of high returns.

Subjective value of the financiers is a function of the expected payoffs and fame. Therefore, the total payoff for a financier in a successful project is more than "without-Fame" investment as given in Equation (15).

$$\frac{\partial \widehat{v_i}}{\partial fame} > 0 \tag{15}$$

The utility function of the entrepreneur is also a function of income/cost as well as additional fame of the project. If he/she can succeed in the project, there is gain in terms of additional fame as given in Equation (16).

$$\pi = \pi(TR, TC, \Delta fame) \tag{16}$$

where $\Delta fame = fame_a - fame_b$.

Therefore, Fame of the project impacts crowdfunding mechanism through two ways.

Firstly, utility function of financiers is impacted by fame, so valuation of a project by financiers is different between Equation (17) and Equation (18) given below:

$$\widehat{v_i} = v(\theta_i, z, f(fame)) \tag{17}$$

$$\widehat{v_i} = v_i + f(fame) \tag{18}$$

Hence, the utility function is represented by Equation (19):

$$\widehat{u_i} = K(\widehat{v_i}, t_i) \tag{19}$$

Funding in a crowdfunding system is by crowd of financiers. Hence, the sum of the utilities is as below:

$$\sum_{i=1}^{n_1} \widehat{u_i} = K.N.\rho. \sum_{i=1}^{n_1} (\widehat{v_i} - t_i) \tag{20}$$

$$\sum_{i=1}^{n_1} \widehat{u_i} = K.N.\rho. \sum_{i=1}^{n_1} (v_i + f(fame) - t_i) \tag{21}$$

$$\sum_{i=1}^{n_1} \widehat{u_i} = \sum_{i=1}^{n_1} u_i + K.N.\rho. \sum_{i=1}^{n_1} f(fame) \tag{22}$$

Projects with zero or negative Fame are rare. Moreover, negative Fame could result in a negative utility function in Equation (22).

There is an assumption of positive fame in the design of the mechanism, as positive fame affect the utility function, $\sum_{i=1}^{n_1} \widehat{u_i} > \sum_{i=1}^{n_1} u_i$. Thus, the payoffs of financiers in fame-augmented crowdfunding are higher than in the usual or conventional (without-fame) system.

Secondly, as mentioned, entrepreneurs know about the impact of their behavior on their fame as the history of their fame is available to all financiers in the system. As a result, even one failure can be troublesome for a famous entrepreneur and thus potentially reduce the amount of funding for his/her future projects. Therefore, higher efforts can be expected from entrepreneurs in order to succeed. Payoff can then be defined as fame plus income minus costs.

$$\hat{\pi} = TR - TC \tag{23}$$

$$\hat{\pi} = K.N.\rho.\sum_{i=1}^{n_1} t_i - TC + \Delta fame \tag{24}$$

$$\hat{\pi} = \pi + \Delta fame \tag{25}$$

This implies that under deficit conditions, entrepreneurs would prefer to invest by themselves and make greater efforts to succeed. Generally, it can be assumed that famous players are bound to select successful strategies. Thus, Equation (26) describes the payoffs that are expected to be positive.

$$\pi = \begin{cases} \pi > 0, \; if \; K.N.\rho.\sum_{i=1}^{n_1} t_i < TC \; because\text{: } \Delta fame > 0 \\ \pi > 0, \; if \; K.N.\rho.\sum_{i=1}^{n_1} t_i > TC \; because\text{: } \Delta fame > 0 \end{cases} \tag{26}$$

It is noted that the with-fame mechanism of crowdfunding can produce better results compared to the without-fame mechanism for players of both sides of the same transactions. These effects may be explained in part with the following reasons.

- The utility of players under the fame-augmented mechanism is higher than that under no-fame mechanism. Thus, there may be stronger motivation for players to enter the crowdfunding system which provides a higher probability of funding.
- Given the availability of the history of participation, risk of cheating, fraud, and moral hazard, the probability of failure is reduced.
- There are clear benefits in the signaling mechanism which is performance-based and amenable to verification. As a result, problems associated with information asymmetry may be expected to decrease.
- There is a stronger incentive for entrepreneurs to succeed in the implementation of projects in order to gain better reputation and fame. This implies that even in cases where funds fall short of required levels, entrepreneurs may devise ways to complete projects successfully in order to avoid damage to personal reputation. It can be stated that success is the dominant strategy for all participants.

- The successful realization of projects may enhance the good reputation or fame for both entrepreneurs and financiers alike. Indeed, both participants are expected to sufficiently fund and effectively manage the projects to achieve the mutual benefits of both sides.

2.4 Aggregate Net Surplus

The aggregate net surplus (ANS) refers to the total payoffs for all participants in the crowdfunding system. It represents the aggregate profits for financiers and entrepreneurs. The Pareto optimality condition is satisfied only if the aggregate net surplus can be maximized. Equation (27) describes the aggregate net surplus as the sum of net suplus under the without-fame system, changes in fame for financiers, and variations in fame for entrepreneurs.

The Pareto optimality condition is satisfied only if the aggregate net surplus of the mechanism can be maximized. Equations of aggregate net surplus in the crowdfunding system encompasses three parts: Aggregate net surplus of a "Fameless" crowdfunding system, changes in the Fame of financiers and the Fame function of entrepreneur as:

$$\hat{S} = S + \Delta fame + K.N.\rho.\sum_{i=1}^{n_1} f(fame) \tag{27}$$

The aggregate net surplus under the with-fame system in higher than that obtained in the absence of fame measurement.

$$\hat{S} \geq S \overset{yields}{\rightarrow} \begin{cases} if\ f(fame) > 0,\ \hat{S} > S \\ if\ f(fame) = 0,\ \hat{S} > S \end{cases} \tag{28}$$

$$if\ f(fame) = 0\ but\ project\ is\ succesful$$

$$\rightarrow\ \Delta fame > 0\ as\ entrepreneur\ collects\ succesful\ feedback$$

2.5 Improvement of Utility under the Fame-based Mechanism

This study argues that a reputation-monitoring mechanism can be useful in reducing information asymmetry. There may be difficulties in the implementation of monitoring mechanisms given the technical requirements for effective credit-scoring platforms, reputation indexes, and comprehensive conditions to cover all users. Crowdfunding is a web 2.0-based platform, which is actually a closed system. Therefore, the implementation of a reputation-monitoring mechanism at the heart of this system may be appropriate through the introduction of the proposed reputation index, Fame, which is function of the banking or financial credit, social credit, participation history, and success and failure rates in previous transactions.

Previous analysis indicates that the fame-augmented mechanism indeed increases the utility level of both financiers and entrepreneurs. The payoffs for entrepreneurs can be expresses as follows.

$$\hat{\pi} = \pi + \Delta fame \tag{29}$$

Similarly, the payoffs for financiers can be expressed as follows

$$\sum_{i=1}^{n_1} \hat{u}_i = \sum_{i=1}^{n_1} u_i + K.N.\rho. \sum_{i=1}^{n_1} f(\text{fame}) \tag{30}$$

Therefore, it can be demonstrated that

$$\hat{\pi} > \pi \text{ and } \sum_{i=1}^{n_1} \hat{u}_i > \sum_{i=1}^{n_1} u_i \tag{31}$$

however, the aggregate payoffs under the fame-augmented crowdfunding are larger than those under crowdfunding without-fame. Thus mathematically, the propensity of a community to participate, collaborate and cooperate under fame-augmented crowdfunding systems is higher than that under without-fame systems.

$$S = \rho.n_1.\left[t(1-n) + \sum_{i=1}^{n_1} v_i\right] - TC \tag{32}$$

$$\hat{S} = S + \Delta fame + K.N.\rho. \sum_{i=1}^{n_1} f(fame) \tag{33}$$

Since $\hat{S} > S$ however, the aggregate payoffs under the fame-augmented crowdfunding are larger than those under crowdfunding without-fame. Thus mathematically, the propensity of a community to participate, collaborate and cooperate under fame-augmented crowdfunding systems is higher than that under without-fame systems.

3 Conclusion

The implementation of reputation mechanism in social networks is not necessarily difficult or unfeasible. There are many popular websites using the concept of reputation in their trading and sales platforms including Google, eBay, Booking.com, and TripAdvisor, among others. The reputation mechanism can be based on explicit feedbacks or implicit analytical methods. The findings of this study differ from other innovative approaches in that the focus is made on the importance of defining a reputation, of fame index for all users of a social network to make personal reputation

Table 15.1: Comparison of the Payoffs of Crowdfunding without-fame and with-fame.

	Financiers pay-off	Entrepreneur pay-off	Net aggregate surplus
Crowdfunding	$\sum_{i=1}^{n_1} u_i = K.\rho.N. \sum_{l=1}^{n_1} (v_i - t_i)$	$\pi = K.N.\rho. \sum_{i=1}^{n_1} t_i - TC$	$S = \rho.n_1. \left[t(1-n) + \sum_{i=1}^{n_1} v_i \right] - TC$
Crowdfunding with "Fame"	$\sum_{i=1}^{n_1} \widehat{u}_i = \sum_{i=1}^{n_1} u_i + K.N.\rho. \sum_{i=1}^{n_1} f(fame)$	$\hat{\pi} = \pi + \Delta fame$	$\hat{S} = S + \Delta fame + K.N.\rho. \sum_{i=1}^{n_1} f(fame)$
Result	$\sum_{i=1}^{n_1} \widehat{u}_i > \sum_{i=1}^{n_1} u_i$	$\hat{\pi} > \pi$	$\hat{S} > S$
Comparison	Crowdfunding with "Fame" *ayoff* > *crowdfunding without fame payoff*		

Source: Authors' own calculation.

systematically measurable and useful for equity-crowdfunding purposes. For instance, as eBay operations have demonstrated, buyers usually provide feedback information on sellers, even as the identity of buyers and personal reputation are not made available. Similarly, the identity and reputation and guests who rate hotels in the case of booking.com are not publicly available.

Generally, in a social network and especially in a crowdfunding platform, a proper definition of reputation or fame for all system users, financiers and entrepreneurs included, provides further clarity about the relevance of timely and accurate information for decision-making the crowdfunding community. Under these conditions, users would be aware and sensitive to the implications of their own activities, as well as of those who vote or blog in social networks. Thus, it is important to develop an effective mechanism for the measurement of reputation in a given community. The index of reputation or fame can reduce the extent of information asymmetry. The analysis demonstrates that once a fame-augemented mechanism is implemented, the aggregate net surplus would be increased. It is important to note that an equity-crowdfunding projects in which participants are aware and compliant with the normative rules of behavior, are conducive to a higher aggregate net surplus than that obtained under in the absence of fame-measurement conditions (see Table 15.1). Thus, the analysis highlights the importance of rule-compliance and taqwa in contractual agreements and its relevance in risk-sharing finance including equity- crowdfunding by a multiple potentially.

References

Ahlers, Gerrit, Douglas Cumming, Christina Günther, and Denis Schweizer. 2015. "Signaling in Equity Crowdfunding." *Entrepreneurship Theory and Practice* 39(4): 955–980.

Bebczuk, Ricardo Néstor. 2003. *Asymmetric Information in Financial Markets: Introduction and Applications*. Cambridge: Cambridge University Press.

Dellarocas, Chrysanthos. 2015. "Reputation Mechanisms." R. H. Smith School of Business University of Maryland.

Iqbal, Zamir and Abbas Mirakhor, 2017. *Ethical Dimensions of Islamic Finance: Theory and Practice*. New York: Palgrave Macmillan.

Mirakhor, Abbas and Hossein Askari. 2017. *Ideal Islamic Economy: An Introduction*. New York: Palgrave Macmillan.

Mohamed, Hazik, Abbas Mirakhor and Nuri Erbas. 2018. *Belief and Rule Compliance*. Cambridge, Massachusetts: Academic Press.

Myers, Stewart. C. and Nicholar S. Majluf. 1984. "Corporate financing and investment decisions when firms have information that investors do not have." *Journal of Financial Economics* 13(2): 187–221.

Ng, Adam, Abbas Mirakhor and Mansor H. Ibrahim. 2015. *Social Capital and Risk sharing*. New York: Palgrave Macmillan.

Ordanini, Andrea, Lucia Miceli, Marta Pizzetti, and Ananthanarayanan Parasuraman. 2011. "Crowdfunding: transforming customers into investors through innovative service platforms." *Journal of Service Management* 22(4): 443–470.

Sabater, J. C. Sierra. 2002. "Reputation and social network analysis in multi-agent systems." *Proceedings of the First International Joint Conference on Autonomous Agents and Multiagent Systems*, Association for Computing Machinery, Bologna, Italy, 475–482.

Schwienbacher, Armin and Benjamin Larralde. 2010. Crowdfunding of small entrepreneurial ventures. Handbook of Entrepreneurial Finance, Oxford University Press.

Voorbraak, K.J.P.M. 2011. *Crowdfunding for financing new ventures: consequence of the financial model on operational decisions*. Eindhoven: Eindhoven University of Technology.

Alaa Alaabed, Mansur Masih, Abbas Mirakhor

Chapter 16: Financial Consumer Protection: Empirical Evidence from Dual Banking Systems

1 Introduction

Amidst a widespread outcry at the disproportionate harm to consumers, financial consumer protection took center stage in policy debates following the Global Financial Crisis (GFC). The original intent of conventional banking is to serve as intermediary between surplus and deficit units in the economy. In this intermediary role, banks transferred risk from the former (depositors) to the latter (borrowers). An edifice of deposit insurance system and supervisory/regulatory structure were introduced to protect the creditor, albeit at the expense of the debtor. Keynes (1930, 1936) had long argued that risk-transfer, through the interest-rate mechanism, leads to two evils of capitalism: worsening income distribution and unemployment. More recently, this is validated by Piketty (2013) through various accounts of worsening income distribution worldwide. As economies grew more prosperous, only the rich became richer. Lower income groups did not share in prosperity. The imbalance was further deteriorated and amplified by the devastating power of risk-transfer enhanced by risk-shifting. Indeed, in the last five decades, advances in information technology and financial innovation gave rise to an immense capacity for rapid regime switching from risk-transfer to risk-shifting, through debt-based contracts. The tendency for banks to shift the risk of losses to external parties, while internalizing gains effectively excludes a majority (depositors) from sharing in the prosperity (Sheng 2009). Worse still, the majority stands to bear the brunt of recurrent risk-shifting-induced crises. The effects of risk-shifting were amply pronounced in the aftermath of the GFC. The fallout from which has intensified calls for financial consumer protection.

Financial consumer protection can be broadly defined as “any activity, action or set of rules that seeks to mitigate risk(s) and harm to the consumer relating to the use of any financial product or service or to the relationship with a “financial institution” (IFC 2015). In the highly regulated banking industry, regulatory measures are theorized to prevent banks from shifting risk and mitigate harm to customers of banking services (Bushman 2016). This is, indeed, the essence of prudential bank regulation (Bushman et al. 2012). For instance, Basel bank guidelines and accords reflect this objective by requiring banks to hold capital in proportion to their risk-weighted assets and reduce leverage. The remaining two pillars of Basel II capital accord, which are supervision and market discipline, exert the same impact. Other regulatory devices include stress tests, disclosure requirements, asset monitoring and prompt corrective actions (Flannery 1998; Furlong and Keeley 1989,

https://doi.org/10.1515/9783110587920-016

1990). However, banks today seem more than capable of amassing risk in spite of regulation, by shifting assets off balance sheet and capitalizing on regulatory arbitrage.[161] This underlies the crucial complementarity of market forces. Though often viewed as the collective responsibility of regulatory and supervisory authorities, financial service-providers, industry associations and private standard-setting bodies, there is an increasing burden laid on consumers to play the role of effective financial consumer protection through "self-protection". The recourse can be made to several measures including taking actions to discipline risk-shifting banks by demanding higher yields commensurate with the risk exposure and/or moving balances to safer banks (Demirguc-Kunt et al., 2009). These are generally applicable and compatible with the aforementioned two pillars of Basel II capital accord, which are supervision and market discipline (Dias 2013).

Over the years, behavioral research has revealed that personal, social, and environmental factors influence individuals' behaviors and decision-making. It is difficult to argue, a priori, that financial decisions are not affected by behavioral factors. Financial behavior cannot be excluded from this observation ex-ante. Given this empirical evidence, this study examines the issue of financial consumer protection through the supervision and market discipline channels in the dual banking systems of the member states of the Organisation of Islamic Cooperation (OIC). An empirical understanding of these channels may better inform policy making to adequately account for the specific characteristics of financial products, providers and consumers of dual systems.

The Islamic banking model, which co-exists with its conventional counterpart in these countries, provides a unique paradigm with risk-sharing at its core (The Kuala Lumpur Declaration 2012). This is to say that the principles and operations of Islamic finance have implications for the distribution of risks and the nature of relationships between consumers and financial institutions (Beck et al. 2013). More specifically, the ideal Islamic banking system is unique in its proposition to separate commercial and investment banking activities, in accordance with the Islamic law of contract. As such, trust-based short-term demand deposits are to be supported with 100% reserves and exclusively maintained for the sole purposes of safe keeping.[162] Investment banks, on the other hand, are to pursue their traditional intermediary function. This will involve accepting surplus funds on a distinct partnership basis (*mudarabah*), and channeling them to the real economy through projects that

---

161 "Some of finance's most abstruse and pernicious activity arises from regulatory arbitrage – restructuring transactions so that they move from a less favorable to a more favorable regulatory rubric" (Heller 2015).

162 This is also the essence of Roman classical law and the Chicago Plan, proposed in the aftermath of the great depression by leading American economists. The proposal advocates a 100% reserve against demand deposits and no deposit insurance for investment deposits (see Mirakhor et al. 2012; Askari et al. 2012; Benes and Kumhof 2012, among others).

match depositors' risk and return profiles (Mirakhor et al. 2012; Askari et al. 2012). Since the principal in *mudarabah* is not protected; no reserve is required for this segment of banking. The risk of capital loss and contingency of profits make depositors residual claimants of Islamic banks (Abedifar et al. 2013); thereby reinforcing the monitoring incentive structure and exposing banks to greater disciplinary withdrawal risk[163] (Beck, Demirgüç-Kunt and Merrouche 2013; Van Wijnbergen et al. 2013; Abedifar et al. 2013; Rosly 1999). Moreover, risk-sharing can potentially contribute to improved transparency and reduce the problems of information asymmetry and power imbalance between providers and users of financial services. Residual claims can also reduce the possibility of adverse wealth transfer (Esty 1997).[164] Theoretical studies have shown that no combination of debt and equity claims can induce the entrepreneur to choose a low risk strategy, except for pure equity (Ozerturk 2002). Given the above economic characteristics and *Shariah* requirement of real sector anchor and restrictions on the sale of debt and short selling, which affect leverage in Islamic banks, it is clear that Islamic banking is axiomatically aligned with greater financial consumer protection (Van Wijnbergen et al. 2013).

It cannot be denied, however, that the present regulatory and supervisory framework for Islamic banks has grown out of conventional wisdom and is geared rather toward risk-transfer (Kammar et al. 2015; Lajis 2015). This is in part an unintended consequence of harmonizing efforts by OIC member countries that were aimed at minimizing regulatory arbitrage and ensuring a level regulatory robustness in dual banking systems. As a result, the legal, administrative, economic, financial and regulatory biases that favor risk-transfer persist, placing risk-sharing at the margin. It is possible to consider, for instance, the adoption of Basel capital adequacy requirements for Islamic banking. These requirements disincentivize the use of risk-sharing based contracts of *mudarabah* and *musharakah* in banks' financing. Moreover, Islamic banks adopt smoothing strategies to mitigate withdrawal risk, such as maintaining profit equalization and investment risk reserves (Van Wijnbergen et al. 2013; IFSB 2010), with adverse effects on information sharing. Taken together, the existing state of affairs may unintendedly undermine financial consumer protection through the same supervision and market discipline channels in Islamic banking.

Whereas the existing literature includes significant work that establishes the theoretical foundations of Islamic banking and its axiomatic characteristics, the empirical assessment of the implications of Islamic banking is relatively limited and often focused on issues of efficiency, profitability and stability. This chapter proceeds as follows. A review of relevant literature is presented in the next section.

---

163 Also known as displaced commercial risk.

164 Ozerturk (2002) shows that no combination of debt and equity claims can induce the entrepreneur to choose a low risk strategy, except for pure equity.

The methodology and estimation model are described in Section 3. The results are reported and discussed in Section 4. Finally, Section 5 concludes the chapter.

2 Review of Relevant Literature

A stream of the literature deems depositors' demand for higher yields and/or the propensity to move balances to safer banks as restraining risk-shifting incentives that are commensurate with self-protection (see, for example, Jagtiani et al. 2000; Flannery and Sorescu 1996; Ellis and Flannery 1992; Benston et al. 1986). For instance, Martinez-Peria and Schmukler (2001) document evidence of deposit withdrawals and demands for higher interest rates with respect to riskier banks in Argentina, Chile and Mexico. Similarly, Gropp et al. (2006), Sironi (2003) and others find subordinated debt to be instrumental in disciplining banks from risk-taking by increasing spreads. However, the existing body of evidence is not conclusive. Omet and Fayyoumi (2004), for example, find that depositor discipline is largely non-existent in Jordan.

The efficiency of market discipline effectiveness has been also the subject of theoretical and applied research. "[M]arket agents must feel at risk and must have sufficient information about bank riskiness (Hamalainen et al. (2005), Baumann and Nier (2006)" (Distinguin et al. 2011). These conditions resonate with the risk-sharing principle underlying Islamic banking and finance and reinforce its theoretical disciplinary advantage. The common practice of income-smoothing, however, defeats this purpose by obscuring the banks' fundamentals and reducing the quality and symmetry of information.

Such an adverse impact is demonstrated empirically in the works of Bushman et al. (2007 and 2012), *inter alia*. The authors document a weakening of outside monitoring and an increasing potential for risk-shifting associated with income-smoothing via discretionary loss provisioning for loans. Using a sample of 27 countries from 1995–2006, discretionary smoothing is shown to intensify risk-shifting incentives in the absence of informational transparency. In contrast, forward-looking provisioning counteracts the potential effects of moral hazard by enhancing transparency and informational symmetry. This is because forward looking provisioning, which mirrors the risk-taking behavior of banks, tends to build up loan loss reserves in good times when more risk is taken. As expected by Bushman et al. (2007), this practice "increase[s] the informativeness of earnings by better reflecting risks of the underlying loan portfolio" (Bushman et al. 2007).

On aggregate, markets and regulators are found to play disciplinary role in a sample of traditional commercial banks in Taiwan (Chang and Chen 2013), in the U.S. (Duan et al. 1992), in Japan (Guizani and Watanabe 2010) and in a mixed sample of large European and American banks (Carbo-Valverde et al. 2011). Bushman et al.

(2007 and 2012) further confirm the empirical results in an international study of banks across 27 countries.[165]

In addition to the above literature, there is evidence of risk-shifting in deposit-taking banks in the United States (Chang and Ho 2017; Hovakimian and Kane 2000) and Australia (Bigg 1999). Among these, this empirical evidence is a testament to the failure of market and regulatory discipline in modern banking architecture to fully eliminate the risk-shifting incentives for banks. In effect, the risk of losses is shifted from banks or informed parties to depositors and uninformed parties leading to unilateral wealth expropriation. The evidence is not, indeed, limited to single-country analyses. For instance, Hovakimian et al. (2003) find significant evidence of risk–shifting for a sample of 56 countries. Interestingly, risk-shifting appears to be particularly strong in poorly capitalized banks (Hovakimian and Kane 2000). Furthermore, cross-country variations exist in the intensity of risk-shifting. Thus, the extent of violation of financial consumer protection have been mainly ascribed to different institutional environments, different deposit insurance design features, and different regulatory and supervisory frameworks. Significant risk-shifting is observed in countries with poor contract enforcement and with property rights rules and governance systems that impede rather the efficient public and private monitoring of financial institutions (Demirgüç-Kunt and Detragiache 2002; Demirgüç-Kunt and Kane 2002).

Moreover, explicit deposit insurance is found to exacerbate risk-shifting in weak institutional environments (Hovakimian et al. 2003). On the other hand, loss-control features such as risk-sensitive premia, loss coverage limits, and coinsurance provisions are found to deter risk-shifting incentives under deposit insurance. In addition, Gropp and Vesala (2004) argue that the exclusion of subordinated debt from financial safety nets improves holders' monitoring and market discipline in systemically unimportant banks with low charter values and considerable base of uninsured subordinated debt holders in the European Union.

Altogether, the empirical literature is dominated by studies related to OECD countries and conventional models of banking. With respect to Islamic banking and finance, Abedifar et al. (2013) investigated some aspects of risk attitudes and the stability of Islamic banks in a cross-country study covering the period between 1999 and 2009. Their findings suggest that leverage disciplines Islamic banks more effectively than their conventional counterparts, despite attempts to mitigate withdrawal risk by offering market-competitive returns. The authors investigate whether Islamic banks are exposed to more or less credit risk compared to conventional banks due to the unique features of their client base. Their findings support the hypothesis that greater withdrawal risk of a unique class of risk-sharing depositors influences the financing

165 In fact, Bushman et al. (2007 and 2012) document eroding discipline when managements distort bank fundamentals through income smoothing. The opposite is found to be true when accurate information is made available to depositors and regulators by forward-looking loan provisioning.

behavior of Islamic banks and is more effective in disciplining them, in comparison to conventional banks. Abedifar et al. (2013, p. 2040) argue that "Islamic depositors are more likely to shift their deposits from poor-performing banks to those offering higher returns or even to conventional banks."

However, the empirical evidence on the behavior of Islamic banks and the comparative disciplinary advantage is still inconclusive. A more recent study by Farooq and Zaheer (2015) shows that Islamic banks in Pakistan were less susceptible to deposit withdrawals during the financial crisis. Moreover, the Islamic windows of mixed banks witnessed an increased demand for their deposit-taking services during the crisis period, suggesting that religiosity and customer loyalty may deter disciplinary withdrawal in the case of Islamic banks.[166] The authors also refer to a recent survey in which 55 percent of respondents (Islamic bank depositors) dismissed withdrawing funds in case of bank losses. A similar response was found in Malaysia (Gerrard and Cunningham 1997), where over 60 percent of Muslim depositors insisted that they would maintain deposits with their Islamic banks even if they did not pay any profit. On aggregate, it seems that risk-shifting incentives intensify, at the expense of financial consumer protection, with reduced monitoring and the presence of information asymmetry and limited liability.

3 The Empirical Model

The chapter employs a variant of an empirical model developed by Duan, Moreau and Sealey (1992) to investigate financial consumer protection under the dual banking systems of OIC member countries. The model provides a suitable empirical framework for the present study. It estimates the dynamics between banks' leverage and volatility, as measured by asset risk, to demonstrate that they are not independent. The model is based on the notion that an increase in risk is expected to be associated with demands to reduce leverage or solicit higher capital in the presence of regulatory and market discipline (Hovakimian et al., 2003; Furlong and Keeley, 1990).

$$\mathrm{D/V} = \alpha_0 + \alpha_1 \sigma_\mathrm{v} \tag{1}$$

where

V is the market value of bank assets,

D is the face value of deposits, and

σ_v is the value of asset risk, represented by standard deviation of returns

166 i.e. banks that operate on both Islamic and conventional bases.

Equation (1) measures the sensitivity of leverage to changes in asset risk. Specifically, α_1 measures the intensity with which regulators and depositors respond to bank risk-taking. α_1 is expected to be negative in the presence of hypothesized market and regulatory discipline (Hovakimian et al. 2003; Berger et al. 2015). Financial consumers are protected when disciplinary pressure forces banks to internalize the full cost of increasing the riskiness of their assets (σ_v) by holding more capital, thereby lowering leverage (D/V) (Bushman et al. 2007).

The standard deviation of annual changes in the market value of assets serves as a measure of asset risk (σ_v). A higher standard deviation indicates higher risk-taking (Distinguin et al., 2013). Leverage, on the other hand, is proxied by the value of deposits (D) divided by the market value of bank assets (V). The standard deviation of asset returns offers a more comprehensive measure of overall ex-ante risk, as compared to the ex-post informative measures of credit and liquidity risks used in the banking literature, such as the ratios of non-performing loans to total assets, risk-weighted assets to total assets, the z-score and others (DeYoung and Rice 2004; Jiménez et al. 2013, 2014). While it may be plausible to use market information in the valuation of banks assets, attention must be paid to the peculiarity of the sample handoff observations and the consequential limitations of market proxies. The majority of OIC banks are unlisted. Therefore, the availability of such data in our sample is a major concern. It is also worth noting that insolvency rules depend on the book value rather than market value of assets (Duan et al. 1992). This reinforces the appeal of using book values. For these reasons, the analysis substitutes the book value of assets and the 3-year rolling window of the standard deviation of annual change in the book value of assets for V and σ_v.

Thus, the model is extended to estimate the impact of Islamic banking on financial consumer protection in a dynamic multi-country setting, as follows:

$$D/V^*_{ijt} = \alpha_0 D/V^*_{ijt-1} + \alpha_1 \sigma_{v\,ijt}^* + \alpha_2 \sigma_{v\,ijt}^* {}^*IB + \alpha_3 \sigma_{v\,ijt}^* {}^*IB + \alpha_4 \sigma_{v\,jit}^* {}^*X^*_{ijt} + \alpha_5 \sigma_{v\,jit}^* {}^*K^*_{jt} + \varepsilon^*_{ijt} \quad (2)$$

where,

D/V^*_{ijt} is leverage, i = bank, j = country and t = time,
$\sigma_v{}^*_{ijt}$ is asset risk,
IB is a binary variable that takes the value of 1 if the bank is Islamic and 0 otherwise, and
X^*_{ijt} is a vector of bank-specific variables
K^*_{ijt} is a vector of country-specific variables
ε^*_{ijt} is an error term.

The coefficient α_2 measures specific protection associated with Islamic banking. To the extent that Islamic banking has disciplinary advantage as envisaged by theory, an estimate of $\alpha_2 < 0$, would suggest that Islamic banking has a superior effect on financial consumer protection. A given increase in risk leads to greater external discipline. The significance of this coefficient will indicate that financial consumer protection is statistically different under Islamic banking as compared to conventional banking.

The use of a single dummy variable (*IB*) may not suffice to make fair statistical inference about the Islamic banking industry at this stage, given the lack of standardization and, at times, widely varying interpretations of Shariah and Islamic legal doctrines. As a result, three-way interaction terms are introduced in the model specification. These terms capture the significance and potentially opposing effects of Islamic banking across the non-standardized industry. However, for the purpose of consistency the estimate of GMM modelling, the analysis proceeds with the interaction terms for Islamic banking in Malaysia and Turkey. These are denoted *MYIB* and *TRKIB*, respectively. All other Islamic banking industries are represented with one dummy variable (*IBxMT*). The choice of interaction terms is based on pre-estimation and statistical testing undertaken by the authors to avoid instrument proliferation.

Monitoring and disciplining incentives are apt to vary with economic, legal and institutional aspects of the respective countries and micro-level banking factors. Therefore, a number of bank-specific and country-specific variables are considered in the empirical model. Estimated coefficients are interpreted in a similar way to α_2. These include the following variables:

- Bank's capital ratio (EQ) measured as the book value of equity reported at the end of the period scaled by end of period total asset as a proxy of bank capital,
- Bank's size (TA) measured as the natural logarithm of total assets,
- Return on assets (RoA) measured as earnings before taxes divided by total assets,
- Real GDP per capita's growth rate,
- Rule of law as proxied by the World Governance Indicators' (WGI) measure,
- Lerner index to measure the market power in the banking industry as reported on Bankscope,
- A stock market dummy that takes the value 1 when the country has a stock market and 0 otherwise, and
- A crisis dummy (GFC) that takes the value of 1 during the recent U.S. financial crisis in 2008 and 0 otherwise.

To estimate the above model, banking data for an unbalanced panel of 272 conventional banks and 75 Islamic banks from 2002 to 2013 were obtained from the Bankscope database. Data represent 19 OIC member countries with dual banking systems countries. These are Bahrain, Bangladesh, Brunei Darussalam, Egypt, Indonesia, Iraq, Jordan, Kuwait, Malaysia, Mauritania, Pakistan, Palestinian Territories, Qatar, Saudi Arabia, Syria, Tunisia, Turkey, United Arab Emirates, and Yemen. The sample is fairly representative of Islamic banking. Country-level data were retrieved from key World Bank global databases, such as the World Development Indicators, and World Governance Indicators.

The analysis benefits from Arellano and Bond's (1991) two-step dynamic difference Generalized Methods of Moments (GMM). The method takes care of fixed effects, dynamics, and endogeneity problems in panel data that could otherwise bias ordinary least squares (OLS) estimates. It also caters for the micro panel properties of our data set.

GMM transforms the equation by taking first difference. This takes care of fixed effects. To address endogeneity, the estimator relies on a set of internal instruments contained within the panel itself. More specifically, it uses lags of the levels as instruments for the first differences. Therefore, past values of leverage and risk can be used as instruments for current realizations of leverage. This overcomes the difficulty of finding external instruments, which are both uncorrelated with the error term and correlated with the independent variables.

There are two variants of the Arellano-Bond estimators: one- and two-step. In the first step, the error terms are assumed to be both independent and homoscedastic across entities and over time. These assumptions are relaxed in the second step, where the residuals obtained in the first step are used to construct a consistent estimate of the variance-covariance matrix.

In general, the consistency of the GMM estimator depends on the validity of the assumption that the error terms do not exhibit serial correlation and on the validity (exogeneity) of its instruments. To validate these assumptions, over-identification and serial correlation tests are undertaken. The null hypothesis of the over identification tests implies that the instruments are orthogonal, whereas the second set of tests examines the hypothesis that the error term is not serially correlated.

Table 16.1 provides summary statistics from the dependent variable and main explanatory variables used in the estimation of the banking model. Islamic banks tend to be less levered and better capitalized, whereas their conventional counterparts seem to be more profitable, less volatile and larger in size.

4 Estimation Results

Table 16.2 reports the estimation results from the relevant difference GMM model. The test of second-order serial correlation (AR (2)) and Hansen J test of over-identification diagnostic tests validate the model estimates. The failure to reject the null hypotheses for both tests validates the choice of model instruments and estimators.

The estimation results reveal the existence of a dynamic process as the one-period lagged leverage ratios have significant and positive effect on current leverage rates. The positive coefficient captures the short-term adjustment costs that arise from information asymmetry and rigidities. Both of which impede instantaneous capital adjustment in response to adverse capital shocks or regulatory and market discipline (Brei and Gambacorta 2014; Stolz 2007; Myers and Majluf 1984).

Table 16.1: Descriptive Statistics.

	Variable	Count	Mean	S.D.	Min	Q25	Mdn	Q75	Max
Conventional Banks	Leverage (D/V)	2779	65.28	15.03	1.43	58.21	68.25	74.93	156.53
	Asset risk (σ_v)	2779	18.26	23.23	0.27	6.95	12.66	20.59	362.4
	Capital ratio (EQ)	2779	11.7	7.68	−95.94	7.69	10.44	14.27	78.97
	Bank size (TA)	2779	8,500	16,000	37	750	2,300	8,200	120,000
	Return on assets (RoA)	2734	1.39	2.43	−72.44	0.81	1.44	2.15	13.2
	Return on equity (RoE)	2731	13.62	34.06	−534.93	7.57	13.74	20.4	850.24
	Governance	2779	11.84	3.25	2.43	8.82	11.32	14.03	18.74
	Rule of Law	2779	1.78	0.59	0.08	1.23	1.89	2.37	3.04
	GDP Growth	2712	22.67	3.85	2.94	21.18	23.54	24.82	70.03
	Lerner Index	2045	2.28	0.15	1.81	2.19	2.24	2.4	2.62
	Crisis	2697	45.34	27.38	1.27	26.76	35.99	55.52	123.88
Islamic Banks	Leverage (D/V)	571	60.29	20.41	1.3	51.63	65.23	74.47	111.08
	Asset risk (σ_v)	571	21.6	33.34	0.36	7.19	13.09	23.73	453.57
	Capital ratio (EQ)	571	14.06	12.6	−77.21	7.52	11.19	17.53	82.61
	Bank size (TA)	571	5,300	9,100	20	620	2,200	5,500	75,000
	Return on assets (RoA)	563	1.36	2.35	−12.72	0.55	1.13	1.91	21.39
	Return on equity (RoE)	563	10.09	31.63	−573.3	5.26	11.19	17.02	101.22
	Governance	571	12.64	3.78	3.88	8.68	13.65	16.02	18.74
	Rule of Law	571	1.96	0.68	0.16	1.23	2.26	2.51	3.04
	GDP Growth	553	21.66	4.44	2.94	19.83	22.74	24.37	37.49
	Lerner Index	372	2.33	0.15	1.81	2.22	2.35	2.46	2.62
	Crisis	548	52.69	33.21	2.68	29.11	43.85	71.44	123.88

Source: Authors' calculations.
Note: Count indicates the number of observations. S.D. indicates standard deviation. Min, Q25, Mdn, Q75 and Max represent the minimum value, the 25th percentile, the median, the 75th percentile and the maximum value in the sample, respectively. Variables are as defined above.

Furthermore, the magnitude of the estimated coefficients is below unity in all model estimates, implying that banks have a target leverage ratio that acts as a long-term drift. Convergence occurs over 2.2 years, on average, from the time of a shock. This further confirms the existence of time dependence in bank leverage decision, which justifies the importance of incorporating lagged variables in the derivation of consistent estimates. The findings are in congruence with the work by Brei and Gambacorta (2014), de Mooij et al. (2013), Keen and de Mooij (2012), among others. They also lend support to the argument by Admati et al. (2012) that leverage is "addictive".

The four estimated coefficients of the risk measure (σ_v) are found to be positive and statistically significant across all specifications. The positive sign stands in conflict with the evidence from Duan et al. (1992) and the necessary condition that regulators, depositors and other market forces react to banks' efforts to increase risk

Table 16.2: The Impact of Islamic Banking on the Sensitivity of Leverage (D/V) to Risk (σ_v).

	(1)	(2)	(3)	(4)	(5)	(6)
Bank-specific variables						
Lagged leverage (D/V_{it-1})	0.628***	0.552***	0.533***	0.528***	0.508***	0.532***
	(0.0923)	(0.107)	(0.107)	(0.0956)	(0.0869)	(0.0953)
Asset risk (σ_v)	0.0178*	0.437***	0.341**	0.272**	0.259**	0.279**
	(0.00996)	(0.154)	(0.138)	(0.128)	(0.124)	(0.142)
Size* σ_v		−0.00662	0.00258	0.00922	0.0109*	−0.0025
		(0.00387)	(0.00664)	(0.00561)	(0.00645)	(0.00471)
Capital* σ_v		−0.0425	−0.0328	−0.0383*	−0.0361*	−0.0378*
		(0.0326)	(0.0244)	(0.0228)	(0.0204)	(0.0226)
ROA* σ_v		−0.0328*	−0.0353*	−0.0333**	−0.0357**	−0.0282*
		(0.0153)	(0.0143)	(0.0156)	(0.0139)	(0.0169)
Islamic banking sector Variables						
$IB_{xMY\&TRK}$*σ_v	0.0502	0.0582	0.0338	0.0171	0.00466	0.0199
	(0.0683)	(0.0675)	(0.0601)	(0.0548)	(0.0421)	(0.0490)
MY*IB*σ_v	−0.00428	0.0239	0.0400	0.0393	0.0547	0.0963
	(0.0678)	(0.0580)	(0.0389)	(0.0396)	(0.0470)	(0.0660)
TRK*IB*σ_v	0.00846	0.171	0.142	0.0660	0.0285	−0.0028
	(0.0629)	(0.194)	(0.154)	(0.102)	(0.165)	(0.0929)
Country-specific variables						
GDP Growth* σ_v			−0.00719	−0.0033	−0.0031	−0.0048
			(0.00566)	(0.00645)	(0.00721)	(0.00613)
Rule of Law* σ_v			−0.0821*	−0.0657**	−0.0669**	−0.0692*
			(0.0324)	(0.0249)	(0.0249)	(0.0336)
Stock Market* σ_v				−0.0161	−0.0215	0.0190
				(0.0373)	(0.0389)	(0.0404)
Lerner Index* σ_v				−0.00514	−0.0100	0.126*
				(0.0320)	(0.0384)	(0.0674)
Crisis-related variables						
$IB_{xMY\&TRK}$*Crisis*σ_v					−0.0662	
					(0.0416)	
MY_{IB}* Crisis* σ_v					−0.0285*	−0.0272*
					(0.0166)	(0.0155)
TRK_{IB}*Crisis* σ_v					0.0126	0.00102
					(0.0124)	(0.0181)
CB*Crisis* σ_v						0.0111*
						(0.00620)
F	9.387***	7.583***	8.410***	5.791***	5.572***	4.898***
No. of observations	1776	1846	1846	1769	1769	1769
No. of banks	287	283	283	286	286	286

Table 16.2 (continued)

	(1)	(2)	(3)	(4)	(5)	(6)
No. of instruments	84	150	192	227	230	230
AR(2) test	1.47	1.12	1.03	−0.95	−1.00	−0.90
Hansen test	96.96	147.48	183.17	206.97	208.32	198.99

Source: Authors' calculations.

Note: This table reports the results from Arellano and Bond's (1991) two-step difference GMM estimation of: $D/V^*_{ijt} = \alpha_0 D/V^*_{ijt-1} + \alpha_1 \sigma_v{}^*_{ijt} + \alpha_2 \sigma_v{}^*_{ijt} * IB + \alpha_3 \sigma_v{}^*_{ijt} * IB + \alpha_4 \sigma_v{}^*_{ijt} * X^*_{ijt} + \alpha_5 \sigma_v{}^*_{ijt} * K^*_{jt} + \varepsilon^*_{ijt}$, t= 2002, 2003 ... 2013. Following Merton (1977) and Duan et al. (1992), D/V is the face value of deposits (D) divided by the market value of bank assets (V). All other variables are as defined before. Windmeijer-corrected standard errors are in parentheses. AR(2) is a test for second-order serial correlation in the first-differenced residuals, under the null of no serial correlation. The Hansen test of over-identification is under the null that all instruments are valid. ***, **, * represent significance at the 1%, 5% and 10% level, respectively. The instruments used in the GMM estimation are the lagged levels of IPPijt, σvijt, σvijt*IB, σvjit*Xijt and σvjit*Kjt.

by pressuring them to reduce leverage and maintain equity positions commensurate with risks undertaken. The results don't only point at the failure of external discipline to restrain excessive risk-taking and protect financial consumers. They also indicate that risky banks were allowed to accumulate even more financial leverage along the way. This evidence is consistent with the debt overhang effect (Admati et al. 2012) and recent experience in banking and finance. There is in effect a massive build-up of financial leverage in the balance sheet of the banks in tandem with enormous risk-taking (Turner 2010; Reinhart and Rogoff 2009).

The inefficacy of external risk controls validates their failure to protect financial consumers. This could be partially attributed to regulatory forbearance and distortions in the present regulatory and supervisory framework that contribute to excessive risk-taking and risk-shifting (Garcia et al. 2004). Also, regulatory forbearance allows banks' assets to deteriorate to threshold levels below the face value of deposits before declaring bankruptcy (Duan et al. 1992). The same argument can be extended to accommodative measures adopted by policy makers during financial crises, including bailouts and other crisis intervention policies that keep faltering banks afloat and shift the burden of losses to taxpayers (Claessens et al. 2011; Poole 2007; Frankel 2007). In addition, the lender of last resort facilities and deposit insurance tend to "displace more private discipline than official oversight can generate" (Hovakimian et al. 2003). Thus, the current regulatory framework creates a distortive perception regarding its substitutability with bank capital (Carbo-Valverde et al. 2011). As a result of market misperceptions and ineffective government guarantees, depositors and other bank creditors are seldom on a constant "watch" and cease to impose discipline on excessive risk-taking (Admati and Hellwig 2013; Admati et al. 2013).

Indeed, this evidence lends support to arguments that raise doubts about the ability of market participants to discipline banks amidst the distortions of the current regulatory framework. For instance, Billett, Garfinkel, and O'Neal (1998) document the increased use of insured deposits (i.e. leverage) following increase in bank risk. Furthermore, Admati et al. (2012) argue that leverage is subsidized, whether through lender of last resort facilities, deposit insurance or the too-big-to-fail subsidies. Therefore, any external deleveraging pressure entails a loss of these subsidies and a much-resisted wealth transfer to depositors and other bank creditors (Musgrave 2014).

Moreover, external discipline requires informed decision-making on the part of depositors and regulators as well as timely access to accurate information on bank actions and returns (Admati and Hellwig 2013). However, informational opacity plagues the operation of Middle Eastern banks, in general, as suggested by Lee and Hsieh (2013). In general, the bulk of the countries in the sample lacks the crucial prerequisites for external discipline. In comparison to the majority of OECD countries covered in earlier studies, these countries have substantially different levels of financial development, financial literacy, consumer awareness and empowerment, inter alia. It is possible that these invariably lower levels of development, literacy and awareness are not sufficient to allow for effective external discipline. By way of example and not limitation, more than three-quarters of adults in OIC member countries did not have accounts at formal financial institutions, as of 2011 (Mohseni-Cheraghlou 2015; COMCEC 2014).

Furthermore, instruments frequently used for external discipline are almost inexistent in the sample countries. For instance, the use of stock-market-based indicators is constrained by the limited number of publicly listed banks. Similarly, the illiquidity of bond markets hinders the use of subordinated debt (Barth et al. 2003).[167] The failure of external discipline can be understood also in light of the empirical literature on risk-shifting that yields similar results. There is indeed evidence of positive coefficients for the measures of risk for commercial banks in Taiwan (Chang and Chen, 2013), in the U.S. (Chang and Ho 2017 and Hovakimian and Kane 2000), and in Canada (Wagster 2007). The empirical evidence is not conclusive, however, as discussed above.

In the context of Islamic banking, there is insufficient evidence to suggest that the sensitivity of leverage to changes in asset risk is different from evidence based on the conventional model. It is clear from Table 16.2 that Islamic banking regulation and complementary market discipline failed to constrain excessive risk-taking.[168] The insignificance of interaction terms, ($IB_{xMY\&TRK}{}^{*}\sigma_v$) from the Islamic banking runs contrary to the theoretical significance of its disciplinary advantage. The monitoring and disciplining difficulties that present themselves in the conventional sector seem to persist in the current configuration of Islamic banking. They don't seem to be alleviated. To provide

167 The spreads on subordinated debt are arguably reflective of bank riskiness (Sironi 2003).
168 This includes risk-sensitive capital regulation.

an intuition for this implication, it is helpful to consider the following facts and findings, some of which have been discussed earlier.

For external discipline to be effective, banks must convey a degree of informational transparency (Baumann and Nier 2006). Accounting discretion, however, impairs transparency and information quality. Unfortunately, both Islamic and conventional banks in Malaysia managed earnings and capital through loan loss provisioning over the period 1993–2009 (Misman and Ahmad 2011). Similar patterns were observed more widely in seven Middle Eastern countries (Othman and Mersni 2012). More recently, Ashraf et al. (2015) find congruent evidence of income smoothing by Islamic and conventional banks in 12 OIC countries.

Moreover, the Kuala Lumpur-based Islamic Financial Services Board (IFSB) encourages regulators, that don't currently offer explicit Islamic deposit insurance to do so. The standard-setting organization deemed Islamic deposit insurance necessary for the purposes of systemic stability and resilience of the nascent industry (IFSB 2015). Aside from *Shariah* non-compliance risk arising from contentions on the insurability of risk-sharing based deposits, the establishment of such scheme would further deteriorate the conditions of effective external discipline for Islamic banks.

Worse still, the positive sign of $IB_{xMY\&TRK}{}^{*}\sigma_V$, $MY^{*}IB^{*}\sigma_V$ and $TRK^{*}IB^{*}\sigma_V$ coefficients suggest that the present form of Islamic banking may be less susceptible to monitoring and disciplining incentives. This tendency can be explained by a variety of reasons. For one, the religiosity of Islamic bank depositors may influence their disciplinary role, as evident in the study by Farooq and Zaheer (2015). Secondly, the maintenance of profit-equalization and investment risk reserves can potentially distort bank fundamentals (Van Wijnbergen et al. 2013).

Thus, the results are fairly consistent across the sample countries. No disciplinary advantage is evident in the case of Malaysian and Turkish Islamic banking industries either. The estimated coefficient for the Malaysian Islamic banking industry is found to be negative and becomes statistically significant when interacted with the crisis dummy variable. The change in external discipline is reflected by a significant difference in the leverage dynamics of Malaysia's Islamic and conventional banks during the crisis. The increased threat of loss seems to have motivated Islamic banking regulators, depositors and other market forces to restrain excessive risk-taking during the crisis. As a result, Islamic banks' efforts to increase risk were opposed by pressure to reduce leverage and increase equity position. Alternatively, discipline may have been initiated "due to heightened awareness of the risks of bank failures because of the dramatic increase in the numbers of failures and near-failures and the media coverage of them" (Berger and Turk Ariss 2015).

With respect to bank and country-specific variables, asset size appears to be an important determinant of regulatory, supervisory and market disciplinary decisions in OIC countries. Judging from the estimation results of Model (2) in Table 16.2, it appears that large banks are exposed to greater external discipline when only bank-specific variables are taken into consideration. The marginal impact of size on the sensitivity of leverage-to-asset measure of risk is found to be rather positive and statistically insignificant in alternative models (3) and (4), where both bank-specific and country-specific variables are included. The weakened external discipline is consistent with the too-big-to-fail hypothesis. Larger banks enjoy greater regulatory forbearance. As expected, profitability and higher skin-in-the-game alter the benefits of excessive risk-taking, by introducing a negative feedback between leverage and asset risk. The significance of capitalization ratio, in particular, lends credence to regulatory attempts to realign incentives through capital controls.

With respect to the country-specific variables, model specifications (3) to (16) only the rule of law has a consistently significant impact on external discipline and leverage dynamics. The estimated coefficients indicate that stronger confidence and compliance with property rights and terms and conditions of contract induce a negative relationship between leverage and asset risk. At the margin, leverage decreases with additional risk-taking as institutional quality improves. Therefore, institutional development strengthens external discipline and is more conducive to financial consumer protection.

Expectations of accommodative interventions at times of difficulty seem to encourage imprudent behaviour. The recent global financial crisis has, indeed, validated such expectations. At least at the level of conventional banking, regulatory forbearance and intervention policies appear to have rendered government guarantees fully credible (Cubillas et al. 2012). Depositors demand little reduction in leverage in response to increase in riskiness. Meanwhile, it seems that banks have succeeded in raising the level of financial leverage amidst increased volatility. This is consistent with the reduced market discipline widely observed in both the US and the EU during the crisis (Berger et al. 2015). Governments' reactions to the crisis and concerns for bank runs presented no further disciplinary constraints and failed to protect financial consumers. The findings are inconclusive with regards to the influence of the rest of variables on external disciplining incentives.

5 Conclusion

Our findings shed light on the significant implications of Islamic banking reforms and the general framework of regulations and supervision intended for strengthening financial consumer protection. They reaffirm the shortcomings in transparency, deterrence and accountability. Not only do Islamic banks fall short of their axiomatic disciplinary advantage. It is clear that external discipline, more broadly, fails to restrain excessive risk-taking. Worse still, risky banks succeeded in amassing financial leverage along the way. This state of affairs calls for immediate remedial actions and regulatory reforms.

Reform is necessary to correct distortions in the present regulatory and supervisory framework that contribute to excessive risk-taking and risk-shifting (Garcia et al. 2004). Policies ought to be reshaped to ensure that losses are borne by those, who are compensated for their risk bearing during the normal course of business, rather than by depositors and taxpayers.

Despite the significance of capitalization ratio, which lends credence to regulatory attempts to realign incentives through capital controls, its efficacy is not unconditional. It depends on informational, ethical, and economic considerations (Hovakimian et al. 2003; Hovakimian and Kane 2000). Policy makers should refocus on measures that alter the bank attitudes toward risk and increase disciplinary incentives for depositors. Increased capital requirements and stricter disclosure rules in regimes that simultaneously weaken private discipline have not been sufficient. Basel II pillars of capital adequacy, bank supervision and market discipline are potentially more effective collectively (Distinguin et al. 2011). To achieve this, conventional and Islamic financial regulators have to strengthen deterrence, accountability and transparency.

Furthermore, an efficient stock market can effectively complement and supplement the regulatory and supervisory framework and compensate the inadequacy of private discipline. Similarly, information intermediaries, such as rating agencies, research analysts and financial media, can provide valuable means to improve transparency and information flow (Bushman, 2016). But incentives for accurate and independent due diligence must be strengthened and overseen by reinforcing accountability and stressing reputational stake (Čihák et al. 2013).

References

Abedifar, Pejman, Philip Molyneux, and Amine Tarazi. 2013. "Risk in Islamic Banking." *Review of Finance* 17(6): 2035–2096.

Admati, Anat R., Peter M. Demarzo, Martin F. Hellwig, and Paul Pfleiderer. 2012. "Debt Overhang and Capital Regulation." Working Paper, Rock Center for Corporate Governance at Stanford University; and research paper, Stanford Graduate School of Business, Stanford, CA; Preprint 2012/05, Max Planck Institute for Research on Collective Goods, Bonn, Germany.

Admati, Anat R., Peter M. Demarzo, Martin F. Hellwig, and Paul Pfleiderer. 2013. "Fallacies, Irrelevant Facts, and Myths in the Discussion of Capital Regulation: Why Bank Equity Is Not Socially Expensive." Discussion Paper Series of the Max Planck Institute for Research on Collective Goods 2013–23, Max Planck Institute for Research on Collective Goods, Bonn.

Ashraf, Ali and Kabir M. Hassan, and Syed Abul Basher. 2015. "Loan Loss Provisioning in OIC Countries: Evidence from Conventional vs. Islamic Banks." *Journal of King Abdulaziz University: Islamic Economics* 28(1): 23–59.

Arellano, Manuel, and Stephen Bond. 1991. "Some Tests of Specification for Panel Data: Monte Carlo Evidence and an Application to Employment Equations." *Review of Economic Studies* 58: 277–97.

Askari, Hossein, Zamir Iqbal, Noureddine Krichene, and Abbas Mirakhor. 2012. *Risk-Sharing in Finance: The Islamic Finance Alternative*. Singapore: John Wiley & Sons (Asia) Pte.Ltd.

Barth, James R., Daniel E Nolle, Triphon Phumiwasana, and Glenn Yago. 2003. "A Cross-Country Analysis of the Bank Supervisory Framework and Bank Performance." *Financial Markets, Institutions and Instruments 12*(2): 67–120.

Baumann, Ursel, and Erlend Nier. 2006. "Market Discipline, Disclosure and Moral Hazard in Banking." *Journal of Financial Intermediation* 15: 332–361. doi: 10.1016/j.jfi.2006.03.001.

Beck, Thorsten, Asli Demirgüç-Kunt, and Ouarda Merrouche. 2013. "Islamic vs. Conventional Banking: Business Model, Efficiency and Stability." *Journal of Banking and Finance* 37: 433–447.

Benes, Jaromir, and Michael Kumhof. 2012. "The Chicago Plan Revisited." IMF Working Paper WP/12/202, International Monetary Fund, Washington, DC.

Benston, George J., Robert Allen Eisenbeis, Paul M. Horvitz, Edward J. Kane, and George G. Kaufman. 1986. *Perspectives on Safe and Sound Banking: Past, Present, and Future.* Cambridge: MIT Press.

Berger, Allen N., and Rima Turk-Ariss. 2015. "Do Depositors Discipline Banks and Did Government Actions during the Recent Crisis Reduce this Discipline? An International Perspective." *Journal of Financial Services Research* 48: 103–126.

Bigg, Anne M. 1999. "Risk-Shifting Behaviour of Australian Banks 1992–1997." MAFC Research Paper No 21. Applied Finance Centre, Macquarie University, Sydney.

Billett, Matthew. T., Jon A. Garfinkel, and Edward S. O'Neal. 1998. "The Cost of Market Versus Regulatory Discipline in Banking." *Journal of Financial Economics* 48: 333–358.

Brei, Michael, and Leonardo Gambacorta. 2014. "The Leverage Ratio Over the Cycle." BIS Working Papers 471. Bank for International Settlements. Accessed November 1, 2017.

Bushman, Robert M. 2016. "Transparency, Accounting Discretion and Bank Stability." *Economic Policy Review* 22(1): 129–149.

Bushman, Robert M., and Christopher D.Williams. 2007. "Bank Transparency, Loan Loss Provisioning Behavior, and Risk-Shifting." Working Paper, University of North Carolina, Chapel Hill.

Bushman, Robert M., and Christopher D. Williams. 2012. "Accounting Discretion, Loan Loss Provisioning, and Discipline of Banks' Risk-Taking." *Journal of Accounting and Economics* 54: 1–18.

Carbo-Valverde, Santiago, Edward J. Kane, and Francisco Rodriguez-Fernandez. 2011. "Safety-Net Benefits Conferred on Difficult-to-Fail-and-Unwind Banks in The US and EU before and during the Great Recession." NBER Working Paper 16787, National Bureau of Economic Research, Cambridge, MA.

Dias, Denise. 2013. "Implementing Consumer Protection in Emerging Markets and Developing Economies -A Technical Guide for Bank Supervisors." Washington, DC: CGAP. Accessed March 1, 2018.

Chang, Chuang-Chang, and Wei-Ju Chen. 2013. "Risk-Shifting Behavior in Taiwan's Commercial Banks under Different Deposit Insurance Systems." *Journal of Financial Studies* 21(4): 1–24.

Chang, Chuang-Chang, and Ruey-Jenn Ho. 2017. "Risk-Shifting Behavior at Commercial Banks under Different Deposit Insurance Systems: Further Evidence from U.S. Markets." *The Journal of Financial Research* 1: 55–80. doi: 10.1111/jfir.12117.

Čihák, Martin, Asli Demirgüç-Kuntand, and R. Barry Johnston. 2013. "Incentive Audits: a New Approach to Financial Regulation." Policy Research Working Paper Series 6308, The World Bank, Washington, DC.

Claessens, Stijn, Ceyla Pazarbasioglu, Luc Laeven, Marc Dobler, Fabian Valencia, Oana Nedelescu, and Katharine Sealcl. 2011. "Crisis Management and Resolution: Early Lessons from the Financial Crisis." IMF Staff Discussion Notes 11/05, International Monetary Fund, Washington, DC.

Cubillas, Elena, Ana Rosa Fonseca, and Francisco Gonzalez. 2012. "Banking Crises and Market Discipline: International Evidence." *Journal of Banking and Finance* 36: 2285–2298.
Demirgüç-Kunt, Asli, and Edward J. Kane. 2002. "Deposit Insurance around the Globe: Where Does It Work?" *Journal of Economic Perspectives* 16: 175–195.
Demirgüç-Kunt, Asli, and Enrica Detragiache. 2002. "Does Deposit Insurance Increase Banking Stability? An Empirical Investigation." *Journal of Monetary Economics* 49(7): 1373–1406.
Demirgüç-Kunt, Asli, Edward J. Kane, and Luc Laeven (Eds). 2009. *Deposit Insurance Around the World: Issues of Design and Implementation.* Washington, DC: The World Bank
DeYoung, Robert, and Tara Rice. 2004. "How Do Banks Make Money? A Variety of Business Strategies." *Economic Perspectives 28*(4): 52–67.
Distinguin, Isabelle, Tchudjane Kouassi, and Amine Tarazi. 2011. "Deposit Insurance, Moral Hazard and Market Discipline: Evidence from Central and Eastern European Banks." Working Paper Series, University de Limoges, France.
Distinguin, Isabelle, Tchudjane Kouassi, and Amine Tarazi. 2013. "Interbank Deposits and Market Discipline: Evidence from Central and Eastern Europe." *Journal of Comparative Economics* 41 (2): 544–560.
Duan, Jin-Chuann, Arthur F. Moreau, and Calvin William Sealey. 1992. "Fixed-Rate Deposit Insurance and Risk-shifting Behavior at Commercial Banks." *Journal of Banking and Finance* 16: 715–742.
Ellis, David M., and Mark Jeffrey Flannery. 1992. "Does the Debt Market Assess Large Banks' Risk?" *Journal of Monetary Economics* 30: 481–502.
Esty, Benjamin C. 1997. "Organizational Form and Risk-taking in the Savings and Loan Industry." *Journal of Financial Economics* 44: 25–55.
Flannery, Mark Jeffrey. 1998. "Using Market Information in Prudential Bank Supervision: A Review of the U.S. Empirical Evidence." *Journal of Money, Credit and Banking* 30(3): 273–305.
Flannery, Mark Jeffrey, and Sorin M. Sorescu. 1996. "Evidence of Bank Market Discipline in Subordinated Debenture Yields: 1983–1991." *Journal of Finance* 51: 1347–1377.
Farooq, Moazzam, and Sajjad Zaheer. 2015. "Are Islamic Banks More Resilient during Financial Panics?" *Pacific Economic Review* 20 (1): 101–124. doi: 10.1111/1468-0106.12096.
Frankel, Jeffrey. 2007. "Responding to Crises." *Cato Journal*, Cato Institute, 27(2): 165–178.
Furlong, Frederick T., and Michael C. Keeley. 1989. "Capital Regulation and Bank Risk-Taking: A Note." *Journal of Banking and Finance* 13(6): 883–891.
Furlong, Frederick T., and Michael C. Keeley. 1990. "A Reexamination of Mean-Variance Analysis of Bank Capital Regulation." *Journal of Banking and Finance* 14(1): 69–84.
Garcia, Valeriano, Vincent F. Cibils, and Rudolfo Marino. 2004. "Remedy for Banking Crises: What Chicago and Islam Have in Common." *Islamic Economic Studies* 11(2): 23–42.
Gerrard, Phillip, and J. Barton Cunningham. 1997. "Islamic Banking: A Study in Singapore." *International Journal of Bank Marketing* 15(6): 204–216.
Gropp, Reint, and Jukka M. Vesala. 2004. "Deposit Insurance and Moral Hazard: Does the Counterfactual Matter?" *Review of Finance* 8: 571–602.
Gropp, Reint, Jukka M. Vesala, and Giuseppe Vulpes. 2006. "Equity and Bond Market Signals as Leading Indicators of Bank Fragility." *Journal of Money, Credit and Banking* 38(2): 399–428.
Guizani, Brahim, and Wako Watanabe. 2010. "The Deposit Insurance and the Risk-Shifting Incentive Evidence from the Blanket Deposit Insurance in Japan." Keio/Kyoto Joint Global COE Discussion Paper Series 2010-004, Keio/Kyoto Joint Global COE Program.
Hamalainen, Paul, Maximilian Hall, and Barry Howcroft. 2005. "A Framework for Market Discipline in Bank Regulatory Design." *Journal of Business Finance and Accounting* 32:183–209.
Heller, Benjamin. 2015. Review of John Kay's 'Other's People's Money'. *New York Times* (19-6-2015)
Hovakimian, Armen, and Edward J. Kane. 2000. "Effectiveness of Capital Regulation at U.S. Commercial Banks, 1985 to 1994." *Journal of Finance* 55(1): 451–468.

Hovakimian, Armen, Edward J. Kane, and Luc Laeven. 2003. "How Country and Safety-Net Characteristics Affect Bank Risk-Shifting." *Journal of Financial Services Research* 23(3): 177–204.

International Finance Corporation (IFC). 2015. "Promoting Financial Consumer Protection in Cambodia." July 2015. Accessed July 13, 2017. https://www.ifc.org/wps/wcm/connect/6c12edf9-22e9-446f-b025-0c366948b87a/Cambodia+Financial+Consumer+protection-Final.pdf?MOD=AJPERES

Islamic Financial Services Board (IFSB). 2010. "Guidance Note on the Practice of Smoothing the Profits Payout to Investment Account Holders." December 2010. Accessed July 9, 2017. https://www.ifsb.org/standard/eng_GN-3_Guidance_Note_on_the_Practice_of_Smoothing.pdf

Islamic Financial Services Board (IFSB). 2015. "Guidance Note on Quantitative Measures for Liquidity Risk Management in Institutions Offering Islamic Financial Services [Excluding Islamic Insurance (Takâful) Institutions and Islamic Collective Investment Schemes]". April 2015.

Jagtiani, Julapa, George Kaufman, and Catharine Lemieux. 2000. "Do Markets Discipline Banks and Bank Holding Companies? Evidence from Debt Pricing." Emerging Issues Series (Jun), Federal Reserve Bank of Chicago, Supervision and Regulation Department.

Jiménez, Gabriel, Jose A. Lopez, and Jesus Saurina. 2013. "How Does Competition Affect Bank Risk-Taking?" *Journal of Financial Stability* 9(2): 185–195.

Jiménez, Gabriel, Steven Ongena, Jose-Luis Peydro, and Jesus Saurina. 2014. "Hazardous Times for Monetary Policy: What Do Twenty-Three Million Bank Loans Say about the Effects of Monetary Policy on Credit Risk-Taking?" *Econometrica* 82(2): 463–505.

Kammer, Alfred, Mohamed Norat, Marco Pinon, Ananthakrishnan Prasad, Christopher M. Towe, Zeine Zeidane, and IMF Staff Team. 2015. "Islamic Finance: Opportunities, Challenges, and Policy Options." IMF Staff Discussion Note 15/05, International Monetary Fund, Washington, DC.

Keen, Michael, and Ruud de Mooij. 2012. "Debt, Taxes and Banks." IMF Working Paper WP/12/48, International Monetary Fund, Washington, DC.

Keynes, John Maynard. 1930. *A Treaties on Money*. London: Macmillan.

Keynes, John Maynard.1936. *The General Theory of Employment, Interest and Money*. New York: Harbinger.

Kuala Lumpur Declaration, 2012. Available from ISRA's website (20th September, 2012).

Lajis, Siti Muawanah. 2015. "Towards Risk-Sharing Regulatory Framework: A Case for Malaysia (Unpublished doctoral dissertation)." Kuala Lumpur: International Centre for Education in Islamic Finance (INCEIF).

Lee, Chien-Chiang, and Meng-Fen Hsieh. 2013. "The Impact of Bank Capital on Profitability and Risk in Asian Banking." *Journal of International Money and Finance* 32: 251–281.

Martinez Peria, Maria Soledad, and Sergio L. Schmukler. 2001. "Do Depositors Punish Banks for Bad Behavior? Market Discipline, Deposit Insurance, and Banking Crises." *The Journal of Finance* 56(3): 1029–1052.

Merton, Robert Cox. 1977. "An Analytic Derivation of the Cost of Deposit Insurance and Loan Guarantees: An Application of Modern Option Pricing Theory." *Journal of Banking and Finance* 1(1): 3–11.

Mirakhor, Abbas, Noureddine Krichene, and Mughees Shaukat. 2012. "Unsustainability of the Regime of Interest-Based Debt Financing." *ISRA International Journal of Islamic Finance* 4(2): 25–52.

Misman, Farida Najuna, and Wahida Ahmad. 2011. "Loan Loss Provisions: Evidence from Malaysian Islamic and Conventional Banks." *International Review of Business Research Papers* 7(4): 94–103.

Mohseni-Cheraghlou, Amin. 2015. "Islamic Finance, Financial Inclusion and Poverty Reduction in MENA." Chapter 20 in *Routledge Handbook of Religions and Global Development*, edited by Emma Tomalin, 293–314. New York: Routledge.

Mooij De, Ruud, Michael Keen, and Masanori Orihara. 2013. "Taxation, Bank Leverage, and Financial Crises." IMF Working Paper WP/13/48, International Monetary Fund, Washington, DC.

Musgrave, Ralph S. 2014. "The Solution is Full Reserve / 100% Reserve Banking." MPRA Paper No. 57955, University Library of Munich, Germany.

Myers, Stewart C., and Nicholas S. Majluf. 1984. "Corporate Financing and Investment Decisions When Firms Have Information That Investors Do Not Have." *Journal of Financial Economics* 13: 187–221.

Omet, Ghassan. and Nidal Fayyoumi. 2004. "Do Depositors Discipline for Risk and Reward for Cash Prizes: The Case of the Jordanian Banking Sector." Presented at the 11th Annual Conference: Post Conflict Reconstruction, Lebanon.

Othman, Hakin Ben, and Hounaida Mersni. 2012. "The Use of Discretionary Loan Loss Provision by Islamic Banks and Conventional Banks in the Middle East Region: A Comparative Study." Presented at the International Conference on Excellence in Business, Sharjah, United Arab Emirates, 09–10 May 2012.

Ozerturk, Saltuk. 2002. "Risk Sharing, Risk-shifting and Optimality of Convertible Debt in Venture Capital." Working paper, Southern Methodist University.

Piketty, Thomas. 2013. *Capital in the Twenty-First Century*. Paris: Editions du Seuil.

Poole, William. 2007. "Responding to Financial Crises: What Role for the Fed?" *Cato Journal*, Cato Institute, 27(2): 149–155.

Reinhart, Carmen, and Kenneth Rogoff. 2009. *The Time Is Different: Eight Centuries of Financial Folly*. Princeton: Princeton University Press.

Rosly, Saiful Azhar. 1999. "Al-bay' Bithaman Ajil Financing: Impacts of Islamic Banking Performance." *Thunderbird International Business Review* 41: 461–480.

Sheng, Andrew. 2009. *From Asian to Global Financial Crisis*. Cambridge: Cambridge University Press.

Sironi, Andrea. 2003. "Testing for Market Discipline in the European Banking Industry: Evidence from Subordinated Debt Issues." *Journal of Money, Credit, and Banking* 35: 443–472.

Standing Committee for Economic and Commercial Cooperation of the Organization of the Islamic Cooperation (COMCEC). 2014. "Financial outlook of the OIC member countries." Ankara: COMCEC Coordination Office.

Statistical Economics and Social Research and Training Center for Islamic Countries (SESRIC). 2012. "OIC Outlook Series: Islamic Finance in OIC Member Countries." Ankara: SESRIC Publications.

Stolz, Stéphanie M. 2007. *Bank Capital and Risk Taking*. Heidelberg: Springer.

Turner, Adair. 2010. "What Do Banks Do? Why Do Credit Booms and Busts Occur and What Can Public Policy Do About It." Chapter 1 in *The Future of Finance: The LSE Report*, by Adair Turner et al., 5–86. London: London School of Economics and Political Science.

Van Wijnbergen, Sweder J.G., Sajjad Zaheer, and Moazzam Farooq. 2013. "Capital Structure, Risk-shifting and Stability: Conventional and Islamic Banking." Tibergen Institute Discussion paper.

Wagster, John D. 2007. "Wealth and Risk Effects of Adopting Deposit Insurance in Canada: Evidence of Risk-Shifting by Banks and Trust Companies." *Journal of Money, Credit and Banking* 39(7): 1651–1681.

Part V: Financial Institutions and Financial System Stability

Muhammed Habib Dolgun

Chapter 17: Analytical Assessment of Liquidity Risk Management in Islamic Banks

1 Introduction

Liquidity risk can be defined as a shortcoming to cover current financial liabilities. In general, liquidity risk is considered as a determinant of other risks, such as credit risk or determinant of bank performance (Arif and Anees 2012). An examination of the liquidity risk management in an Islamic banking context is crucial to promoting efficiency, growth, and resilience of the Islamic financial industry. While the resilience of the Islamic banking system during the recent Global Financial Crisis highlights its potential contributive role to financial stability, particularly in countries with significant presence of Islamic banks, there remain several concerns. After the 2008 crisis, the global liquidity has been increased by central banks. The central banks injected considerable amount of liquidity and enlarged their reserves several times. For instance, the balance sheet of the Federal Reserve of USA exceeded over 4 trillion US dollars in 2013. Many emerging countries have enjoyed similar levels of liquidity. Islamic banks also have relished much of this liquidity abundance. Since Islamic banks had a more robust mechanism compared to their conventional counterparts, this liquidity helped them to increase the size of their assets. However, global liquidity is pulling back and central banks including Federal Reserve have already started their normalization period. In this new global liquidity environment, Islamic banks may experience serious liquidity problems in foreign currencies in a lower liquidity environment. Furthermore, the Islamic financial markets in many countries are in their infancy stage. Accordingly, they may not be able to withstand the challenges and risks stemming from adverse systemic disturbances and financial shocks.

For sustained real sector financing, the Islamic banking should be protected against financial imbalances and vulnerabilities by introducing relevant sector-specific prudential intruments. A key risk factor relating to financial stability that deserves urgent attention is liquidity risk management. It is well recognized that sustainable liquidity risk management is central to the banks' continuous financing and protection against systemic risks. In this chapter, after literature review, liquidity risk management of Islamic banks will be evaluated and then challenges for proper liquidity risk management are analytically assessed. After that, Basel III and IFSB regulations will be discussed. And then, a model will be employed for analysing the relationship between liquid assets and financing assets of participation banks in Turkey. Lastly, several policy recommendations are developed for regulators.

https://doi.org/10.1515/9783110587920-017

2 Literature Review of Islamic Banks' Liquidity Management

Islamic banks have some structural differences from conventional banks in the context of contracts and the liability side of their balance sheets (Verhoef et al. 2008). Deposits of Islamic banks are composed mainly of three classes of accounts: current account deposits, saving deposits, and investment deposits. Investment accounts are divided into restricted investment accounts and unrestricted investment accounts. Even in the case of the latter, account holders have an option to withdraw their investments before maturity. There is a possibility of premature withdrawal by account holders when there is a mismatch between realized returns and investor expectations. In a perfect liquidity management system, it may be theoretically possible to estimate the likely demand for withdrawal. If this estimation is nearly perfect, banks need to keep only that estimated portion as liquid cash or near-cash items. In practice, however, most Islamic banks hold high levels of excess cash.

The Basel III liquidity coverage ratio (LCR) requirements may lead to implementation challenges for Islamic banks in upcoming years due to the inadequate availability of high-quality liquid assets and difficulties in calibrating the structure to suit the practices of Islamic banks, which have important differences from their conventional counterparts' applications. Unfortunately, the effects of these new standards on Islamic banks have not been well-analyzed by theoretical and empirical research. There are indeed a few studies on these regulatory issues. Even though Islamic banks have to keep significant funds as cash to meet regulatory requirements, Ismal (2010) suggests that Indonesian Islamic banks have historically managed liquidity well, though the industry is too fragile. He shows a trade-off between self-insurance against liquidity risks and opportunity costs of holding liquid assets.

A proper understanding of the macroeconomic situation and regulatory framework is, therefore, important for addressing this trade-off. Mongid (2015) explores the liquidity risk management of small Indonesian Islamic banks and claims that the liquidity risk of Islamic banks is determined by capital adequacy as well as asset management and leverage. But the shortcoming of this study is that the effects of macroeconomic factors or economic environment variables, such as inflation rate, central bank fund rate or interbank rate were not included in the model. Ashraf et al. (2016) studied the impact of the Net Stable Funding Ratio (NSFR) on the financial stability of Islamic banks and found that the modified NSFR will have a positive influence on the financial stability of Islamic banks. Financial stability is a term used for all financial services and regulators do not prefer to use this term for a particular sector. The evidence suggests that the marginal impact of the NSFR on stability weakens as the size of the bank increases. This means that if Islamic banks continue to grow, the positive implications of the NSFR on this sector will diminish.

Among the recent empirical studies, Rashid and Jabeen (2016) examine the bank-specific, financial, and macroeconomic determinants of the performance of Islamic and conventional banks in Pakistan. By using an unbalanced annual panel data and the GLS regression, they showed that the performance of Islamic banks can be explained by operating efficiency, deposits, and market concentration. Rashid and Jabeen (2016) showed that the impact of the lending interest rate on performance is negative for Islamic banks. Many international organizations, supervisory and regulatory authorities, and policy makers have examined various aspects of Islamic financial intermediation, each from their own perspective. Most of this research provides evidence of greater resilience (Bourkhis and Mahmud 2013) and better financial performance of Islamic banks during crises on account of their higher asset quality despite the lack of high-quality liquid instruments. Moreover, this greater degree of resilience may be related to small bank effects (Hasan and Dridi 2010).

Although Basel regulations were developed for internationally active and large banks, most Islamic banks are rather small banks and have been subject to these liquidity standards. The majority of these small banks are scale inefficient in the sense that both profitability and capitalisation were the primary determinants of Islamic banking efficiency (Rosman et al. 2014). In this context, Saeed and Izzeldin (2014) suggest that a decrease in default risk is associated with lower efficiency levels. However, Alam (2013) finds that banking regulations increase the technical efficiency for Islamic banks and suggest that Islamic banks appear to be technically efficient in stricter regulatory conditions. However, tighter regulatory conditions improve the risk-transfer ability of banks, which results in avoiding risk-sharing contracts. Since Alam (2013)'s study covers data for the period 2006–2010, new studies based on more granular data are needed to evaluate the effects of Basel reforms on Islamic banks' efficiency.

Macroeconomic control variables can also influence the behaviour of Islamic banks in managing liquidity according to Mohamad et al. (2013) based on evidence about Malaysian banks. The same evidence is obtained by Krasicka and Nowak (2012) who suggest that Malaysian Islamic banks have responded to economic and financial shocks in the same way as Malaysian conventional banks. Using parametric and non-parametric classification models, Khediri et al. (2015) find that Islamic banks are, on average, more liquid and profitable than conventional banks. Soylu and Durmaz (2013) show that Islamic banks in Turkey have effective and reasonably strong rates of profitability, in light of the lower level of profitability of conventional banks. Islamic banks in Turkey are noticeably influenced by interest rates (Ergec and Arslan 2013). Being influenced by interest rates may relate to being governed by the same banking law and not having any specific money market inclusive for participation banks.

It is accepted that short-term instruments are more liquid than long-term assets. Short-term excess liquidity is managed through the money markets. Several countries have developed money markets for Islamic banks, where Islamic banks can convert assets into liquid ones when needed. These mechanisms allow Islamic banks to manage liquidity while staying profitable. Islamic banks may have excess liquidity because of the regulatory framework that requires achievement of the requirements for of the liquidity coverage ratio (LCR) standards. This excess liquidity can decrease Islamic banks' profits and limit their market share. Variously, for Islamic financial system, Akhtar (2007) suggests that regulators should adopt different approaches. Haan and End (2013) find that most banks hold more liquid assets against liquid liabilities than strictly required. More solvent banks hold less liquid assets against their stock of liquid liabilities, suggesting an interaction between capital and liquidity buffers. However, specific needs of Islamic financial institutions should be taken into consideration when the regulatory framework is developed (Hesse et al. 2008).

It is suggested that the implementation of reforms in emerging markets needs to be sequenced while taking into account several factors. Adam and Thomas (2005) claim that the current regulatory framework should protect the confidence of Muslims in the system as well as their investments. Since this structure punishes Islamic contracts by imposing the current risk-weight system, Islamic banks restrict their activities and are reluctant to introduce new products based on risk-sharing. It is claimed that risk-sharing feature of Islamic banks may facilitate the absorption of external shocks and restrain agains cash outflows because under the risk-sharing system, there would be better transformation between liabilities and assets (Mirakhor 2012; Maghrebi and Mirakhor 2015).

However, Chong and Liu (2009) suggest that most of the deposits are not invested in risk-sharing financing. Instead of questioning the reasons behind this behavior of banks, they conclude that Islamic banks should be regulated and supervised under the same regulations as conventional banks because they are offering similar products (Chong and Liu 2009). In this context, advocates of this position have to answer the following questions: If Islamic banks are offering the same products and they are being regulated in a similar manner as conventional banks, why do we need Islamic banks?

On the other hand, Mirakhor et al. (2012) explore the characteristics, operations, and benefits of a comprehensive risk-sharing financial system for long-term economic and social prosperity and present the development of Islamic finance as a stable financial system. In this mechanism, a free flow of information in the market may increase efficiency (Mirakhor, 2010) and decrease vulnerabilities. To reinforce the efficiency of market operations, trust is needed to be established among participants, transaction costs to be minimized, and rules set up to internalize externalities of two-party transactions by decreasing asymmetric information and providing the regulatory base for different expectations and beliefs of investors. One of the earlier studies on the efficiency of products of Islamic banks was conducted by Rosly and Bakar (2003), who find that Islamic banks that provide markup-based financing products are less likely to outshine mainstream banks in terms of efficiency. They claim that these products lack the necessary moral content and providing these contracts does not increase the efficiency of Islamic banks.

3 Challenges for Islamic Banks

The Islamic banking industry is confronted with several challenges regarding liquidity management. Since an Islamic Financial Institution is not allowed to use interest-based financing resources from interbank money markets or other resources (such as using interest-based central bank's facilities via open market channels) and is not allowed to transfer its debt, Islamic banks have disadvantages concerning liquidity management compared to conventional banks.

After introducing Liquidity Coverage Ratio (LCR) standards by the Basel Committee, the IFSB adopted the LCR for Islamic banks (IFSB, 2015), which requires to hold High-Quality Liquid Assets (HQLA) as reserve. Although the Basel III framework allows local authorities to use discretion power in granting preferential treatment to certain assets, most supervisors of Islamic banks have a tendency to mimic the conventional regulatory framework to avoid non-compliance to Basel standards and possible negative assessment by international organizations and international market players.[169] Mechanical application of the recommended methodology of the BIS and the IFSB standards may not be appropriate especially for risk-sharing and partnership based financial instruments.

The main challenges are discussed below in detail:

(i) There is a dearth of *Shariah*-compliant securities or highly liquid *sukuk* in many jurisdictions (IFSB, 2015). Although there is not any globally systemic important bank in any country, Islamic banking sectors are accepted as systemically important in 12 jurisdictions, in which Islamic banking sector's share in total banking sector has reached 15% (IFSB, 2018) and liquid assets are very vital for liquidity risk management of systemically important banks. Since high quality liquid assets are inadequate for Islamic banks' investment, regulators need to change the regulatory framework for accepting alternative treatments. Although, many countries are issuing *sukuk*, most of these *sukuk* are not accepted as high-quality liquid assets (HQLA) and issuance trend of Sukuk is not stable (Figure 17.1). Islamic banks need more stable issuances of Sukuk that are treated as HQLA for their liquidity risk management.

(ii) In addition, even there are several *Shariah*-compliant sukuk or securities in some jurisdictions, the secondary markets for these assets are thin or underdeveloped. The absence of *Shariah*-complaint lender of last resort (LoLR) facility in many countries places further constraint on Islamic banks' ability to mitigate liquidity risk (Mohammad 2013). Having the relevant lender of last resort facility may promote moral hazard

169 Preferential treatments have been introduced since the introduction of Basel I. Some countries use these treatments for special sectors that are preferred to protect. For example, GCC countries (Bahrain, Kuwait, Oman, Qatar, UAE and Saudi Arabia) decided mutually to apply preferential treatments for credit risk under standardised approach, which do not specifically cover Islamic banks' assets (see RCAP report of Saudi Arabia at http://www.bis.org/bcbs/publ/d335.pdf).

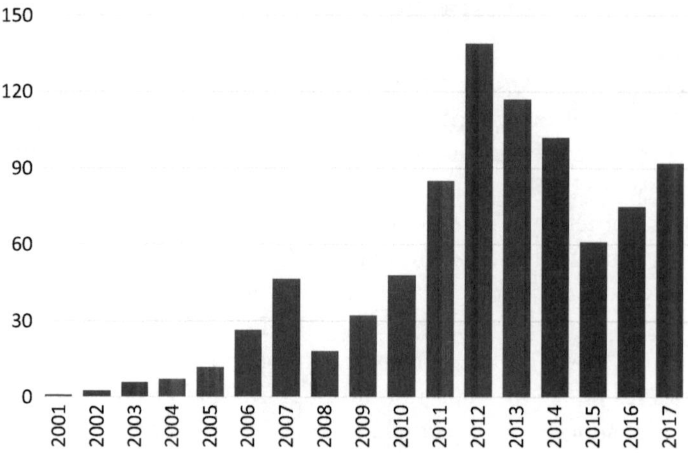

Figure 17.1: Global Sukuk Issuances (USD Billion).
Source: IFSB (2018).

behavior of these banks and consequently attenuate the efficiency of liquidity management. However, without such facility, Islamic banks could not protect themselves against sudden liquidity changes or increasing stress in market liquidity. These factors and many others can impact the performance, growth, and portfolio management of Islamic banks as well as confidence of investors. Moreover, the distinctive behavior of Islamic banks concerning asset-liability management, capital adequacy requirement, loan portfolio risk-taking and interbank demand hinder their capacity to undertake a comparable liquidity transformation as their conventional counterparts.

(iii) Islamic banks hold more cash than normally needed. Table 17.1 shows that cash and cash-equivalent assets of Islamic banks represents 9% of total HQLA assets of these banks in 2014. Total central bank reserves are around 30% of total HQLA stocks. This table shows that Islamic banks place almost 40% of their stocks in accounts that do not generate profits.

(iv) The geographical distribution of Islamic banking suggests that the rates of total sukuk size to total assets ratio differs according to regions. While in some countries more sukuk are issued, and in some countries only few sukuk are available for investors (Table 17.2). In Asia region, the ratio of outstanding sukuk size to total assets exceeds 100%, while in MENA region (excluding GCC) it is only 3%. This shows that there are differences in terms of conditions and market demand across regions.

(v) There is a mismatch between the maturity of assets and liabilities and it seems that Islamic banks are not undertaking maturity transformation. Thus, most Islamic banks are small banks, for which applying the Basel framework is costly. They would have cash-dominated balance sheets if they were forced to apply these standards.

Table 17.1: Islamic Banks HQLA Stocks (World).

Assets Class	Share
Level 1 Assets	**96.83**
Cash and Cash Equivalents	9.01
Total Central Bank Reserves	30.73
% Zero Risk-weighted Assets	21.45
Other Sovereign Assets which don't have % Zero Risk-weight	35.64
Level 2A Assets	**2.97**
Guaranteed by Public Authorities	0.39
Corporate Bonds (AA and higher)	2.58
Covered Bonds (AA and higher)	0
Level 2B Assets	**0.19**
Total 2B Assets	**0.06**
Other 2B Assets	**0.13**

Source: IFSB (2014).

Table 17.2: Islamic Banking Sector.

Region	Banking Assets (billion, $)	Outstanding Sukuk (billion, $)	Islamic Funds (billion, $)	Takaful (billion, $)	Total (billion, $)	Sukuk to Assets Ratio (%)
Asia	232.0	239.5	24.8	3.3	499.6	103%
GCC	683.0	139.2	26.8	12.6	861.6	20%
MENA	569.0	17.8	0.1	9.5	596.4	3%
Africa	27.1	2.0	1.6	0.7	31.4	7%
Others	46.4	1.5	13.3	0.0	61.3	3%
Total	1,557.5	399.9	66.7	26.1	2,050.2	25%

Source: IFSB (2018).

Table 17.3 shows the ratio of liquid assets to short-term deposits for Islamic banks in 14 countries. Unfortunately, it was not possible to arrive at reliable estimates of the the rates for Saudi banks (both Islamic and Islamic Window banks). According to these estimates, several Islamic banks have a chronic shortage of liquid assets whereas some others have high level of liquid assets. It seems that Islamic banks in Oman, UAE, Iran, Nigeria and Indonesia have very low ratios of liquid assets to short term deposit. On the other hand, Islamic banks in Malaysia, Afghanistan and Brunei have estimated ratios of liquid assets to short-term deposits higher than 100%.

Table 17.3: Liquid Asset to Short Term Deposit Ratio (By Country, %).

Country	2013	2014	2015	2016	2017
Qatar				58.9	62.9
Oman	1408.3	360.9	36.4	24.9	22.8
Bangladesh (F &W)	65.2	77.2	62.4	67.8	82.9
Malaysia (F&W)	22	24.3	79.3	112	122.7
Sudan	99.4	95.9	96.3	88.6	82.3
UAE	20.6	19.8	16.8	17.1	17.8
Indonesia (F&W)	25	19.7	21.3	21.3	20
Turkey	86.3	78.4	74.2	63.8	68
Jordan	62.1	63.2	62.2	58.7	58.6
Iran		23.6	18.8	15.7	11.7
Afghanstan (W)	178.6	195.9	152.1	124	152.1
Nigeria	78	52.9	52.8	48.8	18.9
Pakistan	60.4	73.8	68.2	78.7	68.1
Brunei	119.3	119.3	110.2	114.8	113.9

Source: Author's own.

(vi) Lack of globally accepted *Shariah*-compliant liquidity management scheme is another important challenge for Islamic banks. The current regulatory framework for liquidity management has a negative effect on participation banks' credit and a positive effect on their cash positions (see Table 17.4). Therefore, it should be reformulated to allow these banks increase their risk-sharing financing and keep and maintain an optimal and reasonable amount of cash. This means that the current regulatory framework of liquidity based on conventional ontology has direct effects on the portfolio of Islamic banks. Participation banks are not working in an isolated environment. The macro financial and political environment is affected by conventional ontology, epistemology and methodology. All sectors, mainly the government sector, household sector, foreign trade and corporate sector have many rules that are shaped by conventional thinking. Without reforming some parts of this conventional environment, it would not be easy for Islamic banks to pursue their mission.

(vii) High cost of issuing new products or existing instruments compared to conventional ones. Especially in *sukuk* issuances, Islamic banks have to bear some costs which are not seen in conventional bonds issuances, such as Shariah advisory cost or legal costs for preparing related documents.

(viii) Different legal, regulatory and tax frameworks amongst jurisdictions are conducive to problems related to cross-border liquidity markets and infrastructure. Not having enough tradable instruments is another vital challenge for Islamic banks' proper liquidity risk management. Furthermore, the risk-sharing based instruments, i.e. *mudarabah*

Table 17.4: Financing-to-Deposit Ratio (By Country, %).

Country	2013	2014	2015	2016	2017
Qatar	85	87	104	106	110
Oman	110	140	108	106	104
Bangladesh	85	94.8	95	95	96.3
Malaysia	85	88	92	99	96.3
Sudan	106	112	95	88	95.9
UAE	83	88	88	94	92.3
Saudi Arabia	76	79	84	88	88
Indonesia	110	92	92	88	87.9
Turkey	109	96	90	82	83.7
Jordan	84	72	74	74	76.5
Iran	104	85	78	76	74.6
Afghanstan	30	28	26	60	66
Nigeria	34	66	60	64	60
Pakistan	40	42	48	52	58

Source: Author's calculations.

and *musharakah*, contracts, are classified as illiquid instruments. The partnership-based business model of these instruments compels authorities to apply higher risk-weight requirements than mark-up-based products under the Basel II capital requirements. As a result, the risk-sharing based instruments are not preferred by Islamic banks since they have a negative bearing on liquidity management. Although the new Islamic financial products have been developed in recent years, such as esham, GDP-linked sukuk and commodity-based sukuk, these instruments are not accepted yet as high-quality liquid assets in many countries. Furthermore, tax-neutrality conditions are not provided for Islamic banks in many countries.

(ix) Lack of a comprehensive Islamic interbank market with highly rated short-term tradable instruments is another vital challenge for Islamic banks' liquidity management. Only few countries have functional interbank market for Islamic banks. Having interbank money markets for Islamic banks would fasten convergence of Islamic banks to conventional banks, but without such money markets, Islamic banks will continue to face major difficulties in terms of finding liquidity for their daily financial activities.

(x) It is a well-known fact that Islamic banks rely on the wholesale funding markets. After the global financial crisis, several banks had challenges concerning non-performing loans and these banks increased their reliance on wholesale funding markets. Over-reliance on wholesale funding can be a serious problem for Islamic banks during periods of stress in the market. Banks cannot depend too heavily on inflows and, therefore, when designing liquidity stress tests, inflow rates should be calibrated conservatively. By turning to outflows, it appears that uninsured deposit outflows were one of the drivers of liquidity stress. Additionally, off-balance items can add to stress under some circumstances. For example, Islamic banks have certain commitments to non-financial corporations referred to as special purpose vehicles. During the recent financial crisis, it was argued that commitments to asset-backed commercial paper conduits and other capital market instruments could significantly affect banks' liquidity positions. Since sukuk has a similar structure as other asset-backed commercial paper conduits, banks that invest in the sukuk market may face the same problem in stress times.

(xi) Since Islamic banks do not rely on margin calls and pre-funding of FX swaps, these banks are on the safe side regarding the effects of these factors on the bank's liquidity position. Therefore, these factors are not causally significant in creating liquidity gaps for Islamic banks. On the other hand, liquidity risks stemming from off-balance items and derivative transactions should be handled carefully. In order to cope with large net cash outflows, banks hold liquidity buffers. The first buffer is made of cash holdings. The second buffer represents a well-defined operational mechanism, three-party's sale and buy-back agreements. Conventional banks may be able to raise funds through repo with central counterparties (CCPs) if they have such facilities, but Islamic banks do not have this opportunity.

(xii) Research suggests that the market risk is higher for Islamic banks than for their conventional counterparts (Farooqi and O'Brien 2015). Moreover, it is suggested that Islamic banks' assets are exposed to a higher risk than the assets of conventional banks (Ariss 2010). Liquidity risk management requires maintaining an appropriate level of liquid resources for liquidity management purposes.

(xiii) Islamic banking's reliance on cash reserves and use of commodities for collateral makes them comparatively more vulnerable to high inflation rate and changes in real economic activities. From the regulatory perspective, addressing these vulnerabilities in Islamic banking requires having both macroprudential instruments and microprudential tools and applications. As Pagratis et al. (2017) suggest, all classes of liquid assets are dominated by government securities as a liquidity backstop, and time deposits dominates funding vulnerabilities. Since many governments in advanced economies and emerging economies increased the issuance of government bond, *sukuk*, lease certificates and other securities in the last ten years, there are concerns related to the sustainability of massive amounts of public debt. Investigating the main vulnerabilities of Islamic banks necessitates a serious look at potential shocks originating from outside the banking sector, as well as idiosyncratic risks within these banks. Macroeconomic factors may affect the resilience of Islamic banks. The inflation rate, Credit Default Swap (CDS) rate of the country, interbank rate, market liquidity, and regulations have strongly influence on Islamic banks' portfolio selections. Since there is a strong interaction between these banks and financial markets, fire sales of illiquid assets and securities during market stress can especially affect Islamic banking sector in very short periods of time.

(xiv) After the 2008 Global Financial Crisis, the global liquidity has significantly soared. The central banks injected large amounts of liquidity and enlarged their reserves several times. For example, Federal Reserve increased its balance sheet more than four times within six years.[170] This huge amount of market liquidity went to many emerging countries and Islamic banks have enjoyed much of this liquidity abundance. As well as having a more robust mechanism, this abundant global liquidity affected the double-digit rapid growth of Islamic banking after the 2008 crisis. Now global liquidity is pulling back. However, the Federal Reserve has started to decrease its balance sheet size by more than 10%. In 2018, the European Central Bank (ECB) announced that it would start its own normalization period, as well. Islamic banks may experience serious liquidity problems in foreign currency under this new global liquidity environment.

Against these limitations, there is clearly an urgent need to enhance the liquidity management provisions for Islamic banks, especially through the adoption of reasonable applications. At present, *Shariah*-conscious investors are at disadvantage when it comes to participation in the financial services provided by Islamic banks. At the financing end, they face financing rates higher than lending rates offered by conventional banks. Meanwhile, on the other side of the banks' balance sheets, investors receive a lower profit share compared to interest rates paid by conventional banks. In the face of these challenges, *Shariah*-conscious investors may opt out from the Islamic financial system or from the entire financial system. The uneven treatment that these investors receive would likely jeopardize financial inclusion, which is purported to be one of the goals of Islamic finance. Accordingly, there is a need to improve the current regulatory framework including the liquidity standards such that the interests of these investors are protected and financial inclusion is enhanced. In essence, new liquidity standards can be effective in protecting these investors and in strengthening financial inclusion of those unwilling to be bankable under the conventional banking due to religious reasons. The results of this analysis suggest fundamental challenges faced by Islamic banks need to be addressed in order to facilitate liquidity management.

170 See https://www.federalreserve.gov/monetarypolicy/bst_recenttrends.htm.

4 Basel Liquidity Regulations and Liquidity Tools for Islamic Banks' Liquidity Management

The Global Financial Crisis showed that ample liquidity is essential for the proper functioning of financial markets and the banking sector (Bonner 2014; BIS 2013). Before the crisis, thanks to a low levels of monetary policy rate in developed markets, funding rate was very low, and funding liquidity was very high. After the crisis, however, market conditions changed very rapidly, and market liquidity and funding liquidity evaporated within days and hours. According to the BIS (2013), the primary objective of the LCR is to promote the short-term resilience of the liquidity risk profile of banks. The LCR is expected to improve the banking sector's ability to absorb shocks arising from financial and economic stress. The LCR is designed to act as a buffer against liquidity run.

The LCR was developed as a minimum level of liquidity for internationally active banks (BIS 2013). It is proposed that the LCR will contribute to banking liquidity as well as market liquidity. Banks are expected to meet this standard, but national regulatory authorities may set higher minimum levels of liquidity. Many countries including Turkey have already started to implement the LCR since January 1, 2015 with the implementation of a minimum requirement at 60% level, which will rise in equal annual steps to reach 100% by January 1, 2019. This progressive approach was recommended by the Basel Committee though many countries are already applying a higher level of LCR. A bank should have an adequate stock of HQLA for surviving 30 days of the stress scenario, which consists of cash or assets that can be easily converted into cash with acceptable loss. The LCR has been defined by the Basel committee given the following formula:

$$LCR = \frac{High\ Quality\ Liquid\ Assets}{Net\ Cash\ Outflows} \tag{1}$$

HQLA is divided into Level 1 and Level 2 assets. Level 1 assets consist of cash, bank reserves, central bank reserves and securities issued or guaranteed by governments, central banks or multilateral development banks (MDBs). There are two types of Level 2 assets: Level 2A and Level 2B. These assets consist of public sector entities` (PSE) bonds that have high quality, as well as, covered bonds and securities issued or guaranteed by MDBs. Net cash outflows are calculated as the difference between cash outflow and cash inflows. Net cash outflows are related to funding liquidity. There may be some confusion regarding the LCR's implementation which was developed as a minimum level of liquidity for internationally active banks, not for all local banks (BIS 2013). Haan and End (2013) claim that most banks hold more liquid assets than strictly required by these standards. In fact, the minimum LCR is expected to be raised from 60% in January 1, 2015 to 100% by January 1, 2019 with increases of 10% on annual basis.

There are some tools used for the liquidity management of Islamic banks such as *sukuk*, *tawarruq*, participation papers, commodity *murabahah* (Dusuki 2007). These instruments include also Cagamas mudharabah bonds, interbank deposits, interbank financing, interbank *murabahah*, central bank wadiah acceptance, Islamic repo and interbank wakalah (Verhoef et al. 2008). Malaysian Islamic banks are very fortunate to have some liquidity management tools available. However, Islamic banks in Turkey and other countries do not have such a wide choice of instruments. They have to invest in *sukuk*, commodity murabaha or maintain their assets in cash. Obviously, these limited tools are not adequate for ensuring an efficient risk management by Turkish participation banks because of the gap between the supply and demand functions of these instruments.

According to the IFSB (2014), the high-quality liquid assets of seven countries mainly consist of Level 1 assets. This research shows that Islamic banks store 30% of their liquid instruments in central banks accounts or cash accounts. Part of the reason may have to do with protection against market liquidity and constraints related to regulatory standards. Many metrics are used for evaluating the liquidity of assets including bid-ask spread (the difference between demand price and supply price of an asset), turnover ratio (the percentage of an asset that is replaced at a given time) and Amihud illiquidity defined and formulated by Amihud et al. (2005). By applying these metrics, various asset liqidity levels can be determined and assessed from different perspectives. Liquidity shortages may stem from the bank's liability side, due to depositor runs (liquidity issue) or withdrawals of interbank deposits (creditability issue). The recent Global Financial Crisis showed that prevailing market liquidity could evaporate rather very quickly, affecting the market value of banks' assets. This may trigger fire sales (selling assets at heavily discounted prices) and a herding behavior leading to further asset sales. The model of Diamond and Rajan (2005) also focuses on the bank's asset side and shows that a shrinking common pool of liquidity worsens aggregate liquidity shortages. Boss et al. (2006) have developed a system in which models for market and credit risk are brought together and are connected to an interbank network module. This is similar to the framework developed by Alessandri et al. (2009) which also take into account the effects of network spillover risks and asset-price feedback. In consideration of the impact of network spillover risks and liquidity risks, such effects may result in the failure of some banks.

5 Modeling the Relationship between Liquidity Regulations and Banks' Financing

Banerjee and Mio (2014) argue that after the introduction of the LCR which brings together tougher liquidity regulations, banks replaced claims on other financial institutions with cash, central bank reserves and government bonds – and so reduced the interconnectedness of the banking sector without affecting the capacity of lending to the real economy. In this chapter, it is possible to examine whether the Islamic banks follow this pattern or they reduce financing to the real economy. For this specific purpose, this publicly available data on the participation banks in Turkey are used to assess liquidity regulations and financing provided to customers. Following Bonner (2014) and Banerjee and Mio (2014), Tobit regression models can be used for estimation. The base model is as follows:

$$\begin{aligned} LCRY = \alpha_i + \beta_{1it}{}^{*}DUMMY1 + \beta_{2it}{}^{*}RR + \beta_{3it}{}^{*}ROE + \beta_{4it}{}^{*}CAR + \beta_{5it}{}^{*}LINF \\ + \beta_{6it}{}^{*}CDS + \beta_{7it}{}^{*}INTER + \beta_{8it}{}^{*}SUKUK + \beta_{9it}{}^{*}LCRE + \beta_{10it}{}^{*}LDEP \\ + \beta_{11it}{}^{*}SAFS + \varepsilon_{it} \end{aligned} \tag{2}$$

$$i = 1,\ 2,\ 3,\ 4,\ 5 \ and \ t = 1,\ 2,\ \ldots 101$$

In this model, *LCRY* is the liquidity ratio, *RR* is statutory reserves, *ROE* is return on equity, *CAR* is capital adequacy ratio, *INF* is inflation rate, *INTER* is interbank market rate, *SUKUK* is profit rate on lease certificates issued by Turkish Treasury, *CRE* is total financing provided by Participation banks, *DEP* is deposit size, and *SAFS* refers to securities available for sale. The model in Equation 2 is used only for analysing the effects of introducing LCR standards starting from 2013.

A dummy variable is included in Equation 2 for the years between April 2007 and August 2015 to identify the effects of the LCR standards:

$$\theta_i = \beta_{12} + \varepsilon_i \tag{3}$$

where

$$i = efficiency\ scores$$

$$12 = 2013\ LCR\ launch\ day$$

Furthermore, to examine the significance of potential determinants of bank efficiency, the following hypothesis is tested:

$$H_o : \beta x = 0 \tag{4}$$

$$H_i : \beta x = 0$$

where β represents the coefficient associated with explanatory variables included in the country-specific banking systems under study.

Table 17.5 shows that liquidity regulation increased the cash holdings of banks. But there is also a negative significant relationship between introducing new liquidity regulations and financing. The evidence applies their liquidity regulation is associated with a diminished capacity of financing by the participation banks. This is partly consistent with the results of Banerjee and Mio (2014) and fully consistent

Table 17.5: Liquidity Regulation and Bank's Financing.

	Cash	Financing
Regulations	7.51*** (2.96)	−4.84*** (−2.74)
Number of observations	404	
Adjusted-R^2	0.2341	

with findings of Bonner (2014). The fundamental reason behind this negative and statistically significant relation is that liquidity regulation requires banks to permanently maintain certain levels of cash holdings, invest in high-quality liquid assets. Arguably, this implies also an increase in institutional marginal costs of funds, which in turn affect the value of financing. In this context, raising cash is a buffer for these banks against liquidity risk. The incentives for banks to hold cash are different from the incentives to keep other liquid assets. It is very likely that banks with high cash holdings do so because of a lack of other investment opportunities, as opposed to incentives related to liquidity risk. When measuring the impact of liquidity regulation binding, and non-binding liquidity requirements cannot be accurately distinguished (Bonner 2014). Therefore, in this Tobit model, no distinction is made between the effects of binding and non-binding regulations as the overall effects of regulations are rather assessed.

6 Conclusion and Policy Implications

Under the tighter global liquidity conditions and rigid Basel III liquidity requirements, Islamic banking sector may face many challenges in terms of liquidity risk management. As the current Basel regulations and standards are developed for internationally active banks, their application to small local banks or banks that do not pose systemic risk are unlikely fitting. Most of the Islamic banks are small local banks and, as a result, they do not have the capacity to bear such the high costs of international regulations.

Since these banks have close relations with the real sector, there are also important vulnerabilities regarding real-sector financing that should not be ignored. There are indeed counterparty risks and information-sharing problems between banks and companies particulary with respect to partnership-based financing. For these important reasons, a separate and distinct risk assessment of these banks is needed. Regulating cross-sectoral and cross-border linkages and channels necessitates having certain well-formulated tools to identify underlying risks. Otherwise, the overestimation or underestimation of these risks is highly possible. Once these risks are identified, instruments for policy response could be designed and developed. In this context, transparent communication with all stakeholders is very important. Without having transparent and symmetric information, it would not be possible to have appropriate policies and an effective regulatory and supervisory structure. The liquidity management of participation banks should be handled differently from their conventional counterparts'. First of all, these Islamic banks have a shortage of liquidity and shortage of stable funds. If they are forced to keep the same liquidity coverage ratio applicable to conventional banks, they have to keep a large amount of their resources as cash, because there is shortage of high-quality liquid Sukuk. Furthermore, the quantitative study conducted in this chapter shows that there is negative and significant relationship between introducing new liquidity regulations and financing provided by participation banks to the real sector. This result may be explained by the fact that banks have to increase institutional marginal costs of funds, which affect the value of financing. Since liquidity regulation affects the opportunity costs, Islamic banks would be more reluctant to finance large projects.

In addition, many stakeholders in the current financial system are excluded from the decision-making process and are not given the appropriate rights of participation. According to a survey conducted by Ziraat Participation Bank, 25% of investors state that they are excluded from the financial system because of the lack of opportunity to invest deposits in truly *Shariah*-compliant state banks (COMCEC 2016). These investors have trust and confidence problems with private Islamic banking practices after the failure and resolution process of Ikhlas Finans of Turkey in 2001. Introducing a new regulatory framework, or reforming the existing one, will increase the ability of Islamic banks to provide more financing to the real sector and to mitigate liquidity risks. The potential benefits from these would be reduction of costs associated with financial regulation and supervision, and the stability of financial system based on risk-sharing. The unique features of Islamic banks require that the regulatory policies should be redefined and restructured differently from those of their conventional peers.

This chapter includes recommendations for a resilient and sound infrastructure for Islamic banks. In this context, it is proposed that stable funds can be increased and the liquidity risk management for these banks can be properly achieved through the following policies, tools and applications:

- Since there is a chronic shortage of Shariah-compliant securities or highly liquid sukuk in many jurisdictions, public authorities should give priority to the regular issuance of securities and risk-sharing instruments for Islamic banking.
- More liquid instruments within a tailored regulatory framework are required, not only for liquidity purposes but also to increase profitability.
- Every country should be allowed to issue these securities annually both in local currencies and in foreign currency, because in several countries Islamic banks have huge excess foreign currency liquidity.

- The secondary markets should be developed for Shariah-compliant sukuk and securities and central banks should provide relevant tools for Shariah-compliant lender-of-last-resort facility.
- New Shariah-compliant products and assets must be designed by authorities and banks. Also, these assets should be accepted as collateral by central banks for open market operations to increase their acceptance in secondary markets.
- Islamic banks should be supervised differently from the current supervision system. Supervisors should focus not only on specific risks of the model but also review the Shariah aspects with the view of incorporating them into the regulatory supervision procedures.
- Shariah-compliant credit rating, transparency mechanism, special credit rating mechanisms and institutions are also very essential for strengthening liquidity and the asset liability management of Islamic banks.
- International liquidity management initiatives, enhancing cooperation, trust and communication are vital for controlling vulnerabilities, mitigating risks and curtailing regulatory arbitrage. Full transparency is required for each item on both sides of the balance-sheets of Islamic banks.
- Regulators should work towards shaping a risk-sharing packed regulatory framework for Islamic banks.
- To control the cash outflows and mitigate inherent risk in their assets and liabilities, Islamic banks should be more transparent and offer new risk-sharing based channels for investors to place deposits into longer-term investments.

It is also noted that, on the other hand, liquidity risk management cannot be managed properly in a financial system where risks are persistently shifted rather than shared, and regulation is constrained by moral hazards and negative externalities. A new paradigm for financial regulation requires a restructuring of these relations. There are key elements to achieve this objective including a better understanding of the nature of Islamic banking activities, making appropriate changes to the existing regulatory framework for Islamic banking, and levelling the playing field between Islamic banking and conventional banking. These recommendations may be useful for Islamic banks to properly manage liquidity risk and correctly adjust their balance sheet structures to the real economy.

References

Adam, Nathif J. and Abdulkader Thomas. 2005. *Islamic Bonds – Your Guide to Issuing Structuring and Investing in Sukuk*. London, UK: Euromoney Books.

Akhtar, Shamshad. 2007. "Building an effective Islamic financial system." Speech at the Global Islamic Financial Forum, Governor's: Financial Regulators Forum in Islamic Finance, Kuala Lumpur, 27 March 2007.

Alam, Nafis. 2013. "Impact of banking regulation on risk and efficiency in Islamic banking." *Journal of Financial Reporting and Accounting* 11(1): 29–50.

Alessandri, Piergiorgio, Prasanna Gai, Sujit Kapadia, Nada Mora, and Claus Puhr. 2009. "Towards a Framework for Quantifying Systemic Stability". *International Journal of Central Banking* 5(3): 47–81.

Amihud, Yakov, Haim Mendelson, and Lasse Heje Pedersen. 2005. "Liquidity and asset prices." *Foundations and Trends in Finance*, 1, 4, pp.269–364.

Arif, Ahmed, and Ahmed Nauman Anees. 2012. "Liquidity risk and performance of banking system." *Journal of Financial Regulation and Compliance* 20(2): 182–195.

Ariss, Rima Turk. 2010. "Competitive conditions in Islamic and conventional banking: A global perspective." *Review of Financial Economics* 19(3): 101–108.

Ashraf, Dawood, Muhammad Suhail Rizwanb, and Barbara L'Huillier. 2016. "A net stable funding ratio for Islamic banks and its impact on financial stability: An international investigation." *Journal of financial Stability* 25: 47–57.

Banerjee, Ryan N. and Hitoshi Mio. 2014. "The Impact of Liquidity Regulation on Banks." BIS Working Papers, No.470. October 2014.

BIS (Basel Committee on Banking Supervision-BCBS). 2013. *Basel III: The Liquidity Coverage Ratio and liquidity risk monitoring tools*. Download: 6 March 2015, www.bis.org.

Bonner, Clemens. 2014. "Liquidity regulation and bank behaviour." *Tilburg: CentER*, Center for Economic Research.

Boss, Michael, Gerald Krenn, Claus Puhr, Martin Summer. 2006. "Systemic Risk Monitor: A Model for Systemic Risk Analysis and Stress Testing of Banking Systems." *Financial Stability Report* 11: 83–95.

Bourkhis, Khawla, and ahmoud Nabi. 2013. "Islamic and conventional banks' soundness during the 2007–2008 financial crises." *Review of Financial Economics* 22: 68–77.

Chong, Beng, and Ming-Hua Liu. 2009. "Islamic banking: Interest-free or interest-based?" *Pacific-Basin Finance Journal* 17(1): 125–144.

COMCEC. 2016. "Turkey Islamic Finance Report." www.concec.org (last accessed: 01. 07.2018)

Diamond, Douglas W, and Raghuram G. Rajan. 2005. "Liquidity shortages and banking crises." *Journal of Finance* 60(2): 615–647.

Dusuki, Asyraf Wajdi. 2007. "Commodity *Murabahah* programme (CMP): An innovative approach to liquidity management." *Journal of Islamic Economics, Banking and Finance* 3(1): 1–22.

Ergec, Ethem Hakan, and Arslan Bengül Gülümser. 2013. "Impact of interest rates on Islamic and conventional banks: the case of Turkey." *Applied Economics* 45(17): 2381–2388.

Farooqi, Muhammad, and John R. O'Brien. 2015. "A Comparison of the Impact of the Basel Standards upon Islamic and Conventional Bank Risks in the Gulf State Region." Electronic copy available at: http://ssrn.com/abstract=2647562.

Haan, Leo J., and Jan Willem van den End. 2013. "Bank liquidity, the maturity ladder, and regulation." *Journal of Banking and Finance* 37(10): 3930–3950.

Hasan, M, Maher, Jemma Dridi. 2010. "The effects of the global crisis on Islamic and conventional banks: A comparative study." *IMF Working Paper*, WP/10/201.

Hesse, Heiko, Andreas Jobst, and Juan Solé. 2008. "Trend and Changes in Islamic Finance." *World Economics* 9(2): 175–193.

IFSB. 2018. *Islamic Financial Services Industry Stability Report 2018*. Kuala Lumpur: Islamic Financial Services Board.

IFSB. 2015. "Guidance Note on Quantitative Measures for Liquidity Risk Management in Institutions Offering Islamic Financial Services." Kuala Lumpur. IFSB-15. April 2015.

IFSB. 2014. *Islamic Financial Services Industry Stability Report 2014*. Kuala Lumpur: Islamic Financial Services Board.

Ismal, Rifki. 2010. "Assessing the demand and supply of liquidity in Islamic banking (The Case of Indonesia)." *ISRA International Journal of Islamic Finance* 2(1):147–167

Khediri, Karim Ben, Lanouar Charfeddine, and Slah Ben Youssef. 2015. "Islamic versus conventional banks in the GCC countries: A comparative study using classification techniques." *Research in International Business and Finance* 33: 75–98.

Krasicka, Olga and Sylwia Nowak. 2012. "What's in it for me? A Primer on Differences between Islamic and Conventional Finance in Malaysia." IMF Working Paper, WP/12/151, June 2012.

Maghrebi, Nabil, and Abbas Mirakhor. 2015. "Risk-Sharing and Shared Prosperity in Islamic Finance." *Islamic Economic Studies* 23(2): 85–115.

Mirakhor, Abbas. 2010. "Whither Islamic finance? Risk-sharing in an age of crises." The Inaugural Securities Commission Malaysia (SC) – Oxford Centre for Islamic Studies (OCIS) Roundtable "Developing a Scientific Methodology on *Shariah* Governance for Positioning Islamic Finance Globally, 15 March 2010.

Mirakhor, Abbas. 2012. Islamic Finance, Risk-Sharing and Macroeconomic Policies. *MPRA Paper* No. 56338 posted 31. May 2014.

Mirakhor, Abbas, Hossein Askari, Zamir Iqbal, and Noureddin Krichene. 2012. *Risk-Sharing in Finance: The Islamic Finance Alternative*. New York: Wiley.

Mohamad, Ahmad Azam Sulaiman, Mohammad Taqiuddin Mohamad, and Muhamad Lukman Samsudin. 2013. "How Islamic banks of Malaysia managing liquidity? An emphasis on confronting economic cycles." *International Journal of Business and Social Science* 4(7): 253–263.

Mohammad, Sabri. 2013. "Liquidity Risk Management in Islamic Banks: A Survey." *Afro Eurasian Studies* 1(2): 215–230.

Mongid, Abdul. 2015. "Liquidity Risk Management in the Islamic Rural Banking: Evidence from Indonesia." *Banks and Bank systems* 10(3): 61–67.

Pagratis, Spyros, Nikolas Topaloglou, and Mike G. Tsionas. 2017. "System Stress Testing of Bank Liquidity Risk." *Journal of International Money and Finance* 73(A): 22–40.

Rashid, Abdul and Sana Jabeen. 2016. "Analysing Performance Determinants: Conventional versus Islamic Banks in Pakistan." *Borsa Istanbul Review* 16(2): 92–107.

Rosly, Saiful Azhar and Mohd Afandi Abu Bakar. 2003. "Performance of Islamic and mainstream banks in Malaysia." *International Journal of Social Economics* 30(12): 1249–1265.

Rosman, Romzie, Norazlina Abd Wahab, and Zairy Zainol. 2014. "Efficiency of Islamic banks during the financial crisis: An analysis of Middle Eastern and Asian countries." *Pacific-Basin Finance Journal* 28: 76–90.

Saeed, Momna, and Marwan Izzeldin. "Examining the relationship between default risk and efficiency in Islamic and conventional banks." *Journal of Economic Behavior and Organization* 132(28): 127–154.

Soylu, Ali, and Nazif Durmaz. 2013. "Profitability of interest-free versus interest-based banks in Turkey." *The Australian Economic Review* 46(2): 176–88.

Verhoef, Bastiaan, Somia Azahaf, and Werner Bijkerk. 2008. "Islamic Finance and Supervision: An Exploratory Analysis." *DNB Occational Studies* 6(3) (Amsterdam, de Netherlandsche Bank).

Umar Rafi

Chapter 18: Antifragility of Risk-Sharing Finance: A Quantitative Analysis

1 Introduction

Antifragility refers to conditions under which systems become resilient to shocks caused by Black Swans events, which are highly unpredictable outlier events with significant negative or positive implications. According to this concept, the long-term survivability of any system centers exclusively on its antifragile nature, that is, its ability to absorb and potentially benefit from Black Swan-type of shocks. The objective of this study is to examine quantitatively the antifragile nature of Islamic finance, which is based on risk sharing (hereafter referred to as risk-sharing finance).[171]

Antifragility lays down extremely stringent criteria with respect to modeling, as well as empirical analysis. Unlike traditional modeling and econometrics, the analysis of antifragility limits the reliance on standard assumptions for modeling. It doesn't either allow for the recourse to proxy data for empirical analysis. Figure 18.1 gives a detailed account of the quantitative knowledge gap between risk-sharing finance and antifragility, as covered by this study.[172]

The quantitative criteria for Black Swans, as well as for antifragility, are described on the right-side of Figure 18.1. Prominent amongst these are the benchmarks that emerge from Mandelbrot's (2004) analysis of non-Gaussian distributions,[173] from Kahneman's (2011) insights on Prospect Theory,[174] and from Taleb's (2013) 2nd order heuristic[175] for testing antifragility.[176] The techniques used by various researchers in modeling an interest-free economy and financial system are shown on the left side of Figure 18.1. The arrow from the quantitative criteria and tests of antifragility to the

---

171 For a qualitative comparison of antifragility and risk-sharing finance, please see Rafi and Mirakhor (2017)

172 This is a subset of the complete list of characteristics of antifragility. In an effort to keep the scope manageable, the research will concentrate only on this list.

173 A non-Gaussian distribution is a distribution that is not a Normal distribution.

174 Prospect theory is a theory in *cognitive psychology* that describes the way people choose between *probabilistic* alternatives that involve risk, where the probabilities of outcomes are uncertain. The theory states that people make decisions based on the potential value of losses and gains rather than the final outcome, and that people evaluate these losses and gains using some *heuristics*.

175 This is a second order stress test to detect nonlinearities in the tails that can lead to fragility.

176 For a more detailed description of each of the antifragility criteria please see Taleb (2012) and Rafi and Mirakhor (2017).

https://doi.org/10.1515/9783110587920-018

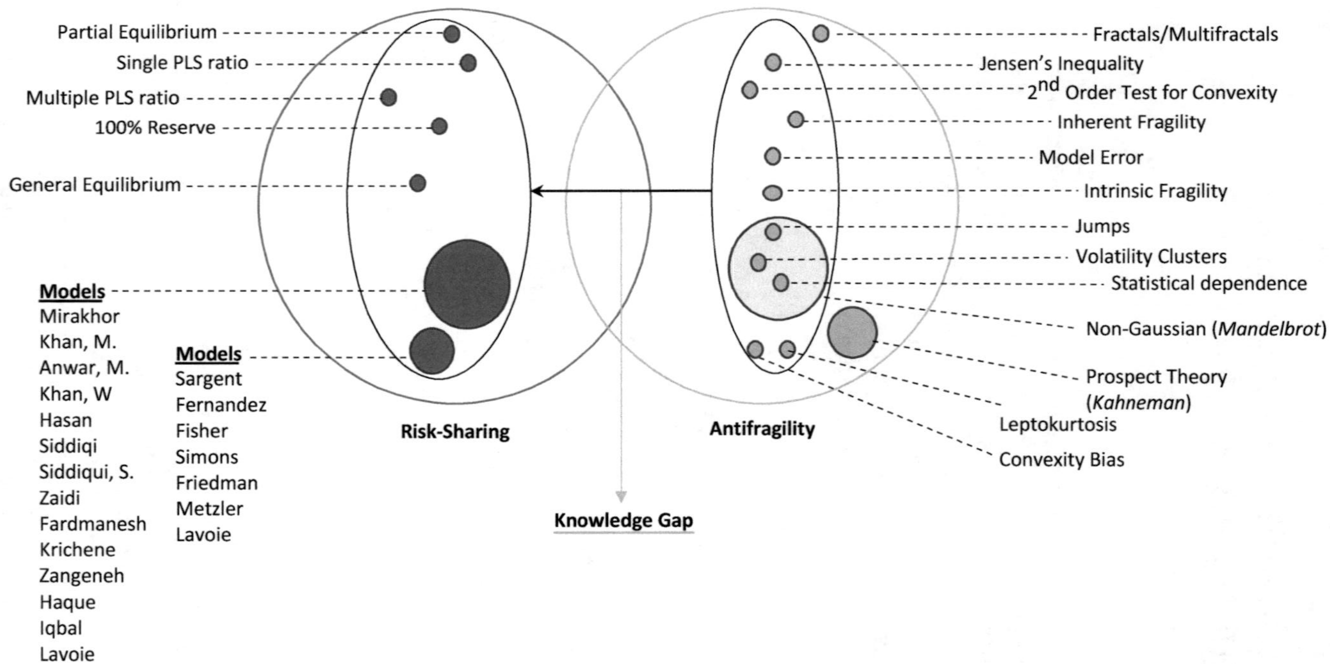

Figure 18.1: Detailed Quantitative Knowledge Gap.
Source: Rafi and Mirakhor (2017).

mathematical models for risk-sharing summarizes the quantitative knowledge gap this research attempts to bridge.

2 Literature Review

The related literature is reviewed under the three domains of risk sharing, antifragility and debt. In the area of risk-sharing and antifragility, both quantitative and qualitative studies are reviewed, while in the area of debt, only a qualitative review is required to fulfill the objectives of the present analysis. Under risk-sharing, primary importance is given to the work by Mirakhor and Askari, while under antifragility, the focus is placed on the work by Taleb and Mandelbrot. Specifically, an attempt is made to review all available qualitative and quantitative literature by Mirakhor on risk-sharing and by Taleb on antifragility and on Black Swans (as well as by Mandelbrot, and, to a lesser extent, by Fama in the area of non-Gaussian probability distributions for price movements).

In this respect, some issues related to statistical dependence, price jumps, volatility clustering and non-Gaussian distribution are extensively covered in Rafi and Mirakhor (2017). This study attempts to summarize certain properties of risk-sharing finance from these models, to rank them within the antifragility triad,[177] and to define a framework under which risk sharing finance can be tested for antifragility.

Many mathematical models based on the notion of risk sharing finance were developed by Abbas Mirakhor and his colleagues over many decades starting from Khan (1986) to Askari et al. (2014a and 2014b). The approach used by Mirakhor (1993) is to create IS-LM[178] models of interest-free economies, defining the equilibrium conditions and then testing the equilibrium status for stability. Stability is a property of economic systems that describe the ability of a system to revert back to tis original state rapidly following exogenous or endogenous shocks. The variables in the equations of interest-free models in order to examine whether and how the variables return to equilibrium, and revert back to the original point of equilibrium. The various tests carried out by Mirakhor reach there important conclusions. Firstly, monetary instruments other than those traditionally used for economic equilibrium. Secondly, interest-free financial systems tend to be more stable than interest-based financial systems. Thirdly, in some cases, certain variables in models of debt-based financial systems do not return to equilibrium after being shocked. Askari et al. (2014a) highlight the first point to establish the practicality of risk-sharing finance, and the third

177 See Section 3 for detailed explained of the antifragility triad.

178 The IS-LM model, which stands for "investment-savings" (IS) and "liquidity preference-money supply" (LM) is a Keynesian macroeconomic model that shows how the market for economic goods (IS) interacts with the loanable funds market (LM) or money market.

point as the cause behind perpetual boom-bust cycles of debt-based economies, regularly requiring external interventions to stabilize the system.

Khan (1986) can be considered as a landmark study in this area. It was the first attempt to bring the interpretation of profit-loss-sharing (PLS) to a western audience. Khan (1986) modifies the model of an equity-based financial system as presented by Metzler (1951). Khan and Mirakhor (1988) and Mirakhor and Zaidi (1988) show how monetary policy can be used to stabilize an economy in which the financial system operates based on the rate of return to equity shares rather than a fixed and pre-determined interest rate. Mirakhor (1987) adds money to the model presented in Khan (1986) and shows that real sector rate of return equilibrates demand and supply of loanable funds. Mirakhor (1993) models a closed economy and open economy with no interest-bearing assets. It establishes that an economy without interest will return to equilibrium. Based on such a model, the returns available on financial assets can be determined (and managed in a more stable manner) by the rate of return from the real sector rather than the interest rate. This solves one of the main issues facing risk-sharing finance – how to replace the interest rate with another variable (the rate of return to the real sector in this case), as per the motivations of Islamic finance. Askari et al. (2014) establishes that an equity-based system moves towards equilibrium, after being shocked, without an interventionist fiscal and monetary policy for a closed economy as well as an open economy.

3 The Antifragility Triad

A *triad* for categorizing systems across the fragility spectrum has been described by Taleb (2012). It divides all systems into three categories as fragile, robust, and antifragile. The qualitative argument for the fragility of conventional finance has been established in detail by Taleb (2012). The qualitative argument for the antifragility of risk-sharing finance has also been established by Rafi and Mirakhor (2017). It becomes essential to quantitatively categorize conventional finance and risk-sharing finance as per the triad.

Quantitatively, this research places the debt-based conventional financial system under the fragile category, as per the triad. Along with his qualitative arguments, Taleb (2012), extending the ideas of Mandelbrot (2004), has mathematically quantified the fragility of conventional finance in a series of studies. In addition, the empirical analysis carried out by Taleb places debt-based conventional finance under the fragile vertical of the triad. Mirakhor, in various publications, has touched upon the instability of conventional finance via mathematical models, as well. This is the inability of the shocked variables in a debt-based system to return back to their respective equilibrium state (or returning to the equilibrium state with difficulty and / or with the assistance of outside interference) indicates the system becomes weaker under shocks (volatility), and is thus fragile.

This research places the stable models of interest-free economies, as defined by Mirakhor (1993), under the robust vertical of the triad; variables modeling risk-sharing finance return to their equilibrium state without being affected one way or the other from shocks (volatility). Since Mirakhor (1993) research pre-dates the categorization of systems under Taleb's triad, thus Mirakhor research on the instability of conventional finance as well as on stability of risk-sharing finance has not been connected to the concepts of fragility. This research attempts to fill this gap by (re) categorizing the quantitative results of Mirakhor's research under the triad. Hence, the aim of this research is to expand the quantitative discussion around interest-free models into the third vertical of the triad – antifragility, within the modeling restrictions defined by Taleb (2012).[179] This can be considered a key contribution of this research, since a similar attempt has yet to be made in academia or in industry. This will extend the discussion one-step beyond what has been shown so far by Mirakhor (1993) through the interest-free models defined over the past three decades.

4 Fragility and Antifragility

Taleb and Douady (2013) provide mathematical definitions underlying the qualitative concepts provided in Taleb (2012). Much like Taleb (2012) can be considered a foundational work in the qualitative domain of risk management, Taleb and Douady (2013) can be considered a landmark paper in the literature about quantitative studies of antifragility. It is the first study to provide the mathematical definition of the fragility spectrum under the triad. In addition, Taleb and Douady (2013) provides the mathematical foundations for a heuristic that can simultaneously test a system for fragility, robustness, and antifragility, along with noticing any exposure to model error and bias.[180] Table 18.1 lists the variables, parameters and constants that are used by Taleb and Douady (2013) for providing mathematical definitions for the fragility spectrum.

179 This is an important point to understand, since the modelling standards defined by Taleb (2011) are significantly more restrictive and stringent that the modelling techniques traditionally used in economics and in finance. In fact, as per Taleb (2012), one of the main causes of fragility in economics and in finance is the incorrect usage of assumptions about models and data.

180 Taleb and Douady (2013) is the final product of Taleb (2011) and Taleb (2012).

Table 18.1: Variables, Parameters and Constants.

Value	Description
F	(Monomodal) Probability distribution
ε	Tail integral (Risk measure)
Z	Tail expectation
K	Threshold (breaking point)
S	Parameter used to measure volatility (STD, MAD, α)
S^-	Left side of own distribution
Δs	Finite perturbation (disturbance) to s
X	Random variable
V	Semi-vega sensitivity
Ω	Distribution center
Λ	Scaling parameter
$S^-(l)$	Sensitivity to disorder cluster
$S^-(\lambda)$	Left semi absolute deviation
F_λ	One parameter family of pdf
ω_A	Convexity bias
ω_B	Missed fragility
$\bar{\alpha}$	Average expected rate
φ	Distribution of α over its domain ϑ_a
Π	Harm function
Z	Stress level

Source: Author's own.

4.1 Fragility

Fragility is defined as how much a system is negatively affected from changes in its surrounding environment to the left (probabilistically) of a certain threshold. It defines how a system suffers from the variability of its environment beyond a certain preset point (K). Taleb and Douady (2013) refer to this as left tail vega sensitivity. V*ega* measures the risk of gain or loss resulting from changes in volatility of the underlying.[181] Within securities trading, vega is a number that provides the direction and extent the option price will move if there is a positive 1% change in the volatility (and only in the volatility). This implies that fragility of a system is dependent on how much the system changes due to the volatility of its environment (not due to its own volatility). Based on this, Taleb and Douady (2013) divides fragility

181 Vega is one of the four Greeks – primary analysis techniques utilized in options trading. These techniques measure the risk involved in an options contract as it relates to the underlying. The other three Greeks are delta, gamma and theta. These measure the sensitivity to the underlying instrument's price, delta in response to price changes in underlying, and time decay of the option, respectively.

into two categories – intrinsic fragility and inherent fragility. Intrinsic fragility refers to the sensitivity of a variable to the left side of its own probability distribution. Inherent fragility refers to the sensitivity of a variable to an external stressor – the probability distribution of the underlying (not to its own environment / surroundings). Within the triad, inherent fragility decides the survival of an object/system.

Moreover, fragility of a fat-tailed system is dependent on tail events only. A system will not be harmed by events within the confidence level (of the environment); irrespective of how many such events occur. However, a system can be devastated by a single tail event of large deviation successfully. K defines the remoteness of the event – the boundary beyond which the distribution is disturbed to check for fragility. An example of left tail vega sensitivity can be the impact of large earthquakes (the environment) on a house (system) existing in an area prone to earthquakes; the house is the system, while the intensity (and number) of the earthquakes is the volatility of the environment. An accumulation of stress from a thousand tiny earthquakes rating low on the Richter scale (events within the confidence level) may not harm the house, while a single big earthquake (Black Swan event beyond a certain threshold point (K) on the Richter scale) may destroy the house.

Based on the above, Taleb and Douady (2013) provides a more formal definition of fragility as, "The sensitivity of the left-tail shortfall (non-conditioned by probability) below a certain threshold K to the overall left semi-deviation of the distribution." Semi deviation evaluates the fluctuations in returns below the mean (or below a defined threshold). It represents the standard deviation of the returns that are lower than the mean (or threshold) return, providing an effective measure of downside risk. It is calculated in the same manner as standard deviation (STD); however, it differs from STD in that semi deviation only looks at periods where the portfolio's return is less than the target level. Mathematically, it is the square root of the semi-variance. Semi variance can be calculated below the mean and / or below a specific target value. If we assume the target value to be K, semi deviation is calculated as:

$$Semi\ deviation = \sqrt{\frac{1}{N} \cdot \sum_{r_T < K}^{N} (K - r_T)^2} \tag{1}$$

where r_t indicates selection return in period t. It should be highlighted here that Taleb (2013) recommends using mean absolute deviation (MAD) in modeling price movements, instead of STD.[182] MAD is a measure of how much the values in the data set are likely to differ from their mean. The absolute value is used to avoid deviations with opposite signs cancelling each other out. It is calculated as:

$$MAD = \frac{1}{N} \sum_{I=1}^{N} |X_I - \bar{X}| \tag{2}$$

182 Taleb (2013) does this to ensure his calculations remain outside of the L^2 norm.

Suppose y and z are random variables with two single-mode probability distributions (f, g), with a volatility of s. F and g are considered the probability distributions of the underlying (environment). The aim is to compare the inherent fragility of a system to f and to g through a comparison of the tail vega sensitivity (V). The two distributions are disturbed at their left tails beyond a breaking point (K). The magnitude of the disturbance is finite and is equal to Δs in both cases. The tail vega sensitivity is calculated at two different lower absolute mean deviations. Exposure to y is more fragile than exposure to z in the tail, if for a given K in the negative domain, the tail vega sensitivity (V) of *f* is higher than that of *g*:

$$V(y, f, K, \Delta s) \; > \; V(z, g, K, \Delta s)$$

$$V(y,f,K,\Delta s) \; \equiv \zeta\left(y,f,K,s+\frac{\Delta s}{2}\right) \; - \zeta\left(y,f,K,s-\frac{\Delta s}{2}\right)$$

$$Z(Y, f, K, s) \equiv \int_{-\infty}^{K} Yf(Y)Dy \tag{3}$$

Figure 18.2 shows the tail vega sensitivity (V) calculated as tail integral (Ɛ) at two different values of left tail semi-deviation (s– and s– + Δ s–). The difference in the areas of the two curves (calculated by the tail integrals Ɛ), beyond K, indicates the effect of the perturbation (Δs–). Thus, fragility is the sensitivity of the tail integral (Ɛ) between – ∞ and K to changes in s.[183]

4.2 Robustness

Taleb and Douady (2013) show it is not possible to (mathematically) define antifragility, without first (mathematically) defining robustness. This is because, unlike a fragile system, which is not impacted by the right tail, an antifragile system has to be robust to volatility of the left tail of the underlying (environment). Robustness is an upper control on the fragility of x that resides on the left side of the distribution beyond K. Upper control implies a value of K beyond which (moving from the left tail towards Ω) the system is not fragile. In this case, K defines the upper bound. As an example, assume Taleb's 80 / 20 barbell portfolio consists of 80% cash and 20% S&P Put options. In this portfolio, K = .8. This implies 80% of the portfolio is not affected by volatility; it is robust to volatility. The remaining 20% is impacted by

183 Taleb & Douady (2013) defines two theorems – fragility transfer theorem and fragility exacerbation theorem – to map nonlinearities to fragility.

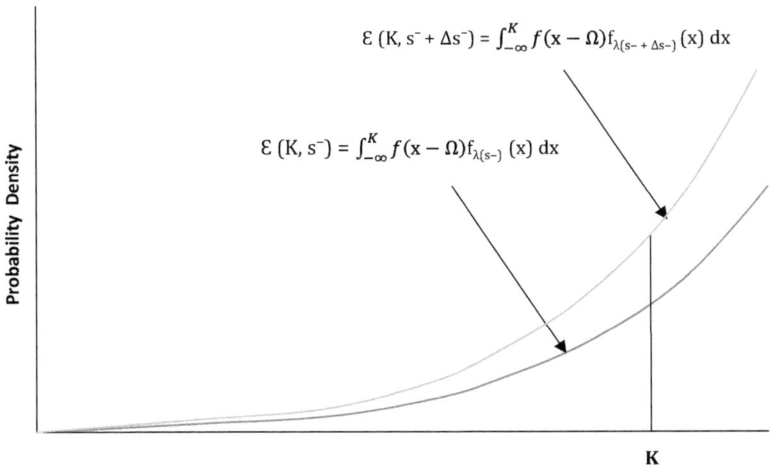

Figure 18.2: Definition of Fragility.
Source: Taleb and Douady (2013).

volatility and should be checked for fragility and antifragility (after which, the combined portfolio should be evaluated under the triad). Mathematically, a payoff y is robust below K for source of randomness x included in determining distribution, if

$$| V(y,f,K,2\Delta s) - V(z,g,K,\Delta s)| < e \tag{4}$$

where f is the monomodal probability distributions for y, V is the tail vega sensitivity, $\zeta(\mathrm{Y},\mathrm{f},\mathrm{K},\mathrm{s})$ Is a payoff below K, and e is a quantity of order that is of negligible utility.

4.3 Antifragility

The above discussion, having mathematically defined fragility and robustness, allows us to quantify the qualitative concepts behind antifragility. Antifragility is defined in the same way as fragility, albeit on the right-hand side of the probability distribution (of the environment), with an addition requirement of control on the robustness of the probability distribution on the left-hand side. Hence, there is a lack of symmetry between antifragility and fragility. This implies that antifragility requires robustness in the left tail, while simultaneously benefiting from right tail vega sensitivity. This is achieved by shrinking the left tail, while simultaneously having unbounded right tail payoffs, thereby causing antifragility to the complete probability distribution (of the environment). This requires a thin left tail and a fat right tail. This results in a distribution that is skewed right. Within the barbell portfolio, the 80% cash corresponds to controlling the robustness of the left tail (by establishing K at .8), while the 20% S&P Put options allow possibility of unbounded right tail payoffs. Mathematically, a payoff y, with a single mode distribution, is locally antifragile over range x = L (lower bound) and x = H (higher bound), if y is robust below L, and:

$$\Lambda\left(Y, f, L, H, s+\frac{\Delta s}{2}\right) - \lambda\left(Y, f, L, H, s-\frac{\Delta s}{2}\right) > 0 \tag{5}$$

4.4 Model Errors and Convexity Bias

Taleb (2011) rejects the contemporary modelling techniques used in conventional finance and economics due to their excessive reliance on standard assumptions. Hence, the mathematical models used by Taleb for antifragility doesn't typically map to the mathematical approach followed by Mirakhor (1933) for interest-free models. The latter is the traditional modeling approach followed in economics and finance, while the former encourages a different (and much more restrictive) approach. This makes it essential to understand the details of the inconsistencies in traditional modeling techniques, prior to testing interest-free economic models for antifragility.

Taleb (2011) highlight two types of errors in traditional approaches to modeling:[184]

1. modelling errors due to missing variables.
2. modelling errors due to the missing or ignorance of convexity effects

The complete missing of stochastic variables in an economic model is conducive to the inconsistency of results, as the effects of the missing variables may not be manifested in the results. However, in general, models tend to include too many variables instead of too few. Hence, this type of model errors may not exert a significant influence on the analysis of interest-free models. As noted by Taleb (2011), the second type of errors may be more significant as it can be conducive to complete model inconsistency. It involves the assumption of stochastic variables to be deterministic for models that are rather concave or convex with respect to those variables. This results in the underestimation or overestimation of the impact of changes in the variables, leading to model errors. For instance, the prince of a call option can be calculated under the Black-Scholes Options Pricing Model (BSOPM) as follows.

$$C(S, K, \bar{\sigma}, t) = e^{-rt} \int_K^{\infty} (S-K) \varnothing\left(S|\mu, \bar{\sigma}\sqrt{t}\right) dS \tag{6}$$

where:

S: asset price

K: strike price

184 Taleb (2013) also describes a third type of error – linear error about the first derivative of the model. However, this is easily detectable, hence not emphasized.

μ: mean
σ: standard deviation
t: time to expiration
$\varnothing$: normal distribution function

The BSOPM model assumes only S to be stochastic while other variables are assumed to be deterministic and measured without estimation errors. This introduces what Taleb (2011) refers to as the convexity bias, which results from the assumption of stochastic variables to be deterministic. into the model, which adds a premium to the initial results from the BSOPM model. This bias increases with the convexity of the payoffs to variations in the standard deviation.

4.5 Convexity Bias via Jensen's Inequality

In light of the previous discussion, it is clear that a system is deemed fragile if it suffers more from large negative shocks than it gains from large positive ones, and vice-versa.

Antifragile => convex; benefits from variability
Fragile => concave; suffers from variability

Thus, the convexity bias of an interest-free system can be tested via Jensen's inequality. For a convex payoff function f and a random variable x, Jensen's inequality implies that

$$E[f(x)] \geq f(E[x]) \tag{7}$$

Jensen's inequality comes into play when transformation is combined with averaging. If a represents the transformation of data and then the averaging of transformed values, and b represents the averaging of data and then the transformation of averages, then if the transformation is linear, a and b will be the same. However, if the transformation is convex, then the value of a will always be higher than the value of b.

4.6 Framework for Testing the Antifragility of Risk-Sharing Finance

Table 18.2 highlights the convexity bias of interest-free models summarized earlier in this study, as well as their position within the fragility triad. The first part lays down the foundations for a quantitative framework that links antifragility to risk-sharing finance. The multiple steps defined in this framework for testing preparedness based on antifragility, can be applied to risk-sharing banks. The framework can also be used to compare debt-based conventional banks with risk-sharing

Table 18.2: Convexity Bias of Risk-sharing Models.

Model	Triad	Convexity Bias
	Liquidity Risk	
$S / P = s = y / r$	Robust	Yes
$m = g(r) * \frac{y}{r}$	Robust	Yes
$\dot{y} = f(r, y; \dot{m})$	Robust	Yes
	Real Sector Rate of Return	
$Q = C + I$	Robust	Yes
$L = N$	Robust	Yes
$E^D = E^S$	Robust	Yes
$i\ (r^m, r) = s\ (r^m)\ y/k$	Robust	Yes
$i\ (r^{*m}, r^*) = i\ (n)$	Robust	Yes
$s\ (r^{*m}, r^*)\ y^*/k^* = i\ (n)$	Robust	Yes
	100% Reserves	
S(k,w) = I®,	Robust	Yes
$m = l(r)k$	Robust	Yes
$\dot{k} = \dot{k}(\tilde{r}, K) \equiv \sigma(k, m)$	Robust	Yes
$\dot{m} \equiv \eta(K, m)$	Robust	Yes

Source: Author's own.

banks with respect to antifragility. As more empirical observations become available, the framework can be useful in evaluating, in a more conclusive manner, how and to what extent ther rate of interest *i* fragilizes the economy while the rate of return from real sector *r* anti-fragilizes it. Thus, future studies may contribute to the empirically estimation of the anti-fragility of interest-free financial systems.

5 Conclusion

This chapter provides an antifragility testing framework for risk-sharing finance. It is important to understand that antifragility is rather a new concept. The qualitative modelling of antifragility is laid down on sound foundations as the quantitative approach may be considered as work-in-progress. Moreover, while the original work has developed within the field of finance, the use of antifragility criteria has extended into other areas. Antifragility may well become a ubiquitous benchmark for risk management across many industries. This study is perhaps the first attempt to extend antifragility into the domain of risk-sharing finance. It provides some explanation of the analytical framework under which risk-sharing can be tested for antifragility.

It is essential to note that the issue is not about the modeling of an interest-free economy, but about the testing of interest-free macroeconomic models for antifragility. The field of antifragility is still in its initial stages of defining and articulating new mathematical approaches that can substitute for standard econometric methods. Mapping a deterministic model to antifragility tests remains an unexplored area in the domains of risk-sharing finance and antifragility. Hence, this chapter constitutes an attempt to provide an analytical framework for the demonstration of the antifragile nature of risk sharing finance and its implications for financial stability and sustainable economic development.

References

Askari, Hossein, Zamir Iqbal, Noureddine Krichene, and Abbas Mirakhor. 2012. *Risk Sharing in Finance: The Islamic Finance Alternative*. Singapore: John Wiley & Sons.

Askari, Hossein, Noureddine Krichene, and Abbas Mirakhor. 2014a. "Understanding Development in an Islamic Framework." *Islamic Economic Studies* 22(1): 1–36.

Askari, Hossein, Noureddine Krichene, and Abbas Mirakhor. 2014b. "On the Stability of an Islamic Financial System." *PLS Quarterly Review* 67(269): 131–167.

Askari, Hossein, Zamir Iqbal, and Abbas Mirakhor. 2009. *Globalization and Islamic Finance Convergence, Prospects and Challenges*. USA: John Wiley & Sons.

Fama, Eugene. 1965. "The Behavior of Stock Market Prices." *The Journal of Finance*. 38(1): 34–105.

Kahneman, Daniel. 2011. *Thinking Fast and Slow*. UK: Penguin Books Limited.

Khan, Mohsin S. 1986. "Islamic Interest Free Banking." *IMF Staff Papers* 33(1): 1–27.

Khan, Mohsin S., and Abbas Mirakhor. 1989. "The Financial System and Monetary Policy in an Islamic Economy." *Journal of King Abdul-Aziz University: Islamic Economics* 1(1): 39–57.

Mandelbrot, Benoit, and Richard Hudson. 2004. *The (Mis) Behavior of Markets*. USA: Basic Books.

Metzler, Lloyd A. 1951. "Wealth, Savings and the Rate of Interest." *Journal of Political Economy* 59: 93–116.

Mirakhor, Abbas. 1987. "Analysis of Short-Term Asset Concentration in Islamic Banking." *IMF Working Paper 87/67*. USA: International Monetary Fund.

Mirakhor, Abbas. 1993. "Equilibrium in a Non-Interest Open Economy." *JKAU: Islamic Econ* 5: 3–23.

Mirakhor, Abbas, and Iqbal Zaidi. 1988. "Stabilization and Growth in an Open Islamic Economy." *IMF Working Papers* 22(88): 1–37.

Taleb, Nassim, and Raphael Douady. 2013. "Mathematical Definition, Mapping, and Detection of (Anti) Fragility." *Quantitative Finance* 13(11): 1677–1689.

Taleb, Nassim. 2012. *Antifragile: Things that Gain from Disorder*. USA: Random House.

Taleb, Nassim. 2011. "A Map and Simple Heuristic to Detect Fragility, Antifragility, and Model Error." New York: Paper presented at JP Morgan.

Umar, Rafi and Mirakhor Abbas. 2017. *Antifragility of Islamic Finance: The Risk Sharing Alternative*. Switzerland: Peter Lang Inc.

Mohamed Ashraf Iqbal

Chapter 19: Modeling Bank Branch Efficiency using Data Envelopment Analysis

1 Introduction

The transition from brick and mortar banking to online banking is certainly gaining momentum, however the choices of which branches that need to be closed or reorganized is not as straight forward as branches are still need to provide products and services to customers. A bank's branch network tends to be the most resource-intensive part of the business where the highest number of employees and capital are employed. While the external challenge of managing the branch network is to ensure that products and services are relevant to the local customer base, the internal challenge is to ensure that all branches are appropriately resourced and the resources are utilized efficiently. This task is shared between the head office, which ensures that branches are correctly resourced and branch managers, who promote the effective use of available resources. Thus, banks are constantly looking for methods to accurately assess the efficiency of their branches to ensure every branch is correctly resourced and the resources are utilized efficiently. According to Paradi and Zhu (2013), parametric and non-parametric analyses, ratios, and other approaches such as the balanced scorecard constitute the four main methods typically used to assess branch network efficiency. Internally, banks rely on ratios and balance scorecards while researchers tend to adopt parametric and non-parametric analyses. Each approach has its own merits and demerits.

Among the various methods, Data Envelopment Analysis (DEA) is one of the most useful for branch network analysis as it overcomes many limitations associated with ratios, parametric analysis and balance scorecards. DEA is able to account for multiple inputs and outputs, does not require a specific relationship between the inputs and outputs to be defined, and it does not depend on pre-defined weights for each variable. It is non-parametric in nature and reports on both the scale characteristics and managerial efficiency of each branch. Because it is a frontier analysis, it provides the targets for each branch to be fully efficient. Yet DEA has not found so far, a broad-based adoption among bank managers, certainly not in Malaysia.

The reasons for the lack of adoption range from the basic challenge of reconciling differences in efficiency scores between branches against established measures of performance to the complex arguments about the modelling process itself. There are reconciliation challenges, as suggested by Drake and Howcroft (1994) study due to contradictory branch efficiency scores and cost-to-income ratios. As for the modelling process, a review of the related literature between 2003 and 2014 identified eleven bank branch level studies. Confirming the concerns of the bank managers around the

https://doi.org/10.1515/9783110587920-019

modelling process, there were no two studies that used the same set of inputs and outputs and all of the studies were based on data for a single year only.

Given the above, this study was undertaken with the objective of proposing a consistent approach to branch network analysis using DEA methodology. The approach is based on defining some criteria for variable selection, the model construction, followed by the analysis of results, including the examination of the relationship between efficiency and profitability. This analysis is done in order to allay concerns by bank managers about the use of efficiency as a measure of performance. To the best of our knowledge, this is the first branch-level DEA study of an Islamic bank with the efficiency characteristics of 115 branches using four models over a five-year time frame spanning the period from 2009 to 2013. Since these data are not publicly available and due to a confidentiality agreement, this study limits the time frame up to 2013. The operating methods of an Islamic and conventional bank branch are the same. Also, the accounting treatment standards for the classification of defaults is the same for both conventional and Islamic banking. The difference is in the underlying contracts that are used. Therefore, conventional banking terms are used in this chapter instead of the Islamic banking terms, such as interest instead of the profit rate, loans instead of financing.

2 Methodology

Based on the idea of Farrell (1957) who originally developed the non-parametric efficiency method, Charnes et al. (1978) were the first to introduce the term DEA to measure the efficiency of each decision-making unit (DMU), obtained as the maximum ratio of weighted outputs to weighted inputs (This approach is hereafter referred to as the CCR model). The more the output produced from a given input, the more efficient is the production. The CCR model is based on the overall technical efficiency (OE) and presupposes that there is no significant relationship between the scale of operations and efficiency and thus assumes the nature of efficiency to be of constant returns to scale (CRS). While the CRS assumption is only justifiable when all DMUs are operating at an optimal scale, in practice, firms or DMUs may face either economies or diseconomies of scale. Thus, if one makes the CRS assumption when not all DMUs are operating at the optimal scale, the computed OE measures may be undermined by scale inefficiency (SE).

The variable returns to scale (VRS) model was first proposed by Banker et al. (1984) and it is an extension of the CCR model, which derives efficiency estimates under the VRS assumption, and relaxes the CRS assumption. The VRS assumption is based on the measurement of pure technical efficiency (PTE). PTE estimates the efficiency of DMUs independent from the scale. Therefore, efficiency results derived from the VRS assumption should provide more reliable information on the efficiency of DMUs (Coelli et al., 1998). A fully efficient DMU under the VRS assumption may or may not be fully efficient under the CRS assumption. When a DMU is fully efficiency under both assumptions, it is also scale efficient and when it is not, then the DMU is also afflicted by scale inefficiency. As noted by Coelli et al. (1998), scale inefficiency represents the difference between the PTE and OE score.

Figure 19.1 provides a brief illustration of different measures of scale efficiency using a single input (*x* axis) and a single output (*y* axis). There are 5 DMU's denoted as DMU1, DMU2, ..., DMU5. A DMU's position on the chart shows its efficiency in converting input X into output Y. The CRS efficiency frontier is a straight line from the origin extending through DMU3, while the VRS efficient frontier connects only the most efficient DMU's which in turn dictate the shape of the line. The vertical line to DMU 1 indicate that no other DMU is able to use less input to produce the same outputs as DMU1 while the horizontal line at DMU 5 indicate that no other DMU is able to produce more outputs for the same level of inputs as DMU 5. Under the CRS assumption, input-oriented overall efficiency of DMU2 is the distance BB_c and measured as AB_c/AB. Under the VRS assumption, however, its technical efficiency would be BB_v measured as AB_v/AB Therefore, the difference between Bc and Bv is attributed to scale inefficiency and measured as AB_c/Ab_v.

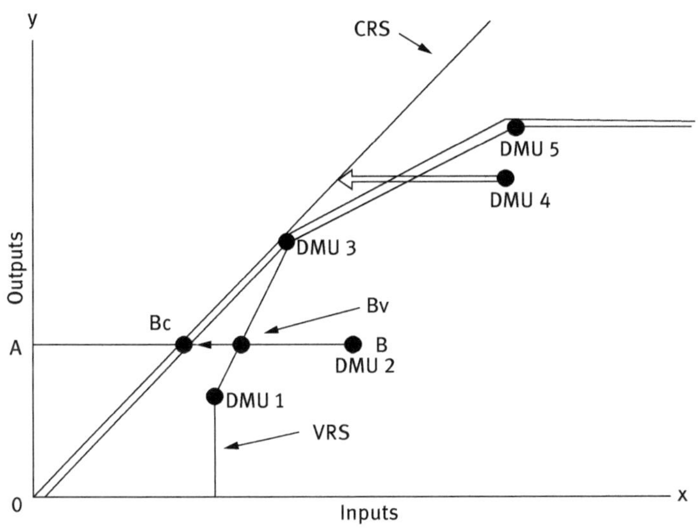

Figure 19.1: Calculation of Scale Economies in DEA.
Source: Coelli (1996).

Farrell (1957) posits that technical efficiency reflects the ability of a firm to obtain maximum output from a given set of inputs. The most basic measurement of efficiency is given as:

$$Efficiency = \frac{output}{input} \tag{1}$$

The above measure is appropriate as long as the production process consumes only one type of input to produce one type of output. In reality, most firms produce multiple outputs using multiple inputs and bank branches are no exception. Hence Equation (1) may be inadequate to capture the full range of production. To address this limitation, Farrell (1957) developed another measure of relative efficiency which involves multiple, possibly incommensurate inputs and outputs. This approach is aimed at defining a frontier of most efficient DMUs, and assessing how far each DMU are from the frontier in order to determine the efficiency of DMUs. The relative efficiency is measured as:

$$efficiency = \frac{weighted\ sum\ of\ outputs}{weighted\ sum\ of\ inputs} \tag{2}$$

Thus, this efficiency measure can be written as:

$$efficiency\ of\ DMU_j = \frac{u_1 y_{1j} + u_2 y_{2j} + \ldots}{v_1 x_{1j} + v_2 x_{2j} + \ldots} \tag{3}$$

where,

u_1 : the weight given to output 1
y_{1j} : the amount of output 1 from *DMUj*
v_1 : the weight given to input 1
x_{1j} : the amount of input 1 to *DMUj*

This function can be applied when there are a common set of weights for the DMUs. However, in practice, it may be difficult to find and agree on a common set off weights for each output and input because each DMU may have its own set of priorities. The difficulty in seeking common weights to determine relative efficiency was recognized by Charnes et al. (1978), who document the importance of different units that value inputs and outputs differently, resulting in different weights. Therefore, they suggested that each DMU be allowed to adopt a set of appropriate weights that are optimal with respect to other DMUs. In order to solve this weighting problem, the DEA method uses DMUs that can properly value inputs or outputs differently such that the efficiency rating of each DMU is maximized.

Thus, the maximization of DMU efficiency is subject to the condition that the efficiency of all other DMUs is less than or equal to 1. This optimization problem can be expressed as follows:

$$\text{maximize efficiency of DMU}_j: \quad \frac{\sum_r u_r y_{rj}}{\sum_r v_i x_{ij}} \tag{4}$$

subject to

$$\frac{\sum_r u_r y_{rk}}{\sum_r v_i x_{ik}} \leq 1 \; for\; each\; DMU_k \; for\; all\; k \neq j$$

$$u_i \geq \varepsilon$$

$$v_i \geq \varepsilon$$

where, ε is a small number that ensures neither input nor output is given zero weight, generally taken to be 1.0E-6.

The optimization equation above represents the fractional linear of the DEA method, and linear programming can be used to solve this model by setting the denominator to be equal to a constant. Therefore, the resulting linear programming can be rewritten as follows:

$$\text{maximize efficiency of DMU}_j\text{:} \quad \frac{\sum_r u_r y_{rj}}{\sum_r v_i x_{ij}} \tag{5}$$

subject to

$$\sum_{i=1}^{m} v_i x_{ij} = 1$$

$$\sum_{i=1}^{m} v_i x_{ik} - \sum_{i=1}^{m} u_r y_{rk} \leq 1, k = 1,\ 2, \ldots, N \; and \; k \neq j$$

$$u_r \geq \varepsilon, r = 1,\ 2, \ldots, s$$

$$v_i \geq \varepsilon, r = 1,\ 2, \ldots, m$$

where,

v_i : the weight assigned to input *i*
x_{ij} : the level of input *i* used by DMU_j
u_r : the weight assigned to output *r*
y_{rj} : the level of output r produced by DMU_j

If the value of efficiency of DMU unit *j* is equal to,1 then it will be considered "efficient" in the sense that no other DMU or combination of DMUs can produce more of one output without worsening other output levels and without utilizing higher input levels. In other words, the DMU is deemed as efficient if it fully utilizes its inputs to produce maximum outputs. However, if the value is less than 1, then the DMU is considered relatively inefficient. Hence, this model can be used to find the optimal combination of inputs and outputs weights which can maximize the efficiency of a DMU.

A brief illustration is presented hereafter to provide a better understanding of the DEA method. Assume that the data A represents inputs and B outputs for each of the N branches. For the jth branch, these are represented by the vectors of x_1 and y_1 respectively. Thus, $A \times N$ input matrix – X, and $B \times N$ output matrix – Y include data for all N branches. To measure the efficiency of each branch, the ratios of all outputs over all inputs are calculated as $u'y_j/v'x_j$ where u is a $B \times 1$ vector of output weights and v is a $A \times 1$ vector of input weights. To select the optimal weight, the following mathematical programming is adapted:

$$max_{u,v}\left(\frac{u'y_j}{v'x_j}\right) \tag{6}$$

subject to,

$$\left(\frac{'y_k}{v'x_k}\right) \le 1,$$

$$u, v \ge 0.$$

However, according to Coelli et al. (1998), there is an infinite number of solutions in the sense that, if (u^*, v^*) is a solution, then $(\alpha u^*, \alpha v^*)$ is also a solution for any scalar α. Therefore, it is possible to impose the constraint $v'x_j = 1$, which leads to:

$$max_{\mu,v}\mu' y_j \tag{7}$$

subject to,

$$v'x_k = 1, k = 1, 2, \ldots, N$$

$$\mu, v \ge 0.$$

The changing of notation from (u, v) to (μ, v) is used to reflect transformation to different linear programming problem. Hence, it is possible to derive an equivalent envelopment form using the dual form as follows:

$$max_{\theta,\lambda}\theta \tag{8}$$

subject to

$$y_i + y\lambda \ge 0,$$

$$\theta x_i - y\lambda \ge 0,$$

$$\lambda \ge 0.$$

where: θ: a scalar value of the efficiency score for the *jth* DMU, ranging between 0 and 1

λ: a $N \times 1$ vector of scalars

This envelopment form involves fewer constraints than the multiplier form ($A+B<N+1$), and therefore, is generally the preferred form to solve the programming problem of efficiency (Coelli et al. 1998).

3 Modeling Bank Branch Efficiency

The first step in DEA analysis is to determine the choice of inputs and outputs and the selection criteria and number of branches to be examined in the model. In considering the input and output variables to be used, Avkiran (1999) states the models should reflect the variables that are of concern to management, while Sufian (2009) suggests that the variables should be parsimonious. With respect to sample size, Cooper et al. (2006) suggest that for proper discrimination, the number of branches in the study should be more than three times the sum of inputs and outputs to ensure proper discrimination, while Dyson et al. (2001) argue that the branches selected should be homogeneous.

This section is sub-divided into nine sub-sections addressing the various steps and issues related to the modelling process ranging from the main business of branches to the reconciliation of branch efficiency and profitability.

3.1 The Main Business of a Branch

It is assumed that the business of a branch is to pursue profits, and the most efficient of branches are those capable of achieving the most profit using the least resources. The path to profitability is through balance sheet growth by undertaking financing activities (assets), which need to be matched by the collection of deposits (liabilities). To match assets and liabilities, branches may earn income by lending surplus funds to, or incur costs by borrowing funds from the head office. In addition, branches may earn income which is not related to financing activities through the selling of ancillary products and provision of services.

While the business of branches may seem to be rather smooth and straightforward, there is a degree of uncertainty stemming from customer defaults. Current accounting standards require an aggressive write-down of non-performing loans, which in turn can severely depresses branch profitability while the regularization of defaulted loans may cause significant one-off spikes in branch profitability. These accounting treatments constitute the pitfalls and windfalls of branch performance, and timing, therefore, is critical. A full year of profitable business can be wiped out by end-year defaults or suppressed performance can turn good with write-backs resulting from default recoveries.

Given the above outline of a bank's branch business, the next step is to determine the choice of variables that provide the best representation of branch efficiency. With parsimony in mind and to help managers focus, the goal is to find the fewest input and output variables that sufficiently capture the whole of the business. Operationally, the main difference between a conventional and an Islamic bank's branch is in the workflow and to a lesser extent the latter focus on non-finance income rather than finance income. As this may be the very first extensive branch level DEA study of an Islamic bank, we hope that it will provide another perspective into the discussions on Islamic banking.

3.2 Branch Inputs and Outputs

Given that the choice of input and output variables must be of interest to management, it is possible to consider the degree to which the head office is able to correctly resource branches and the effectiveness of each branch manager in using those resources in the pursuit of profits. Based on discussions with the bank's management, the variables in Table 19.1 are deemed to be key measures of branch performance.

Table 19.1: Description of Inputs and Outputs.

Outputs	Description
Loan Balance (Y1)	total outstanding financing recorded in the balance sheet
Savings Balance (Y2)	total savings deposits recorded in the balance sheet
FD Balance (Y3)	total fixed deposits (term deposits or certificate of deposits) recorded in the balance sheet
Net Operating Income (Y4)	net income from financing less expenses recorded in the income statement
Non-Finance Income (Y5)	non-finance income recorded in the income statement
Inputs	**Description**
Cost of Savings (X1)	profit paid to savings depositors
Cost of FD (X2)	profit paid to fixed deposit depositors
Cost of HQ Funds (X3)	profit earned or paid to HQ for surplus or shortfall in deposits
Number of Staff (X4)	number of employees on branch payroll on 31st Dec fiscal year
Cost of Staff (X5)	all cost directly related to the employment of staff
Cost of Opex (X6)	all other branch costs excluding staff cost
Cost of Impairment (X7)	cost of impaired financing taken as a write-down against income

Source: Author's own.

Note: The variables are expressed as units of 1000RM, except for the Number of Staff (X4)

While the variables reported in Table 19.1 are under the control of the branch managers there are some relationships between variables that need to be considered. The bank's financing rate, deposit rate and rate to borrowing/lending of funds from/to HQ are prescribed by the head office and these three rates are uniform across all branches with very little discretion given to branch managers to influence the rates. These rates dictate the relationship between the output variables Y1 and Y4, Y2 and X1, Y3 and X2 and Y1, Y2, Y3 and X3. This implies that at the branch level, outputs cannot be raised or inputs lowered simply by changing rates. To understand how all variables relate to each other, it is helpful to run a correlation analysis (Table 19.2). With the exception of X3, all variables have a positive relationship.

3.3 Model Construction

For the purpose of model construction and interpretation, it is important that the combination of variables and efficiency results be grasped intuitively by the managers. It is also useful to estimate a set of model variables so that managers are able to compare and contrast differences in efficiency results and understand the significance of different input and output variables. These four competitive models are estimated and reported with Model I serving as the baseline reference model where no variable lies under the control of branch managers while the other three models II, III, IV represent production models where all variables are under the control of the respective branch managers (see Table 19.3).

Model I (CE) focuses on capital efficiency and it is constructed using outputs from the balance sheet while inputs reflect the costs of the savings and fixed deposits as well as costs of funds borrowed/loaned from/to HQ. The relationships between outputs and inputs are dictated by three rates determined by the head office, including the financing rate, deposit rate, and HQ funds. As noted earlier, these are all beyond the authority of branch managers. Therefore, under this baseline model, the overall efficiency of all branches is expected to be high with negligible managerial inefficiency as there are no factors under the control of branch managers.

In contrast, Model II (BE) considers balance sheet efficiency by retaining the outputs included in Model I but replaces the inputs with factors under the control of branch managers. It measures the efficiency of each branch with the growth in assets relative to the resources made available to the branch manager. Some degree of variability in efficiency measurement across branches is expected. Given the individual impact of branch managers and the resources available to them, if two branches have similar levels of outputs, the one using lesser inputs in generating observed outputs is deemed to be more efficient.

The next transition is from the BE to the PE model whereby the inputs of the BE model are retained while the outputs are changed from balances to income. The model is now assessing the efficiency of the branch in generating income from the

Table 19.2: Pearson Correlation Coefficients between Variables.

	Loan Balance (Y1)	Savings Balance (Y2)	FD Balance (Y3)	Net Operating Income (Y4)	Other Income (Y5)	Cost of Saving (X1)	Cost of FD (X2)	Cost of HQ Funds (X3)	Number of Staff (X4)	Cost of Staff (X5)	Opex (X6)	Impairment (X7)
Loan Balance (Y1)	1.00											
Savings Balance (Y2)	0.75*	1.00										
FD Balance (Y3)	0.53	0.29	1.00									
Net Operating Income (Y4)	0.95*	0.72*	0.64	1.00								
Other Income (Y5)	0.59	0.46	0.48	0.69	1.00							
Cost of Saving (X1)	0.76*	0.97*	0.34	0.71*	0.47	1.00						
Cost of FD (X2)	0.54	0.30	0.97*	0.64	0.46	0.36	1.00					
Cost of HQ Funds (X3)	−0.38	−0.20	−0.96*	−0.52	−0.37	−0.26	−0.98*	1.00				
Number of Staff (X4)	0.78*	0.77*	0.27	0.77*	0.53	0.74*	0.25	−0.15	1.00			
Cost of Staff (X5)	0.83*	0.80*	0.34	0.79*	0.56	0.77*	0.36	−0.24	0.89*	1.00		
Opex (X6)	0.82*	0.68	0.45	0.78*	0.54	0.68	0.44	−0.32	0.80*	0.80*	1.00	
Impairment (X7)	0.47	0.28	0.42	0.57	0.78*	0.31	0.39	−0.31	0.42	0.43	0.45	1.00

Source: Author's own.

Note: * Statistical significance with $p < 0.001$.

Table 19.3: Models, Inputs and Outputs.

Model	Outputs	Inputs	Remarks
Model I: CE (Capital Efficiency)	Loan Balance (Y1) Savings Balance (Y2) FD Balance (Y3)	Cost of Savings (X1) Cost of FD (X2) Cost of HQ Funds (X3)	The CE model reflects the balance sheet on the outputs and cost of the balance sheet as inputs. It is free of any managerial influence and serves as a reference model. The efficiency of all branches should be relatively high.
Model II: BE (Balance Sheet Efficiency)	Loan Balance (Y1) Savings Balance (Y2) FD Balance (Y3)	Number of Staff (X4) Cost of Staff (X5) Opex (X6)	The BE model retains the outputs of the CE model but swaps the inputs with factors under the control of the branch manager. The difference in efficiency between the CE and BE model can be attributed to the effectiveness of the manager.
Model III: PE (Profit Efficiency)	Net Operating Income (Y5) Other Income (Y6)	Number of Staff (X4) Cost of Staff (X5) Opex (X6)	The PE model retains the inputs of the BE model but the outputs change from the balance sheet to the financial income generated by the balance sheet and other non-financing income. Any difference in efficiency between the BE and PE model should be attributable to the branch's ability to earn income from non-financing activities.
Model IV: RE (Risk Efficiency)	Net Operating Income (Y5) Other Income (Y6)	Number of Staff (X4) Cost of Staff (X5) Opex (X6) Impairment (X7)	The RE models retain all variables of the PE model but add impairment as an additional input to reflect the inherent risk of doing business. Thus, the difference between the PE and RE models can be attributed to the degree at which the branch is able to manage credit risk.

Source: Author's own.
Note: Regression analysis was conducted to test the validity and relationship between each model input and outputs against profit. The results found all models to be significant at the 0.001 level with each having an adjusted R2 > 0.90.

resources available to the manager. In the final transition, the PE model morphs into the RE model by the addition of one additional input which reflects how well credit risk is being managed. This study at the onset has no expectation of what the differences in efficiency will be like among the three production models. Having determined the model, the next step is to ensure the branches in the study are homogeneous.

3.4 Branch Selection

The importance of homogenous decision-making units for the implementation of the DEA approach is well established. In the analysis of bank branches, homogeneity needs to be considered in terms of location (urban-rural), type of local market (commercial-residential), and branch setup (full service-automated), among other factors. Following Doyle et al. (1979) and Boufounou (1995), branch age is used as the criterion for branch selection with five years of operation.[185] In total, 115 branches, the population of the study, met this requirement. The inclusion of branches below 5 years of age has the effect of tightening the envelopment curve and affecting the aggregate network efficiency, given the time new branches required to achieve profitability and business maturity.

The descriptive statistics reported in Appendix 1a and 1b. There is evidence from net operating income (Y4) and other income (Y5) of bank growth from 2009 to 2012, followed by a contraction in 2013. There is also an increase in the cost of savings (X1) and drop in the cost of HQ funds (X3) which suggest that branches have switched from being net borrowers to net lenders of funds to HQ. Table 19.4 provides a brief summary of the overall performance in terms of profitability. There is evidence of some discrepancy in the distribution of profits across branches.

Table 19.4: Distribution of Branches Based on Profit.

Profit Range (RM Million)	2009	2010	2011	2012	2013
Profit < 10	17.4%	12.2%	8.7%	2.6%	4.3%
10 ≤ Profit < 20	59.1%	55.7%	53%	35.7%	53.9%
20 ≤ Profit < 30	15.7%	22.6%	27%	43.5%	27.8%
30 ≤ Profit < 40	6.1%	7.0%	8.7%	11.3%	9.6%
40 ≤ Profit	1.7%	2.6%	2.6%	7.0%	4.3%

Source: Author's own.

The percentage of branches in the lower class of profitability has decreased over the years, while that of branches in the higher profits have increased. The share of branches achieving levels of profit between these classes has steadily grown from 51% to 91%. This evidence suggests that despite variations in the distribution of profits across branches, there is a tendency for a concentration of profits between the lower and higher branches, with a lower frequency of extremely low and extremely high profits.

185 five years ≈ mean branch age of the population minus one standard deviation

3.5 Implementation of DEA Methodology

The DEA analysis is conducted using PIMS-DEA software, which reports the overall efficiency (OE), managerial efficiency (PTE) and scale efficiency (SE) scores for each branch with respect to benchmark branches. The analytical results include also the total factor productivity (TFP) and input/output targets in order for each branch to be fully efficient. The DEA analysis can be run either to maximize outputs while holding inputs constant (output orientation) or to minimize inputs while holding outputs constant (input orientation). This study is based on input orientation in order to understand the efficiency of branches in relation to the existing business. Output orientation is rather useful for the assessment of the upside business potential.

In order to make rational decisions about resource-allocation across the branch network, it is essential to understand whether the returns to scale are constant or variable. In the case where the network is operating at variable returns to scale, it is imperative to determine if it is managerial efficiency (PTE) or scale efficiency (SE) that dominates. This assessment of returns to scale is necessary in light of the conflicting evidence from the literature, where some studies suggest that networks tend to operate at VRS[3] while others operate at CRS[4]. As suggested by Banker et al. (2010), it is possible to use the parametric paired t-test and non-parametric Kolmogorov-Smirnov (KS) to determine if the network is operating at CRS or VRS. Failure to reject the null hypothesis of no difference between OE and PTE efficiency suggests that the branch network is operating at CRS while rejecting the null is evidence of VRS-operating network.

3.6 Analytical Results

The estimation of the four DEA models based on capital efficiency (Model I), balance sheet efficiency (Model II), profit efficiency Model (III) and risk efficiency (Model IV) and their summary statistics are reported in Appendix 2a, 2b, 2c, and 2d, respectively. As noted earlier, the sample consists of 115 branches but the number of branches is reduced to 113 because of the absence of feasible solutions with respect to two branches. Three immediate observations can be made from these analytical results.

First, as predicted, Model I based on capital efficiency has the highest levels of efficiency relative to the other models with loss of efficiency attributable to scale (SE) rather than managerial efficiency (PTE). From the estimates of standard deviation, it appears that PTE remains high and stable over the years. There is a significant drop in both scale and managerial efficiency as the focus shifts from the capital efficiency model to the balance sheet efficiency (Model II), where inputs are replaced with factors under the control of branch managers. The evidence lends support to the notion that PTE is indeed a measure of managerial effectiveness as postulated by Berger et al. (1997), Camanho and Dyson (2005), and Li (2007).

Second, the branch network is found to be operating at variable returns to scale (VRS) for all models and time periods. Scale efficiency (SE) is found indeed to be significantly lower than managerial efficiency (PTE). In other words, while branch managers seem to be capable of operating with similar levels of efficiency, it is the head office that may be resourcing branches below their optimal size. This is an important result that may be useful in making optimal decisions about resource-allocation across branches.

Third, while there is evidence of increasing branch profitability over the period of study, none of the models showed improvements in efficiency. This finding is a source of concern for managers given that the cost-to-income ratios are conducive to higher efficiency. This concern can be addressed in the course of the discussion about branch efficiency and branch profitability.

3.7 Testing for Similarity

The results reported in Table 19.5 suggests that there are differences in efficiency across the different models. In the CE Model I, overall efficiency and scale efficiency

Table 19.5: Mean Efficiency Variations Over Time.

	2009	2010	2011	2012	2013
CE					
Overall Efficiency	95.79	94.92	95.97	95.91	95.52
Pure Technical Efficiency	99.55	99.42	99.41	99.19	99.07
Scale Efficiency	96.21	95.47	96.53	96.68	96.41
BE					
Overall Efficiency	79.42	75.56	74.46	70.61	68.22
Pure Technical Efficiency	95.59	95.81	95.70	96.16	95.04
Scale Efficiency	83.00	78.81	77.71	73.34	71.63
PE					
Overall Efficiency	74.51	69.28	70.55	69.44	70.94
Pure Technical Efficiency	94.39	94.52	94.89	95.69	94.84
Scale Efficiency	78.80	73.25	74.21	72.45	74.63
RE					
Overall Efficiency	75.05	73.93	74.21	70.50	72.43
Pure Technical Efficiency	95.59	95.72	96.11	96.44	95.10
Scale Efficiency	78.44	77.28	77.17	73.04	76.05

Source: Author's own calculations.

fluctuate over in a W-shaped movement, while technical efficiency exhibits a linear decline. In the balance sheet efficiency Model II, overall efficiency and scale efficiency are associated with straight decline but technical efficiency appears to be M-shaped. With respect to the profit efficiency Model III, technical efficiency takes an inverted tick, rising for the first 4 years then declining in 2013, while overall efficiency and scale efficiency are W-shaped. Finally, with respect to the risk efficiency Model IV, it is noted that both the overall and scale efficiencies are W-shaped whereas technical efficiency follows and inverted tick.

Asides from the description of the shape taken by efficiency curves, there is also a need to examine if the rank order of branches within a particular model is similar over the years. From the perspective of branch managers, there is more interest in the ranking of branches in relation to others rather than the actual efficiency score of individual branches. Between a top-ten branch with low-efficiency score and bottom-ten branch with a higher score, maybe a straightforward choice for managers whose preference would be for the former over the latter, hence rank order is important.

The assessment of branch rank-order is performed out using the Wilcoxon Signed-Rank test with the ranking criterion based on the managerial efficiency score. The objective is to test whether the rank order of branches, based on the PTE score, are similar from year to year. The results of rank tests indicate that the rank order of branches is not stable and tends to vary over the years depending on the efficiency models. Comparisons are within the model and not across models.

3.8 Branch Level Analysis

It is possible to examine the managerial efficiency scores of branches at the top, at the bottom, and mid-ranks based on the balance sheet efficiency, profitability efficiency and risk efficiency models.

Using the efficiency scores, branches can be ranked from 1 to 115 with the branch associated with the higher efficiency score of 100 ranked 1, and those with the lowest score ranked 115. Table 19.6 presents the evolution of ranking for the sample of branches over the years.

It is noted that branch 1 is ranked first with respect to the balance sheet efficiency model for the last three years, while it was 53rd in the initial year. Judging from their efficiency score of 98.19 in 2010, the lower ranking may not be however the sign of significant management ineffiiciency Branch 19 stands out among all branches, with the highest score of efficiency for all models and all-time periods. There is no consistency however in the performance of Branch 4, while ranks top only under the balance sheet efficiency model. Similarly, Branch 64 is associated with the higher efficiency score under the balance sheet efficiency score, but it ranks consistently first under both the profitability efficiency and risk efficiency models.

Table 19.6: Branch Ranking Based on PTE Efficiency Score.

Branch No:	Balance Sheet Efficiency (BE)					Profit Efficiency (PE)					Risk Efficiency (RE)				
	2009	2010	2011	2012	2013	2009	2010	2011	2012	2013	2009	2010	2011	2012	2013
1	53	35	1	1	1	86	96	98	40	1	1	1	106	38	1
2	98	103	64	111	106	113	114	97	112	110	114	115	109	114	108
3	56	92	105	112	112	90	99	112	114	111	105	109	115	41	110
4	1	1	1	1	1	70	71	66	60	58	40	47	79	66	56
5	60	47	48	24	39	81	61	58	19	38	94	69	69	23	39
18	57	45	70	76	57	47	43	78	73	42	54	49	92	72	40
19	1	1	1	1	1	1	1	1	1	1	1	1	1	1	1
20	102	113	112	113	109	97	101	101	105	102	108	110	111	110	99
63	59	61	51	39	37	46	58	53	59	26	55	70	66	70	30
64	43	1	32	34	41	1	1	1	1	1	1	1	1	1	1
65	54	1	23	1	44	67	33	33	21	21	71	39	42	1	1
114	1	32	1	1	20	1	24	1	1	23	1	23	1	1	24
115	1	1	1	1	24	15	1	1	1	32	1	1	1	1	33

Source: Author's own calculations.

Thus, it is clear that the efficiency and rank of individual branches do vary over time and depending on efficiency model estimations it may not be sufficient to examine the overall characteristics of the network, the individual branch characteristics are also important. While the overall characteristics reflect the extent to which head office is efficiently allocating resources across the branch network, individual branch analysis provides insights on how efficiently each branch is administered by its local manager.

3.9 Branch Efficiency and Branch Profitability

It was noted earlier that higher profitability of bank branches is not necessarily associated with higher efficiency, and this may send conflicting signals to branch managers. There are two main explanations related to the concepts of relative efficiency and rational inefficiency. Since DEA is a measure of relative efficiency rather than absolute efficiency, for a branch to improve its efficiency, it needs to improve more than the improvements in all other branches. Absolute efficiency may improve with better cost to income ratios, but if the pattern applies to all other branches, then relative efficiency may very remain the same for all branches.

With respect to rational inefficiency, Bogetoft and Hougaard (2003) argue that there is no economic rationale for branches to carry inefficiencies. Yet studies show that together with growth in profitability, branches tend to show increased inefficiency. It is argued that branches are willing to trade-off marginal efficiency for incremental profits. Hence the term "rational inefficiency" which implies a meaning conscious managerial preference for higher profits even under conditions of inefficiency. Typically, the branch would be allocated additional resources if it can be demonstrated that the marginal income remains higher than marginal costs. This managerial strategy may not improve efficiency but it contributes to higher profitability. This may explain in part why many studies have found a U-shape relationship between branch profitability and branch efficiency with the smallest and largest branches often being the most efficient. Appendix 3 describes the relationship between efficiency and profitability, and it appears that managerial efficiency under the three models based on the balance sheet, portfolio, and risk efficiency models (BE, PE, RE) tend to be U-shaped. Scale efficiency, however, is likely to follow a straight line rising from the smallest to the largest branches.

It is possible to understand these results using Figure 19.2, which shows the relationship between managerial efficiency and profitability, and Figure 19.3, which describes the linkage between profitability and scale efficiency. It is clear that managerial efficiency does indeed take a U-shape while scale efficiency rises in tandem with branch profitability. Both models of balance sheet efficiency and risk efficiency exhibit similar patterns. This empirical evidence lends credence to the theory of rational inefficiency.

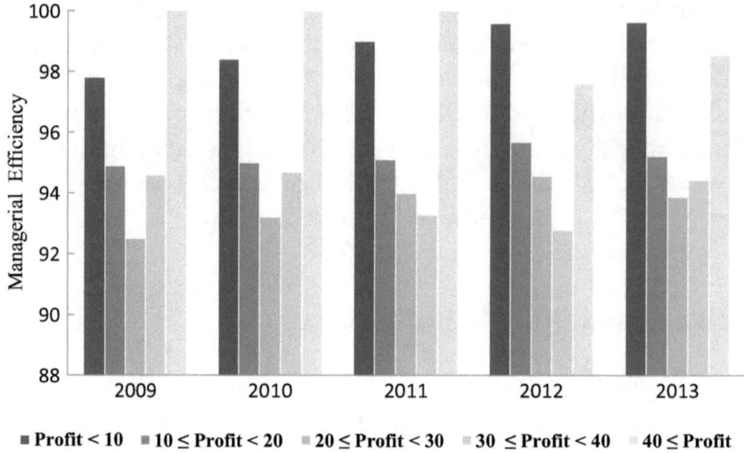

Figure 19.2: Risk Efficiency (Model IV) – Mean Managerial Efficiency by Profit Range. Source: Author's own calculations.

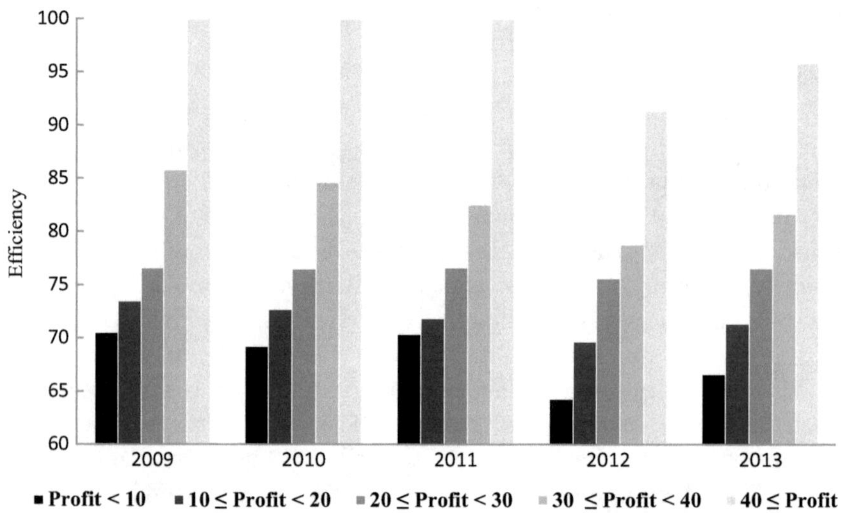

Figure 19.3: Profit Efficiency (Model iii) – Mean Scale Efficiency by Profit Range. Source: Author's own calculations.

4 Conclusion

This chapter provides evidence on the usefulness of data envelopment analysis. The examination of branch networks in Islamic banking addresses some of the concerns raised by bank managers with respect to the methodological approach by explaining the various steps of implementation. There are two main steps in the DEA analysis, including the estimation of efficiency score, and examination of the determinants of efficiency. DEA can provide managers with profound insights on the efficiency of both branch networks and individual branches. It identifies different levels of inefficiency thereby enabling managers to focus on the significant factors that determine efficiency and profitability. In the case of the bank's branch network estimation results of efficiency, models suggest that it is optimal to improve scale efficiency rather than managerial efficiency. Since DEA reports the distribution of returns to scale by branch, managers can reallocate resources from branches operating at decreasing returns to scale to those operating at increasing returns to scale, hence improving efficiency without increasing total resources. If the network is still operating at variable returns to scale after reallocation then additional resources shall be provided to branches with increasing returns to scale. However, managers need to ensure that additional resources are not associated with decreasing managerial efficiency. Due to the indivisibility of some resources, the ultimate objective is not to eliminate all inefficiency but to ensure that branches operate within a predetermined threshold of efficiency.

The results are robust to different models of efficiency and estimation periods but they may be sample dependent. Furthermore, the DEA approach has its own limits including the reliance on data, which may not be very accurate, and the potential underestimation of inefficiencies. These difficulties may be due to the dependence of the frontier on the set of DMUS. Measurement problems may also derive from difficulties in distinguishing outputs from other outcomes.

As the Islamic banking sector continues to develop as an integral part of the financial system, efficiency and profitability will grow in importance as reliable gauges of its maturity. It is crucial to understand differences in inputs and outputs between conventional banks and Islamic banks. The social and economic objectives of Islamic banks and their modus operandi also necessitate a redefinition of the concepts of profitability and risk measurement under the risk-sharing principle of Islamic finance. Future analytical studies should focus on the implications of this paradigm shift on the performance of Islamic banks. Modus operandi requires also a redefinition of the concepts of profitability and the measures of risk under the risk-sharing principle of Islamic finance. Future analytical studies should focus on the implications of the paradigm shift on the performance of Islamic banks.

References

Avkiran, Necmi K. 1999. "An application reference for data envelopment analysis in branch banking." *International Journal of Bank Marketing* 17(5): 206–220.

Banker, Rajiv D., Abraham Charnes, and William Wager Cooper. 1984. "Some models for estimating technical and scale inefficiencies in data envelopment analysis." *Management Science* 30(9): 1078–1092.

Banker, Rajiv D., Zhiqiang Eric Zheng, and Ram Natarajan. 2010. "DEA-based hypothesis tests for comparing two groups of decision-making units." *European Journal of Operational Research* 206(1): 231–238.

Berger, Allen N., John H. Leusner, and John J. Mingo. 1997. "The efficiency of bank branches." *Journal of Monetary Economics* 40: 141–162.

Bogetoft, Peter, and Jens Leth Hougaard. 2003. "Rational inefficiencies." *Journal of Productivity Analysis* 20(3): 243–271.

Boufounou, Paraskevi V. 1995. "Evaluating bank branch location and performance: A case study." *European Journal of Operational Research* 87(2): 389–402.

Camanho, Ana S., and Robert G. Dyson. 2005. "Cost efficiency measurement with price uncertainty: a DEA application to bank branch assessments." *European Journal of Operational Research* 161(2): 432–446.

Charnes, Abraham, William W. Cooper, and Edwardo Rhodes. 1978. "Measuring the efficiency of decision making units." *European Journal of Operational Research* 2(6): 429–444.

Coelli, Tim. 1996. *A guide to DEAP version 2.1: a data envelopment analysis (computer) program*. Centre for Efficiency and Productivity Analysis, University of New England.

Coelli, Tim, DS Prasada Rao, and G. E. Battese. 1998. *An Introduction to Efficiency and Productivity Analysis*. Boston: Kluwer Academic Publishers.

Cooper, William W., Lawrence M. Seiford, and Kaoru Tone. 2006. *Introduction to Data Envelopment Analysis and Its Uses*. New York: Springer US.

Doyle, P., I. Fenwick, and G. P. Savage. 1979. "Management planning and control in multi-branch banking." *Journal of the Operational Research Society* 30(2): 105–111.

Drake, Leigh, and Barry Howcroft. 1994. "Relative efficiency in the branch network of a UK bank: an empirical study." *Omega* 22(1): 83–90.

Dyson, Robert G., Rachel Allen, Ana S. Camanho, Victor V. Podinovski, Claudia S. Sarrico, and Estelle A. Shale. 2001. "Pitfalls and protocols in DEA." *European Journal of Oerational Research* 132(2): 245–259.

Farrell, Michael James. 1957. "The measurement of productive efficiency." *Journal of the Royal Statistical Society: Series A (General)* 120(3): 253–281.

Li, Chu-Fen. 2007. "Problems in bank branch inefficiency: management, scale and location." *Asian Journal of Management and Humanity Sciences* 1(4): 523–538.

Paradi, Joseph C., and Haiyan Zhu. 2013. "A survey on bank branch efficiency and performance research with data envelopment analysis." *Omega* 41(1): 61–79.

Sufian, F. 2009. Total Factor Productivity Change of the Malaysian Islamic Banking Sector: An Empirical Study. *Journal of Islamic Economics, Banking and Finance* 5(1): 73–88.

Sufian, Fadzlan. 2006. "The efficiency of non-bank financial institutions: empirical evidence from Malaysia." *International Journal of Finance and Economics* 6: 49–65.

Appendices

Appendix 1a: Descriptive Statistics for Outputs.

Outputs	2009	2010	2011	2012	2013
Loan Balance (Y1)					
Min	78,769.97	123,697.00	145,517.00	168,973.00	189,151.39
Mean	300,614.17	347,238.68	371,826.63	407,292.37	422,852.63
Max	766,010.25	972,271.00	989,272.00	1,098,543.00	1,119,962.60
Standard deviation	130,453.04	142,559.68	144,440.95	151,692.178	152,903.07
Savings Balance (Y2)					
Min	3,492.31	5,19300	6,511.00	9,525.00	8,654.00
Mean	20,051.31	21,723.43	23,053.83	28,007.98	26,713.60
Max	77,785.42	80,664.00	82,539.00	101,694.00	107,069.00
Standard deviation	12,462.35	12,334.01	12,565.57	15,216.63	15,509.39
FD Balance (Y3)					
Min	21,862.29	26,617.00	49,743.00	68,462.00	34,758.00
Mean	215,650.10	265,479.68	357,007.50	366,080.35	356,486.76
Max	1,412,818.63	2,001,538.00	2,691,383.00	2,813,519.00	2,751,624.00
Standard deviation	270,692.57	328,965.64	431,532.835	405,700.15	409,467.97
Net Operating Income (Y4)					
Min	3,307.23	4,525.70	7,293.03	9,002.29	7,976.22
Mean	20,299.91	24,300.17	25,268.34	27,794.91	24,343.56
Max	58,511.19	69,657.02	75,316.94	79,653.13	73,796.53
Standard deviation	9,883.91	12,132.86	11,706.08	12,146.17	11,161.68
Other Income (Y5)					
Min	179.81	338.53	355.78	416.63	379.52
Mean	1,540.01	1,804.869	2,093.38	2,048.04	1,447.09
Max	8,483.25	7,913.74	9,385.85	7,543.44	6,179.70
Standard deviation	1,375.18	1,327.00	1,515.05	1,287.02	989.76

Source: Author's own calculations.

Appendix 1b: Descriptive Statistics for Inputs.

Inputs	2009	2010	2011	2012	2013
Cost of Savings (X1)					
Min	29.75	55.75687	64.88549	96.98274	110.032
Mean	229.03	257.92	265.24	314.08	369.23
Max	1,048.56	1,032.50	1,041.29	1,203.47	1,858.89
Standard deviation	160.45	170.53	163.77	191.73	247.60
Cost of FD (X2)					
Min	224.50	760.9497	1,296.33	2,030.90	1,739.70
Mean	4,949.35	6,430.00	10,548.18	12,582.56	12,661.45
Max	41,867.67	46,498.23	77,485.12	95,915.97	95,335.26
Standard deviation	6,606.77	7,924.69	12,837.59	14,394.90	14,267.24
Cost of HQ Funds (X3)					
Min	−36,220.55	−46,542.17	−77,341.84	−99,220.89	−102,692.67
Mean	−387.41	−527.56	−3,820.74	−5,965.30	−5,721.81
Max	6,974.57	8,450.44	9,349.47	8,545.74	8,968.74
Standard deviation	6,725.36	8,732.03	13,836.45	15,856.92	15,871.91
Number of Staff (X4)					
Min	11	12	14	14	13
Mean	26	26	26	25	27
Max	51	48	47	44	43
Standard deviation	9	8	8	7	7
Cost of Staff (X5)					
Min	587	635	739	882	874
Mean	1,314	1,423	1,541	1,749	1,745
Max	2,848	2,889	2,918	3,162	3,099
Standard deviation	491	522	511	545	512
Opex (X6)					
Min	572	589	585	650	632
Mean	1,087	1,042	1,046	1,151	1,190
Max	2,513	2,151	2,029	2,135	2,113
Standard deviation	387	289	311	326	329
Cost of Impairment (X7)					
Min	40	314	447	418	−4,616
Mean	3,740	5,565	4,918	3,797	3,159
Max	18,338	31,617	24,062	20,393	13,449
Standard deviation	3,774	5,292	4,085	3,147	2,255

Source: Author's own calculations.

Appendix 2a: Estimation Results for Capital Efficiency (CE) Model I.

	Mean	Min.	Max.	Std. Dev.	Number of efficient branches	Returns to Scale
2009						
Overall Efficiency	95.79	83.38	100.00	3.51	15	
Pure Technical Efficiency	99.55	97.95	100.00	0.51	40	VRS
Scale Efficiency	96.21	84.89	100.00	3.23	15	
2010						
Overall Efficiency	94.92	85.57	100.00	3.15	11	
Pure Technical Efficiency	99.42	96.81	100.00	0.73	42	VRS
Scale Efficiency	95.47	87.52	100.00	2.81	11	
2011						
Overall Efficiency	95.97	83.84	100.00	3.45	22	
Pure Technical Efficiency	99.41	96.73	100.00	0.75	44	VRS
Scale Efficiency	96.53	83.84	100.00	3.10	22	
2012						
Overall Efficiency	95.91	79.77	100.00	3.67	21	
Pure Technical Efficiency	99.19	95.27	100.00	1.02	42	VRS
Scale Efficiency	96.68	83.73	100.00	3.13	21	
2013						
Overall Efficiency	95.52	84.55	100.00	3.66	20	
Pure Technical Efficiency	99.07	94.11	100.00	1.34	44	VRS
Scale Efficiency	96.41	85.97	100.00	3.19	20	

Source: Author's own calculations.
Note: The number of branches is reduced from 115 to 113 for model estimation based on observations for the year 2009 because of the failure to reach feasible solutions for two branches.

Appendix 2b: Estimation Results for Balance Sheet Efficiency (BE) Model II.

	Mean	Min.	Max.	Std. Dev.	Number of efficient branches	Returns to Scale
2009						
Overall Efficiency	79.42	59.88	100.00	9.09	8	
Pure Technical Efficiency	95.59	86.85	100.00	3.30	18	VRS
Scale Efficiency	83.00	65.52	100.00	8.09	8	
2010						
Overall Efficiency	75.56	58.13	100.00	9.77	6	
Pure Technical Efficiency	95.81	86.93	100.00	3.30	20	VRS
Scale Efficiency	78.81	62.60	100.00	9.17	6	

Appendix 2b (continued)

	Mean	Min.	Max.	Std. Dev.	Number of efficient branches	Returns to Scale
2011						
2011Overall Efficiency	74.46	56.23	100.00	10.18	6	
Pure Technical Efficiency	95.70	86.50	100.00	3.32	21	VRS
Scale Efficiency	77.71	57.69	100.00	9.42	6	
2012						
Overall Efficiency	70.61	51.91	100.00	10.76	5	
Pure Technical Efficiency	96.16	86.90	100.00	3.22	21	VRS
Scale Efficiency	73.34	57.44	100.00	10.15	5	
2013						
Overall Efficiency	68.22	51.51	100.00	11.66	6	
Pure Technical Efficiency	95.04	87.47	100.00	3.61	16	VRS
Scale Efficiency	71.63	55.38	100.00	10.75	6	

Source: Author's own calculations.

Appendix 2c: Estimation Results for Profit Efficiency (PE) Model III.

	Mean	Min.	Max.	Std. Dev.	Number of efficient branches	Returns to Scale
2009						
Overall Efficiency	74.51	54.34	100.00	10.00	4	
Pure Technical Efficiency	94.39	84.22	100.00	4.00	12	VRS
Scale Efficiency	78.80	54.34	100.00	8.70	4	
2010						
Overall Efficiency	69.28	49.66	100.00	10.91	4	
Pure Technical Efficiency	94.52	84.10	100.00	4.05	15	VRS
Scale Efficiency	73.25	50.55	100.00	10.55	4	
2011						
Overall Efficiency	70.55	44.80	100.00	11.24	4	
Pure Technical Efficiency	94.89	83.69	100.00	3.91	16	VRS
Scale Efficiency	74.21	51.12	100.00	10.35	4	
2012						
Overall Efficiency	69.44	45.88	100.00	10.38	3	
Pure Technical Efficiency	95.69	85.98	100.00	3.52	18	VRS
Scale Efficiency	72.45	52.09	100.00	9.54	3	
2013						
Overall Efficiency	70.94	51.41	100.00	10.53	4	
Pure Technical Efficiency	94.84	86.10	100.00	4.00	19	VRS
Scale Efficiency	74.63	57.34	100.00	9.18	4	

Source: Author's own calculations.

Appendix 2d: Estimation Results for Risk Efficiency (RE) Model IV.

	Mean	Min.	Max.	Std. Dev.	Number of efficient branches	Returns to Scale
2009						
Overall Efficiency	75.05	54.34	100.00	9.94	4.00	
Pure Technical Efficiency	95.59	86.64	100.00	3.47	20.00	VRS
Scale Efficiency	78.44	54.34	100.00	9.19	4.00	
2010						
Overall Efficiency	73.93	60.33	100.00	9.22	4.00	
Pure Technical Efficiency	95.72	87.53	100.00	3.41	22.00	VRS
Scale Efficiency	77.28	60.73	100.00	9.30	4.00	
2011						
Overall Efficiency	74.21	55.36	100.00	10.17	6.00	
Pure Technical Efficiency	96.11	87.33	100.00	3.15	21.00	VRS
Scale Efficiency	77.17	55.36	100.00	9.77	6.00	
2012						
Overall Efficiency	70.50	52.92	100.00	10.07	3.00	
Pure Technical Efficiency	96.44	87.19	100.00	3.09	22.00	VRS
Scale Efficiency	73.04	53.92	100.00	9.61	3.00	
2013						
Overall Efficiency	72.43	53.58	100.00	10.37	4.00	
Pure Technical Efficiency	95.10	86.87	100.00	3.89	22.00	VRS
Scale Efficiency	76.05	59.77	100.00	9.45	4.00	

Source: Author's own calculations.

Appendix 3: Mean Efficiency by Profit Range.

Profit in RM Mil		Profit < 10	10 ≤ Profit < 20	20 ≤ Profit < 30	30 ≤ Profit < 40	40 ≤ Profit
2009	***No of branches***	***20***	***68***	***18***	***7***	***2***
BE	OE	63.01	65.64	72.64	87.82	100
	PTE	97.62	94.48	93.16	96.53	100
	SE	64.55	69.36	77.51	90.71	100
PE	OTE	68.77	69.69	70.81	81.32	100
	PTE	97.58	94.63	92.17	94.51	100
	SE	70.5	73.44	76.56	85.77	100
RE	OTE	70.07	70.68	74.78	82.2	100
	PTE	97.83	94.9	92.52	94.58	100
	SE	71.62	74.31	80.74	86.67	100
2010	***No of branches***	***14***	***64***	***26***	***8***	***3***
BE	OE	61.37	64.52	71.24	88.08	100
	PTE	98.12	94.56	93.45	96.85	100
	SE	62.55	68.13	75.99	90.73	100
PE	OTE	67.94	68.92	71.34	80.2	100
	PTE	98.23	94.67	92.92	94.62	100
	SE	69.17	72.64	76.48	84.57	100
RE	OTE	67.94	70.24	74.4	81	100
	PTE	98.39	94.97	93.21	94.72	100
	SE	69.05	73.83	79.65	85.36	100
2011	***No of branches***	***10***	***61***	***31***	***10***	***3***
BE	OE	61.36	64.02	70.72	83.42	100
	PTE	98.36	94.86	93.84	95.11	100
	SE	62.44	67.41	75.12	87.26	100
PE	OTE	69.51	68.19	72.03	77.09	100
	PTE	98.74	94.82	93.7	93.1	100
	SE	70.35	71.79	76.61	82.51	100
RE	OTE	69.51	69.23	74.72	79.48	100
	PTE	98.95	95.11	93.98	93.28	100
	SE	70.21	72.67	79.35	85.06	100

Appendix 3: (continued)

Profit in RM Mil		Profit < 10	10 ≤ Profit < 20	20 ≤ Profit < 30	30 ≤ Profit < 40	40 ≤ Profit
2012	***No of branches***	***3***	***41***	***50***	***13***	***8***
BE	OE	57.66	61.89	67.7	75.94	95.34
	PTE	99.32	95.61	94.08	93.64	98.86
	SE	58.04	64.69	71.82	80.75	96.31
PE	OTE	63.86	66.49	71.54	73.02	89.33
	PTE	99.34	95.39	94.33	92.39	97.56
	SE	64.27	69.64	75.59	78.79	91.36
RE	OTE	63.86	67.57	72.97	76.84	89.97
	PTE	99.6	95.67	94.57	92.78	97.62
	SE	64.11	70.56	76.99	82.69	92
2013	***No of branches:***	***5***	***62***	***32***	***11***	***5***
BE	OE	60.04	63.72	69.52	79.12	100
	PTE	99.5	94.98	93.65	95.19	100
	SE	60.32	67.01	74.04	82.95	100
PE	OTE	66.26	67.88	71.81	77.06	94.59
	PTE	99.47	94.98	93.5	94.16	98.56
	SE	66.6	71.34	76.54	81.66	95.82
RE	OTE	66.26	68.41	75.19	79.68	94.8
	PTE	99.63	95.22	93.87	94.43	98.56
	SE	66.5	71.75	79.93	84.25	96.04

Source: Author's own calculations.

Mohsin Ali

Chapter 20: An Empirical Analysis of Income Structure and Profitability of Islamic and Conventional Banks in South Asia

1 Introduction

Sustainable economic growth rests on a well-functioning financial system. Generally, it is believed that the banking sector affects economic growth positively by bridging the gap between surplus units and deficit units. The empirical literature suggests that the development of the banking system is crucial for economic growth (Rajan and Zingales 1998; Bertocco 2008; Jalil et al. 2010; Rahaman 2011; Law et al. 2013). Despite the evidence about the importance of an efficient banking sector, an over-leveraged and fragile banking system can also be conducive to major financial crises (Beck et al. 2009).

Although the main role of conventional banks is to act as intermediaries between depositors and borrowers (Yun Zhang 2010), intense and ever-increasing competition has paved the way for the banking system to gradually decrease the share of intermediation activities in total banking activities (Allen and Santomero 2001). Given the increasing degree of competition, expanding the share of non-intermediary banking activities is a necessity, rather than an option. Such structural shifts in business activities imply greater diversification of the sources of income. At the micro level, diversified sources of income smooth out total operating income because non-traditional activities are assumed to be uncorrelated with intermediation-based traditional banking activities (Chiorazzo et al. 2008). However, as argued by DeYoung and Roland (2001), income from non-traditional activities may be associated with larger variations because the switching from these activities is rather easier as compared to traditional intermediation activities.

In recent periods, non-intermediation banking activities were the subject of a broad strand of studies focusing on the linkages between non-intermediation income and bank profitability, as well as, non-intermediation income and risk management. Most of the existing literature focuses on the U.S. and European banks, but the role of non-intermediary income on banks' business activities has not been extensively examined for banks in South Asia, where banks represent the predominant source of financing (Deesomsak et al. 2004, Ito 2006). Although the main business of banks is still lending, an increasing number of banks have shifted into investment banking and other related activities in South Asia. It is this structural shift towards non-intermediation activities that warrants further analysis of its potential implications on bank performance as well as on economic performance in South Asian countries.

https://doi.org/10.1515/9783110587920-020

Another feature of South Asian countries is the emergence of Islamic banking, which indeed, has played a leading role in the overall expansion of Islamic finance. Islamic banking promotes an alternative form of financing in the region. In addition to financial intermediation, Islamic banks also offer fee-based services including *kafalah* (guarantee), *amanah* (safe keeping), *wakalah* (agency) and *joalah* (promise of reward). These non-intermediation activities have the potential to affect the risk-return profile of Islamic banks differently as compared to the intermediation-based activities. In light of these developments, there is however still a scant literature about the impact of non-traditional activities on Islamic banks in South Asia. The existing literature focuses on other Asian countries, including the study by Shahimi et al. (2006), which examines the characteristics of Islamic banks in Malaysia that determines the development of non-traditional banking activities. Also, Karakaya and Er (2013) analyze the relation between non-interest income and performance of commercial and participation banks in Turkish banking system. Other studies focus also on the determinants of bank risk and profitability including Bashir (2003), Al-Kassim (2005), Haron and Azmi (2004), Smaoui and Salah (2011), Masruki et al. (2010), Ashraf and Rehman (2011). Although part of the literature employs non-interest income as control variable, the impact of non-traditional activities on Islamic banks *per se* has rarely been the subject of empirical analysis.

The importance of these new activities in comparison with traditional financial intermediation has increased over time since financial institutions have intensified their risk diversification efforts (Demirguc-Kunt and Huizinga, 2010; Baele et al., 2007). Arguably, bank activities based on financial intermediation and non-intermediation are meant to serve different purposes and functions, and may have different effects on economic growth and volatility. The existing literature does not focus on the effects of non-interest and financing income on growth and volatility (Beck et al., 2014). Thus, the objective of the present study is to examine the significance of non-interest income and fee income financing activities and the effect of non-traditional banking activities on the performance of Islamic banks *vis-à-vis* their conventional counterparts in South Asia. The chapter is organized as follows. The next section includes a brief literature review. The third section provides a description of the econometric model and data. The analysis is based on the estimation of empirical models using the generalized method of moments (GMM) estimator developed by Arellano and Bond (1991) (i.e. the difference GMM) and the system-GMM estimator suggested by Blundell and Bond (1998) both for dynamic panel data. The fourth section discusses the empirical results and the final section concludes the chapter.

2 Literature Review

There is mixed evidence form the existing literature on the effects of non-intermediary sources of income on several bank indicators. Early studies include, for instance, Demsetz and Strahan (1997), who employ market-based data to study bank holding companies (BHCs) listed in the U.S. markets and find that diversification gains are positive associated with the size of bank assets. Kwan (1998) examines the BHC subsidiaries and suggests that higher risk does not guarantee higher profitability due to the fact that the correlation of returns is low. Cornett et al. (2002) use accounting information on a sample of BHCs in the U.S. and find an improvement in operating pre-tax cash flow returns. There is no evidence however of an increase in risks attributed to migration toward investment banking activities. Smith et al. (2003) employ accounting data from Bankscope on a large sample of financial institutions from fifteen EU member countries, and provide evidence that non-interest income tends to be more volatile than interest-based income. It is suggested that there is an indirect relationship between non-interest based income activities and interest-generating activities, and that venturing into some types of activities may cause a decrease in earnings volatility. In addition, the studies by Ramasastri et al. (2004) on Indian banks, and Lin et al. (2005) on Taiwanese banks provide further evidence on the benefits of diversification.

Stiroh and Rumble (2006) examine the effects of a shift towards non-interest income based activities such as fees and trading on the performance of financial holding companies (FHCs) in the U.S. from 1997 to 2002. The results indicate that there are potential benefits from diversification, but they are not significant enough to compensate for the increased risk associated with non-interest activities. These activities are found to be relatively more volatile but not necessarily more lucrative than interest-based activities. It is suggested that the marginal increase in non-interest returns are associated with lower risk-adjusted profits, hence revenue diversification does not necessarily lead to better performance. Also, Hirtle and Stiroh (2007) use both accounting and market data on a sample of U.S. financial institutions to examine the effects of financing retail clients on the relation between risk and return. It is found that the degree of retail banking is negatively related to market return, particularly for small and mid-size financial institutions. There is no clear evidence about the sign of this association for large financial institutions as there is no significant impact on earnings volatility.

Chiorazzo et al. (2008) use annual data from Italian banks, to examine the relationship between non-interest income and profitability. It is found that income diversification increases risk-adjusted returns. The empirical evidence is in line with other studies on European banks, but it is not consistent with studies on U.S banks. The relation between non-interest income and profitability is stronger for large banks, but there are limits to the benefits of diversification as bank size increases. Smaller banks can only make profits from non-interest income, if they have limited initial share of non-interest income. Thus, the level of non-interest income seems to be more important than its source. Demirgüc-Kunt and Huizinga (2010) use a world-wide sample of banks to examine the impact of different bank activities and short-term funding strategies on the relation between risk and return prior to the U.S. financial crisis. It is found that expansion into non-interest-based activities increases the return on assets, and at very low levels it can also result in risk diversification benefits. In contrast, non-deposit funding decreases the return on assets, and may offer some level of risk reduction. Banking strategies based on non -interest income or non-deposit funding are found to be rather risky, a result which may explain the decline of the U.S. investment banking sector.

Geyfman and Yeager (2009) examine the impact of universal banking on the risks of financial holding companies and banks prior and after the passage of the 1999 Gramm-Leach-Bliley Act. Using equity data for public listed banks, it is found that institutions involved in universal banking had higher total and systematic risks as compared to banks focusing on traditional activities. Following Gramm-Leach-Bliley regulation, universal banking is conducive to moderate benefits from risk diversification. It is found that fee-generating banking activities are inversely related to traditional banking activities, and that BHCs with investment banking activities are associated with greater total and idiosyncratic risks, but with the same systematic risks as banks focused on traditional activities only. The authors argue also that Gramm-Leach-Bliley Act allowed for universal banks to takeover independently operating investment banks, preventing thereby a total failure of the U.S. financial system during the financial crisis.

In contrast, there are others studies providing little evidence in support of the hypothesis of positive effects of income diversification. For instance, DeYoung and Roland (2001) suggest that revenue diversification is associated with negative effects. To test the impact of bank product diversity on earnings volatility, the authors use a measure of the theoretical linkage between earnings volatility and revenue volatility, as well as diversification and variability of expenses for a sample of U.S. commercial banks. The results suggest that that moving from intermediation activities towards fee-based activities is associated with higher volatility of revenues as well as higher total leverage, which implies higher earnings volatility.[186]

Insofar that Islamic banks are concerned, the literature on the impact of non-traditional activities by Islamic banks are rather scant. In additon to the results of previous studies by Shahimi et al. (2006) and Karakaya and Er (2013) addressed above, it is noted that Molyneux and Yip (2013) also examine the linkage between income diversification and performance of Islamic banks. This study is based on accounting data for a sample of conventional and Islamic banks in Muslim majority

186 The empirical findings by DeYoung and Roland (2001) were verified by many other studies including Stiroh (2004), Stiroh (2006b), Baele et al. (2007), Lepetit et al. (2008), Chiorazzo et al. (2008), Sanya and Wolfe (2011) and DeJonghe (2010).

countries including Malaysia, Saudi Arabia, Kuwait, United Arab Emirates, Bahrain and Qatar. The evidence suggests that the focus of Islamic banks on non-financing income has positive effects on their risk-adjusted performances. Higher income diversification, however, increases volatility, which negatively affects risk-adjusted returns. The authors provide also evidence that Islamic banks are less diversified in comparison to their conventional counterparts, and more reliant on deposit/loan financing. Given their lower reliance on non-interest income-generating activities, Islamic banks tend to be less vulnerable to earnings volatility. They are also found to be less profitable on a risk-adjusted basis as compared to conventional banks. In addition to these empirical studies on Islamic banking, the literature has generally focused on the determinants of bank risk and profitability.[187] Some of these empirical studies include non-interest income as control variable, but the need remains for the empirical testing of its significance.

3 Data and Methodology

3.1 Data Description

The empirical analysis is based on a sample of Islamic banks, conventional banks and investment banks from South Asia over the period 2005–2013. The data are obtained from Bankscope database of the Bureau van Dijk's company and Worldbank World Governance Indicators. Banks are selected under the condition of the availability of a minimum period of four years of data observations. The final sample covers a total of 84 banks from four South Asian countries, including Afghanistan, Bangladesh, Pakistan and Maldives, including 60 conventional banks, 16 Islamic banks, and 8 investment banks.

3.2 Variable Definitions and Empirical Model

Given the objectives of the present study, the dependent variable is represented by a measure of bank profitability and risk, respectively. Bank profitability is measured by the return on assets (ROA) and return on equity (ROE), whereas risk is measured by the z-score. For this purpose, it is possible to follow previous studies such as Cihak and Hesse (2008), and Demirgüç-Kunt and Detragiache (2011). The z-score measures the number of standard deviations by which ROA has to decline below its expected value before equity is exhausted and the bank becomes insolvent. The ratio of net

187 See for instance, Bashir (2003); Hassan and Bashir (2003); Al-Kassim (2005); Karim et al. (2010); Smaoui and Salah (2011); Masruki et al. (2010); Ashraf and Rehman (2011).

non-interest/financing income to net operating income (LNIIOI) is used as proxy for non-interest/financing income, which consists of trading, fees and commission activities. It is noted also that Lepetit et al. (2008) and Laeven and Levine (2007) measure other operating income as the combination of net fee, net commission, and net trading income. Similar proxies have been used by DeYoung and Roland (2001) and Stiroh and Rumble (2006).

With respect to control variables, it is possible to include the bank size, measured by log of total assets (LTA), ratio of loans to total assets (LNTA), ratio of deposits to total assets (LCDTA), ratio of equity to total assets (EA), and ratio of loan/financing loss provisions to total assets (LLPTA). In addition to these bank-specific control variables, some macro-level control variables are used as well, including the Gross Domestic Product (LGDP) and inflation rates (LINF). The analysis relies also on the use of some dummy variables including ISL representing Islamic banks, and INVEST representing investment banks. The interactive dummy ISL-LNIIOI is used to capture the impact of LNIIOI on the dependent variable with respect to Islamic banks.

Thus, the following dynamic panel data model is used to empirically examine the relation between bank profitability or risk measures and accounting ratios.

$$Profitabilty_{kt} = \alpha_0 + \alpha_1 Profitabilty_{kt-1} + \alpha_2 NFI_{kT} + \alpha_3 Control_{kt} + \in_{kt} \tag{1}$$

$$Risk_{kt} = \beta_0 + \beta_1 Risk_{kt-1} + \beta_2 NFI_{kt} + \beta_3 Control_{kt} + \mu_{kt} \tag{2}$$

where k and t refer to bank number and time, respectively. Profitability refers to the return on assets (ROA) and return on equity (ROE), whereas *Risk* is measured by z-score. Finally, NFI refers to non-financing income and *Control* represents the list of control variables.

3.3 Methodology

The dynamic panel data exhibit two important features, including the autocorrelation function reflecting the presence of lagged dependent variables, as well as the specific effects associated with the unobserved heterogeneity problems. The latter can be addressed using the generalized method of moments (GMM) analysis by Arellano and Bover (1995) and Blundell and Bond (1998), including regressions both in the levels and differences. Using the GMM estimator, the instruments for the level equations are the lagged differences of the corresponding variables.

The system GMM method is conducive to more consistent and efficient estimators of model coefficients, and provides remedies for the problems of endogeneity, heteroscedasticity, and autocorrelation (Arellano and Bover, 1995). The dynamic panel technique is also helpful in amending the bias induced by omitted variables in cross-sectional estimates and the inconsistency caused by endogeneity. In addition, the dynamic panel analysis is appropriate for the present study, with a rather short sample period and a large number of cross-sections per year particularly for Islamic banks. The robustness tests are performed by repeating the same estimations using two-step system GMM with robust standard errors.

4 Results and Discussion

Table 20.1 presents descriptive statistics of the variables related to our study. The banks on average remain profitable over the sample period, though the variability remains high. The descriptive statistics of Z-score, which is a measure of bank stability, suggest that on average banks from South Asia remain fairly stable. The descriptive statistics of our main variable NIIOI suggest that 47% of the operating income of the banks in the sample comes from non-intermediation activities. NIIOI also seems to have high level of variability.

Table 20.1: Descriptive Statistics.

Variables	Mean	Standard Deviation
ROA	0.448	6.417
ROE	12.651	70.420
Z-Score	2.326	1.114
NIIOI	47.441	174.012
TA	1,613.09	2,370.61
LTA	6.400	1.630
CDTA	72.210	19.907
EA	13.596	17.998
GLTA	54.660	22.685
LLPTA	1.007	2.157
GDP	96,747.5	38,793.4
LGDP	11.240	0.966
Inf	9.434	4.508

Source: Author's own.

The estimation results reported in Table 20.2 shows the impact of non-intermediation activities on bank risk and return. The evidence from the estimation of Model 1 and Model 2 based on the ROA and ROE variables, respectively, suggests that non-intermediation income has positive and significant effects on bank profitability in the South Asian region. This result is consistent with the descriptive statistics reported earlier where non-interest/financing income to net operating income amounts to 47.44% for South Asian banks. With respect to control variables, the ratio of equity to total assets appears to be positively related with the return on assets, but negatively

Table 20.2: Significance of Non-Intermediation Income for South Asian Banks.

	Model 1 ROA	Model 2 ROE	Model 3 z-score
L.ROA	0.442***		
	(4.53)		
L.ROE		0.480***	
		(4.18)	
L.Z-score			0.872***
			(15.84)
NIIOI	0.194*	0.285*	0.00933
	(1.71)	(1.66)	(0.15)
EA	0.206*	−0.444***	0.325***
	(1.68)	(−4.23)	(3.71)
GLTA	0.461***	0.352***	0.237**
	(4.00)	(3.14)	(2.05)
LTA	0.121**	0.131**	0.0701***
	(2.33)	(2.50)	(2.63)
LGDP	−0.150**	−0.112*	−0.0153
	(−2.46)	(−1.83)	(−0.34)
INF	0.0658	0.00326	0.0215
	(0.54)	(0.03)	(0.43)
CDTA	−0.245	−0.425**	0.0881
	(−1.05)	(−1.99)	(1.24)
LLPTA	−0.163***	−0.175***	−0.0604***
	(−3.38)	(−3.08)	(−3.53)
ISL	−0.722	−0.357	−0.351
	(−0.80)	(−0.41)	(−0.97)
ISLxNIIOI	0.194	0.0887	0.0812
	(0.81)	(0.38)	(0.73)
Constant	−1.266	1.888	−2.174***
	(−0.97)	(1.45)	(−2.79)
AR(1) p-value	0.00675	0.00893	0.121
AR(2) p-value	0.404	0.431	0.540
Hansen test statistic	0.255	0.0418	0.0820

Source: Author's own calculations.
Notes: t-statistics in parentheses. *, ** and *** denote significance at 10%, 5% and 1%, respectively.

related with return on equity. The bank size seems also to exert positive and significant effects on bank profitability.

The evidence suggests also that gross financing and loan-loss provision are useful in explaining bank profitability. Whereas the gross financing, which is a proxy for bank intermediation, increases bank profitability, the loan-loss provision used to measure bank credit risk is rather associated with a negative and significant sign. These empirical results are in line with the theoretical arguments, as an increase in bank financing is expected to raise bank profitability as suggested by Molyneux et al. (2013) and Chiorazzo et al. (2008). However, lower loan quality is expected to reduce bank returns as documented by Chiorazzo et al. (2008) and DeYoung and Rice (2004). Also, the explanatory variable GDP appears to be negatively related to bank profitability in South Asia, whereas other control variables remain statistically insignificant. Judging from the insignificance of the interaction term based on the ratio of non-interest financing income to net operating cots, it is difficult to distinguish Islamic banks from their conventional counterparts in the South Asian region in terms of income structure.

The estimation results of Model 3 based on the z-score risk measure indicate that non-interest/financing income does not impact bank's risk. There is evidence that the ratio of equity to total assets is significant at the 1% level and has a positive relationship with z-score. This implies that an increase in capitalization is likely to decrease bank risk. Also, an increase in gross financing seems to reduce bank risk. Total assets are also found to be positively and significantly related to the z-score, implying that increase in bank size is conducive to lower bank risk. Also, an increase in credit risk increases banks' default risk in the South Asian region. It is noted that other control variables have no significant impact on bank risk. The dummy variables and interactive terms remain also insignificant. This evidence implies that Islamic and conventional banks have similar business structures and that non-intermediation income is not associated with asymmetric effects.

5 Conclusion

The objective of this analytical study is to examine the growing tendency towards bank product diversification and the potential effects on the levels of risk and return for South Asian banks. The aim is to understand also the significance of these trends with respect to Islamic banks as compared to conventional counterparts. The empirical evidence suggests that non-interest financing income has the potential of improving the profitability of banks in the South Asia region without affecting their risk levels. In addition, it is difficult to distinguish between the income structure of Islamic banks and conventional banks.

Future research may shed more light on the nature of non-interest income activities by distinguishing between proprietary trading and other fee-based income activities. This may provide some insights on the usefulness of these income-generating activities for the riskiness and profitability of Islamic banks in particular. The focus on Islamic banking is important because of its reliance on risk-sharing activities, which offer a viable alternative to interest-based financing and have the potential of contributing toward a stable financial system and sustainable economic growth.

References

Alkassim, Faisal A. 2005. “The profitability of Islamic and conventional banking in the GCC countries: A comparative study.” *Journal of Review of Islamic Economics* 13(1): 5–30.

Allen, Franklin, and Anthony M. Santomero. 2001. “What do financial intermediaries do?.” *Journal of Banking & Finance* 25(2): 271–294.

Arellano, Manuel, and Stephen Bond. 1991. “Some tests of specification for panel data: Monte Carlo evidence and an application to employment equations.” *The review of economic studies* 58(2): 277–297.

Arellano, Manuel, and Olympia Bover. 1995. “Another look at the instrumental variable estimation of error-components models.” *Journal of econometrics* 68(1): 29–51.

Ashraf, Mian Muhammad, and Zia-ur Rehman. 2011. “The performance analysis of Islamic and conventional banks: The Pakistan’s perspective.” *Journal of Money, Investment and Banking* 22: 99–113.

Baele, Lieven, Olivier De Jonghe, and Rudi Vander Vennet. 2007. “Does the stock market value bank diversification?.” *Journal of Banking & Finance* 31(7): 1999–2023.

Bashir, Abdel-Hameed M. 2003. “Assessing the performance of Islamic banks: Some evidence from the Middle East.” *Islamic Economic Studies* 11(1): 31–57.

Beck, Thorsten, Hans Degryse, and Christiane Kneer. 2014. “Is more finance better? Disentangling intermediation and size effects of financial systems.” *Journal of Financial Stability* 10: 50–64.

Beck, Thorsten, and Asli Demirguc-Kunt. 2009. *Financial institutions and markets across countries and over time-data and analysis*. Washington D.C.: The World Bank.

Bertocco, Giancarlo. 2008. “Finance and development: Is Schumpeter’s analysis still relevant?.” *Journal of Banking & Finance* 32(6): 1161–1175.

Blundell, Richard, and Stephen Bond. 2000. “GMM estimation with persistent panel data: an application to production functions.” *Econometric reviews* 19(3): 321–340.

Chiorazzo, Vincenzo, Carlo Milani, and Francesca Salvini. 2008. “Income diversification and bank performance: Evidence from Italian banks.” *Journal of Financial Services Research* 33(3): 181–203.

Čihák, Martin, and Heiko Hesse. 2010. “Islamic banks and financial stability: An empirical analysis.” *Journal of Financial Services Research* 38(2–3): 95–113.

Cornett, Marcia Millon, Evren Ors, and Hassan Tehranian. 2002. “Bank performance around the introduction of a Section 20 subsidiary.” *The Journal of Finance* 57(1): 501–521.

De Jonghe, Olivier. 2010. “Back to the basics in banking? A micro-analysis of banking system stability.” *Journal of financial intermediation* 19(3): 387–417.

Deesomsak, Rataporn, Krishna Paudyal, and Gioia Pescetto. 2004. “The determinants of capital structure: evidence from the Asia Pacific region.” *Journal of multinational financial management* 14(4–5): 387–405.

Demirgüç-Kunt, Asli, and Enrica Detragiache. “Basel Core Principles and bank soundness: Does compliance matter?.” *Journal of Financial Stability* 7(4): 179–190.

Demirgüç-Kunt, Asli, and Harry Huizinga. 2010. “Bank activity and funding strategies: The impact on risk and returns.” *Journal of Financial Economics* 98(3): 626–650.

Demsetz, Rebecca S., and Philip E. Strahan. 1997. “Diversification, size, and risk at bank holding companies.” *Journal of Money, Credit, and Banking* 29(3): 300–313.

DeYoung, Robert, and Tara Rice. 2004. “Noninterest income and financial performance at US commercial banks.” *Financial Review* 39(1): 101–127.

DeYoung, Robert, and Karin P. Roland. 2001. “Product mix and earnings volatility at commercial banks: Evidence from a degree of total leverage model.” *Journal of Financial Intermediation* 10(1): 54–84.

Geyfman, Victoria, and Timothy J. Yeager. 2009. "On the Riskiness of Universal Banking: Evidence from Banks in the Investment Banking Business Pre-and Post-GLBA." *Journal of Money, Credit and Banking* 41(8): 1649–1669.

Haron, S., and W. N. Azmi. 2004. "Profitability Determinants of Islamic Banks: A Cointergration Approach." Islamic Banking Conference, Union Arab Bank. Beirut, Lebnon: Kuala Lampur Business School.

Hassan, M. Kabir, and Abdel-Hameed M. Bashir. 2003. "Determinants of Islamic banking profitability." In *10th ERF annual conference, Morocco*, vol. 7, pp. 2–31.

Ito, Hiro. 2006. "Financial development and financial liberalization in Asia: Thresholds, institutions and the sequence of liberalization." *The North American Journal of Economics and Finance* 17 (3): 303–327.

Jalil, Abdul, Mete Feridun, and Ying Ma. 2010. "Finance-growth nexus in China revisited: New evidence from principal components and ARDL bounds tests." *International Review of Economics & Finance* 19(2): 189–195.

Karakaya, Aykut, and Bünyamin Er. 2013. "Noninterest (nonprofit) income and financial performance at Turkish commercial and participation banks." *International Business Research* 6(1): 106–117.

Karim, Ben Khediri, Ben Ali Mohamed Sami, and Ben-Khedhiri Hichem. 2010. "Bank-specific, industry-specific and macroeconomic determinants of African Islamic banks' profitability." *International Journal of Business and Management Science* 3(1): 39–56.

Kwan, Simon. 1998. "Securities activities by commercial banking firms' section 20 subsidiaries: risk, return, and diversification benefits." Working Papers in Applied Economic Theory 98–10, Federal Reserve Bank of San Francisco.

Laeven, Luc, and Ross Levine. 2007. "Is there a diversification discount in financial conglomerates?." *Journal of Financial Economics* 85(2): 331–367.

Law, Siong Hook, W. N. W. Azman-Saini, and Mansor H. Ibrahim. 2013. "Institutional quality thresholds and the finance–growth nexus." *Journal of Banking & Finance* 37(12): 5373–5381.

Lepetit, Laetitia, Emmanuelle Nys, Philippe Rous, and Amine Tarazi. 2008. "Bank income structure and risk: An empirical analysis of European banks." *Journal of banking & finance* 32(8): 1452–1467.

Lin, Shu Ling, Soushan Wu, Jack HW Penm, and Richard Deane Terrell. 2005. "The relationship and causality testing between diversification, risk and financial performance: empirical examination in Taiwan's banking industry." *IJSTM* 6(6): 556–575.

Masruki, Rosnia, Norhazlina Ibrahim, Elmirina Osman, and Hishamuddin Abdul Wahab. 2011. "Financial performance of Malaysian founder Islamic banks versus conventional banks." *Journal of Business and Policy Research* 6(2): 67–79.

Molyneux, Philip, and John Yip. 2013. "Income diversification and performance of Islamic banks." *Journal of Financial Management, Markets and Institutions* 1(1): 47–66.

Rahaman, Mohammad M. 2011. "Access to financing and firm growth." *Journal of Banking & Finance* 35(3): 709–723.

Rajan, Raghuram, and Luigi Zingales. 1998. "Financial development and growth." *American Economic Review* 88(3): 559–586.

Ramasastri, A. S., Achamma Samuel, and S. Gangadaran. 2004. "Income stability of scheduled commercial banks: Interest vis-à-vis Non-interest income." *Economic and Political Weekly* 39(12): 1311–1319.

Sanya, Sarah, and Simon Wolfe. 2011. "Can banks in emerging economies benefit from revenue diversification?." *Journal of Financial Services Research* 40(1–2): 79–101.

Shahimi, Shahida, Abd Ismail, B. Ghafar, and Sanep B. Ahmad. 2006. "A panel data analysis of fee income activities in Islamic banks." *Journal of King Abdulaziz University: Islamic Economics* 19(2): 23–35.

Smaoui, Houcem, and Ines Ben Salah. 2012. "Profitability of Islamic banks in the GCC region." *Global Economy and Finance Journal* 5(1): 85–102.

Smith, Rosie, Christos Staikouras, and Geoffrey Wood. 2003. "Non-interest income and total income stability." Bank of England Working Paper No. 198.

Stiroh, Kevin J., and Adrienne Rumble. 2006. "The dark side of diversification: The case of US financial holding companies." *Journal of banking & finance* 30(8): 2131–2161.

Stiroh, Kevin J. 2004. "Diversification in banking: Is noninterest income the answer?." *Journal of Money, Credit, and Banking* 36(5): 853–882.

Trichet, Jean-Claude. 2010. "What role for finance." *Lecture at Universidade Nova de Lisboa, Lisbon.*

Turner, Adair. 2010. "What do banks do? Why do credit booms and busts occur and what can public policy do about it." In *The ?Future of Finance: The LSE Report*. London: London School of Economics and Political Science.

Zhang, Yun. 2010. "Analysis of the Systematic Risk of Financial Institution in Modern Finance Evolution." *International Journal of Economics and Finance* 2(3): 234–238

Part VI: Risk-Sharing Finance, Income Inequality and Asset-based Redistribution

Tarık Akın, Obiyathulla Ismath Bacha, Abbas Mirakhor, Zamir Iqbal

Chapter 21: Risk-Sharing Asset-based Redistribution in Public Finance: A Stock-Flow Consistent Analysis

1 Introduction

Increasing inequalities is one of the defining social, economic, and political challenges of the post-Global Financial Crisis (GFC) era. Apart from the negative social, public finance, and short-run growth effects of high inequality, the compelling evidence indicates that inequality is an important cause for the financial crises (Kumhof, Rancière, and Winant 2015; Rajan 2010; de Haan and Sturm 2016; Turner 2016) and low long-term economic growth (World Economic Forum 2017; OECD 2015; IMF 2017).[188] The inequality problem and its visible repercussions on economic growth and financial crises have spurred interest in the economics of inequality. Historically, the literature on the economics of inequality focused exclusively on income inequality. However, the fact that the deterioration of the distribution of wealth is much worse than that of income and the evidence that trends in wealth distribution have dissociated from the trends in income distribution, have placed wealth inequality at the core of the economics of inequality. The literature provides a number of important determinants of wealth inequality ranging from the share of top-income classes to the heterogeneity of saving rates. These determinants can be defined under two main entries of meritocracy and saving behavior (Akin and Mirakhor 2019). However, these determinants cannot satisfactorily explain the observed trends in wealth inequality. Indeed, recent literature suggests that it is the wealth residual, defined as the increase in wealth without a concomitant increase in capital, that is mainly responsible for higher wealth inequality (Basu and Stiglitz 2016). Interest-based debt contracts are arguably the main driver of the formation of wealth residual. Furthermore, the rate of return on capital is persistently higher than the growth rate of output and income, which implies that increased income inequality is an inevitable by-product of capitalism

These two recent findings that increasing inequality is an inherent feature of market economies and interest-based debt contracts are intimately related to wealth inequality, should give rise to reconsideration of the redistribution tools, which are still the main ammunition for the policy-makers to fight against the increasing

188 For a comprehensive review on drivers, patterns, and current trends of the wealth inequality see Akın and Mirakhor (2019).

https://doi.org/10.1515/9783110587920-021

wealth inequality. Indeed there is also heightened interest in research on equitable growth and redistribution in line with the changing mindset in the academia and policy-making that addressing the inequality problem is a priority for securing strong, sustainable and inclusive growth of the economies.[189] In the post-GFC era, the redistribution policies to address wealth inequality roughly fall in two categories: i) income-based redistribution, which aims at mitigating income inequality as an important driver of the wealth inequality and ii) asset-based redistribution, which targets the wealth per se (Akın and Mirakhor 2019). Proposals under the income-based redistribution involve "hard" income-based redistribution such as the taxing income and wealth at high rates. OECD (2017) concludes that less distributive tax and benefits system as one of the important causes of increasing inequalities. One such concrete income-based redistribution policy proposal is coordinated progressive wealth tax at the global level (Piketty 2014; Piketty 2015; Piketty, Saez, and Stantcheva 2014). Political viability and coordination problems, as well as, compliance by the rich are the main impediments of implementing such a tax, though. There are also "soft" income-based redistribution proposals such as the notion of shared prosperity asserted by the World Bank (2016). This type of redistribution proposals take the current distribution of income and wealth as given and focus on attenuating the consequences of market operations by distributing the additional income more equally through public investment, financial inclusion, transfers and wage adjustments. Since wealth has command over use of resources, leaving current asset concentration intact means that market-determined rewards which go to the concentrated wealth will be still very unequal. In turn, implementation of the soft income-based redistribution tools may have adverse effects in achieving more equitable distribution of wealth. Income-based redistribution tools, either hard or soft, may also have perverse incentive effects such as less participation in labor markets (OECD 2017) and distorting investment decisions (Seshadri and Yuki 2004). Moreover, keeping the current asset inequality intact means leaving the governance structures that give rise to emergence of inequality intact, too. The proposals addressing weakness in the income-based redistribution tools include wholesale change of economic rules of the game (Stiglitz 2015), changing the underlying property right claims such as the asset-based approach (Bowles 2012) and risk-sharing redistribution (Askari et al. 2012).

This chapter focuses on asset-based redistribution and discusses the proposition that risk-sharing asset-based redistribution can address the shortcoming of

189 A search at ideas.repec.org website reveals that total number of studies with the keyword "redistribution" was 9,382 between 2000 and 2014; it rose to 2,676 between 2015 and 2017. In other words, average number of studies on redistribution until the publication of *Capital in the Twenty-First Century* by Thomas Piketty was 670; it increased to 1,338 in the post-Piketty era.

income-based redistribution. It examines also two recent findings in wealth inequality related to interest-based debt contracts and increasing inequalities, which constitute an inherent feature of modern market economies. It examines also two recent findings in wealth inequality, namely, that the increasing inequalities constitute an inherent feature of the market economy, and that interest-based debt contracts are intimately related to wealth inequality. This study provides a blueprint for implementing the risk-sharing asset-based redistribution in public finance, which is typically the most important redistributive mechanism in a country, through GDP-linked *sukuk* and gauges prospective gains in inequality by employing a simple stock-flow consistent macroeconomic model. The chapter consists of four sections. Section 1 provides a succinct discussion of the inequality problems and the redistribution proposals in the literature. Section 2 reviews the literature on asset-based redistribution and then states that risk-sharing is an important missing element in the current asset-based redistribution literature. Section 3 develops a stock-flow consistent macroeconomic model to gauge distributional effects of financing public sector by means of GDP-linked *sukuk* compared to interest-based debt instruments. Section 4 concludes and makes concrete policy recommendations in public finance based on the risk-sharing framework.

2 Risk-Sharing Asset-Based Redistribution: A Literature Review

The main feature of the asset-based redistribution is the change in contractual framework of economic exchange rather than implementing hard redistribution tools. Bowles (2012) argues that highly unequal distribution of assets hinder implementation of productivity-enhancing[190] governance structure through three main channels. Firstly, asset-poor households cannot enter contracts available to asset-rich ones. To give an example, the asset-poor is typically constrained by fixed-price loan contracts rather than equity-based financing contracts which may fit better to the opportunity cost of their economic activity. Indeed, fixed-price contracts impede productivity-enhancing behavior, such as putting full effort to work, providing full information, risk-taking, and cooperation, in many respects. One feature of the fixed-price contracts, such as debt contracts, is that productivity-enhancing behavior can't be internalized in these types of contracts because there is high monitoring cost. In effect, fixed-price contracts don't incentivize the borrower to elicit maximum levels of

190 Bowles (2012) defines a governance structures as productivity-enhancing "*if the winners could compensate the losers (which would make the change a Pareto improvement), except that the implied compensation need not be carried out or even be implementable under the informational conditions and other incentive problems in the economy*".

efforts. Secondly, it is difficult to decrease principal-agent and coordination problems in case of high inequality because there is a trade-off between high inequality and incentive for productivity-enhancing behavior. Thirdly, maintaining high level of inequality in the society is costly for the wealthy because it requires expensive supportive institutional structure, such as security forces. These costs divert resources away from productive activities thus involve allocative inefficiencies.

It is the contention of the asset-based redistribution that there is a class of contractual relationships in economic exchange that is incentive-compatible, enhances productivity and generates higher economic growth (Bowles 2012). The chief characteristic of this class of contracts is that they reduce or eliminate the distinction between principal and agent. Asset-based redistribution rewrites the property rights by allowing agents to share in the three crucial dimensions of property rights: (a) right to control access to the asset; (b) right to control the disposition over its use; and (c) right of claim on the residual income produced by the asset (Bowles 2012). An example of these forms of contracts is a joint-partnership where the ownership of an economic venture is shared between two or more partners. They share the property rights claim and residual income jointly. Each has residual claim but also the control that is involved in the property rights claim. These types of contracts are referred to as risk-sharing contracts. Although Bowles' (2012) asset-based redistribution proposal represents a compelling substitute for income-based redistribution proposals, it does not provide a blueprint of policies and procedures for its implementation. However, he suggests a roadmap by "first identifying those aspects of concentrated ownership of assets that can give rise to perverse incentive and costly enforcement strategies and then to devise asset redistributions that can attenuate the resulting co-ordination failures without introducing their own costly incentive problems." (Bowles 2012).

Islam gives a concrete blueprint for asset-based redistribution through risk-sharing, which is the essence of Islamic finance as confirmed by Kuala Lumpur Declaration of 2012 (ISRA 2012). Risk-sharing basically can be defined as a contractual or societal arrangement whereby the outcome of a random event is borne collectively by a group of economic agents involved in a contract, a transaction or a community (Askari et al. 2012). Parties in the contractual or social arrangement undertake risk-sharing with the expectation that involvement of many participants, resources and skills result in lesser individual risk, as well as, greater output. Instances of risk-sharing arrangements range from purchasing stocks of domestic or foreign business entities, participating in cooperatives to insuring against idiosyncratic risks. As opposed to the debt-based system, risk-sharing financial arrangements render the financial system counter-cyclical due to its inherent nature that the returns depend on contingent realizations (Askari et al. 2012). In this sense, risk-sharing can overcome the equitable economic growth and financial stability trade-off of the debt-based system. Another advantage of risk-sharing is to secure allocative efficiency with equitable growth (Akın and Mirakhor 2019).

One important asset-based and risk-sharing instrument in Islamic finance is *sukuk*, which has important advantages over debt-based instruments in corporate and public finance. *Sukuk* is a prospective candidate for Shiller's (1993) "macro-market" securities, which are issued by the public sector and can help people to mitigate their risks to their income (Askari, Iqbal, and Mirakhor 2014). A type of *sukuk*, which also resembles the macro-market securities, is GDP-linked *sukuk*. The notion of the GDP-linked *sukuk* is based on the idea of sharing of a country's output (Bacha, Mirakhor, and Askari 2015; Bacha, Lahsasna, and Diaw 2014; Ismath Bacha and Mirakhor 2017). The governments can easily issue *sukuk* for revenue generating projects for their investments. It is more difficult to design risk-sharing instruments for non-revenue generating projects as indicated by Bacha and Mirakhor (2017):

> As there obviously is no revenue to be shared, the funding will have to be based on some other benchmark or index which is in some way linked to the earnings capacity of the obligor, the borrowing government. As the GDP is a measure of a country's output of goods and services, it is an obvious indicator of income to the government. Furthermore, as an increasing number of developing countries move towards a goods and services tax (GST) framework, GDP becomes even more closely linked with government income.

Three advantages of the GDP-linked *sukuk* is specifically related to the asset-based redistribution to mitigate wealth inequality (Bacha, Mirakhor, and Askari 2015). Firstly, investors prospectively have higher and more stable returns that co-moves with the national output growth. This is an important alternative to the debt-based instruments which are pro-cyclical. Secondly, these instruments reduce the systematic risks stemming from public sector debt, which is an important cause of financial crises, because they are equity in the balance sheet of the public sector. Thirdly, inherently regressive feature of the debt contracts, which is a primary reason for increasing inequality, is eliminated (Akın and Mirakhor 2019).

The GDP-linked *sukuk* and its variants, such as revenue generating *sukuk* for the infrastructure projects, can be designed as an effective risk-sharing asset-based redistribution policy tool. The risk-sharing features of the GDP-linked *sukuk* are already discussed. This instrument can be used as an asset-based redistribution tool in many ways. One idea to use GDP-linked *sukuk* as an asset-based redistribution tool is the mass issuance of the GDP-linked *sukuk* in small denominations to fund the public finance needs and to distribute the *sukuk* certificates to the middle-class as an investment instrument and to the (asset) poor as a complement or substitute for the regular transfer payments. Since there are not many alternative financial investment opportunities and/or rate of return to the financial instruments, which are mostly consist of bank deposits, are usually not high, the demand for the GDP-linked *sukuk* is expected to be high for the middle-class in many OIC countries. In addition, the poor will benefit from having the GDP-linked *sukuk* as a transfer tool because the will have income generating assets to surpass the problems caused by being the asset-poor.

3 The Model

Given the proposal in Part 2 that the GDP-linked *sukuk* can be used as a risk-sharing asset-based redistribution tool, Part 3 develops a simple stock-flow consistent (SFC) macroeconomic model to measure the distributional implications of using the GDP-linked *sukuk* compared to traditional debt instruments in public finance.[191] Part 3 consists of three sections. Section 3.1 gives the base model, in which we develop an interest-based closed economy with four sectors (the households, the firms, the banking sector and the government). Section 3.2, alternatively, construct an economy in which the public sector is financed by the GDP-linked *sukuk*, as a proxy for risk-sharing public finance. In the alternative SFC model, we keep the changes in the equation developed in the base model at a minimum. Section 3.3 shows how to calculate inequality indices and then simulates evolution of the inequality in the base and the alternative model.

3.1 Base Model

In our simple macroeconomic setup, there are four interrelated sectors, namely, the households, the real sector (firms), the banking sector and the public sector. Since the banking sector in the model has power to provide unlimited supply of credit to the rest of the economy by construction, we prefer not to add a central bank to the model. Thanks to the interrelated model equations in the base model and stock-flow consistent constraints, each household income quantile ends up with disposable income and net wealth in the end of each period; based on the disposable income and net wealth level we then calculate inequality indices for every period. The base model assumes an interest-based economy. Thus, the public sector uses interest-based debt contracts, as well as, other sectors in the economy to finance their net lending requirement in each period.

---

191 A SFC model coherently integrates all stocks and flows in an economy through an accounting framework, which reproduces the balance sheets and transaction matrices of the sectors in the economy. In other words, the SFC models integrate national accounting data into dynamic macroeconomic modelling through interconnections between sectoral stocks (balance sheets) and flows (transaction matrices). The approach is based on the precept that every transaction by a sector must have an equivalent transaction by another sector and every change in the balance sheet of a sector must give rise to an equivalent change in the balance sheet of another sector. In effect, there is always a counter-party change in the flow and stock of a sectoral transaction. This "*everything comes from somewhere and everything goes somewhere*" principle allows describing evolution of the whole economic system in a consistent way, linking real and financial sector and setting up linkages between income and wealth (Dafermos and Papatheodorou 2015). For a detailed review of the SFC modeling, see Godley and Lavoie (2007) and Akın and Mirakhor (2019).

The household sector consists of five 20% income quintiles, in which the first quintile (i=1) stands for the poorest 20% of the population and the fifth quintile (i=5) represents the richest top 20% of the population. We assume that each household has one unit of labor and there is no unemployment; labor supply always equal to labor demand. In addition, we assume a very stable population setup with no growth in population and no reshuffling of the individuals among the income quintiles. The sectoral equations are closed by the current deposits, which then equates expectations to the ex-post realizations.

We assume a demand-led economic setup so that the real sector in the economy supplies all demand instantly. The demand-led economy assumption makes total production in the economy always equal to total consumption by the households, total investment by the real sector and total expenditure by the public sector. Thus, total production is equal to the gross domestic product (GDP). The real sector resorts to their internal funds and/or bank loans to finance their negative net lending in the end of each period. We also assume that all the household income quintiles receive dividend payments from the real sector.

The public sector receives income tax from the households and corporate tax from the real sector and makes expenditures through transfer payments to the households, public investment and interest payments on public securities. Negative net lending is financed through new public borrowing. In the base model, we only consider interest payments for the bonds, while in the simulations we assume there is no interest payment but non-interest rate of return on Islamic instruments. It should be noted here that we use the terms bonds and bills interchangeably in the model. The interest-based government securities can be regarded as zero-coupon paying perpetual bond.

The banking sector instantly supplies all loans demanded by the households and the firms because it has the power of create money and credit.[192] The banking sector buys (sells) government securities in case the demand of government securities by the households is short of (exceed) supply by the government. The closure item for the banking sector is equity issuance.

This study follows adaptive expectations assumption throughout the model as it is the general form of the expectations in the SFC modeling literature. The adaptive expectations for the variable (X) at time t is formed as follows:

$$X_t^e = \beta \cdot X_{t-1} + (1-\beta) \cdot X_{t-1}^e$$

192 Money creation by banks is an area of big debate in the literature. Compelling evidence and, even the official documents by the central banks in advanced economies, indicate that banks indeed create money and credit. We will not discuss this important topic in this study. Yulek, Mahmud and Yamaguchi (2017), and Kumhof, Rancière, Winant (2015) gives a comprehensive and up-to-date review of the topic.

3.1.1 Households

Household sector is composed of five 20% income quintiles.[193] Each of the household groups has the same set of equations but they differ from each other with respect to their parameter and initial values. Equation (1) gives the components of disposable income (YD_{ih}) for the ith household income quintile. Total disposable income is composed of wages net of taxes, which is calculated as the ongoing wage rate net of progressive taxes $(wb_{ih}.(1-\tau_{ih}))$ multiplied by the number of people in each income quintile (N_{ih}). The household sector receives transfer payments from the government (TR_{ih}), dividend income from the real sector (FD_{ih}) and banking sector (BD_{ih}). Each period the households also pay out amortization (LR_{ih}) and interest $(i_l.L_{ih-1})$ for their bank loans outstanding They have interest income from government securities $(i_g.B_{ih-1})$ and time deposits $(i_d.DT_{ih-1})$.

$$YD_{ih} = wb_{ih}.(1-\tau_{ih}).N_{ih-1} + TR_{ih} + FD_{ih} + BD_{ih} - LR_{ih} + i_g.B_{ih-1} + i_d.DT_{ih-1} - i_l.L_{ih-1} \quad (1)$$

Equation (2) shows the dynamic evolution of the wage rates over time. The quintile-specific wage rate grows at the exogenous rate of quintile-specific productivity (θ_{ih}). The productivity parameter implies that institutional and economic factors make the wage rate growth differ among the household income quintile groups. Transfer payments are fixed proportion of expected disposable income since the transfer amount is determined by the government in the beginning of each period within the budget preparation process as given in Equation (3).

$$wb_{ih} = \theta_{ih} \cdot wb_{ih-1} \quad (2)$$

$$TR_{ih} = tr_{ih} \cdot YD^{e}_{ih} \quad (3)$$

Equation (4) states that amortization of the bank loans by each household quintile in each period is a constant share (rep) of the loans outstanding in the previous period. Equations (5) and (6) indicate that the dividends disbursed by the real sector (FD) and the banking sector (BD) are distributed among the household income quintiles with respect to income quintile specific parameters, which are held constant all over the periods.

$$LR_{ih} = rep.L_{ih-1} \quad (4)$$

$$FD_{ih} = \gamma_{if} \cdot FD, \ where \sum_{i=1}^{5} \gamma_{if} = 1 \quad (5)$$

193 In the equations, the subscript i stands for the ith income quintile. (i=1: first income quintile, i=2: second income quintile, i=3: third income quintile, i=4: fourth income quintile, i=5: fifth income quintile).

$$BD_{ih} = \gamma_{ib} \cdot BD, \; where \sum_{i=1}^{5} \gamma_{ib} = 1 \tag{6}$$

Equation (7) describes the Haig-Simons type consumption function which relates consumption of each household income quintile to expected disposable income (YD^{e}_{ih}) and gross wealth (GW_{ih-1}) accrued up to the previous period. The marginal propensity to consume out of disposable income (mpc_{ih}) and wealth (mpw_{ih}) are assumed to be constant in all periods.

$$C_{ih} = mpc_{ih}.YD^{e}_{ih} + mpw_{ih}.GW_{ih-1} \tag{7}$$

Equation (8) defines net lending as the difference between disposable income and consumption. Primary balance in Equation (9) is defined as the net lending net of interest payments and amortization of debt. Primary balance checks whether the households are still eligible for make extra borrowing.

$$NL_{ih} = YD_{ih} - C_{ih} \tag{8}$$

$$PBAL_{ih} = YD_{ih} - C_{ih} + i_{l}.L_{ih-1} + LR_{ih} \tag{9}$$

Equations (1) and (9) provide an account of how the amount of net lending is determined in each period. The next step is to design how the net lending is financed and how the stock variables evolve in response to the change in the flow variables.

The first task in determination of how financial assets changes in the household sector in response to the given net lending level is to determine how the total amount of available financial sources is allocated among different financial instruments. In the beginning of each period, households decide on a target portfolio level. Equation (10) shows that the target portfolio is composed of the stock values of government securities (B_{ih-1}), time deposits (DT_{ih-1}), equities (EQ_{ih-1}) and a constant share of net lending.[194]

$$PORT_{ih} = B_{ih-1} + DT_{ih-1} + EQ_{ih-1} + ncd.NL_{ih} \tag{10}$$

Equations (11–13) allocate target portfolio among the financial assets with respect to the *Tobinesque* portfolio choice principles (see Godley and Lavoine (2007) for a detailed review of the *Tobinesque* Portfolio Choice Model). We assume that the share of each financial asset in total portfolio is a linear function of a constant coefficient, reflecting institutional and behavioral patterns in portfolio formation, own rate of return, rate of return of other financial assets, and ratio of expected disposable income to expected portfolio size. In each of these equations, constant coefficients, own rate

194 It is assumed that households are risk-averse, and that a certain proportion of wealth is held in the form of liquid assets.

of returns and disposable income have positive and the rate of returns of other financial assets have negative coefficient signs.

$$\frac{B_{ih}}{PORT_{ih}} = \lambda_{i10} + \lambda_{i11}.i_g + \lambda_{i12}.i_d + \lambda_{i13}.i_e + \lambda_{i14} \cdot \left(\frac{YD^e_{ih}}{PORT_{ih}}\right) \tag{11}$$

$$\frac{DT_{ih}}{PORT_{ih}} = \lambda_{i20} + \lambda_{i21}.i_g + \lambda_{i22}.i_d + \lambda_{i23}.i_e + \lambda_{i24} \cdot \left(\frac{YD^e_{ih}}{PORT_{ih}}\right) \tag{12}$$

$$\frac{EQ_{ih}}{PORT_{ih}} = \lambda_{i30} + \lambda_{i31}.i_g + \lambda_{i32}.i_d + \lambda_{i33}.i_e + \lambda_{i34} \cdot \left(\frac{YD^e_{ih}}{PORT_{ih}}\right) \tag{13}$$

Given the allocation share of each of the financial assets in the total portfolio, the flows in government securities, time deposits and equities are calculated as the difference between ex-ante target level of these assets and their realized value in the end of the previous period, as given in Equation (14), (15) and (16), respectively. The primary balance checks whether the households deal with the financial asset accumulation through an indicator variable as given in Equation (17). The indicator variable guarantees that the households cannot accumulate financial assets if they fall under Minsky's (1992; 1982) well-known taxonomy of speculative and Ponzi finance.

$$\Delta B_{ih} = z1_{ih} \cdot (B_{ih} - B_{ih-1}) \tag{14}$$

$$\Delta DT_{ih} = z1_{ih} \cdot (DT_{ih} - DT_{ih-1}) \tag{15}$$

$$\Delta EQ_{ih} = z1_{ih} \cdot (EQ_{ih} - EQ_{ih-1}) \tag{16}$$

$$z1_{ih} = \begin{cases} 1, \ if \ PBAL_{ih} > 0 \\ 0, \ otherwise \end{cases} \tag{17}$$

The financial sources for asset accumulation and financing of the net lending by households are secured through bank loans or change in current deposits (see Equation (18)). Although banks are assumed to create money and can provide unlimited supply of bank loans, there is a maximum amount of bank loans that households can borrow. As given in Equation (21), the limit of borrowing is determined by the loan-to-value ratio (*ltv*), which stands for collateral requirements or macroprudential policy tools. There are also two further conditions shown through the indicator variables in Equation (21). The indicator variable $(z2_{ih})$ in Equation (19) indicates that sum of current deposits and net lending must be greater than the collateral required. If not, the households can't use loans. Furthermore, indicator variable $(z3_{ih})$ in Equation (20) puts the condition that if the current deposits (internal funds) is bigger than the borrowing requirement, there is no need for resorting to loans. All financing required can be met by the internal funds.

$$BoR_{ih} = (\Delta B_{ih} + \Delta DT_{ih} + \Delta EQ_{ih} - NL_{ih}) \tag{18}$$

$$z2_{ih} = \begin{cases} 1, \; if \; DC_{ih-1} + NL_{ih} > (1 - ltv) \cdot BoR_{ih} \\ 0, \; otherwise \end{cases} \tag{19}$$

$$z3_{ih} = \begin{cases} 1, \; if \; BoR_{ih} > \; DC_{ih-1} \\ 0, \; otherwise \end{cases} \tag{20}$$

$$\Delta L_{ih} = z2_{ih}.z3_{ih}.ltv.BoR_{ih} \tag{21}$$

The current deposits are the closure item of the household sector. Equation (22) indicates that change in current deposits equals to the loan usage minus the borrowing requirement.

$$\Delta DC_{ih} = \Delta L_{ih} - BoR_{ih} \tag{22}$$

The rest of the equations in this part defines how the financial stocks accumulate. The stocks in the current period are calculated as the sum of the stock level in previous period and the flow in the current period.

$$DC_{ih} = DC_{ih-1} + \Delta DC_{ih} \tag{23}$$

$$DT_{ih} = DT_{ih-1} + \Delta DT_{ih} \tag{24}$$

$$B_{ih} = B_{ih-1} + \Delta B_{ih} \tag{25}$$

$$EQ_{ih} = EQ_{ih-1} + \Delta EQ_{ih} \tag{26}$$

$$L_{ih} = L_{ih-1} + \Delta L_{ih} \tag{27}$$

Gross wealth is defined as the sum of all financial assets in Equation (28) and net wealth is the difference between gross wealth and loans in Equation (29).

$$GW_{ih} = DC_{ih} + DT_{ih} + B_{ih} + EQ_{ih} \tag{28}$$

$$NW_{ih} = GW_{ih} - L_{ih} \tag{29}$$

3.1.2 Real Sector

The real sector in the model makes investment decisions but production level is determined by the households since we assume a consumption-led economy. Employment is also exogenous to the firm decisions. These assumptions aim at simplifying the real sector as much as possible in order to solely focus on the income and wealth distribution of the household sector. On the financing side, the firm decides on how much to borrow and to make dividend payments with respect to the financing constraints and stock-flow consistent sectoral balance sheet.

Equation (30) indicates that the economy is consumption-led by equating total production to the GDP. Equation (31) states that total household consumption is sum of the level of consumption in each household income quintile. Similarly, Equation (32) indicates that total investment is the sum of private sector and public sector investments.

$$Y = GDP = C + I + G \tag{30}$$

$$C = C_{1h} + C_{2h} + C_{3h} + C_{4h} + C_{5h} \tag{31}$$

$$I = I_f + I_g \tag{32}$$

Equation (33) shows that investment by the real sector is a linear function of capital stock, capacity utilization and interest rates. The ratio of the GDP to the capital stock, which is a proxy for capacity utilization, is an indicator of the aggregate demand with positive coefficient. On the other hand, the interest rates, as a proxy for the cost of capital for the firms, enter the equation with a negative coefficient. Equation (34) shows that the total labor cost to the real sector is the sum of wage payments to each household income quintile. Equation (35) states that the real sector makes amortization payments at an amount of a fixed proportion of the outstanding loans in the previous period.

$$\left(\frac{I_f}{K_{-1}}\right) = \alpha_0 + \alpha_1.\left(\frac{Y_{-1}}{K_{-1}}\right) - \alpha_2.i_l \tag{33}$$

$$WB = \sum_{i=1}^{5}[wb_{ih}.N_{ih-1}] \tag{34}$$

$$LR_f = rep.L_{f-1} \tag{35}$$

Total real sector profits (FT) in Equation (36) equals to total production minus corporate taxes, wage payments, dividend payments, loan amortization and interest expense. Equation (37) gives a rule for dividend payments: If the profit is positive in the previous period, then a fixed portion of it distributed to the households, else there is no dividend payments. Equation (38) states that the net lending for the real sector is then equal to the difference between retained earnings and private sector investments.

$$FT = Y - \tau_f \cdot FT_{-1} - WB - FD - LR_f - i_l.L_{f-1} \tag{36}$$

$$FD = \begin{cases} \kappa.FT_{-1} \text{ } if \text{ } FT_{-1} > 0 \\ 0 \text{ } if \text{ } FT_{-1} \leq 0 \end{cases} \tag{37}$$

$$NL_f = FT - I_f \tag{38}$$

Equations (39)–(42) show how the net lending affects the financing side of the transaction matrix. Equation (39) indicates that the real sector issues new equities (ΔE_f) at expected equity price (P_e^e) to finance a fixed share (ψ_e) of its investment expenditure. Equation (40) shows that the total number of equities is updated every period as per the new equity issuance. Equation (41) indicates that rest of the investment expenditure is financed by the new bank loans. However, total amount of bank loans available to the real sector in each period is constrained by the loan-to-value ratio. Equation (42) shows change in the bank deposits owned by the real sector. The equations states that any remaining investment spending which can't be financed by equities and bank loans is financed by current deposits, which is a proxy for the internal funds.

$$\Delta E_f = \frac{1}{P_e^e} \cdot (\psi_e \cdot I_f) \tag{39}$$

$$E_f = E_{f-1} + \Delta E_f \tag{40}$$

$$\Delta L_f = ltv \cdot ((1 - \psi_e) \cdot I_f) \tag{41}$$

$$\Delta DC_f = NL_f + P_e \cdot \Delta E_f + \Delta L_f \tag{42}$$

Equation (43)–(48) shows how the balance-sheet of the real sector evolves. Total volume of the equity stock is calculated as the multiplication of the price of the equity with the total number of equities. Other financial stocks in Equation (44)–(46) are calculated as the sum of the stock level in previous period and the flow in the current period. Gross wealth is defined as the sum of current deposit balance and total capital stock in Equation (47) and net wealth is the difference between gross wealth and equities and loans in Equation (48).

$$EQ_f = P_e \cdot E_f \tag{43}$$

$$DC_f = DC_{f-1} + \Delta DC_f \tag{44}$$

$$L_f = L_{f-1} + \Delta L_f \tag{45}$$

$$K = K_{-1} + I_f + I_g \tag{46}$$

$$GW_f = DC_f + K \tag{47}$$

$$NW_f = GW_f - EQ_f - L_f \tag{48}$$

3.1.3 Public Sector

The public sector in the base model is simple and composed of only several equations. Equations (49–51) state that government consumption (G), government investment (I_g) and government transfers (TR) are calculated as a fixed proportion of expected GDP. Equation (52) shows that total tax income consists of income tax and corporate taxes from the firms and the banks. Net lending in Equation (53) is the difference between tax income and expenditures, as well as, the interest expense of the government securities.

$$G = tc.Y^e \tag{49}$$

$$I_g = ig.Y^e \tag{50}$$

$$TR = \sum_{i=1}^{5} \left[tr_{ih} \cdot YD^e_{ih}\right] \tag{51}$$

$$TAX = \sum_{i=1}^{5} [tr_{ih} \cdot wb_{ih} \cdot N_{ih-1}] + \tau_f \cdot FT_{-1} + \tau_b \cdot BT_{-1} \tag{52}$$

$$NL_g = TAX - I_g - G - TR - i_g.B_{-1} \tag{53}$$

The public sector issues bonds to finance its budget deficit as given in Equation (54). Equation (55) states that total bond stock in the current period is the sum of previous period's bond stock and bond flow in the current period. Finally, the net worth, which equals to net worth by construction, is defined as negative of the bond stock (see Equation 56).

$$\Delta B = -NL_g \tag{54}$$

$$B = B_{-1} + \Delta B = B_{1h} + B_{2h} + B_{3h} + B_{4h} + B_{5h} + B_b \tag{55}$$

$$GW_g = NW_g = -B \tag{56}$$

3.1.4 Banking Sector

By construction, the banking sector is the closure sector in the sense that most of the transaction matrix items are closed in the banking sector. This means the banking sector doesn't make strategic decisions on lending, borrowing and asset management but how much it will extend bank loan is exclusively determined by other sectors.

Equation (57) calculates total banking sector profits as loan repayments, interest income from bonds and loans minus interest payments for the deposits, dividends distributed and corporate tax payment. are calculated as the difference between revenues and expenditures. Equation (58) gives a rule for dividend payments: If the profit is positive in the previous period, then a fixed portion of it distributed to the households, else there is no dividend payments. Total loan amortization is the sum of sectoral loan amortization payments (see Equation (59)). Net lending in Equation (60) equals to total profits, by construction. In the banking sector, equity issuance closes the sector so it is a residual item in capital account of the banks, as given in Equation (61). Equations (62–65) calculate the loan repayments, transactions in current deposits and time deposits as the sum of their equivalent definitions in other sectors. Equations (66–71) calculate the stocks of the financial assets held by the banks. Equation (72) and (73) calculate gross and net wealth of the banking sector, respectively. Equation (74) indicates that there is a fixed difference between lending and loan interest rates. Equation (75) shows how the return on stock market is calculated; it is simply the expected return of the equity price change. Equation (76) calculates the equity price as the division of equity demand by the households in their portfolio by the number of equities issued by the firms and the banks. This equation implicitly allows rise in equity price stemmed from demand by the household, which is affected by expected equity prices.

$$BT = LR + i_g \cdot B_{b-1} + i_l \cdot L_{-1} - i_d \cdot DT_{-1} - BD - \tau_b \cdot BT_{-1} \tag{57}$$

$$BD = \begin{cases} \kappa.BT_{-1} \text{ if } BT_{-1} > 0 \\ 0 \text{ if } BT_{-1} \leq 0 \end{cases} \tag{58}$$

$$LR = LR_{1h} + LR_{2h} + LR_{3h} + LR_{4h} + LR_{5h} + LR_f \tag{59}$$

$$NL_b = BT \tag{60}$$

$$\Delta E_b = (\Delta B_b + \Delta L - \Delta DC - \Delta DT - BD_b)/P_e^e \tag{61}$$

$$\Delta B_b = \Delta B - \Delta B_{1h} - \Delta B_{2h} - \Delta B_{3h} - \Delta B_{4h} - \Delta B_{5h} \tag{62}$$

$$\Delta DC = \Delta DC_{1h} + \Delta DC_{2h} + \Delta DC_{3h} + \Delta DC_{4h} + \Delta DC_{5h} + \Delta DC_f \tag{63}$$

$$\Delta DT = \Delta DT_{1h} + \Delta DT_{2h} + \Delta DT_{3h} + \Delta DT_{4h} + \Delta DT_{5h} \tag{64}$$

$$\Delta L = \Delta L_{1h} + \Delta L_{2h} + \Delta L_{3h} + \Delta L_{4h} + \Delta L_{5h} + \Delta L_f \tag{65}$$

$$DC = DC_{1h} + DC_{2h} + DC_{3h} + DC_{4h} + DC_{5h} + DC_f \tag{66}$$

$$DT = DT_{1h} + DT_{2h} + DT_{3h} + DT_{4h} + DT_{5h} \tag{67}$$

$$L = L_{1h} + L_{2h} + L_{3h} + L_{4h} + L_{5h} + L_f \tag{68}$$

$$B_b = B_{b-1} + \Delta B_b \tag{69}$$

$$E_b = E_{b-1} + \Delta E_b \tag{70}$$

$$EQ_b = P_e.E_b \tag{71}$$

$$GW_b = L + B_b \tag{72}$$

$$NW_b = L + B_b - DC - DT - EQ_b \tag{73}$$

$$i_l = spr + i_d \tag{74}$$

$$i_e = \frac{P_e^e}{P_{e-1}} - 1 \tag{75}$$

$$P_e = \frac{\sum_{i=1}^{5} EQ_{ih}}{E_f + E_b} \tag{76}$$

3.2 Risk-Sharing (RS) Model

Section 3.1 sets up an interest-based economy in which the public sector finances its deficit through bond issuance. In this section, we modify the base model and introduce a hypothetical GDP-linked *sukuk* as the sole instrument of public finance. It should be noted here that use of the GDP-linked *sukuk* for all of the public finance is not realistic. Even in an ideal risk-sharing world, the public sector has other alternative means for public sector financing requirement, such as *ijarah sukuk* and profit-and-loss sharing instruments for investment projects. The idea for using GDP-linked *sukuk* is that the rate of return for the GDP-linked *sukuk* converges to the national output and real sector activity. Thus, rate of return to the national output provides a good approximation for other risk-sharing instruments, as well as, simplifies the modeling exercise.

The counterfactual setup of this section makes minimal changes in the equations compared to the base model of Section 3.1. This will allow us to compare the simulation results without much changes in the parameter values and behavioral equations. In an ideal simulation process, a typical way to compare the two states of the world is to change the parameter values. Here, we also introduce new equations. In case of the major change in the equations and parameter values would render the comparison of the base model and the risk-sharing model useless. Keeping the two models as much similar as possible makes the comparison will be free from the Lucas critique.[195] In the risk-sharing model, we attempt to devise a counterfactual world in which there is no new issuance of bonds. Instead, all public investment and consumption is financed by GDP-linked *sukuk*.

In the equations below, we only give the equations which differ from the base model. All other equations will be the same. We insert the suffix "+" to the equation number given in the base model to indicate that we use the alternative equation in place of the original equation given in the base model.

Equation (1') states that the first three income quintiles now have extra income $\left(r_g \cdot S_{ih-1}\right)$ due to the *sukuk* stock they are redistributed by the public sector. Transfer payments $\left(TR_{ih}^{rs}\right)$ are also different from the base model due to the reasons explained in Equation (4') below. Equation (2') shows that the *sukuk* stock accumulates over

195 The Lucas critique states that the economic agents take the policy regime into account. In turn, "*estimates of economic parameters for one policy regime may well not be valid if the policy regime changes*" (Caballero 2010).

time. Equation (3') calculates amount of *sukuk* received by each household income quintile. As the redistributed *sukuk* is assumed to substitute the transfer payments of the same amount, each household quintile takes a portion of the *sukuk* issued in tandem with their share of transfers in total transfers in the base model. Equation (4') indicates that there is one to one correspondence and substitution between transfer payments and redistributed *sukuk* assets. Equation (4') allows us to keep the amount of fiscal burden between the transfer payments and the redistribution through *sukuk* constant. Transfers are just replaced by the GDP-linked *sukuk* if transfer payments in the base model are bigger than the *sukuk* issues. If transfer payments in the base model is smaller than the *sukuk* issued, there is no transfer payments in the risk-sharing model.

$$\begin{aligned} YD_{ih} = {} & wb_{ih}.(1-\tau_{ih}).N_{ih-1} + TR^{rs}_{ih} + FD_{ih} + BD_{ih} - LR_{ih} + i_g.B_{ih-1} \\ & + r_g.S_{ih-1} + i_d.DT_{ih-1} - i_l.L_{ih-1} \end{aligned} \tag{1'}$$

$$S_{ih} = S_{ih-1} + \Delta S_{ih} \tag{2'}$$

$$\Delta S_{ih} = \frac{TR_{ih-1}}{\sum_{i=1}^{3} TR_{ih-1}} \cdot \Delta S \tag{3'}$$

$$TR^{rs}_{ih} = \begin{cases} TR_{ih} - \Delta S_{ih} \; if \; TR_{ih} \geq \Delta S_{ih} \\ 0 \; if \; TR_{ih} < \Delta S_{ih} \end{cases} \tag{4'}$$

There are also modifications in the public sector following introduction of the GDP-linked *sukuk*. As *sukuk* is an equity item in the balance sheet of the public sector by construction, net lending in Equation (5') now consists of only taxes, modified transfer payments and interest payments to the bonds (the rich and the banking sector still have outstanding bond stock). As before, net lending equals to the bond flows. Indeed, the introduction of the GDP-linked *sukuk* only changes the magnitude of the net lending and subsequent issuance of the bonds from the lens of the conventional side of the public finance. Finally, *sukuk* issuance equals to public investment and government expenditure.

$$NL_g = TAX - TR^{rs} - i_g.B_{-1} \tag{5'}$$

$$\Delta S = I_g + G \tag{6'}$$

4 Simulations

Section 4 simulates the base and the risk-sharing models to gauge how inequality evolves over time in these models. The aim of the simulation exercise is to understand whether a shift from interest-based debt instruments to risk-sharing instruments in public finance and to use the risk-sharing instrument as an asset-based redistribution tool help income and wealth inequalities decline over time.

Before executing the simulations, we explain how to transform the disposable income and gross wealth figures into inequality indices based on which we run the simulations. We measure income and wealth inequalities by using the Gini coefficients for each period. As the most commonly used measure of inequality, Gini index takes value between 0 (indicating absolute equality) and 1 (indicating absolute inequality where one individual takes all). The index is calculated as the ratio of the area between the Lorenz curve of the distribution and the uniform distribution line to the area under the uniform distribution line. In line with the literature, we calculate Gini coefficients as follows:

$$Gini_{income} = \frac{1}{2.N^2 \cdot \mu} \cdot \sum_i \sum_j \left| YD_i - YD_j \right| \cdot N_i \cdot N_j$$

$$Gini_{wealth} = \frac{1}{2.N^2 \cdot \mu} \cdot \sum_i \sum_j \left| GW_i - GW_j \right| \cdot N_i \cdot N_j$$

where (N), (μ), (YD_i), (GW_i) represent population size, mean income (wealth), disposable income of the ith quintile and gross wealth of the *ith* income quintile, respectively.

The base model is calibrated and solved based on key data and ratios representing a hypothetical developing country with low level of financialization. Once initial values and parameters of the equations are determined, the dynamic model iteratively solves the equations for each period and the stock variables are updated in the end of each period. The iterations last for 100 periods. As there is no inheritance rule and real estate gains in the model by construction, change in the wealth inequality should be considered as the lower bound.

The risk-sharing model of asset-based redistribution is designed as follows:

- From the first period on, the public decides to finance all its future investment and consumption expenditures through GDP-linked *sukuk*.
- Outstanding stock of bonds still exist and pays interest to the current bond holders. However, there is no new issuance of the new interest-bearing bonds throughout the simulation period.
- Due to redistributive policy priorities, new issuance of *sukuk* can only be purchased by low and middle income households, that is, household income quintiles of 1, 2, and 3.
- As a reflection of the policy choice, there is no portfolio choice for the *sukuk* since all the issuance is redistributed to the eligible households in equal amounts.
- The ongoing transfer payments are replaced by the GDP-linked *sukuk*. This secures that here is no extra budget cost to the government for implementing the asset-based redistribution policy. Now the households have income generating assets which can also be used as collateral.

- The rate of return to the GDP-linked *sukuk* is no more fixed but equals to the GDP growth ex-post. In order to keep the model as simple as possible, we do not apply any *sukuk* pricing formula.

Figure 21.1 shows the evolution of the income Gini coefficients in the base and the risk-sharing models. Interestingly, income inequality is higher in the risk-sharing model compared to the interest-based base model. Although it might seem to be an unexpected and confusing output at the first sight, it is compliant with the risk-sharing asset-based redistribution policy framework hypothesized here.

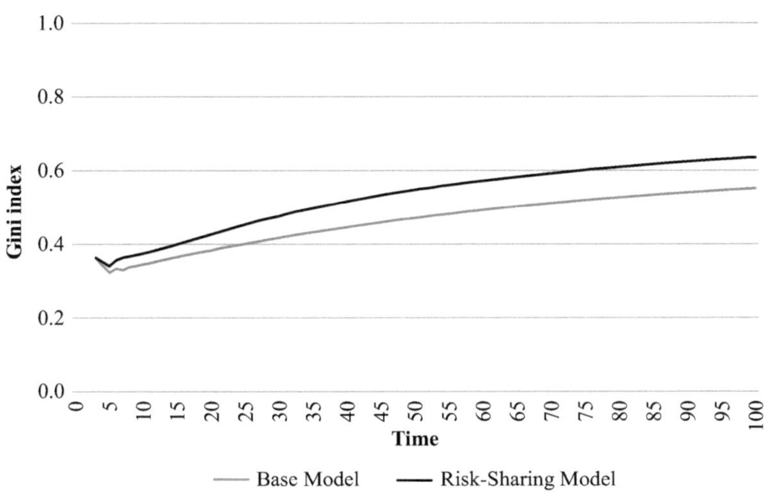

Figure 21.1: Income Gini Coefficient (Base Model vs Risk-Sharing Model).
Source: Authors' calculations.

The public sector allows for the lowest 40% of the population to hold risk-sharing instrument but there is no secondary market in which the household transact the GDP-linked *sukuk* in case they need money. Since the GDP-linked *sukuk* substitute for the transfer payments, which are an income class by definition, in the model setup, the households give up some of their income in exchange for having new risk-sharing assets. The simulation results in income distribution underlines the need for secondary market or other complementary income redistribution tools in implementing an asset-based redistribution policy.[196]

196 The question may arise as to why income inequality increases in the model while there is a clear reduction in wealth inequality and which mechanisms should be introduced in order to

On the contrary, Figure 21.2 shows that there is a significant decline in wealth inequality in the risk-sharing models compared to the base model.

Finally, we evaluate how the main public finance figures evolve between the base and the risk-sharing models. Figure 21.3 gives the public deficit to GDP figures in the base and the risk-sharing models. By design, the model is developed in a way to keep the total payments to the household at similar levels from the side of the public sector. Indeed, as shown in Figure 21.3, public deficit to GDP levels are quite similar between the base and the risk-sharing model. Figure 21.4 compares the public debt figures in the base and the risk-sharing models. Figure 21.4 confirms that public debt is lower in the risk-sharing model. This mainly stems from the counter-cyclical benefits of the risk-sharing mechanism in public finance.

reduce the income inequality after implementing the risk-sharing asset-based redistribution proposal. We attribute the increase in the income inequality to the lack of secondary markets that do not allow the monetization of the public transfers in the form of *sukuk*. While a secondary market would indeed allow for monetization, it also allows the targeted group to sell off the *sukuk* and use the proceeds on consumption. Such action would put the policy implementation back at zero with no impact on inequality reduction. However, it is important to note that the structure of a capital market is governed by Islamic rules with no culture of risk-transfer-driven speculative behavior, no leverage, no short sales, and no-margin-stock-purchase. In other words, a capital market driven by an investment culture will serve purely as a mechanism of transfer of property rights and of liquidity creation through transfer of ownership shares. In a risk-sharing world, one imagines three possible ways in which the phenomenon of 'rushing-to-sell' in the secondary market may not be motivated either as a result of need, presumably because workers move to higher income bracket, due to profit sharing, that obviates the need to sell for immediate consumption, or as result of speculative behavior which would be costly, because of the loss of voting power in the management of corporation which would serve as a deterrent to "rush-to-sell. A third way that one can imagine that "rush-to-sell" may happen under risk-sharing arrangement is neither consumption smoothing nor speculative behavior, but motivated for hedging against future risk and uncertainty. While this motivation cannot be ruled out, given that selling shares of a corporation in which one is employed is costly, one can imagine an internal institutional structure, such as those already in existence, such as matched retirement funds, credit unions or similar programs, like *takaful* arrangements that would be helpful in managing future risks. Another complementary policy could be imposing conditions like the transferred *sukuk* cannot be sold for a certain number of years or can only be sold to certain category of buyers. It should also be noted here that an asset-based redistribution proposal should also take into account the possibility that the GDP-linked *sukuk* owned by the poor can be purchased by the institutional investors over time by worsening the inequality. Thus, appropriate and complementary policy tolls should also be introduced in such a framework.

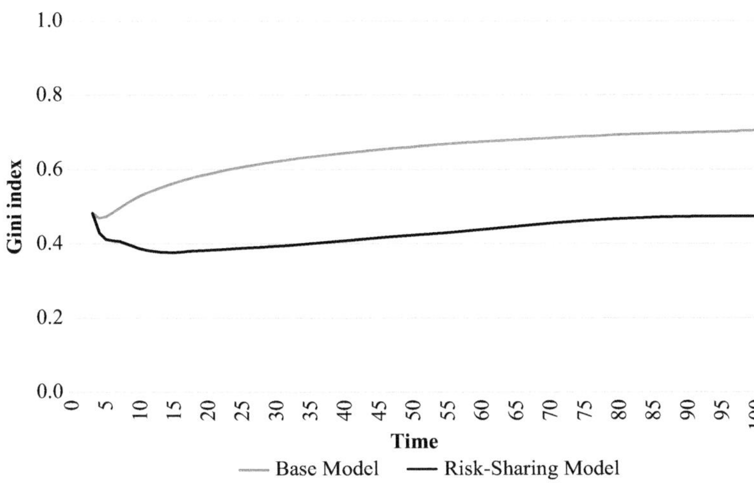

Figure 21.2: Wealth Gini Coefficient (Base Model vs Risk-Sharing Model).
Source: Authors' calculations.

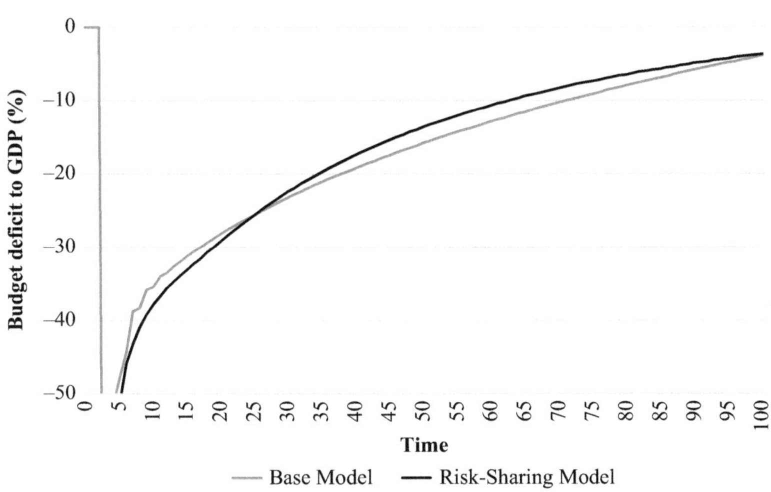

Figure 21.3: Public Deficit to GDP (%) (Base Model vs Risk-Sharing Mode).
Source: Authors' calculations

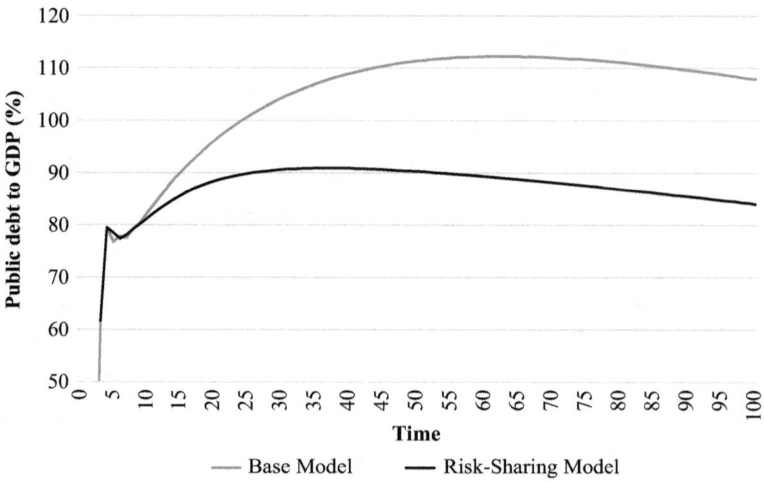

Figure 21.4: Public Debt to GDP (%) (Base vs Risk-Sharing Model).
Source: Authors' calculations

5 Conclusion

The simulation results indicate that GDP-linked *sukuk* constitute an important risk-sharing instrument that can play the important role of asset-based redistribution and prevent wealth inequality from further worsening. The simulation outputs can be confidently considered as lower bounds for a potential decrease in wealth inequality because the model still includes interest-based debt contracts such as the deposits and bonds. The model outputs also highlight the importance of using the GDP-linked *sukuk* as a redistribution mechanism, which should be supported and complemented by other policy tools, such as the effective use of zakah and the existence of secondary markets for *sukuk* trading.

Given the apparent benefits of implementing risk-sharing policies in public finance for distributional purposes, the natural question then arises as to how to implement such risk-sharing framework. The current social, political and economic realities make it almost unfeasible to immediately switch the entire public finance system into risk-sharing mode, even within the OIC countries. However, one good starting point is to issue *sukuk* for the purposes of revenue-generating public expenditures, and to issue GDP-linked *sukuk* for the purposes of non-revenue-generating public finance. Risk-sharing finance is particularly easier to implement for development projects with the potential of generating future revenues. Infrastructure projects such as highways, railroads, mass rapid-transit systems, and airports, can indeed be financed with risk-sharing public finance instruments. Furthermore, around 30–40% of government budgets in the developing world are devoted to development projects.

Thus, there is a good opportunity for a broader use of risk-sharing instruments in developing economies. The issuance of such instruments in low denominations for poor and middle-income households can also provide remedies to wealth inequality because these initiatives increase the proportion of risk-sharing instruments in investment portfolios but also provide good substitutes for traditional instruments such as gold. As the OIC countries need to invest heavily in future infrastructure and alternative development projects, financing such projects with risk-sharing instruments should be considered very seriously given the potential benefits of risk-sharing and its implications for financial stability and equitable economic growth.

References

Akın, Tarık. 2017. "Financialization, Risk-Sharing and Wealth Inequality in A Stock-Flow Consistent Model." The International Centre for Education in Islamic Finance (INCEIF).

Akın, Tarık, and Abbas Mirakhor. 2019. *Wealth Inequality, Asset Redistribution and Risk-Sharing Islamic Finance*. Berlin: De Gruyter Oldenbourg.

Askari, Hossein, Zamir Iqbal, Noureddine Krichene, and Abbas Mirakhor. 2012. *Risk Sharing in Finance: The Islamic Finance Alternative*. Singapore: John Wiley & Sons.

Askari, Hossein, Zamir Iqbal, and Abbas Mirakhor. 2014. *Challenges in Economic and Financial Policy Formulation: An Islamic Perspective*. 1st ed. New York: Palgrave Studies in Islamic Banking, Finance, and Economics. Palgrave Macmillan.

Bacha, Obiyathulla Ismath, Ahcene Lahsasna, and Abdou Diaw. 2014. "Public Sector Funding and Debt Management: A Case for GDP-Linked Ṣukūk." *Islamic Economic Studies* 22(1): 185–216.

Bacha, Obiyathulla Ismath, Abbas Mirakhor, and Hossein Askari. 2015. "Risk Sharing in Corporate and Public Finance: The Contribution of Islamic Finance." *PSL Quarterly Review, Economia Civile* 68(274): 187–213.

Basu, Kaushik, and Joseph E. Stiglitz. 2016. *Inequality and Growth: Patterns and Policy Volume I: Concepts and Analysis*. London, UK: Palgrave Macmillan UK.

Bowles, Samuel. 2012. *The New Economics of Inequality and Redistribution (Federico Caffè Lectures)*. New York, NY: Cambridge University Press.

Caballero, Ricardo J. 2010. "Macroeconomics after the Crisis: Time to Deal with the Pretense-of-Knowledge Syndrome." *Journal of Economic Perspectives* 24 (4): 85–102.

Dafermos, Yannis, and Christos Papatheodorou. 2015. "Linking Functional with Personal Income Distribution: A Stock-Flow Consistent Approach." International Review of Applied Economics 29(6): 787–815.

de Haan, Jakob, and Jan-Egbert Sturm. 2016. "Finance and Income Inequality: A Review and New Evidence." *DNB Working Paper No.530*. De Nederlandsche Bank.

Godley, Wynne, and Marc Lavoie. 2007. *Monetary Economics: An Integrated Approach to Credit, Money, Income, Production and Wealth*. New York: Palgrave Macmillan US.

IMF. 2017. *Fiscal Monitor: Tackling Inequality. Fiscal Monitor*. Washington, D.C.: International Monetary Fund.

Ismath Bacha, Obiyathulla, and Abbas Mirakhor. 2017. “Funding Development Infrastructure without Leverage: A Risk-Sharing Alternative Using Innovative *Sukuk* Structures.” *The World Economy* 41(3): 752–762.

ISRA. 2012. “Kuala Lumpur Declaration.” In *The Second Strategic Roundtable Discussion ISRA-IRTI-DURHAM University*, 1–3. Kuala Lumpur, Malaysia.

Kumhof, Michael, Romain Rancière, and Pablo Winant. 2015. “Inequality, Leverage, and Crises.” *American Economic Review* 105(3): 1217–45.

Maghrebi, Nabil, and Abbas Mirakhor. 2015. “Risk Sharing and Shared Prosperity in Islamic Finance.” *Islamic Economic Studies* 23(2): 85–115.

Mahmud, Syed F., Kaoru Yamaguchi, and Murat A. Yülek. 2017. *Money Matters: Some Puzzles, Anomalies and Crises in the Standard Macroeconomic Model*. Frankfurt: Peter Lang GmbH, Internationaler Verlag der Wissenschaften.

Minsky, Hyman Philip. 1982. “The Financial-Instability Hypothesis: Capitalist Processes and the Behavior of the Economy.” In *Financial Crises: Theory, History, and Policy*, edited by Charles P. Kindleberger and Jean-Pierre Laffargue. New York, NY: Cambridge University Press.

Minsky, Hyman Philip. 1992. “The Instability Hypothesis.” Working Paper No. 74. NY.

OECD. 2017. *Bridging the Gap: Inclusive Growth 2017 Update Report*. Paris: OECD Publishing.

OECD. 2015. *In It Together: Why Less Inequality Benefits All*. Paris: OECD Publishing.

Piketty, Thomas. 2015. “Capital and Wealth Taxation in the 21st Century.” *National Tax Journal* 68(2): 449–58.

Piketty, Thomas. 2014. *Capital in the Twenty-First Century*. Cambridge, MA: Belknap Press of Harvard University Press.

Piketty, Thomas, Emmanuel Saez, and Stefanie Stantcheva. 2014. “Optimal Taxation of Top Labor Incomes: A Tale of Three Elasticities.” *American Economic Journal: Economic Policy* 6(1): 230–71.

Rajan, Raghuram G. 2010. *Fault Lines: How Hidden Fractures Still Threaten the World Economy*. Princeton: Princeton University Press.

Seshadri, Ananth, and Kazuhiro Yuki. 2004. “Equity and Efficiency Effects of Redistributive Policies.” *Journal of Monetary Economics* 51(7): 1415–47.

Shiller, Robert J. 1993. *Macro Markets: Creating Institutions for Managing Society’s Largest Economic Risks (Clarendon Lectures in Economics)*. Oxford: Oxford University Press.

Stiglitz, Joseph E. 2015. *Rewriting the Rules of the American Economy: An Agenda for Growth and Shared Prosperity*. New York: W. W. Norton & Company.

Turner, Adair. 2016. *Between Debt and the Devil: Money, Credit, and Fixing Global Finance*. 1st ed. Princeton, New Jersey: Princeton University Press.

World Bank. 2016. *Poverty and Shared Prosperity 2016: Taking on Inequality*. Washington, D.C.: World Bank.

World Economic Forum. 2017. *The Inclusive Growth and Development Report*. Geneva: World Economic Forum.

Appendices

Appendix 21.1: Balance Sheet

	Households First 20% (1h)	Households First 20% (2h)	Households First 20% (3h)	Households First 20% (4h)	Households First 20% (5h)	Firms (f)	Government (g)	Banks (b)	Total
Current Deposits	$+DC_{1h}$	$+DC_{2h}$	$+DC_{3h}$	$+DC_{4h}$	$+DC_{5h}$	$+DC_f$		$-DC$	0
Time Deposits	$+DT_{1h}$	$+DT_{2h}$	$+DT_{3h}$	$+DT_{4h}$	$+DT_{5h}$			$-DT$	0
G. Securities	$+B_{1h}$	$+B_{2h}$	$+B_{3h}$	$+B_{4h}$	$+B_{5h}$		$-B$	$+B_b$	0
Equities					$+EQ_{5h}$	$-EQ_f$		$-EQ_b$	0
Loans	$-L_{1h}$	$-L_{2h}$	$-L_{3h}$	$-L_{4h}$	$-L_{5h}$	$-L_f$		$+L$	0
Capital Stock						$+K$			$+K$
Net Worth	$+NW_{1h}$	$+NW_{2h}$	$+NW_{3h}$	$+NW_{4h}$	$+NW_{5h}$	$+NW_f$	$+NW_g$	$+NW_b$	$+HV+K$

Appendix 21.2: Transaction Matrix

	Households First 20%	Households First 20%	Households First 20%	Households First 20%	Households First 20%	Firms (Current)	Firms (Capital)	Public	Banks (Current)	Banks (Capital)	Total
Consumption	$-C_{1h}$	$-C_{2h}$	$-C_{3h}$	$-C_{4h}$	$-C_{5h}$	$+C$					0
Investment						$+I$	$-I_f$	$-I_g$			0
G. Consumption						$+G$		$-G$			0
Wages	$+wb_{1h} \cdot N_{1h-1}$	$+wb_{2h} \cdot N_{2h-1}$	$+wb_{3h} \cdot N_{3h-1}$	$+wb_{4h} \cdot N_{4h-1}$	$+wb_{5h} \cdot N_{5h-1}$	$-WB$					0
Transfers	$+TR_{1h}$	$+TR_{2h}$	$+TR_{3h}$					$-TR$			0
Taxes	$-wb_{1h}.\tau_{1h}.N_{1h-1}$	$-wb_{2h}.\tau_{2h}.N_{2h-1}$	$-wb_{3h}.\tau_{3h}.N_{3h-1}$	$-wb_{4h}.\tau_{4h}.N_{4h-1}$	$-wb_{5h}.\tau_{5h}.N_{5h-1}$	$-\tau_f \cdot FT_{-1}$		$+TAX$	$-\tau_b \cdot BT_{-1}$		0
Firm Profits					$+FD_{5h}$	$-FT$	$+FD_f$				0
Bank Profits					$+BD_{5h}$				$-BT$	$+BD_b$	0
Loan Repayment	$-LR_{1h}$	$-LR_{2h}$	$-LR_{3h}$	$-LR_{4h}$	$-LR_{5h}$	$-LR_f$			$+LR$		0
Return on deposits	$+i_b.DT_{1h-1}$	$+i_d.DT_{2h-1}$	$+i_d.DT_{3h-1}$	$+i_d.DT_{4h-1}$	$+i_d.DT_{5h-1}$				$-i_d.DT_{-1}$		0

Return on bonds	$+i_g.B_{1h-1}$	$+i_b.B_{2h-1}$	$+i_b.B_{3h-1}$	$+i_b.B_{4h-1}$	$+i_b.B_{5h-1}$			$-i_b.B_{-1}$	$+i_b.B_{b-1}$		0
Return on loans	$-i_l.L_{1h-1}$	$-i_l.L_{2h-1}$	$-i_l.L_{3h-1}$	$-i_l.L_{4h-1}$	$-i_l.L_{5h-1}$	$-i_l.L_{f-1}$			$+i_l.L_{-1}$		0
Net Lending	NL_{1h}	NL_{2h}	NL_{3h}	NL_{4h}	NL_{5h}	*0*	NL_f	NL_g	*0*	NL_b	*0*
Current Deposits	$-\Delta DC_{1h}$	$-\Delta DC_{2h}$	$-\Delta DC_{3h}$	$-\Delta DC_{4h}$	$-\Delta DC_{5h}$		$-\Delta DC_f$			$+\Delta DC$	0
Time Deposits	$-\Delta DT_{1h}$	$-\Delta DT_{2h}$	$-\Delta DT_{3h}$	$-\Delta DT_{4h}$	$-\Delta DT_{5h}$					$+\Delta DT$	0
Bonds	$-\Delta B_{1h}$	$-\Delta B_{2h}$	$-\Delta B_{3h}$	$-\Delta B_{4h}$	$-\Delta B_{5h}$			ΔB		$-\Delta B_b$	0
Equities					$-P_e \cdot \Delta E_{5h}$		$+P_e \cdot \Delta E_f$			$+P_e \cdot \Delta E_b$	0
Loans	$+\Delta L_{1h}$	$+\Delta L_{2h}$	$+\Delta L_{3h}$	$+\Delta L_{4h}$	$+\Delta L_{5h}$		$+\Delta L_f$			$-\Delta L$	0
Sum	*0*	*0*	*0*	*0*	*0*	*0*	*0*	*0*	*0*	*0*	*0*

Mohamed Wail Aaminou, Tarık Akın

Chapter 22: Risk-Sharing Finance and Inequality in a Benchmark Agent-Based Model

1 Introduction

The Global Financial Crisis (GFC) has shown that the stylized facts stated by Nicholas Kaldor (1961) on the patterns of economic growth and national income accounts are no more valid in many of the advanced and developing countries.[197] On the contrary, growing inequalities, surge in rate of return to wealth, declining share of labor in national income and historically high wealth to income ratios have been the new norm (Stiglitz 2015d; Jones and Romer 2010). Arguably, increasing income and wealth inequality, as a defining feature of the world economy in the post-GFC era, is one of the underlying reasons for the divergence between the current reality and the Kaldorian stylized facts. Although role of inequality on social conflict, higher public finance requirement and slower short-run growth has well-studied in the literature, new evidence adds that:

- Inequality is one of the underlying drivers of global imbalances and financial crises (Kumhof, Rancière, and Winant 2015; Rajan 2010; de Haan and Sturm 2016; Goda, Onaran, and Stockhammer 2016; Turner 2016);
- Inequality undermines long-term economic growth (Islam and McGillivray 2015; Ostry, Berg, and Tsangarides 2014; World Economic Forum 2017; OECD 2015; Bagchi and Svejnar 2015; Cynamon and Fazzari 2016; IMF 2017).

In the post-GFC Era, the new evidence on the effects of inequality on financial crises and long-term growth have spurred hightened interest in economics of inequality in the academia. Moreover, policy-makers have also realized that addressing inequality is a key policy ingredient to achieve strong and sustainable economic growth. Within the economics of inequality literature, wealth inequality is increasingly becoming an important field of research. Publication of Thomas Piketty's *Capital in the Twenty-First Century* in 2014 is arguably one of the pushing factors that have given rise to heightened interest towards wealth inequality. In his book, Piketty sketches out the long-run dynamics of income and wealth inequality in

197 Jones and Romer (2010) summarize these stylized facts as follows: i) growth of labor productivity is sustained, ii) growth of capital per worker is sustainable, iii) interest rates and return to capital is stable, iv) capital to output ratio is stable, v) shares of capital and labor income in national accounts is stable, and vi) rate of economic growth is stable around 2%–5% among the fast-growing economies.

https://doi.org/10.1515/9783110587920-022

many advanced and developing countries going as far back as the 18th century. He shows that wealth inequality has been increasing at an unsustainable pace in the last several decades. One of the core arguments in his book is that the rate of return to wealth is higher than the rate of economic growth, which he calls as the "fundamental inequality", an inevitable by-product of capitalism. The subsequent question is which forces cause the wealth inequality to increase.

There are many social, political, institutional and economic drivers of high wealth inequality in historical perspective (Scheidel 2017). In the mainstream economics, wealth distribution is considered as the outcome of two underlying factors, namely, meritocracy and saving behavior. Indeed, many determinants of the wealth distribution in the mainstream model, such as top income shares, entrepreneurship, and heterogeneity in saving rates, derive from these underlying drivers. It can then be argued that the underlying causes of the wealth distribution are more or less justifiable since they are in compliant with a well-functioning market economy. However, recent studies on wealth inequality highlight the fact that the wealth inequality can be explained, to a large extent, by neither the capital accumulation models nor the notion of meritocracy. This is because the bulk of the wealth inequality stems from rents which should not exist in a well-functioning market system. Some studies suggests that interest-based debt contracts might be one of the important drivers of existence of high level of rents in debt-based economic systems. This study takes this view and attempts to answer whether there is indeed a relationship between interest-based debt contracts and wealth inequality by resorting to agent-based modelling.

The ABM, which aims at explaining the behavior of a complex system based on behaviors of autonomously interacting agents within it, is gaining popularity and becoming one of the workhorse family of models in economics and finance (Turrell 2016; Janssen and Ostrom 2006). The key feature of the ABM is that the agent-based models "show how even very simple behaviors can combine from the 'bottom up' to recreate the more complex behaviors observed in the real world." (Turrell 2016). The Segregation model (Schelling 1971) is a typical ABM implementation case. In this model, individuals' small preferences to live next to similar neighbors (eg. based on ethnicity or on income) could lead to total city segregation. According to Macal and North (2010), an agent-based model is composed of the agents, the environment, and the interactions. Agents are self-contained and uniquely identifiable individuals. An agent can function independently and has attributes (e.g. age, gender, preferences) and a decision-making process (e.g. utility maximization). In Schelling's model, every individual is either "Red" or "Blue" (attributes) and moves from or stays in a given neighborhood depending on the percentage of similar neighbors (decision making). The Environment represents the setting in which the modeling (market, geographic area, ...) takes place. In Schelling's segregation case, the city environment is modeled as a grid where inhabitants, or agents, are located each within a separate cell. An inhabitant's neighbors are the ones located in immediate surrounding boxes. Finally, the Interactions take place within the different agents, and between the agents and the environment.

This chapter argues that interest-based debt contracts are one of the main drivers of the existence of rents and ensuing high wealth inequality. An agent-based model is constructed to show that the bulk of the wealth inequality in a debt-based economic system stems from the interest-based debt contracts. Subsequently, a counterfactual model based on substitution of interest-based debt contracts with risk-sharing contracts is also constructed to show that the wealth inequality tapers off to acceptable levels.

Section 1 introduces the chapter. Section 2 reviews the literature on the nexus between the interest-based debt contracts and inequality from the lens of the notion of the wealth residual. Section 3 develops a benchmark agent-based macroeconomic model to show that wealth inequality in a debt-based economic system is associated with the interest-based debt contracts. Subsequently, a counterfactual model is introduced derived from the benchmark agent-based macroeconomic model. The main difference between the benchmark and counterfactual models is that interest-based debt contracts in the former model is replaced with risk-sharing instruments in the latter one. The simulation outputs from the benchmark and the counterfactual models indicate that resorting to the risk-sharing finance both reduces wealth inequality and increases economic output. Section 4 concludes and makes concrete policy recommendations based on the risk-sharing framework.

2 Interest-Based Debt Contracts and Wealth Residual

As underlined in Section 1, the mainstream literature considers wealth inequality as a function of heterogeneity in meritocracy and saving behavior among economic agents. Since meritocracy plays a direct role on the level of savings and marginal propensity to save for economic agents, it is the saving behavior that determines wealth inequality in a well-working market economy. Thus, the mainstream economics argues that why people save should be the main field of research on wealth inequality (De Nardi and Fella 2017). In this regard, the Bewley models, which set up a link from saving behavior to wealth inequality, have become the workhorse frameworks on wealth inequality studies. The Bewley models seek to understand "which mechanisms generate saving behavior that leads to a distribution of asset holdings consistent with the data" (De Nardi 2015). However, the Bewley models don't perform well in matching data with the model outputs if the wealth inequality stems from factors other than accumulation of capital and savings. In case of dominancy of non-market factors in the formation of wealth inequality, such as rents, explanatory power of the Bewley models is diluted.

As stated by Stiglitz (2015b), "much of the increase in wealth has little to do with savings in the usual sense. Rather it is the result of capital gains – especially the increased value of land – and an increase in the capitalized value of other rents”. A natural extension of this view is that income inequality, as a function of the meritocracy and the saving behavior, explains only one part of the wealth inequality. The bulk of the wealth inequality which can’t be explained by the factors that explain income inequality is named as “wealth residual” (Basu and Stiglitz 2016). Alternatively, the wealth residual can be defined as part of the wealth inequality which can’t be explained by the capital accumulation and/or savings. It is the increase in wealth without concomitant increase in capital. The wealth residual concept is analogous to the Solow residual, which is the measure of growth that is not explained by factors of production (Solow 1957). Similar to the notion of the wealth residual, this chapter defines wealth residual as the bulk of the wealth inequality, which can’t be explained by ‘factors of’ income inequality.

Stiglitz (2015c) argues that there are four main factors for the existence of the wealth residual, namely, asset boom in real estate, increase in the value of positional goods which are price inelastic to supply, intellectual property, and exploitation rents. There are two main underlying factors for the asset boom in real estate prices for the last few decades. Firstly, most of the real estate purchased by the super-rich can be counted as positional goods, which stand for luxury spending (Stiglitz 2015a). Since the real estate is in fixed supply, higher demand for the real estate as a positional good, its price increases over time. Secondly, low interest rate policies recently implemented by the central banks have played a significant role in the formation of the real estate bubble (Stiglitz 2015a). Increase in the value of positional goods occurs because higher wealth level increases the demand for positional goods, which derive their value from the fact that consumers prefer them to demonstrate their status (Stiglitz 2015c). These goods are also related to the interest rate mechanism since their cost is linked to their opportunity cost, the interest rate. As another source of wealth inequality, changes in the property rights regimes, patents and intellectual property rights have contributed to the wealth of the economic agents who hold rights of the intellectual property (Stiglitz 2015c). Finally, exploitative rents, which are defined by Stirati (2016) as the market power stemming from ownership of an asset and cannot be in any way eliminated by competition, are an important driver of wealth inequality. Exploitative rents lead to the prices that are quite different from optimal market prices, which are determined by marginal product of capital in a competitive economy. These rents are not considered in the traditional growth and distribution models, however, since the notion of rents play no role in traditional mainstream models (Stiglitz 2015c). The exploitative rents can take many forms, some of which are specified by Stiglitz (2015c) as follows:

- *Changes in market power and exploitation*: There is a rising monopoly and concentration trend among the firms in the world. To give an example, a recent finding, which is based on a dataset of 28,000 firms formed by the McKinsey Global Institute, indicates that the ratio of average market capitalization of the top 100 firms to that of the bottom 2,000 firms was 7,000 in 2015. This ratio was only 31 in 1995 (UNCTAD 2017). Besides explicit forms of exploitation (privatizations, tax evasion, market manipulation, etc.), subtle forms of exploitation also matter such as bail outs by the government in the form of shifting the risk to the public.

- *Exploitation of consumers*: These rents include taking advantage of the consumers due to their limitations to process information and irrationalities in behaviors. Corporations and financial institutions have extensively used behavioral techniques to exploit the customers.
- *Knowledge and information rents*: These rents occur due to abuse of information asymmetries by the informed party such as insider trading and market manipulations.
- *Changes in discount rates and risk management*: For instance, fall in the rate of discount and subsequent relative price changes induce important wealth gains for the holders of certain assets.
- *Improved risk management*: Improved risk management has changed wealth income ratios.

This analytical chapter regroups forms of the exploitative rents under two main rubrics. The first one, which is called as 'malfunctioning rents', are the ones that can be eliminated by implementing appropriate regulation and enforcement of the rules of the game. For instance, consumer protection measures can eliminate knowledge and information rents. Securing rules of the game in privatization can impede formation of excessive market power. The second one, which is named as 'inherent rents', cannot be eliminated by better implementation of rules or elimination of tax evasion in the system since they exist inherently in the financial system. For instance, capital gains in real estate and risk-shifting through bail-outs are inherent features of the interest-rate based systems (Askari et al. 2012).

The interest-based debt contracts, due to their inherent features, are one of the underlying factors that give rise to formation of the 'inherent rents'. In effect, the interest-based debt contracts are as important as, in some cases even more important than, the income inequality as a driver of the wealth inequality. Theoretically, the interest rate should go in line with the rate of return to capital, which is then a reflection of the marginal productivity of capital. The theoretical nexus between the interest rates and real sector activity through the marginal productivity of capital forms the basics of economic theory (For instance, see Ljungqvist and Sargent (2012), and Wickens (2008). A natural extension of this assumption is that rate of return to capital should be associated with the growth rate of the economy. In such a world, there should be no significant rents, especially inherent rents, in the system and the wealth grows in line with the growth rate of capital and economic activity. On the contrary, the fundamental inequality $(r > g)$ concept argued by Piketty (2014), which simply states that rate of return to wealth (not capital) outstrips rate of return to economic growth, is the norm in the capitalist system and this inequality is the main cause of increasing wealth inequality. But how the interest-based debt contracts lead to the fundamental inequality to persist? There are indeed two main channels between interest-based debt contracts and wealth residual that paves the way for higher wealth inequality. The first one is called "volume channel", which covers formation of wealth inequality stemming from differed access to credit, credit expansion/contraction and level of debt. The second one is called "price channel", which covers repercussions of interest rate mechanism and capital gains through asset price booms. These two channels, which are then determined by the interest-based contracts, affect wealth inequality through wealth residual.

2.1 Volume Channel

The volume channel is a source of wealth residual stemming from wealthy individuals' better access to interest-based debt contracts compared to less wealthy individuals at more favorable terms due to the higher level of wealth of the former group. There are arguably two main pillars of the volume channel, namely, credit constraints and collateral, and the level of debt. It should be noted here that these pillars are highly interrelated.

In an ideal economic setting, the contracts are complete and fully enforceable. The level of the initial wealth does not constrain the type of the contract an economic agent can take part and there is no systematic discrimination against the poor in harnessing the contractual opportunities (Bowles 2012). The income and/or wealth level determines only the budget constraint. On the contrary, the contracts are incomplete and not fully enforceable in the real world.[198] Hence, the level of the initial wealth both constrains the size of the transactions in a contract and affects whether to take part in specific class of contracts for economic agents. In sum, the level of initial wealth determines whether the terms of the contracts are favorable to the contracting parties.

With the existence of the incomplete and unenforceable contracts, access to credit constraints increase wealth inequality through several channels (Bowles 2012). Firstly, impediments in access to credit usually prevent high-quality projects from being implemented. Secondly, credit-constrained economic agents typically have lower expected returns from their financial contracts. Thirdly, more access to credit means less risk-aversity from the lens of the economic agents since they there is a positive relationship between their initial wealth and expected returns. Fourthly, credit-constraints increase economic agents' degree of impatience, which is negatively associated with their propensity to save and to invest. Although, these

198 Wang (2013) defines complete contract as: "a contract in which the income-sharing rule is capable of handling all possible contingencies so that additional mechanism are unnecessary."

channels are also at work in the risk-sharing contracts, it is the existence of the collateral that amplifies the nexus between credit constraints and the wealth inequality (Akın and Mirakhor 2019). Since collateral increases odds of the repayment of the loans, it is a key determinant of access to credit (Serra-Garcia 2010). As indicated by Bowles (2012) "among those who do borrow, those with more wealth borrow on better terms. ... This is the case, for example, when the borrower has sufficient wealth to post collateral or put her own equity in a project ...". An important area that feeds the wealth inequality is the real estate. The economic agents with higher initial wealth level can purchase real estate with credit at more favorable conditions and enjoy the capital gains stemming from incessant increase in real estate prices.

Besides credit constraints and collateral, accumulation of debt is another element of volume channel that gives rise to increasing wealth inequality over time. As underscored by Buiter and Rahbari (2015) "[t]he academic literature has emphasized that debt, particularly when it is relatively large, can cause either underinvestment (the debt overhang problem of Myers (1977) or excessive risk-taking. ... Debt, particularly if it is large enough, can, therefore, systematically induce adverse behavioral distortions in the decisions of individual households and businesses." The literature shows that there is a nexus between the volume of the debt, especially household debt, and severity of following recessions and decline in national income, which have important distributional repercussions (Mian and Sufi 2018).

2.2 Price Channel

The price channel is a source of wealth residual stemming from capital gains due to the interest rate mechanism and leverage. Thanks to the price channel, asset booms work to the benefit of the economic agents with high level of initial wealth. Interest-based debt contracts is the underlying driver of leverage, which allows debt claims to be multiplied by several times of the current output (Bezemer 2011).

Speculation and asset bubbles are inherent features of debt-based economic system. Unlimited power of the banks and other financial institutions, at least theoretically, to create debt is an important driver for the increasing asset prices, such as stocks, real estate, and precious commodities. Since the demand comes from easy credit conditions as a fallout of the debt creation, not from income generation, the prices can keep increasing independent of the developments in the real sector activity. During asset booms, rational economic agents also play role through their expectation that the prices will continue to increase (Askari and Mirakhor 2015).

Changes in asset prices in a debt-driven economy have different impacts on the wealth levels of heterogeneous economic agents. As indicated by Turner (2016), "superior access to credit in volatile economic circumstances has often been crucial to the accumulation of large fortunes". Asset prices typically affect "the accumulation of large fortunes" with two main mechanisms (Akın and Mirakhor 2019). Firstly, composition of the asset portfolios differs among the income and wealth segments. There is positive correlation between being at the higher tail of the wealth distribution and having more diversified asset portfolios in which share of equity is typically higher. Moving towards the lower end of the wealth distribution (to the lower percentile) increases the probability of having higher share of real estate and deposits in the portfolio of financial assets. (Domanski, Zabai, and Scatigna 2016). For instance, the fifth quintile in the wealth distribution in the U.S. has 15.1% of their financial assets in equities. This number is only 0.6% for the second quintile of the wealth distribution (Domanski, Zabai, and Scatigna 2016). Secondly, economic agents at the top of the wealth distribution have typically much better access to their internal funds to finance their projects or needs. It means they are less likely to be inflicted by the repercussions of leverage and over-borrowing. This mechanism is especially relevant to the real estate market. Real estate is typically most important asset for households and it is usually financed by bank credit. It is also a fact that most of the credit extended for real estate goes to purchase of already existing buildings, not new constructions. Once real estate prices increase due to asset boom, the rich disproportionally benefits from ever increasing prices because are benefitted from not only easier access to credit in favorable terms but also having higher level of internal funds. On the other hand, ever increasing real estate prices means resorting to more bank credit, higher collateral and lower net worth for the rest of the society. Furthermore, it is the highly-leveraged poor who have big losses during the fall of the asset prices. This is mostly because debt magnifies the repercussions of the fall in asset prices through foreclosures and concentration of losses on the indebted economic agents. As a result, wealth inequality exacerbates the fallouts of financial crises and recessions by exposing borrowers (those whose capital ownership is small) and protecting lenders (the fortunate ones with positive net capital) (Askari and Mirakhor 2015).

3 Wealth Inequality in a Risk-Sharing World

Section 2 discusses that the interest-based debt contracts are one of the drivers of the wealth residual through the volume and the price channels. It is arguably the state independent nature of the ex-ante interest rate mechanism from the economic output that lead to higher wealth inequality. If this is the case, state contingent contracts, such as the risk-sharing contracts, should end up with comparably lower level of wealth inequality. Indeed, "the essence of risk sharing derives from the imperative of taking different states of nature into account, not all of which are necessarily favorable and associated with positive returns. It can be argued that debt financing requires the payment of future cash flows inclusive of principal and interest, irrespective of future states of nature." (Maghrebi and Mirakhor 2015).

Risk-sharing is a contractual arrangement in which the outcome of a random event is borne collectively by the economic agents who are involved in the contract (Askari et al. 2012). Economic agents who are involved in the risk-sharing contract expect that the outcome will result in lesser idiosyncratic risk and higher level of output (Akın and Mirakhor 2019). As stated by Maghrebi and Mirakhor (2015),

> Arrow-Debreu competitive economy, is also the defining principle of Islamic finance. As noted by Cowen (1983), it is difficult however to accommodate pre-determined rates of interest in Arrow-Debreu-Hahn into the system of equations for general equilibrium. The foundations of optimal allocation of resources in a competitive economy are laid indeed on the concept of state-dependent payoffs, and interest-bearing fixed-income securities would be inconsistent with the definition of pure contingent claims. Under Islamic finance, the return on capital is determined on ex post basis, which implies that future payoffs on contingent claims are function of variables in the real economy. It is the intrinsic interdependencies between time, cash flows and risks that forces future cash-flows to be defined by economic activities under a world of uncertainty. This provides the basis for stronger linkage between the financial sector and the real economy.

Since the notion of risk-sharing is based on contingent claims, as reflected in the Arrow-Debreu-Hahn general equilibrium models, risk-sharing contracts work in line with the market forces and not against them (Bacha and Mirakhor 2013). One of the reasons for the fact that the wealth residual is becoming the bulk of the wealth inequality is the notion of the fundamental inequality $(r > g)$ as discussed at length by Piketty (2014). Indeed, the fundamental inequality reflects the divergence between return to financial wealth and real sector activity. Since, the interest rate mechanism is state independent, it does not move in tandem with the realizations of the economic activity.

An alternative mechanism is the risk-sharing contracts in which return to capital is a function of the productive capital and is determined ex-post. If the rate of return to wealth is an ex-post function of the productive capital, the rate of return to wealth (r) cannot overgrow the rate of return to economic growth (g) in the long-run. In other words, $(r = f(g))$ in such a risk-sharing-based counterfactual world. As highlighted by Maghrebi and Mirakhor (2015),

> Since the payoffs are contingent on the realization of a particular state of nature, the realized return on real investment is known only on ex post basis. The growth rate can be positive or negative depending on the realization of favorable or unfavorable states of nature. This implies that capital is not allowed to increase irrespective of growth rates, and that it is bound to decrease with negative growth. The systematic risks entailed by economic activities are thus shared by investors in capital markets insofar that equity markets, rather than bond markets, are concerned.

The ABM model given in Section 4 follows the same counterfactual assumption to show that such a risk-sharing economy would prevent formation of the fat tails in the distribution of wealth. The relationships between debt, financialization and inequality is an active field of research in the ABM literature, especially in the post-GFC period.

However, general direction of research in the ABM literature on this field of research is to understand repercussions of high inequality on several macroeconomic variables, especially financial fragility. In the ABM literature, Cardaci (2018), and Cardaci and Saraceno (2016) argue that growing inequality combined with loose monetary policy is an important driver of the financial crises. Palagi et al. (2017) focus on credit-constrained households and effects of fiscal policy to show that inequality shocks pave the way for financial crises through income dynamics. Russo (2017) looks into the effects of the social classes on the formation of the income and wealth inequalities and concludes that social structure plays a role on the formation of the business cycles and financial crises by affecting the macroeconomic dynamics. Russo et al. (2016) conclude that introduction of consumer credit to their agent-based model with financially fragile heterogeneous economic agents increases the probability of a financial crisis in their model. Dosi et al. (2013) investigate the interactions between income distribution and key macroeconomic variables based on an agent-based Keynesian model and find that income distribution plays role in severity of business cycles fluctuations, unemployment rates, and financial crises.

The agent-based model in Section 4 diverges from the aforementioned studies in the literature on the ground that the model examines the prospective role that the interest-based debt contracts might play on income and wealth inequalities.

4 The Model

Section 4 constructs a benchmark agent-based macroeconomic model to investigate the interplay between debt-based economy and increasing inequalities. Calibrating the benchmark model, another model is introduced, which is based on a risk-sharing economy in which ex-ante interest rate in the benchmark model is replaced by ex-post rate of return to real sector activities. Only a few equations and parameter values differ between the benchmark and the modified models. The aim is to simulate the interest-based benchmark economy (the base model) and the risk-sharing economy (the RS model) in an agent-based framework and then to compare the simulation outputs to see whether there is a pronounced divergence between these two hypothetical worlds with respect to the levels of inequality in the household sector.

The dynamic nature of these two economies evolve over a time span of $t = 1, 2, \ldots, T$. Both the base and the RS models are composed of three sectors, namely, the households, the real sector and the banking sector. The household sector encompasses many interacting heterogeneous agents (households) who differ from each other with respect to several characteristics such as wage income, dividend income and consumption. The real sector and the banking sector are kept as simple as possible. Thus, there is only a representative firm and a bank in the base and the RS economies. The inequality indicators in both of the models are based on evolution of the income and net wealth levels of the heterogeneous household agents. Although the literature offers many inequality indicators, such as Atkinson index and coefficient of variation, only the Gini index is employed in this study.[199] Section 4.1 explains the details of the sectors and equations which form the base model. Section 4.2 introduces the RS model, which is a slightly modified version of the base model. Section 4.3 succinctly explains how the Gini index is calculated for each of the models. Section 4.4 runs the simulations and shows that there is a pronounced divergence in evolution of inequality between the base model and the RS model.

4.1 The Base Model in a Debt-Based Economy

There are three sectors, namely, the households, the real sector, and the banking sector in the benchmark model. Since having many firms and banks in the model do not lead to significant changes in the evolution of the household inequality and change in the behavioral patterns among the agents, there is a representative firm and a bank in the economy. Net income and wealth of each sector, and intersectoral relationships are modeled through simple macroeconomic equations. The main line of difference between the base model and the risk-sharing economy is that ex-ante interest rate in the base economy is replaced with ex-post rate of return to economic activity. Although, many macroeconomic variables and behavioral parameters should differ between interest-based and risk-sharing economies, such as direct and indirect effects of debt, even solely focusing on ex-ante interest rate vs. ex-post rates of return can result in big differences in the evolution of the macroeconomic variables between these two hypothetical setups. Once one can show that existence of the ex-ante interest rate gives rise to higher level of inequality compared to an economy in which the interest rate is replaced by the ex-post rate of return, the benchmark model can be expanded further. Thus, the focus of this study is to show that even a change in the nature of the economy from interest-based contracts to rate of return to the economic activity might have significant implications on the inequality indicators. Two features of the hypothetical economy make the model compatible with application of the ABM. Households are heterogeneous and there is a direct interaction through catching up with the Joneses effect.

199 A thorough analysis of inequality should include analyzing different inequality indices concurrently. Due to space limitations, this study solely focus on the Gini index, which measures the change in the middle segments of a distribution better compared to many other popular inequality indices.

4.1.1 Households

The model consists of $h = \{1, \ldots, H\}$ infinitely lived and heterogeneous households which differ in their level of income, consumption and stock of indebtedness. There is no population growth in the economy, so the total number of households is fixed in every period. It should also be noted from the outset that there is no government and tax in this economy. Thus, total income equals to disposable income by definition.

Equation (1) defines ex-ante household income (Y^{*}_{ht}), which consists of wage income (W_{ht}), dividends from firm profits (PF^{dist}_{ht}), dividends from bank profits (PB^{dist}_{ht}), interest income from deposits $(i_{dt}.D_{ht-1})$, interest payments to loans $(i_{lt}.L_{ht-1})$ and amortization payments for the outstanding loans $(amort.L_{ht-1})$. Ex-ante household income is equal to realized (ex-post) household income under certain conditions: If the sum of the interest payments and amortization of the outstanding debt is more than other components of the ex-ante household income, then the ex-ante household income become negative. Equation (2) then identifies realized (ex-post) household income based on the sign of the ex-ante household income. If the ex-ante household income is positive, realized (ex-post) household income equals to the ex-ante household income. If the ex-ante household income is negative, it means the household h is unable to pay out its interest and amortization payments at time t. In such a case, the household h defaults and the bank has to forgive the outstanding loan stock. However, the bank seizes the collateral as given in Equation (17). Equation (1) and (2) guarantee that the realized (ex-post) household income is always non-negative.

$$Y^{*}_{ht} = W_{ht} + PF^{dist}_{ht} + PB^{dist}_{ht} + i_{dt}.D_{ht-1} - i_{lt}.L_{ht-1} - amort.L_{ht-1} \tag{1}$$

$$Y_{ht} = \begin{cases} W_{ht} + PF^{dist}_{ht} + PB^{dist}_{ht} + i_{dt}.D_{ht-1} - i_{lt}.L_{ht-1} - amort.L_{ht-1}, & if\ Y^{*}_{ht} \geq 0 \\ W_{ht} + PF^{dist}_{ht} + PB^{dist}_{ht} + i_{dt}.D_{ht-1}, & if\ Y^{*}_{ht} < 0 \end{cases} \tag{2}$$

The model states that wage income of each household is a constant share of total wage payments to the households. The total wage payments to the households *vis-à-vis* capital income in the economy can change over time. However, assuming a constant share within wage income is not unrealistic. The implicit assumption is that wage income of each household is a linear function of productivity and total amount allotted to the wage payments in the economy. Since, by assumption, relative productivity doesn't change among the workers over time (but not the total productivity), it can be assumed that the initial distribution of the wages stays constant over time.

Hence, according to Equation (3), the total wage payments to the household sector is distributed among the households as per an income distribution parameter (η_j), which is the main source of income inequality among the households. The one-parameter exponential distribution function (η_{ht}) gives a weight to each household in line with the wage level in the current period. The income distribution parameter can be regarded as the weight from an 'exponential distribution' assigned to each household in the economy and it adds up to 1 for all households.[200] An implicit result of using the income distribution parameter is that wage inequality lasts more or less stable over the simulation period.

$$W_{ht} = \eta_{ht}.W_t \tag{3}$$

Following König and Größl (2014), Equation (4) shows that income distribution parameter follows a unit root process to account for uncertainty in wage setting process. Equation (4) points out that income distribution weight assigned to each household includes a stochastic element which is a correction factor for slight changes in the circumstances at the individual level such as increasing individual productivity level in a period.

$$\eta_{ht} = \eta_{ht-1} + \varepsilon_{ht} \tag{4}$$

Total wage payments to the labor force in the economy is determined by institutional and market forces. Following Dosi et al. (2013), the total wage payments is set according to labor productivity (*lprod*), as a proxy for institutional factors, and growth rate of the GDP in the previous year ($\Delta dGDP_{t-1}$), as a proxy for unemployment and other market forces. The labor productivity variables are set fixed throughout the simulation period and the growth rate of the GDP in the previous year is calculated given in Equation (35). Hence, Equation (5) indicates that total wage payments to the households in the model is calculated as the total wage payments in the previous period multiplied by the combined coefficient of institutional and market factors.

$$W_t = W_{t-1}.\left[1 + \theta_1^w.lprod + \theta_2^w.\Delta dGDP_{t-1}\right] \tag{5}$$

$$where\ \Delta dGDP_{t-1} = \frac{(GDP_{t-1} - GDP_{t-2})}{GDP_{t-2}}$$

In calculation of each household's dividend income from banking and real sector, same income distribution parameter as the one given in Equation (4) is used. This is due to the assumption in the model that higher wage income earners are expected to receive higher dividend income in proportion to their wage income. Thus, Equation (6) and (7) indicate that each household has a dividend income $\left(PF_{ht}^{dist},\ PB_{ht}^{dist}\right)$ in

200 As argued by Tao et al. (2019), pattern of income inequality typically follows power distribution for the top income class and exponential distribution for the rest of the population. Since this study assumes that the population is more or less egalitarian in the initialization of the simulations, only exponential distribution is used in the model.

proportion to their wage income given total amount of distributed firm and bank profits $\left(PF_t^{dist},\ PB_t^{dist}\right)$ at time *t*.

$$PF_{ht}^{dist} = \eta_{ht}.PF_t^{dist} \tag{6}$$

$$PB_{ht}^{dist} = \eta_{ht}.PB_t^{dist} \tag{7}$$

After households receive their income at the beginning of the period, they decide on their desired consumption level $\left(C_{ht}^{*}\right)$. As given in Equation (8), desired consumption is composed of two parts: a regular consumption part which is a function of income in the previous period and average economy-wide consumption per capita in the previous period (see Equation 9). The regular consumption part is similar to the Keynesian consumption function and the average economy-wide consumption is a reflection of the "Catching up with the Joneses" effect.[201]

$$C_{ht}^{*} = mpc_d.Y_{ht-1} + cuj_d.Cbar_{t-1} \tag{8}$$

$$Cbar_{t-1} = \frac{1}{H}\cdot\sum_{1}^{H} C_{ht-1} \tag{9}$$

In the model, it is assumed that there are different marginal propensity to consume and Catching up with the Joneses effect parameter values for different segments of the population. One way to define such parameter values at the individual level similar to the income distribution parameter. Instead, we divide the households into 5 equal deciles, each of which represent 20% income group in the population, in ascending order with respect to their income level. The first 20% income group is then composed of the household with the lowest income share, the rest is formed accordingly. Then a different parameter value is assigned to each of these groups. Equation (10) shows the intervals of each of the parameter values of the consumption equation given in Equation (8).

$$mpc_d = \begin{cases} mpc_1, & if\ h \in \left[0, \overline{H_1}\right) \\ mpc_2, & if\ h \in \left[\overline{H_1}, \overline{H_2}\right) \\ mpc_3, & if\ h \in \left[\overline{H_2}, \overline{H_3}\right) \\ mpc_4, & if\ h \in \left[\overline{H_3}, \overline{H_4}\right) \\ mpc_5, & if\ h \in \left[\overline{H_4}, \overline{H_5}\right] \end{cases} \quad \text{and} \quad cuj_d = \begin{cases} cuj_1, & if\ h \in \left[0, \overline{H_1}\right) \\ cuj_2, & if\ h \in \left[\overline{H_1}, \overline{H_2}\right) \\ cuj_3, & if\ h \in \left[\overline{H_2}, \overline{H_3}\right) \\ cuj_4, & if\ h \in \left[\overline{H_3}, \overline{H_4}\right) \\ cuj_5, & if\ h \in \left[\overline{H_4}, \overline{H_5}\right] \end{cases} \tag{10}$$

201 Ulph (2014) explains the "Catching up with the Joneses Effect" as follows: "... there is an extensive literature on conspicuous consumption whereby individuals lose esteem if their consumption of some good(s) which signal their status is below the average of the reference/peer group and gain esteem if their consumption exceeds the average. It is recognized that this can lead to a "rat race" in which individuals over-consume ..."

However, financial constraints may impede some or all of the households to realize their desired consumption level $\left(C^*_{ht}\right)$. Thus, actual and desired consumption levels may diverge. In Equation (11) actual consumption level is calculated as follows: If income level of a household is higher than its desired consumption, actual consumption equals to desired consumption. As long as outstanding loan stock of the household (L_{ht}) is less than or equal to the threshold level, which can be defined as pre-determined multiple of her/his level of income in the previous period $(\ell_t.Y_{ht-1})$, s/he can still realize the desired consumption thanks to availability of credit extended by the banking sector. If outstanding stock of loan stock surpasses this threshold, the household partly defaults on his loan. Hence, the banking sector will not extend new credit line to the defaulted household. In such a case, the household has to allocate some portion of his consumption for debt repayment. Until paying back the debt or having sufficient primary balance, the household consumes the subsistence level $\left(C^{min}_{ht}\right)$, which is given in Equation (12)

$$C_{ht} = \begin{cases} C^*_{ht}, \ if \ Y_{ht} > C^*_{ht} \\ C^*_{ht}, \ if \ Y_{ht} < C^*_{ht} \ and \ L_{ht-1} \leq \ell_t.Y_{ht-1} \\ C^{min}_{ht}, \ if \ Y_{ht} < C^*_{ht} \ and \ L_{ht-1} > \ell_t.Y_{ht-1} \end{cases} \tag{11}$$

$$C^{min}_{ht} = \theta^{min}_h.C_{ht-1} \tag{12}$$

Net lending of each household is defined as the difference between current income and current consumption, as given in Equation (13).

$$NL_{ht} = Y_{ht} - C_{ht} \tag{13}$$

Each household has either positive or negative net lending at the end of each period. For simplicity, we assume in the model that positive net lending increase deposits of the households held in the banking system while negative net lending is financed through new credits from the banking system (see Equation (14) and (15)).[202] It is also assumed that all deposits are in the form of time deposit, which earn interest income. It should also be noted here that even if a household defaults due to negative income, the household is not excluded from the credit market. Instead, the defaulted household transfers the collateral to the banking sector. In effect, the gross wealth of the household is reduced by the amount of the collateral.

$$\Delta L_{ht} = \begin{cases} |NL_{ht}|, \ if \ NL_{ht} \leq 0 \\ 0, \ if \ NL_{ht} > 0 \end{cases} \tag{14}$$

202 Since the effect of the amortization payments are realized through new loan usage, a counterparty entry item for the amortization in the banking balances is not introduced in the model framework.

$$\Delta D_{ht} = \begin{cases} |NL_{ht}|, \ if \ NL_{ht} \geq 0 \\ 0, \ if \ NL_{ht} < 0 \end{cases} \tag{15}$$

Final step for the household sector macroeconomic balances is to define the stock variables. Equation (16) defines the accumulation of the loan stock. As long as the ex-ante household income is positive, the total loan stock at time t equals to the sum of the loan stock in the previous period and new acquisition of the loans. On the other hand, outstanding loan stock is forgiven for the defaulted households if the ex-ante household income is negative. Hence, the loan stock in the previous period becomes zero for the defaulted households. Equation (17) indicates that if the ex-ante household income is positive, the total deposits at time t equals to the sum of the deposits in the previous period and net accumulation of new deposits. If the household is defaulted, the bank seizes the collateral and the deposit stock is reduced by the collateral.[203] However, the deposit stock can't be negative. Finally, Equation (18) and (19) give the gross and net wealth of each household, respectively.

$$L_{ht} = \begin{cases} L_{ht-1} + \Delta L_{ht}, \ if \ Y^*_{ht} \geq 0 \\ 0 + \Delta L_{ht}, \ if \ Y^*_{ht} < 0 \end{cases} \tag{16}$$

$$D_{ht} = \begin{cases} D_{ht-1} + \Delta D_{ht}, \ if \ Y^*_{ht} \geq 0 \\ max\left[0, D_{ht-1} + \Delta D_{ht} - L_{ht-1}\right], \ if \ Y^*_{ht} < 0 \end{cases} \tag{17}$$

$$GW_{ht} = D_{ht} \tag{18}$$

$$NW_{ht} = D_{ht} - L_{ht} \tag{19}$$

4.1.2 Firms

The economy consists of one representative firm which is responsible for all investment and production activities and pays out the wages, as well as, the dividends to the households.

The firm's total profits in Equation (20) equals to gross domestic product (GDP_t), minus total wage payments (W_t), interest payments on stock of bank loans $(i_{lt}.L_{ft-1})$ and amortization of loans outstanding $(amort.L_{ft-1})$.

$$PF_t = GDP_t - W_t - i_{lt}.L_{ft-1} - amort.L_{ft-1} \tag{20}$$

203 In practice, collateral level is usually equal to the amount of credit extended. Since the loan stock is the sum of all of the extended new credits (we assume that the amortization is very small compared to the new credit extended), loan stock approximately equals to the collateral.

Total wage payments to the households are already defined in Equation (5), and interest and amortization payments are determined in the previous period. Hence, the only missing element in determination of the level of the total firm profits in each period is the gross domestic product (GDP), which is defined as the sum of total consumption and private investment. Total consumption is already defined in Equation (11). The next step is to define total investment. Following Burgess et al. (2016), Equation (21) indicates that the level of "desired" investment (I_{ft}^{*}) depends on the cost of financing the investment, interest rate.

$$\frac{I_{ft}^{*}}{K_{t-1}} = \alpha_{0b} - \alpha_{1b}.i_{lt} \tag{21}$$

However, financing constraints may impede the firm to reach at its desired level of investment. Similar to the desired and actual consumption distinction given in Equation (8) and Equation (11), it is assumed that actual investment equals to desired investment only if the firm meets the leverage constraints. There are two leverage constraints, namely, the Ponzi condition and the target leverage. Equation (22) indicates that if the firm meets the Ponzi condition and does not surpass the target leverage, which can be considered as a break put by the banking system to prevent from over-leverage, it has full access to finance to meet its desired level of investment. If the firm can meet the Ponzi condition but exceeds the level of maximum leverage, it decreases its level of investment to the minimum investment level. Similarly, if the firm can't even meet the Ponzi condition, its actual level of investment equals to minimum investment level. Equation (23) defines the minimum investment as a pre-defined share of the GDP in the previous period.

$$I_{ft} = \begin{cases} I_{ft}^{*}, \ if \ L_{ft-1} \le \ell_f.GDP_{t-1} \\ I_{ft}^{min}, \ if \ L_{ft-1} > \ell_f.GDP_{t-1} \end{cases} \tag{22}$$

$$I_{ft}^{min} = \theta_f^{min}.GDP_{t-1} \tag{23}$$

Accumulation of the capital stock in the current period is calculated as the sum of the capital stock in the previous period and level of actual investment in the current period (see Equation 24). We assume depreciation is zero for simplicity.

$$K_t = K_{t-1} + I_{ft} \tag{24}$$

At the end of each period, the firm distributes a fixed share of their profits (ϕ_f) to the households if its profits are positive in the previous period as given in Equation (25). The equation also implies that the firm keeps undistributed profits and use it as own capital to finance investment as a perfect substitute for the bank loans. This also saves us from introducing bank deposits for the firm sector. Equation (26) indicates that net lending is equal to the undistributed profits (PF_t^{undist}).

$$PF_t^{dist} = \begin{cases} \phi_f.PF_{t-1}, \text{ if } PF_{t-1} \geq 0 \\ 0, \text{ if } PF_{t-1} < 0 \end{cases} \tag{25}$$

$$PF_t^{undist} = NL_{ft} = PF_t - PF_t^{dist} \tag{26}$$

Equation (27) calculates the amount of bank loan borrowed by the firm at time t. The gap between actual investment requirement and net lending is filled through the credit from the banking sector. Outstanding loan stock to the banking sector evolves according to the Equation (28). Finally, net worth of the firm sector equals to the sum of capital stock minus loan stock (see Equation (29)).

$$\Delta L_{ft} = I_{ft} - PF_t^{undist} \tag{27}$$

$$L_{ft} = L_{ft-1} + \Delta L_{ft} \tag{28}$$

$$NW_{ft} = K_t - L_{ft} \tag{29}$$

4.1.3 Banks

As indicated in the previous sections, there is one representative bank in the economy. The bank can create unlimited credit supply to the other sectors. Hence, the constraint to the credit supply solely stems from insufficient credit demand. Although the assumption of power to create unlimited credit supply seems to be unrealistic in the first sight, the economic literature out of the orthodox economic tradition provides compelling evidence that banks indeed create money and credit (Akın and Dolgun 2015; Burgess et al. 2016). In this regard, the assumption that the banking sector in our model can create unlimited credit supply is both realistic and simplifies the model itself to a great extent.

Equation (30) shows that the total profits of the banking sector is the sum of interest income from the loans extended to the households and the real sector minus the interest paid to the deposits owned by the households. At the end of each period, the bank distributes a fixed share of their profits (ϕ_f) to the households if its profits are positive in the previous period as given in Equation (31). Equation (32) gives the net worth of the banking sector.

$$PB_t = i_{lt}.\sum_{h=1}^{H} L_{ht-1} + i_{lt}.L_{ft-1} - i_{dt}.\sum_{h=1}^{H} D_{ht-1} \tag{30}$$

$$PB_t^{dist} = \begin{cases} \phi_f.PB_{t-1}, \text{ if } PB_{t-1} \geq 0 \\ 0, \text{ if } PB_{t-1} < 0 \end{cases} \tag{31}$$

$$NW_{bt} = \sum_{h=1}^{H} L_{ht} + L_{ft} - \sum_{h=1}^{H} D_{ht} + \left(PB_t - PB_t^{dist}\right) \tag{32}$$

Since, interest rates are not totally insensitive to the economic conditions even in the interest-based economy model; we also define how the interest rates evolve over time. In the real world, the Taylor rule is an important benchmark to determine interest rate movements in the economic models. Following this tradition, we assume that interest rates evolve in line with the deviation of the previous period's GDP from its historical average. That is, interest rate slightly increases in the model if the previous period's GDP is above its historic average because above-the-historical-average GDP is an indication for overheating. The reverse happens if the GDP is below its average. Although there is no central bank in the model, there is still an implicit interest rate correction mechanism as given in Equation (33). We assume that the amount of correction is stochastically determined by an indicator of uniform distribution between 0 and $1(U(0,1))$.

$$i_{lt} = \begin{cases} i_{lt-1}.(1+\alpha.U(0,1)), & if\ GDP_{t-1} \geq \overline{GDP_{t-2}} \\ i_{lt-1}.(1-\alpha.U(0,1)), & if\ GDP_{t-1} < \overline{GDP_{t-2}} \end{cases} \tag{33}$$

Finally, we define rate of interest on deposits. It depends on rate of interest on loans as follows:

$$i_{dt} = 0.9.i_{lt} \tag{34}$$

4.2 Risk-Sharing (RS) Model

Section 3.1 constructs an interest-based economy which forms our benchmark model. Section 3.2 instead designs a counterfactual world in which the ex-ante interest rate is replaced by the ex-post rate of return to real sector activity. The aim here is to show that even change in the price in making economic decisions has pronounced effects in the evolution of the economic activity and inequality. The counterfactual RS model, similar to the base model, starts with the same initial and parameter values in sectoral equations. Since most of the equations of the RS model are the same as the base model, we only discuss several new equations specific to the RS model in this section.

In the RS model, there is no ex-ante interest rate in the equations so that Equation (31) is eliminated from the RS model equations altogether. Interest rate in other equations is also replaced by the ex-post rate of return to real sector activity. Firstly, Equation (33) is replaced with Equation (35), which states that ex-post rate of return now equals to percentage change in GDP in previous year. Using the percentage change in the GDP of previous year as a proxy for the ex-post rate of return to real sector activity secures one-to-one matching between financial and real sector returns.

It is also assumed that there is still difference between the rate of returns to the participation accounts, which is a replacement for the time deposits, and financing provided by the banking sector, which is a replacement for the bank loans, as given in Equation (36).

$$r_{lt} = \frac{(GDP_{t-1} - GDP_{t-2})}{GDP_{t-2}} \tag{35}$$

$$r_{dt} = 0.9.r_{lt} \tag{36}$$

Another important change in the RS model compared to the base model is that the structure of the desired investment equation already given in Equation (19). In the RS model, there should be a positive association between desired investment and ex-post rate of return to capital because higher ex-post rate of return to the real sector activity exhorts the firm to increase its desired investment level in the subsequent periods. The modified desired investment equation then becomes as given in Equation (37):

$$\frac{I^{*}_{ft}}{K_{t-1}} = \alpha_{0r} + \alpha_{1r}.i_{lt} \tag{37}$$

It should also be noted here that there are slightly different distributed profits equations of the firm and the banking sectors because of profit-and-loss sharing structure of the RS model. Equation (38) and Equation (39) show that there is an implicit risk-sharing assumption with respect to the firm and banking sector profits.

$$PF^{di}_{t} = \phi_f.PF_{t-1} \tag{38}$$

$$PB^{dist}_{t} = \phi_f.PB_{t-1} \tag{39}$$

Appendix 1 gives the full RS model with the slight difference between the base and RS models.

5 Simulations

Section 4 discusses the ABM simulation outputs on the base and the RS models. Calculation of the inequality levels over time in the base and the RS models are based on self-calculated inequality indices obtained from the household income level and net wealth. Although there are many inequality indices in the literature, such as Atkinson index and coefficient of variation, we use Gini coefficient to measure and to evaluate the evolution of the inequality in the simulations. The main reason for using the Gini index is that the Gini index captures the change in the average inequality rather than change in inequality at the tails of the distribution. Given that the focus of this analytical chapter is wealth inequality, only Gini coefficients based on wealth are provided and discussed.

In line with the literature, we calculate the Gini coefficient as follows:

$$Gini_{wealth} = \frac{1}{2.H^2 \cdot \mu} \cdot \sum_i \sum_j \left| GW_{it} - GW_{jt} \right| \cdot H_i \cdot H_j \tag{40}$$

where (H), (μ), (GW_m) represent quintile size, mean level of wealth in the economy, and gross wealth of the *mth* quintile, respectively. By the help of the Gini coefficients, Lorenz curve and deviations from the completely egalitarian state can be calculated.

Figure 22.1 shows that Gini coefficient based on wealth inequality is higher in the interest-based base model compared to the risk-sharing (RS) model in the medium to long-run. The Gini coefficient gap between the base and RS model is also increasing, indicating that the RS alternative is getting better over time without any external disruption.

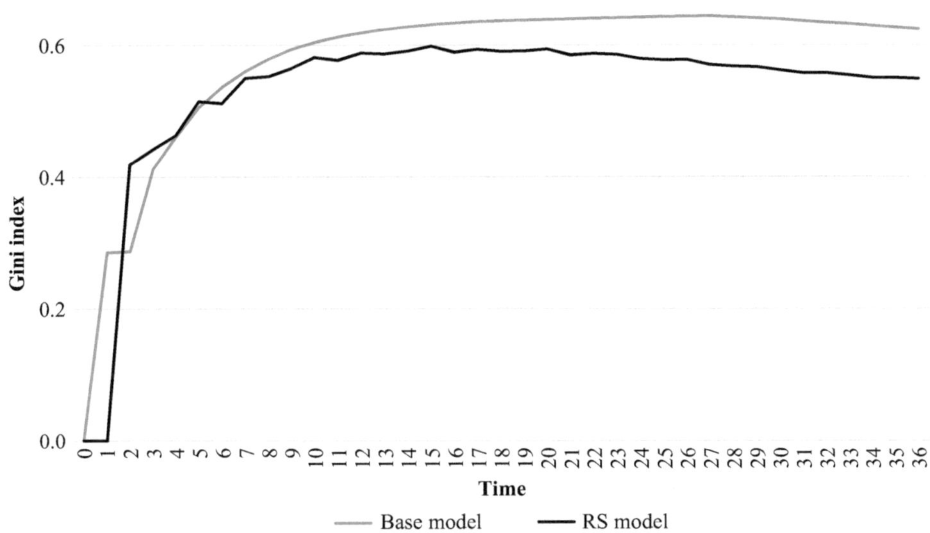

Figure 22.1: The Evolution of the GINI Index in Interest and Risk Sharing Models.
Source: Authors' calculations.

According to Figure 22.2, the Lorenz curve, which compares wealth inequalities between the base and the RS models in the last simulation period, is closer to the equality line under the RS model.

Given the simulation outputs in Figures 22.1 and 22.2, a subsequent question is at what cost the improvement in wealth distribution is achieved in the RS model. If decline in the Gini coefficient in the RS model is achieved with lower national income growth or higher unemployment, such an improvement in inequality may not be

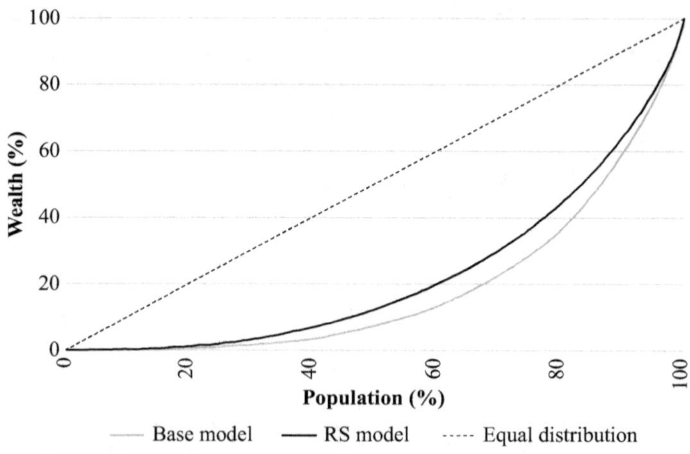

Figure 22.2: Lorenz Curve Comparing Wealth Inequalities between the Base and RS Models. Source: Authors' calculations.

politically and economically viable. Although this is an appropriate concern, two other factors in understanding the extent of inequality and redistribution should be also taken into account.

- Inequality is one aspect of the shared prosperity. Another aspect is the growth rate of the economy, which generates extra income and wealth to be shared among the households.
- The model does not contain any soft or hard redistribution policy, such as tax policy, existence of *zakah*, or other pro-poor redistribution mechanisms.

Simulation results show that the GDP growth, consumption and investment diverge, to a large extent, between the base and RS models. Before delineating these variables, it should be noted that the rate of return to the real sector differs much in the base and RS models. As given in Figure 22.3, interest rate in the base mode follows a smooth path and seemingly does not respond much to the developments in the real economy as given in Figures 22.4–22.6. In contrast, real rate of returns in the RS model go in tandem with the real rate of growth in the economy. Hence, it follows a much volatile path compared to the interest rate. The real rate of returns in the RS model revolves around a trend level, which is higher than the rate of interest in the base model. In conventional economic setup, such a higher rate of return is expected to go with suppressed investment level and lower GDP growth.

As opposed to ex-ante expectation that higher rate of return in the RS model goes with lower investment level, Figure 22.4 shows that both the level and rate of growth of the investment is higher in the RS model compared to the base model. This is due to a fundamental difference between the definitions of the rate of returns in these two models. Investment in the base model is an ex-ante and negatively associated function of

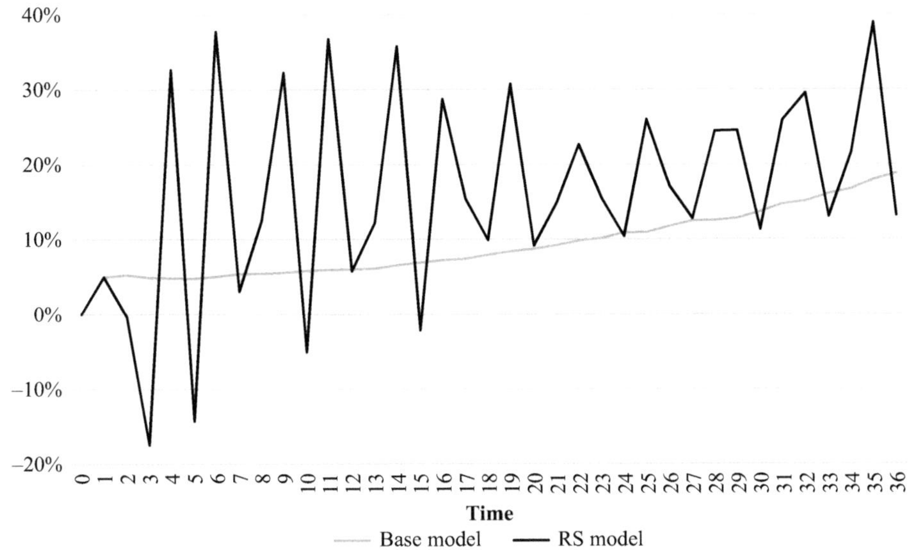

Figure 22.3: The Evolution of Rates of Returns in the Base and RS Models.
Source: Authors' calculations.

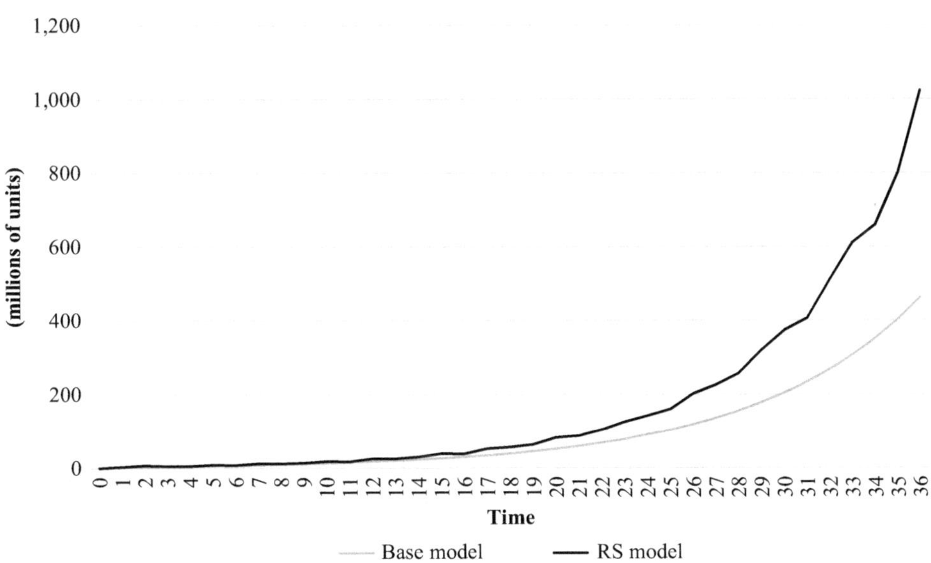

Figure 22.4: The Evolution of Investment in the Base and RS Models.
Source: Authors' calculations.

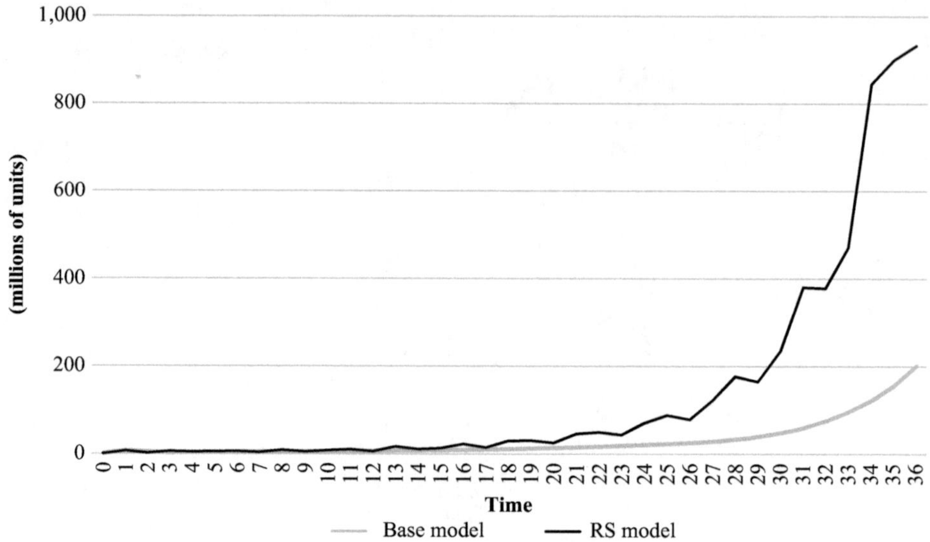

Figure 22.5: The Evolution of Consumption in the Base and RS Models.
Source: Authors' calculations.

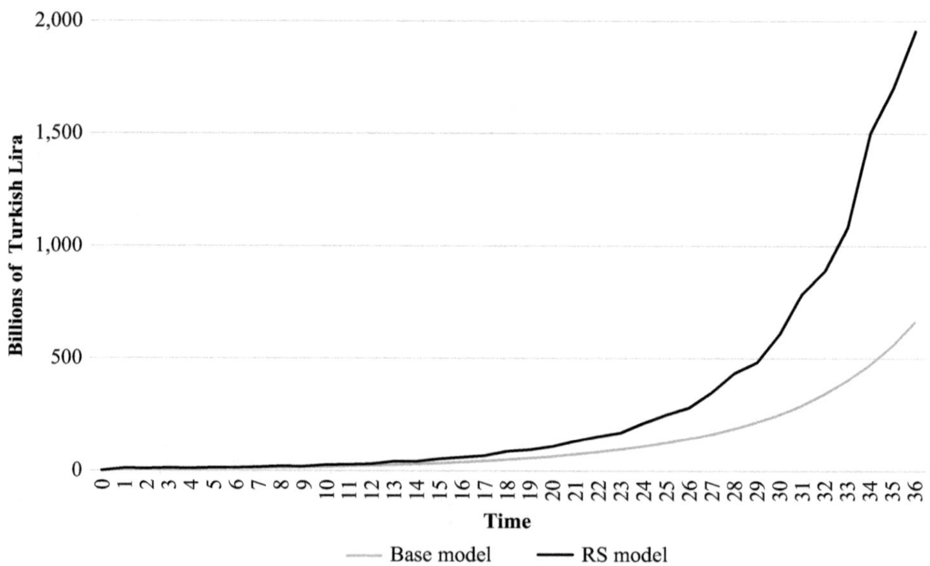

Figure 22.6: The Evolution of GDP Growth in the Base and RS Models.
Source: Authors' calculations.

the interest rate, which is determined by the monetary authorities in conventional economies and typically does not move in tandem with the real sector. Rate of return in the RS model, however, is determined ex-post and reflects the real growth in the economy. As the rate of return is higher in the previous period, the firms consider it as an opportunity for higher profits in the future and invest more in the current period.

Similarly, consumption is higher in the RS model compared to the base model as given in Figure 22.5. Higher consumption is reflection of higher household income and wealth, higher economic growth and lower indebtedness of the household sector.

As a result of better performance in macroeconomic variables, GDP growth is much higher in the RS model compared to the base model. This result is very important in the sense that slightly better wealth inequality level is achieved in the RS model without any disruption in the rate of GDP growth in the economy. Indeed, the GDP growth is much better even under lower inequality level.

Neither of the models contain any type of soft or hard redistribution policy. Indeed, wealth inequality can be reduced more under the RS model due to the fact that much higher GDP growth in the RS model provides an opportunity for redistribution of the extra income generated by higher GDP growth through redistribution policies. For instance, income tax revenues by the public sector will be higher under the RS model and these tax revenues can further be redistributed to the poor. Similarly, level of wealth subject to *zakah* will be higher in the RS model.

In sum, from the perspective of the shared prosperity, which takes both inequality and growth into account, converting from interest-based system to risk-sharing system bring considerable benefits even without implementing any redistribution policy.

6 Conclusion

This chapter investigates whether converting from an interest-based economy to a risk-sharing economy can reduce wealth inequality in a simple agent-based macroeconomic setup. This is the first agent-based modeling attempt in the literature that investigates whether interest rate mechanism is an important generator of in equality in the long-run.

The simulations are based on comparing the wealth Gini coefficients and other pertinent macroeconomic variables in a base model, which replicates an interest and debt-based economy, and a risk-sharing economy in which the ex-ante interest rate is replaced by ex-post rate of return to real sector activity. The simulation results indicate that even using the ex-post rate of return instead of ex-ante interest rate can have pronounced effects on level of inequality and real GDP growth. It should be noted that the current model setup does not have any redistribution policy, the evolution of the inequality in both of the scenarios are based self-correction of the market forces in a market economy. It should also be assumed from the outset that achieving lower inequality and higher GDP growth means that the inequality levels could be reduced to much lower levels by implementing appropriate redistribution tool, such as tax policy.

It can be argued that the current redistribution policies are based on sharing the output, which is produced through interest-based modes of production and services, among the citizens. This is because the interest-based economy self-generates higher inequality without using the redistribution policies. Thus, implementing redistribution policies is a necessity in interest-based economies. This chapter instead proposes that transforming into the risk-sharing finance and economy can have pronounced effects on reducing wealth inequality even without resorting to redistribution policies. This is because a risk-sharing economy is inherently balanced and sustainable for all segments of the society.

References

Akın, Tarık, and Muhammed Habib Dolgun. 2015. "The Chicago Plan from the Lenses of Islamic Finance: Implications for Financial Stability and Indebtedness." *International Journal of Islamic Economics and Finance Studies* 1(2): 87–112.

Akın, Tarık, and Abbas Mirakhor. 2019. *Wealth Inequality, Asset Redistribution and Risk-Sharing Islamic Finance*. Berlin: De Gruyter Oldenbourg.

Askari, Hossein, Zamir Iqbal, Noureddine Krichene, and Abbas Mirakhor. 2012. R*isk Sharing in Finance: The Islamic Finance Alternative*. Singapore: John Wiley & Sons.

Askari, Hossein, and Abbas Mirakhor. 2015. *The Next Financial Crisis and How to Save Capitalism*. New York: Palgrave Macmillan US.

Bacha, Obiyathulla Ismath, and Abbas Mirakhor. 2013. *Economic Development and Islamic Finance*. In *Economic Development and Islamic Finance*, edited by Zamir Iqbal and Abbas Mirakhor. The World Bank.

Bagchi, Sutirtha, and Jan Svejnar. 2015. "Does Wealth Inequality Matter for Growth? The Effect of Billionaire Wealth, Income Distribution, and Poverty." *Journal of Comparative Economics* 43(3): 505–30.

Basu, Kaushik, and Joseph E. Stiglitz. 2016. *Inequality and Growth: Patterns and Policy Volume I: Concepts and Analysis*. London, UK: Palgrave Macmillan UK.

Bezemer, Dirk J. 2011. "Causes of Instability: Don't Forget Finance." *Levy Economics Institute Working Papers No. 665.*

Bowles, Samuel. 2012. *The New Economics of Inequality and Redistribution (Federico Caffè Lectures)*. New York, NY: Cambridge University Press.

Buiter, Willem H., and Ebrahim Rahbari. 2015. "Why Economists (and Economies) Should Love Islamic Finance." *JKAU: Islamic Economics* 28(1): 139–62.

Burgess, Stephen, Oliver Burrows, Antoine Godin, Stephen Kinsella, and Stephen Millard. 2016. "A Dynamic Model of Financial Balances for the United Kingdom." *Staff Working Paper No. 614*. London, UK: Bank of England.

Cardaci, Alberto. 2018. "Inequality, Household Debt and Financial Instability: An Agent-Based Perspective." *Journal of Economic Behavior & Organization* 149(C): 434–458.

Cardaci, Alberto, and Francesco Saraceno. 2016. “Inequality, Financialisation and Credit Booms: A Model of Two Crises.” *Working Paper 2/2016*. LUISS Guido Carli / School of European Political Economy.
Cynamon, Barry Z., and Steven M. Fazzari. 2016. “Inequality, the Great Recession and Slow Recovery.” *Cambridge Journal of Economics* 40 (2): 373–99.
Domanski, Dietrich, Anna Zabai, and Michela Scatigna. 2016. “Wealth Inequality and Monetary Policy.” *BIS Quarterly Review, March 2016.*
Dosi, Giovanni, Giorgio Fagiolo, Mauro Napoletano, and Andrea Roventini. 2013. “Income Distribution, Credit and Fiscal Policies in an Agent-Based Keynesian Model.” *Journal of Economic Dynamics and Control* 37(8): 1598–1625.
Goda, Thomas, Özlem Onaran, and Engelbert Stockhammer. 2016. “Income Inequality and Wealth Concentration in the Recent Crisis.” *Development and Change* 39 (3): 935–58.
Haan, Jakob de, and Jan-Egbert Sturm. 2016. “Finance and Income Inequality: A Review and New Evidence.” *DNB Working Paper No.530*. De Nederlandsche Bank.
IMF. 2017. “Fostering Inclusive Growth – Background Note for G-20 Leaders’ Summit.” Hamburg, Germany.
Islam, Rabiul, and Mark McGillivray. 2015. “Wealth Inequality and Economic Growth: A Macroeconomic Perspective.” In *Australian Conference of Economists*, 1–23. Brisbane.
Janssen, Marco A., and Elinor Ostrom. 2006. “Empirically Based, Agent-Based Models.” *Ecology and Society* 11(2): 37–56.
Jones, Charles I., and Paul M. Romer. 2010. “The New Kaldor Facts: Ideas, Institutions, Population, and Human Capital.” *American Economic Journal: Macroeconomics* 2(1): 224–245.
Kaldor, Nicholas. 1961. “Capital Accumulation and Economic Growth.” In *The Theory of Capital*, edited by F. A. Lutz and D. C. Hague, 177–222. London: Palgrave Macmillan UK.
König, Nadja, and Ingrid Größl. 2014. “Catching up with the Joneses and Borrowing Constraints: An Agent-Based Analysis of Household Debt.” Macroeconomics and Finance Series 201404, University of Hamburg, Department of Socioeconomics.
Kumhof, Michael, Romain Rancière, and Pablo Winant. 2015. “Inequality, Leverage, and Crises.” *American Economic Review* 105(3): 1217–45.
Ljungqvist, Lars, and Thomas J. Sargent. 2012. *Recursive Macroeconomic Theory*. Cambridge: MIT Press.
Macal, C M, and M J North. 2010. “Tutorial on Agent-Based Modelling and Simulation.” *Journal of Simulation* 4 (3): 151–62. https://doi.org/10.1057/jos.2010.3.
Maghrebi, Nabil, and Abbas Mirakhor. 2015. “Risk Sharing and Shared Prosperity in Islamic Finance.” *Islamic Economic Studies* 23(2): 85–115.
Mian, Atif, and Amir Sufi. 2018. “Finance and Business Cycles: The Credit-Driven Household Demand Channel.” *Journal of Economic Perspectives* 32(3): 31–58.
Nardi, Mariacristina De. 2015. “Quantitative Models of Wealth Inequality : A Survey.” *NBER Working Paper No. W21106*. NBER Working Paper No. 21106. Cambridge, Massachusetts.
Nardi, Mariacristina De, and Giulio Fella. 2017. “Saving and Wealth Inequality.” *Review of Economic Dynamics* 26: 280–300.
OECD. 2015. *In It Together: Why Less Inequality Benefits All*. Paris: OECD Publishing.
Ostry, Jonathan, Andrew Berg, and Charalambos Tsangarides. 2014. “Redistribution, Inequality, and Growth.” *Staff Discussion Notes* 14(02): 1–30.
Palagi, Elisa, Mauro Napoletano, Andrea Roventini, and Jean Luc Gaffard. 2017. “Inequality, Redistributive Policies and Multiplier Dynamics in an Agent-Based Model with Credit Rationing.” *Working Paper 02/2017 January*.
Piketty, Thomas. 2014. *Capital in the Twenty-First Century*. Cambridge, MA: Belknap Press of Harvard University Press.

Rajan, Raghuram G. 2010. *Fault Lines: How Hidden Fractures Still Threaten the World Economy*. New Jersey: Princeton University Press.

Russo, Alberto. 2017. "An Agent Based Macroeconomic Model with Social Classes and Endogenous Crises." *Italian Economic Journal* 3(3): 285–306.

Russo, Alberto, Luca Riccetti, and Mauro Gallegati. 2016. "Increasing Inequality, Consumer Credit and Financial Fragility in an Agent Based Macroeconomic Model." *Journal of Evolutionary Economics* 26(1): 25–47.

Scheidel, Walter. 2017. *The Great Leveler: Violence and the History of Inequality from the Stone Age to the Twenty-First Century*. New Jersey: Princeton University Press.

Schelling, Thomas C. 1971. "Dynamic Models of Segregation†." *The Journal of Mathematical Sociology* 1(2): 143–86.

Serra-Garcia, Marta. 2010. "Moral Hazard in Credit Markets: The Incentive Effect of Collateral." Tilburg University Working Paper.

Solow, Robert M. 1957. "Technical Change and the Aggregate Production Function." *The Review of Economics and Statistics* 39(3): 312–20.

Stiglitz, Joseph E. 2015a. "New Theoretical Perspectives on the Distribution of Income and Wealth among Individuals: Part IV: Land and Credit." *NBER Working Paper Series No. 21192*. Cambridge, MA.

Stiglitz, Joseph E. 2015b. "The Origins of Inequality, and Policies to Contain It." *National Tax Journal* 68 (2): 425–48.

Stiglitz, Joseph E. 2015c. "New Theoretical Perspectives on the Distribution of Income and Wealth among Individuals: Part I. The Wealth Residual." NBER Working Paper Series No. 21189. Cambridge, MA.

Stiglitz, Joseph E. 2015d. "New Theoretical Perspectives on the Distribution of Income and Wealth among Individuals: Part II: Equilibrium and Wealth Distributions." NBER Working Paper Series No. 21190. Cambridge, MA.

Stirati, Antonella. 2016. "Piketty and the Increasing Concentration of Wealth: Some Implications of Alternative Theories of Distribution and Growth." Centro Sraffa Working Papers No: 18.

Tao, Yong, Xiangjun Wu, Tao Zhou, Weibo Yan, Yanyuxiang Huang, Han Yu, Benedict Mondal, and Victor M. Yakovenko. 2019. "Exponential Structure of Income Inequality: Evidence from 67 Countries." *Journal of Economic Interaction and Coordination* 14(2): 345–76.

Turner, Adair. 2016. *Between Debt and the Devil: Money, Credit, and Fixing Global Finance*. New Jersey: Princeton University Press.

Turrell, Arthur. 2016. "Agent-Based Models: Understanding the Economy from the Bottom Up." *Quarterly Bulletin of the Bank of England* Q4(1): 173–88.

Ulph, David. 2014. "Keeping up with the Joneses: Who Loses Out?" *Economics Letters* 125(3): 400–403.

UNCTAD. 2017. *Trade and Development Report 2017: Beyond Austerity: Towards A Global New Deal*. New York, NY.

Wang, Susheng. 2013. *Organization Theory and Its Applications (Routledge Studies in Business Organizations and Networks)*. New York, NY: Routledge.

Wickens, Michael. 2008. *Macroeconomic Theory A Dynamic General Equilibrium Approach*. New Jersey: Princeton University Press.

World Economic Forum. 2017. *The Inclusive Growth and Development Report*. Geneva: World Economic Forum.

Appendices

Appendix 1: Equations in the RS Model

$$Y^*_{ht} = W_{ht} + PF^{dist}_{ht} + PB^{dist}_{ht} + r_{dt}.D_{ht-1} - r_{lt}.L_{ht-1} - amort.L_{ht-1} \tag{41}$$

$$Y_{ht} = \begin{cases} W_{ht} + PF^{dist}_{ht} + PB^{dist}_{ht} + r_{dt}.D_{ht-1} - r_{lt}.L_{ht-1} - amort.L_{ht-1}, \ if \ Y^*_{ht} \geq 0 \\ W_{ht} + PF^{dist}_{ht} + PB^{dist}_{ht} + r_{dt}.D_{ht-1}, \ if \ Y^*_{ht} < 0 \end{cases} \tag{42}$$

$$W_{ht} = \eta_{ht}.W_t \tag{43}$$

$$\eta_{ht} = \eta_{ht-1} + \varepsilon_{ht} \tag{44}$$

$$W_t = W_{t-1}.\left[1 + \theta^w_1.lprod + \theta^w_1.\Delta dGDP_{t-1}\right] \tag{45}$$

$$PF^{dist}_{ht} = \eta_{ht}.PF^{dist}_t \tag{46}$$

$$PB^{dist}_{ht} = \eta_{ht}.PB^{dist}_t \tag{47}$$

$$C^*_{ht} = mpc_d. \ Y_{ht-1} + cuj_d.Cbar_{t-1} \tag{48}$$

$$Cbar_{t-1} = \frac{1}{H} \cdot \sum_1^H C_{ht-1} \tag{49}$$

$$mpc_d = \begin{cases} mpc_1, \ if \ h \in [0, \overline{H_1}) \\ mpc_2, \ if \ h \in [\overline{H_1}, \overline{H_2}) \\ mpc_3, \ if \ h \in [\overline{H_2}, \overline{H_3}) \\ mpc_4, \ if \ h \in [\overline{H_3}, \overline{H_4}) \\ mpc_5, \ if \ h \in [\overline{H_4}, \overline{H_5}] \end{cases} \quad \text{and} \quad cuj_d = \begin{cases} cuj_1, \ if \ h \in [0, \overline{H_1}) \\ cuj_2, \ if \ h \in [\overline{H_1}, \overline{H_2}) \\ cuj_3, \ if \ h \in [\overline{H_2}, \overline{H_3}) \\ cuj_4, \ if \ h \in [\overline{H_3}, \overline{H_4}) \\ cuj_5, \ if \ h \in [\overline{H_4}, \overline{H_5}] \end{cases} \tag{50}$$

$$C_{ht} = \begin{cases} C^*_{ht}, \ if \ Y_{ht} > C^*_{ht} \\ C^*_{ht}, \ if \ Y_{ht} < C^*_{ht} \ and \ L_{ht-1} \leq \ell_t.Y_{ht-1} \\ C^{min}_{ht}, \ if \ Y_{ht} < C^*_{ht} \ and \ L_{ht-1} > \ell_t.Y_{ht-1} \end{cases} \tag{51}$$

$$C^{min}_{ht} = \theta^{min}_h.C_{ht-1} \tag{52}$$

$$NL_{ht} = Y_{ht} - C_{ht} \tag{53}$$

$$\Delta L_{ht} = \begin{cases} |NL_{ht}|, \ if \ NL_{ht} \leq 0 \\ 0, \ if \ NL_{ht} > 0 \end{cases} \tag{54}$$

$$\Delta D_{ht} = \begin{cases} |NL_{ht}|, \ if \ NL_{ht} \geq 0 \\ 0, \ if \ NL_{ht} < 0 \end{cases} \tag{55}$$

$$L_{ht} = \begin{cases} L_{ht-1} + \Delta L_{ht}, \; if \; Y^*_{ht} \geq 0 \\ 0 + \Delta L_{ht}, \; if \; Y^*_{ht} < 0 \end{cases} \tag{56}$$

$$D_h = \begin{cases} D_{ht-1} + \Delta D_{ht}, \; if \; Y^*_{ht} \geq 0 \\ max[0, D_{ht-1} + \Delta D_{ht} - L_{ht-1}], \; if \; Y^*_{ht} < 0 \end{cases} \tag{57}$$

$$GW_{ht} = D_{ht} \tag{58}$$

$$NW_{ht} = D_{ht} - L_{ht} \tag{59}$$

$$PF_t = GDP_t - W_t - r_{lt}.L_{ft-1} - amort.L_{ft-1} \tag{60}$$

$$\frac{I^*_{ft}}{K_{t-1}} = \alpha_{0r} + \alpha_{1r}.i_{lt} \tag{61}$$

$$I_{ft} = \begin{cases} I^*_{ft}, \; if \; L_{ft-1} \leq \ell_f.GDP_{t-1} \\ I^{min}_{ft}, \; if \; L_{ft-1} > \ell_f.GDP_{t-1} \end{cases} \tag{62}$$

$$I^{min}_{ft} = \theta^{min}_f.GDP_{t-1} \tag{63}$$

$$K_t = K_{t-1} + I_{ft} \tag{64}$$

$$PF^{dist}_t = \phi_f.PF_{t-1} \tag{65}$$

$$PF^{undist}_t = NL_{ft} = PF_t - PF^{dist}_t \tag{66}$$

$$\Delta L_{ft} = I_{ft} - PF^{undist}_t \tag{67}$$

$$L_{ft} = L_{ft-1} + \Delta L_{ft} \tag{68}$$

$$NW_{ft} = K_t - L_{ft} \tag{69}$$

$$PB_t = r_{lt}.\sum_{h=1}^{H} L_{ht-1} + r_{lt}.L_{ft-1} - r_{dt}.\sum_{h=1}^{H} D_{ht-1} \tag{70}$$

$$PB^{dist}_t = \phi_f.PB_{t-1} \tag{71}$$

$$NW_{bt} = \sum_{h=1}^{H} L_{ht} + L_{ft} - \sum_{h=1}^{H} D_{ht} + \left(PB_t - PB^{dist}_t\right) \tag{72}$$

$$r_{lt} = \frac{(GDP_{t-1} - GDP_{t-2})}{GDP_{t-2}} \tag{73}$$

$$r_{dt} = 0.9.r_{lt} \tag{74}$$

Appendix 2: Initial Values of the Variables

Symbol	Definition	Initial Value
Y_{ht-1}	Total income of household *h* at time *t-1*	900
C_{ht-1}	Actual consumption by household *h* at time *t-1*	700
C_{t-1}	Actual total consumption at time *t-1*	7,000,000
W_{t-1}	Total wage payments at time *t-1*	6,000,000
K_{t-1}	Capital stock at time *t-1*	25,000,000
L_{ht-1}	Loan stock outstanding indebted by household *h* at time *t*	200
L_{ft-1}	Loan stock outstanding indebted by the firm at time *t-1*	2,000,000
D_{ht-1}	Deposit stock owned by household *h* at time *t-1*	200
GDP_{t-1}	Gross domestic product at time *t-1*	10,000,000
$\overline{GDP_{t-2}}$	Rolling five years average GDP	9,750,000
PF_{t-1}	Firm's total profit at time *t*	0
PB_{t-1}	Bank's total profit at time *t*	0
i_{lt-1}	Interest rate on loan at time *t-1*	0.05

Appendix 3: Parameter Values

Symbol	Definition	Value
H	Number of households in the economy	10,000
$amort$	Amortization of loan	0.1
θ_1^w	Sensitivity of wage growth to labor productivity	0.9
θ_2^w	Sensitivity of wage growth to GDP growth	0.5
$lprod$	Labor productivity value	0.01
θ_h^{min}	Proportion of subsistence level compared to the actual level of consumption	0.7
θ_f^{min}	Proportion of minimum investment level	0.75
mpc_1	Marginal propensity to consume out of income for lowest 20%	0.9
mpc_2	Marginal propensity to consume out of income for second 20%	0.8
mpc_3	Marginal propensity to consume out of income for third 20%	0.6
mpc_4	Marginal propensity to consume out of income for fourth 20%	0.5
mpc_5	Marginal propensity to consume out of income for highest 20%	0.4
cuj_1	Marginal propensity to consume out of average cons. for lowest 20%	0.1
cuj_2	Marginal propensity to consume out of average cons. for second 20%	0.1
cuj_3	Marginal propensity to consume out of average cons. for third 20%	0.1
cuj_4	Marginal propensity to consume out of average cons. for fourth 20%	0.1
cuj_5	Marginal propensity to consume out of average cons. for highest 20%	0.1
α_{0b}	Constant term in the desired investment (base model)	0.15
α_{1b}	Sensitivity of capacity utilization to desired investment (base model)	0.6
α_{0r}	Constant term in the desired investment (RS model)	0.09
α_{1r}	Sensitivity of capacity utilization to desired investment (base model)	0.6
ϕ_f	Share of firm profits distributed to the households	0.7
ℓ_h	Leverage target by households	10
ℓ_f	Leverage target by firms	10

Maznita Mokhtar, Mohamed Ariff, Obiyathulla Ismath Bacha

Chapter 23: People's Wellbeing: A Strive to Meet *Maqasid al-Shariah*

1 Introduction

There is wide consensus that the ultimate objective of government policies is to improve the quality of people's lives. The reality, however, is that the impact of government policies tends to be measured rather in terms of GDP growth as proxy for progress. The debate about growth vs. development is not new as the distinction between these concepts was recognized since the 1970s. GDP growth has often been understood in terms of improvement in the quality of life. However, further research is indicating that inequality affects sustainable growth (Berg and Ostry 2011), which in turn reduces the ability to improve the quality of life. This is the case of many OECD nations where household income of the richest segments grew faster than that of the poorest (OECD 2011a). Thus, the redistribution of income and wealth should not be regarded as a substitute but a complement to economic growth (Mat Zin 2008).

The fundamental principles of Islamic economics should be based on the abundance not scarcity of resources. Allah (swt) has enriched the world with unlimited resources. Verse 2:245 of the Holy Quran states:

> Who is he that will loan to Allah a beautiful loan, which Allah will double unto his credit and multiply many times (in abundance)? It is Allah that gives, (you) want or plenty, and to Him shall be your return. (Yusof Ali 2004)[204]

To achieve the *Maqasid al-Shariah* for each individual, human wellbeing (*falah*) is to be fulfilled. The ultimate objective is to protect and preserve religion (*din*), life (*nafs*), progeny (*nasl*), property (*mal*), and intellect (*'aql*) based on Al-Ghazali's theoretical framework (Chapra 2008b). Chapra (2008b) further extends each objective to produce multi-dimensional effects. For example, the preservation and enrichment of progeny involves the institution of family, moral upbringing and intellectual advancement of offspring, which are linked to the levels of consumption, savings and investment by current generations, as well as the preservation of environment for future generations.

There is no consensus on the validity of GDP per capita as a measure of people's wellbeing (Atkinson 2012). In 2006, UK's Prime Minister James Cameron argued for a

204 All translations of Quranic verses in this dissertation are based on Abdullah Yusof Ali, *An English Interpretation of Holy Quran* (2004).

https://doi.org/10.1515/9783110587920-023

shift in focusing on general wellbeing rather than merely on the GDP. The shift was reflected by the frequent use of wellbeing in evidence-based policy-making, and the increased reference to Wellbeing Economics (Berry 2014). The 2010 Report by the Stiglitz-Sen-Fitoussi Commission lend further support to the notion that the measurement of people's wellbeing was more significant than that of economic production and that material living standards can be better tracked through measures of household income (Stiglitz, Sen, and Fitoussi 2009). The United Nations organized its first high level meeting on happiness and wellbeing in 2012, and the first World Happiness Report was published soon after (J. Helliwell, Layard, and Sachs 2013).

This institutional focus on wellbeing is reflected by the development of many socio-economic indices to assess whether economic development is concurrent with improvement in people's lives. The wellbeing indices include the United Nations' World Happiness Index (WHI), OECD's Better Life Index, and Quality of Life Index (QOL) by the Economist Intelligence Unit, inter alia. The government of Bhutan is using its own holistic Gross National Happiness (GNH) Index as an alternative to GDP.

In so far as Islamic economics is concerned, new wellbeing indices have been also developed to benchmark growth and development against *Maqasid Al-Shariah*, such as the Integrated Development Index (I-Dex) by Yusof et al. (2015), the Maqasid Benchmark Index by Alaabed et al. (2014), and the *Maqasid Al-Shariah* Based Development Index by Ali and Hasan (2014).

2 Literature Review

The term wellbeing is interchangeably used with similar terms such as quality of life, happiness and life satisfaction. The OECD Guidelines on Measuring Subjective Well-being (2013) gives the following broad definition:

> good mental states, including all of the various evaluations, positive and negative, that people make of their lives, and the affective reactions of people to their experiences.

In Islamic economics, the concept of human wellbeing (*falah*) is referred to the fulfilment of *Maqasid Al-Shariah* for each individual (Chapra 2008a). In light of this definition, the present study examines the empirical issue of what the wellbeing of the people functions not only of inclusive growth ensuring equitable income distribution, but also of other socio-economic functions that reflect the requirements of *Shariah*.

2.1 The Determinants of Wellbeing

It is important to understand the extent to which wellbeing is reflected by economic factors. There is evidence that economic globalization tends to make rich countries richer, and contributes to poverty reduction (Krongkaew and Mat Zin 2007; Dollar and Kraay 2004). The poor may not have benefited proportionately, however. The need to ensure broader participation and benefit from growth is reflected by the general agreement within international policy circles about the definition of "inclusiveness" in terms of pro-poor growth to reduce poverty and inequality (Ramos, Ranieri and Lammens 2013; Kakwani and Pernia 2000). The empirical analysis performed by Ramos, Ranieri, and Lammes (2013) using poverty and inequality as proxies for benefits, and employment for participation for a sample of 43 developing countries reveals significant progress in levels of inclusiveness between mid-1990s and mid-2000s.

This chapter examines the empirical question of how growth affects people's lives and their wellbeing. From the perspective of the average person, the GDP per capita measure is essentially an indicator of production, and not income and consumption (Stiglitz, Sen, and Fitoussi 2009). The OECD reports note that wellbeing is a complex concept and that many determinants of wellbeing are strongly correlated with each other. Hence, assessing wellbeing involves a multi-dimensional approach, which requires the input of several components (OECD 2013). In line with the proposal by Stiglitz et al. (2009), the OECD framework lists three major pillars of wellbeing: (i) economic (material) wellbeing reflected by income, consumption and wealth; (ii) quality of life based on non-monetary enhancement to people's lives with intrinsic value; and (iii) the sustainability of the socio-economic system and natural ecosystem in which people live. The sustainability of the overall level of wellbeing depends on the preservation of natural, economic, human and social capital.

2.2 An Islamic Perspective on Wellbeing

The Islamic view of development centers around the ultimate purposes and objectives of Shariah, or *Maqasid Al Shariah*. The three fundamental goals include the institution of effective education, the establishment of justice, and the statement of wellbeing in terms of achieving *Maslahah*.[205] Some recent studies have demonstrated it is possible to consider these *Shariah* values in the development of a theoretical framework for economic development and human wellbeing.

Yusof et al. (2015) construct the Integrated Development Index (I-Dex), a benchmark encompassing both of the physical and spiritual dimensions of human development identified from the five conceptual components of *Maqasid Al Shariah*. For example, the preservation of property (*hifdh al-mal*) can be defined from different perspectives. The early Islamic scholars including Ibn Ashur, Al Juwayni and Al

205 Ghazali (d.505H./1111CE) categorised Maslahah into three: necessities (*daruriyyat*), complements (*hajjiyat*), embellishments (*tahsiniyyat*) (Yusof et al. 2015).

Ghazali define *hifdh al-mal* as the protection of the community's wealth from ruin without compensation, and protection of individual possessions from theft. The definition adopted by more recent literature tends to be more holistic, including the (i) protection of ownership and property; (ii) acquisition and development of property or wealth; and (iii) preservation of wealth. The classical definition of *Maslahah* by Al Ghazali can be understood in terms of essential wealth availability (*darruriyah*), circulation of wealth as complements (*hajiyyah*), and investment and wealth growth as embellishment (*tahsiniyyah*) (Ng 2008). Also, Chapra (2008b) stresses the importance of promoting an equitable distribution of wealth and income that ensures justice for all levels of community.

The construction of the I-Dex considers two dimensions for the preservation of property and wealth including the protection of ownership and property, as measured by the International Property Rights Index and the acquisition and development of property and wealth as measured by the Inclusive Wealth Index (Yusof et al. 2015). It is argued that the I-Dex is more integrated than the E-HDI (Dar 2004) and I-HDI (Anto 2009), which do not take into account the various dimensions embedded in each *Maqasid* component.

In order to measure social development for the *Maqasid* based Development Index, Ali and Hasan (2014) consider the following three elements: (i) faith or iman (*tazkiyah & taqwa*), referring to individual's achievement of spiritual purity and development of good character; (ii) The Holy Book revelation from Allah (swt); and (iii) wisdom (*hikmah*), leading to higher moral values that translate *Shariah* principles into practice. The grouping of survey questions follows the methodology developed in the World Values Survey (WVS),[206] which takes into consideration each dimension of *Maqasid Al Shariah*. The level of faith (*tazkiyah and taqwa*) is omitted in light of its spiritual nature and measurement problem.

Rehman and Askari (2010) develop the Islamicity Index (EI^2), which measures the level of adherence to Islamic principles.[207] The top five countries with more developed "Islamic" systems are represented by Ireland, Denmark, Luxembourg, Sweden, and United Kingdom, whereas the average ranking of the 56 OIC nations is 133. Among the OIC countries Malaysia ranks highest (33rd) followed by Kuwait (42nd), Kazakhstan (54th), Brunei (55th), Bahrain (61st), United Arab Emirates (64th), and Turkey (71st). Thus, these findings expose the dismal lack of compliance to Islamic values and departure from *Maqasid Al-Shariah* and ideal Islamic economic systems.

The development of Maqasid Benchmark Index (MI) is based on a set of 13 indicators that reflect the multi-faceted dimensions with respect to the socio-economic

206 The World Values Survey (VWS) has relevant indicators, which were mapped to the *Maqasid al-Shariah* dimensions, of which survey data is made available on public domain (www.worldsurveyvalues.org) (Ali and Hasan 2014).

207 The EI^2 is part II of their larger ongoing work that entails an overall Islamicity Index (I^2). Part I of this series was published in an earlier issue of the same journal (Vol. 10, Issue 2, May 2010).

behavior of Muslims and the compliance with the axioms of *tawheed* (unity of creation), *nubuwwah* (Prophethood), and *ma'ad* (accountability), as well as, adherence to the Islamic values and moral virtues (*akhlaq*). The scores of the MI index showed similar results to the Islamicity Index (EI^2) as the OIC countries fall under poor and unacceptable levels of development (Alaabed et al. 2014).

It is noted that factors that may explain the decline of Muslim civilizations were rationalised several centuries ago in the seminal work by Ibn Khaldun on the theory of development. Ibn Khaldun (1332–1406) provided the first analytical study of social and economic development in the *Muqaddimah*, which is part of *Kitab al-Ibar* or "The Book of Lessons (of History)".[208] As argued by Chapra (2008b), Ibn Khaldun considers five circular factors affecting the rise and fall of civilizations, including: people's wellbeing or misery (N); development (d); justice (j); rules of behavior (S); political authority or state (G); and wealth (W). The economic literature refers to the study of political authority (G) in terms of good governance, and the study of rules of behavior (S) in terms of Institutional economics.

Ibn Khaldun notes that Muslim societies suffered from the failure of political authority that led to the misuse of public resources and injustice. These conditions further led to the lack of development and deterioration of general wellbeing. This functional relationship among the different factors of development can be explained as:

$$G = f(S, N, W, j \text{ and } d)$$

Where the survival of authority (G) depends ultimately on the wellbeing of people (N). The government authority (G) must ensure that resources for development (d) and administrative justice (j), through the implementation of Shariah (S) are provided. Ibn Khaldun suggests that the rise and fall of a nation is fully dependent on the strength or weakness of the government, and that corrupt and incompetent governments are not bound to the necessary development functions conscientiously for the good of the people. Most scholars agree the interdependence of the factors of development but present different arguments about the trigger mechanism. For example, social decline may be attributed to poor family upbringing and lack of well-educated citizens (N), lack of reinforcement of the institutions (S), absence of justice (j), and lack of educational and health facilities for the people.

An extension of Ibn Khaldun's model of development for modern Muslim societies is provided by Chapra (2008b), who refers to the works of some Western scholars that examines the importance of Islam in the development history of Muslim societies. As Islam (S) provides the foundations of the rules of behavior, a development-friendly environment with good moral values to uplift the people (N) with a strong sense of purpose in life. At the same time the political system of *khalifah*

208 The full name of the book in Arabic is "The Book of Lessons and Record of Cause and Effects in the History of Arabs, Persians, and Berbers and their Powerful Contemporaries." (Ibn Khaldun 1672)

(caliph) elected by the people allows for broad participation, including the establishment of the *shura* (advisory council). Good governance is, in turn, conducive to justice, equality, and self-respect. History of Muslim societies includes clear evidence of all-rounded economic development covering agriculture, crafts and trade, and putting strong emphasis on education and research, as well as, the role of women in society. It is on the basis of this historical evidence that Shatzmiller acknowledges importance of the classical age of Islam, and argues that "all the factors which enabled Europe to succeed were available in Islam much earlier" (Shatzmiller 1994).

3 Research Methodology

The principal proposition in this empirical study is that the wellbeing of people within an economy is not merely reflected in the measure of GDP per capita alone but it is highly influenced by several other determinants. The literature suggests that the level of wellbeing is a function of the inclusiveness of growth, material or economic standing, and quality of life. Many studies, if not most, provide evidence on the crucial importance of good governance and institutional framework that sustain human development. In Islam, it can be argued that wellbeing (*falah*) is achieved with the fulfilment of *Maqasid Al-Shariah* for each individual (Chapra 2008a).

Thus, this study explores two main research questions. The first issue is whether there is a relationship between GDP growth and people's wellbeing. The second question arises as to which of the four determinants, including quality of GDP growth, economic wellbeing, quality of life, and fulfilment within Islamic needs is significantly related to the wellbeing of people.

3.1 Model Specification

It is possible to model wellbeing as a function of variables that reflect *Maqasid Al-Shariah* as follows:

$$WB_{it} = \alpha + \beta.QY_{it} + \gamma.E_{it} + \delta.QL_{it} + \theta.S_{it} + \xi_{it} \tag{1}$$

where WB, QY, E, QL and S represent wellbeing, economic growth rates, individual economic wellbeing, quality of life, satisfaction through Islamic lifestyle, respectively. The relationship between wellbeing and explanatory variables is subject to the disturbance term ξ_{it}. In light of *Maqasid Al-Shariah*, wellbeing ensures the preservation of faith as the foundation of religion (*din*), intellect (*'aql*), life (*nafs*), progeny or lineage (*nasl*), and wealth or income (*mal*). As with the *Maqasid* benchmarks suggested by many studies in the literature, including Yusof et al. (2015), Alaabed et al. (2014), Ali and Hasan (2014) there are overlaps between the four components (QY, E, QL and S).

The first variable, QY_{it} represents the intrinsic nature of economic growth, reflected by its (i) significance, measured by annual change in real GDP per capita; (ii) its stability, measured by the inverse of the coefficient of variation (CV). Economic growth can be also described by (iii) the degree of diversification in the sources of growth as measured by export data;[209] and the degree of (iv) outward orientation measured by net external demand as a percentage of GDP; as discussed by Mlachila et al. (2014). Thus, the explanatory variable QY_{it} reflects the extent to which *Maqasid Al-Shariah* is achieved in terms of the preservation of wealth and income (*hifdh al mal*), and preservation of progeny (*hifdh al nasl*).

The second explanatory variable E_{it} represents the economic characteristics of the people, which include: (i) income levels; (ii) distribution of income measured by the median income level (Stiglitz, Sen, and Fitoussi 2009);[210] (iii) income inequality measured by Gini coefficient, ratio of top and bottom quintiles, Palma ratio of top 10% to bottom 40%, and population below poverty line. The income characteristics include also the (iv) purchasing power parity (PPP); (v) inflation measured with the consumer price index; and (vi) housing prices (Malik 2014); OECD 2013; Stiglitz, Sen and Fitoussi 2009; Chapra 2008a). Thus, this explanatory variable reflects the fulfilment of *Maqasid Al-Shariah* in terms of the preservation of life (*hifdh al nafs*) and preservation of wealth (*hifdh al mal*).

The third variable QL_{it} represents the quality of life reflected by socio-economic factors as well as living standards. The quality of life depends on: (i) health, measured by infant mortality rate, and public expenditure on health; (ii) education quality measured by pupil-teacher ratio, and education attainment measured by enrolment levels, as well as public expenditure on education; (iv) security and safety; (v) environmental sustainability measured by CO_2 emissions, and (vi) technological advancement measured by rate of internet / broadband usage (Human Development Index by UNDP, Better Life Index by OECD; Maqasid Al-Shariah by Chapra, 2008a). The set of variables represents the preservation of intellect (*hifdh al 'aql)*, progeny or lineage (*hifdh al nasl*), and life (*hifdh al nafs*).

209 The diversification of sources of growth is measured using export data, i.e. Export Diversification database developed by IMF staff (Henn, Papageorgiou and Spatafora). The rationale here is that export diversification is linked to stronger growth while lowering output volatility (Papageorgiou and Spatafora 2012). This database is accessible at data.imf.org/?sk=A093DF7D-E0B8-4913-80E0-A07CF90B44DB.

210 Stiglitz, Sen, and Fitoussi (2009) stress a number of considerations, such as (i) reflecting wealth (in terms of "stock" or capital) together with income in one's goal pursuit to satisfy needs, to ensure one's life can be sustained; (ii) giving prominence to the distribution of income and wealth, i.e. using average and median measures; and (iii) broadening the measures to non-market activities, looking at time spent on housework, paid work and leisure, which requires the use of purchasing power parity (PPP).

Finally, the explanatory variable S_{it} represents the level of satisfaction achieved through the fulfillment of Islamic lifestyle (Setia 2009; Chapra 2008a). The *Maqasid* elements relevant to this variable relate to the preservation of life (*hifdh al nafs*), religion (*hifdh al din*) and wealth (*hifdh al mal*).

3.2 Estimation Methodology

The theoretical model of wellbeing described above is estimated using two pooled ordinary least squares (OLS) models under the assumption that both the intercept and slope are the same across countries. The disturbance terms (ξ) are identically and independently distributed uncorrelated with the explanatory variables.

It is important also to examine the likelihood of heterogeneity with different intercepts or slopes across countries. It is possible to use the Breusch-Pagan Lagrange Multiplier (BP-LM) test to examine whether the GLS regression with random effects or the pooled OLS is more appropriate for model estimation (Baltagi 2008). The null hypothesis of homogeneity implies the absence of country-specific effects in the data with zero variance indicating no panel effects.

$$H_0\colon \sigma_\lambda^2 = 0 \qquad (2)$$

$$H_0\colon \sigma_A^2 \neq 0$$

The rejection of the model by the null hypothesis implies that the panel model with random effects is more appropriate than the pooled one. There is evidence in this case of country-specific effects in the data.

There are several advantages of panel data estimation: it is possible to increase the sample size to produce better estimates. The problem of omitted variables which might cause biased estimates in single individual regression may be also reduced in the panel data analysis. With panel data estimation, the disturbance term is decomposed into two independent components, $\xi_0 = \lambda_i + \mu_{it}$, where λ_i is country-specific and time-invariant, and μ_{it} is time dependent and differs across countries. To examine the individual country effects, it is possible to apply two estimation methods: The random effects, in which assuming λ_i is drawn independently, whereas the analysis based on Fixed Effects considers λ_i to be constant.

If the country-specific effects are uncorrelated with the explanatory variables, the random effects approach results in a consistent estimator that is also efficient. The modeling approach based on the fixed effects is conducive to estimators, which may be inefficient if the country-specific effects are uncorrelated with the explanatory variables. Thus, the merit of the estimation model based on fixed effects lies in the ability to remove the effects of time-invariant disturbances, allowing thereby for the assessment of the net effects of the explanatory variables only (Schmidheiny 2014; Baltagi 2008; Wooldridge 2002).

The Hausman specification test is to be used to determine whether the modelling with random effects or fixed effects is appropriate, based on the following hypotheses:

$$H_0\colon \sigma_{\lambda_i,\, X_{it}} = 0 \text{ (Random effects)} \tag{3}$$

$$H_A\colon \sigma_{\lambda_i,\, X_{it}} \neq 0 \text{ (Fixed effects)}$$

Where $\sigma_{\lambda_i, X_{it}}$ represents the covariance between the disturbance terms and explanatory variables. The rejection of the null (H_0) indicates the preference for modelling the relation with fixed effects (Greene 2012).

3.3 Data Description

For the purpose of the empirical analysis, annual data observations are used for 22 countries over the period 1980–2013. These countries are selected on the basis that their economic conditions in 1980 were comparable to Malaysia, which had a GDP per capita level of $1,803 (World Bank, in current USD prices). The sample includes Algeria, Belize, Bulgaria, Colombia, Cote d'Ivoire, Costa Rica, Cuba, Fiji, Hungary, Iran, Jamaica, Jordan, Korea, Malaysia, Namibia, Panama, Paraguay, Seychelles, Suriname, Syria, Tunisia, and Turkey. The sample also allows for 30% dispersion in GDP per capita level ranging from Namibia (1980: $2,404) to Cote d'Ivoire (1980: $1,231).

Our proxy for the overall wellbeing is the Human Development Index (HDI) developed by the United Nations (UNDP), which focuses on health, education and income. Mlachila et al. (2014) propose a new Quality of Growth Index (QGI) that focused on the nature of growth rather than the HDI's measure of the level of income.

4 Research Methodology

The empirical analysis of the determinants of wellbeing is performed through the estimation of the different models of wellbeing. The results of the cross-country analysis of the relation between the overall wellbeing and quality of growth are reported in Table 23.1. There is evidence from Model I in estimation of a significant relation between wellbeing and both growth persistence and external demand. It seems that the stability of growth rates is more associated with the wellbeing compared to the magnitude of growth rates. This result is consistent with the findings by Guillaumont-Jeanneney and Kpodar (2005) and Ames et al. (2001). The evidence from the estimations of Model 1 suggests that the effects of net external demand and export diversification are statistically significant. This is consistent with the findings by (OECD 2011b).

Table 23.1: Cross-Country Analysis: Wellbeing and Quality of Growth (QY).

	Model 1	Model 2	Model 3	Model 4
constant	−12.98*	−10.47	−14.05***	−14.63***
	(−1.82)	(−1.55)	(−12.91)	(−13.55)
strength	1.722	1.272		
	(1.71)	(1.33)		
stability	0.0984***	0.0148		
	(3.21)	(0.51)		
sectoral	−0.164	−0.142**		
	(−1.61)	(−2.12)		
demand	0.0825**	0.0916**		
	(2.44)	(2.44)		
gdppc		0.101***		
		(5.72)		
c			−0.0908***	
			(−2.90)	
fdi			0.0242*	0.0218
			(1.71)	(1.56)
i			0.00507	0.00576
			(0.56)	(0.61)
g			0.0392***	0.0329**
			(3.04)	(2.56)
xm			0.0204	0.0276
			(1.06)	(1.48)
s				0.0302*
				(1.79)
ppp			0.00385	0.00353
			(0.61)	(0.56)
cpi			−0.00132	−0.00101
			(−0.37)	(−0.26)
u			−0.0127**	−0.0111**
			(−2.45)	(−1.96)
year			0.00687***	0.00690***
			(12.25)	(12.32)
Estimation	FE robust se	FE robust se	RE robust se	RE robust se
Adjusted R2	0.177	0.566		
Observations	559	559	169	169
Model p-value	0.0083	0.0000	0.0000	0.0000

Source: Author's own calculations.

Note: Model 1 represents the following estimation model WBit = α + βQYit + ξit where the proxy (HDI) for wellbeing is regressed on the four Quality of Growth (QY) variables; Model 2 adds GDP per capita (lgdppc) as the fifth explanatory variable. Model 3 and 4 represent variants where the wellbeing proxy is regressed on different components of GDP. The reported results refer to the most appropriate models after testing for panel estimation (Breush-Pagan Lagrange Multiplier test), selection for random or fixed effects (Hausman test) and robust standard errors (Modified Wald test for heteroskedasticity). All variables are log-transformed. Figures in parentheses are t-statistics. *, ** and *** indicate statistical significance at the 10%, 5% and 1% levels, respectively.

With reference to Models 4 and 5, there is evidence that wellbeing is also a function of different compositions of the GDP. An increase in foreign direct investments, government expenditures and savings are likely to improve wellbeing. These results are consistent with the idea of the HDI, which measures standard of living component of wellbeing using GDP per capita and purchasing power parity (Malik 2014). Consumption and savings affect differently and then led to have opposite effects on wellbeing, as well. It is also noted that unemployment may have long-term impacts on wellbeing far beyond the immediate loss of income (Berry, 2014).

The focus can now be shifted to the association between wellbeing and other economic variables such as income level. Table 23.2 reports the estimation results of various models of wellbeing using the explanatory variables in Equation (1).

Economic variables (E): Interpreting from the estimated coefficients associated with income variables, it appears that the results are in agreement with Mlachila et al. (2014) in their emphasis on inclusiveness of growth and the development of the Quality of Growth Index (QGI). Indeed, the evidence suggests that higher income improves overall wellbeing. This result contravenes many previous studies including income inequality (Stiglitz, Sen, and Fitoussi 2009; J. F. Helliwell et al. 2009; Deaton 2007; inter alia). With respect to income inequality, the Palma Ratio is positively linked to HDI, but statistically insignificant. It is noted that this coefficient of inequality is also included as one of the components of HDI (Malik 2014). The results suggests also that housing affects wellbeing negatively, lending support to the evidence by Cesa-bianchi, Cespedes, and Rebucci (2015) that the volatility of house prices affect emerging economies more significantly than advanced ones. Naturally, it is high-quality rather than poor-quality housing that is associated with higher levels of wellbeing (Stoll, Michaelson, and Seaford 2012).

With respect to explanatory variables related to the quality of life, the results reported in Table 23.2 indicate the significance of proxies for health, education, and IT savviness. As expected, infant mortality is negatively related to overall wellbeing. Lower infant mortality is an indicator of better health conditions and human development (Malik 2014; J. Helliwell, Layard, and Sachs 2013; Stiglitz, Sen, and Fitoussi 2009; Kenny 2005; etc). The evidence is also consistent with previous studies such as Cutler et al. (2006), who suggests that improvement in health technologies and healthcare conditions and not just income, is an important determinant of mortality. The evidence from Legatum Institute (2014) indicates also that the effectiveness of health expenditure depends on the quality and level of governance.

With respect to the variables related to education, it appears that pupil-teacher ratio at primary schools is associated with the expected negative sign, as higher ratios are indicative of poorer quality of education and thus lower levels of wellbeing. The impact of education on wellbeing is also conditional on other factors. According to research by Duflo, Dupas, and Kremer (2007), the reduction in classroom sizes is only effective when it is combined with teaching incentives. The results indicate also that higher enrollment ratios exact positive effects on wellbeing as suggested by the

Table 23.2: Cross-Country Analysis: Wellbeing and Economic (E), Quality of Life (QL) and Shariah fulfilment (S) factors.

	Model 5	Model 6	Model 7	Model 8	Model 9	Model 10
constant	−0.235	0.0319	−0.976***	−0.929**	−1.423***	−0.982**
	(−1.07)	(−0.04)	(−3.00)	(−2.58)	(−4.45)	(−2.68)
mediangni	0.0659***					
	(−9.99)					
gini		−0.381	0.0153			
		(−1.36)	(−0.44)			
ratiolh		−0.00824		−0.00887		
		(−0.13)		(−0.62)		
poverty		−0.00479			0.0051	
		(−0.35)			(−0.71)	
ratio1040		0.236*				0.00231
		(−1.88)				(−0.11)
housing	−0.0940***					
	(−10.66)					
lnfantm	−0.0944***					
	(−9.59)					
healthg		−0.0275*	−0.0252	−0.0221	−0.0101	−0.0241
		(−1.88)	(−1.49)	(−1.23)	(−0.63)	(−1.41)
ptsecondary	0.0217					
	(−1.43)					
ptprimary	−0.0645***					
	(−4.78)					
nenrol	−0.00403					
	(−0.15)					
genrol	0.225***					
	(−4.94)					
internet	0.000467					
	(−0.49)					
broadband		0.0112*	0.0315***	0.0312***	0.0173**	0.0306***
		(−1.79)	(−5.88)	(−5.67)	(−2.31)	(−5.56)
cc		0.0295	0.013	0.01	0.0132	0.0143
		(−1.17)	(−0.58)	(−0.43)	(−0.47)	(−0.64)
ge		0.0892**	0.0692*	0.0574	0.0559	0.0731*
		(−2.51)	(−1.77)	(−1.48)	(−1.37)	(−1.90)
psav		−0.0057	−0.00872	−0.00647	0.00294	−0.0105
		(−0.38)	(−0.67)	(−0.49)	(−0.18)	(−0.80)
rl		0.0802**	0.0706**	0.0779**	0.0845**	0.0691**
		(−2.63)	(−2.26)	(−2.50)	(−2.39)	(−2.21)

Table 23.2 (continued)

	Model 5	Model 6	Model 7	Model 8	Model 9	Model 10
rq		−0.092	−0.165**	−0.146**	−0.143*	−0.171***
		(−1.05)	(−2.64)	(−2.04)	(−1.95)	(−2.75)
va		−0.00779	0.0370*	0.0363*	0.0330**	0.0401**
		(−0.39)	(−1.94)	(−1.87)	(−2.13)	(−2.15)
propr		−0.0171	−0.00116	0.00135	−0.0374	−0.000854
		(−0.57)	(−0.06)	(−0.07)	(−1.37)	(−0.04)
frc		−0.0864*	−0.00483	−0.00561	−0.0156	−0.00755
		(−1.79)	(−0.12)	(−0.13)	(−0.25)	(−0.18)
fiscalfr		0.267***	0.347***	0.335***	0.307***	0.347***
		(−3.41)	(−6.03)	(−5.81)	(−4.19)	(−6.02)
govtx		0.0182	−0.0765***	−0.0746***	−0.101***	−0.0724***
		(−0.47)	(−3.15)	(−3.17)	(−3.42)	(−3.15)
bizfr		0.00493	−0.0526	−0.0528	0.0452	−0.0465
		(−0.10)	(−1.24)	(−1.23)	(−0.90)	(−1.09)
labfr		0.0126	0.00518	0.00359	0.0173	0.00596
		(−0.43)	(−0.24)	(−0.16)	(−0.74)	(−0.28)
monfr		−0.0162	−0.0291	−0.0188	0.0276	−0.0263
		(−0.20)	(−0.39)	(−0.25)	(−0.35)	(−0.36)
trfr		−0.0393	−0.140***	−0.132***	−0.0252	−0.137***
		(−0.82)	(−4.27)	(−3.91)	(−0.61)	(−4.17)
invfr		0.0593*	0.0362	0.018	0.0185	0.0371
		(−1.85)	(−0.99)	(−0.49)	(−0.45)	(−1.01)
finfr		0.0347	0.0730**	0.0750**	0.0175	0.0724**
		(−1.07)	(−2.58)	(−2.58)	(−0.58)	(−2.55)
Estimation	RE robust se	OLS	OLS	OLS	OLS	OLS
Adjusted R2		0.987	0.953	0.952	0.971	0.953
Observations	84	36	58	58	38	58
Model p−value	0.0000	0.0000	0.0000	0.0000	0.0000	0.0000

Source: Author's own calculations.

Note: The models above represent regression $WB_{it} = \alpha_t + \beta E_{it} + YQL_{it} + \delta S_{it} + \xi_{it}$ where each of the wellbeing proxy is regressed with Economic (E), Quality of Life (QL) and Shariah fulfilment (S) variables. Model 5 is estimated on the set of observations over the sample period 1980–2013. Models 6–10 are estimated over the sample period 1995–2013. These models are found to be appropriate only for OLS estimation based on the BP-LM test.

The reported results refer to the most appropriate models after testing for panel estimation (Breush-Pagan Lagrange Multiplier test), selection for Random or Fixed Effects (Hausman test) and robust standard errors (Modified Wald test for heteroskedasticity).

All variables are log-transformed. Figures in parentheses are t-statistics. *, ** and *** indicate statistical significance at the 10%, 5% and 1% levels, respectively.

Table 23.3: Description of Explanatory Variables.

Variable	Description	Source
Quality of Growth (QY) factors		
strength	**Strength of growth** Annual change in real GDP per capita.	World Bank
stability	**Stability of growth** Inverse coefficient of variation (CV) of the change in growth above. The CV is the ratio of standard deviation over the average.	World Bank
sectoral	**Sectoral composition** Export diversification index (Papageorgiou and Spatafora 2012).	IMF
demand	**Demand composition** Net external demand, difference between export and import of goods and services, as a percentage of GDP.	World Bank data
gdppc	**GDP per capita** Gross domestic product divided by midyear population. GDP is the sum of gross value added by all resident producers in the economy plus any product taxes and minus any subsidies not included in the value of the products. It is calculated without making deductions for depreciation of fabricated assets for depletion and degradation of natural resources.	World Bank
Quality of Life (QL) factors		
Health		
infantm	**Infant Mortality rate** Infant mortality (per 1000 births)	UNESCO
healthg	**Health expenditure** Health expenditure as a percentage of GDP	World Bank
Education		
ptsecondary	**Pupil-teacher ratio** Pupil-teacher ratio for secondary school level.	UNESCO Institutes of Statistics (via World Bank)
ptprimary	Pupil-teacher ratio for primary school level.	
nenrol	**Enrolment** Net enrolment rate for primary level.	
genrol	Gross enrolment ratio for all levels combined (except pre-primary).	
IT savviness		
internet	**Internet users** Internet users (per 100 people).	World Bank
broadband	**Broadband subscription** Fixed broadband Internet subscribers (per 100 people).	World Bank

Table 23.3 (continued)

Variable	Description	Source
Components of GDP growth		
lc	**Consumption** Total consumption expenditure (household /private and general government consumption)	World Bank
lfdi	**Foreign Direct Investment (FDI)** Foreign direct investment refers to direct investment equity flows in the reporting economy (inclusive of equity capital, reinvestment of earnings, other long-term capital and short-term capital shown in the balance of payments).	World Bank
li	**Investment** Gross capital formation (or gross domestic investment) consists of outlays on additions to the fixed assets of the economy plus net changes in the level of inventories.	World Bank and OECD national accounts
lg	**Government expenditure** All government current expenditures for purchases of goods and services (including compensation of employees), as well as most expenditures on national defence and security	World Bank and OECD national accounts
lxm	**Trade openness** The sum of exports and imports of all goods and services in terms of % of GDP. They include the value of merchandise, freight, insurance, transport, travel, royalties, license fees, and other services such as communication, construction, financial, information, business, personal and government services. They exclude compensation of employees and investment income and transfer payments.	World Bank and OECD national accounts
ls	**Savings** Gross domestic savings, calculated as GDP less total consumption.	World Bank and OECD national accounts
lppp	**Purchasing Power Parity (PPP)** Purchasing power parity conversion factor for private consumption – the number of units of a country's currency required to buy the same amounts of goods and services in the domestic market as US dollar would buy in the US.	World Bank, International Comparison Programme
Lcpi	**Inflation, Consumer Price Index** Inflation reflects the annual percentage change in the cost to the average consumer of acquiring a basket of goods and services that may be fixed or changed at specified intervals, e.g. annually.	World Bank, IMF

Table 23.3 (continued)

Variable	Description	Source
Components of GDP growth		
lu	**Unemployment** Total unemployment i.e. the share of the labour force that is without work but available for and seeking employment.	World Bank, International Labour Organisation
Economic (E) factors		
Distribution of income		
mediangni	**Median of GNI per capita** The median of GNI per capita, calculated at five-year rolling window. Time series of GNI per capita (2011 PPP constant) is used.	World Bank, IMF, UN data (via World Bank)
Inequality		
gini	**Gini index** Gini index (also known as Gini coefficient or Gini ratio) measures the deviation of the distribution of income (or consumption) among individuals within a country from a perfectly equal distribution. The values 0 and 100 correspond with absolute equality and absolute inequality, respectively.	World Bank
ratiolh	**Ratio of bottom and top quintiles** The ratio of income share held by lowest 20% to highest 20%; data retrieved from income quintile share data.	World Bank
poverty	**Poverty headcount** Poverty headcount below US$2 a day PPP (% population)	UNESCO
ratio1040	**Ratio of top 10% to bottom 40%, i.e. the Palma Ratio** The ratio of income share held by top 10% to the combined total of income share held by lowest 20% and fourth 20%; data retrieved from income percentage share data. The **Palma Ratio** focuses on the locus of inequality, and is also sensitive to extreme inequality unlike the Gini (OECD).	World Bank
Housing		
housing	**Housing** Stockbuilding or dwelling housing property; the value of stocks of outputs that are still held by the units that produced them and stocks of products acquired from other units for immediate consumption or for resale.	Datastream

Table 23.3 (continued)

Variable	Description	Source
Shariah fulfilment (S) factors		
Political Governance		
cc	**Control of Corruption** Captures perceptions of the extent to which public power is exercised for private gain, including both petty and grand forms of corruption, as well as "capture" of the state by elites and private interests.	
ge	**Government effectiveness** Captures perceptions of the quality of public services, the quality of the civil service and the degree of its independence from political pressures, the quality of policy formulation and implementation, and the credibility of the government's commitment to such policies.	
psav	**Political stability and absence of violence/terrorism** Measures perceptions of the likelihood of political instability and/or politically motivated violence, including terrorism.	World Governance Index (World Bank)
rl	**Rule of law** Captures perceptions of the extent to which agents have confidence in and abide by the rules of society, and in particular the quality of contract enforcement, property rights, the police and the courts, as well as the likelihood of crime and violence.	
rq	**Regulatory Quality** Captures perceptions of the ability of the government to formulate and implement sound policies and regulations that permit and promote private sector development.	
va	**Voice and accountability** Captures perceptions of the extent to which a country's citizens are able to participate in selecting their government, as well as freedom of expression, freedom of association, and free media.	

Table 23.3 (continued)

Variable	Description	Source
Shariah fulfilment (S) factors		
Freedom		
propr	**Property rights** An assessment of the ability of individuals to accumulate private property, secured by clear laws that are fully enforced by the state. It measures the degree to which a country's laws protect private property rights and the degree to which its government enforces those laws.	
frc	**Freedom from corruption** Corruption introduces insecurity and uncertainty into economic relationships, eroding economic freedom. This is derived primarily from Transparency International's Corruption Perception Index (CPI), which measures the level of corruption in 178 countries.	Index of Economic Freedom (Heritage Foundation)
fiscalfr	**Fiscal freedom** A measure of the tax burden imposed by government. It includes both the direct tax on individuals and corporate income and the overall amount of tax revenue as a percentage of GDP.	
govtx	**Government expenditure** The level of government expenditure as a percentage of GDP, including consumption and transfers.	
bizfr	**Business freedom** A quantitative measure of the ability to start, operate and close a business that represents the overall burden of regulation as well as the efficiency of gover nment in the regulatory process.	
labfr	**Labour freedom** A quantitative measure that looks into various aspects of the legal and regulatory framework of a country's labour market. This includes regulations concerning minimum wages, laws inhibiting layoffs, severance requirements, and measurable regulatory burdens on hiring, hours, etc.	Index of Economic Freedom (Heritage Foundation)
monfr	**Monetary freedom** Monetary freedom combines a measure of price stability with an assessment of price controls. Price stability without microeconomic intervention (inflation and price controls) is the ideal state for the free market.	

Table 23.3 (continued)

Variable	Description	Source
Shariah fulfilment (S) factors		
trfr	**Trade freedom** A composite measure of the absence of tariff and non-tariff barriers that affect imports and exports of goods and services.	
invfr	**Investment freedom** A score of 100 would mean there would be no constraints on the flow of investment capital; and firms and individuals would be allowed to move resources into and out of specific activities, internally and across borders without restriction.	
finfr	**Financial freedom** A measure of banking efficiency as well as a measure of independence from government control and interference in the financial sector. In an ideal environment, minimum level of government interference exists, independent central bank supervision and regulation of financial institutions are limited to enforcing contractual obligations and preventing fraud; credit is allocated on market terms; government does not own financial institutions; financial institutions provide various types of services; banks are free to extend credit, accept deposits and conduct operations in foreign currencies; foreign financial institutions operate freely and are treated the same as domestic institutions.	

evidence on the relationship between high attainment levels in education and wellbeing (World Bank 2012; Coyle 2011; Stiglitz, Sen, and Fitoussi 2009; Barro 2002). The Legatum Prosperity Index 2014 finds that further key factors that affect this relationship including low gender inequality and the quality of teaching and curriculum (Legatum Institute 2014). There is also strong evidence from the estimated models in Table 23.2 that broadband subscription levels are reflective of the overall level of wellbeing. This is consistent with the impact of technological advances on life styles and the quality of life (OECD 2013; EPU 2013; "Numbeo.Com" n.d.). It is noted that Barro (2002) explains the relation between the level of education and economic development in terms of the diffusion process of technologies.

Finally, the estimation results for variables including *Shariah* fulfilment are reported in Table 23.2. There is evidence of strong relationships between overall wellbeing and explanatory variables representing governance and freedom. The impact of government effectiveness, rule of law, accountability, as well as fiscal and financial freedom are likely to be positive. In contrast, the effects of regulatory quality, government expenditure and trade freedom are expected to be negative. This may be reflective of the ability of governments to formulate and implement sound social and economic policies, and their efficient allocation of public expenditure to promote the private sector. As reflected by the negative sign associated with trade freedom, the lowering of tariffs and trade barriers is conducive to increased quality of growth. This empirical evidence is also consistent with the previous results on the impact of export diversification.

5 Conclusion and Policy Implications

This empirical study examines the relation between wellbeing and various measures of economic growth, economic distribution, quality of life and level of Shariah fulfillment. The evidence from a sample of developing economies including some Muslim countries suggests that higher level of wellbeing depends on inclusive economic growth, as well as, improvement in the economic conditions and quality of life.

These findings are in line with the properties of similar indicates of wellbeing mapped out by the WHI, OECD, Economist Intelligence Unit. Our results are augmented with the Shariah fulfilment category, explored in terms of governance and freedom, which is found to be of vital importance to people's wellbeing. Broader income distribution, lower housing costs, lower infant mortality, increased educational opportunities, and better connectivity can significantly improve the levels of overall wellbeing.

The estimated models are augmented with explanatory variables closely related to Shariah fulfilment in terms of governance and freedom, which represent dimensions of social and economic justice. There is evidence of positive effects from effective government, rule of law, transparency and accountability as well as from fiscal and financial freedom. Measures of the quality of regulation, government expenditure and trade freedom seem to be, however, associated with negative effects. This may be negative reflection of the public perceptions about the ability of the government institutions to promote the social and economic justice.

Thus, it is important for Muslim countries to promote wellbeing by addressing the chronic issues related to accountability, governance, and efficiency. Economic policies that focus solely on the immediate short-term effects on economic growth may bring little remedy to the long-term social effects of income inequality. Only a coherent approach to development that encompasses not just the economic dimensions but the human perspectives as well has the potential to improve welfare and wellbeing. Our recommended policy objectives to enhance and sustain wellbeing of the people, would be two-pronged – firstly to address development and secondly its sustainability. The priorities of development should be human development as well as non-income perspectives of development, of which the latter is to ensure that the environment also fosters sustainable growth. One of the fundamental characteristics illustrated by nations with sustained growth over an extended period is effective leadership and governance, as clearly illustrated by our findings (World Bank and IMF 2015).

References

Alaabed, Alaa, Hossein Askari, Zamir Iqbal, and Adam Ng. 2014. "Developing Benchmark Index for Monitoring Compliance with Maqasid Al-Shari'ah."

Ali, Salman Syed, and Hamid Hasan. 2014. "Towards a Maqasid Al-Shariah Based Development Index." *IRTI Working Paper Series* 18: 1–22.

Ames, Brian, Ward Brown, Shatayanan Devarajan, and Alejandro Izquierdo. 2001. "Macroeconomic Policy and Poverty Reduction." Washingtonj, D.C., International Monetary Fund and World Bank.

Anto, MB Hendrie. 2009. "Introducing an Islamic Human Development Index (I-HDI) to Measure Development in OIC Countries." *Islamic Economic Studies* 19(2): 69–95.

Atkinson, Anthony B. 2012. "Putting People First and Macro-Economic Policy." *European Commission. Economic Papers* 481(PartIII): 39–64.

Baltagi, Badi. 2008. *Econometric Analysis of Panel Data*. Chichester: John Wiley & Sons.

Barro, Robert J. 2002. *Education as a Determinant of Economic Growth. Education in the Twenty-First Century*. In *Education in the Twenty-First Century*, edited by Edward P. Lazear, 9–24. Stanford: Hoover Institution Press.

Berg, Andrew G., and Jonathan D. Ostry. 2011. "Inequality and Unsustainable Growth: Two Sides of the Same Coin ?" *IMF Staff Discussion Note* SDN/11/08.

Berry, Christine. 2014. *Wellbeing in Four Policy Areas*. London: New Economics Foundation.

Cesa-bianchi, Ambrogio, Luis Felipe Cespedes, and Alessandro Rebucci. 2015. "Capital Flows, House Prices, and the Macroeconomy: Evidence from Advanced and Emerging Market Economies." *IMF Working Paper* WP/15/23: 1–53.

Chapra, M. Umar. 2008a. *The Islamic Vision of Development in the Light of Maqasid Al-Shariah. The International Institute of Islamic Thought*. London: The International Institute of Islamic Thought (IIIT).

Chapra, M. Umer. 2008b. "Ibn Khaldun's Theory of Development: Does It Help Explain the Low Performance of the Present-Day Muslim World?." *The Journal of Socio-Economics* 37(2): 836–63.

Coyle, Diane. 2011. *The Economics of Enough: How to Run the Economy as If the Future Matters*. Princeton, New Jersey: Princeton University Press.

Cutler, David, Angus Deaton, and Adriana Lleras-Muney. 2006. "The Determinants of Mortality." *Journal of Economic Perspectives* 20(3): 97–120.

Dar, Humayon A. 2004. "On Making Human Development More Humane." *International Journal of Social Economics* 31(11/12): 1071–1088.

Deaton, Angus. 2007. "Income, Aging, Health and Wellbeing around the World: Evidence from the Gallup World Poll." NBER Working Paper Series No. 13317.

Dollar, David, and Aart Kraay. 2004. "Trade, Growth, and Poverty." *The Economic Journal* 114 (February): 22–49.

Duflo, Esther, Pascaline Dupas, and Michael Kremer. 2007. "Peer Effects, Teacher Incentives, and the Impact of Early Tracking: Evidence from a Randomized Evaluation in Kenya." *American Economic Review* 101(5): 1739–1774.

EPU. 2013. "Malaysian Well-Being Report 2013." Putrajaya.

Greene, William. H. 2012. "Chapter 11. Models for Panel Data." In *Econometric Analysis*, Seventh, Harlow, UK: Pearson Education, Inc.

Guillaumont-Jeanneney, Sylviane, and Kangni Kpodar. 2005. "Financial Development, Financial Instability and Poverty." University of Auvergne CSAE WPS/2: 1–35.
Helliwell, John F., Christopher P. Barrington-leigh, Anthony Harris, and Huang Haifang. 2009. "International Evidence on the Social Context of Well-Being." NBER Working Paper Series No. 14720.
Helliwell, John, Richard Layard, and Jeffrey Sachs. 2013. *World Happiness Report 2013*. New York: United Nations.
Ibn Khaldun,. 1672. *The Muqaddimah*. Translated by Abd Ar Rahman Muhammed
Kakwani, Nanak, and Ernesto M. Pernia. 2000. "What Is Pro-Poor Growth?" *Asian Development Review* 18(1): 1–16.
Kenny, Charles. 2005. "Why Are We Worried about Income? Nearly Everything That Matters Is Converging." *World Development* 33(1): 1–19.
Krongkaew, Medhi, and Ragayah Mat Zin. 2007. "Income Distribution and Sustainable Economic Development in East Asia: A Comparative Analysis." *Journal of Development Studies* 45(7): 1209–1210.
Legatum Institute. 2014. *The 2014 Legatum Prosperity Index*. London, UK.
Malik, Khalid. 2014. *Human Development Report 2014 – Sustaining Human Progress: Reducing Vulnerabilities and Building Resilience*. New York, USA.
Mat Zin, Ragayah. 2008. "Income Inequality in Malaysia." *Asian Economic Policy Review* 3: 114–32.
Mlachila, Montfort, René Tapsoba, and Sampawende J. A. Tapsoba. 2014. "A Quality of Growth Index for Developing Countries : A Proposal." IMF Working Paper, WP/14/172.
Ng, Boon Ka. 2008. "Maqasid Al-Shariah – an Objective from a Prism of Wealth." *Berita Kijang, BNM*, 2008.
Numbeo.com. n.d. Accessed October 19, 2015. http://www.numbeo.com/quality-of-life.
OECD. 2013. *OECD Guidelines on Measuring Subjective Well-Being*. Paris: OECD Publishing.
OECD. 2011a. "An Overview of Growing Income Inequalities in OECD Countries: Main Findings." In *Divided We Stand: Why Inequality Keeps Rising*: 21–45. Paris: OECD Publishing.
OECD. 2011b. "Special Focus : Inequality in Emerging Economies (EEs)." In *Divided We Stand: Why Inequality Keeps Rising*: 47–82. Paris: OECD Publishing.
Papageorgiou, Chris, and Nikola Spatafora. 2012. "Economic Diversification in LICs : Stylized Facts and Macroeconomic Implications." SDN/12/13. IMF Staff Discussion Note. International Monetary Fund.
Ramos, Almeida, Rafael Ranieri, and Jan-Willem Lammens. 2013. "How Inclusive Has Growth Been in the Last Decade ?" UNDP Working Paper, International Policy Centre for Inclusive Growth (IPC-IG), no. 189.
Ramos, Raquel Almeida, Rafael Ranieri, and Jan-Willem Lammes. 2013. "Mapping Inclusive Growth." UNDP Working Paper, International Policy Centre for Inclusive Growth (IPC-IG) No. 105 (March).
Rehman, Scheherazade S., and Hossein Askari. 2010. "An Economic IslamicityIndex (EI^2)" *Global Economy Journal* 10(3): 1–37.
Schmidheiny, Kurt. 2014. "Short Guides to Microeconomics, Panel Data : Fixed and Random Effects." *Lecture Notes*. Basel. http://kurt.schmidheiny.name/teaching/panel2up.pdf.
Setia, Adi. 2009. "The Islamic Gift Economy : A Brief Conceptual Outline." In *Islamic Gift Economy and Selected Articles, and Waqf Institutions*. Durban, South Africa: Adi Setia & National Awqaf Foundation of South Africa.
Shatzmiller, Maya. 1994. *Labour in the Medieval Islamic World*. Vol. 4. Leiden: Brill.
Stiglitz, Joseph E., Amartya Sen, and Jean-Paul Fitoussi. 2009. "Report by the Commission on the Measurement of Economic Performance and Social Progress." Paris.
Stoll, L, J Michaelson, and C Seaford. 2012. *Well-Being Evidence for Policy: A Review*. London: New Economics Foundation.

Wooldridge, Jeffrey M. 2002. *Econometric Analysis of Cross Section and Panel Data*. Cambridge, Massachusetts: The MIT Press.

World Bank. 2012. *Putting Higher Education to Work: Skills and Research for Growth in East Asia*. Washington, D.C: World Bank.

World Bank. 2015. *Global Monitoring Report 2015/2016: Development Goals in an Era of Demographic Change*. Washington, DC: World Bank

Yusof Ali, Abdullah. 2004. *An English Interpretation of the Holy Quran*. Pennsylvania State University: Sh. Muhammad Ashraf.

Yusof, Selamah Abdullah, Ruzita Mohd Amin, Mohamed Aslam Haneef, A O Muhammad, and G Oziev. 2015. "The Integrated Development Index (I-Dex): A New Comprehensive Approach to Measuring Human Development." Islamic Economic: Theory, Policy and Social Justice. Bloomsbury Qatar Foundation Doha.

Part VII: Islamic Finance, Economic Growth and Human Development

Patrick Amir Imam, Kangni Kpodar

Chapter 24: Is Islamic Banking Good for Growth?

1 Introduction

Since the modern birth of Islamic banking in the 1960s in Egypt, it has expanded rapidly across the globe. As illustrated by Imam and Kpodar (2013), such expansion has taken place, in particular – though not exclusively –in countries with larger Muslim populations. From an insignificant beginning, the industry has grown to over USD 1.6 trillion in assets in 2012, and is expected to reach USD 6.1 trillion by the end of this decade (Gewal, 2013). Not only have local banks in Muslim countries adopted Islamic banking principles, but large multinational banks have established Islamic windows. Islamic finance has spread beyond commercial banks, and now spans investment banks, insurance companies, as well as investment (e.g. asset management) and financial companies (e.g. leasing). The development of new products, such as sukuk (Islamic bonds), has also broadened the range of products available.

There is mounting evidence – at least for lower and middle income countries – that financial sector development is good for growth (see for instance the seminal paper of Levine, Loayza, and Beck, 2000). A developed financial sector helps mobilize savings, facilitates the allocation of capital to where returns are expected to be highest, monitors the use of capital once invested, and allows for diversification of risk. Moreover, there is a growing consensus among economists that it does not matter much for economic growth whether the financial system is more bank-based or market-based (Allen and Gale, 2000; Levine, 2002). The particular institutional arrangements that provide financial services to the economy are not so important; what matters is the level of overall financial development.

However, do these findings of financial sector deepening impacting growth also apply to systems where Islamic banking plays a significant role: Is the development of Islamic banking good for growth? This is an important question to answer, as Islamic banking has unique characteristics that differ from conventional banking; they appear better adapted to characteristics prevailing in poorer countries of the Middle-East, sub-Saharan Africa and Asia. In addition, with a few exceptions, countries with large Islamic populations are typically not highly developed (see Figure 24.1), and have often not performed well in economic terms, one of the reasons being an underdeveloped financial system. This chapter is not attempting to answer the question of whether the development of Islamic banking would contribute more to financial sector development than conventional banks, an altogether different question. It is simply asking the question of whether Islamic banking is good for growth. There are parallels to the Information Technology Revolution. As

https://doi.org/10.1515/9783110587920-024

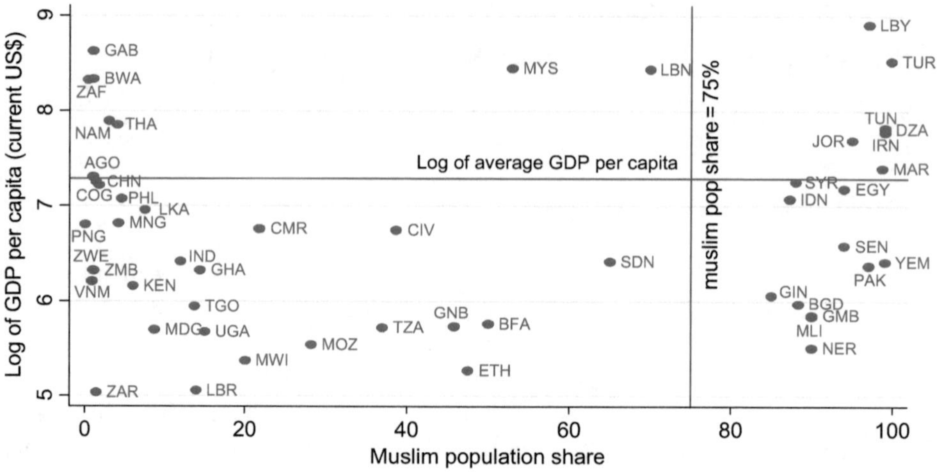

Figure 24.1: Average GDP per Capita in Islamic and Other Countries (1990–2010).
Source: IMF, Alesina, et al. (2003).
Note: See Appendix 4 for country names.

Information and Communication Technology was becoming ubiquitous in the 1980s, Robert Solow famously quipped "You can see the computer age everywhere but in the productivity statistics". A whole niche within the economics profession emerged, to help explain this apparent paradox. Similarly, Islamic banking has made inroads into many countries, reaching a critical threshold. It is therefore valid to ask whether Islamic banking is becoming visible in the statistics, or whether explanations need to be found to explain why it is not visible (yet).

Growth in Islamic countries, while not spectacular, has not been dismal compared to other countries with a similar level of development. The widely held perception is that Islamic countries have performed poorly in economic terms since the 1950s, but this does not hold. After an initial strong growth spurt following independence – in sync with other low-income countries (LICs) – growth rates were sub-par following the lost decades of the 1980s and 1990s. While it is true that Islamic countries and sub-national regions with large Muslim populations are characterized by low incomes and a low level of social development, with the exception of oil-producing Gulf countries, they are in fact not much different from other emerging markets (EMs) and LICs (Figure 24.2). In fact, once adjustments for low education levels, poor institutions, commodity prices, etc., are made, evidence is mounting that Islam *per se* is not holding back these countries (Nolan, 2003).

Similarly, Islamic countries do not currently stand out in terms of private sector credit to GDP (Figure 24.3). However, as Islamic banking becomes more acceptable to a large swath of the population, it could expand faster, as it would not necessarily be a substitute for conventional banking, but it would provide financial products to a part of the population that otherwise would not use the financial system, potentially

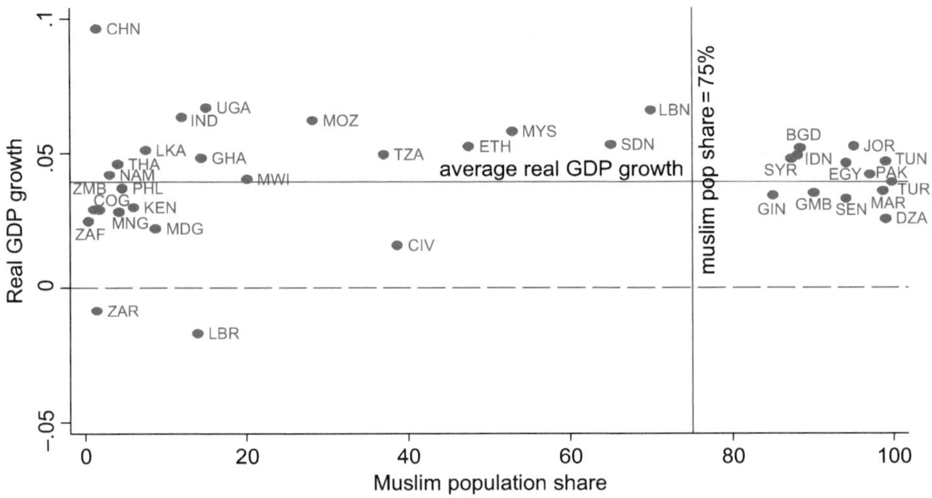

Figure 24.2: Average Real GDP Growth: How do Islamic Countries Compare to Others (1990–2010)?.
Source: IMF, Alesina, et al. (2003).
Note: See Appendix 4 for country names.

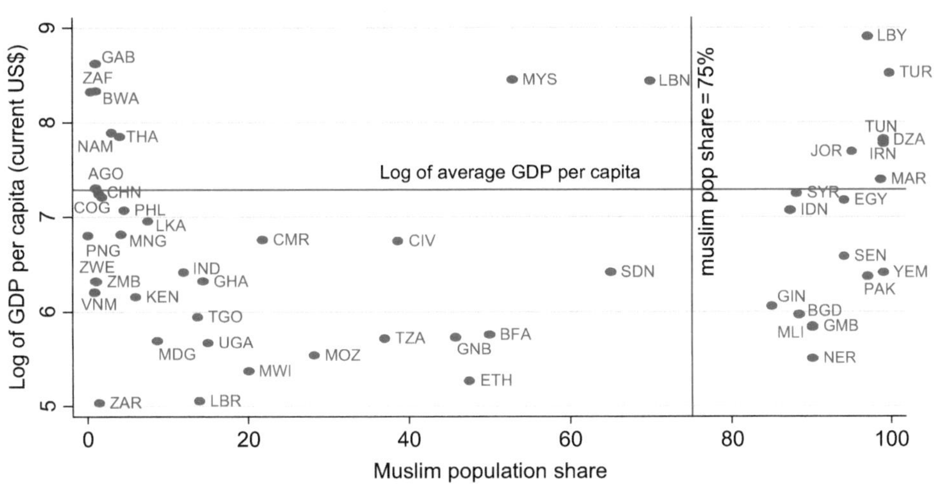

Figure 24.3: Average Private Sector Credit Ratio to GDP in Islamic and Other Countries (1990–2010).
Source: Beck, Demirguc-Kunt and Levine, (2000), Alesina, et al. (2003).
Note: See Appendix 4 for country names.

leading to higher financial inclusion and an acceleration of economic growth in these countries. Currently, while many Muslims use conventional banking services, a large swath of the population– pious individuals who want to adhere to the principles of Islam – are significantly less likely than non-Muslims to own a formal account or save at a formal financial institution after controlling for other individual- and country-level characteristics (Demirguc-Kunt, 2013).

Thus, the rapid diffusion of Islamic banking represents a growth opportunity for Islamic countries, as much of the empirical evidence suggests a strong link between financial sector development and growth (see Levine (2005) for a summary). However, the empirical literature has only looked at conventional banking, not Islamic banking. The aim of this study is to examine the positive relationship between Islamic banking and economic growth, and not to answer the question of whether the growth-enhancing effect of Islamic banking goes beyond that of conventional banking, an issue that is important in its own right. Using a sample of low- and middle-income countries with data over the period 1990–2010, we investigate the impact of Islamic banking on growth and discuss the policy implications. The results show that, notwithstanding its relatively small size compared to the economy or the overall size of the financial system, Islamic banking is positively associated with economic growth even after controlling for various determinants, including the level of financial depth. The results are robust across different measures of Islamic banking development, econometric estimators (pooling, fixed effects and System GMM), and to the sample composition and time periods.

The chapter is structured as follows. Section 2 reviews the literature, with a focus on how Islamic banking could help financial deepening, and ultimately growth. Section 3presents the sample, the econometric model, and estimators, as well as the results. Section 4 concludes with the policy implications.

2 Literature Review

Although the finance–growth nexus continues to be heavily debated in the literature, the main thrust is that financial development has, by and large, a favorable impact on economic growth. Financial intermediaries carry out five basic functions that serve growth: they (i) facilitate the trading, hedging, diversifying, and pooling of risk; (ii) allocate resources; (iii) monitor managers and exert corporate control; (iv) mobilize savings; and (v) facilitate the exchange of goods and services (see Levine, 1997). In performing their functions, financial intermediaries mitigate the effects of information and transaction costs, and improve the allocation of resources, thus influencing saving rates, investment decisions, technical innovation, and ultimately long-run growth rates. In turn, economic activity can also influence financial development. It is worth noting that this whole literature implicitly refers to conventional banking. An interesting question is: does this also apply to Islamic banks?

The literature has evolved overtime, however, and depicted alternating periods of optimism and skepticism on the benefits of finance for growth. It began early with the work of Schumpeter (1934), who highlighted the essential role of banks in financing innovative businesses and increasing productivity. Robinson (1952) challenges this view, arguing that financial development simply follows economic growth. Although Gurley and Shaw (1960) share Schumpeter's view on the importance of finance for growth, they stress instead the role of financial innovation for economic development, as it facilitates better risk management and a reduction in intermediation costs.

However, following the work of McKinnon (1973) and Shaw (1973), mixed country experiences from the wave of financial liberalization policies in the 1970s and 1980s raised uncertainties on the potential benefits of finance for growth. The studies of King and Levine (1993a, 1993b and 1993c) and Levine (1997) gave a new impetus to the finance–growth literature. The authors thoroughly documented the channels through which financial development positively impacted economic growth and undertook convincing theoretical and empirical investigation to support their hypothesis. Subsequent studies confirmed their findings (e.g. Rajan and Zingales, 1998; Levine, Loayza, and Beck, 2000), although some more recent studies – especially since the global financial crisis – cast doubt on the strength of the positive relationship between financial development and growth (see for instance Andersen and Tarp, 2003, Arcand, Berkes and Panizza, 2012 and Panizza, 2014). There is also evidence that by increasing the likelihood of banking crisis, the positive relationship between financial sector development and growth may be conditional (see Guillaumont Jeanneney and Kpodar, 2006).

Following the Miller and Modigliani (1958) capital structure irrelevance theory, it is likely that Islamic banking and conventional banking will not have different impacts on growth per se, if they finance the same projects. Although the benefits/risks of the project are distributed differently for conventional banks than for Islamic banks, the overall return on the project is the same. On the other hand, while Islamic banks perform similar functions to conventional banks, they have distinct features. While some view Islamic banking as being indistinguishable in practice from conventional banking (e.g. Khan, 2010), most scholars think that there are differences, even in practice (see Iqbal and Mirakhor, 2013). In fact, Islamic banking has many advantages, not only in Islamic countries, but also in low- and middle-income countries in general, that could make it better adapted to the local environment and could be better at stimulating growth compared conventional banking, under certain circumstances. As we will show, while Islamic banking could, at the macroeconomic level, contain features that may stimulate growth, at the microeconomic level, given that it is still a nascent industry, it still faces hurdles that may make it difficult to fully maximize this advantage. Therefore, we are only looking at whether the development of Islamic banking has a positive impact on growth, not whether it is more "efficient" than conventional banks is raising growth. What are these distinct attributes of Islamic banking?

– *Encourages lending (to individuals without assets).* Conventional banks in most countries lend based on some form of guarantee/collateral. The *risk-sharing* characteristic of Islamic banking means that the borrower and the bank share the risk of any investment on agreed terms, and divide any profits or losses between them, without recourse to guarantees. Risk-sharing leads providers of financial capital and entrepreneurs to share business risks in return for a share of profits, suggesting that borrower liabilities are state-contingent, in contrast to conventional banks. This should in principle encourage more investment – notably by individuals who could not otherwise borrow because of a lack of assets that could act as a guarantee – and thereby growth.[211] Ben Naceur et al. (2015) find that although physical access to financial services has grown more rapidly in member countries of the Organization for Islamic Cooperation, the use of these services has not increased as quickly. Through the prohibition of *riba* (interest rates), the incentives of lenders and borrowers are aligned, thus reducing moral hazard. At the same time, it helps to spur investment that would otherwise not take place, and thereby growth, and also acts as a shock absorber for countries subject to large shocks.

- *Raises savings (capital accumulation).* In Islamic countries, large segments of the Muslim population do not have access to adequate banking services–often because devout Muslims are unwilling to put their savings into a traditional financial system that runs counter to their religious principles. Therefore, Islamic banking can raise the savings of pious individuals who refrain from using conventional banks. This could thereby increase financial intermediation. Demirguc-Kunt et al. (2013) explore the difference between Muslims and non-Muslims within the same country, and find that in the 64 countries they cover, 24 percent of Muslim adults report having a bank account, in contrast to 44 percent of non-Muslims who have one. This under-banking of an important segment of the population leads to savings not being channeled to the formal sector, and therefore not being used efficiently, leading to sub-optimal financial intermediation.[212]

211 Most Islamic financial instruments can be thought of as falling into one of two general families. First, contracts can be classified as venture financing, where the provider of funds to a venture expects a return conditional on the success of the venture (profit-and-loss sharing, PLS). Contracts that are most common include equitable participation (*musharakah*) in a venture such as an import consignment and a sleeping partnership (*mudarabah*) in a defined venture. Second, and rising in importance are payment smoothing arrangements, where an intermediary's client has a lumpy cash need in order to accomplish some project (e.g. housing, productive investment). The intermediary enters into an arrangement which, while profitable to it, enables the client to smooth their cash outlay. For example, the provider of funds may acquire a productive asset and make it available to the user of funds for a fee, as in installment sale (*murabahah*), leasing (*ijarah*) or hire-purchase arrangements (see Honohan, 2001). These innovations should help economic development in Islamic countries, by providing access to financing that is acceptable to the (pious) population.

212 Growing evidence (see Demirguc-Kunt and Levine, 2009) suggests that better functioning financial systems exerts a disproportionately positive impact on the relatively poor.

Bringing Muslims into the formal sector, by providing them with suitable products, would increase access to finance, with savings increasing commensurately.

- *Enhances financial stability*. Most boom-bust cycles witnessed across the world in recent decades have exposed several underlying factors that highlight the vulnerability of conventional banking, namely high leveraging, wholesale financing, and utilization of complex instruments.[213] In Islamic finance, balance sheet mismatches are absent, as banks do not have asset-liability mismatches, given that short-term deposits finance short-term trading, while for longer-term investments, longer-term deposits are used (Mirakhor, 2010). There is also consistent evidence of higher capitalization of Islamic banks, and this capital cushion combined with higher liquidity reserves explains the relatively better performance of Islamic banks during the recent crisis. Derivatives and other non-transparent products are also disallowed.[214] This, combined with the sharing of profits and losses, creates a less crisis prone system (Cihak and Hesse, 2010; Hasan and Dridi, 2010). It is probably fair to say that banking systems that are diversified, through including Islamic banks as a complement to conventional banks, are likely to contribute to financial stability (Imam and Kpodar, 2013).[215]
- *Quality of "Modern Institutions" less relevant in Islamic Banking*. It has long been established that the quality of modern institutions – legal systems for instance – is a major determinant of financial sector development, which is a key input into growth (Levine, 2005). Islamic countries often do not have strong legal systems; but as Imam and Kpodar (2013) have shown, the spread of Islamic banking is not dependent on the quality of these institutions, presumably because Islam has its own institutions that can resolve conflicts among parties.
- *Finances morally acceptable projects*. Islamic banking is based on a moral system of Islam, which only allows for the financing of assets that are not harmful to society. Islamic banks are not allowed to finance casinos and other activities that are deemed harmful to society and the poor in particular. While the standard of 'morally' acceptable projects might seem subjective to some outsiders, the gray areas are few, and an Islamic scholar will in case of doubt be able to provide an answer. This aspect is difficult to quantify, but could be growth enhancing by reducing negative externalities imposed on society by undesirable projects. If conventional banking and Islamic banking co-exist, this aspect is

---

213 Islamic banking prohibits speculative products, which are deemed *gharar* – contracts and transactions that contain excessive uncertainty. This reduces the probability of fraud, for instance. Derivative products are generally viewed as unacceptable under Shariah, as they involve speculation.

214 While some financial innovations may add to financial stability risks it may not necessarily be a first-best response to abstain from such financial innovations altogether, but this falls beyond the scope of this study.

215 Minsky moments, whereby periods of calm create the seeds for financial instability (endogenous financial instability) are absent in Islamic banking.

unlikely to matter much, as *haram* activities can be financed by conventional banking.

All these factors are, in principle, conducive to higher growth and poverty alleviation. Moreover, if Islamic banking is more likely to develop in Islamic countries because it is more acceptable to pious Muslims, growth is likely to accelerate more rapidly in these countries than it would if only conventional banking were available.[216] However, Islamic banks have certain structural weaknesses that counterbalance the positive aspects, something that is partly going to improve as the industry matures.

- *Difficulty of Managing Risk/Operational Risk.* As Islamic banks are not allowed to use derivatives, it is simply harder to mitigate and diversify risk. In addition, given their size, most Islamic banks have high geographical and sector concentration, accentuating the lack of diversification. Lack of proper accounting standards, clearing and settlement processes, coupled with the lack of stakeholder participation in governance of financial institutions offering Islamic products which lead to lack of transparency render banks risky (see Abedifar et al., 2013, Beck et al., 2013). Again, all these hurdles should gradually become less constraining as the industry matures and grows in size.
- *Lack of Economies of Scale.* Islamic banks are often newer, and therefore smaller, than conventional banks. This means that they are often still below optimal scales and thus have higher cost structures (Hasan and Dridi, 2010).[217] We should expect that, with continued growth, the disadvantage of scale will disappear over time as the industry grows. Comparing conventional and Islamic banks and controlling for other bank and country characteristics, Beck et al. (2013) find few significant differences in business orientation, efficiency, asset quality, or stability. While Islamic banks seem more cost-effective than conventional banks in a broad

---

216 There is sometimes a distorted view that Islamic banks are not profit maximizing institutions, which is erroneous. Like conventional banks, they try to be as profitable as possible, but are simply subject to different constraints than conventional banks.

217 Smallness of the financial system has obvious, though not necessarily visible, costs to the macro-economy. In the academic literature, micro-studies such as Rajan and Zingales (1998) and macro-level studies such as Levine (2005) have illustrated the causality of financial sector development on economic growth. A small financial system implies a *lack of economies of scale*, as there are significant fixed costs in setting up operations. As more individuals and firms use financial intermediaries, the *information flow* on customers improves, but a small financial system reduces the information flow function of financial intermediaries (Greenwood and Jovanovic, 1990). Smallness of the financial system also suggests *limited risk-diversification* options for savers and investors alike. In addition, a small financial system implies that profitable investment opportunities will be forgone, thereby limiting *growth below potential*. However, the lack of easily available financing reduces the resilience of the economy to shocks, smoothing consumption over time – a feature particularly important for many LICs/EMs that lack flexibility.

cross-country sample, this finding reverses in a sample of countries with both Islamic and conventional banks. However, conventional banks that operate in countries with a higher market share of Islamic banks are more cost-effective but less stable.

- *Lack of Liquid Instruments*. There is no secondary market for Islamic fixed-income products, forcing Islamic banks to have large liquidity buffers, putting them at a disadvantage relative to conventional banks (Moody's, 2009). This is because Islamic banks are prohibited from engaging in activities that include interest, but the way central banks function is through a repo that includes interest bearing assets. The establishment in 2010 of the "International Islamic Liquidity Management Corporation" (IILM), whose objective is to issue *Shariah*-compliant financial instruments that facilitate more efficient and effective liquidity management solutions for institutions offering Islamic financial services should help address this problem.[218] However, this is still a work in progress.

Thus, Islamic banks have features that can promote growth, but at the same time are disadvantaged by the lack of economies of scale and liquid instruments – though work is ongoing to address these shortcomings. This suggests that the answer to the question as to whether Islamic banking promotes growth lies in the empirical evidence. While there is a plethora of empirical studies on the impact of financial development on growth,[219] studies on how Islamic banking development affects growth are virtually nonexistent, a void that this study attempts to fill in the next section.

3 Econometric Estimation

3.1 The Data and Model

In this section, we empirically attempt to assess the impact of Islamic banking on growth. We construct a panel of 52 developing economies, of which 29 belong to the Organisation of Islamic Cooperation (OIC), with data spanning the period 1990–2010, and averaged over 3-year intervals. The sample size is constrained by data availability, in particular on variables capturing Islamic banking expansion and the quality of the institutional environment. In addition, we restricted the sample to low and middle income countries as the macroeconomic variables included

218 www.ifsb.org/preess_full.php?id=149&submit=more

219 Levine (2005) offers an overview of empirical studies on financial development and growth. For a more recent survey, see Panizza (2014).

in the growth model are more relevant to them, and also because this helps reduce sample heterogeneity. With regard to the length of the time period, the 3-year average represents a good balance between the need to smooth business cycle fluctuations and that of ensuring an adequate number of observations for the regressions.

We rely on a standard growth model, with a set of variables of interest measuring broad financial development and Islamic banking development, and control variables conventionally utilized in the growth literature. The data sources for the variables are found in Appendix 1. The variables of interest consist of:

- *Development of Islamic banking.* As discussed above, there are theoretical grounds for expecting a positive impact of Islamic banking development on growth. This makes Islamic banking indicators good candidates for explaining cross-country growth. We measure Islamic banking development by the amount of loans extended by these banks to the private sector divided by nominal GDP. While this indicator gives an idea on the size of the Islamic banking sector, it may not accurately measure the indirect channels through which Islamic banks could ignite growth (facilitate risk sharing, enhance financial stability, and mobilize savings). However, it is reasonable to assume that the larger the Islamic banking sector, the better it can perform its functions, a common hypothesis also made for conventional banking in past studies. We also use two alternative indicators of Islamic banking development: the ratio of Islamic banking assets to GDP and the ratio of deposits in Islamic banks to GDP, the latter being a useful indicator to gauge the ability of Islamic banks to mobilize savings.[220] As a robustness check we also used an indicator of capitalization (the capital-to-asset ratio), and the standard ratios of Return on Equity (ROE) and Return on Assets (ROA) to measure the financial strength and profitability of Islamic banks.
- *Development of the overall banking system.* There is a general acceptance in the economic literature that financial deepening stimulates growth (for a literature review, see Levine, 2005). As a result, we include in the model the ratio of private sector credit by commercial banks in percent of GDP as a measure of the development of the banking sector. Since both conventional and Islamic banking coexist in many countries and evolve together, it is important to control growth for the overall size of the banking system in order to properly isolate the growth impact of Islamic banking. Alternative measures of financial development considered include the ratio of private sector credit by bank and non-bank financial institutions in percent of GDP, the total assets of financial institutions as a ratio of GDP and finally the total financial system deposits as a ratio to GDP.

220 The lack of data availability prevents us from considering Islamic bond ("sukuk") market development. The market is still in its infancy and has low volumes.

The control variables include:

- *Initial real GDP per capita*: This variable is intended to control for growth convergence as the neoclassical model points out that lower income countries, with lower initial levels of technology and capital, will tend to grow faster than more advanced countries.
- *Inflation*: It has long been argued that inflation uncertainty lowers real output growth. Inflation uncertainty increases the variability of prices, which distorts the price signal and thereby harms economic efficiency and productivity. In addition, high inflation is likely to be associated with weaker growth as it is often a reflection of weak quality and unsustainable macroeconomic policies.
- *Government consumption*. The issue of government spending and its effect on economic growth is still widely debated in the economic literature. While government spending is necessary, and has a growth-enhancing impact when it finances public goods such as infrastructure, it can deter growth when excessively dominated by current spending. The hypothesis is that rising government consumption (as a percent of GDP) encourages poor quality spending, leads to an oversized government and often results in a waste of public resources, which crowd out private investment when government relies on domestic resources to finance growing deficits.
- *Education*: Human capital accumulation, as proxied by the primary school enrolment rate, is expected to have a positive impact on growth through improved labor productivity.
- *Trade Openness*: It is to be expected that countries that are more open will experience higher economic growth, as they can take better advantage of economies of scale in production, benefit from technological transfer, promote efficient allocation of resources, and encourage competition in domestic markets. At the same time, trade openness can make countries more vulnerable to exogenous shocks when export concentration is high, making growth more volatile, which ultimately can result in lower long-term growth.
- *Terms of Trade*: Improvements in terms of trade are often associated with economic growth. Conversely, deteriorating terms of trade would hamper growth, especially in developing countries where financial markets are shallow.
- *Quality of Institutions*: Institutional quality matters for long-term growth, as it determines the incentives of and the constraints on economic actors, fosters better policy choices, and shapes economic outcomes (Acemoglu, Johnson and Robinson, 2004). However, measuring accurately institutional development remains a challenge. While, no perfect or comprehensive indicator exists, we opted for the indicator of rule of law as a proxy for the quality of institutions, as compiled by the International Risk Country Guide (ICRG), which is widely used in the literature.

The baseline regression looks as follows:

$$G_{it} = \alpha + \beta IslBank_{it} + \delta FD_{it} + \varphi X_{it} + u_i + \varepsilon_{it} + v_t \quad (1)$$

where : G is the growth rate of real GDP per capita; *IslBank* is the indicator of Islamic banking development (ratio of loans, assets, or deposits in Islamic banks to GDP); *FD* is the measure of overall financial development (ratio of private sector credit by commercial banks to GDP); X is the set of control variables described above; u is the country-specific effect, ε the error term and v is the time-specific effect (see Appendix 1 for the source and description of data).

3.2 Methodology

Estimating the growth impact of Islamic banking poses several econometric challenges. First, while Islamic banking is fast growing, the size of Islamic banking development in relation to GDP or banking assets is often zero, or very small in the majority of countries, including Islamic ones. This makes it challenging to identify any statistically significant impact. Second, like for conventional banking, there may be a reverse causality from growth to Islamic finance, raising an endogeneity issue that needs to be addressed in the regressions. Third, the indicators of Islamic bank development are subject to measurement errors as only pure Islamic banks are covered by statistics while Islamic windows (of conventional banks) are not included, due to lack of data. This is because conventional banks often do not separate in their balance sheets and financial reports activities related to Islamic finance from those of conventional banking. The underestimation of Islamic banking development would lead to a downward bias of the estimated coefficient.

In light of the challenges outlined above, we use a range of econometric techniques which include pooling and fixed effects estimator to control for country-specific effects, and the System GMM estimator to control for endogeneity bias. In the following section, we will provide the rationale behind each econometric estimator, as well as what issues they address and what they don't. Before that, we look at the two-way relationship between real GDP per capita growth and each of the three indicators of Islamic banking development. This simple illustration suggests a positive correlation between Islamic banking development and economic growth (Figure 24.4 and Appendix 2). This result holds for the whole sample as well as for the sub-sample of countries with Islamic banks (Figure 24.4).

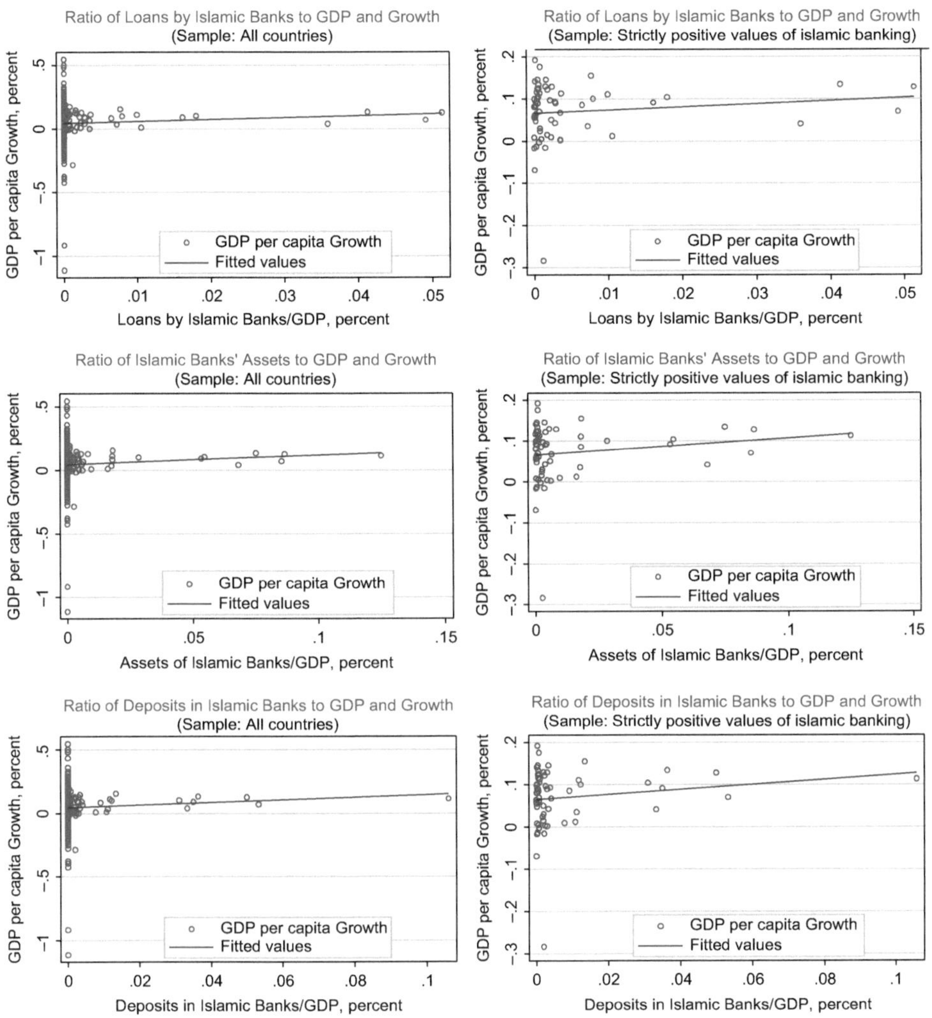

Figure 24.4: Islamic Banking Development and Economic Growth (1990–2010).
Sources: Beck, Demirguc-Kunt and Levine, (2000), Alesina, et al. (2003).
Note: Data are 3-year average over the period 1990–2010.

3.3 Main Results

3.3.1 Pooling and Fixed-effects

Table 24.1 presents the results from the estimations using a pooling and fixed-effect estimator. The pooling estimator runs ordinary least squares (OLS) with the panel data, without regard to which countries they belong. Unlike the pooling estimator,

Table 24.1: Islamic Banking and Growth: Pooling and Fixed Effect Regressions.

	Pooling						Fixed effects					
	(1)	(2)	(3)	(4)	(5)	(6)	(7)	(8)	(9)	(10)	(11)	(12)
Initial GDP per capita	−0.001	−0.012	−0.013	−0.014	−0.014	−0.014	−0.034	−0.102	−0.110	−0.102	−0.101	−0.102
	[0.005]	[0.006]*	[0.006]**	[0.006]**	[0.006]**	[0.006]**	[0.034]	[0.037]***	[0.039]***	[0.037]***	[0.037]***	[0.037]***
Education	0.062	0.059	0.060	0.062	0.062	0.061	0.153	0.165	0.171	0.167	0.166	0.167
	[0.020]***	[0.019]***	[0.019]***	[0.019]***	[0.019]***	[0.019]***	[0.049]***	[0.048]***	[0.048]***	[0.048]***	[0.048]***	[0.048]***
Inflation (log)	−0.084	−0.078	−0.078	−0.080	−0.080	−0.079	−0.085	−0.080	−0.077	−0.080	−0.081	−0.080
	[0.007]***	[0.011]***	[0.011]***	[0.010]***	[0.009]***	[0.010]***	[0.008]***	[0.009]***	[0.008]***	[0.008]***	[0.008]***	[0.008]***
Government consumption/GDP	−0.252	−0.330	−0.328	−0.319	−0.318	−0.321	−0.517	−0.685	−0.670	−0.673	−0.673	−0.671
	[0.101]**	[0.117]***	[0.118]***	[0.118]***	[0.118]***	[0.118]***	[0.218]**	[0.242]***	[0.242]***	[0.241]***	[0.242]***	[0.241]***
Trade openness	−0.026	−0.033	−0.032	−0.030	−0.031	−0.031	0.011	0.007	0.009	0.004	0.004	0.005
	[0.014]*	[0.015]**	[0.015]**	[0.015]**	[0.015]**	[0.015]**	[0.043]	[0.041]	[0.040]	[0.041]	[0.041]	[0.041]
Terms of trade growth	0.119	0.185	0.182	0.180	0.181	0.180	0.111	0.107	0.106	0.107	0.107	0.107
	[0.068]*	[0.067]***	[0.067]***	[0.067]***	[0.067]***	[0.067]***	[0.057]*	[0.056]*	[0.058]*	[0.057]*	[0.057]*	[0.057]*
Quality of Institutions	0.027	0.022	0.022	0.021	0.021	0.021	0.010	0.008	0.008	0.008	0.008	0.008
	[0.004]***	[0.004]***	[0.004]***	[0.004]***	[0.004]***	[0.004]***	[0.006]*	[0.005]	[0.006]	[0.005]	[0.005]	[0.005]
Overall financial development		0.001	0.001	0.001	0.001	0.001		0.002	0.001	0.002	0.002	0.002
		[0.000]***	[0.000]***	[0.000]***	[0.000]***	[0.000]***		[0.001]**	[0.001]**	[0.001]**	[0.001]**	[0.001]**
Loans by Islamic Banks/GDP			0.857						5.254			
			[0.475]*						[2.748]*			

Assets of Islamic Banks/GDP				0.673						0.711		
				[0.202]***						[0.269]**		
Deposits of Islamic Banks/GDP					1.001						0.801	
					[0.233]***						[0.279]***	
Composite indicator of Islamic Banking						0.006						0.008
						[0.002]***						[0.003]**
Constant	−0.024	0.051	0.054	0.059	0.060	0.060	0.172	0.587	0.628	0.584	0.580	0.588
	[0.030]	[0.037]	[0.038]	[0.038]	[0.038]	[0.038]	[0.201]	[0.222]**	[0.232]***	[0.218]**	[0.219]**	[0.219]**
Observations	286	252	252	252	252	252	286	252	252	252	252	252
Number of countries	52	45	45	45	45	45	52	45	45	45	45	45
R-squared	0.34	0.33	0.33	0.34	0.34	0.34	0.32	0.37	0.38	0.37	0.37	0.38

Note: Robust standard errors in brackets; * significant at 10%; ** significant at 5%; *** significant at 1%.

a fixed-effect estimator allows to control for unobservable country-specific effects invariant over time, and which affect a country's economic growth. The results from the pooling estimation are presented in columns 1 to 6, while those of the fixed-effect estimator are shown in columns 7 to 12. For each series of regressions, the first specification runs the baseline model only with the control variables (columns 1 and 7), while the second specification controls for overall financial development (columns 2 and 8) measured by the ratio of private sector credit by commercial banks in percent of GDP. Subsequent specifications (column 3 to 6, 9 to 12) add in turn the 3 indicators of Islamic banking development, as well as a composite indicator constructed as the first principal component of the above 3 indicators of Islamic banking development using the principal component analysis (PCA).

The findings confirm the well-known result found in the economic literature that financial deepening matters for growth. The coefficient is positive and significant in all specifications at least at the 5 percent significance level. More interestingly, for a given level of financial development, Islamic banking is found to stimulate growth. The coefficients for all the indicators of Islamic banking development, including the composite index, are positive and enter the regressions in a statistically significant way, confirming the theoretical predictions, despite the fact that Islamic banking has been small relative to GDP.[221] This result suggests that Islamic banking responds to the specific needs of households and firms, which would have been otherwise unmet and the associated incremental growth would have been forgone. This result also provides evidence that Islamic banking does not appear to crowd out traditional finance – it complements, rather than substitutes for conventional banking – as for a given level of financial development, more Islamic banking raises economic growth.

Regarding the control variables, as expected, accumulation of human capital stimulates economic growth, with the coefficient for primary school enrollment rate highly significant in all regressions. We also tested the secondary school enrollment rate, which gives similar results but missing values on this variable reduce the sample size. Countries with sound macro-economic policies, characterized by low inflation and subdued government current spending, tend to grow faster. This also seems to be the case for countries with positive terms of trade changes and good institutional quality. Further, the hypothesis of economic convergence is supported by the negative and significant sign of the variable initial GDP per capita. In contrast, trade openness seems to have an ambiguous effect on growth, often with a counterintuitive sign, which is not surprising given the contrasting results in previous studies focusing on the growth dividend of trade openness (see Winters, 2004,

221 A cross-country regression averaging the dependent and explanatory variables over the entire period also shows that Islamic banking is positively and significantly correlated with economic growth.

for an overview). Overall, the model helps explain 33 to 38 percent of the variability in economic growth rates.

Although the pooling and fixed effect estimators provide interesting results, the coefficients may be biased in the presence of the endogeneity of the right-hand side variables, in particular with regard to the financial sector indicators. This is particularly relevant for Islamic banking indicators, as their potential endogeneity does not only result from the reverse causality to growth, but also from measurement errors when the full size of Islamic banking development is not captured in the data.[222]

3.3.2 System Generalized Method of Moment

To address the endogeneity issue, not only for the banking indicators, but also for some other explanatory variables, we rely on the System-GMM estimator (dynamic panel Generalized Method-of-Moment) developed by Blundell and Bond (1998). They show that the System-GMM estimator, which simultaneously uses both the difference in the panel data and the data from the original levels specification, produces dramatic increases in both consistency and efficiency relative to the first-differenced GMM developed by Arellano and Bond (1991).[223] We use the one-step System GMM estimator while controlling for sample heterogeneity.[224] Further, to minimize over-fitting of the model, careful attention is paid to the selection of the instruments. For variables considered as predetermined or endogenous, only the first relevant lag is used.[225] To test the validity of the lagged

222 Indeed, measurement errors on Islamic banking indicators would be captured by the error term, which will then be correlated with the Islamic banking variable. This violates the assumption of the fixed-effect estimator whereby the error term is orthogonal to right-hand side variables.

223 For a useful guide on the application of the System GMM estimator to growth models, see Bond, Hoeffler and Temple (2001).

224 The two-step method with the Windmeijer's correction produces comparable results.

225 As commonly done in the literature, we assume that the initial GDP per capita is pre-determined, which rules out contemporaneous correlation with the error term but not feedbacks from past shocks. The variables of inflation, government spending, and more importantly financial sector development and Islamic banking development are treated as endogenous. This allows to address reverse causality issues, measurement errors and omitted variable bias. Given the small size of the sample, not all the variables can be assumed to be endogenous, as the number of instruments grows very quickly to the point that they can weaken the Hansen test. For practical and theoretical reasons, the variables of primary school enrollment, quality of institutions, terms of trade, and trade openness are considered exogenous. Since the first two variables vary little over time, the high persistence makes lagged values poor instruments for the equations in first differences. Although the System GMM is meant to reduce this bias, the use of these instruments leads to a noticeable increase in the Hansen test probability towards the maximum value of 1. For the other two variables, terms of trade and trade openness, we assume that these are likely to be exogenous considering that our sample consists of relatively small and developing countries. All that said, it is worth noting that the quality of the

variables as instruments, we use the standard Hansen test of over-identifying restrictions, where the null hypothesis is that the instrumental variables[226] are not correlated with the residual, and the serial correlation test, where the null hypothesis is that the errors exhibit no second-order serial correlation.

The results from the System GMM estimator presented in Table 24.2 are comparable to those from the fixed-effect estimator.[227] Once again, both overall financial system development and Islamic banking development appear to have a meaningful positive impact on economic growth. The coefficients on financial variables should be interpreted with caution, however, given the relatively small size of Islamic banking compared to the overall financial development, which makes them not directly comparable. One way to make the coefficients more informative by taking into account the scale effect is to estimate the coefficients for the standardized financial variables.[228]

The results (in Appendix 5) suggest that a one standard deviation increase in the overall financial development would lead to about 3.4 percent increase in real GDP per capita growth. For a one standard deviation increase in the ratio of loans by Islamic banks to GDP, the impact on growth would be of 0.5 percent compared to about 0.8 percent for the ratios of assets and deposits of Islamic banks to GDP. However, even with the standardized variables, the regressions do not allow for reliable inference on the magnitude of the growth impact of Islamic banking, although they provide strong evidence on the positive effect of Islamic banking on growth. From that perspective, the fixed effects and GMM System results are quite encouraging, especially given the concern that a significant number of countries in the sample are reported as not having Islamic banking activities (although they might have banks with Islamic finance windows), while in countries where Islamic banks are present, their relative importance in the economy or the banking system is still far from significant.

---

results from the regressions are not affected when all the right-hand side variables are assumed endogenous, except for the Hansen test probability which suffers from the high ratio of the number of instruments over the number of observations.

226 To control for the potency of Islamic-specific law and institutions is inherently difficult, as one wants to make sure that the effect of growth comes from the developments of Islamic banking, as opposed to the evolution of the state and its institutions in general. A good instrumental variable must therefore incorporate a change in institutions when Islamic banks were first incorporated, and could include natural experiments. In this study, we use not only an internal instrument, but also external ones, such as number of Islamic scholars.

227 In addition, neither the Hansen test nor the serial correlation test rejects the null hypothesis of the validity of the instruments.

228 The regressions are rerun with the financial variables rescaled to have a mean of zero and a standard deviation of one

Table 24.2: Islamic Banking and Growth: Dynamic Panel System GMM estimations.

	(1)	(2)	(3)	(4)	(5)	(6)
Initial GDP per capita	0.014	−0.020	−0.025	−0.017	−0.012	−0.014
	[0.019]***	[0.011]***	[0.011]***	[0.011]***	[0.011]***	[0.011]***
Education	0.038	0.072	0.080	0.070	0.063	0.064
	[0.038]	[0.029]**	[0.028]***	[0.029]**	[0.030]**	[0.030]**
Inflation (log)	−0.235	−0.213	−0.219	−0.208	−0.203	−0.203
	[0.104]**	[0.114]*	[0.118]*	[0.107]*	[0.102]**	[0.103]**
Government consumption/GDP	−0.718	−0.713	−0.633	−0.561	−0.666	−0.657
	[0.468]	[0.360]**	[0.353]*	[0.312]*	[0.331]**	[0.337]*
Trade openness	−0.040	−0.048	−0.043	−0.047	−0.048	−0.046
	[0.024]*	[0.023]**	[0.024]*	[0.024]*	[0.025]*	[0.024]*
Terms of trade growth	0.108	0.167	0.175	0.162	0.158	0.159
	[0.082]	[0.078]**	[0.079]**	[0.078]**	[0.079]**	[0.077]**
Quality of Institutions	0.017	0.016	0.015	0.015	0.015	0.015
	[0.007]***	[0.006]***	[0.006]**	[0.006]***	[0.005]***	[0.005]***
Overall financial development		0.002	0.002	0.002	0.002	0.002
		[0.000]***	[0.000]***	[0.000]***	[0.000]***	[0.000]***
Loans by Islamic Banks/GDP			1.395			
			[0.518]***			
Assets of Islamic Banks/GDP				0.900		
				[0.336]***		
Deposits of Islamic Banks/GDP					1.300	
					[0.522]**	
Composite indicator of Islamic Banking						0.007
						[0.003]**
Constant	0.027	0.169	0.188	0.140	0.127	0.134
	[0.070]	[0.062]***	[0.063]***	[0.059]**	[0.057]**	[0.056]**

(continued)

Table 24.2 (continued)

	(1)	(2)	(3)	(4)	(5)	(6)
Observations	286	252	252	252	252	252
Number of countries	52	45	45	45	45	45
AR2 test prob.	0.35	0.70	0.70	0.67	0.75	0.73
Hansen test prob.	0.07	0.36	0.64	0.67	0.67	0.76

Note: Robust standard errors in brackets; * significant at 10%; ** significant at 5%; *** significant at 1%. AR(2): Arellano and Bond test of second order autocorrelation.

3.4 Robustness Analysis and Alternative Specifications

Table 24.3 presents additional regressions to test the robustness of the relationship between Islamic banking development and economic growth using alternative indicators of Islamic Banking. In column 1, we use a step dummy taking 1 for strictly positive values of the composite indicator if Islamic banking and zero otherwise to measure the presence of Islamic banking in a given country. The associated coefficient is positive and significant confirming the above results that for countries with similar level of financial development, those with Islamic banking would experience faster economic growth.

In the subsequent regressions, we test the impact of variables related to the soundness and profitability of Islamic banks on economic growth (columns 2 to 5). It emerges that well-capitalized Islamic banks may have a favorable impact on economic growth, probably because healthy banks are less prone to crisis. With profitability measured by the standard ratios of Return on Equity (ROE) and Return on Assets (ROA), we find that Islamic banks' profitability also benefit economic growth.

Using alternative measures of overall financial development does not change the conclusion that Islamic banking matters for growth. The coefficient for Islamic banking indicators retains its sign and statistical significance when bank and non-bank private credit ratio, a broader measure of financial development, is controlled for (Table 24.4, column 1 to 3).

In addition, we introduce as a measure of overall financial development the ratio of total financial sector assets to GDP and the ratio of total financial sector deposit to GDP respectively in the specification using the corresponding measure for Islamic banking (Table 24.4, column 4 and 5). Both the indicators of overall financial development and Islamic banking continue to be positively and significantly correlated with economic growth.

To test the robustness of the results it is worthwhile to assess their sensitivity to sample composition and the time period. As Islamic banks are likely to emerge and expand in countries with large Muslim population, we restricted the sample to countries with more than 50 percent Muslim population share (column 1 to 3, Table 24.5). In subsequent regressions, this threshold is increased to 75 percent (column 4 to 6, Table 24.5). The results are broadly in line with those obtained for the whole sample and the magnitudes of the coefficients are also comparable,[229] suggesting that countries with smaller share of Muslim population can potentially benefit from Islamic banking. The regressions are rerun with a sample restricted to net oil importer countries (column 7 to 9, Table 24.5) in order to exclude potential outlier countries where

229 The difference is not statistically significant. We cross-checked this by introducing the interaction between Islamic banking development indicators and the share of Muslims in the population in the baseline model, without any conclusive results.

Table 24.3: Dynamic Panel System GMM Estimations with Alternative Indicators of Islamic Banking Development.

	(1)	(2)	(3)	(4)	(5)
Initial GDP per capita	−0.027	−0.026	−0.030	−0.028	−0.028
	[0.012]***	[0.011]***	[0.012]***	[0.012]***	[0.011]***
Education	0.087	0.088	0.089	0.085	0.089
	[0.029]***	[0.027]***	[0.028]***	[0.028]***	[0.027]***
Inflation (log)	−0.219	−0.221	−0.217	−0.218	−0.221
	[0.117]*	[0.119]*	[0.118]*	[0.116]*	[0.117]*
Government consumption/ GDP	−0.683	−0.610	−0.298	−0.667	−0.615
	[0.350]*	[0.327]*	[0.277]	[0.326]**	[0.316]*
Trade openness	−0.043	−0.043	−0.036	−0.042	−0.041
	[0.023]*	[0.022]**	[0.025]	[0.024]*	[0.023]*
Terms of trade growth	0.163	0.180	0.195	0.143	0.161
	[0.078]**	[0.077]**	[0.074]***	[0.080]*	[0.078]**
Quality of Institutions	0.015	0.016	0.014	0.014	0.015
	[0.006]**	[0.006]***	[0.006]**	[0.006]**	[0.006]**
Overall financial development	0.002	0.001	0.001	0.002	0.001
	[0.000]***	[0.000]***	[0.000]***	[0.000]***	[0.000]***
Dummy variable for strictly positive values of Islamic Banking					
Composite indicator of Islamic Banking	0.036				
	[0.017]**				
Soundness and profitability of Islamic banks					
Total capital ratio		0.002			0.001
		[0.001]***			[0.001]*
Return on equity			0.004		
			[0.001]***		
Return on assets				0.026	0.016
				[0.012]**	[0.007]**
Constant	0.200	0.186	0.167	0.207	0.200
	[0.069]***	[0.063]***	[0.063]***	[0.072]***	[0.067]***
Observations	252	252	252	252	252
Number of countries	45	45	45	45	45
AR2 test prob.	0.77	0.77	0.77	0.96	0.91
Hansen test prob.	0.42	0.71	0.68	0.55	0.82

Note: Robust standard errors in brackets; * significant at 10%; ** significant at 5%; *** significant at 1%. AR(2): Arellano and Bond test of second order autocorrelation.

Table 24.4: Use of Different Indicators of Overall Financial Development (System GMM Estimations).

	(1)	(2)	(3)	(4)	(5)
Initial GDP per capita	−0.019	−0.009	−0.007	−0.010	−0.014
	[0.010]***	[0.011]***	[0.011]***	[0.011]***	[0.013]***
Education	0.076	0.065	0.062	0.062	0.069
	[0.029]***	[0.030]**	[0.031]**	[0.030]**	[0.029]**
Inflation (log)	−0.238	−0.221	−0.220	−0.222	−0.227
	[0.134]*	[0.118]*	[0.116]*	[0.098]**	[0.122]*
Government consumption/ GDP	−0.574	−0.588	−0.558	−0.538	−0.321
	[0.267]**	[0.245]**	[0.242]**	[0.263]**	[0.267]
Trade openness	−0.028	−0.031	−0.033	−0.031	−0.058
	[0.021]	[0.020]	[0.022]	[0.020]	[0.024]**
Terms of trade growth	0.169	0.159	0.157	0.158	0.166
	[0.079]**	[0.079]**	[0.078]**	[0.074]**	[0.074]**
Quality of Institutions	0.017	0.018	0.017	0.016	0.010
	[0.006]***	[0.006]***	[0.005]***	[0.005]***	[0.006]*
Overall financial development (banks and nonbanks)	0.001	0.001	0.001		
	[0.000]**	[0.000]*	[0.000]*		
Assets of banks and other financial institutions/GDP				0.050	
				[0.029]*	
Financial system deposits/ GDP					0.134
					[0.037]***
Loans by Islamic Banks/GDP	1.593				
	[0.683]**				
Assets of Islamic Banks/GDP		0.873		1.067	
		[0.373]**		[0.401]***	
Deposits of Islamic Banks/ GDP			1.385		1.507
			[0.616]**		[0.538]***
Constant	0.152	0.103	0.089	0.102	0.111
	[0.062]**	[0.058]*	[0.055]	[0.061]*	[0.065]*
Observations	258	258	258	258	258
Number of countries	45	45	45	45	45
AR2 test prob.	0.38	0.43	0.42	0.39	0.20
Hansen test prob.	0.67	0.65	0.65	0.58	0.60

Note: Robust standard errors in brackets; * significant at 10%; ** significant at 5%; *** significant at 1%. AR(2): Arellano and Bond test of second order autocorrelation.

Islamic banking development might have been fueled by oil money. While the three indicators of Islamic banking remain positively correlated with economic growth, the asset and deposit ratios are significant but not the loan ratio. This probably is a reflection that Islamic banks in net oil importer countries may not enjoy the benefits of large oil money deposits that could be used to scale-up loans compared to net oil exporting countries.

We also run the regressions over different time periods to see if the results hold. First, we considered the period 1996–2010, leaving out the first half of the 1990s where Islamic banks were at the nascent stage. Second, we choose to run the regressions over 1990–2007, excluding the 2008–2010 period which might be affected by structural breaks associated with the 2008 global financial crisis. The conclusion that Islamic banking is favorable to economic growth holds regardless of the period considered (Table 24.6). The regressions over the period 1996–2007 yield similar results.

4 Conclusion

The objective of this chapter was to assess whether the development of Islamic banking is good for economic growth. This is the first study, to our knowledge, that comprehensively assesses this empricial question using robust empirical testing methods. We find that, holding constant the level of financial development and other growth determinants, countries where Islamic banking is developing and hence its impact on growth is measurable, experience faster economic growth than others. This is a powerful result, and robust to various specifications: we use different measures of Islamic banking development, econometric estimators (pooling, fixed effects and System GMM), and control for country and time-specific dummies. This finding is also encouraging as, despite its rapid growth, Islamic banking still represents a relatively small share of the economy and of the overall size of the financial system, and it has yet to reap the benefits from economies of scale. Although our study does not suggest that Islamic banking provides more "bang for the buck" compared to conventional banks; it does, however, establish the positive impact on growth. As indicated, there are uncertainties on the magnitude of the growth effect of Islamic banking, which calls for further research as Islamic banks diffuse further and become larger. Should future studies confirm this finding, the policy implications would be significant. One further avenue of research going forward will be to look at the development of Islamic banking at the local level – comparing localities where Islamic banks are present from those where they are lacking – to confirm more robustly our findings.

As the global crisis has illustrated, conventional banking has many weaknesses – its excessive dependence on leverage being one of them. However, Islamic banking, which is one of the fastest growing segments of global finance, has unique features

Table 24.5: Sensitivity to Sample Composition (System GMM Estimations).

	Muslim population share > 50 percent			Muslim population share > 75 percent			Net oil importer countries		
	(1)	(2)	(3)	(4)	(5)	(6)	(7)	(8)	(9)
Initial GDP per capita	−0.001	−0.001	0.011	0.001	0.003	0.010	−0.014	−0.010	−0.008
	[0.010]***	[0.009]***	[0.010]***	[0.012]***	[0.008]***	[0.009]***	[0.013]***	[0.011]***	[0.012]***
Education	0.051	0.059	0.027	0.071	0.074	0.055	0.090	0.087	0.085
	[0.042]	[0.034]*	[0.037]	[0.049]	[0.036]**	[0.042]	[0.029]***	[0.029]***	[0.029]***
Inflation (log)	−0.143	−0.136	−0.129	−0.131	−0.142	−0.151	−0.179	−0.174	−0.173
	[0.104]	[0.048]***	[0.055]**	[0.109]	[0.049]***	[0.051]***	[0.080]**	[0.076]**	[0.075]**
Government consumption/GDP	−0.760	−0.728	−0.675	−0.710	−0.736	−0.669	−0.561	−0.535	−0.556
	[0.240]***	[0.253]***	[0.206]***	[0.303]**	[0.347]**	[0.282]**	[0.261]**	[0.225]**	[0.243]**
Trade openness	−0.033	−0.028	−0.039	−0.038	−0.030	−0.039	−0.048	−0.046	−0.047
	[0.042]	[0.035]	[0.040]	[0.050]	[0.046]	[0.046]	[0.023]**	[0.024]*	[0.024]*
Terms of trade growth	0.207	0.188	0.204	0.079	0.061	0.062	0.144	0.140	0.140
	[0.107]*	[0.098]*	[0.102]**	[0.077]	[0.065]	[0.071]	[0.099]	[0.096]	[0.096]
Quality of Institutions	0.008	0.008	0.007	0.007	0.007	0.006	0.019	0.019	0.019
	[0.008]	[0.008]	[0.007]	[0.006]	[0.006]	[0.005]	[0.006]***	[0.006]***	[0.006]***
Overall financial development	0.001	0.001	0.001	0.001	0.001	0.001	0.001	0.001	0.001
	[0.001]**	[0.000]**	[0.001]**	[0.001]**	[0.000]**	[0.001]*	[0.001]**	[0.001]**	[0.001]**
Loans by Islamic Banks/GDP	1.196			1.307			2.286		
	[0.440]***			[0.352]***			[4.091]		
Assets of Islamic Banks/GDP		0.650			0.733			1.110	
		[0.302]**			[0.320]**			[0.606]*	
Deposits of Islamic Banks/GDP			0.921			1.252			1.310
			[0.637]			[0.583]**			[0.758]*
Constant	0.091	0.083	0.032	0.058	0.047	0.012	0.097	0.074	0.067
	[0.065]	[0.063]	[0.065]	[0.061]	[0.056]	[0.058]	[0.073]	[0.066]	[0.067]

(continued)

Table 24.5 (continued)

	Muslim population share > 50 percent			Muslim population share > 75 percent			Net oil importer countries		
	(1)	(2)	(3)	(4)	(5)	(6)	(7)	(8)	(9)
Observations	101	101	101	92	92	92	213	213	213
Number of countries	19	19	19	17	17	17	36	36	36
AR2 test prob.	0.12	0.13	0.11	0.13	0.14	0.12	0.38	0.40	0.41
Hansen test prob.	0.99	0.94	0.94	0.98	0.98	0.98	0.90	0.91	0.90

Note: Robust standard errors in brackets; * significant at 10%; ** significant at 5%; *** significant at 1%. AR(2): Arellano and Bond test of second order autocorrelation.

Table 24.6: Sensitivity to Time Periods (System GMM Estimations).

	1996–2010			1990–2007		
	(1)	(2)	(3)	(4)	(5)	(6)
Initial GDP per capita	−0.018	−0.015	−0.010	−0.021	−0.008	−0.008
	[0.011]***	[0.010]***	[0.010]***	[0.013]***	[0.013]***	[0.013]***
Education	0.079	0.078	0.071	0.071	0.052	0.052
	[0.031]**	[0.028]***	[0.030]**	[0.025]***	[0.029]*	[0.029]*
Inflation (log)	−0.218	−0.191	−0.191	−0.221	−0.207	−0.207
	[0.098]**	[0.081]**	[0.076]**	[0.121]*	[0.107]*	[0.107]*
Government consumption/GDP	−0.771	−0.626	−0.744	−0.395	−0.417	−0.387
	[0.369]**	[0.328]*	[0.351]**	[0.332]	[0.305]	[0.304]
Trade openness	−0.046	−0.049	−0.052	−0.040	−0.043	−0.044
	[0.025]*	[0.024]**	[0.026]**	[0.027]	[0.027]	[0.027]
Terms of trade growth	0.255	0.239	0.235	0.172	0.155	0.155
	[0.072]***	[0.070]***	[0.071]***	[0.079]**	[0.080]*	[0.079]*
Quality of Institutions	0.023	0.021	0.021	0.014	0.014	0.014
	[0.007]***	[0.007]***	[0.007]***	[0.007]**	[0.006]**	[0.006]**
Overall financial development	0.002	0.002	0.002	0.001	0.001	0.001
	[0.000]***	[0.000]***	[0.000]***	[0.001]***	[0.000]**	[0.000]**
Loans by Islamic Banks/GDP	1.065			1.504		
	[0.523]**			[0.544]***		
Assets of Islamic Banks/GDP		0.868			0.923	
		[0.371]**			[0.349]***	
Deposits of Islamic Banks/GDP			1.308			1.482
			[0.570]**			[0.573]***
Constant	0.133	0.103	0.093	0.146	0.085	0.079
	[0.062]**	[0.062]*	[0.061]	[0.070]**	[0.067]	[0.065]
Observations	182	182	182	224	224	224
Number of countries	45	45	45	45	45	45
AR2 test prob.	0.60	0.51	0.57	0.70	0.80	0.82
Hansen test prob.	0.62	0.63	0.61	0.28	0.27	0.26

Note: Robust standard errors in brackets; * significant at 10%; ** significant at 5%; *** significant at 1%. AR(2): Arellano and Bond test of second order autocorrelation.

that are highly appropriate for developing countries. In particular, it is based on risk-sharing, making its activities more closely related to the real economy than conventional finance; it is also more flexible against shocks and more inclusive with regards to growth. Not only does Islamic finance help to stimulate growth, but it also appears less prone to risks such as bubbles (Hasan and Dridi, 2010).

This means that many countries that currently suffer from low growth – a feature often present in Muslim countries – may want to further develop this segment of finance. As an initial step, it is essential to develop proper legislation and regulation, as well as the supporting infrastructure, including the necessary skill set. Future areas of research include measuring better Islamic banking development and assessing the impact of Islamic banking on inequality and social development.

References

Abedifar, Pejman, Philip Molyneux, and Amine Tarazi. 2013. "Risk in Islamic Banking." *Review of Finance* 17: 2035–2096.

Acemoglu, Daron, Simon Johnson, and James Robinson. 2004. "Institutions as a Fundamental Cause of Long-Run Growth," NBER Working Paper 10481. National Bureau of Economic Research, Cambridge, MA.

Alesina, Alberto., Arnaud Devleeschauwer, William Easterly, Sergio Kurlat, and Romain Wacziarg. 2003. "Fractionalization." *Journal of Economic Growth* 8(2): 155–94.

Allen, Franklin and Douglas Gale. 2000. *Comparing Financial Systems.* Boston: MIT Press.

Amin Gutiérrez de Piñeres, Sheila and Michael Ferrantino. 2000. *Export Dynamics and Economic Growth in Latin America: A Comparative Perspective.* UK: Ashgate.).

Andersen, Thomas, and Finn Tarp. 2003. "Financial Liberalization, Financial Development and Economic Growth in LDCs." *Journal of International Development* 15(2): 189–209.

Arcand, Jean-Louis, Enrico Berkes, and Ugo Panizza. 2012. "Too Much Finance?" IMF Working Paper No. 12/161. Washington DC: IMF.

Arellano, Manuel and Stephen Bond. 1991. "Some Tests of Specification for Panel Data: Monte Carlo Evidence and an Application to Employment Equations." *Review of Economic Studies* 58: 277–297.

Arellano, Manuel and Olympia Bover. 1995. "Another Look at the Instrumental-Variable Estimation of Error-Components Models." *Journal of Econometrics* 68(1): 29–52.

Beck, Thorsten, Asli Demirguc-Kunt and Ross Levine. 2000. "A New Database on Financial Development and Structure." *World Bank Economic Review* 14: 597–605

Beck, Thorsten, Asli Demirguc-Kunt and Ouarda Merrouche. 2013. "Islamic vs. conventional banking: business model, efficiency and stability." *Journal of Banking and Finance* 37: 433–447.

Benhabib, Jess and Mark Spiegel. 1994. "The role of human capital in economic development: evidence from aggregate cross-country data." *Journal of Monetary Economics* 34: 143–174.

Ben Naceur, Sami, Adolfo Barajas and Alexander Massara. 2015. "Can Islamic Banking Increase Financial Inclusion?" IMF Working Paper No. 31. Washington DC: IMF.

Blundell, Richard and Stephen Bond. 1998, "Initial Conditions and Moment Restrictions in Dynamic Panel Data Models." *Journal of Econometrics* 87(1): 115–143.

Bond, Stephen, Anke Hoeffler and Jonathan Temple. 2001. "GMM Estimation of Empirical Growth Models." CEPR Discussion Paper No. 3048.

Cihak, Martin and Heiko Hesse. 2010. "Islamic Banks and Financial Stability: An Empirical Analysis." *Journal of Financial Services Research* 38: 95–113.

Cleveland, William. 1979. "Robust Locally Weighted Regression and Smoothing Scatterplots." *Journal of the American Statistical Association* 74: 829–836.

Demirguc-Kunt, Asli and Ross Levine. 2009. "Finance and Inequality: Theory and Evidence," NBER Working Paper No. 15275. Cambridge, MA: National Bureau of Economic Research.

Demirguc-Kunt, Asli, Leora Klapper, and Douglas Randall. 2013. "Islamic Finance and Financial Inclusion: Measuring Use of and Demand for Formal Financial Services among Muslim Adults." World Bank Policy Research Paper No. 6642. Washington DC: World Bank.

DiNardo, John and Justin Tobias. 2001. "Nonparametric Density and Regression Estimation," *Journal of Economic Perspectives* 15(4):11–28.

Easterly, Willaim and Aart Kraay. 2000. "Small States, Small Problems? Income, Growth, and Volatility in Small States." *World Development* 28: 2013–27.

Easterly, William, Ariell Reshef, and Julia M. Schwenkenberg. 2009. "The Power of Exports." World Bank Policy Research Working Paper Series 5081.

Gewal, Baljeet Kaur. 2013, "Overview of the Islamic Financial Landscape: Globally and in Europe." Kuwait Finance House mimeo, accessed June 15, 2018

Greenwood, Jeremy and Boyan Jovanovic. 1990, "Financial Development, Growth, and the Distribution of Income," *Journal of Political Economy* 98(5): 1076–1107.

Guillaumont Jeanneney, Sylviane, and Kangi Kpodar. 2006. "Développement financier, instabilité financière et croissance économique," *Économie et Prévision* 174 (3): 87–111.

Gurley, John and Edward Shaw. 1960. *Money in a Theory of Finance*. Washington D.C.: The Brookings Institution.

Hassan, Maher and Jemma Dridi. 2010. "The Effects of the Global Crisis on Islamic and Conventional Banks: A Comparative Study." IMF Working Paper No. 201 (Washington DC: IMF)

Honohan, Patrick. 2001. "Islamic Financial Intermediation: Economic and Prudential Considerations." *Development Research Group and Financial Sector Strategy Department mimeo*, Washington DC: World Bank.

Ichimura, Hidehik and Petra Todd. 2007. "Implementing Nonparametric and Semiparametric Estimators." In *Handbook of Econometrics*, edited by J.J. Heckman and E.E. Leamer, Vol. 6, Chap. 74.

Imam, Patrick and Kangi Kpodar. 2013. "Islamic Banking: How has it Expanded?" *Emerging Markets Finance and Trade* 49: 112–137.

Iqbal, Zamir and Abbas Mirakhor. 2013. Economic Development and Islamic Finance. Washington DC: World Bank.

Jansen, Marion. 2004. "Income Volatility in Small and Developing Economies: Export Concentration Matters." WTO Discussion Paper 3. Geneva: World Trade Organization.

King Robert and Ross Levine. 1993a. "Finance and Growth: Schumpeter Might Be Right," *Quarterly Journal of Economics* 108: 717–738.

King Robert and Ross Levine. 1993b. "Finance, Entrepreneurship, and Growth: Theory and Evidence," *Journal of Monetary Economics* 32: 513–542.

King Robert and Ross Levine. 1993c. "Financial Intermediation and Economic Development," In *Financial Intermediation in the Construction of Europe*, edited by Mayer Colin and Xavier Vives: 156–189. London: Centre for Economic Policy Research.

Khan, Feisal. 2010. "How 'Islamic' is Islamic Banking?" *Journal of Economic Behavior and Organization* 76: 805–820.

Levine, Ross. 1997. "Financial Development and Economic Growth: Views and Agenda," *Journal of Economic Literature* 35(3): 688–726.

Levine, Ross, Norman Loayza, and Thorsten Beck. 2000. "Financial Intermediation and Growth: Causality and Causes." *Journal of Monetary Economics* 46(1): 31–77.

Levine, Ross. 2002. "Bank-based or Market-based Financial Systems: Which is Better?" NBER Working Paper No. 9138. Cambridge, MA: National Bureau of Economic Research.

Levine, Ross. 2005. "Finance and Growth: Theory and Evidence" In *Handbook of Economic Growth* Vol, edited by Philippe Aghion and Steven Durlauf: 865–934. Amsterdam: North-Holland Elsevier.

McKinnon Ronald. 1973. *Money and Capital in Economic Development*. Washington D.C.: The Brooking Institution.

Mirakhor, Abbas. 2010. "Whither Islamic Finance? Risk Sharing in An Age of Crises," MPRA Paper 56341, University Library of Munich, Germany.

Modigliani, Francesco and Merton Miller. 1958. "The Cost of Capital, Corporation Finance and the Theory of Investment." *American Economic Review* 48: 261–297.

Moody's. 2009. "The Liquidity/Leverage Trade-Off for Islamic Banks – and its Impact on Their Ratings" New York: Moody's Investors Service.

Nolan, Marcus. 2003. "Religion, Culture, and Economic Performance" Peterson Institute Working Paper Series WP03-8. Washington DC: PIIE.

Panizza, Ugo. 2014. "Financial Development and Economic Growth: Known Knowns, Known Unknowns, and Unknown Unknowns," *Revue d'Economie du Développement* 22(2): 33–66.

Pritchett, Lant. 1997. "Where Has All the Education Gone?" Working Paper No. 1581. Washington D.C: World Bank.

Rajan, Raghuram, and Luigi Zingales. 1998. "Financial Dependence and Growth." *American Economic Review* 88(3): 559–86.

Robinson, Joan. 1952. "The Generalization of the General Theory," in *the Rate of Interest and Other Essays*. London: Macmillan.

Schumpeter, Joseph. 1934. *Theory of Economic Development: An Inquiry into Profits, Capital, Credit, Interest, and the Business Cycle*. Cambridge, MA: Harvard University Press.

Shaw, Edward. 1973. "Financial Deepening in Economic Development," New York: Oxford University Press.

Winters, Alan. 2004. "Trade Liberalisation and Economic Performance: An Overview," *Economic Journal* 114: 4–21.

Appendices

Appendix 1: Variable Definition and Sources.

Variables	Definitions	Sources
GDP per capita growth	Change in the ratio of real Gross Domestic Product (GDP) divided by the size of the population.	
Inflation (log)	Change in consumer price index (CPI).	
Government consumption/GDP	General government current expenditure divided by GDP.	International Monetary Fund
Terms of trade growth	Change in terms of trade index calculated as the percentage ratio of the export unit value indexes to the import unit value indexes, measured relative to the base year 2000.	
Education (primary)	The ratio of total enrollment in primary education, regardless of age, to the population of the age group that officially corresponds to the primary education level.	World Bank (Word Development Indicators)
Trade openness	The sum of exports and imports of goods and services measured as a share of GDP.	
Rule of law	The confidence of citizens in law, and the extent that they abide by the rules of the society, such as contract enforcement, property rights, police, and court.	World Bank (World Bank Governance Indicators)
Overall financial development (Bank private credit ratio)	Credit by deposit money banks to the private sector divided by GDP.	
Private credit by banks and other financial institutions/GDP	Demand, time and saving deposits in deposit money banks and other financial institutions as a share of GDP	Beck, Demirgüç-Kunt and Levine (2000); 2013 Financial Development and Structure Dataset
Assets of banks and other financial institutions/GDP	Credit by deposit money banks and other financial institutions to the private sector as a percentage of GDP	

Appendix 1 (continued)

Variables	**Definitions**	**Sources**
Financial system deposits/GDP	Claims on domestic real nonfinancial sector by deposit money banks and other financial institutions as a share of GDP	
Share of Muslims in the population	Numbers of muslims divided by the size of the population.	Alesina, et al. (2003)
Loans by Islamic Banks/GDP	Total loans by Islamic Banks divided by GDP	
Assets of Islamic Banks/GDP	Total assets of Islamic Banks divided by GDP	
Deposits in Islamic Banks/GDP	Total deposits in Islamic Banks divided by GDP	
Capital ratio of Islamic banks	Capital of Islamic banks as of share of their total assets	Bankscope database
Return on equity of Islamic banks	Net income of Islamic Banks as a percentage of shareholders equity	
Return on assets of Islamic banks	Net income of Islamic Banks as a percentage of their assets	

Appendix 2: Correlation Matrix.

		(1)	(2)	(3)	(4)	(5)	(6)	(7)	(8)	(9)	(10)	(11)	(12)	(13)	(14)	(15)	(16)	(17)
GDP per capita growth	(1)	1.00																
Education (primary)	(2)	0.21	1.00															
Inflation (log)	(3)	−0.35	−0.07	1.00														
Government consumption/GDP	(4)	−0.06	0.06	−0.10	1.00													
Trade openness	(5)	0.04	0.29	−0.14	0.22	1.00												
Terms of trade growth	(6)	0.15	0.06	−0.08	−0.02	0.12	1.00											
Rule of law	(7)	0.36	0.19	−0.18	0.27	0.09	−0.01	1.00										
Overall financial development (Bank private credit ratio)	(8)	0.28	0.21	−0.16	0.22	0.42	0.01	0.27	1.00									
Loans by Islamic Banks/GDP	(9)	0.10	0.04	0.00	0.03	−0.02	0.06	0.12	0.10	1.00								
Assets of Islamic Banks/GDP	(10)	0.11	0.01	0.06	0.00	−0.05	0.05	0.11	0.05	0.78	1.00							
Deposits in Islamic Banks/GDP	(11)	0.11	0.01	0.07	0.00	−0.04	0.04	0.11	0.05	0.62	0.97	1.00						
Capital ratio of Islamic banks	(12)	0.16	0.03	−0.05	0.10	0.19	−0.01	0.14	0.35	0.43	0.36	0.29	1.00					
Return on equity of Islamic banks	(13)	0.22	0.03	−0.02	−0.12	−0.03	−0.05	0.07	0.22	0.39	0.36	0.31	0.56	1.00				
Return on assets of Islamic banks	(14)	0.12	0.05	−0.01	0.12	0.03	0.10	0.16	0.18	0.48	0.41	0.35	0.27	0.24	1.00			
Private credit by banks and other financial institutions/GDP	(15)	0.21	0.22	−0.14	0.27	0.32	0.02	0.21	0.94	0.10	0.05	0.05	0.26	0.17	0.15	1.00		
Assets of banks and other financial institutions/GDP	(16)	0.20	0.23	−0.14	0.27	0.26	0.04	0.21	0.90	0.07	0.03	0.03	0.25	0.17	0.13	0.97	1.00	
Financial system deposits/GDP	(17)	0.29	0.25	−0.16	0.20	0.40	0.06	0.34	0.89	0.13	0.08	0.07	0.41	0.26	0.17	0.79	0.83	1.00

Appendix 3: Summary Statistics.

Variables	Obs.	Mean	Std. Dev.	Min	Max
GDP per capita growth	286	0.05	0.09	−0.39	0.33
Education (primary)	286	0.93	0.24	0.26	1.56
Inflation (log)	286	0.13	0.35	−0.05	4.48
Government consumption/GDP	286	0.14	0.05	0.04	0.41
Trade openness	286	0.71	0.35	0.14	2.14
Terms of trade growth	286	0.00	0.07	−0.37	0.28
Rule of law	286	3.23	1.13	0.14	6.00
Overall financial development (Bank private credit ratio)	252	23.1	21.5	0.4	103.8
Loans by Islamic Banks/GDP	286	0.001	0.005	0.000	0.051
Assets of Islamic Banks/GDP	286	0.002	0.011	0.000	0.125
Deposits in Islamic Banks/GDP	286	0.001	0.008	0.000	0.106
Capital ratio of Islamic banks	286	2.18	8.15	0.00	66.17
Return on equity of Islamic banks	286	1.59	5.71	−13.06	47.12
Return on assets of Islamic banks	286	0.10	0.64	−4.07	3.34
Private credit by banks and other financial institutions/GDP	286	28.1	30.7	0.4	168.2
Assets of banks and other financial institutions/GDP	286	0.34	0.35	0.00	2.08
Financial system deposits/GDP	286	0.32	0.25	0.01	1.15

Appendix 4: Country Sample.

DZA	Algeria*	MWI	Malawi
AGO	Angola	MYS	Malaysia*
BGD	Bangladesh*	MLI	Mali*
BWA	Botswana	MNG	Mongolia
BFA	Burkina Faso*	MAR	Morocco*
CMR	Cameroon*	MOZ	Mozambique*
CHN	China	NAM	Namibia
ZAR	Congo, Dem. Rep.	NER	Niger*
COG	Congo, Rep.	PAK	Pakistan*
CIV	Côte d'Ivoire*	PNG	Papua New Guinea
EGY	Egypt, Arab Rep.*	PHL	Philippines
ETH	Ethiopia	SEN	Senegal*
GAB	Gabon*	ZAF	South Africa
GMB	Gambia, The*	LKA	Sri Lanka
GHA	Ghana	SDN	Sudan*
GIN	Guinea*	SYR	Syrian Arab Republic*
GNB	Guinea-Bissau*	TZA	Tanzania
IND	India	THA	Thailand
IDN	Indonesia*	TGO	Togo*

Appendix 4 (continued)

IRN	Iran, Islamic Rep.*	TUN	Tunisia*
JOR	Jordan*	TUR	Turkey*
KEN	Kenya	UGA	Uganda*
LBN	Lebanon*	VNM	Vietnam
LBR	Liberia	YEM	Yemen, Rep.*
LBY	Libya*	ZMB	Zambia
MDG	Madagascar	ZWE	Zimbabwe

Note: *Organization of Islamic Cooperation (OIC) members.

Appendix 5: Islamic Banking and Growth: Dynamic Panel System GMM estimations with Standardized Coefficients for the Financial Variables.

	(1)	(2)	(3)	(4)
Initial GDP per capita	−0.025	−0.016	−0.011	−0.018
	[0.011]***	[0.011]***	[0.011]***	[0.011]***
Education	0.079	0.068	0.061	0.070
	[0.029]***	[0.029]**	[0.031]**	[0.028]**
Inflation (log)	−0.218	−0.204	−0.199	−0.189
	[0.118]*	[0.105]*	[0.100]**	[0.090]**
Government consumption/GDP	−0.641	−0.581	−0.681	−0.491
	[0.354]*	[0.318]*	[0.339]**	[0.286]*
Trade openness	−0.043	−0.046	−0.048	−0.051
	[0.024]*	[0.024]**	[0.024]**	[0.025]**
Terms of trade growth	0.174	0.159	0.155	0.172
	[0.077]**	[0.077]**	[0.078]**	[0.075]**
Quality of Institutions	0.016	0.015	0.015	0.015
	[0.006]**	[0.006]***	[0.005]***	[0.006]***
Standardized coefficients				
Overall financial development	0.034	0.032	0.032	0.034
	[0.009]***	[0.008]***	[0.009]***	[0.008]***
Loans by Islamic Banks/GDP	0.005			
	[0.002]***			
Assets of Islamic Banks/GDP		0.008		
		[0.003]***		
Deposits of Islamic Banks/GDP			0.008	
			[0.003]**	
Composite indicator of Islamic Banking				0.007
				[0.003]***
Constant	0.223	0.171	0.160	0.171
	[0.067]***	[0.062]***	[0.059]***	[0.067]**
Observations	252	252	252	252
Number of countries	45	45	45	45

Appendix 5 (continued)

	(1)	(2)	(3)	(4)
AR2 test prob.	0.70	0.69	0.75	0.63
Hansen test prob.	0.73	0.74	0.76	0.63

Note: Robust standard errors in brackets; * significant at 10%; ** significant at 5%; *** significant at 1%. AR (2): Arellano and Bond test of second order autocorrelation.

Adama Dieye

Chapter 25: An Alternative Model of Economic Stabilization and Growth for Developing Countries

1 Introduction

Since the mid-1990s and due to the worsening financial, economic, and social conditions in IMF and World Bank program countries, there is a constant search for alternative model to orthodox economic stabilization models. These alternative models reflect a shift in policy choices (Blanchard 2010; Stiglitz 2011). There are indeed calls for rethinking macroeconomic policy.[230] A major component of this debate has been the fact that past stabilization policies designed and financed by the IMF and the World Bank as well as other bilateral/multilateral donors have not been effective in achieving stabilization and promoting growth for developing and emerging market economies. Particularly, many Muslim countries still suffer poor economic growth rates, declining infrastructure, critical unemployment rates, and unsustainable external debt (Chapra 1995, 2007, 2008; Ahmed 2002; Mirakhor and Krichene 2009; Rehman and Askari 2010; Askari et al. 2015).

There are strong concerns about the efficiency of IMF policy prescriptions following the onset of financial crises leading to economic downturns excessive fiscal deficits, financial imbalances, rising unemployment rates and worsening poverty[231] (Edwards 1989; Easterly 1999, 2002, 2003; Agenor 2002; Barro and Lee 2002; Krugman 2009; Niels and Brigitte 2009; Blanchard and Dell'Ariccia 2010). The IMF policies are based on fiscal and monetary austerity, and they are conducive to the aggravation of financial crises and even debt-deflation and depression (Wolfson 2002). Even though IMF consensus is officially expressed about short-term structural constraints, stabilization policies remain dominant in financial program operations. The focus is indeed made only on some financial variables such as the external current account, fiscal balance, inflation, monetary aggregates, and public debt.

There is clear evidence that many Muslim countries, including Senegal, on which this analytical study is based, suffer from similar problems of economic fragility, related to the IMF programs. Countries that manage their economies under the IMF and World Bank regime are in dire need of finding alternative economic

230 In the wake of the U.S. credit crisis, the IMF organized a series of international conferences on the broad theme of "Rethinking Macro Policy".

231 Critics raise also issues with the IMF organization and mandate, reform in the 1970s, political-influence on programs design, conditionality and patterns of policy lending, (Mills and Nallari 1992; Steiwand and Stone 2008; Reinhart and Trebesch 2016).

https://doi.org/10.1515/9783110587920-025

models that have the potential to achieve higher and sustainable economic growth, and to improve social justice and human development. A system based on the economic principles derived from the Qur'an and the Sunnah of the Prophet (sawa) can provide an ideal model of macroeconomic stability and economic growth for Muslim and non-Muslim countries (Mirakhor and Askari 2017).

The objective of this empirical study is to demonstrate that it is possible to consider the conceptualization and operationalization of macroeconomic policy adjustment from the perspective of Islamic economics. The proposed model falls within the class of traditional models of adjustment policies. The remainder of the chapter is structured as follows. Section 2 reviews the literature about economic growth and its linkages with institutions, macroeconomic policies and social issues. Section 3 addresses the methodological issues related to the estimation and simulation of stabilization and growth in an Islamic economic system. The empirical illustration of these results is based on the macroeconomic framework of stabilization and growth for Senegal. Some policy recommendations are discussed in Section 4. The final section concludes and provides suggestions for the modelling of macroeconomic policies from the perspective of Islamic economics.

2 Literature Review confrmed

The *Qur'an* is the source of all Islamic paradigms. The *Qur'an* prescribes the general rules of behavior for individuals and societies that cover the principle facets of life, including economic and financial achievements. In particular, the *Qur'an* (S7: 96) defines the necessary and sufficient condition for economic prosperity in terms of compliance with the set of religious and behavioral norms prescribed in the *Quran*:[232]

> S 7: 96: "And if only the people of the cities had believed and feared Allah, We would have opened upon them blessings from the heaven and the earth; but they denied [the messengers], so We seized them for what they were earning."

The focus of Islamic economics are behavioral rules and the role of institutions in consistence with the development of the new field of studies referred to as New Institutional Economics (NIE) (Williamson 2000; North 1993). According to Ahmed (2002) and Mirakhor and Idris (2009), there are issues that are shared between conventional and Islamic economics including property rights and contracts. From the methodological perspective, these issues may be rather challenging but they remain important for a better understanding of the impact of institutions on economic performance. The focus is made on property rights institutions, protection of political rights and the quality of institutions, which are conducive to economic growth. With respect

232 The English translation of verses is from Sahih International.

to institutions, research has found evidence that leaders have a large causative influence on the economic outcomes of their nations (World Bank 2002; Acemoglu and Johnson 2005; Jones and Olken 2004; Aghion, et al. 2005; Acemoglu 2009; Afonso and Aubyn 2011; Cristina and Levieuge 2013). From a panel data analysis, Asimakopoulos and Karavias (2015) find a significant and non-linear relationship between public expenditure and economic growth, which can be derived by an inverted "U-shaped" curve.[233] This suggests that an increase in government spending beyond which the impact on growth would turn negative can only be effective until a certain threshold.[234]

The design of macroeconomic policies remains also a controversial issue (IMF 1987, 2006, 2012; Bruno 1988; Rana and Lim 1999; Ghosh et al. 2005; Kentikelenis et al. 2016). The design of fiscal policies and the examination of related issues including the pace, composition, sequence and timing of reforms are the subject of many debates (Portes and Wren-Lewis 2014; Alesina and Ardagna 2012; Jonung 2014; Blot et al. 2015; Yang et al. 2015). Alesina and Ardagna (2012) suggest that pro-growth policies can reduce the likelihood of downturns associated with expenditure-based adjustments. In contrast, Blot et al. (2015) argue that until short-term nominal interest rate reach the zero-lower-boundary spending-based consolidations are likely to be less effective than tax-based ones. This is bound to affect public finance sustainability and make economic growth more costly.

Following the seminal work of Aschauer (1989), the emphasis still remains on the impact of public investment on growth and output. Empirical evidence suggests that public expenditures in infrastructure is likely to be associated with higher returns to private sector productivity, GDP growth, and even shrinking fiscal deficits (Belloc and Vertova 2006; Bello 2006; Bivens 2012; Duran-Fernandez and Santo 2014; Estache and Garsous 2012; Pereira and Andraz 2013; Creel and Saraceno 2015). In particular, Duran-Fernandez and Santo (2014) provide evidence about the positive elasticities of aggregate output with respect to public infrastructure expenditure that are close to the estimates by Bivens (2014).

The related literature includes also some empirical studies that suggest the existence of a relation between infrastructure development and income growth as well as distributive equity. Indeed, material progress and growth show that overall, studies find positive effects of infrastructure development on income growth and,

---

233 The "U-shaped" curve is widely referred to as the "Barro, Armey, Rahn, and Scully (BARS)" curve.

234 Asimakopoulos and Karavias (2015) estimate the optimal level of government size defined as general government final expenditure as a share of output that maximizes economic growth at 18.04%. It amounts 19.12% for developing countries, and 17.96% for developed ones. The thresholds from panel data analyses are 16% and 17.3% according to Karras (1997) and Gunalp and Dincer (2005), respectively. The evidence from the country-specific studies by Chen and Lee (2005), and Altunc and Aydin (2013) show that the threshold estimation ranges between 11% to 25%.

more tentatively, on distributive equity. Results of recent studies Hooper et al. (2017) suggest that there are causal effects associated with the growth in infrastructure spending and education leading to a reduction in inequality. Still, the precise mechanisms through which these effects accrue, and their full impact on welfare, remain relatively unexplored (Raychaudhuri and Prabir 2010; Odondo and Kalu 2016).

From the practical perspective, there are also important issues related to the design of macroeconomic policies, and the financial inclusion-growth nexus as well as the link between economic growth, inequality, and poverty. There are indeed some studies that examine the nexus between growth and financial development (Rioja et al. 2004; Demirguc-Kunt et al. 2009, 2011; Levine 2005, 2011; Beck 2012). In a broad survey of theoretical and empirical literature, Levine (2005) notes the existence of a positive link between the functioning of the financial system and long-term growth. However, more recent studies using panel threshold methods suggest that financial development is favorable to growth only up to a certain level, beyond which further development turns negative (Law et al. 2013, 2014). With respect to social issues, the empirical literature places a growing emphasis on the association between access to finance, including financial inclusion and inequality (Demirguc-Kunt et al., 2009, 2011; Stijn and Enrico, 2007; World Bank, 2014).[235,236] Honohan (2004) suggests that growth driven by banking depth is empirically associated with lower poverty ratios. However, it can be also argued that financial depth alone needs to be supplemented with other important institutional environment such as the legal and regulatory framework, and ownership rules. Mookerjee and Kalipioni (2010) provide evidence that leads support to the proposition that financial development and broader access to the financial system help to mitigate income inequality.

From the perspective of Islamic finance, it is noted that the risk-sharing principle promotes the distribution and allocation of risk according to individual levels of risk tolerance rather than its concentration among borrowers and the needy segments of the society. Many studies using panel approach suggest that the development of Islamic banking favors macroeconomic efficiency (Gheeraert and Weill 2014) and economic growth (Gudarzi and Dastan 2013; Imam and Kpodar 2015, Abedifar et al. 2016). In contrast, other studies based on cointegration analysis provide conflicting evidence about the association between Islamic finance and economic growth (Furqani and Mulyany 2009; Abduh and Chowdhury 2012; Nejib and Amine 2015). With respect to the issue of financial inclusion, recent empirical studies related to the OIC countries offer rather weak evidence about the potentially positive impact of Islamic finance on financial inclusion. The weak evidence may be

235 Financial inclusion can be broadly defined as the economic state where individuals and firms are not denied access to basic financial services based on motivations other than efficiency criteria.
236 Earlier conceptual studies (Galor and Zeira 1993; Banerjee and Newman 1993) suggest a strong negative relationship between inequality and financial sector development.

partially reflective of data issues (Demirguc-Kunt et al. 2013; Naceur et al. 2015) as well as deviations from risk-sharing Islamic finance (Alaabed 2016). Other works by Mohieldin et al. (2012) and Mirakhor (2012) argue that Islamic finance could offer a large spectrum of instruments and unconventional approaches which, if implemented according to the Islamic tenets, can lead to poverty alleviation and reduction of inequality, promote financial inclusion, and provide viable modes of interest-free financing for capital accumulation.

At the macro level, there are several early studies focused on the modelling of the Islamic economy and assessing its consistency (Khan 1984; Khan 1986; Mirakhor and Iqbal 1988; Mirakhor 1993; Naqvi 1997). A review of the conceptual models of Islamic economy, Tahir (2009) points out the main limitations such as the narrow focus on closed economy, and lack of analysis of long-run dynamics to the steady state and economic stability.[237]

Further, studies extend the analysis to open economy models. Mirakhor (1993) and Askari et al. (2014) examine the short-term and long-term equilibrium conditions for the general cases of closed economy, open economy with trading in goods only, and complete open Islamic economy with trading in goods and equity shares. The major implications of the latter model are as follows. Firstly, the rate of return in the real sector plays a determinant role in the equilibrium market conditions in an Islamic economy.[238] Secondly, the economy moves from short-run equilibrium to a stable long-run equilibrium from any initial point as a result of the absence of interest and debt, and the full flexibility of markets. Also, Shaukat et al. (2013) demonstrate the viability of a risk-sharing model based on Islamic finance, which constitutes an alternative to the debt-based models.

There are also attempts to translate the Qur'anic injunctions into general rules that govern aggregate consumption (Khan 1984; 2013; Iqbal 1985; Hasan 1997, 2007) and aggregate investment (Sattar 1991). There is scant literature, however, about the components of aggregate demand and the consumption and investment functions.

From the perspective of macroeconomic policy-making, the conduct of fiscal and monetary policies in an Islamic system is the subject of increasing interest. With respect to fiscal policy, recent studies (Othman and Mirakhor 2013; Askari et al. 2015) underscore the importance of simplicity, as well as efficiency and fairness in revenue

237 It is noted that early studies of Islamic economic models used the standard analytical framework IS-LM to examine the equilibrium conditions of an Islamic economy where interest is replaced by the rate of return to the real sector.

238 Askari et al. (2014) underscore that: "*In an Islamic financial system, the rate of return to capital is neither a purely monetary phenomenon determined in the money market by the demand and supply of money, as in a Keynesian model, nor is it purely determined by the real demand for and supply of real savings, as in the Classical model. Instead, the rate of return to capital is determined by the rate of return to ownership position (equity) related to marginal product of capital as well as to the portfolio balance equilibrium*".

collection. These studies suggest a tax structure with a mixture of income tax (20%) and wealth tax (2.5%). Regarding the conduct of monetary policy in an Islamic economy, earlier conceptual works by Mirakhor and Iqbal (1988), and Khan and Mirakhor (1989) address the monetary transmission mechanism based on the rate of return of capital to real sector as policy anchor. More recent studies examine these issues in dual financial systems where Islamic and conventional institutions coexist (Solê 2007; Cevik and Joshua 2011; Basu et al. 2015; Zulkhibri 2016; Khatat 2016).

Thus, the empirical literature on Islamic macroeconomic models is rather scant. This observation stands in contrast to the growing empirical studies in Islamic finance, which address the relation between theory and practice (Iqbal and Muljawan 2007; Askari et al. 2014). Since the macroeconomic variables used in the examination of adjustment modeling for many IMF and World Bank country programs have not been effective, this chapter proposes a different policy framework where the standard variables representing macroeconomic adjustment policy are substituted by their respective proxies in Islamic economics.

3 Simulation Analysis and Data Description

The empirical modelling of an Islamic economy faces several challenging issues. Firstly, historical data on some macroeconomic variables do not exist, precluding thereby the examination of empirical relationships. Secondly, since the rules of behavior are internalized by individuals, their formalization and quantification for modelling purposes are constrained by the lack of appropriate methodologies that can handle subjective variables. Due to these measurement problems, the recourse can be made to simulation techniques which are widely used to analyze the effects of macroeconomic policies (Bourguignon et al. 1989; Caivano et al. 2011; Orphanides and Williams 2011; Pesaran and Smith 2014).

It is possible to perform the simulation exercise with respect to an Islamic economy on the basis of the two most important and quantifiable rules regarding the prohibition of interest rate and debt-based financing and their substitution with the rate of return to the real sector and risk-sharing equity financing, respectively. Hence, it can be assumed that the rules of conduct require only an appropriate legal framework, adequate policies and policy-legislative actions, effective structure of incentives. These behavioral rules are also considered within the set of policy recommendations.

The optimal conditions for macroeconomic stability and growth in an Islamic economy can be modelled through programming methods. The conditions of macroeconomic stability are considered under assumption of appropriate levels of domestic inflation fiscal deficit and external current account. According to Mikelsen

(1998), the target growth rate must remain sustainable over the long term, and this implies that fiscal and monetary policies should contain the short-term fluctuations of output growth within the boundaries of its long-term drift.

In the absence of well-functioning financial markets, the rate of return on capital i(t) is used as proxy for investment return to the real sector, following Bai Chong-En et al. (2006). The macroeconomic nominal return $i(t)$ is computed as:

$$i(t) = \frac{\alpha(t)}{(P_K(t).K(t))/(P_Y(t).Y(t))} - \delta(t) + \hat{P}_K(t) \tag{1}$$

where the numerator $\alpha(t)$ represents capital share in total output calculated as unity minus the labor share, $P_Y(t)$ denotes the price of aggregate output $Y(t)$, $P_K(t)$ refers to the price of aggregate capital stock $K(t)$, and $\delta(t)$ its average depreciation rate, $\hat{P}_K(t)$ the average growth rate of the price of aggregate capital stock. Assuming a constant price of capital, the rate of return can be extracted as the ratio of capital share in total income divided by the ratio of capital output minus the depreciation rate.

The rate of capital depreciation is calculated using the geometric form used in previous studies of asset depreciation including Fraumeni (1997), and Baldwin et al. (2005). The periodic depreciation (D_t) term can be expressed as:

$$D_t = \delta.(1 - \delta)^{t-1} \tag{2}$$

where δ represents a constant rate of depreciation. Given the focus of this analysis and developing economies, the simulation is based on the economic conditions of Senegal, which is a developing African country with predominantly Muslim population. Thus, the parameter δ is set to 5% following Issoufou et al. (2014).

The design of the macroeconomic analysis requires the specification and estimation of reduced-form models that relates real GDP growth rate (GYR) to the investment rate of return (IRR), and the investment rate of return to the policy variables (PV). The reduced-form equations are specified and estimated using the Autoregressive Distributed Lag (ARDL) model in its following functional form (Pesaran and Smith 2014)[239]

$$GYR = f(IRR,\ IEV) \tag{3}$$

$$IRR = f(PV,\ IEV) \tag{4}$$

where PV represents a given policy variable and IEV is a proxy variable for external environment such as capital inflows, terms of trade, or economic growth rate

239 The design of the macroeconomic model involves the identification of a set of endogenous variables that constitute the policy targets and the definition of instrumental variables that fall under the control of policy-makers.

(World or Euro Zone). Given its membership in the West African Economic and Monetary Union (WAEMU), monetary and exchange rate policies are addressed at regional level. Thus, the policy variables in Equation (4) are reduced to fiscal policy, represented by the ratio of public investment to the GDP.

The simulation of short-term economic conditions is conducted in three steps. The calibration of model parameters is needed to test the extent to which the historical economic and financial patterns can be replicated. The setting the medium-term baseline scenario (2015–2019) is made under the assumption that previous macroeconomics policies remain unchanged and that there are no fundamental external shocks. The simulation of economic policy experiments for the same period allows for the analysis of possible outcomes compared to the baseline scenario projections, and the examination of the expected results from the implementation of the IMF policies.

The main economic data are available from the Ministry of Economic and Finance, the Central Bank of West African States (BCEAO), the International Monetary Fund, the World Bank and the Penn World Tables (Feenstra et al. 2013).

4 Modelling Macroeconomic Conditions

4.1 Analytical Framework

As noted earlier, it is possible to analytically examine the properties of an Islamic open economy with fixed exchange rate and trading commodities, and equity assets following the seminal work of Askari and Mirakhor (2014). Under the assumptions that the forces of demand and supply operate freely leading to market clearing, and that the rate of return to capital equilibrates investment and savings, the theoretical framework proposed by Askari and Mirakhor (2014) can be also adopted to include the public sector account, reduced-form equations for the real GDP growth rate and for the investment rate of return expressed as a function of fiscal policy in terms of public investment. It is possible to include also the behavioral relations for consumption, import and export of goods and nonfactor services, fiscal revenues and money demand.

With all macroeconomic variables expressed in real terms, the equilibrium conditions in the goods and services market can be described as follows:

$$Y = C + I + (X - M) \tag{5}$$

$$C = C_P + C_G \tag{6}$$

$$I = I_P + I_G \tag{7}$$

where Y is the real gross domestic product (GDP), C denotes total consumption (C_P and C_G represent private and government consumption, respectively), I is the value of the total gross investment (with I_P representing gross private investment, and I_G gross government investment), and the differential $(X - M)$ denotes the net exports of goods and nonfactor services.

The reduced functional form used to estimate the target medium- and long-term rates of growth can be expressed as follows:

$$GYR = \alpha_0 + \alpha_1 . IRR + \alpha_2 . NODA + \alpha_3 . TTR + \alpha_4 . DUM \tag{8}$$

where GYR is the rate of real economic growth, IRR is the computed investment rate of return, and the controlling variables include the Net Official Development Assistance (NODA) expressed as a ratio to the real GDP, and the Terms of Trade Index (TTR) used to proxy external shocks to the economy. The dummy variable (DUM) is included to take into account the effects of the sharp 1994 currency devaluation of the common currency CFA with respect to the French Franc. The short-run dynamics of real GDP (Y) can be expressed as:

$$Y = Y_{-1} . (1 + GYR) \tag{9}$$

The reduced form equation of the investment rate of return can be expressed as follows:

$$IRR = \beta_0 + \beta_1 . RI_G + \beta_2 . TTR + \beta_3 . DUM \tag{10}$$

where RIG represents the policy variable and is calculated as the ratio of public investment to real GDP. The constraint of fiscal balance (FB) can be expressed as:

$$T - C_G - I_G = FB \tag{11}$$

where C_G, I_G represent fiscal revenues, current public expenditures, and public capital expenses, respectively.

The restrictions on the balance of payments can be described as follows:

$$Z + FCA = \Delta R \tag{12}$$

$$Z = X - M + NCT \tag{13}$$

where Z is the external current account, FCA denotes the external financial and capital account, and NCT represents the net current transfers (including net foreign income payments).

The market equilibrium conditions for financial assets imply that

$$\Delta M^S = \Delta M^D \tag{14}$$

where ΔM^S and ΔM^D represent the flow of money supply, and the flow of money demand, respectively.

The behavioral relationships describe private consumption and demand from exports, which can be respectively expressed by Equations (15) and (16) as follows:

$$C_P = c.(Y - T) \tag{15}$$

where $(Y - T)$ represents the level of disposable income.

The demand for imports is expressed as follows:

$$M = \lambda_1 . Y + \lambda_2 . RPM \qquad (\lambda_1 > 0, \lambda_2 < 0) \tag{16}$$

where *RPM* represents the relative price of imports and λ_1 and λ_2 denote the sensitivity of the demand for imports to fluctuations in GDP and import prices, respectively. For practical purpose, the following reduced-form equation can be used in the definition of the demand for imports in the case of developing countries:

$$M = m.Y \tag{17}$$

The growth rate of real exports supply can be expressed as:

$$GXR = \delta_1 . GYR + \delta_2 . \Delta REER \qquad (\delta_1 > 0, \delta_2 < 0) \tag{18}$$

where *GXR* represents the rate of growth in the real exports supply of goods and non-factor services. The volume of exports can thus be derived from Equation (18) as follows:

$$X = X_{-1}.(1 + GXR) \tag{19}$$

The demand form money can be expressed as a function of variations in real GDP following the Cambridge equation for money demand:

$$\Delta M^D = k.\Delta Y \tag{20}$$

The fiscal revenue is also defined as a function of the level of real GDP:

$$T = t.Y \tag{21}$$

Macroeconomic sustainability can be examined with the Islamic economic model by adopting macroeconomic secondary targets. The fiscal constraints are reflected by the ratio (*f*) of fiscal balance to GDP to ensure fiscal sustainability and, the ratio (R_{IG}) of public investment to GDP to raise the capacity of public investment while improving its efficiency:

$$FB = f.Y \tag{22}$$

$$I_G = RI_G.Y \tag{23}$$

From Equations (10), (22) and (23), it is possible to determine C_G as follows:

$$C_G = T - I_G - FB \tag{24}$$

From Equations (5), (9), (10), (12), the level of investment that is consistent with the long-term rate of economic growth can be described as follows:

$$I = Y - C - X + M \tag{25}$$

$$I_P = I - I_G \tag{26}$$

With respect to external exchange targets, it is important to ensure that the ratio (z) of external current account to GDP is sustainable and international reserve coverage of imports remains also appropriate levels:

$$Z = z.Y \tag{27}$$

$$R = r.\frac{M}{12} \tag{28}$$

Finally, net current transfers (*NCT*), financial and capital account (*FCA*), and variation in international reserves (ΔR) are calculated as follow:

$$NCT = Z - (X - M) \tag{29}$$

$$FCA = \Delta R - Z \tag{30}$$

$$\Delta R = R - R_{-1} \tag{31}$$

4.2 Calibration of Model Parameters

The macroeconomic model parameters are calibrated with the annual observations available from the dataset described above. The long-term $\propto_i i = 0, \ldots, 4$ coefficients are associated with real economic growth and $\beta_j\ j = 0, \ldots, 3$ coefficients in the investment rate of return, which are obtained from the ECM estimation based on the ARDL approach.[240]

The table reports also the average ratio of consumption (C) to the real GDP Y, and k representing inverse of money velocity. The baseline values of external current account are computed from the observed level of real GDP. The same method of computation is used to simulate the values of the baseline fiscal balance.

In light of the theoretical setup, it is possible to assess the extent to which the simulated baseline results are consistent with historical observations. Figure 25.1 describes the relative behaviors of the variables including the real economic growth, consumption, public investment, and current account balance, among others.

240 Econometric investigation pointed out positive and statistically significant long-run impacts of: (i) the public investment policy on the investment rate of return that supports the design of a spending-based fiscal policy; and (ii) the investment rate of return on the real economic growth appears consistent with the expected results from the conceptual research.

Table 25.1: Structural Parameters for Calibration.

Parameters	Value	Parameters	Value	Parameters	Value
$\propto_0$	−2.32	δ_1	1.24	β_0	5.77
$\propto_1$	0.32	δ_2	0.12	β_1	0.09
$\propto_2$	−0.03	k	0.26	β_2	21.04
$\propto_3$	0.41	t	0.23	β_3	−26.63
$\propto_4$	2.63	r.	3		
c	0.89	m	0.36		

Source: Dieye (2017), Olofin and Babatunde (2007).

The evidence suggests that the model baseline reproduces the historical macroeconomic trends reasonably well. The simulated long-run real economic growth (LTGYR) baseline shows lower levels of volatility and, more sustained pattern toward the end of the simulation period compared to the historical observations. The simulated trend for real GDP seems to diverge from historical observations. For private investment and export growth, baselines display notable differences during the period from 1993 to 2004, which can be associated with various shocks, including the FCFA devaluation, power supply failure, increase in oil price, and sharp decline in crop production, among others. From 2005 onward, however, it seems that the baseline estimates for these economic aggregates fits the patterns of historical data rather well. It is also noted that the simulated patterns for the remaining economic variables reflect closely the historical tendencies.

4.3 Simulation of an Islamic Model of Stability and Growth

In light of the calibration results, it is possible to perform the model simulations with the estimation of the five-year economic baseline projections (2015–2019) under the assumption that current policies and recent economic trends would persist. These projections are followed by the simulation of policy scenarios. The simulated baseline projections include a moderate increase in real GDP growth from 4% in 2015 to 5.1% in 2019, and an average growth rate of 3.5% from exports. There is a likelihood however for higher deficit of the current account balance as well as the balance. In light of these projections, scenarios of policy experiments are considered. The first scenario involves the resorption of the fiscal deficit, and reallocation of public expenditures toward real investment and adjustment of the current account. The main assumptions include the adjustment of current account deficit from 8% in 2015 to 4% in 2019, the incremental resorption of the fiscal deficit relative to GDP, from 4% in 2015 to 1% in 2019, and gradual reallocation of public expenditures, with an increase in the ratio of public investment to GDP from 11% in 2015 to 15% in 2019. The ratio of fiscal revenue to GDP is maintained at the 25% level reached in 2014. The foreign

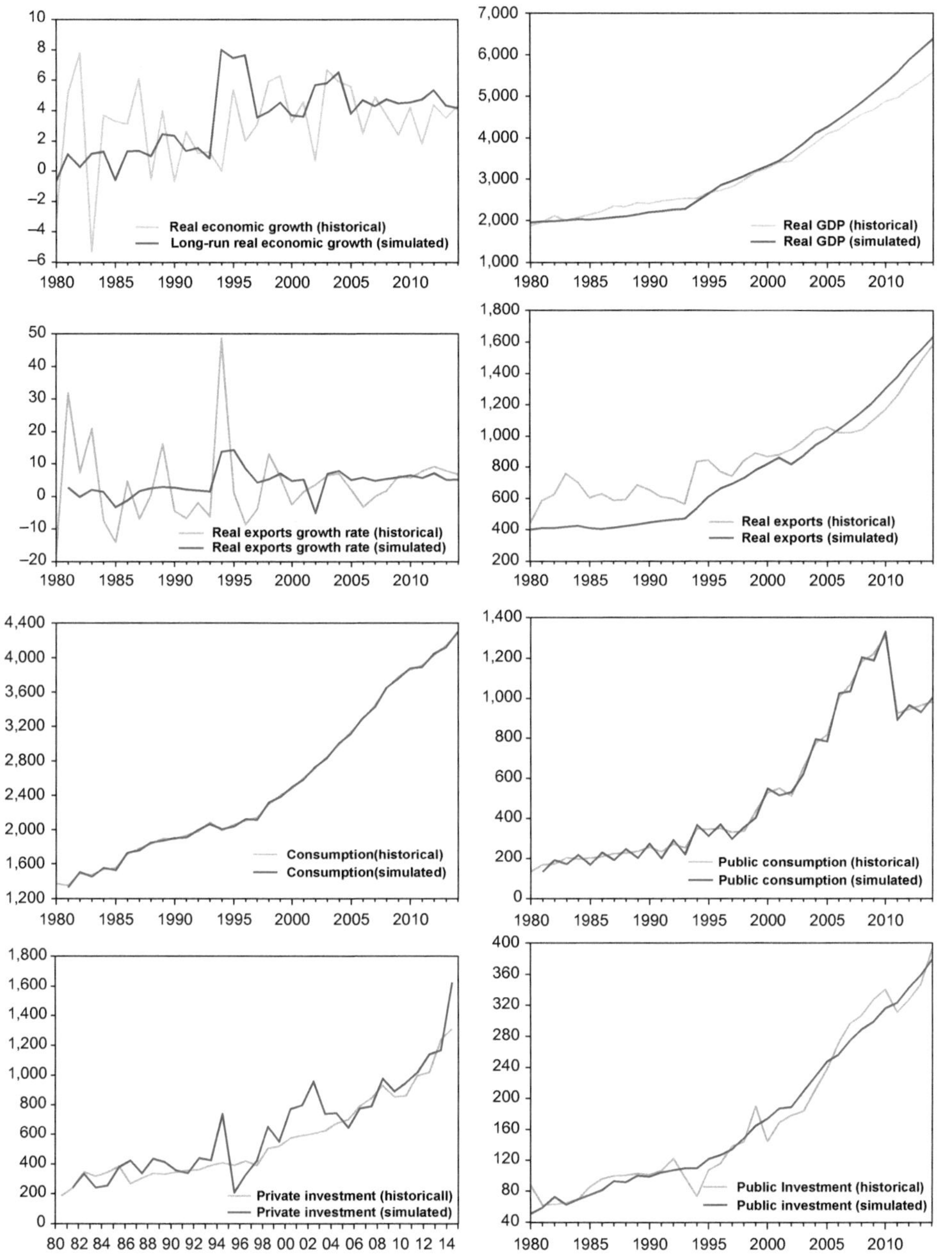

Figure 25.1: Senegal, Counterfactual Replication of Historical Data (1980–2014).
Source: Dieye (2017), Government of Senegal/ANSD (2014).

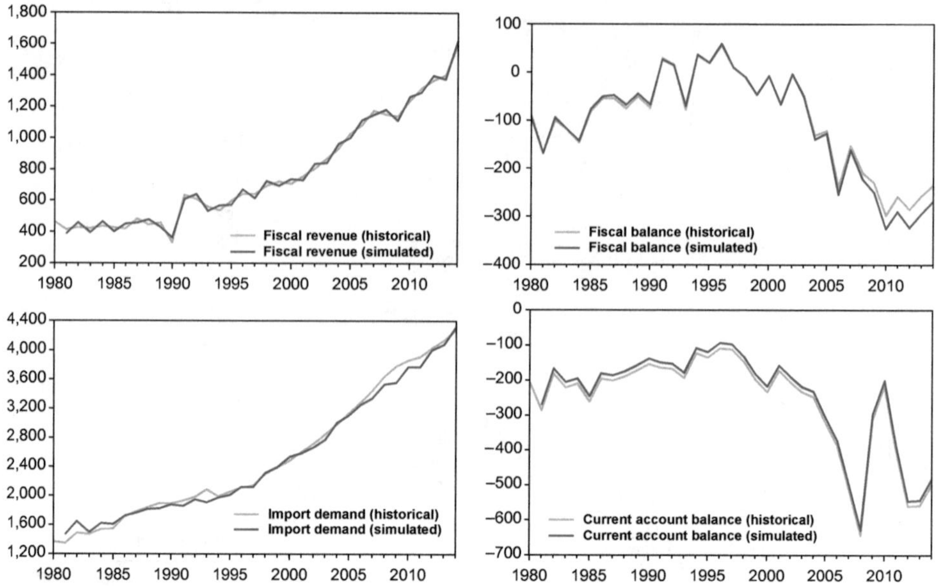

Figure 25.1 (continued)

reserves are set to cover three months of imports, and the real effective exchange rate remains unchanged at the level observed in 2014.

Compared to the baseline, this scenario allows for a fiscal adjustment based on expenditure rather than taxation, and it is expected to lead to higher projected real GDP, total investment, and exports than the baseline estimates (Figures 25.1 and 25.2).

It appears also from Figures 25.3 and 25.4 that the model of stability and growth is associated with better prospects for macroeconomic stability and growth compared to actual observations. It is noted also that this evidence does not depend on the efficient use of public resources.

The second scenario includes policy actions that address the high propensities to consume and to import. It is based on the adjustment of increased agricultural production to achieve national self-sufficiency for local food products in 2019 including cereals and dairy products. This policy may induce a reduction in the propensity to import by 1% annually between 2015 and 2019. It is assumed also that the average propensity to consume is reduced by 1% annually from its estimated value of 89% in 2014. This is in line with the Islamic rules of moderation in consumption behavior.

In comparison with the first scenario, it appears from Figure 25.5 that, ceteris paribus, the effects of macroeconomic policies include an increase in investments and a reduction in the current account deficit from 7% to 3% of GDP. However, the evidence suggests also that the average propensity to consume should fall under 80% to induce a significant rise in the ratio of total investment to GDP.

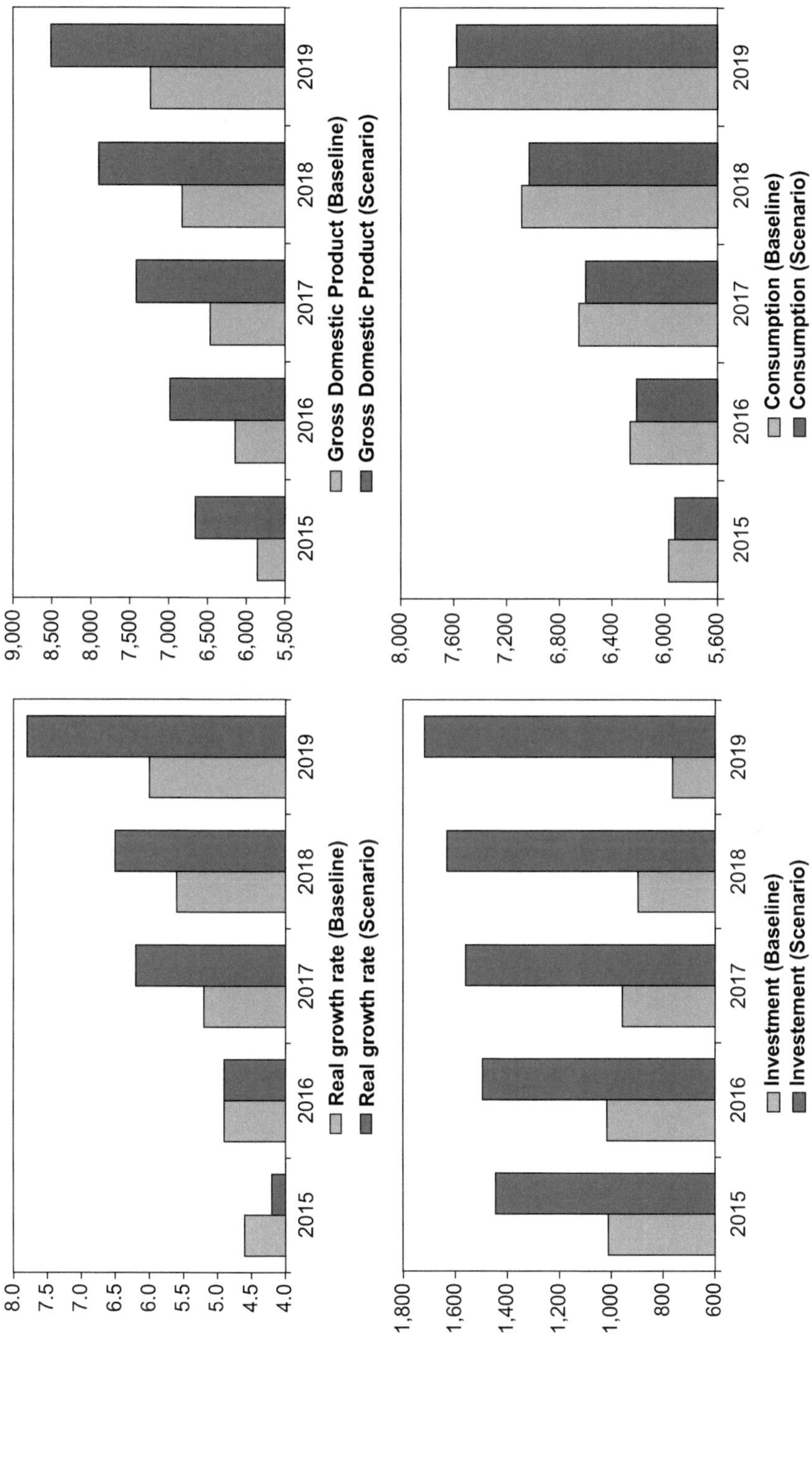

Figure 25.2: Macroeconomic Response to Fiscal and External Policy Shocks (2015 – 2019).
Source: Dieye (2017).

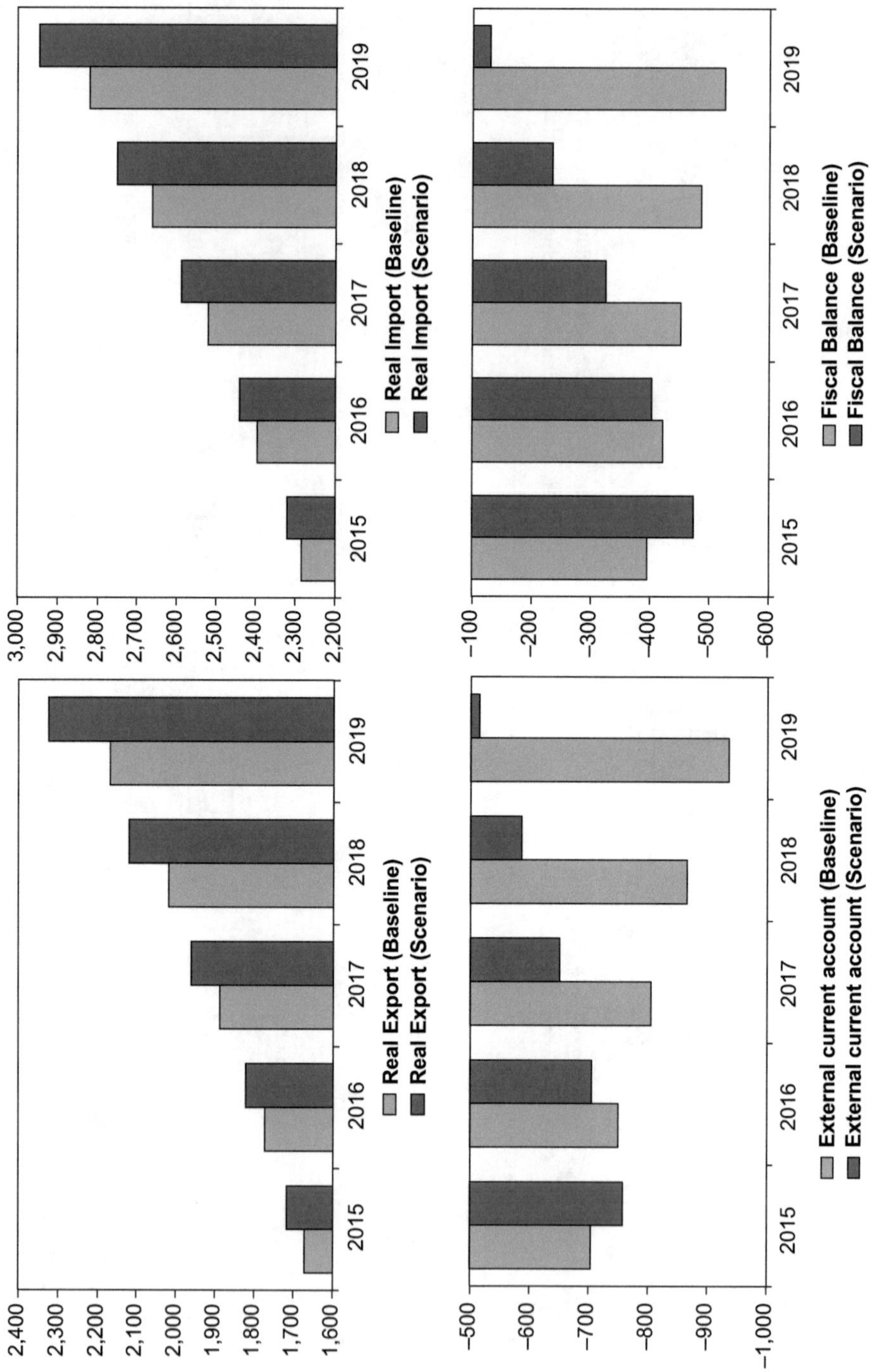

Figure 25.2 (continued)

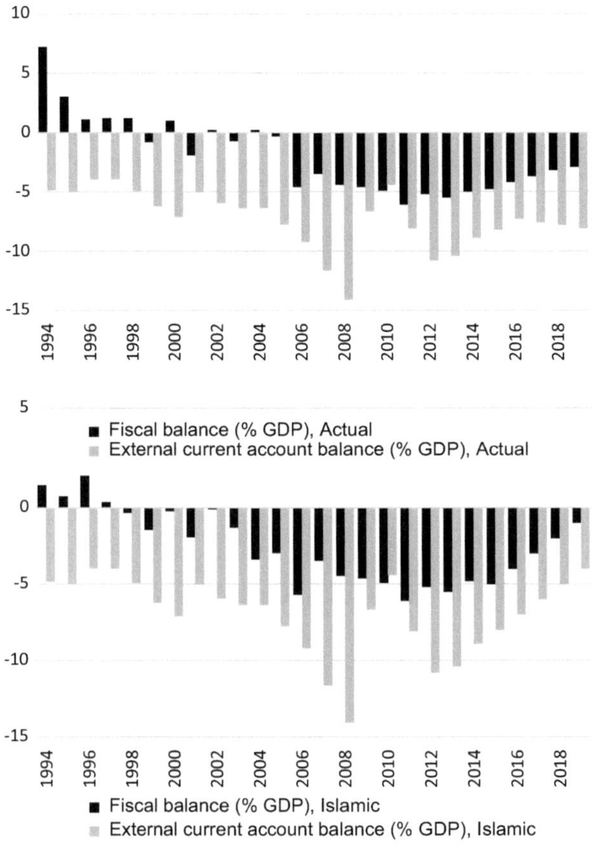

Figure 25.3: Senegal. Macroeconomic Stability Adjustment (% GDP).
Source: Dieye (2017), IMF WEO (2016).

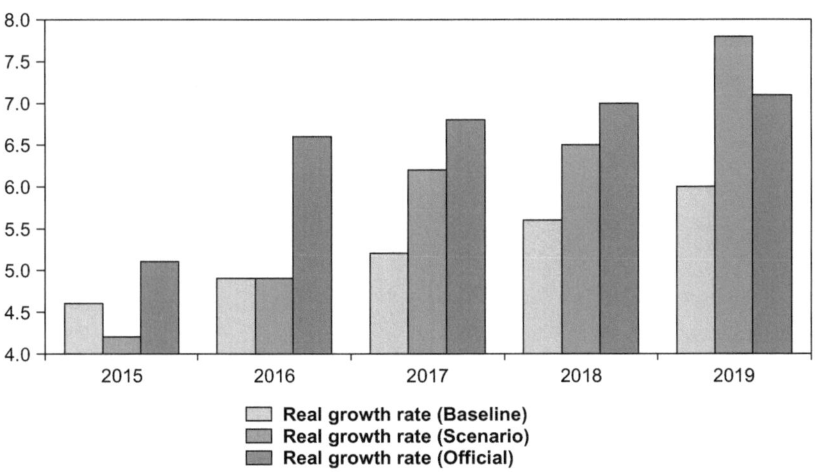

Figure 25.4: Senegal. Economic Growth Projections: Islamic Scenario vs Official (2015–2019).
Source: Author's calculations, IMF Senegal Staff Report (2017).

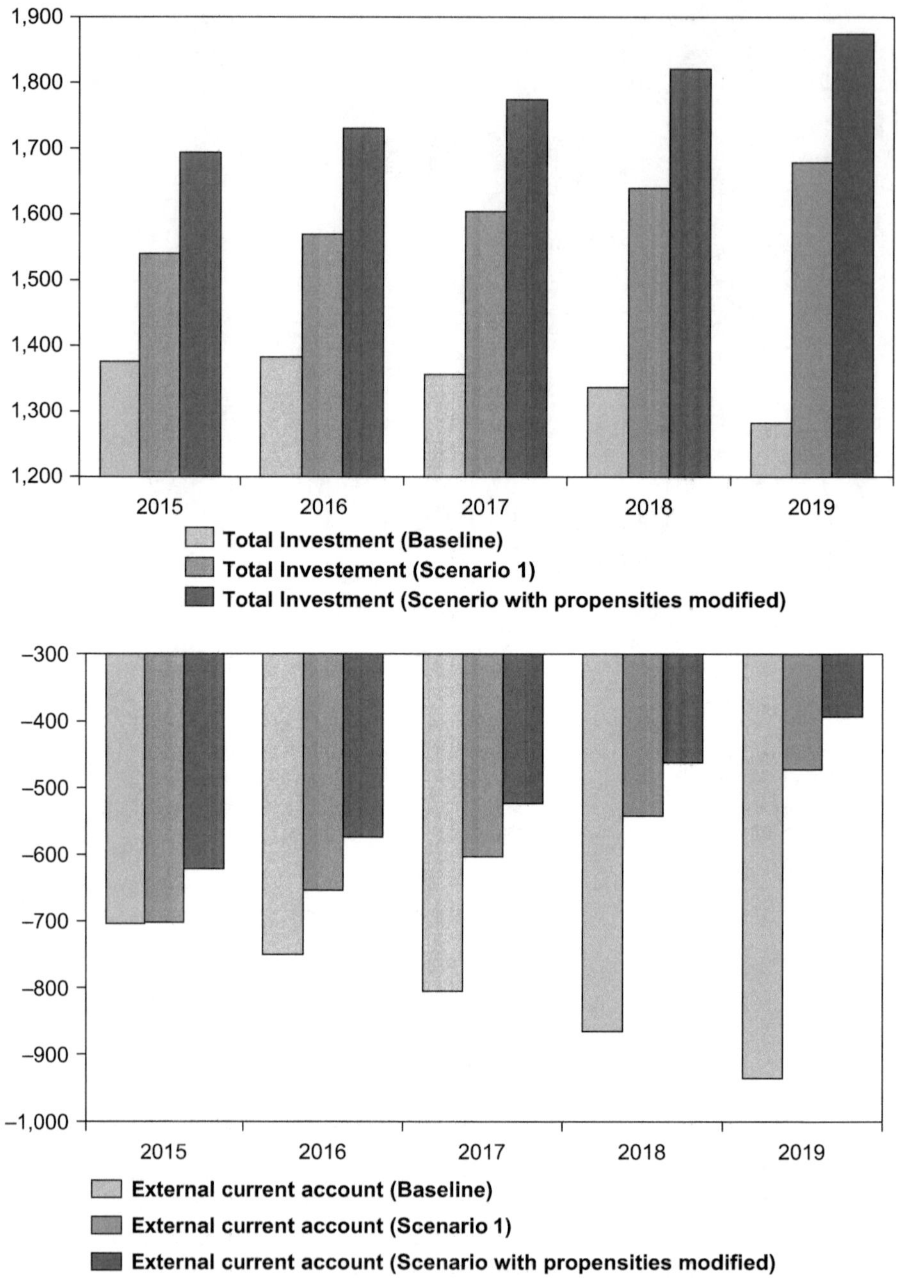

Figure 25.5: Senegal. Macroeconomic Response to Policy Shocks on Propensities (2015–2019).
Source: Author's calculations, IMF Senegal Staff Report (2017).

5 Conclusion

This chapter provides an empirical analysis of economic stability and growth for developing Muslim countries. Standard economic policies are based on monetary and fiscal solutions that tend to perpetuate the cycles of indebtedness and austerity. Under the different paradigm of an Islamic economy, alternative economic solutions may be possible. The principles of risk-sharing and prohibition of interest may provide the basis for a different set of policy recommendations. Economic policies based on these guiding principles may be conducive to different short and long-run effects on macroeconomic indicators.

For illustrative purposes, the simulation exercise is based on the economic conditions of the African and predominantly Muslim country Senegal, which offers an interesting example of a developing country with rich resources that can be optimally leveraged to address the economic and social challenges. The analytical framework for Islamic economics can be also extended to examine the significance of the rate of return in the real sector for monetary and financial policies. It can shed light also on the behavioral factors affecting private investment and the determinants of "moderate consumption".

Thus, the macroeconomic Islamic model presents a more comprehensive alternative to conventional models that allowing for the formalization and quantification of the rules of conduct, including the institutional and individual rules of behavior. It permits also the assessment of the impact of these rules of behavior on economic performance. Islamic economics offers new perspectives on institutional rules and behavior, which can contribute to the further development of new institutional economics and on the rules governing individual consumption and investment. It is these rules of conduct and behavior that have the potential to improve the long-term effectiveness of economic policies.

References

Abduh, Muhamad and Chowdhury Nazreen. 2012. "Does Islamic Banking Matter For Economic Growth In Bangladesh?." *Journal of Islamic Economics, Banking and Finance* 8(3): 104–113.

Abedifar, Pejman, Hasan, Iftekar, and Taraziet Amine. 2016. "Finance-Growth Nexus and Dual-Banking Systems: Relative Importance of Islamic Banks." *Journal of Economic Behavior & Organization* 132: 98–215.

Acemoglu, Daron. 2009. *Introduction to Modern Economic Growth*. Princeton: Princeton University Press.

Acemoglu, Daron, Simon Johnson and James Robinson. 2005. "Institutions as a Fundamental Cause of Long-Run Growth." In *Handbook of Economic Growth* Vol, edited by Philippe Aghion and Steven Durlauf: 386–472. Amsterdam: North-Holland Elsevier.

Afonso António and João Tovar Jalles. 2011. "Economic Performance and Government Size." European Central Bank Working Paper 1399.

Agenor, Pierre-Richard. 2002. "Macroeconomic Adjustment and the Poor: Analytical Issues and Cross-Country Evidence." World Bank Working Paper 2788.

Aghion, Philippe, Alberto Alesina and Francesco, Trebbi. 2007. "Democracy, Technology, and Growth." NBER Working Paper 13180.

Ahmed, Adulrahman Yousri. 2002. "The Scientific Approach to Islamic Economics: Philosophy, Theoretical Construction and Applicability." In *Theoretical Foundations of Islamic Economics*, edited by Habib Ahmed. Jeddah: Islamic Development Bank.

Alaabed, Alaa. 2016. "Risk Shifting and Islamic Banking." *International Centre for Education in Islamic Finance PhD*. Kuala Lumpur.

Alesina, Alberto and Ardagna, Silvia. 2012. "The Design of Fiscal Adjustments." NBER Working Paper 18423. Cambridge: National Bureau of Economic Research.

Altunc, Omer Faruk and Celil Aydın. 2013. "The relationship between optimal size of government and economic growth: Empirical evidence from Turkey, Romania and Bulgaria." *Procedia – Social and Behavioral Sciences* 92: 66–75.

Aschauer, David Alan. 1989. "Is public expenditure productive?." *Journal of Monetary Economics* 23 (2): 177–200.

Asimakopoulos, Stylianos and Yiannis Karavias. 2015. "The Impact of Government Size on Economic Growth: A Threshold Analysis." Granger Centre Discussion Paper. University of Nottingham, 15(02).

Askari, Hossein, Zamir Iqbal, and Abbas Mirakhor. 2014. "Understanding Development in An Islamic Framework." *Islamic Economic Studies* 22 (1): 1–36.

Askari, Hossein, Zamir Iqbal, and Abbas Mirakhor. 2015. *Introduction to Islamic Economics. Theory and Applications*. Singapore: John Wiley & Sons.

Askari, Hossein, Noureddine Krichene, and Abbas Mirakhor. 2014. "On the stability of an Islamic financial system." *PSL Quarterly Review* 67(269): 131–167.

Bai, Chong-En, Chang-Tai Hsieh, and Yingvi Qian. 2006. "The Return to Capital in China". NBER Working Paper 12755. Cambridge: National Bureau of Economic Research.

Baldwin, John, Guy Gellatly, Marc Tanguay, and André Patry. 2005. "Estimating Depreciation Rates for the Productivity Accounts". Unpublished. Statistics Canada, Ottawa.

Banerjee, Abhijit, and Newman Andrew. 1993. "Occupational Choice and the Process of Development." *Journal of Political Economy* 101(2): 274–298.

Barro, Robert. J., and Jong-Wha Lee. 2002. "IMF Programs: Who is Chosen and What Are the Effects?." NBER Working Paper 8951. Cambridge: National Bureau of Economic Research.

Basu, Ritu, Anantharishnan Prasad and Sergio Rodriguez. 2015. "Monetary Operations and Islamic Banking in the (GCC): Challenges and Options." IMF Working Paper, 15/234. Cambridge: National Bureau of Economic Research.

Beck, Thorsten. 2012. "Finance and Growth – Lessons from the Literature and the Recent Crisis". Prepared for London School of Economics Growth Commission.

Belloc, Marianna and Pietro Vertova. 2006. "Public Investment and Economic Performance in Highly Indebted Poor Countries: An Empirical Assessment." *International Review of Applied Economics* 20(2): 151–170.

Bivens, Josh. 2012. "Public Investment: The Next 'New Thing' For Powering Economic Growth." Economic Policy Institute, Briefing paper, 338.

Blanchard, Olivier, Giovanni Dell'Ariccia, and Paolo Mauro. 2010. "Rethinking Macroeconomy Policy." *Journal of Money, Credit and Banking* 41(1): 199–215.

Blot, Christophe, Jerome Creel, Bruno Ducoudré, and Xavier Timbeau. 2015."Back To Fiscal Consolidation in Europe and Its Dual Tradeoff: Now Or Later, Through Spending Cuts Or Tax Hikes?." Working Paper NO: 11. Sciences Po publications.

Bourguignon, Francois, William H. Branson, and Jaime de Melo. 1989. "Adjustment and Income Distribution: A Counterfactual Analysis." NBER Working Paper 2943. Cambridge: National Bureau of Economic Research.

Bruno, Michael. 1988. "Econometrics and the design of economic reform". NBER Working Paper, 2718. Cambridge: National Bureau of Economic Research.

Caivano, Michele, Lisa Rodano and Stefano Siviero. 2011. "The transmission of the global financial crisis to the Italian economy". *Giornale degli Economisti e Annali di Economia* 70(3): 1–32.

Cevik, Serhan and Joshua Charap. 2011. "The Behavior of Conventional and Islamic Bank Deposit Returns in Malaysia and Turkey". IMF Working Paper 11/156. Washington, D.C.: International Monetary Fund.

Chapra, Muhammad Umar. 2008. *Muslim Civilization: The Causes of Decline and the Need for Reform*. Leicestershire, UK: The Islamic Foundation.

Chapra, Muhammad Umar. 2007. *Islam and Economic Development: A Strategy for development with justice and stability*. New Delhi: Adam Publishers.

Chapra, Muhammad Umar. 1995. "Islam and the Economic Challenge." The Islamic Foundation and the International Institute of Islamic Thought Islamic Economics Series, 17.

Chen, Sheng-Tung and Chien-Chiang Lee. 2005. "Government size and economic growth in Taiwan: A threshold regression approach." *Journal of Policy Modeling* 27(9): 1051–1066.

Creel, Jérôme, Hubert Paul and Saraceno Francesco. 2015. "An Empirical Analysis of the Link between Public and Private Investment in Four OECD Countries." 17th Banca d'Italia Workshop on Public Finance.

Cristina, Jude and Gregory Levieuge. 2013. "Growth Effect of FDI In Developing Economies: The Role Of Institutional Quality". Banque de France Working paper, 559.

Demirguc-Kunt, Asli, Erik Feyen, and Ross Levine. 2009. "Finance and Inequality: Theory and Evidence" NBER Working Paper 15275. Cambridge: National Bureau of Economic Research.

Demirguc-Kunt, Asli. 2011. "Optimal Financial Structures and Development: The evolving importance of banks and markets." World Bank Policy Research Working Paper 5805.

Demirguc-Kunt, Asli, Leora Klapper, and Douglas Randall. 2013. "Islamic finance and financial inclusion: measuring use of and demand for formal financial services among Muslim Adults". World Bank Policy Research Working Paper 6642.

Dieye, Adama. 2017. *Riba-free model of stability and growth: an application to Senegal.* International Centre for Education in Islamic Finance PhD. Kuala Lumpur.

Duran-Fernandez, Roberto and Georgina Santo. 2014. "An empirical approach to public capital, infrastructure, and economic activity: A critical review". *Research in Transportation Economics* 46(C): 3–16.

Easterly, William. 1999. "The Ghost Of Financing Gap: Testing The Growth Model Used In The International Financial Institutions." *Journal of Development* Economics 60(2): 423–438.

Easterly, William. 2002. "An Identity Crises? Testing IMF Financial Programming." Center for Global Development Working Paper 9.

Easterly, William. 2003. "IMF and World Bank Structural Adjustment and Poverty." In *Managing currency crisis in emerging markets*, edited by Michael P. Dooley, and Jeffrey A. Franke. Chicago: University of Chicago Press

Edwards, Sebastian. 1989. "The International Monetary Fund and the Developing Countries: A Critical Evaluation." Carnegie-Rochester Conference Series on Public Policy No: 31: 7–68.

Estache, Antonio and Gregoire Garsous. 2012. "The impact of infrastructure on growth in developing countries." IFC/World Bank Economics Notes. Note 1.

Farahani, Yazdan Gudarzi and Masood Dastan. 2013. "Analysis of Islamic Banks' Financing and Economic Growth: A Panel Cointegration Approach." *International Journal of Islamic and Middle Eastern Finance and Management* 6(2): 156–172.

Feenstra, Robert C., Robert Inklaar, and Marcel R Timmer.2013. "The Next Generation of the Penn World Table." NBER Working Paper 19255. Cambridge: National Bureau of Economic Research.

Feizi, Mehdi. 2008. "A New Keynesian Small Open Economy DSGE Model in Islamic Economic Framework: The Case of Iran." Working Paper.

Fraumeni, Barbara M. 1997. "The Measurement of Depreciation in the U.S. National Income and Product Accounts." *Survey of Current Issues* 77: 7–23.

Furqani, Hafas and Ratna Mulyany. 2009. "Islamic Banking and Economic Growth: Empirical Evidence from Malaysia." *Journal of Economic Cooperation and Development* 30(2): 59–74.

Galor, Oded and Joseph Zeira. 1993. "Income distribution and macroeconomics." *Review of Economics Studies* 60: 35–52.

Gheeraert, Laurent and Laurent Weill. 2014. "Does Islamic Banking Development Favour Macroeconomic Efficiency? Evidence on the Islamic Finance Growth Nexus." University of Strasbourg Working paper, 2014–04.

Ghosh, Atish R., Charis Christofides, Jun Kim, Laura Papi, Uma Ramakrishnan, Alun Thomas, and Juan Zalduendo. 2005. "The Design of IMF-Supported Programs". IMF Occasional Paper, 241.

Government of Senegal/ANSD. 2015. *"National accounts"*. ANSD.

Gourinchas, Pierre-Olivier and Maurice Obstfeld. 2011. "Stories of the Twentieth Century for the Twenty-First". NBER Working Paper No: 17252. Cambridge: National Bureau of Economic Research.

Gunalp, Burak and Oguzhan Dincer. 2005. "The Optimal Government Size in Transition Countries". Department of Economics, Hacettepe University Beytepe, Ankara and Department of Commerce, Massey University, Auckland.

Hall, Robert E. and Dale W. Jorgenson. 1967. "Tax Policy and Investment Behavior." *American Economic Review* 57(3): 391–414.

Hasan, Zubair. 1997. "Fulfilment of Basic Needs: Concepts, Measurement and Muslim Countries Performance." *IIUM Journal of Economics & Management* 5(2).

Hasan, Zubair. 2007. "Treatment of Consumption in Islamic: Economics: An Appraisal." *Munich Personal RePEc Archive Paper (MPRA)*, 3089.

Honohan, Patrick. 2004. "Financial Development, Growth and Poverty: How Close Are The Links?" World Bank Policy Research Working Paper, 3203.

Hooper, Emma, Sanjay Peters,and Patrick A. Pintus. 2017. "To What Extent Can Long-Term Investment in Infrastructure Reduce Inequality?." Banque de France Working Paper, 624.

Imam, Patrick and Kpodar Kagni. 2015. "Is Islamic Banking Good for Growth?." IMF/Working Paper, 15/81.

IMF. 1987. "Theoretical Aspects of the Design of Fund-Supported Adjustment Programs." Occasional Paper No. 55. Washington DC: International Monetary Fund.

IMF. 2017. "Senegal: Staff Report for the Article IV Consultation and Third Review under the Policy Support Instrument Request for a Three-Year Policy Support Instrument." Washington DC: International Monetary Fund.

IMF. 2016. *World Economic Outlook*. Washington DC: International Monetary Fund.

IMF. 2013. "Evaluation of the Prolonged Use of Fund Resources." IMF Independent Evaluation Office. Washington DC: International Monetary Fund.

IMF. 2012. "Review of Conditionality Background Paper 2: Design of Fund-Supported Programs." Washington DC: International Monetary Fund.

IMF. 2006. *IMF Supported Program: Recent Staff Research*, edited by Ashoka Mody and Alessandro Rebucci. Washington DC: International Monetary Fund.

IMF. 2002. "Evaluation of the Prolonged Use of Fund Resources." IMF Independent Evaluation Office. Washington DC: International Monetary Fund.

Iqbal, Munawar. 2007. *Advances in Islamic economics and finance: proceedings of 6th International Conference on Islamic Economics and Finance*, edited by Munawar Iqbal, Salman Syed Ali, and Dadang Muljawan. Jeddah: Islamic Development Bank.
Iqbal, Munawar. 1985. "Zakah, Moderation and Aggregate Consumption in an Islamic Economy." *Journal of Research in Islamic Economics* 3(1): 45–61.
Iqbal, Zamir and Abbas Mirakhor. 2017. *Ethical Dimensions of Islamic Finance: Theory And Practice*. Cham: Palgrave Macmillan
Islamic Development Bank Group. 2013. "Senegal: Supporting Competitiveness Enhancement, Increased Agricultural Production and Productivity for an Emergent Nation". Member Country Partnership Strategy.
Jones, Benjamin F., and Benjamin A. Olken. 2004. "Do Leaders Matter? National Leadership and Growth since World War II." *Quarterly Journal of Economics* 120(3): 835–864.
Jonung, Lars. 2014. "Reforming the Fiscal Framework: The Case of Sweden 1973–2013." Knut Wicksell Centre for Financial Studies Working Paper, 26.
Karras, Georgios. 1997. "On the Optimal Government Size in Europe: Theory and Empirical Evidence." *The Manchester School of Economic & Social Studies* 65(3): 280–94.
Kentikelenis, Alexander E., Thomas H. Stubbs, and Lawrence P. King. 2016. "IMF Conditionality and Development Policy Space, 1985–2014." *Review of International Political Economy* 23(4): 543–582.
Khan, M. Fahim. 1984. "Macro Consumption Function in an Islamic Framework." *Journal of Research in Islamic Economics* 1 (2): 3–25.
Khan, Mohsin S. 1986. "Islamic interest free banking". *IMF Staff Papers* 33(1): 1–27
Khan, Mohsin S., and Abbas Mirakhor. 1989. "Islamic Banking: Experiences in the Islamic Republic of Iran and in Pakistan". IMF Working Paper, 89/12
Khatat, Mariam *El* Hamiani. 2016. "Monetary Policy in the Presence of Islamic Banking". IMF Working Paper 16/72.
Krugman, Paul. 2009. "How Did Economists Get It So Wrong? New York Times." In: www.nytimes.com/2009/09/06/magazine/06Economic-t.html. (last accessed August 8, 2018).
Law, Siong Hook, and Nirvikar Singh. 2014. "Does Too Much Finance Harm Economic Growth?." *Journal of Banking & Finance*- 37: 36–44.
Law, Siong Hook, W.N.w Azman-Saini, and Mansor Ibrahim 2013. "Institutional Quality Thresholds and the Finance-Growth Nexus." *Journal of Banking & Finance* 37: 5373–5381.
Levine, Ross. 2005. "Finance and Growth: Theory and Evidence" In *Handbook of Economic Growth* Vol, edited by Philippe Aghion and Steven Durlauf: 865–934. Amsterdam: North-Holland Elsevier.
Levine, Ross. 2011. "Regulating Finance and Regulators to Promote Growth." *Jackson Hole symposium on "achieving maximum long run growth"*. Federal Reserve Bank of Kansas City, August 25–27.
Mikkelsen, Jan Giehm. 1998. "A model For Financing Programming". IMF Working Paper, 98/80. Washington DC: International Monetary Fund.
Mills, Cadman Atta and Raj Nallari. 1992. "Analytical Approaches To Stabilization And Adjustment Programs." World Bank seminar paper, 44. Washington D.C.: World Bank.
Mirakhor, Abbas and Idris Samawi Hamid. 2009. *Islam and Development: The Institutional Framework*. New York: Global Scholarly Publications.
Mirakhor, Abbas and Iqbal Zaidi. 1988. "Stabilization and Growth in an Open Islamic Economy." *IMF Working Paper*, 22. Washington DC: International Monetary Fund.
Mirakhor, Abbas. 1993. "Equilibrium in a Non-Interest Open Economy". *Journal of King Abdulaziz University Islamic Economics* 5: 3–23.
Mirakhor, Abbas and Noureddine Krichene. 2009. "The Recent Crisis: Lessons for Islamic Finance". *Second lecture*. Kuala Lumpur: IFSB.

Mirakhor, Abbas and Hossein Askari. 2017. *Ideal Islamic Economy: An Introduction*. New York: Palgrave Macmillan.

Mohieldin, Mahmoud, Zamir Iqbal, Ahmed Rostom, and Fu Xiaochen. 2012. "The Role of Islamic Finance in Enhancing Financial Inclusion in Organization of Islamic Cooperation (OIC) Countries." *Islamic Economic Studies* 20(2): 55–120.

Mookerjee, Rajen and Paul Kalipioni. 2010. "Availability of financial services and income inequality: the evidence from many countries." *Emerging Markets Review* 11: 404–408.

Naceur, Sami Ben, Adolfo Barajas, and Alexander Massara. 2015. "Can Islamic Banking Increase Financial Inclusion?" IMF Working Paper 15/31. Washington DC: International Monetary Fund.

Nader, Yasmine F. 2008. "Microcredit and the socio-economic wellbeing of women and their families in Cairo." *The Journal of Socio-Economics* 37(2): 644–656.

Naqvi, Syed Nawab Haider. 1997. "The Dimension of an Islamic Economic Model". *Islamic Economies Studies* 4 (2): 1–23.

Nejib, Hachicha and Ben Amar Amine. 2015. "Does Islamic Bank Financing Contribute To Economic Growth? The Malaysian Case." *International Journal of Islamic and Middle Eastern Finance and Management* 8(3): 349–368.

Niels, Gilbert and Unger Brigitte. 2009. "Do Loans Harm? The Effect of IMF Programs on Inequality." Tjalling C. K. Research Institute Discussion Paper Series, 09–26.

North, Douglas C. 1993. "The New Institutional Economics and Development." Economic History 9309002, University Library of Munich, Germany.

Kodongo, Odongo and Kalu Ojah. 2016. "Does Infrastructure Really Explain Economic Growth in Sub-Saharan Africa?" Economic Research Southern Africa (ERSA) Working Paper, 653. National Treasury of South Africa.

Olofin, Sam and M. Adetunji Babatunde. 2007. "Estimating Price and Income Elasticities of Sub-Saharan African Exports." *African Journal of Economic Policy* 16(2): 1–39.

Orphanides, Athanasios and John C. Williams. 2011. Monetary Policy Mistakes and the Evolution Of Inflation Expectations. *NBER Working Paper*, 17080.

Othman, Azura and Abbas Mirakhor. 2013. "An Islamic Solution to the Present Policy Dilemma." *New Horizon*, January.

Pereira, Alfredo Marvão and Jorge M. Andraz. 2013. "On the Economic Effects of Public Infrastructure Investment: A Survey of the International Evidence." *Journal of Economic Development* 38(4): 1–37.

Pesaran, M. Hashem and Ron P. Smith. 2014. "Counterfactual Analysis in Macroeconometrics: An Empirical Investigation into the Effects of Quantitative Easing." Birbeck University Working Paper No. 1406.

Portes, Jonathan and Simon Wren-Lewis. 2014. "Issues in the Design of Fiscal Policy Rules." Oxford Discussion Paper Series, 704. Department of Economics, University of Oxford.

Rana, Pradumna B. and Joseph Anthony Lim. 1999. "The East Asian Crisis: Macroeconomic Policy Design and Sequential Issues.". In *Rising to the Challenge in Asia: A Study of Financial Markets*, edited by S. Ghon Rhee Manila: Asian Development Bank.

Raychaudhuri, Ajitava and Prabir De. 2010. "Trade, Infrastructure and Income Inequality in Selected Asian Countries: An Empirical Analysis." Asia-Pacific Research and Training Network on Trade Working Paper Series, 82.

Rehman, Scheherazade S., and Hossein Askari. 2010. "An Economic IslamicityIndex (EI^2)" *Global Economy Journal* 10(3): 1–37.

Reinhart, Carmen M. and Christoph Trebesch. 2016. "The International Monetary Fund: 70 Years of Reinvention." *Journal of Economic Perspectives* 30(1): 3–28.

Rioja, Felix and Valev Neven. 2004. "Finance and the Sources of Growth at Various Stages of Economic Development". *Economic Inquiry* 42(1): 127–140.

Sattar, Zaidi. 1991. "Interest-Free Banking, Profit-Sharing and the Islamic Macroeconomic System." In *Essays in Islamic Economic Analysis*, edited by F.R. Faridi: 82–101. New Delhi: Genuine Publications.

Senhadji, Abdelhak S. and Claudio Montenegro. 1999. "Time Series Analysis of Export Demand Equations: A Cross-Country Analysis". *IMF Staff Papers* 46(3).

Shatzmiller, Maya. 2011. "Economic Performance and Economic Growth in the Early Islamic World." *Journal of the Economic and Social History of the Orient* 54: 132–184.

Shaukat, Mughees, Zubair Hasan, and Datuk Syed Othman Alhabshi. 2013. "Financing Economic Growth with Stability from Islamic Perspective." *Journal of Islamic Business and Management* 4(2): 15–62.

Slesman, Ly, Ahmad Zubaidi Baharumshah, and Wahabuddin Ra'ees. 2015. "Institutional Infrastructure and Economic Growth in Member Countries of the Organization of Islamic Cooperation (OIC)." *Economic Modelling* 5(1): 214–226.

Solé, Juan. 2007. "Introducing Islamic Banks into Conventional Banking Systems." IMF Working Paper, WP7/175.

Steinwand, Martin and Randal Stone. 2008. "The International Monetary Fund: A review Of the Recent Evidence." *The Review of International Organizations* 3(2): 123–149.

Stiglitz, Joseph E. 2011. "Rethinking Macroeconomics: What Failed, And How To Repair It." *Journal of the European Economic Association* 9(4): 591–645.

Stijn, Claessens and Perotti Enrico. 2007. "Finance and Inequality: Channels and Evidence." *Journal of Comparative Economics* 35: 748–773.

Tahir, Sayyid. 2009. "Macroeconomics in Islamic Economy: A Theoretical Perspective." 10th Distance Learning Program of IRTI, Kuala Lumpur: International Islamic University Malaysia.

United Nations Development Programme. 2016. *Briefing note for countries on the 2016* Human Development Report: *Senegal*. UNDP.

Williamson, Olivier E. 2000. "The New Institutional Economics: Taking Stock, Looking Ahead". *Journal of Economic Literature* 38(3): 595–613.

Wolfson, Martin H. 2002. "Minsky's Theory of Financial Crises in a Global Context". *Journal of Economic issues* 36 (2): 393–99.

World Bank. 2002. "Building Institutions for Markets". In *World Development Report*. New York: Oxford University Press.

World Bank. 2014. "Financial Inclusion". In *Global Financial Development Report*. New York: World Bank.

Yang, Weonho, Jan Fidrmuc, and Sugata Ghosh. 2015. "Macroeconomic Effects of Fiscal Adjustment: A Tale of Two Approaches". *Journal of International Money and Finance* 57(C): 31–60.

Zulkhibri, Muhamed. 2016. *Islamic Financing and Monetary Policy in a Dual Banking System: Experience and Evidence from Malaysia*. Jeddah: Islamic Development Bank

Md Akther Uddin, Buerhan Saiti, Mansur Masih

Chapter 26: Are Finance and Human Development Important for Economic Growth? International Evidence from Dynamic GMM Approach

1 Introduction

A great number of theoretical and empirical studies have been carried out to identify the determinants of economic growth in developing countries. While many nations have emerged as developed economies since the end of World War II, most of the Muslim majority countries entangled in wars, foreign invasions, coups, ethnic rivalries and sectarian violence. In spite of showing tremendous economic performance, many emerging Muslim countries have lost their growth trajectory in the last two decades or so. At one end of the spectrum, there is extreme poverty, poor healthcare, illiteracy and low levels of human capital accumulation. There is also political instability, rampant corruption, underdeveloped financial sector, absence of property rights, lack of rule of law and resource curse restrain sustainable growth in most of the OIC countries. Are these countries poor because of their religious affiliation? The reality is that most Muslim societies do not embrace efficient institutions, rules and rule-compliance to promote development (Askari and Rehman 2013). Thus, a humble attempt is made here to find some answers to the following questions: Are human development and financial development important for economic growth in member countries of the Organization for Islamic Conference (OIC)? How are they different from other developing countries? In addition to that we investigate how financial development affects growth indirectly.

The OIC countries represent one of the world's largest markets with around 1.3 billion consumers who roughly constitute 25% of the world population. The OIC was established in 1969 with the purpose of promoting closer cooperation among Islamic countries in the economic, political and cultural fields. Currently, there are 57 member countries throughout the world with great diversity in terms of economic structure, political system, development level, ethnic background as well as social and cultural environment.

To the best of our knowledge, this study is the first attempt to fill the gap in the existing growth literature by integrating human, institutional, environmental factors in determination of in real income for OIC countries with other developing countries. Five adjusted indicators of human and financial development are used in a large panel of OIC and non-OIC countries with observations spanning the sample

https://doi.org/10.1515/9783110587920-026

period from 1996 to 2014. The two-step Dynamic System Generalized Method of Moments (GMM) is used in the analysis of this empirical relationship.

The study finds that in general human development affects economic growth positively in developing countries. The effect of health spending on economic growth is significantly higher in OIC countries. The average years of schooling, a proxy for human capital accumulation, contributes toward economic growth more significantly at higher level in Asian OIC countries. Primary school enrollment affects economic growth in Asian and African OIC countries less significantly than other developing countries. For lower and middle-income OIC countries the effect of schooling is significantly less than developing countries. The opposite effect is found for upper income countries, oil dependent countries and countries with the strong presence of Islamic finance. At the same time, there is evidence of significant negative and non-linear negative relationships between financial development, as well as, various measures of financial depth. A positive relationship between bank cost to income and growth is also identified. Financial development affects economic growth significantly at lower level in all OIC countries and country groups than developing countries except countries with a strong presence of Islamic finance, where the relationship remains positive and significant. Moreover, financial development affects economic growth in developing countries through capital formation and the macroeconomic environment, the combined effects of which are found to be negative. Also, higher unemployment is found to be detrimental to economic growth for developing countries. The CO_2 emissions used a proxy for industrialization, affects economic positively. Economic institutions are also found to have a significant impact on economic growth in developing countries. In line with that we recommend some policy measures for developing countries in general and OIC countries in particular.

The remainder of this chapter is organized as follows: In the next section, an overview of related studies. Section 3 introduces the empirical model and methodology. Section 4, describes the data. The estimation results and discussion in the fifth section and the final section presents the conclusion of the study.

2 Literature Review

2.1 Human Development and Growth

The theory of endogenous growth argues that economic growth is generated from within the economic system as a direct result of internal processes (Romer 1994; Aghion et al. 1998; Solow 2000). More specifically, the theory argues that an enhancement of human capital will lead to economic growth by means of the development of new forms of technology as well as efficient and effective means of production. According to the United Nations Development Programme (UNDP), human development can be defined as enlarging people's choices in ways that enable them to lead longer, healthier and fuller lives. This chapter refers to the human development with respect to the health and education albeit this is arguably a reductionist interpretation. There are two approaches in the examination of this nexus. The standard approach is to treat human capital, or the average years of schooling for the labor force, as an ordinary input in the production function (Mankiw, Romer and Weil 1992). Another approach is associated with the endogenous growth theory, which is to treat the growth of total factor productivity as a function of the level of education, human capital, and life expectancy. The underlying assumption is that an educated and healthy labor force is better at creating, implementing, and adopting new technologies, thereby generating high economic growth.

The role of human capital in economic development is examined in the seminal work by Benhabib and Spiegel (1994). The significance of this growth model is better understood in terms of its empirical implications and the notion that human capital is assured the levels rather than growth rates now play a role in the determination of the growth rate of per capita income. A number of empirical studies support the strong linkage between human development and economic growth (Pischke 1997; Sianesi and Van Reeenen 2003; Gennaioli et al. 2011; Lee and Hong 2011; Suri et al. 2011). The direction of the relationship is important and there is evidence from Mustafa et al. (2017), for instance, that human development contributes positively to economic growth. In the case of our Asian sample, economic growth does not appear to have, however, a positive influence on human development.

On the other hand, a negative albeit statistically insignificant relationship between human capital and economic growth is also reported (Pritchett 2001). Holmes (2013) also does not find a significant relationship between higher education and GDP growth using a range of cross-country regression models. It is also argued that the results of cross-country regression estimates, such as those pointed in Gemmell (1996), should be viewed with caution, as the results are sensitive to the sample period and country coverage. In another study, using continuously-updated fully modified panel estimation, Chen and Zhang (2017) found that industrial electricity consumption has a significantly larger impact on economic prosperity than physical and human capital investment.

It is noted, however, that with respect to OIC countries, there are almost no empirical studies on the relationship between human development and economic growth. Thus, the objective of this study is to fill the literature gap by examining 118 developing countries, with the focus on 54 OIC member countries.

2.2 Financial Development and Growth

The finance-growth nexus is a complex phenomenon and many theories have been developed to explain this dynamic relationship after the seminal theoretical work of

Schumpeter (1934) and empirical work by Goldsmith (1969). The following studies found a significant positive relationship between finance and growth at the both macro and micro levels (King and Levine 1993; Demirguc-Kunt and Levine 2004; Beck et al. 2000, 2014). On the other hand, many economists argue that finance is a relatively unimportant factor in economic development. Particularly, Robinson (1952) contends that financial development simply follows economic growth and later, Lucas (1988) terms the relationship between financial and economic development is "overstressed" (as cited in King and Levine 1993). A number of studies find a negative relationship between finance and growth at the macro and micro levels for developing countries (De Greogorio and Guidotti 1995; Shan 2005; Hao 2006; Djalilov and Piesse 2011; Hasan et al. 2009; and Xu 2016). Cecchetti and Kharroubi (2012) outlines that there is a negative link between the finance and growth, after a certain point. They further argue that when an economy is immature and the financial sector is small, an incremental growth in the latter is useful (Cecchetti and Kharroubi 2012). Arcand et al. (2012) suggests that finance starts having a negative effect on growth when credit to private sector reaches the threshold of 100% of GDP. Narayan and Narayan (2013) find that the banking sector variable (domestic credit) has a negative and statistically significant impact effect on economic growth in the sample of 65 developing countries except for the Middle Eastern countries. Using dynamic panel threshold technique on 87 developed and developing countries, Law and Singh (2014) find that more finance is not necessarily good for economic growth, and highlight that an optimal level of financial development is more crucial in facilitating growth.

More recently, the evidence from Batuo et al. (2018) suggests that financial development and financial liberalization have positive effects on financial stability. The findings also reveal that economic growth reduces financial instability in the pre-liberalization period compared to post-liberalization period. In another study, Lim (2017) suggests that economic growth during housing booms is greater in countries with less developed financial systems. Ruiz (2017) argues that countries below the finance threshold grow less and those above the threshold grow faster.

There are few empirical studies that examine financial development and economic growth by focusing on regional country groups like the Middle East and North Africa (Darrat et al. 2006), Commonwealth of Independent States and Central Asian Countries (Cojocaru et al. 2016; Djalilov and Piesse, 2011), Sub-Saharan Africa (Inoue and Hamori 2016; Ahmed 2016). Therefore, it can be argued that the finance-growth relationship remains an open empirical question despite the vast literature that contributed toward a better understanding of this dynamic relationship.

2.3 Theoretical Foundation of Growth in Islam

It is important to understand economic development in Islam in terms of raising the absolute income levels of the poor to eradicate poverty, meeting material or non-material human needs, the conservation of natural resources, protection of property rights, wildlife, and ecological environment (Mannan 1989; Mirakhor and Askari 2010). In other words, the principal foundational elements of development in Islam reflect individual self-development, physical earth development including natural resources, and collective human development (Askari and Rehman 2013; Mirakhor and Askari 2010). In addition, the goals that derived the Islamic concept of development must be expressed in terms of the preservation of moral and spiritual values, as reflected in the notion of *tazkiyah* (moral purification).

Despite the conceptual clarity, the evidence from Askari and Rehman (2013) suggests that in most Muslim societies, efficient institutions, rules and rule-compliance to promote development are not embraced and practiced. Therefore, many countries that profess Islam and are labeled as Islamic today rather represent clear examples of injustice and underdevelopment. It is further argued that despite the fact that the Islamic basis for development is multidimensional with its moral, social, political and economic dimensions. There is still a need to integrate the elements of moral and spiritual development into the very concept of economic development right from the beginning.

The establishment of an Islamic financial system is one of the most pressing needs to reform all economic institutions in accordance with the principles of Islamic Economics. Anwar (1987) argues that the advantages of financial markets include greater portfolio diversification, alteration in risk-tolerance levels, and the transfer of resources from savers to investors, all of which permit increased investment opportunities and higher levels of economic development. The importance of finance for economic growth in Muslim countries is also emphasized by Bacha and Mirakhor (2014), and Çizakça (2014), and empirically supported by Imam and Kpodar (2016).

In such context, it is imperative to analyze the relationship among finance, human development and economic growth in the case of OIC countries, which include many Muslim countries. The empirical model follows Goldsmith (1969), Mankiw et al. (1992), Beck et al. (2000), Demirguc-Kunt and Levine (2004) and integrates Islamic development principles explained by Anwar (1987), Mannan (1989), and Mirakhor (1993).

3 Empirical Model and Methodology

In order to examine empirical relationship among finance, economic growth and human development, it is possible to consider the following growth equation:

$$Y_{it} = \alpha_i Y_{it-1} + \beta_i \; Initial\ GDP\ per\ capita_{it} + \gamma_i X_{it} + \delta_{it} FD_{it} + \lambda_{it} HD_{it} + v_i + \varepsilon_{it} \quad (1)$$

where i indicates the country $(i = 1, \ldots N)$ and t indicates the time period $(t = 1 \ldots T_i)$.

The dependent variable Y_{it} stands for the economic growth of country i at the end of period t. FD_{it} represents financial development and HD_{it} does human development. The coefficients α, β, γ, δ, and λ are the parameters and vectors of parameters to be estimated. The country-specific effects are represented by v_i and, ε_{it} is the error term. The main control variables comprise the log of initial GDP per capita, and X_{it} is a vector of control variables hypothesized to affect output growth including capital investment to GDP, savings to GDP, CO_2 emission per capita (metric tons), and unemployment rate.

Aisen and Veiga (2013) thoroughly discussed the limitations of estimating the dynamic model (Equation (1)) by using OLS. As our sample has only 6 non-overlapping 3-year periods, the dynamic panel bias may remain. Arellano and Bond (1991) suggest the recourse to first differences of the variables to eliminate the fixed effects. This approach which is also referred to the Standard or Difference GMM. The first difference formulation of Equation (1) can be rewritten as follows:

$$\Delta Y_{it} = \alpha_i Y_{it-1} + \beta_i \textit{ Initial GDP per capita}_{it} + \gamma_i \Delta X_{it} + \delta_{it} \Delta FD_{it} + \lambda_{it} \Delta HD_{it} + \Delta v_i + \varepsilon_{it} \quad (2)$$

However, the problem of correlation between the lagged dependent variable and the error term remains and this requires the use of instruments. As remedy to this problem, Arellano and Bond (1991) advocate the use of appropriate lags of dependent and independent variables as instruments. The lagged levels of regressors may be however weak instruments for the differenced variables. More specifically, first difference GMM estimators may behave poorly and lead to large sample biases when the independent variables are persistent over time (Blundell and Bond 1998). Finally, it is noted that the absence of information about the variables of interest in the level form may result in the loss of substantial parts of total variance (Arellano and Bover 1995).

To solve the above problems with Difference GMM models, Arellano and Bover (1995) and Blundell and Bond (1998) propose System GMM estimator. This is a combination of system with the regression in first differences and with the regression in levels. To estimate the GMM system, variables in differences are instrumented with lags of their own levels, while variables in levels are instrumented with lags of their own differences (Bond et al. 2009). In other words, the first differenced moment conditions in Difference GMM are augmented by level moment conditions in System GMM estimates for more efficiency in estimation (Blundell and Bond, 1998). In the System GMM modeling, even though the levels of the explanatory variables are essentially correlated with the country-specific fixed effects, the differences are not serially correlated. In addition, time dummies may be included to control for the time-specific effects and to eliminate cross-sectional dependence. Country or unit dummies may be also used to control for country-specific or unit effects. One more argument in favor of using System GMM is that for unbalanced panel data, as in the proposed case, it is better to use System GMM rather than Difference GMM estimation, which is associated with the potential of magnifying gaps (Roodman 2009b).

While System GMM may be appropriate in unbalanced panel data, it suffers also from its own weaknesses. Though asymptotically more efficient, the two-step GMM is based on the estimation of standard errors that tend to be critically downward biased. However, it is possible to overcome this estimator problem using the finite-sample correction to the two-step covariance matrix developed by Windmeijer (2005). This two-step robust GMM estimates more efficiently than one-step robust estimates especially for the System GMM (Roodman 2009b).[241] The second weakness of system GMM estimation is the possibility of having too many instruments. Roodman (2009b) develops a detailed analysis of this issue and emphasizes the symptoms of an excessive use of instruments. The idea is that as time dimension increases, the number of instruments can be too large compared to the sample size, therefore invalidating some asymptotic results and specification tests. Too many instruments can overfit endogenous variables and fail to wipe out their endogenous components, resulting in biased coefficients (Roodman 2009a, 2009b). Another argument is that the Hansen J-test and difference-in -Hansen test can be weak in the presence of over-identification. It is possible to proceed with the system GMM estimation following two empirical strategies that deal with the issue of too many instruments (Roodman 2009b). The first one is to use the 'collapse' sub-option for the *xtabond2* command in STATA. The second empirical strategy (lag limits) forces the use of only certain lags instead of all available lags as instruments. Both empirical choices have something in common, which is the reduction of the number of instruments and linearity in t (Vieiraet al. 2013). It is the second strategy that is followed in this study.

As noted above, the xtabond2 command (Roodman 2009a) is used to run System GMM estimation in Stata 13. With respect to post-estimation specification tests, it is the Hansen J-test test for over-identifying restrictions that is used after applying Weinjmier correction to correct the issue of standard deviation. This is achieved by by using syntax robust in STATA and the Arellano and Bond (1991) test, AR(2), for no autocorrelation in the second-differenced errors.

4 Data and Empirical Results

Based on the empirical model Equation (2), the dynamic linkages among finance, economic growth, and human development are estimated using two-step system GMM methodology for an unbalanced panel data of 118 countries of which 54 belong to the OIC countries over the sample period from 1996 to 2014 (for the full list of countries, please refer to Appendix 2). The variables are averaged over 3-year non-overlapping intervals, to smooth out business cycle fluctuations, a measurement approach that is common in current growth literature (Imam and Kpodar

241 After specifying the Windmeijer corrected standard errors (WC-robust) it is Hansen J-test rather than Sargan test that is applied for validating the instruments, particularly in the presence of heteroscedasticity.

2016; Slesman et al. 2015). It is noted that the sample size is constrained by data availability, in particular with regard to the variables capturing human development, and that the natural logarithm is taken for all financial development indicators. CO_2 emissions and all human development indicators are expressed in their original units for better and clear interpretation of the results. The data used in the analysis were collected from The World Development Indicators (WDI), Barro and Lee (2013), UNESCO Institute for Statistics, Global Financial Development Database (GFDD), and The Heritage Foundation (see Appendix 1 for variable definitions, sources and their expected signs based on the existing literature). First, line graphs are plotted for only selected key variables in Figure 26.1 to give a broad view about different patterns over time. It is clear that OIC countries are lagging behind in terms of human development and financial development. No significant difference between OIC and non-OIC countries is observed in terms of growth, however, OIC countries have lower levels of GDP per capita.[242]

The first set of results from the dynamic System-GMM estimations on financial development, human development and economic growth are presented in 45 models in 8 different Tables. The diagnostic tests performed with respect to the dynamic System-GMM models display the following: i) Only variables statistically significant at the conventional level are included in the final models. ii) All the models passed the AR (2) tests, as indicated by p-value showing that the serial correlation in the error terms is not second order. The number of instruments remain below the number of groups (i.e., countries). On the whole, the validity of the instruments is confirmed using Hansen J test as a necessary condition for the estimation of System-GMM models. Accordingly, in consideration of these test statistics, it can be concluded that all estimated models are adequately specified.

For the available sample of developing countries and sample time period, the evidence suggests that human development significantly affects economic growth positively (Table 26.1) at the conventional level. It can be further argued that investment in human capital (primary school enrollment) and health care spending Granger-causes economic growth. This result is strongly supported by the existing literature (Gennaioli et al., 2011; Pischke 2017; Abubakar et al., 2015). Financial development is found to have significant negative effects on economic growth for developing countries, and this evidence is consistent for all four financial development variables as evidenced in Table 26.2. Similar results have been reported in previous studies (De Greogorio and Guidotti, 1995; Shan, 2005; Djalilov and Piesse, 2011; Xu, 2016). However, the efficiency of the financial sector, as measured by bank cost to income, is positively correlated with economic growth, and it is found

242 To calculate the average GDP per capita, the high-income OIC countries (Bahrain, Brunei, Oman, Qatar, Kuwait, Saudi Arabia, UAE) are excluded to avoid biased average GDP numbers for the OIC group. For descriptive statistics and correlation analysis please refer to the Appendix 3.

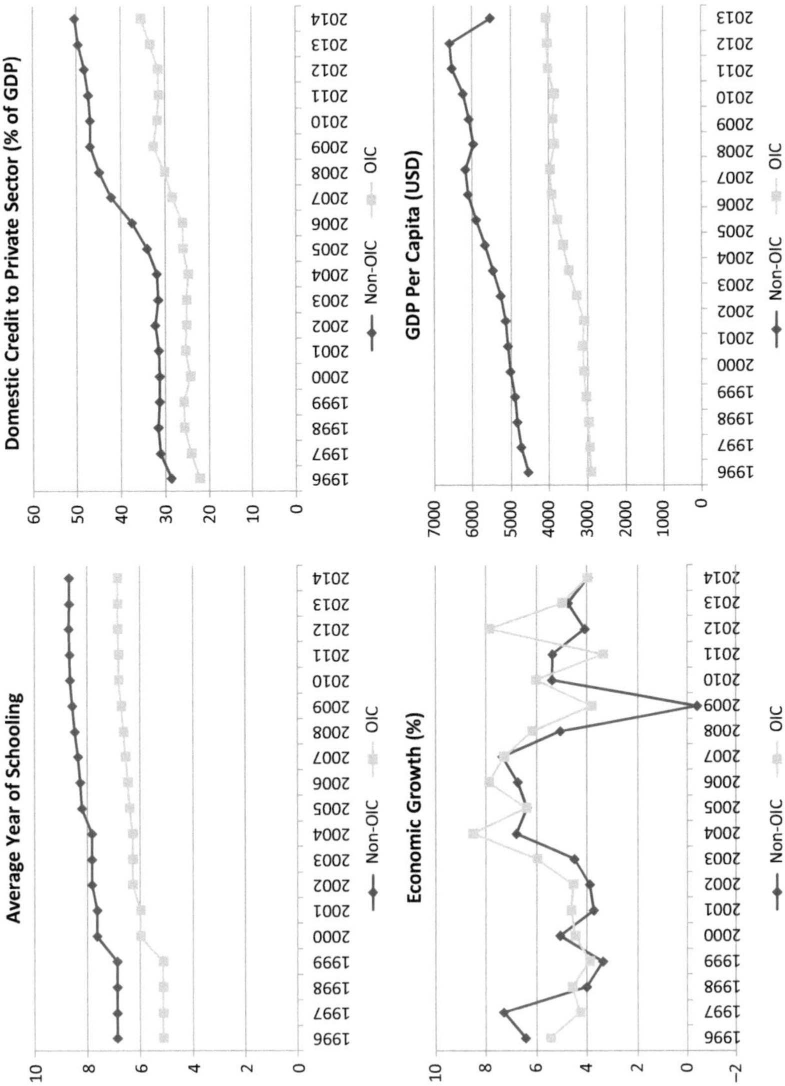

Figure 26.1: Human Development, Finance and Economic Growth in OIC and Non-OIC Countries.
Source: Authors' calculations.
Note: Variables are expressed as yearly averages for each of the 55 OIC and 65 non-OIC countries.

Table 26.1: Human Development and Economic Growth: Developing Countries 1996–2014.

	(1)	(2)	(3)	(4)	(5)	(6)
Economic Growth (t-1)	0.156***	0.254***	0.202***	0.166***	0.216***	0.144***
	[0.04]	[0.04]	[0.05]	[0.04]	[0.04]	[0.04]
GDP per capita	−1.637***	−3.088***	−2.091***	−2.499***	−1.559***	−1.299***
	[0.44]	[0.69]	[0.54]	[0.45]	[0.48]	[0.38]
Capital investment (% of GDP)		4.622***	6.206***	6.229***	4.850***	6.812***
		[1.69]	[1.67]	[1.77]	[1.47]	[1.59]
CO_2 emissions per capita (m.ton)	0.163***	0.175***	0.192**	0.183***	0.132**	0.127***
	[0.06]	[0.06]	[0.08]	[0.05]	[0.06]	[0.04]
Savings (% of GDP)	10.690***	8.962*	10.003	11.246**	10.045*	13.091***
	[4.05]	[4.74]	[6.41]	[4.34]	[6.00]	[4.61]
Unemployment rate (%)	−1.521*	−0.864	−1.077	−0.571	−0.662	−1.492**
	[0.83]	[0.81]	[0.93]	[0.64]	[1.07]	[0.62]
Capital investment (% of GDP) (t-1)	3.376*					
	[1.75]					
Institutional Quality						
Economic Freedom (t-1)	2.995**					
	[1.38]					
Human Development						
Secondary School Enrollment		0.085***				
		[0.03]				
Tertiary School Enrollment			0.037*			
			[0.02]			
Average Year of Schooling				0.460***		
				[0.13]		

Primary School Enrollment (t-1)					0.044**	
					[0.02]	
Health spending (% of GDP) (t-1)						0.577***
						[0.19]
Observations	525	445	420	467	489	526
Instruments	94	94	94	94	94	94
Number of Groups	107	104	104	100	106	108
Arellano-Bond: AR(1)	0.00	0.002	0.006	0.001	0.002	0.001
Arellano-Bond: AR(2)	0.14	0.268	0.073	0.138	0.319	0.417
Hansen test (p-val)	0.225	0.13	0.172	0.156	0.24	0.258

Notes:
- The System-GMM estimation for dynamic panel-data observations based on three-year non-overlapping averages from the sample period 1996 to 2014.
- All explanatory variables are treated as endogenous. The two-period lagged values are used as instruments in the first-difference equations and the one-period lagged first-differences are used in the levels equations.
- Two-step estimations are based on robust standard errors corrected for finite samples. Windmeijer correction and Hansen J tests support the validity of over-identifying restrictions.
- Second order autocorrelation of residuals is rejected for all estimation models.
- Standard errors are in brackets.: ***, 1%; **, 5%, and *, 10%.

Table 26.2: Financial Development and Economic Growth: Developing Countries 1996–2014.

	(7)	(8)	(9)	(10)	(11)	(12)	(13)
Economic Growth (t-1)	0.145***	0.140***	0.127***	0.128***	0.128***	0.145***	0.142***
	[0.03]	[0.03]	[0.04]	[0.04]	[0.03]	[0.03]	[0.03]
GDP per capita	−1.042**	−0.820*	−1.185***	−1.171***	−1.632***	−0.907**	−0.948**
	[0.44]	[0.43]	[0.40]	[0.40]	[0.39]	[0.44]	[0.42]
Capital investment	5.902***	5.744***	5.741***	5.859***	7.094***	6.172***	5.369***
(% of GDP)	[1.30]	[1.52]	[1.57]	[1.56]	[1.51]	[1.26]	[1.54]
CO_2 emissions per capita (m.ton)	0.110**	0.049	0.095*	0.093*	0.175***	0.106**	0.059
	[0.05]	[0.05]	[0.05]	[0.05]	[0.05]	[0.05]	[0.05]
Savings (% of GDP)	8.129**	9.756**	10.287***	10.247***	10.264*	6.966*	9.911**
	[3.63]	[4.29]	[3.84]	[3.80]	[5.77]	[3.75]	[4.29]
Unemployment rate (%)	−1.708**	−2.323***	−2.019***	−2.011***	−1.104	−1.727**	−2.446***
	[0.72]	[0.82]	[0.76]	[0.75]	[0.68]	[0.71]	[0.86]
Financial Development							
Domestic Credit to Private Sector	−1.472**						
	[0.74]						
M3 (% of GDP)		−1.831**					
		[0.72]					
Financial System Deposit			−1.303**				
(% of GDP) (t-1)			[0.65]				
Bank Deposit				−1.254*			
(% of GDP) (t-1)				[0.64]			
Bank Cost to Income					8.073**		
					[3.90]		

Non-linearity of Financial Development							
Domestic Credit to Private Sector (Squared)						−0.257**	
						[0.11]	
M3 (% GDP) (Squared)							−0.254**
							[0.10]
Observations	528	523	518	518	518	528	523
Instruments	94	94	94	94	94	94	94
Number of Groups	108	107	106	106	106	108	107
Arellano-Bond: AR(1)	0.001	0.001	0.001	0.001	0	0.001	0.001
Arellano-Bond: AR(2)	0.371	0.231	0.156	0.158	0.203	0.416	0.221
Hansen test (p-val)	0.256	0.12	0.192	0.192	0.194	0.277	0.148

Notes:
- The System-GMM estimation for dynamic panel-data observations based on three-year non-overlapping averages from the sample period 1996 to 2014.
- All explanatory variables are treated as endogenous. The two-period lagged values are used as instruments in the first-difference equations and the one-period lagged first-differences are used in the levels equations.
- Two-step estimations are based on robust standard errors corrected for finite samples. Windmeijer correction and Hansen J tests support the validity of over-identifying restrictions.
- Second order autocorrelation of residuals is rejected for all estimation models.
- Standard errors are in brackets.: ***, 1%; **, 5%, and *, 10%.

to be statistically significant. In addition, a non-linear negative relationship between financial sector development, (namely domestic credit to private sector and M3 to GDP) and economic growth for developing countries. These findings are also supported by the existing literature (Huang and Lin 2009; Cecchetti and Kharroubi 2012; Law and Singh 2014).

As discussed earlier, there are two major views and findings in empirical literature on the finance-growth nexus. The first one is the positive contribution of financial development toward economic growth (Demirguc-Kunt and Levine 2004; Beck et al. 2000; Beck et al. 2014) and the second one is the negative and non-linear effect of financial development on growth (Deidda and Fattough 2002; Huang and Lin 2009; Arcand 2012; Narayan and Narayan 2013; Law and Singh 2014). Interestingly, Adu et al. (2013) argue whether financial development is good or bad for growth depends on the choice of indicator used to proxy for financial development. Using four financial development indicators, there is either a significantly negative or non-linear negative relationship between finance and growth. There is a convergence among the sample developing countries, for which a negative and significant relationship between economic growth and GDP per capita (Barro 1991). There is also evidence economic freedom, a proxy for economic institutional quality, affects economic growth positively for all developing countries (Aisen and Veiga 2013).

The empirical analysis is extended to address the question of whether human development and financial development are important for OIC countries. If so, how do they differ from non-OIC countries and whether the effect differs across OIC countries? In applying System-GMM on unbalanced panel estimation, there is concern about number of missing values. Moreover, it is very critical to maintain a sufficient number of cross-section observations. If there is an insufficient number of cross-section observations, the estimation may suffer from consistency problems and the coefficients of the independent variables may become critically downward biased. Therefore, it is important to introduce interaction terms rather than running separate regressions with a small number of countries or only OIC countries.[243] Although Figure 26.1 provides no evidence for the significant differences, System-GMM estimation reported in Table 26.3 shows that economic growth is significantly lower in OIC countries compared to non-OIC countries. As expected, upper-income OIC countries are associated with higher growth rates than other developing countries.[244] Asian OIC countries tend to have significantly higher growth rates while African OIC countries suffer from lower growth compared to other developing countries. Interestingly, countries with an Islamic banking sector grow significantly

243 For robustness tests, we have extensively use categorical by continuous and continuous by continuous interaction terms by dividing OIC countries into: Asian, African, lower income, lower middle-income, upper income, oil-dependent, presence of Islamic banking groupings.

244 The graph of other developing countries include rest of the developing OIC and non-OIC countries

Table 26.3: Economic Growth: OIC Countries 1996–2014.

	(14)	(15)	(16)	(17)	(18)
Economic Growth (t-1)	0.121***	0.138***	0.147***	0.102***	0.136***
	[0.04]	[0.03]	[0.03]	[0.03]	[0.03]
GDP per capita	−1.433***	−1.822***	−1.793***	−2.779***	−1.725***
	[0.39]	[0.44]	[0.52]	[0.66]	[0.45]
Capital investment (% of GDP)	5.839***	6.707***	7.592***	5.963***	5.756***
	[1.69]	[1.23]	[1.47]	[2.02]	[1.77]
CO_2 emissions per capita (m.ton)	0.153***	0.187***	0.118**	0.250***	0.212***
	[0.06]	[0.05]	[0.06]	[0.07]	[0.07]
Savings (% of GDP)	10.955**	8.133**	9.307**	11.072**	10.162**
	[4.22]	[3.15]	[4.26]	[4.98]	[4.82]
Unemployment rate (%)	−1.568*	−1.273*	−1.283	−0.508	−1.164
	[0.85]	[0.77]	[1.02]	[0.90]	[0.79]
Economic Freedom (t-1)	2.796*				
	[1.48]				
OIC Dummies					
OIC Dummy	−1.500*				
	[0.90]				
Upper Income OIC Dummy		2.990***			
		[0.91]			
Asian OIC Dummy			2.355**		
			[1.07]		
African OIC Dummy				−4.714**	
				[2.03]	
Countries with Islamic Bank Presence Dummy					−2.039*
					[1.17]
Observations	525	528	528	528	528
Instruments	98	85	85	85	85
Number of Groups	107	108	108	108	108
Arellano-Bond: AR(1)	0.001	0.001	0.001	0.001	0.001
Arellano-Bond: AR(2)	0.186	0.312	0.362	0.202	0.281
Hansen test (p-val)	0.249	0.343	0.208	0.079	0.164

Notes:
- The System-GMM estimation for dynamic panel-data observations based on three-year non-overlapping averages from the sample period 1996 to 2014.
- All explanatory variables are treated as endogenous. The two-period lagged values are used as instruments in the first-difference equations and the one-period lagged first-differences are used in the levels equations.
- Two-step estimations are based on robust standard errors corrected for finite samples. Windmeijer correction and Hansen J tests support the validity of over-identifying restrictions.
- Second order autocorrelation of residuals is rejected for all estimation models.
- Standard errors are in brackets.: ***, 1%; **, 5%, and *, 10%.

lower than other developing nations. It is not clear whether the lower growth rates are achieved despite or because of the presence of Islamic banking sector.

To examine how the relationship between human development and economic growth in OIC regions differs from other developing countries, it is possible to include categorical-by-continuous interaction terms as presented in Tables 26.4 and 26.5.[245] Health spending has significant effects on economic growth in OIC countries (Model 19 Table 26.4). Judging from Models 20 to 23 (Table 26.4), there is evidence that human capital accumulation, measured by the average number of years of schooling, affects economic growth significantly in Asian OIC countries than other developing countries. It is also found that tertiary school enrollment matters less for economic growth. It can be argued with respect to Asian OIC countries with lower levels of schooling, increase in one additional year of schooling can contribute greatly toward economic growth in the long run through an improvement in labor productivity. Sianesi and Van Reenen (2003) find similar results in their empirical study. Primary school enrollment has small but significant effect on economic growth in African countries while tertiary school enrollment affects economic growth with greater extent in African countries than other developing countries. The results reported in Table 26.5 (Models 24 to 27) suggest that an increase in primary school enrollment has significantly less effects on economic growth for lower and lower-middle-income OIC countries. As expected, secondary school enrollment affects economic growth more significantly in upper-income OIC countries than in other developing countries.

The evidence suggests also that an increase in health spending has significantly higher effects on economic growth in oil-dependent OIC countries and those associated with Islamic financial sector (Table 26.6). Similarly, primary and secondary school enrollment has lesser effect on economic growth for oil dependent countries and those associated with Islamic banking. Thus, it can be argued that undeveloped economies cannot absorb large number of graduates due to the lack of weak infrastructure, which cause brain drain, migration of qualified personnel from developing to developed countries. This has been a problem for many Muslim countries and it may be more acute for Asian and African Muslim countries. As education increases the quality of labor, higher education leads to higher productivity, thus higher growth. Therefore, in addition to the need to increase health spending, most developing OIC countries should focus on increasing average years of schooling and create employment opportunities to avoid brain drain.

The impact of how financial development affects economic growth in OIC countries compared to non-OIC developing countries is assessed with the estimation

245 To get the interaction term we multiply the variables originally included in the models. So interaction terms with human development variables are in their original form while financial development variables are in log form.

Table 26.4: Human Development and Economic Growth: OIC Regional Difference 1996–2014.

	(19)	(20)	(21)	(22)	(23)
Economic Growth (t-1)	0.250***	0.163***	0.296***	0.361***	0.260***
	[0.07]	[0.03]	[0.09]	[0.05]	[0.09]
GDP per capita	−1.975***	−2.060***	−3.181***	−2.799***	−3.326***
	[0.61]	[0.38]	[0.56]	[0.67]	[0.61]
Capital investment (% of GDP)	7.412***	5.926***	6.684***	4.240**	6.901***
	[1.93]	[1.52]	[1.89]	[1.66]	[2.34]
CO_2 emissions per capita (m.ton)	0.283***	0.134***	0.210**	0.202**	0.226***
	[0.07]	[0.05]	[0.09]	[0.08]	[0.07]
Savings (% of GDP)	14.218***	10.642***	14.875**	14.079**	14.596**
	[3.94]	[3.88]	[7.40]	[5.67]	[6.22]
Average Year of Schooling		0.175			
		[0.16]			
Primary School Enrollment (t-1)				0.117***	
				[0.03]	
Tertiary School Enrollment			0.087***		0.027
			[0.03]		[0.03]
Health Spending (% of GDP)	−0.29				
	[0.35]				
OIC Dummy	−8.868***				
	[2.53]				
Asian OIC Dummy		−3.374	4.960***		
		[2.47]	[1.61]		
African OIC Dummy				6.843*	−6.232***
				[3.57]	[1.99]
OIC Dummy and Human Development Interactions					
OIC x Health Spending	1.152***				
	[0.39]				
OIC Regional Dummies and Human Development Interactions					
Asian OIC Dummy x Average Year of Schooling		0.576*			
		[0.33]			
Asian OIC Dummy x Tertiary School Enrollment			−0.117**		
			[0.05]		
African OIC Dummy x Primary School Enrollment				−0.085**	
				[0.04]	
African OIC Dummy x Tertiary School Enrollment					0.207**
					[0.09]
Observations	532	470	425	480	425
Instruments	71	98	71	71	71
Number of Groups	109	101	105	106	105

Table 26.4 (continued)

	(19)	(20)	(21)	(22)	(23)
Arellano-Bond: AR(1)	0.002	0.001	0.006	0.005	0.009
Arellano-Bond: AR(2)	0.833	0.151	0.133	0.445	0.16
Hansen test (p-val)	0.092	0.198	0.11	0.209	0.125

Notes:
- The System-GMM estimation for dynamic panel-data observations based on three-year non-overlapping averages from the sample period 1996 to 2014.
- All explanatory variables are treated as endogenous. The two-period lagged values are used as instruments in the first-difference equations and the one-period lagged first-differences are used in the levels equations.
- Two-step estimations are based on robust standard errors corrected for finite samples. Windmeijer correction and Hansen J tests support the validity of over-identifying restrictions.
- Second order autocorrelation of residuals is rejected for all estimation models.
- Standard errors are in brackets.: ***, 1%; **, 5%, and *, 10%.

results in Models (33) to (39), which are reported in Table 26.7. It appears that the effect of M3 to GDP ratio has become insignificant but the interaction term is significant. This implies that financial development has significantly lesser effect on OIC countries than on non-OIC countries with the inclusion of the significant negative effects of M3 to GDP ratio in sample countries. At the same time, the ratios of domestic credit to private sector, bank deposit to GDP, and financial system deposits to GDP have significantly lesser effects on Asian OIC countries. However, for countries with Islamic finance sector, financial development brings significantly higher growth than for other developing countries (Model 39 Table 26.7). As argued earlier, the theoretical and empirical relationship between finance and growth is controversial with many studies confirm significant negative and negative non-linear relationship. In other words, the impact of finance on growth may be reversed after reaching a certain threshold. However, it can be also argued that financial development based on the genuine application of Islamic principles can stimulate economic growth as it encourages real sector connectivity and risk-sharing principles (Anwar 1987; Mirakhor 1993; Bacha and Mirakhor 2014).

4.1 Robustness Tests and Financial Development Transmission Channel

To further the analysis through robustness tests it is necessary to perform separate regressions by excluding high income OIC countries and Global Financial Crisis period 2008–2009. The results are consistent with previous evidence, especially when

Table 26.5: Human Development and Economic Growth: OIC Country Groups 1996–2014.

	(24)	(25)	(26)	(27)
Economic Growth (t-1)	0.344***	0.374***	0.340***	0.328***
	[0.05]	[0.05]	[0.03]	[0.05]
GDP per capita	−3.011***	−3.105***	−2.800***	−3.102***
	[0.70]	[0.88]	[0.75]	[0.73]
Capital investment (% of GDP)	4.988**	5.294**	3.487	4.052**
	[2.22]	[2.22]	[2.18]	[1.79]
CO_2 emissions per capita (m.ton)	0.244***	0.128	0.260***	0.180**
	[0.09]	[0.09]	[0.08]	[0.09]
Savings (% of GDP)	12.485*	9.02	12.489***	8.385*
	[6.41]	[6.18]	[4.65]	[4.92]
Unemployment rate (%)		−0.391		−0.657
		[0.94]		[0.87]
Secondary School Enrollment		0.097***		0.064**
		[0.03]		[0.03]
Primary School Enrollment (t-1)	0.114***		0.113***	
	[0.03]		[0.03]	
Lower Income OIC	7.623*			
	[4.45]			
Lower Middle Income OIC		6.830*		
		[3.61]		
Upper Income OIC			37.656**	−6.38
			[17.18]	[4.42]
OIC Country Dummies and Human Development Interactions				
Lower Income OIC x Primary School Enrollment	−0.101**			
	[0.05]			

(continued)

Table 26.5 (continued)

	(24)	(25)	(26)	(27)
Lower Middle Income OIC x Secondary School Enrollment		−0.109** [0.05]		
Upper Income OIC x Primary School Enrollment			−0.337* [0.17]	
Upper Income OIC x Secondary School Enrollment				0.097* [0.06]
Observations	480	445	480	445
Instruments	71	80	71	80
Number of Groups	106	104	106	104
Arellano-Bond: AR(1)	0.006	0.002	0.004	0.002
Arellano-Bond: AR(2)	0.478	0.415	0.447	0.394
Hansen test (p-val)	0.255	0.073	0.126	0.061

Notes:
- The System-GMM estimation for dynamic panel-data observations based on three-year non-overlapping averages from the sample period 1996 to 2014.
- All explanatory variables are treated as endogenous. The two-period lagged values are used as instruments in the first-difference equations and the one-period lagged first-differences are used in the levels equations.
- Two-step estimations are based on robust standard errors corrected for finite samples. Windmeijer correction and Hansen J tests support the validity of over-identifying restrictions.
- Second order autocorrelation of residuals is rejected for all estimation models.
- Standard errors are in brackets.: ***, 1%; **, 5%, and *, 10%.

Table 26.6: Human Development and Economic Growth: OIC Oil Dependent and Islamic Finance Presence 1996–2014.

	(28)	(29)	(30)	(31)	(32)
Economic Growth (t-1)	0.152***	0.388***	0.286***	0.375***	0.268***
	[0.04]	[0.04]	[0.07]	[0.05]	[0.06]
GDP per capita	−2.424***	−2.457***	−1.369**	−2.971***	−1.461**
	[0.44]	[0.67]	[0.60]	[0.72]	[0.66]
Capital investment (% of GDP)	5.748***	4.516**	9.402***	6.008***	8.319***
	[1.70]	[2.21]	[1.79]	[2.20]	[2.54]
CO_2 emissions per capita (m.ton)	0.165***	0.166***	0.203***	0.219***	0.258***
	[0.05]	[0.05]	[0.07]	[0.07]	[0.08]
Savings (% of GDP)	12.143***	18.485***	12.202***	7.506*	12.279**
	[4.08]	[6.37]	[3.47]	[4.36]	[4.84]
Average Year of Schooling	0.25				
	[0.17]				
Unemployment rate (%)				−0.9	
				[1.03]	
Primary School Enrollment (t-1)		0.115***			
		[0.03]			
Secondary School Enrollment				0.098***	
				[0.03]	
Health spending (% of GDP)			−0.01		−0.32
			[0.32]		[0.29]
Oil-dependent OIC Dummy	−4.866*	17.959*	−6.468*		
	[2.83]	[9.27]	[3.34]		
Islamic Bank Presence OIC				6.345**	−10.210***
				[2.97]	[3.53]
Human development and oil dependent and Islamic finance presence OIC					
Oil dependent OIC Dummy x Average Year of Schooling	0.713* [0.37]				
Oil dependent OIC Dummy x Primary School Enrollment		−0.178* [0.10]			
Oil dependent OIC Dummy x Health spending			1.189* [0.64]		
Islamic Bank Presence OIC x Secondary School Enrollment				−0.086** [0.04]	
Islamic Bank Presence OIC x Health spending					1.015* [0.59]
Observations	470	480	532	445	532
Instruments	98	71	71	80	71
Number of Groups	101	106	109	104	109

Table 26.6 (continued)

	(28)	(29)	(30)	(31)	(32)
Arellano-Bond: AR(1)	0.001	0.004	0.001	0.002	0.001
Arellano-Bond: AR(2)	0.123	0.527	0.904	0.365	0.747
Hansen test (p-val)	0.18	0.067	0.078	0.058	0.052

Notes:
- The System-GMM estimation for dynamic panel-data observations based on three-year non-overlapping averages from the sample period 1996 to 2014.
- All explanatory variables are treated as endogenous. The two-period lagged values are used as instruments in the first-difference equations and the one-period lagged first-differences are used in the levels equations.
- Two-step estimations are based on robust standard errors corrected for finite samples. Windmeijer correction and Hansen J tests support the validity of over-identifying restrictions.
- Second order autocorrelation of residuals is rejected for all estimation models.
- Standard errors are in brackets.: ***, 1%; **, 5%, and *, 10%.

the observations related to the Global Financial Crisis. Moreover, interaction terms between financial developments with control variables such as M3 × unemployment rate as additional explanatory variables apart from the standard variables used in the growth equation.[246] The financial development and macroeconomic indicators are included independently in the regression for two primary reasons. First, the significance of the interaction terms may be the result of the omission of these variables. It is possible to test jointly whether these variables affect growth directly or through the interaction terms. Second, these variables ensure that the interaction term do not proxy for financial development indicators or macro variables. These variabls are included in the estimation models independently. From the model specifications 40 to 45, reported in Table 26.8, it is clear that upon including interaction terms, all indicators of financial development change sign and become statistically significant at the conventional level, except for domestic credit to the private sector (model 40) and the ratio of bank deposits to GDP (model 44). The coefficient of the interaction term between M3 and Unemployment rate (model 40) is found to be statistically significant and negative, but the individual coefficients are associated with positive sign and are significant at the conventional levels. In other words, the effects of financial development and unemployment rate are not weakened when the interaction terms are included in the model.

246 Given the evidence of significantly negative relationship between financial development and economic growth in sample developing countries, it is important to investigate how financial development could affect economic growth indirectly.

Table 26.7: Financial Development and Economic Growth: OIC Countries 1996–2014.

	(33)	(34)	(35)	(36)	(37)	(38)	(39)
Economic Growth (t-1)	0.263***	0.235***	0.255***	0.254***	0.271***	0.233***	0.221***
	[0.07]	[0.06]	[0.06]	[0.06]	[0.07]	[0.07]	[0.07]
GDP per capita	−1.378**	−2.926***	−2.252***	−2.225***	−1.209**	−1.254**	−1.199**
	[0.61]	[0.68]	[0.56]	[0.56]	[0.59]	[0.56]	[0.51]
Capital investment	7.805***	5.114**	6.427***	6.468***	8.556***	8.280***	7.912***
(% of GDP)	[2.08]	[2.04]	[2.16]	[2.14]	[2.14]	[2.18]	[1.95]
CO_2 emissions per capita (m.ton)	0.113	0.243***	0.171***	0.167***	0.045	0.064	0.057
	[0.08]	[0.07]	[0.06]	[0.06]	[0.09]	[0.08]	[0.07]
Savings (% of GDP)	12.501***	14.244***	12.995***	12.991***	11.797**	12.521**	13.050***
	[4.24]	[4.13]	[3.45]	[3.43]	[4.77]	[4.77]	[3.83]
Lag M3 (% of GDP) (t-1)	0.63				0.558		
	[0.85]				[0.82]		
Domestic Credit to Private Sector		1.569*					
		[0.82]					
Bank Deposit			1.136				
(% of GDP) (−1)			[1.04]				
Bank Deposit (% of GDP)						−0.655	−2.514*
						[1.38]	[1.51]
Financial System Deposit				1.087			
(% of GDP)				[1.04]			
OIC Dummy	8.286*						
	[4.95]						
Asian OIC Dummy		14.249**	15.813**	15.748**			

(continued)

Table 26.7 (continued)

	(33)	(34)	(35)	(36)	(37)	(38)	(39)
		[7.18]	[7.05]	[7.13]			
Lower Middle Income OIC					15.639**	12.111*	
					[7.20]	[7.09]	
Islamic Bank Presence OIC							−10.109**
							[4.71]
Financial Development and growth in OIC							
OIC Dummy x	−2.570*						
M3 (% of GDP)	[1.35]						
Asian OIC Dummy x		−3.758*					
Domestic Credit to Private Sector		[2.18]					
Asian OIC Dummy x			−3.984*				
Bank Deposit (% of GDP)			[2.21]				
Asian OIC Dummy x				−3.949*			
Financial System Deposit (% of GDP)				[2.23]			
Lower Middle Income OIC x					−5.028**		
M3 (% of GDP)					[2.12]		
Lower Middle Income OIC x						−4.022*	
Bank Deposit (% of GDP)						[2.11]	
Islamic Bank Presence OIC x							3.028**
Bank Deposit (% of GDP)							[1.46]
Observations	528	533	523	523	528	523	523
Instruments	71	71	71	71	71	71	71
Number of Groups	108	109	107	107	108	107	107

Arellano-Bond: AR(1)	0.002	0.001	0.001	0.001	0.002	0.002	0.002
Arellano-Bond: AR(2)	0.921	0.558	0.733	0.723	0.986	0.779	0.566
Hansen test (p-val)	0.091	0.275	0.078	0.078	0.06	0.092	0.067

Notes:

- The System-GMM estimation for dynamic panel-data observations based on three-year non-overlapping averages from the sample period 1996 to 2014.
- All explanatory variables are treated as endogenous. The two-period lagged values are used as instruments in the first-difference equations and the one-period lagged first-differences are used in the levels equations.
- Two-step estimations are based on robust standard errors corrected for finite samples. Windmeijer correction and Hansen J tests support the validity of over-identifying restrictions.
- Second order autocorrelation of residuals is rejected for all estimation models.
- Standard errors are in brackets.: ***, 1%; **, 5%, and *, 10%.

Table 26.8: Transmission Channels Financial Development and Economic Growth: Developing Countries 1996–2014.

	(40)	(41)	(42)	(43)	(44)	(45)
Economic Growth (t-1)	0.238***	0.280***	0.200***	0.201***	0.216***	0.221***
	[0.06]	[0.07]	[0.06]	[0.06]	[0.07]	[0.06]
GDP per capita	−1.092**	−2.053**	−1.030*	−1.070*	−1.091**	−0.917
	[0.48]	[0.80]	[0.54]	[0.55]	[0.47]	[0.61]
Capital investment	8.092***	6.585***	9.966***	9.907***	8.381***	20.215***
(% of GDP)	[1.72]	[2.15]	[2.20]	[2.16]	[2.04]	[7.44]
CO_2 emissions per capita (m.ton)	0.021	1.204*	0.048	0.05	0.031	0.032
	[0.08]	[0.65]	[0.06]	[0.06]	[0.07]	[0.07]
Savings (% of GDP)	12.640***	13.752***	21.302***	20.889***	11.963***	9.495*
	[3.89]	[4.89]	[5.49]	[5.51]	[4.02]	[4.93]
Unemployment rate (%)	8.741***	−0.619	−1.145	−1.147	6.911**	−1.811*
	[3.29]	[0.95]	[0.97]	[0.96]	[3.48]	[1.00]
M3 (% of GDP)	0.656*					
	[0.37]					
Domestic Credit to Private Sector		0.235				
		[0.20]				
Financial System Deposit			1.553***			
(% of GDP)			[0.53]			
Bank Deposit (% of GDP)				1.469***	0.522	1.455*
				[0.51]	[0.39]	[0.83]
Transmission Channels						
M3 x Unemployment rate	−2.709***					
	[0.88]					
Domestic Credit to Private Sector x CO_2		−0.287*				
		[0.17]				
Financial System Deposit x Savings (% of GDP)			−2.547***			
			[0.81]			

Bank Deposit x Savings				−2.406***		
(% of GDP)				[0.78]		
Bank Deposit x Unemployment rate					−2.359**	
					[0.96]	
Bank Deposit x Capital Investment						−3.145*
(% of GDP)						[1.83]
Observations	523	528	518	518	518	518
Instruments	76	76	76	76	76	76
Number of Groups	107	108	106	106	106	106
Arellano-Bond: AR(1)	0.002	0.001	0.002	0.002	0.002	0.002
Arellano-Bond: AR(2)	0.703	0.741	0.557	0.553	0.56	0.607
Hansen test (p-val)	0.082	0.056	0.066	0.07	0.064	0.056

Notes:
- The System-GMM estimation for dynamic panel-data observations based on three-year non-overlapping averages from the sample period 1996 to 2014.
- All explanatory variables are treated as endogenous. The two-period lagged values are used as instruments in the first-difference equations and the one-period lagged first-differences are used in the levels equations.
- Two-step estimations are based on robust standard errors corrected for finite samples. Windmeijer correction and Hansen J tests support the validity of over-identifying restrictions.
- Second order autocorrelation of residuals is rejected for all estimation models.
- Standard errors are in brackets.: ***, 1%; **, 5%, and *, 10%.

In contrary, the evidence suggests that we observed that when the interaction terms between domestic credit to private sector and CO2 emissions are included, the coefficient is negative and significant at 10% level. The positive coefficient on domestic credit to private sector is insignificant. In other words, the direct effects of financial development on growth seems to be suppressed or weakened when the interaction terms are included, whereas industrialization still plays a significant role in economic development. The interaction terms between financial system deposit and savings are found to be negative and statistically significant whereas the coefficients on financial system deposit and savings to GDP remain statistically significant. Moreover, the effects of savings to GDP increase in association with the inclusion of the interaction term. In other words, financial development has positive effects on economic growth with the inclusion of the interaction terms.

Therefore, it can be argued that though the indirect effects of financial development, macroeconomic stability, industrialization, and capital formation are negative, the direct contribution of financial development on growth is positive and significant and magnitude of macroeconomic stability, industrialization, and capital formation increases significantly. It is often argued in the related literature that a developed financial system contributes toward channeling savings from surplus units to deficit units, which increases efficiency and ensures the allocation of resources for securing economic growth. However, most developing countries have low levels of financial development in terms of depth and access to finance. Thus, without therefore without macroeconomic stability, a mere increase in labor productivity through human capital accumulation, technological innovation, industrialization and strong capital base these countries may not be effective. Financial development alone may not be enough to spur economic growth in the long run.

5 Conclusions

The principal factors that deter economic growth in Muslim countries may not be different from those undermining development in non-Muslim countries. But most OIC countries have long been suffering from extreme poverty, rampant corruption, high political instability, civil wars and foreign invasions and they are naturally lagging behind other developing countries in terms of economic growth.[247] At the same time, many Muslim countries have failed to develop human capital, one of the most fundamental Islamic development indicators. Lower levels of financial development in OIC countries are also evident from the evidence presented in this study. The results indicate also that the development of Islamic finance contributes

247 Many Muslim countries are suffering from political turmoil and rise of extremism, greatly affected and somewhat lost their growth trajectory.

positively to economic growth (Imam and Kpodar 2016). Financial development seems to affect economic growth more significantly at higher level in countries with the stronger presence of Islamic finance. It is difficult, however, to draw strong claims from weak inferences limited to a small number of countries and still very insignificant compared to its conventional counterpart.

By estimating dynamic system-GMM on 118 countries including 54 OIC countries between 1996 and 2014, this study empirically analyzed whether human development and financial development have contributed to economic growth in developing countries in general and OIC countries in particular. The estimation results indicated that there is a positive relationship between human development indicators (average year of schooling, primary, secondary and tertiary school enrollment and health spending to GDP) and economic growth. Most importantly, from the beginning of the twenty-first century, the per capita real GDP growth rates in OIC Asian countries have been rising significantly but still at slower rates than other developing countries. On the other hand, financial development (domestic credit to private sector, M3, banking deposit and financial system deposits to GDP) and economic growth are found to be negatively correlated but bank cost to income, which is a measure of financial system efficiency, is found to be positively correlated with economic growth. Our empirical evidence is consistent with the results of Hao (2006), Hasan et al. (2009) and Xu (2016). Furthermore, there is evidence that non-linear negative relationships between domestic credit to private sector and economic growth, and M3 and economic growth. As most of the OIC countries, besides oil rich GCC,[248] Malaysia and Turkey, have rather weak financial sector and relatively weaker capital markets in terms of depth, access and efficiency (Beck et al. 2000; Demirguc-Kunt and Levine 2004). Beck et al. (2007) argue that if financial development increases average growth only by increasing the incomes of the rich and hence by increasing income inequality, then financial development will not help those with lower incomes.

Therefore, in addition to an increase in health spending, most developing OIC countries should focus on increasing investment in human capital accumulation. They should also develop production and services industry to create employment opportunities for graduates to avoid brain drain. At the same time, OIC countries should develop the Islamic finance industry based on the principles of risk-sharing and close relationship with the real economy instead of pursuing rent-seeking activities similar to conventional finance. The focus should be made also on institutional development, macroeconomic stability, capital formation, and industrialization, which are crucial for growth in Muslim countries.

248 GCC stands for Gulf Cooperation Council and consists of Bahrain, Kuwait, Oman, Qatar, Saudi Arabia, and UAE.

References

Abubakar, Abdulsalam, Salina HJ Kassim, and Mohammad B. Yusoff. 2015. "Financial Development, Human Capital Accumulation and Economic Growth: Empirical Evidence from the Economic Community of West African States (ECOWAS)." *Procedia-Social and Behavioral Sciences* 172: 96–103.

Adu, George, George Marbuah, and Justic Tei Mensah. 2013. "Financial development and economic growth in Ghana: Does the measure of financial development matter?." *Review of Development Finance 3*(4): 192–203.

Aghion, Philippe, Peter W. Howitt, Maxine Brant-Collett, and Cecillia García-Peñalosa. 1998. *Endogenous Growth Theory*. Cambridge: MIT Press.

Ahmed, Abdullahi D. 2016. "Integration of financial markets, financial development and growth: Is Africa different?" *Journal of International Financial Markets, Institutions and Money* 42: 43–59.

Aisen, Ari, and Francisco Jose Veiga. 2013. "How does political instability affect economic growth?." *European Journal of Political Economy* 29: 151–167.

Anwar, Muhammad. 1987. "Modelling Interest-Free Economy: A Study in Macroeconomics and Development (No. 4)." International Institute of Islamic Thought (IIIT).

Arcand, Jean Louis, Enrico Berkes, and Ugo Panizza. 2012. "Too Much Finance?." IMF Working Papers, 12: 161.

Arellano, Manuel, and Stephen Bond. 1991. "Some tests of specification for panel data: Monte Carlo evidence and an application to employment equations." *Review of Economic Studies* 58: 277–297.

Arellano, Manuel, and Olympia Bover. 1995. "Another look at the instrumental variables estimation of error component models." *Journal of Econometrics* 68: 29–51.

Askari, Hossein, and Scheherazade Rehma. 2013. "A Survey of the Economic Development of OIC Countries." In *Economic Development and Islamic Finance*, edited by Zamir Iqbal and Abbas Mirakhor: 299–324. Washington, DC: The World Bank Group.

As-Sadr, Kazem. 1989. "Money and Monetary Policies in Early Islamic Period." In *Essays on Iqtisad: The Islamic Approach to Economic Problems*, edited by Dalam Al-Hasani and Abbas Mirakhor, 199–217. Silver Spring: Nur Corp,

Bacha, Obiyathulla Ismath and Abbas Mirakhor. 2013. "Islamic Capital Markets and Development." In *Economic Development and Islamic Finance*, edited by Zamir Iqbal and Abbas Mirakhor: 253–273. Washington, DC: The World Bank Group.

Barro, Robert J. 1991. "Economic Growth in a Cross Section of Countries." *The Quarterly Journal of Economics* 106(2): 407–443.

Barro, Robert J., and Jong Wha Lee. 2013. "A new data set of educational attainment in the world, 1950–2010." *Journal of Development Economics* 104: 184–198.

Batuo, Michael, Kupukile Mlambo, and Simplice Asongu. 2018. "Linkages between financial development, financial instability, financial liberalisation and economic growth in Africa." *Research in International Business and Finance* 45(October):168–179.

Beck, Thorsten, Hans Degryse, and Christiane Kneer. 2014. "Is more finance better? Disentangling intermediation and size effects of financial systems." *Journal of Financial Stability* 10: 50–64.

Beck, Thorsten, Asli Demirgüç-Kunt, and Ross Levine. 2007. "Finance, inequality and the poor." *Journal of Economic Growth* 12(1): 27–49.

Beck, Thorsten, Ross Levine, and Norman Loayza. 2000. "Finance and the Sources of Growth." *Journal of Financial Economics* 58(1): 261–300.

Benhabib, Jess, and Mark M. Spiegel. 1994. "The role of human capital in economic development evidence from aggregate cross-country data." *Journal of Monetary economics* 34(2): 143–173.

Blundell, Richard, and Stephen Bond. 1998. "Initial conditions and moment restrictions in dynamic panel data models." *Journal of Econometrics* 87: 115–143.

Bond, Stephen R, Anke Hoeffler, and Jonathan RW Temple. 2000. "GMM estimation of empirical growth models." CEPR Discussion Papers no. 3048.

Cecchetti, Stephen G., and Enisse Kharroubi. 2012. "Reassessing the impact of finance on growth." BIS Working Papers No 381.

Chen, Yang, and Zheng Fang. 2018. "Industrial electricity consumption, human capital investment and economic growth in Chinese cities." *Economic Modelling* 69: 205–219.

Çizakça, Murat. 2013. "Finance and Development in Islam: A Historical Perspective and a Brief Look Forward." In *Economic Development and Islamic Finance*, edited by Zamir Iqbal and Abbas Mirakhor: 299–324. Washington, DC: The World Bank Group.

Cojocaru, Laura, Evangelos M. Falaris, Saul D. Hoffman, and Jeffrey Miller. 2016. "Financial system development and economic growth in transition economies: new empirical evidence from the CEE and CIS countries." *Emerging Markets Finance and Trade 52*(1): 223–236.

Darrat, Ali F., Khaled Elkhal, and Brent McCallum. 2006. "Finance and macroeconomic performance. Some evidence for emerging markets." *Emerging Markets Finance and Trade 42*(3): 5–28.

De Gregorio, Jose, and Pablo E. Guidotti. 1995. "Financial development and economic growth." *World Development 23*(3): 433–448.

Deidda, Luca, and Bassam Fattouh. 2002. "Non-linearity between finance and growth." *Economics Letters* 74(3): 339–345.

Demirgüç-Kunt, Asli, and Ross Levine. 2004. *Financial Structure and Economic Growth: A Cross-Country Comparison of Banks, Markets, and Development*. Cambridge: The MIT Press.

Djalilov, Khurshid, and Jenifer Piesse. 2011. "Financial development and growth in transition countries: A study of Central Asia." *Emerging Markets Finance and Trade 47*(6): 4–23.

Gemmell, Norman. 1996. "Evaluating the impacts of human capital stocks and accumulation on economic growth: some new evidence." *Oxford Bulletin of Economics and Statistics* 58(1): 9–28.

Gennaioli, Nicola, Rafael La Porta, Florencio Lopez-de-Silanes, and Andrei Shleifer. 2011. "Human capital and regional development." *The Quarterly Journal of Economics* 128 (1): 105–164.

Goldsmith, Raymond William. 1969. *Financial Structure and Development*. New Haven and London: Yale University Press.

Chen, Hao. 2006. "Development of financial intermediation and economic growth: The Chinese experience." *China Economic Review* 17 (4): 347–362.

Hasan, Iftekhar, Paul Wachtel, and Mingming Zhou. 2009. "Institutional development, financial deepening and economic growth: Evidence from China." *Journal of Banking & Finance* 33(1): 157–70.

Holmes, Craig. 2013. "Has the expansion of higher education led to greater economic growth?," *National Institute Economic Review* 224(1): 29–47.

Huang, Ho-Chuan, and Shu-Chin Lin. 2009. "Non-linear finance–growth nexus." *Economics of Transition* 17: 439–466.

Imam, Patrick, and Kangni Kpodar. 2016. "Islamic banking: Good for growth?" *Economic Modelling* 59: 387–401.

Inoue, Takeshi, and Shigeyuki Hamori. 2016. "Financial Access and Economic Growth: Evidence from Sub-Saharan Africa." *Emerging Markets Finance and Trade* 52(3): 743–753.

King, Robert. and Ross Levine. 1993. "Finance and growth: Schumpeter might be right." *The Quarterly Journal of Economics* 108(3): 717–737.

Law, Siong Hook, and Nirvikar Singh. 2014. "Does too much finance harm economic growth?." *Journal of Banking & Finance* 41: 36–44.

Lee, Jong-Wha, and Kiseok Hong. 2012. “Economic growth in Asia: Determinants and prospects.” *Japan and the World Economy* 24(2): 101–113.

Lim, Taejun. 2018. “Growth, financial development, and housing booms.” *Economic Modelling* 69: 91–102.

Mankiw, N. Gregory, David Romer and David N. Weil. 1992. “A contribution to the empirics of economic growth.” *The Quarterly Journal of Economics* 107(2): 407–437.

Mannan, Muhammad Abdul. 1989. *Economic Development and Social Peace in Islam: An Analytical Study of the Process of Economic Development in the Muslim Community of Today.* Bangladesh: Ta-Ha Publication.

Mirakhor, Abbas. 1993. “Equilibrium in a non-interest open economy.” *Journal of King Abdulaziz University: Islamic Economics* 5: 3–23.

Mirakhor, Abbas, and Hossein Askari. 2010. *Islam and the Path to Human and Economic Development.* New York: Palgrave Macmillan.

Mustafa, Ghulam, Marian Rizov, and David Kernohan. 2017. “Growth, human development, and trade: The Asian experience.” *Economic Modelling* 61: 93–101.

Narayan, Paresh Kumar, and Seema Narayan. 2013. “The short-run relationship between the financial system and economic growth: New evidence from regional panels.” *International Review of Financial Analysis* 29: 70–78.

Von Pischke, J. D. 1997. “Poverty, human development and financial services.” Human Development Occasional Papers (1992–2007) HDOCPA-1997–04, Human Development Report Office (HDRO), United Nations Development Programme (UNDP).

Pritchett, Lant. 2001. “Where has all the education gone?” *The World Economic Review* 15(3): 367–391.

Romer, Paul M. 1994. “The origins of endogenous growth.” *The Journal of Economic Perspectives* 1: 3–22.

Roodman, David. 2009a. “How to do xtabond an introduction to difference and system GMM in Stata.” *Stata Journal* 9: 86–136.

Roodman, David. 2009b. “A note on the theme of too many instruments.” *Oxford Bulletin of Economics and Statistics* 71: 135–158.

Ruiz, Jose L. 2017. “Financial development, institutional investors, and economic growth.” *International Review of Economics & Finance* 54: 218–224.

Schumpeter, Joseph. 1934. *Theory of Economic Development: An Inquiry into Profits, Capital, Credit, Interest, and the Business Cycle*. Cambridge, MA: Harvard University Press.

Shan, Jordan. 2005. “Does financial development ‘lead’economic growth? A vector auto-regression appraisal.” *Applied Economics* 37(12): 1353–1367.

Sianesi, Barbara, and John Van Reenen. 2003. “The returns to education: Macroeconomics.” *Journal of Economic Surveys* 17 (2): 157–200.

Slesman, Ly, Ahmad Zubaidi Baharumshah, and Wahabuddin Ra’ees. 2015. “Institutional Infrastructure and Economic Growth in Member Countries of the Organization of Islamic Cooperation (OIC).” *Economic Modelling* 5(1): 214–226.

Solow, Robert M. 2000. *Growth Theory: An Exposition*. New York: Oxford University Press.

Suri, Tavneet, Michael A. Boozer, Gustav Ranis, and Frances Stewart. 2011. “Paths to success: The relationship between human development and economic growth.” *World Development* 39(4): 506–522.

Vieira, Falvio V., Marcio Holland, C. Gomes da Silva, and Luiz C. Bottecchia. 2013. “Growth and exchange rate volatility: a panel data analysis.” *Applied Economics* 45(26): 3733–3741.

Windmeijer, Frank. 2005. “A finite sample correction for the variance of linear efficient two-step GMM estimators.” *Journal of Econometrics* 126(1): 25–51.

Xu, Haifeng. 2016). “Financial Intermediation and Economic Growth in China: New Evidence from Panel Data.” *Emerging Markets Finance and Trade* 52(3): 724–732.

Appendices

Appendix 1: Variable definition, source and expected coefficient sign

	Definition and Source	Expected sign
Dependent Variable		
Economic Growth	Annual percentage growth rate of GDP at market prices based on constant local currency. Aggregates are based on constant 2010 U.S. dollars. Source: The World Bank	(+)
Independent Control Variable		
Log GDP Per Capita	GDP per capita is gross domestic product divided by midyear population. Data are in constant 2010 U.S. dollars. Source: The World Bank	(+/–)
Log Capital Investment to GDP	Gross capital formation (formerly gross domestic investment) consists of outlays on additions to the fixed assets of the economy plus net changes in the level of inventories. Source: The World Bank	(+)
CO_2 Emission Per Capita	Carbon dioxide emissions are those stemming from the burning of fossil fuels and the manufacture of cement. They include carbon dioxide produced during consumption of solid, liquid, and gas fuels and gas flaring. Source: The World Bank	(+/–)
Log Savings (% of GDP)	Gross savings are calculated as gross national income less total consumption, plus net transfers. Source: The World Bank	(+)
Unemployment rate (%)	Unemployment refers to the share of the labor force that is without work but available for and seeking employment.	(–)
Log Economic Freedom Index	The Overall index of economic freedom has ten components grouped into four broad categories: Rule of Law; Limited Government; Regulatory Efficiency and Open Markets. The overall economic freedom is scored on a scale of 0 to 100, where 100 represents the maximum freedom. Source: The Heritage Foundation	(+)
Financial development indicators (Financial depth)		
Log Domestic credit to private sector (% of GDP)	Domestic credit to private sector refers to financial resources provided to the private sector. Source: Global Financial Development Database (GFDD)	(+/–)

Appendix 1 (continued)

	Definition and Source	**Expected sign**
Log M3 (% of GDP)	Ratio of liquid liabilities to GDP. They are the sum of currency and deposits in the central bank (M0), plus transferable deposits and electronic currency (M1), plus time and savings deposits, foreign currency transferable deposits, certificates of deposit, and securities repurchase agreements (M2), plus travelers checks, foreign currency time deposits, commercial paper, and shares of mutual funds or market funds held by residents. Source: GFDD	(+/–)
Log Bank deposits (% of GDP)	The total value of demand, time and saving deposits at domestic deposit money banks as a share of GDP. Deposit money banks comprise commercial banks and other financial institutions that accept transferable deposits, such as demand deposits. Source: GFDD	(+/–)
Log Financial system deposits (% of GDP)	Demand, time and saving deposits in deposit money banks and other financial institutions as a share of GDP. Source: GFDD	(+/–)
Financial development indicators (Financial System Efficiency)		
Log Bank cost to income ratio (%)	Operating expenses of a bank as a share of sum of net-interest revenue and other operating income. Source: GFDD	(+/–)
Human development indicators		
Average Year of Schooling[249]	Average number of years of education received by people ages 25 and older, converted from education attainment levels using official durations of each level. Source: Barro and Lee (2013).	(+)
Primary School Enrollment	Gross enrolment ratio (GER). Primary. Total is the total enrollment in primary education, regardless of age, expressed as a percentage of the population of official primary education age. GER can exceed 100% due to the inclusion of over-aged and under-aged students because of early or late school entrance and grade repetition. Source: UNESCO	(+)

249 Average Year of Schooling data is available from 1980 but with an interval of 5 years till 2005 after that yearly data are available. When calculating 3 year average, for the period of 1996 and 2002, we take the average of 1990 and 2000, 2000 and 2005, respectively.

Appendix 1 (continued)

	Definition and Source	**Expected sign**
Secondary School Enrollment	Gross enrolment ratio. Secondary. All programmes. Total is the total enrollment in secondary education, regardless of age, expressed as a percentage of the population of official secondary education age. GER can exceed 100% due to the inclusion of over-aged and under-aged students because of early or late school entrance and grade repetition. Source: UNESCO	(+)
Tertiary School Enrollment	Total enrollment in tertiary education (ISCED 5 to 8), regardless of age, expressed as a percentage of the total population of the five-year age group following on from secondary school leaving. Source: UNESCO	(+)
Health spending (% of GDP)	Total health expenditure is the sum of public and private health expenditure. It covers the provision of health services (preventive and curative), family planning activities, nutrition activities, and emergency aid designated for health but does not include provision of water and sanitation. Source: The World Bank	(+)

Appendix 2: List of countries in the study

Non-OIC		**OIC**	
Andorra	Lesotho	Afghanistan	Libya
Angola	Liberia	Albania	Malaysia
Argentina	Macedonia	Algeria	Maldives
Armenia	Malawi	Azerbaijan	Mali
Bahamas	Malta	Bahrain	Mauritania
Barbados	Mexico	Bangladesh	Morocco
Belarus	Moldova	Benin	Mozambique
Belize	Mongolia	Brunei	Niger
Bhutan	Montenegro	Burkina Faso	Nigeria
Bolivia	Namibia	Cameroon	Oman
Bosnia and Herzegovina	Nepal	Chad	Pakistan
Botswana	Nicaragua	Comoros	Qatar
Brazil	Panama	Djibouti	Saudi Arabia
Burma (Myanmar)	Papua New Guinea	Egypt	Senegal
Cambodia	Paraguay	Gabon	Sierra Leone
Chile	Peru	Gambia	Sudan
China	Philippines	Guinea	Suriname
Colombia	Puerto Rico	Guyana	Syria
Croatia	Romania	Indonesia	Tajikistan

Appendix 2 (continued)

Non-OIC		OIC	
Dominican Republic	Russia	Iran	Togo
Ecuador	Rwanda	Iraq	Tunisia
El Salvador	Samoa	Ivory Coast	Turkey
Eritrea	Serbia	Jordan	Turkmenistan
Fiji	South Africa	Kazakhstan	Uganda
Ghana	Sri Lanka	Kuwait	United Arab
Honduras	Tanzania	Kyrgyzstan	Emirates
Hungary	Thailand	Lebanon	Uzbekistan
India	Ukraine		Yemen
Jamaica	Uruguay		
Kenya	Venezuela		
Kiribati	Vietnam		
Laos	Zambia		
Oil Dependent OIC		**OIC Islamic Bank Presence**	
Albania	Libya	Bahrain	Maldives
Algeria	Malaysia	Bangladesh	Mauritania
Azerbaijan	Mauritania	Brunei	Nigeria
Bahrain	Nigeria	Egypt	Oman
Brunei	Oman	Gambia	Pakistan
Cameroon	Qatar	Indonesia	Qatar
Chad	Saudi Arabia	Iran	Saudi Arabia
Egypt	Sudan	Iraq	Senegal
Gabon	Suriname	Ivory Coast	Sudan
Indonesia	Syria	Jordan	Syria
Iran	Tunisia	Kuwait	Tunisia
Iraq	Turkmenistan	Lebanon	Turkey
Ivory Coast	United Arab Emirates	Malaysia	United Arab Emirates
Kazakhstan	Uzbekistan		Yemen
Kuwait	Yemen		

Appendix 3: Descriptive statistics and correlation matrix

	(1)	(2)	(3)	(4)	(5)	(6)	(7)	(8)	(9)	(10)	(11)	(12)	(13)	(14)	(15)	(16)	(17)
OIC																	
Mean	4.95	6887.70	22.82	5.04	20.42	9.20	55.00	5.84	95.19	58.38	17.77	5.09	27.77	44.44	36.10	36.18	51.76
Std. Dev.	6.47	12830.83	8.66	9.53	14.77	6.16	8.99	2.79	20.43	29.80	14.52	2.07	24.53	35.42	34.09	34.09	16.56
Minimum	−62.08	207.78	−2.42	0.01	−24.92	0.30	16.00	0.70	22.20	5.13	0.21	1.87	0.56	6.06	1.84	1.84	0.00
Maximum	104.49	74632.24	60.16	68.70	73.91	32.50	78.00	11.20	144.10	111.15	78.98	13.73	158.51	252.72	245.43	245.43	120.14
Observations	996	988	958	876	767	1026	912	595	828	679	628	1013	950	921	925	925	897
Non-OIC																	
Mean	4.44	5561.17	23.62	2.50	19.89	9.54	57.62	7.44	105.70	72.91	29.66	6.11	38.64	44.09	35.62	35.84	56.18
Std. Dev.	5.85	6954.61	8.27	2.48	10.46	7.43	9.41	2.43	14.37	23.51	21.77	1.98	32.50	29.80	23.40	23.37	16.94
Minimum	−30.15	122.49	1.53	0.06	−37.34	0.10	21.00	2.05	45.43	5.22	0.30	1.56	1.39	7.24	1.94	1.94	0.00
Maximum	106.28	48195.41	74.82	12.65	60.27	39.30	79.00	11.70	165.65	110.76	91.03	14.39	268.05	182.73	140.61	140.61	218.09
Observations	1200	1209	1101	996	1018	1159	1093	657	993	840	728	1210	1127	1114	1104	1104	1103
Economic Growth (1)	1.000																
GDP per capita (2)	−0.121	1.000															
Capital Investment (3)	0.135	0.108	1.000														
CO_2 (4)	0.028	0.629	0.109	1.000													
Savings (5)	0.052	0.410	0.366	0.420	1.000												
Unemployment rate (6)	−0.076	0.136	0.058	−0.195	−0.067	1.000											
Economic freedom (7)	0.125	−0.457	−0.053	−0.267	−0.105	0.084	1.000										
Average Year of Schooling (8)	−0.086	0.662	0.161	0.334	0.207	0.233	−0.357	1.000									

(continued)

Appendix 3 (continued)

	(1)	(2)	(3)	(4)	(5)	(6)	(7)	(8)	(9)	(10)	(11)	(12)	(13)	(14)	(15)	(16)	(17)
Primary School Enrollment (9)	0.005	0.283	0.115	0.086	0.079	0.003	−0.161	0.225	1.000								
Secondary School Enrollment (10)	−0.136	0.773	0.052	0.422	0.207	0.132	−0.389	0.851	0.377	1.000							
Tertiary School Enrollment (11)	−0.161	0.574	0.015	0.191	0.062	0.169	−0.239	0.706	0.205	0.724	1.000						
Health spending (12)	−0.050	−0.079	−0.015	−0.220	−0.397	0.197	−0.040	0.020	0.138	0.144	0.273	1.000					
Domestic Credit to Private Sector (12)	−0.115	0.515	0.156	0.247	0.187	−0.023	−0.506	0.459	0.230	0.530	0.392	0.134	1.000				
M3 (13)	−0.143	0.447	0.204	0.243	0.251	−0.045	−0.345	0.259	0.138	0.358	0.202	0.050	0.762	1.000			
Bank Deposits (14)	−0.174	0.532	0.180	0.278	0.227	−0.019	−0.481	0.343	0.227	0.444	0.271	0.082	0.788	0.927	1.000		
Financial System Deposits (15)	−0.176	0.529	0.175	0.276	0.227	−0.018	−0.476	0.341	0.230	0.442	0.269	0.083	0.790	0.926	0.999	1.000	
Bank Cost to Income Ratio (16)	0.048	−0.248	−0.181	−0.258	−0.347	0.044	0.006	−0.037	−0.003	−0.022	0.097	0.195	−0.107	−0.255	−0.179	−0.180	1.000

Liza Mydin, Abbas Mirakhor

Chapter 27: Resource Curse in Muslim Countries

1 Introduction

The Organisation of the Islamic Cooperation (OIC) comprises 57 countries including Palestine, and members typically have significant Muslim populations and adopt Islam as official religion. The OIC is deemed to represent the collective voice of Muslims all over the world and to espouse the importance of safeguarding the interests of Muslims. Its primary objectives include the promotion of Islamic teachings and safeguard of Islamic heritage. Many OIC members are also endowed with rich natural resources, with Saudi Arabia ranking among the world's top oil producers and contributing with the United Arab Emirates to approximately 20% of the world oil production. In theory wealth from natural resources should position these oil-producing OIC countries on a steady path of economic growth and sound development. However, Askari and Rehman (2013) provide compelling evidence that the economic performance of OIC countries has declined over the last 30 years.

The dismal economic performance of OIC countries may be attributed to the decade old economic puzzle of resource curse, which describes poor economic growth despite endowment with rich natural resources. The dependence on natural resources is conducive to in efficiencies and counterproductive behavior that affect many aspects of economic life, leading ultimately to people's sufferance.

Arguably the principle cause of the resource curse lies in the lack of compliance of the rules of Islam. Indeed, the *Qur'an* provides clear guidance and proper injunctions about the distribution of income and wealth in order to achieve economic and social justice. According to Askari, et al. (2012), dynamic and vibrant economies should promote social justice, unity, trust and social cohesiveness. Indeed, sustainable development can only be achieved in the absence of deceit, greed and wealth misappropriation.

The *Qur'an* regards wealth simply as one of the many blessings from the Allah (swt), the Creator of all things on earth and heavens. Thus, the ultimate ownership of wealth rests with the Creator, and people are the custodians of these worldly resources and they are expected to toil, manage, distribute and redistribute wealth derived from the use and allocation of resources according to the rules prescribed by Allah (swt). The guiding principle in the management of wealth in Islam is moderation, which allows people to achieve a decent level of living standards and allocate a significant part to the less able members of society.

The *Qur'an* provides clear guidelines on consumer behavior, with rules that prohibit overspending (*israf*), waste (*itlaf*), and ostentatious and opulent spending (*itraf*). All segments of the society should benefit from the sharing of wealth and the interests

https://doi.org/10.1515/9783110587920-027

of future generations should be protected, as well. Allah (swt) has created an abundance of resources for mankind and the benefits should be rendered to all members of the society a fair and equitable manner. It is the efficient transformation of the resources into productive capital that allows for the equal sharing of economic benefits.

The act of professing Islam as the official religion should compel OIC countries to provide strong example of efficient implementation of rules and principles ordained in the Qur'an. These are however strong indications to the contrary given the high levels of corruption and the lack of economic and social justice. The failure to alleviate poverty and reach decent levels of economic and social development despite the rich endowment of natural resources in indicative of OIC economies suffering from prolonged periods of resource curse. The remainder of the chapter is organized as follows. The next section briefly discusses the theory of resource curse. Section 3 presents an empirical model of resource curse for a sample of OIC countries. Section 4 proposes an institutional framework based on Islamic economic principles in order to address the chronic problems of the resource curse. Section 5 concludes the chapter.

2 The Theory of Resource Curse

Economic theory refers to the concept of resource curse to describe the economic conditions of countries that fail to achieve sustainable levels of economic growth and development despite abundant natural resources. The notion that resources represent a curse rather than blessing may seem counterintuitive, but it is difficult to ignore the theoretical and empirical evidence. This important issue is discussed by Sachs and Warner (1997 and 2001). The theoretical proposition is that an increase in resources is conducive to a reduction in economic growth and that countries with rich resources lag in economic performance compared to those with poor resources. The evidence suggests an inverse relationship between natural resources and economic growth for a sample of countries over the 1970s and 80s after controlling for investment rates, global commodity shocks, government expenditure ratios and long run external terms of trade changes. It is found also that the resource-rich Asian countries, Malaysia and Thailand, were not able to outperform resource-poor countries such as Singapore, Hong Kong and Korea. The literature suggests also that the oil-rich GCC countries present an even stronger negative association between growth and natural resources.

Sachs and Warner provide some plausible explanations for the resource curse. The Dutch Disease theory implies that the new discovery of natural resources has negative effects on export-oriented economies as the appreciation of domestic currency renders the allocation of labor and capital is ultimately affected by the shrinking manufacturing sector. It is noted also that resource abundance affects growth gives the lower degree of trade openness. Most importantly, the authors argue that the natural resources generate higher economic rents as a result of government exploitation. There is evidence of positive association between the quality of legal and government institutions and economic growth. Similarly, Apergis and Payne (2014) suggest that improvement in the quality of institutions contributes to the mitigation of the adverse effects of the resource curse. Further evidence from Everhart (2010), Kolstad and Søreide (2009), and Bjorvatn et al. (2012) shed light on the impact of corruption. It is shown that resource-rich countries can experience sustainable economic growth under the condition of strong governance. Robinson et al. (2014) argue that there is an incentive for governments to distribute resources as patronage to dictate the outcome of elections. The allocation of special favors is conducive to imbalances in public finance.

Thus, the significance of the resource curse depends on the quality of institutions as poor governance and lack of accountability ultimately lead to perverse political incentives and weaker economic performance. The literature provides compelling evidence on the determinants and effects of the resource curse, including inefficiencies in redistribution of income from natural resources and corruption stemming from governmental promotion of narrow interests. It is important to address these institutional failures and shortcomings with structural and institutional reforms that have the potential of transforming the curse into blessing.

There is scant literature on the resource curse in oil-producing OIC countries. The focus of these countries is important as they typically share common beliefs, tend to follow similar structural forms, and achieve comparable economic performances. It is possible to address the effects of the resource curse through the guiding principles of Islamic economics and finance that can ensure economic justice and the equitable distribution of resources. The objective of the present study is to determine whether there is strong evidence of the resource curse in oil-producing OIC countries and to discuss the conditions required to achieve sustainable economic growth and poverty alleviation, which are consistent with the concept of economic justice in Islam. From the economic principles derived from the *Qur'an* and *Sunnah* constitute the basis for policy recommendations in terms of structural reform and institution building.

3 Modelling the Resource Curse in OIC Countries

This empirical study tests for the evidence of resource curse in oil-producing OIC countries, including Algeria, Bahrain, Cameroon, Côte d'Ivoire, Egypt, Indonesia, Malaysia, Nigeria, Oman and Saudi Arabia. The following growth model is typically used in the empirical literature on resource curse. The Pooled Mean Group (PMG) estimation method for dynamic heterogeneous panels. The procedure is introduced by Pesaran, Shin, and Smith (1999) permits the linear variables and short-term coefficients to vary across groups but imposes coefficients on the long-term coefficients to be identical.

The PMG method is adopted for the purpose of robustness. According to Bassanini and Scarpetta (2001), the advantage of a panel data for the analysis of growth equations is that country-specific effects can be controlled for by employing methods such as the Dynamic Fixed Effects and Generalized Methods of Moments (GMM). However, the author states that these approaches generally impose homogeneity of all slope coefficients allowing only the intercepts to vary across countries. They further highlight that past research has found under slope heterogeneity these estimates become affected by a potentially serious heterogeneity bias, especially in small country samples. To this effect, the authors found that PMG was a suitable method to suit their sample country size of 21 countries. Due to the small country sample in this thesis, the PMG estimator is also employed for testing of the results. The method allows short-run coefficients, speed of adjustment and error variances to differ across countries but impose homogeneity on long-run coefficients (Bassanini and Scarpetta 2001).

The following PMG model is estimated for the sample period from 1984 to 2012:

$$lnY_{it} = \mu_i + \beta_1.lnOilR_{it} + \beta_2.INST_{it} + \beta_3.lnFD_{it} + \theta.X_{it} + e_{it} \tag{1}$$

where lnY_{it} represents the log of GDP per capita, $lnOilR_{it}$ represents the log of oil rent. The variable $INST_{it}$ is a measure of various institutional factors and governance qualities from the International Country Risk Guide (ICRG). It represents the average of six indicators from the ICRG including political stability, corruption, law and order, democratic accountability and bureaucratic quality indexes. The variable $lnFD_{it}$ represents the log of financial development, measured in terms of money supply and domestic credit to private sector. The control variables X_{it} include investment, government expenditure and trade openness. The disturbance terms are represented by e_{it}, which are assumed to be independently and identically distributed. The basic model specification (Model 1) allows for tests of the resource curse depending on the significance of inverse relationship between oil rent and GDP. It is also possible to estimate an alternative model specification (Model 2) the dependent variable represented by the quality of institutions. This model allows for the examination of the relation between the quality of institutions and oil rent. Evidence of significant and positive relations suggests that resource abundance contributes to better quality of institutions whereas negative relation indicates that higher income from oil resources is conducive to the erosion of institutions. In contrast, evidence of negative linkage between resource abundance and institutional quality is indicative of resource curse rather than blessing.

$$INST_{it} = \mu_i + \beta_1.lnOilR_{it} + \beta_2.lnY_{it} + \beta_3.lnINV_{it} + \beta_4.lnTRADE_{it} + \theta.X_{it} + e_{it} \tag{2}$$

where $lnINV_{it}$ and $lnTRADE_{it}$ represent log of investment and trade openness, respectively. The control variables X_{it} include unemployment rate, school enrolment at the tertiary level and population size as measures of equal opportunity.

Appendix 1 provides a description of the different variables used in the estimation of Models I and II. It is noted in particular that oil rent is measured as the difference between the value of crude oil at world prices and production costs. There may be, thus, some measurement problems due to oil price volatility and fluctuations in foreign exchange rates. The estimation results of both Models I and II are reported in Table 27.1. The evidence from Model I suggests that the resource curse is indeed present given the significant and negative relationship between oil rent and GDP. With the exception of financial development, the estimated coefficients associated with all variables are found to be significant. The variable representing institutional quality is significant, albeit at 10% level, indicating that institutions play an important role in economic development. With respect to Model II, the results indicate that the relation between oil rent and quality of institutions is rather negative. This evidence implies that resource abundance is likely to induce counterproductive behavior including corruption and rent-seeking activities. It is noted that trade openness has the potential of improving the quality of institutions and attenuate thereby, the adverse effects of rent-seeking activities.

There is also evidence of strong positive contribution to GDP from investment and government expenditures. The impact of financial development is found to be significant and associated with the negative sign.

Table 27.1: PMG Estimation Results for Model I and Model II.

Independent variable	Model I	Model II
Oil rent	−1.141***	−0.504***
	(−3.43)	(−4.11)
Investment	1.887***	0.323
	(3.69)	(0.10)
GCE	3.101***	
	(3.37)	
Institutional quality	0.186*	
	(2.44)	
Financial development	−0.369	
	(−1.68)	
Trade openness		1.824***
		(3.39)
GDP		−0.550
		(−1.74)
Unemployment		−0.560
		(−1.44)
Tertiary education		0.253
		(1.01)
Population		0.920
		(1.13)
N	280	280

Note: t statistics in parentheses *, **, *** indicate significance at 10%, 5% and 1% respectively.

4 The Issue of Resource Curse in an Islamic Institutional Framework

This empirical chapter provides evidence that lends support to the proposition of resource curse in a sample of oil-producing OIC countries. The natural question arises as to why these dismal economic performances are associated with countries that profess allegiance to Islamic faith, and how can Islamic economics provide remedies to the repeated failures in managing the immense natural and human resources, in accordance with the teachings of *Qur'an* and *Sunnah*. The moral and economic principles are conducive to economic justice, greater transparency, equitable distribution of resources and, significant capital of trust and mutual cooperation. Rather demonstrating models of dynamic and thriving economies, oil-producing OIC countries remain notorious principally for good education and social justice. This the result of deep misconceptions about the teachings of Islam and the importance of Islamic economics.

Thus, the long-term solution to the structural problems reflected by the resource curse is to redirect education toward a better understanding of the relationship between The *Creator* and creation. It is important to reorient and to arrange their daily lives in accordance with Islamic teachings. It is noted in this respect that Mirakhor (2009) introduces the notion of *walayah* to describe the relationship between the Creator and believers. This relationship is based on divine love and affection as Allah (swt) is in close proximity to all human beings. The manifestation of *walayah* can be evident in the fondness, attachment and devotion to Allah (swt). The status of conflict and serenity can be achieved by believers who reflect and actively strive in strengthening the relationship of *walayah*. Allah (swt) provides protection, guardianship and authority at one end of the relationship while believers strive to follow Islamic teachings on the other. The bound between Allah (swt) and the believer depends on the intensity of love and human devotion.

Mirakhor (2009) argues that believers are required to act upon the *walayah* toward all of humanity. The love and affection from the Creator should be the basis of all relationship with the Creator. The ultimate objective of those relations is the satisfaction of Allah (swt). Thus, it is Allah (swt) alone that one should seek help from, and to whom one should attach and pledge ultimate allegiance (Mirakhor & Hamid, 2009b).

It can be further argued that the initialization of *walayah* and awareness of the profound Love of Allah (swt) on His creation can avoid unjust action and unruly behavior. It is the behavior of losing the divine love that can prevent transgressions and violations of the *walayah* bounds. It is also the hope of benefiting from the divine love that provides the strongest incentive for believers to observe the rules ordained by Allah (swt), in all aspects of daily life. It is clear that corruption is the natural result of a scant understanding of the *walayah* of Allah (swt). The pledge and deviations are not made to Allah (swt) but to any authority that promises worldly benefits. The poor understanding of *walayah* can be regarded as the deep root cause of the problems that often arise the resource curse. It is the love of power rather than the love of Allah (swt) that is conducive to abuse of power, corruption and rent-seeking activities. It is unrestrained pursuit of material wealth that results in the unjust and inefficient allocation of resources.

There is an urgent need for the believers to be fully aware and cognizant that *walayah* of Allah (swt) supersedes any other worldly satisfactions and that trust in the power of the Almighty takes precedence over every source of authority. A better understanding of *walayah* should be also reflected in the kindness and fairness toward all creations, and in the moderation in consumption and use of available resources. It is sufficient that Muslim children are taught how to recite and make *tajwid* of *Qur'an* a without properly understanding its endearing messages, including the moderate behavior and balanced lifestyle.

With reference to Mydin, Askari, and Mirakhor (2018), it is also important to establish an independent supervisory body in the public repository to oversee the allocation of resources in oil-producing OIC countries. The authors argue that the notion of supervision is not new in Islam and it can be traced back to the Medinan period. The Prophet (sawa) created indeed several means for enhanced supervision to oversee the market practices in Medina, and the important role of supervision was undertaken by *muhtasib* (market supervisor), whose presence in the marketplace was meant to curb any malpractices and irregularities.

The importance of *muhtasib* can be adopted for the purpose of supervising the oil resources. National corporate entities involved in oil-production should be transparent and disclose all relevant information about their activities. This independent authority can be composed of representatives from political and non-governmental organizations to ensure that proper checks and balances as well as regulatory measures are observed in the strategic decisions and daily operations.

The authors suggest the establishment of a national authority of *muhtasib* that can operate with the full mandate to ensure the full compliance to Islamic rules and teachings in the management of national resources. The *muhtasib* authority should also ensure full transparency in the resource revenues. Thus, the *muhtasib* should represent the collective action to 'enjoin good and forbid evil'. No ruling power should be left unaccountable for the conduct of the economic and political affairs of millions of individuals. The absence of supervision would perpetuate unjust oppression, corrupt practices and other unscrupulous acts.

Finally, additional checks and balances require the transfer of oil revenues to a special fund subject to management rules independent from regular government budget spending. This optimal solution is proposed by Askari et al. (2006), who argues for the establishment by oil-producing countries. The entire oil revenues should be placed this fund and annual payouts made to all segments of the society.

To avoid the moral hazard associated with unconditional entitlement behaviors from receiving the funds, it is possible to impose limits related to social factors such as the attainment of education proficiency. The management of fund liquidity can be also assured by an independent entity responsible for investment activities and portfolio optimization with risk diversification based on a mixture of Islamic financial investments. It is imperative that fund administration remains independent and transparent with sound governance. The long-term viability of the fund is also intrinsically linked to an efficient and effective taxation system.

5 Conclusion

Poverty in oil-rich countries is rampant. There is clear evidence of corrosion in the quality of institutions, misallocation of resources and imbalanced socio-economic conditions. It is difficult to ignore these chronic conditions as institutional weakness is associated with corruption, wastefulness, economic underdevelopment, and eventually internal conflicts. The poor institutional scaffolding is conducive to economic imbalance and it is the poorest and weakest segments of the society that are bound to suffer from the effects of policy failures and economic mismanagement.

The Islamic institutional framework offers comprehensive and just solutions for countries that profess Islam and seek prosperity in this life and hereafter. Muslims need to look no further than the divine teachings of *Qur'an* and *Sunnah*. Therein lies a wealth of remedies to the resource curse and plight of oil-rich countries. It is important to understand that the evidence of resource curse documented in this study points toward fundamental problems of faith and attitudes. Given the concentration of power, poor governance and lack of accountability, no amount of written rules and regulations can be effective without a significant change in attitudes toward wealth accumulation and wealth redistribution. Indeed, Allah (swt) does not change people's condition unless they change what is their hearts (Al- Qur'an 13:11).

References

Askari, Hossein, Faranghees Abbas, George Jabbour, and Dohee Kwon. 2006. "An Economic Manifesto for the Oil Exporting Countries of the Persian Gulf." *Banca Nazionale Del Lavoro Quarterly Review* 59(239): 363–388.

Askari, Hossein, Zamir Iqbal, Noureddine Krichene, and Abbas Mirakhor. 2012. R*isk Sharing in Finance: The Islamic Finance Alternative*. Singapore: John Wiley & Sons.

Apergis, Nicholas, and James E. Payne. 2014. "The oil curse, institutional quality, and growth in MENA countries: Evidence from time-varying cointegration." *Energy Economics* 46(C): 1–9.

Bassanini, Andrea, and Stefano Scarpetta. 2001. "Does human capital matter for growth in OECD countries? Evidence from pooled mean-group estimates." OECD Economic Department Working Papers No. 282. Paris: Organisation for Economic Cooperation and Development (OECD).

Bjorvatn, Kjetil, Mohammad Reza Farzanegan, and Friedrich Schneider. 2012. "Resource Curse and Power Balance: Evidence from Oil-Rich Countries." *World Development* 40(7): 1308–1316.

Everhart, Stephen S. 2010. "The Resource Curse and Private Investment: A Theoretical Model of the Impact of Corruption." *Contemporary Middle Eastern Issues* 3(2): 117–135.
Kolstad, Ivar, and Arne Wiig. 2012. "Testing the Pearl Hypothesis: Natural resources and trust." *Resources Policy* 37(3): 358–367.
Kolstad, I., and Søreide, T. 2009. Corruption in natural resource management: Implications for policy makers. *Resources Policy* 34(4), 214–226. https://doi.org/10.1016/j.resourpol.2009.05.001
Mirakhor, Abbas. 2009. Islamic Economics and Finance: An Institutional Perspective. *IIUM Journal of Economics and Management* 17(1): 31–72.
Mirakhor, Abbas and Idris Samawi Hamid. 2009. *Islam and Development: The Institutional Framework.* New York: Global Scholarly Publications.
Mydin, L., Askari, H., and Mirakhor, A. 2018. Resource Rich Muslim Countries and Islamic Institutional Reforms. Resource Rich Muslim Countries and Islamic Institutional Reforms. *Peter Lang US.* https://doi.org/10.3726/b11157
Pesaran, M. H., Pesaran, M. H., Shin, Y., and Smith, R. P. 1999. Pooled Mean Group Estimation of Dynamic Heterogeneous Panels. *Journal of the American Statistical Association* 94(446), 621–634. https://doi.org/10.1080/01621459.1999.10474156
Robinson, James, Ragnar Torvik, and Thierry Verdier. 2014. "Political foundations of the resource curse: A simplification and a comment." *Journal of Development Economics* 106(C): 194–198.
Sachs, Jeffrey D., and Andrew M. Warner. 1997. "Natural Resource Abundance and Economic Growth." mimeo, Centre for International Development, Harvard University.
Sachs, Jeffrey D., and Andrew M. Warner. 2001. "The curse of natural resources." *European Economic Review* 45(4–6): 827–838.

Appendix

Appendix 1: Data Description

Notation	Variable	Definition	Source
Y	GDP	Gross Domestic Product in US Dollars. GDP at purchaser's prices is the sum of gross value added by all resident producers in the economy plus any product taxes and minus any subsidies not included in the value of the products.	World Bank Database
Oilrent	Oil Rent	Oil rent Oil rents are the difference between the value of crude oil production at world prices and total costs of production.	World Bank Database
INST	Institutional Quality	Institutional Quality Indicator comprising the average of 5 Indicators which include Government Stability, Corruption Quality, Law and Order, Democratic Accountability and Bureaucratic Quality taken from International Country Risk Guide.	International Country Risk Guide Database

Appendix 1 (continued)

Notation	Variable	Definition	Source
FD	Financial Development	Domestic Credit to Private Sector. It measures financial resources provided to the private sector by financial corporations, such as through loans, purchases of non-equity securities, and trade credits and other accounts receivable, that establish a claim for repayment. Money supply as a percentage of GDP. Money and quasi money comprise the sum of currency outside banks, demand deposits other than those of the central government, and the time, savings, and foreign currency deposits of resident sectors other than the central government.	World Bank Database
Inv	Investment	Gross capital formation (formerly gross domestic investment) consists of outlays on additions to the fixed assets of the economy plus net changes in the level of inventories.	World Bank Database
GCE	Government Consumption and Expenditure	General government final consumption expenditure (formerly general government consumption) includes all government current expenditures for purchases of goods and services (including compensation of employees). It also includes most expenditure on national defense and security, but excludes government military expenditures that are part of government capital formation.	World Bank Database
Trade	Trade	Trade is the sum of exports and imports of goods and services measured as a share of gross domestic product.	World Bank Database
Un	Unemployment	Unemployment refers to the share of the labor force that is without work but available for and seeking employment.	World Bank Database
Te	Tertiary Enrolment	Total is the total enrollment in tertiary education), regardless of age, expressed as a percentage of the total population of the five-year age group following on from secondary school leaving.	World Bank Database

Source: Author's own.

List of Figures

https://doi.org/10.1515/9783110587920-028

List of Tables

https://doi.org/10.1515/9783110587920-029

Author Biographies

Abbas Mirakhor is a retired professor of economics and finance. His current research interests are Islamic economics and finance.

Adama Dieye is a former Director of Department of the Central Bank of West African States (BCEAO). He was recruited as a senior executive in 1978. From 1998 to 2006, Dr. Adama has been seconded to the Government of Senegal as Technical Adviser in the Cabinet of the Minister of Economy and Finance of the Government of Senegal, in charge of macroeconomic policy and financial system. During this period, Dr. Adama represented the State of Senegal at Central Bank Board and participated in several high-level international meetings on financial and economic policy issues. Since his retirement in 2008, Dr. Adama Dieye is a part-time instructor in Islamic Economics and Finance at IFACE/University Cheikkh Anta Diop/Dakar and at Business Schools in Dakar (CESAG/DAKAR, BEM-DAKAR). Also, he is appointed as member of the Waqf High Authority Commission set up by the Senegalese Government in 2018. Dr. Adama holds a master's degree in Applied Mathematics at University of Dakar in 1978, a doctorate in economics at University of Auvergne-Clermont Ferrand in 1996, and PhD in Islamic Finance at INCEIF in 2017.

Alaa Alaabed has earned her PhD in Islamic finance from INCEIF, Malaysia where she also won the President's Award in 2012 and 2016. She qualified as a Chartered Islamic Finance Professional (CIFP) in 2011. Alaa was awarded Bachelor of Commerce; major in Finance from Macquarie University, Australia in 2007. Her work experience includes Treasury products' development in HSBC Amanah, Malaysia, buy-side research analysis in SICO investment bank, Bahrain, education in the College of Banking and Financial Studies, Oman, rating in the Islamic International Rating Agency (IIRA), Bahrain, and FinTech focused research and advisory in Finocracy and Wethaq Capital Markets. Alaa has presented in a number of international Islamic banking and finance fora and has published a number of research papers in journals of repute. In 2018, Alaa was recognized among the "100 Most Influential Women in Global Islamic Banking & Finance" by Cambridge IF Analytica's WOMANi Index.

Azura Othman graduated with a degree in Accounting and Finance from the London School of Economics and Political Science. She is also a Fellow of ACCA (UK), a member of Malaysian Institute of Accountant and a chartered member of the Chartered Institute of Islamic Finance Professionals (CIIF). She received her PhD in Islamic Finance from the International Centre of Education in Islamic Finance (INCEIF). Currently, Dr Azura is the CEO of the Chartered Institute of Islamic Finance Professionals (CIIF), an Independent Non-Executive Director of Bank Muamalat Malaysia Berhad since 2015, where she is the chairman of the Nomination and Remuneration Committee, and an Independent Non-Executive Director of Malaysia Debt Ventures Berhad (chairman of its Board Audit Committee). Prior to this, she was an Executive Director of PricewaterhouseCoopers Taxation Services, Malaysia with over 19 years of experience as a tax consultant and in engagements relating to Islamic Finance. Among her major assignments include formulating the tax incentives for Malaysia as the International Islamic Financial Centre (MIFC).

Barbara L'Huillier currently serves as Associate Chair for the Department of Accounting and Finance and Interim Associate Chair for the Department of Business Administration and Management Information Systems at Prince Mohammad Bin Fahd University in Saudi Arabia. She is an accountant by "trade", initially working in public practice before turning to teaching. Theoretical direction for her doctoral and post-doctoral research comes from critical theory and the use of

https://doi.org/10.1515/9783110587920-030

power for transformational intent. She is particularly interested in Islamic Finance, notions of justice, equity, and "good" governance, ethics, globalization and accreditation.

Belal Ehsan Baaquie has been trained as a theoretical physicist at Caltech (BS) and Cornell University (PhD), specializing in quantum field theory. He has pioneered the application of quantum mathematics to economics and finance and has written three books and numerous research papers on the subject. He has also written books on science and physics for undergraduates. Over the years he has extended his research interests to the social sciences including religion, history and politics.

Buerhan Saiti is currently an Associate Professor of Department of Islamic Economics and Finance of the Istanbul Sabahattin Zaim University. Recently, he earned Outstanding Young Researcher Award by Turkey Academy of Sciences (TÜBA) (2018–2021). Previously, he was full-time Associate and Assistant Professor of Institute of Islamic Banking and Finance of the International Islamic University Malaysia (IIUM) where he won the highest number of publications in citation-indexed journals in social science category in the year 2017. As a young academician, he has published 2 books, 7 book chapters, almost 50 refereed journal publications (most of them are citation-indexed journals) and attended more than 35 Intentional and local conferences. He teaches both at the Post Graduate and Undergraduate levels. His research interest is both theoretical and empirical studies of Islamic Banking and Finance.

Dawood Ashraf is a Senior Researcher at Islamic Research and Training Institute (IRTI) of Islamic Development Bank Group. Before joining IRTI in 2014, he was working as faculty member at the College of Business of Prince Mohammad Bin Fahd University in the Kingdom of Saudi Arabia. Dr. Ashraf holds a PhD in Banking and Finance from the University Wales in the UK and a Masters of Economics in International Business and Economy from the Kyushu University Japan. He is also a charter holder and member of the CFA Institute. Dr. Ashraf has also worked in the banking industry in Canada and Pakistan. Dr. Ashraf's research interests are in portfolio management, banking, corporate finance, Islamic capital markets, and Islamic banking with special focus on the interaction of incentive structure and risk-taking behavior of financial institutions. Dr. Ashraf's research is published in international journals and has presented his research work in various international conferences. Dr. Ashraf has also contributed as the team leader for the first two Global Report on Islamic Finance jointly prepared by the Islamic Development Bank and the World Bank in 2016 and 2018.

Hazik Mohamed is a well-rounded professional with 20+ years varied experience in strategic, problem-solving, project management and operational leadership roles. He began his career in engineering and having spent 10 years building significant experience in problem-solving, strategy and operational leadership. He currently spends his time building start-ups and in business consulting, where he has consulted for MSMEs and regional/international organizations on various business-related issues. Prior to consulting for UNCDF and ASEAN, Hazik worked on an array of consulting projects including behavioral applications for financial regulations as well as digital transformation at several organizations (Malaysia, Singapore), multi-dimensional approach to poverty-alleviation and sustainability (Jakarta), development of rules-based socio-development index and financial inclusion (Islamabad), early warning indicators in macro-prudential policy (Manama) that recommend solutions to pro-cyclical economic behaviors. He is currently working on business growth strategies for start-ups and digital applications in various sectors using AI, blockchain, data analytics and IoT integration. He also finds time to teach Business Economics at Putra Business School. Hazik has a PhD in Islamic Finance, with research in Behavioral Economics and decision-making analysis, an MSc in Finance from Baruch College at the City University of New York, and a BSc in Mechanical Engineering from the University of Arkansas.

Idris Samawi Hamid is a Professor of Philosophy at Colorado State University. Prof Hamid's areas of specialization are Islamic Philosophy, Cosmology, Metaphysics, and Mysticism; his research includes software development for scholarly Arabic typesetting. He has served as the editor-in-chief of International Journal of Shīʿī Studies. He is the author of Islam, Sign and Creation: the Cosmology of Walāyah (Global Scholarly Publications); Islam, Stations, and Process: the Spirituality of Walāyah (Global Scholarly Publications); and coauthor of Islam and Development: The Institutional Framework (Global Scholarly Publications). His articles include the book chapter The Cosmological Journey of Neo: an Islamic Matrix, in More Matrix and Philosophy (Open Court Press).

Kaoru Yamaguchi is Director at Japan Futures Research Center. He holds a PhD degree in Economics, University of California, Berkeley (1985). He held academic posts (do you mean "he has taught") in the USA at California State University, Hayward, the University of San Francisco, the University of Hawaii, Manoa, and then in Japan at Osaka Sangyo University, and Doshisha University (Business School) in Kyoto. He was visiting scholar at Sloan School of Management, MIT (1998, 1999), Hawaii Futures Research Center, University of Hawaii (2001), Haas School of Business, University of California, Berkeley (2003), and Victoria Management School, Victoria University of Wellington, New Zealand (2009). He served as the president of the Economics Chapter of the System Dynamics Society (2008) and received the Advancement of Monetary Science and Reform Award from the American Monetary Institute (2010).

Liza Mydin is currently the Head of Corporate Strategy at one of the leading Islamic Banks in ASEAN. She received her PhD in Islamic Finance from INCEIF, Malaysia and in 2016 was a Visiting Scholar at George Washington University in Washington, DC. Liza is also the country partner for the Islamicity Index project. She is co-author of the books Resource Rich Muslim Countries and Islamic Institutional Reforms and Reformation and Development in the Muslim World.

Mahfuzul Alam Taifur is a research assistant and PhD candidate at Department of Shariah and Economics, Academy of Islamic Studies, University of Malaya, 50603 Kuala Lumpur, Malaysia. He received his Bachelor of Commerce in Accounting from National University, Bangladesh and Master in Accounting from International Islamic University Malaysia. He conducted research on management and accountability of waqf and wrote his Master's thesis on it. He has four years work experience as an assistant accountant at Alliance IFA (M) Sdn. Bhd. (Forensic Accounting Firm), Kuala Lumpur, Malaysia. He also participated and presented in conferences in Malaysia.

Mansur Masih was educated at Manchester (M.A. Econ) and Leeds (Ph.D.) Universities. Professor Masih is currently holding a 'Senior Professor' position in Finance/Islamic Finance at UniKL Business School, Malaysia, held the Chair Professorship of Finance at the UKM, UUM and KFUPM. He taught at INCEIF, Malaysia for 9 years and at the Australian (New South Wales and Edith Cowan) and British (Leeds) Universities for a total of 27 years. On econometric testing of issues in Finance and Economics, he got 152 refereed "applied" papers published (of which 141 papers are in European/American international scholarly journals). A total of 117 published papers are in top four publishers' journals (including 83 ISI/SSCI Journals). During the last five years (2015–2019), he had 66 papers published in mostly top-tier ISI/SSCI/Elsevier journals (on top of 5 papers currently under revisions and 27 working papers completed). His REPEC country rank is 1 (top authors by country, Malaysia) and REPEC global rank is 11 (top authors by field, South East Asia), Research Gate score (above 95% global researchers' scores). He presented 151 refereed papers at international conferences and got 6,935 citations (Googles). He sits on the editorial/advisory board of 11 international refereed journals including three top-tier ISI/SSCI Journals such as, the 'Subject

Editor' of JIFMIM, 'Guest Editor' of EMFT and 'Associate Editor' of IJIMEFM. His h-index is 38 and i10-index is 86 (Googles).

Masudul Alam Choudhury presently holds the position of Professor and Dean, Faculty of Business Administration, University of Science and Technology Chittagong, Bangladesh and is International Chair in Islamic Economics and Finance at the Faculty of Economics, Trisakti University, Jakarta, Indonesia. He continues as annual summer visiting professor in the Ontario Institute for Studies in Education in Social Economics, University of Toronto. Professor Choudhury is one of a handful of academic scholars in the field of Islamic Economics and Finance whose work has been recognized in both Western as well as Muslim academic circles as playing an influential role in defining the discipline of Islamic Finance and Economics. He is the first academic in his field to address the original methodology of tawhid as ontological law in the development of a theory of meta-science within the Qur'anic epistemological framework of Unity of Monotheistic Knowledge, by way of his seminal works, mathematical formalism, and inferential approach. His works span over 30 books published by highly-rated publishing outlets (i.e. Routledge, Macmillan, Springer-Verlag, Kluwer Academic, Sage, Kegan Paul, World Scientific, Taylor & Francis, New Palgrave, Edwin Mellen, Cambridge Scholars Publishing, IGI-Inc., among various others). He is the Editor-in-Chief of the SCOPUS-listed, Australian Deans Ranking, Web of Science (ESCI), and JEL-catalogued journal HIJSE (Humanomics: International Journal of Systems & Ethics). His published works have been reviewed by the Times Higher Education Supplement, Economic Journal, Southern Economic Journal, Middle East Review and the Journal of Economic Literature. He has also been a contributor to the Harvard University Islamic Finance and Investment Program at their annual gatherings in Cambridge, Massachusetts. Although an Economist and Mathematician by training, Professor Choudhury has contributed to the associated fields of Qur'anic studies, Philosophy of Science, Finance, Business Studies, Maqasid as-Shari'ah and, most recently, Computer Science (neural networks and complexity in the light of Tawhidi methodological worldview) and the diverse areas of Sociology within Economics (participative dynamics, circular causation, Ethics, systems and wellbeing). Professor Choudhury obtained his PhD in the field of Human Capital Theory and Economic Growth (Canada) from the University of Toronto in 1977.

Maznita Mokhtar's professional career began as a Chartered Accountant (ICAEW) trained in an accounting firm in the United Kingdom. In Malaysia, she gained valuable corporate finance consultancy experience with PriceWaterhouseCoopers (PWC), servicing large government projects and multinational corporations. She has conducted Islamic Finance training and consultancy services for several companies in Malaysia, Singapore and Brunei. Maznita was an active practitioner in the Islamic Financial Planning industry. She was a speaker for a number of wealth management seminars, not limited to client corporations, and was responsible as a module writer-cum-trainer-cum-examiner of the IFP (Islamic Financial Planning) certification. She has jointly written one book published by the Islamic Banking and Finance Institute of Malaysia (IBFIM). She contributed articles in her free time; she has written articles for AKPK (published in the STAR newspaper), 4E Journal (industry newsletter for CFPs) and leisure magazine Sur La Terre. Maznita graduated from London School of Economics, UK. She pursued higher academic qualifications to enhance her consultancy work and completed the CIFP (Chartered Islamic Finance Practitioner) qualification, a Masters equivalent, as well as the PhD at INCEIF (International Centre for Education in Islamic Finance).

Mohamed Ariff, a specialist in International Economics, is currently a Professor of Economics and Governance at INCEIF (International Centre for Education in Islamic Finance). Concurrently, he also holds the titles of Professor Emeritus at the Faculty of Economics and Administration (FEA), University of Malaya, and Distinguished Fellow at the Malaysian Institute of Economic Research

(MIER). Ariff was the Executive Director of MIER from June 1997 until December 2009. Previously he had held the Chair of Analytical Economics at the University of Malaya where he had also served as the Dean of FEA. He was conferred emeritus professorship by the University of Malaya in August 2004 and "Datukship" by His Majesty the King in June 2007. Ariff obtained his B.A. with First Class Honours and M.Ec. from the University of Malaya. He completed his PhD programme at the Lancaster University, England, in 1970, as Commonwealth Scholar. He has authored, co-authored and edited 18 books and monographs, in addition to publishing numerous articles in academic journals and mass media. His book "The Malaysian Economy: Pacific Connections – published by Oxford University Press – won the prestigious Tun Razak Award in 1993. He is a Correspondent Editor of Asian-Pacific Economic Literature (Canberra), Associate Editor of Asian Economic Policy Review (Tokyo).

Mohamed Ashraf Mohamed Iqbal is the founder director of MindSpring Sdn Bhd, independent non-executive director in Bank Pembangunan Malaysia Berhad, and Shari'ah Committee Member in HSBC Amanah, Malaysia. He examines organisations and the problems within it from the perspective of an engineer. His fixation is on improving the efficiency of organisations through the reduction of chaos. He believes the most efficient path to efficiency improvement is to help managers reframe. However reframing can only happen when managers free themselves from being victims of the system and instead recognise that they are the system. Ashraf's PhD thesis "Determinants of Variability in Branch Efficiency within the Branch Network of and Islamic Bank" was the formalisation of some of his methods used in turning around under-performing organisations. Ashraf is currently focused on examining Islamic banking from a non-theological perspective, arguing that countries which adopt a dual banking system ought to ensure the second system is equally, if not, more efficient than the first. Ashraf has a PhD in Islamic finance from INCEIF, Malaysia. He did his BSc in Mechanical Engineering and MBA from California State University. He also has a post-graduate diploma in Islamic Studies from International Islamic University, Malaysia.

Mohsin Ali has a diverse background of academia and professional Islamic banking. Currently, he is working as Senior Lecturer at Taylor's Business School, Taylor's University, Malaysia. His research interests include conventional and Islamic economics and finance. He has a PhD in Islamic finance from INCEIF, Malaysia. He did his bachelor and master in business administration from International Islamic University, Islamabad.

Md. Akther Uddin is a young multidisciplinary-educator with teaching and learning experience from Russia, Malaysia, the UK, and Bangladesh. Currently, he is working as Assistant Professor and Program Coordinator of School of Business and teaching Accounting, Finance and Economics at the undergraduate and post-graduate level. He has already published a great number of scholarly articles in ISI, Scopus, and refereed international journals. He has participated in many conferences, workshops, certificate courses, and seminars in many countries. He has already visited Russia, England, Malaysia, Lithuania, Belarus, Egypt, Thailand, and Maldives. His current research interests include students' motivation, Islamic economics, Islamic banking and finance, human capital and institutions in developing countries, emerging capital markets, and Blockchain technology.

Muhammed Habib Dolgun has a PhD in finance from INCEIF. The main objective of his dissertation is to critically examine the factors that affect liquidity risk management of Islamic banks. He has been working in the Central Bank of the Republic of Turkey since 2006. He worked as a secondee at International Islamic Liquidity Management Corporation between 2013 and 2015. His research areas are related with banking sector, Islamic banks' capital and liquidity risk management, derivatives. He wrote several papers in many journals, including Emerging Markets Finance and Trade,

Emerald Group-ISRA Journal, International Journal of Islamic Economics and Finance Studies, International Journal of Islamic and Middle Eastern Finance and Management. He wrote one chapter of a book on "Sukuk Market" published by Edward Elgar Publishing. Similarly, he wrote a chapter of a book on "Turkish banking industry: A CAMELS Analysis" which was published by Springer International Publishing. He is dealing with peer review of papers in many international journals, including the Afro-Asian J. of Finance and Accounting (AAJFA), Islamic Studies, Central Bank Review, Emerald Group-ISRA Journal, International Journal of Islamic Economics and Finance Studies, Journal of Economic Cooperation and Development.

Muhammad Wajid Raza is assistant professor of finance. Currently he is serving as head of department of management sciences at Shaheed Benazir Bhutto University Dir, Pakistan. He has done his PhD from the Vrije University Brussels, Belgium (2018). He is an expert in Islamic finance in general and Shariah-compliant equity investing in particular. He has published his research work in top ranking finance journals such as, Journal of Portfolio Management, International Review of Financial Analysis, International Review of Economics and Finance, and Journal of International Financial Markets, Institution & Money. He was awarded a Gold medal by University of Malakand, Pakistan. For his excellence in teaching, he received the faculty development award from the Higher Education Commission in Pakistan. He is also working as financial advisor with ADCO Stoller, Pakistan. He is also working as social activist in the field of education and is passionate about oil painting.

Murat A. Yülek has recently joined Ostim Technical University as rector. He has also served as professor of economics at Istanbul Ticaret University and the Director of the Center for Industrial Policy and Development. He is also a partner at PGlobal Global Advisory and Training Services Inc. Previously, he served as Vice Rector and Dean of the Faculty of Business Administration at THK University. He has also served as member and chairman of several boards of directors, as well as CEO of financial and non-financial institutions. He has taught at various universities, including Georgetown University and served as consultant at the World Bank, Islamic Development Bank and UNCTAD, among others. These responsibilities have exposed him to various development issues, and he has published widely in that field, as well as books and articles on economic and financial development. He holds PhD and M.A. degrees in economics from Bilkent University, an MBA degree from Yale University, an MSM (Management) degree from Boston University and a B.Sc. degree (mechanical engineering) from Boğaziçi University.

Nabil ElMaghrebi is currently serving as dean of the *Faculty of Economics*, and head of the *Graduate School of Economics*, Wakayama University, Japan. He is Professor of Finance at Wakayama University, visiting professor at the *Center for Mathematical Modeling and Data Science*, Osaka University. He is also associate editor of *ISRA International Journal of Islamic Finance*. He served as research fellow at the *International Institute for Advanced Studies*, Kyoto, visiting scholar at the *International Centre for education in Islamic Finance*, Kuala Lumpur, and visiting professor at the *Center for International Financial and Economic Research*, Loughborough University, United Kingdom. He has more than 25 years of experience in education and research in Japanese national universities. The focus of his research is placed on financial stability, asset pricing, market volatility, risk analysis, and Islamic finance. He developed the VXJ volatility index for the Japanese financial markets, and co-authored several articles on empirical finance and economics as well as the first analytical reference and textbook, Intermediate Islamic Finance. He graduated from *Institut des Hautes Etudes Commerciales, IHEC-Carthage*, Tunisia, and earned his PhD in Economics from *Osaka University*, Japan.

Nuri S. Erbaş was a Senior Economist at the IMF. He also held academic positions at the Universities of Hawaii, Houston, Maryland and INCEIF. His most recent research is on Saudi Arabia's labor markets and decision-making in ambiguity. He holds a PhD in Economics from Columbia University in New York and is the recipient of 1975 Rectorate Award from Boğaziçi University, Istanbul.

Obiyathulla Ismath Bacha is currently a Professor of Finance at the International Centre for Education in Islamic Finance ("INCEIF"), a post graduate university specialising in Islamic Finance, established by Bank Negara Malaysia. Prior to joining INCEIF, he has held several key positions at the International Islamic University Malaysia, including as Director of the university's Management Center. Professor Obiyathulla began his working career at Malayan Banking Berhad. Subsequent, to completing his doctoral studies, he was appointed an Assistant Professor of Finance at Boston University, where he taught at both the MBA and undergraduate levels. Professor Obiyathulla was President of the Malaysian Finance Association for 5 years,2013–2017. He has also been a trainer at several institutions such as the Securities Commission of Malaysia and the Central Bank of Malaysia. Internationally, he has conducted training programs in Islamic Capital Markets at the University of Luxembourg where he is an Adjunct Professor, The Chinese University of Hong Kong, Waseda University, Japan, Seoul National University, Korea and several other institutions. He has published scholarly articles in numerous local and international journals and has presented papers at several international and Islamic finance conferences. He is author of a course textbook on Financial Derivatives, currently in its 4th edition and another on Islamic Capital Markets. He received his Doctor of Business Administration (Finance), Master of Business Administration (High Honours) and Master of Arts (Economics) from Boston University and Bachelor of Social Science from the Science University of Malaysia in Penang.

Omid Torabi is currently VP of Sales and Customer Affairs of TOSAN; one of the largest FinTech companies in Iran, being active for the last twenty years specialized in provisioning of Islamic banking, banking and payment software solutions for financial, banking and payment institutions. He was formerly CEO of IDCORP (Innovation and Development Sdn. Bhd., Malaysia), TOSAN Data miners (TIDM), a software specialist company in knowledge discovery and financial Business Intelligence solutions. He has worked also for around 20 years in the field of banking software and in different positions such as Product manager of Islamic core banking solution, banking dashboards, Trade finance solutions, Islamic banking researches and etc. He is also part time researcher in the fields of Islamic banking and digital banking at MBRI (Monetary and Banking Research Institute of Central Bank of Iran). Omid graduated with computer engineering degree from Polytechnic of Tehran, and holds an MBA in Information Technology from IMI of Iran. He achieved the PhD degree in Islamic finance at INCEIF, Malaysia.

Patrick Amir Imam is currently the representative of the IMF in Zimbabwe and has been with the institution since 2005. Prior to joining the Fund, he worked as an investment banker at Credit Suisse First Boston in London. Since joining the Fund, he has worked on IMF programs, carried out technical assistance and done surveillance in the Middle East and Central Asia department and the African Department, the IMF Institute, and more recently the Monetary and Capital Markets Department. He was also the IMF Resident Representative in Madagascar from 2014 – 2018. His publications have focused on issues related to financial stability, macro-prudential policies, and financial sector development. He was educated at the University of Oxford, at the University of Warwick, and has a PhD in Economics from Cambridge University.

Rasim Mutlu worked at Borsa Istanbul research department as specialist and at the World Bank Global Islamic Finance Development Center as consultant. At Borsa Istanbul, his responsibilities included performing statistical analysis daily, monthly movements in financial markets and taking part in various projects Istanbul Global Financial Center, optimal investment strategies in clearing and settlement services for stock markets. At the World Bank, he contributed to first Global Financial Development Report in Islamic Finance and Utilizing Islamic Finance for Long Term financing. In addition to these, he conducted academic research testing whether Islamic finance enhances financial inclusion and risk sharing. Rasim Mutlu holds MA degree in economics from Johns Hopkins University and is currently pursuing PhD in economics.

Reza Gholami is a last year PhD candidate in Money and Finance at the National University of Malaysia. Before starting his PhD and after completion of his Master's degree in Economics at Shahid Beheshti University, for a decade he worked as a team leader and provides economic advices to the governmental agencies. During his PhD, he worked in Islamic finance specifically on profit-loss sharing contracts. He is currently working as an economic consultant for governmental and different private advisories institutions in Iran.

Roland Kangni Kpodar is Deputy Unit Chief in the Strategy, Policy and Review Department at the International Monetary Fund and Senior Fellow at the Foundation for Studies and Research on International Development (FERDI). He graduated with a PhD in economics from the CERDI in Clermont-Ferrand (France) and has worked on a number of developing and emerging economies since joining the Fund in 2006. He has published extensively on financial development, poverty reduction, and fiscal issues, including fuel subsidies. Roland is a national of Togo.

Sami Al-Suwailem is currently Acting Director General of the Islamic Research and Training Institute (IRTI), the Islamic Development Bank Group, Jeddah, Saudi Arabia. Before joining IRTI in 2004, Dr. Al-Suwailem managed the Research and Development Center at Al-Rajhi Bank, Riyadh, Saudi Arabia. He worked at the Institute of Islamic and Arabic Sciences in America, Virginia; Southern Illinois University, Carbondale, Illinois, USA; and King Saud University, Riyadh, Saudi Arabia. Dr. Al-Suwailem held membership in several professional committees, including the Technical Committee of the Islamic Financial Services Board; Economic Committee of Awqaf at the Ministry of Islamic Affairs in Riyadh; Academic Committee in Islamic Fiqh Academy of Muslim World League; Liquidity Risk Management Working Group at IFSB; and Task Force for Islamic Finance and Global Financial Stability at IsDB, among others. He obtained his M.A. from Southern Illinois University in 1990, and his PhD from Washington University, St. Louis, Missouri, in 1995. He authored many books and published several papers on Islamic economics and finance.

Seyed Kazem Sadr has been a faculty member at the Shaid Beshti University, Tehran Iran for more than 30 years. He also has served at the International Center for Education in Islamic Finance in Kuala Lumpur, Malaysia during the 2013–2016 years. He is a research fellow at the Shahid Beheshti University at present. He has been a member of the Islamic Banking drafting committee at the Finance Ministry, a member of the Economic curriculum program at the Ministry of Higher Education and also consultant at the Agricultural Bank, all in Iran. He is the author of books and refereed Journal articles on Islamic Economics and Banking, Agricultural and Natural Resource Economics. He is a member of editorial board of national and international journals. He received his PhD from the Ohio State University.

Seyid F. Mahmud is a professor of economics at Social Sciences University of Ankara. He also had a long association with Bilkent University as a faculty member in the department of economics. He holds a PhD degree in economics from McMaster University (1986) in Canada, and has over 35 years of experience in both teaching and academic research. He has held his faculty position at

Bilkent University since 1989. During his tenure at Bilkent University, he has taught many courses both at graduate and undergraduate level and supervised Masters and Ph.D theses. In recent years, his research has been primarily focused on banking and finance. Applied microeconomics, using both parametric and non-parametric econometric techniques, has been one of his leading fields of specialization. He has published many papers in leading journals of economics. He has a keen interest in developing macroeconomic models based on the System Dynamic Approach and using it to evaluate the workings of alternative banking proposals, including an equity-based financial system.

Siti Raihana Hamzah is a Senior Lecturer of Islamic Science University of Malaysia (USIM) and the 6th SC-OCIS Visiting Fellow in Islamic Finance of Oxford Centre for Islamic Studies (OCIS). She holds a PhD degree in Islamic finance from the International Centre for Education in Islamic Finance (INCEIF) and postgraduate studies in Mathematics from the University of New South Wales (UNSW) Australia. She is currently active in conducting research, particularly in Sukuk Market with the theoretical and mathematical application. Raihana is the Principal Investigator of USIM internal research project that examines the comparative approach of few types of sukuk and bonds in the Malaysian market. In addition, with ten years backgrounds in Pure mathematical studies, she has become the co-investigator for two government research grants in Numerical Solution for Islamic Pricing Option Using a Modified 2 Point Block Backwards Difference Method and The Stochastic Asset Investment Model for Insurer.

Tarık Akın is SC-OCIS Visiting Fellow in Islamic Finance at University of Oxford and division director in Finance Office of the Presidency of the Republic of Turkey. Dr. Tarık worked at the Ministry of Treasury and Finance, Islamic Financial Services Board (IFSB), and the World Bank. His work experience also includes consultant positions at the United Nations Development Programme (UNDP), and Silatech-Qatar. He also worked as research assistant in the Center for International Development at Harvard University and INCEIF. Dr. Tarık has earned his bachelor's degree in economics from Bilkent University, master's degree in international development from Harvard University and PhD degree in Islamic finance from INCEIF. His research interests include Islamic capital markets, economics of inequality, redistribution policies, and SME finance.

Thorsten Beck is professor of banking and finance at Cass Business School in London. He is also a research fellow of the Centre for Economic Policy Research (CEPR) and the CESifo. He was professor of economics from 2008 to 2014 at Tilburg University and the founding chair of the European Banking Center from 2008 to 2013. Previously he worked in the research department of the World Bank and has also worked as consultant for – among others – the European Central Bank, the Bank of England, the BIS, the IMF, the European Commission, and the German Development Corporation. He holds a PhD from the University of Virginia and an MA from the University of Tübingen in Germany.

Umar Rafi specializes in the field of Information Technology in the Financial Services domain. He is currently working as a computer scientist in Silicon Valley. He has a BS in Mathematics from the United States Air Force Academy, and MS in computer science from Wichita State University, and a PhD in Islamic Finance from INCEIF. His areas of research include Black Swan risks, antifragility and how they impact equity-based financing.

Wail Mohamed Aaminou is an international consultant in impact finance. He particularly focuses on fintech and on integrating sustainable development into the business model of financial institutions. In this capacity, he has been advising banks, capital markets' institutions and international organizations. Dr. Wail Mohamed Aaminou also lectured in many academic institutions including the University of Istanbul Sabahattin Zaim, the University of Sunderland, Toulouse Business School and Paris Dauphine University and contributed to several articles in international journals. His research specializes in agent-based simulation, consumer behavior and sustainability financing. In 2016, he won the award for the best application of agent-based simulation by the Islamic Development Bank. Dr. Wail Mohamed Aaminou holds a Ph.D. in financial engineering from Ecole Mohammadia d'ingénieurs (Morocco). He also holds an MBA in Finance with an academic excellence award from Duke University (U.S) and an IT state engineering degree from ENSIAS (Morocco).

Zamir Iqbal is currently serving as the Vice President, Finance and CFO of the Islamic Development Bank. Prior to joining the Islamic Development Bank, he served as head of the World Bank Global Islamic Finance Development Center in Istanbul. He has more than 25 years of experience of capital markets, asset management, risk management, and financial sector at the World Bank. Islamic finance has been his research focus and he has co-authored several articles and books on Islamic finance on the topics of banking risk, financial inclusion, economic development, financial stability, and risk-sharing. He played an instrumental role in the publication of World Bank and IsDB's first Global Report on Islamic Finance. He earned his PhD in international finance from the George Washington University and served as Professional faculty at Carey Business School of Johns Hopkins University.

Index

https://doi.org/10.1515/9783110587920-031